NINE[illegible] CENTURY BRITISH DRAMA

An Anthology of Representative Plays

Edited by
Leonard R.N. Ashley
Brooklyn College
The City University of New York

UNIVERSITY
PRESS OF
AMERICA

for ALAN S. DOWNER in appreciation

University Press of America,® Inc.

4720 Boston Way
Lanham, MD 20706

Printed in the United States of America

Library of Congress Cataloging-in-Publication Data

Nineteenth-century British drama : an anthology of representative
plays / edited by Leonard R.N. Ashley
p. cm.
Reprint. Originally published: Glenview, Ill. : Scott, Foresman, ©1967.
Bibliography: p.
1. English drama—19th century. I. Ashley, Leonard R.N.
PR1271.N56 1988
822'.7'08—dc 19 88–8487 CIP
ISBN 0–8191–7107–7 (pbk. : alk. paper)

All University Press of America books are produced on acid-free paper.
The paper used in this publication meets the minimum requirements of
American National Standard for Information Sciences—Permanence of
Paper for Printed Library Materials, ANSI Z39.48–1984.

CONTENTS

PREFACE

This book presents thirteen of the best, most influential, or most significant British plays of the nineteenth century. Since 1900 the drama of the last century has been largely ignored; most students think that between Sheridan and Shaw there was no British drama at all—that modern drama sprang full-grown from nowhere. This volume explains and illustrates what occurred between the "laughing comedy" of the late eighteenth century and Shaw's "drama of ideas." A general introduction to the dramaturgy and stage of the time, brief introductions to the plays, and pertinent biographical and bibliographical information provide the historical and critical context for the drama of this important and much-neglected period.

The author wishes to thank those who introduced him to the study of drama, especially Professor Elmer Hall, formerly of McGill University, and George Ian Duthie, D. Litt., formerly of McGill University and now of the University of Aberdeen; his mentors at Princeton University, especially Professor Gerald Eades Bentley and Professor Alan S. Downer; his students and colleagues at the University of Utah, the University of Rochester, the New School for Social Research, and Brooklyn College of the City University of New York; and Professor Stuart L. Astor of Adelphi University, for bibliographical advice, and Mr. Hundley Thompson, Jr., for assistance in preparing the typescript.

L. R. N. A.

PREFACE TO THE 1988 EDITION

Nineteenth-Century British Drama helped to correct the bad habit of literary and theatre critics and historians of jumping from Sheridan to Shaw, from Laughing Comedy to The Drama of Ideas, as if there had been no comedy and no drama at all in between. It encouraged the inclusion of representative Victorian plays in critical surveys; it led to the establishment of courses in Victorian drama. It was in print as a textbook for a dozen years.

University Press of America now has given *Nineteenth-Century British Drama* a new lease on life. I am grateful.

I have not been permitted to alter the text printed in 1967, though I should have liked to correct a few minor errors, such as the date of Oscar Wilde's birth. (He often lied about his age, and I made him two years younger than he was, misled like some others.) I have been given the opportunity, however, to create a limited addendum. The updated bibliographical information will, I trust, document the fact that interest in these selected plays continues and I hope that the bibliography will assist students and encourage researchers of these authors, their theatre, and their literary period.

Thanks are due to Fred Bogin and William Gargan for assistance with that selective bibliographical update. "A more comprehensive bibliography is simpler to compile" wrote G. O. Sayles as he updated his *Medieval Foundations of England* (1963), "but correspondingly less useful." I hope everything in this new edition will be found useful.

Feast of St. Botolph, 1988 *L. R. N. A.*

Nineteenth-Century British Drama:

AN INTRODUCTION

WHEN THE RESTORATION (1660) brought the merry monarch Charles II back to the throne, he granted Sir William D'Avenant and Thomas Killigrew letters patent "for the presentation of tragydies, comedyes, plays, operas, and all other entertainments of that nature." At the beginning of the nineteenth century these monopolies (strengthened by the Licensing Act of 1737 that Henry Fielding's satires had brought down upon the stage) were still in effect. The Theatre Royal in Drury Lane and that in Covent Garden, along with the Haymarket[1] (supposedly confined to opera), were the only "legitimate" theatres. Originally established to preserve the drama, they were now strangling it. Though the patent theatres had been adequate for the aristocratic audiences and the lackeys who attended them on their afternoons of leisure, they had inevitably become outmoded. As the population of the capital trebled in the first half of the nineteenth century and a whole new class of society clamored for entertainment, the old theatres not only failed to meet the public's needs but positively contributed to the decline of the drama in quality as it increased in quantity.

1. The Haymarket still operated under a revocable license granted to the comedian Samuel Foote in 1766. It was supposed to supply entertainment during the summer months when the patent theatres were dark; in 1840 the Haymarket's "summer season" ran ten months.

The theatre in Drury Lane, simply designed by Sir Christopher Wren in 1674—"A bare convenience only is design'd," said Dryden—was elaborated by Robert Adam a century later but still accommodated no more than a thousand persons. However, when it burned in 1792, Henry Holland erected a new theatre (for Sheridan) to seat 3611; and when that was also consumed by fire in 1809, the new Drury Lane, built in 1812, was so grand that the actor on stage was "lost in an immense space." Covent Garden underwent similar changes over the years and after a fire in 1808 was redesigned at a cost of £150,000, and without "a particle of taste," to hold approximately 3000. The Haymarket, the first opera house in London (1705), from the start has been cavernous. It was built by Sir John Vanbrugh along the same "vast, triumphal" lines as Blenheim Palace and sacrificed acoustics to grandeur, so that Colley Cibber damned its "extraordinary, and superfluous Space" in his *Apology* (1740): "For what could their vast Columns, their gilded Cornices, their immoderate high Roofs avail, when scarce one Word in ten, could be distinctly heard in it?"[2]

Small wonder that Sarah Siddons, "The Tragic Muse," complained of having to howl to be heard. She dubbed Drury Lane "the tomb of the drama," and plays had to be acted ever more broadly, tragedy ranted and comedy mugged, to carry to the back of these immense, candlelit barns. The word *ham* to describe a posturing, grimacing, wildly gesturing actor, striving for crude and large effects, is said to have been derived from the way everyone, from established stars to "infant Ros-

---

2. *On the other hand, the architect of the 1812 Drury Lane, Benjamin Wyatt, in his observations on the design of the Theatre Royal, Drury Lane, compared his new theatre favorably with the older ones:*

> *Drury-lane Theatre, consisting of three-fourths of a circle, with a Proscenium limiting the Stage-opening to 33 feet, contains, in four different heights, 80 Boxes, holding 1098 persons; with four Boxes—of larger size than the rest—next to the Stage, on each side of the Theatre, capable of containing 188 [more]... amounting in an aggregate to 1286 persons. A Pit capable of containing 920 persons, a Two-Shilling Gallery for 550 persons, a One-Shilling Gallery for 350 persons, exclusive of four Private Boxes in the Proscenium, and 14 in the Basement of the Theatre, immediately under the Dress Boxes.... I confined the distance from the front of the Stage to the back wall of the Boxes, facing the Stage, to 53 feet 9 inches... 38 feet 6 inches laterally. ... In the late Theatre in Drury Lane it [the distance from the front of the stage to the back of the boxes] was 74 feet, or 20 feet 3 inches more than at present; in the Old Theatre in Covent Garden (I mean as it was built about the year 1730), the distance between the front of the Stage, and the back wall of the front Boxes, was 54 feet 6 inches, or 1 foot 3 inches more than in my design.... [I]n the Haymarket, it was 66 feet, or 12 feet 3 inches more than in my design.... In the present Theatre at Covent Garden it is 69 feet 8 inches, or fifteen feet eleven inches more.*

ciuses," had to play *Hamlet* in such halls. People no longer spoke of going to hear a play: they went to see one. The spectacle counted most. The actors tried not to impersonate convincingly but to declaim impressively, the management draped them in togas and backed them with effects that proved that "the *Play-House* is an Inchanted Island, where nothing appears in Reality what it is, nor what it should be." As scene painters became more important than poets, it began to seem that Thomas Carlyle was right in dismissing the stage for attempting to achieve by mechanical means what poetic genius alone could accomplish on the printed page.

The classical repertory was still played, that being one of the justifications of the patents, but playwrights succumbed increasingly to mountebanks, managers, and "scenes, machines, and dancing." If scenery had been "the soul of masque" in the days of Inigo Jones (1573–1652), it was now the *raison d'être* of many plays. Plays became vehicles for egotistical actor-managers who appeared in tailored versions of scripts, "supported" by inferior actors and superior stage and lighting technicians. Such as John Philip Kemble stalked in tragedy, "precise in passion,"

> Stiff, pompous, stern, each haggard feature gloom'd;
> Each step predestin'd, and each look foredoom'd,

meticulously arranging their mantles, their grand pauses, and their artificial effects.

These tedious ceremonies had to be relieved with what Sir Richard Steele had much earlier called "non-rational" trappings, because of the stiff competition from the unlicensed theatres. At the beginning of the nineteenth century half a dozen of these challenged the "legitimate drama" with musical concerts and ballets, aquatic and equestrian spectacles, Gothic thrillers, gripping melodramas, parodies, pantomimes, and burlettas. (The burlettas, from the Italian *burlare,* "to mock or jest," were dramas which contained a minimum of six songs and were therefore technically musical rather than dramatic.) Thus did the unlicensed theatres evade the restrictions of the Lord Chamberlain, by law the absolute master and "Examiner of all Plays, Tragedies, Comedies, Operas, Farces, Interludes, or any other entertainment for the stage, of what denomination whatsoever."[3] Their success led to a major boom in "minor" theatres such as the Lyceum (1809), which featured the

---

3. As late as 1892 Parliamentary committees were still declaring this sort of censorship neither unworkable nor unfair.

immensely popular plays of Edward Fitzball (or Ball, 1792-1873); the Surrey (1810), bringing gilt and red velvet elegance to the south side of the Thames; the Sans Pareil (1806), later renowned for melodramas as the Adelphi; and the Coburg (1816, after 1833 the Royal Victoria), which seated nearly four thousand persons.

As the century wore on these theatres and many others, in which Lottie Venne and Edward Terry played, in which Charles Wyndham and the Bancrofts and the Kendals acted and produced, drew patrons from the "legitimate" houses and compelled the patent theatres to mount splendiferous and prodigiously expensive spectacles "Where all that's wond'rous occupies the stage." Having thrice failed to get Parliament to license a third house—the Haymarket didn't count—the "minors" changed their tack and began to steal the thunder of the "legitimate" houses. *The Theatrical Observer* (May 28, 1831) wryly commented on the turnabout that competition and imitation had created:

> At the theatre royal, Drury Lane, we have *Timour the Tartar* and the horses. At the theatre royal, Covent Garden, we have the *Life and Death of Buonaparte,* as a mere spectacle accompanied by every kind of catch-shilling gee-gaw, and some horses, while, on the other hand [at the "minors"], we find at Sadler's Wells, *Romeo and Juliet, Katharine and Petruchio* [*The Taming of the Shrew* "pictorialized" with scenery]; at the Surrey, *Richard III* [Colley Cibber's adaptation of Shakespeare], several other of Shakespeare's plays and [Richard] Cumberland's *Jew* [*of Mogadore,* with music by M. Kelly], with Elliston [a leading actor]; and finally at the new City Theatre in Milton Street (alias Grubb) ["among the more respectable of the 'minors' "—Nicoll] the *Merchant of Venice;* Shylock, Mr. [Edmund] Kean! ! !

It was strange that the minor theatres seemed to be taking over the serious drama from the licensed houses. In 1832 the future Lord Lytton, then a young member of Parliament, introduced a bill to remove the restrictions on the minor theatres. It failed of passage in the House of Lords; but thereafter the laws were very loosely applied, and a bill to free the theatres was successfully carried in 1843. The well-schooled companies of the patent theatres almost immediately dispersed to the "minors" where there was room for new stars:

Portia. I say you're free to act where'er you please, no longer pinioned by the patentees.

. . . .

Drama. O joyful day! Then I may flourish still!
Punch. May—well, that's something.
Let us hope you will.

(*The Drama at Home,* 1844)

But there was little change. For the next twenty years the "vast profound" patent theatres were likely to be doing "gilt-gaud" spectacles on the largest scale—the stage at Drury Lane, 92 feet deep, lent itself to such things. The smaller theatres introduced more plays, generally domestic, into long and varied bills which combined melodramas, burlettas and burlesques, skits and spectacles; the programs amounted to modern television, radio, cinema, and theatre all rolled into one. For a few shillings one could have up to five or six hours of live and lively entertainment. The intellectuals could stay home and read poetry and novels: the middlebrows and lowbrows got Sir Walter Scott and other novelists in dramatic adaptations and Lord Byron with fireworks. The influential new reviews might thunder, but the public was content with simple pleasures and delighted to find "some useful moral for the feeling mind" included now and again.

When Kemble had reopened Covent Garden in 1809, the famous "Old Price" riots that raged for sixty-seven nights were occasioned perhaps as much by the pit's resentment of the private boxes as by the sixpenny hike in admission charges. "The many-headed monster of the pit" was determined to rule, and did. The mob (or, more politely, the general public) won that battle and also dictated that action and thrills, slapstick and sentiment, the merchant's ethics and the machinist's effects were to prevail.

But the public could be impressed by the classics, too, and Dion Boucicault's pronouncement that "Shakespeare spells ruin and [Lord] Byron bankruptcy," was an exaggeration. Between 1844 and 1862 Samuel Phelps transformed Sadler's Wells from a hippodrome to a stage for Shakespeare. William Cheswick produced the Bard (as well as transpontine melodrama) at the Surrey in the 1850's. Charles Kean, a pedant and antiquary as well as an actor and manager, brought archeological accuracy to revivals of Shakespeare at the Princess' from 1850 to 1859, though Charles Macready complained that "the accessories swallow up the poetry and the action." [4] Even at the end of the century Sir Herbert Beerbohm Tree at Her Majesty's was noted "for his partiality for real livestock in Shakespeare."

But "The Drama's law's the Drama's patrons give," and the newly emancipated and rambunctious audiences generally could not stomach Shakespeare without some mitigating novelty. As for the verse tragedies of Coleridge and Shelley or, later, Tennyson and Swinburne, they were found unpalatable indeed. Macready hoped that such vampire-cold reanimations of Elizabethan verse tragedy as Browning's *Strafford* (1837) would elevate the stage, but they only succeeded in depressing the audience.[5] The best poets would not stoop to theatricality and deplored the vulgarity of the theatre. Mediocre or bad poets, with jog-trot rhetoric and old-fangled devices, were given short shrift. The public, offered *Virginius* (1820) and *The Love-Chase* (1837), at first were respectful; but their later reactions to his plays forced James Sheridan Knowles (1784-1862) off the stage and into the Baptist pulpit. Sir Thomas Noon Talfourd (1795-1854), the author of *Ion* (1835), and Sir Henry Taylor (1800-1886), the author of *Philip van Artevelde* (1834), were likewise unable to create a permanent audience for verse tragedy. The gap between literature and drama only widened when talented hacks succeeded, serious mediocrities failed, and acknowledged writers would not risk their reputations in the popular theatre. After all, some important

---

4. *As actor-manager at Covent Garden (1837-1839, and at Drury Lane 1841-1843), Macready himself had boasted that "the costume of the piece [it was* Coriolanus *meticulously mounted] is strictly realized. All is correct. . . ." Careful costuming was an advertisable novelty in those days.*

5. *Robert Browning, master of the dramatic monologue, could not handle the deft dramaturgy made popular by Eugène Scribe and perfected by Victorien Sardou, two immensely popular French masters of machine-made plays, with their ingenuity, economy, precision tooling, and inevitability—they were written backwards. Browning was interested in character more than mechanism and disinclined to provide what had become popular in the "well-made" play: artificiality of structure, stereotyped psychology, pedestrian morality, minimum passion and maximum unreality. Plot was Browning's weakest point, a fact best illustrated in a play which he dashed off in five days, called* A Blot in the 'Scutcheon. *Macready opened it to great applause at Drury Lane in 1843, Phelps played it at Sadler's Wells, Lawrence Barrett toured with it in America, but finally not even Browning's immense reputation could disguise its faults. The author boasted it had "*action *in it, drabbing, stabbing, et autres gentillesses," but it was basically literature, not dramatic literature. The heroine's coy excuse "I was so young—I had no mother" moved Charles Dickens and others to tears, but today we are more critical and liable to compare Browning's gallant attempt at poetry in the theatre (as opposed to poetry of the theatre) to the expansive verse dramas of Victor Hugo of which it was said that they were admirable in every respect save only that of fitness for the stage.*

writers were boasting that their plays were unstageable and critics were commending Shakespeare's *King Lear* as being unactable.

A real poet of the theatre might have won them over, but the general public would have no truck with the pseudo-Elizabethan and neo-Greek verse dramas they were offered. They wanted engaging and more or less realistic pictures of the "glad, confident morning" of their own age of prosperity and progress. The increasingly influential middle class believed in self-help, the gospel of work, stable institutions at home and economic influence and empire abroad; they celebrated Martin Tupper's "common humble multitudinous Man." No one wanted to write a verse drama about that, nor a high tragedy based on decent, common middle-class virtues, solid middle-class standards, restrained middle-class emotions. Not for John Bull, shopkeeper, nor for his lower-class contemporaries

> A dull romantic whining play,
> Where poor frail woman's made a deity,
> With senseless amorous idolatry,
> And sniveling heros sigh, and pine, and cry.

Unless, of course, the author also threw in "A Domestic, Melo-dramatic, Choreographic, Fantastique, Traditionary Tale of Superstition," or something equally attractive.

Such plays as Bulwer-Lytton's comedy *Money* (1839) proved that literary merit and theatrical success were not entirely incompatible in Victorian England, but most of the plays of the period only prove how unreadable a smash hit can be. The public welcomed a lot of trash as well as the easy, entertaining plays of the journalist Douglas William Jerrold (1803-1857), the lucky author of *Black-Ey'd Susan,* the success of 1829. Public taste was still inclined toward German romance and native sentimentalism, first in vogue in the preceding century. Thomas Holcroft's *A Tale of Mystery* (1802), the first melodrama so-called, signaled the beginning of a whole new school of theatrical thrills for theatricality's sake, ushering in the era of the vampire trap, the real waterfall, and the simulated holocaust. Holcroft borrowed his play from Guilbert de Pixérécourt's *Coelina; ou, l'enfant du mystère* (1800). After the phenomenal success of Holcroft's play it is scarcely surprising that a large percentage of British plays was taken from the French. John Maddison Morton (1811-1891) based his popular farce *Box and Cox* (1847) on *Une chambre à deux lits.* James Robinson Planché (1796-1880), a herald turned hack, made a long and busy career out of adapting innumerable French imports.[6]

Native English dramatists went into a decline and either abandoned the stage or were compelled to sell their wares in a market glutted with stolen goods. Who would pay £250 for "a new, original" play when a "logical" success by Eugène Scribe (1791-1861) or Victorien Sardou (1831-1908) could be translated for £50? Scribe especially was easily adapted for foreign audiences: the machine ran as well in London or Berlin as it did in Paris. His were not studies of society, close observations of private little worlds one had to live in to understand or appreciate. Scribe's *Adrienne Lecouvreur* (written with Gabriel Legouvé, 1849) was not a French play in the way that Wilde's *The Importance of Being Earnest* was an English play. Scribe's liberal ideas, his bourgeois morality, his theatrical tricks were internationally acceptable. A play by Scribe was an eminently exportable machine, like a Swiss watch.

It was also possible to steal closer to home and to succeed without a knowledge of foreign languages. Many undertook "the task of compressing Tales of three volumes into Plays of three Acts . . . merely technical and mechanical drudgery" and pillaged the Waverley novels of Scott, condensed Dickens, went back to Smollett, or dramatized the newest novel. Charles Reade (1814-1884), the author of many a "matter of fact romance," even reversed the trend. With Tom Taylor (1817-1880), a jack-of-all literary trades, Reade wrote a play about the eighteenth-century theatre, *Masks and Faces* (1852). Reade tells us how they did it:

> While Taylor was away at his office, I wrote, and when he came back at night, he cut. Then he wrote a bit and I cut. [It was this necessity of cutting that would have defeated Dickens as a playwright.] It was snip, snap, slish, slash.

The next year Reade wrote a novel, *Peg Woffington,* based on the play. He put back everything that had been cut out of the playscript.

Some writers, however, had a peculiar knack for the theatre, quite

6. *"Planché, being introduced to Scribe at the Garrick Club," reported Harley Granville-Barker in 1929, "with the bland recommendation* 'Encore un qui vous a pillé,' *capped it in compliment by* 'Impossible de faire même du nouveau sans piller Monsieur Scribe.' *And Scribe smiled politely." In 1852 Parliament passed an act to give foreign writers a five-year copyright on their works, but not until 1875 did a limit on adaptation make it difficult to evade the restrictions imposed, and not until 1887 were foreign works placed under full copyright protection in England.*

often enhanced by personal experience of the stage. Holcroft (1745-1809) had been a stage manager in Dublin and a strolling player in England. Dion Boucicault (1822?-1890) put his expertise into more than one hundred plays. Careful production made a hit of his *London Assurance* (1841) when Boucicault was still in his teens. Though it was basically Goldsmith and Sheridan with a new middle-class tone, and though William Archer pronounced it "probably the shallowest and flashiest production that ever passed for serious comedy," its effect was immediate and lasting. Boucicault was a hack, writing not for posterity but for Wednesday, yet his *Corsican Brothers* (1852), *The Octoroon* (1861), and various Irish melodramas helped to free stage diction and to advance theatrical technique.[7] Henry James Byron (1834-1884) also knew the stage from acting experience. He confected many farces and burlesques and set the record for a long run with *Our Boys*, which filled houses from January 16, 1875, to April 18, 1879. His friend and colleague Tom Taylor owed much of the effect of his famous character Lord Dundreary in *Our American Cousin* (1858) to the help of the actor E. A. Sothern.

Thomas William Robertson (1829-1871) attempted to break away from caricatures and combined Boucicault's tricks with a new realism. In this he was assisted by Madame Vestris and Charles Matthews (with whom he worked, as a prompter, at the Olympic) and, expecially, Marie Wilton, who took over the management of a broken down theatre called "The Dust Hole" and made it famous as the Prince of Wales. There tasteful, thoughtful staging became the rule:

> No attempt is made by any one of its members to eclipse his fellows, or to monopolize either the space on the boards, or the attention of the audience. No piece is presented in such a state of unpreparedness that the first dozen performances are no better than rehearsals; no slovenliness in the less important accessories of the play is permitted. (*The Athenaeum*, May 18, 1872)

To a dedicated ensemble company Robertson contributed a fresh modern comedy of natural dialogue, eschewing the eccentric and the grotesque. Robertson is Tom Wrench, hero of Pinero's *Trelawney of the 'Wells':*

---

7. *Boucicault also improved the position of the playwright financially.* London Assurance *made him little money, considering its success, but twenty years later he demanded and got a "percentage of the take" for* The Colleen Bawn *(1860), and his profits approached £10,000 on that play. Thomas Dibdin (1771-1841), who wrote about eight hundred theatre pieces under the old system, died poor, glad of a £50 subscription a year in his old age.*

Imogen. You know, the speeches were so short and had such ordinary words in them, in the plays you used to read to me—no big opportunity for the leading lady, Wrench.

Tom. M'yes, I strive to make my people talk and behave like live people, don't I—?

Imogen. I suppose you do.

Tom. To fashion heroes out of actual, dull, every-day men—the sort of men you see smoking cheroots in the club windows in St. James's Street; the heroines from simple maidens in muslin frocks. Naturally, the managers won't stand that.

. . . .

Tom. . . . Windows on the one side, doors on the other—just where they should be, architecturally. And locks on the doors, *real* locks, to work; and handles—to turn! Ha, ha! You wait—wait—!

Robertson's "cup-and-saucer" realism created radically new styles of acting and staging in the box set (introduced 1832) which had, a critic averred in *The Examiner,* "the appearance of a private chamber, infinitely better than the old contrivance of [backdrop and] wings." From then on, the actors were to perform in practicable scenery and more plausible plots, not posing on the apron and using the proscenium-framed picture (and the play itself) as mere background. The actors began to be costumed more thoughtfully rather than in rummage and to move under the lights (after 1817 gas, after 1825 limelight too[8]) in more natural ways, speaking a more human language.

The dramatists of the new school of Robertson shared credit with

8. In the previous century candles, in chandeliers and sconces, and lanterns, both with candles and with oil, lit the auditorium and the stage. In the hands of De Loutherbourg and Capon both subtle and spectacular effects were possible, especially when oil lamps and transparent scenery were used. The Lyceum installed gas early in the nineteenth century. The patent theatres followed in 1817, returning briefly to older methods in 1828 until the dangerous and evil-smelling gas lamps could be perfected. Calcium or limelight was invented in 1825 and over the next quarter century gradually came into general use. Limelight gave an intense white light (or slightly greenish one), but it was unreliable and required constant attention. Lighting was not subtle; the "glare" of which Gainsborough complained in the theatre of Garrick's time increased enormously. Then in 1880 the Paris Opera employed electric lighting and the next year D'Oyly Carte installed electric light throughout the Savoy, the new theatre he had erected for Gilbert and Sullivan.

the "good taste and sound policy" that Planché tells us Madame Vestris introduced at the Olympic:

> In a time of unexampled peril to the best interests of the Drama—whilst theatrical property was at the lowest ebb, the larger theatres changing hands continually, and the ruin of their lessees involving that of hundreds of their unfortunate dependents—the little Olympic, the most despised nook in the dramatic world, became not only one of the most popular and fashionable theatres London ever saw, but served as a life-boat to the respectability of the stage, which was fast sinking in the general wreck.

Marie Wilton and her husband, Sir Squire Bancroft, who built a tradition, a repertory, and an audience at the Prince of Wales' also were representative of the managers who helped reform the stage. But in general the actor-managers were contributors to the decline of the drama. The star system, which had caused London to react to Edmund Kean's frenzied performances,

> Holding in high disdain all sort of action
> That does not evidence complete distraction,

as it had not reacted to any theatrical personality since it had gone "horn mad" over David Garrick, was invidious. Kean reintroduced the small, nervous, jerky Richard III of Colley Cibber and played him, as he also played Shylock, so fitfully and hypnotically that Coleridge said "to see him act is like reading Shakespeare by flashes of lightning." His son Charles Kean, though handicapped by an insignificant figure and a shrill, nasal voice, also established himself as a Shakespearian actor and manager, taking over the mantle from his father's rival, William Charles Macready, probably the most intelligent and reliable and possibly the most striking actor of the first half of the century. Macready presented good plays written for him by Bulwer-Lytton and Browning, and he carefully presented Shakespeare. Unfortunately, however, most actor-managers were not this conscientious. In the 1820's, said Robertson, who pretty much invented the stage-manager's job, the actor-manager was "an intensely clever, bustling, wrong-headed, highly appreciative fellow, fond of his authors, his company, his orchestra, his scene-shifters, his supernumeraries, and all that belonged to the little world he ruled." But then came the commercial manager:

> The Commercial Manager is a very common type [wrote Robertson in sketches in the *Illustrated Times,* 1850] . . . willing to exploit opera, ballet, equestrianism, and Shakespeare . . . . He takes an entirely commercial view of all things . . . prides himself greatly upon his practical commonsense, distrusts manuscripts, fears authors, but places great reliance upon his costumier and property-man. . . . Although he professes a high respect for dramatic literature, he judges the merit of the drama like a butterman—by its weight in paper.
> . . . The Actor Manager is a good second or third rate sort of artist, who forces himself into a prominent position by taking a theatre, and, by carefully stewing down the abilities of the authors and actors he employs, and mixing with his own their mental and artistic porridge, makes his weak water-gruel talents thick and slaby. . . .There is your Tragedian Manager, who kindly puts Shakespeare right, and explains what that erring author really meant; and there is your High Comedy Manager, who knows three Lords to speak to, and once met a Countess at a ball, and is in consequence a great authority on fashionable life; and, like Goldsmith's bear-leader, can't abide anything that is low.

The most influential actor-manager of all was probably Sir Henry Irving, who attempted to enlist Tennyson's aid in making the drama respectable. Irving's knighthood honored the whole profession, and his personality dominated it.[9] In him were met the best and the worst of that tyrannous breed of actor-managers. Bernard Shaw wrote of Irving:

> To the author, Irving was not an actor: he was either a rival or a collaborator who did all the real work [as in *The Bells*]. Therefore, he was anathema to master authors, and a godsend to journeymen authors.

---

9. "It is only within the last few years," wrote Bernard Shaw in 1898, "that some of our younger actor-managers have been struck with the idea, quite novel in their profession, of performing Shakespear's plays as he wrote them, instead of using them as a cuckoo uses a sparrow's nest. In spite of the success of these experiments, the stage is still dominated by Garrick's conviction that the manager and actor must adapt Shakespear's plays to the modern stage by a process which no doubt presents itself to the adapter's mind as one of masterly amelioration, but which necessarily be mainly one of debasement and mutilation whenever, as occasionally happens, the adapter is inferior to the author."

The playwright began to assume his proper place when smaller theatres, more tasteful production, and more concern with realism than rant appeared. The new drama borrowed dramaturgy from the French *pièce bien faite,* seriousness from the "thesis play," and, especially after visits to London by the Comédie Française inspired native troupes, led to Jones and Pinero and Shaw. But first there was to be an era of "Fairy Extravaganzas, Classical Burlesques, New and Original Burlesque Pantomimes, Operatic Extravaganzas," and the excruciating puns of Planché's parodies, Burnand and Brough's buffooneries:

Henry. Where's Suffolk?
Suffolk. Here, my liege, in waiting.
Henry. My loving Suffolk, I feel *suffoc*-ating.
I am so ill.
Suffolk. Nay, Sire, cheer up I pray;
You were so brave and jolly yesterday.
Henry. Yesterday all was fair—a glorious Sunday,
But this *sick transit* spoils the *glory o' Monday.*
(William Brough, *The Field of the Cloth of Gold,* 1868)[10]

This tradition did, nonetheless, produce Sir W. S. Gilbert (1836-1911), who wrote his first piece, *Dulcamara* (1866), according to this rule:

Each speech should have a pun in it, with very foolish fun in it
And if you can't bring one in it—you'd better stop away.

Had he not turned to masterpieces of comic opera with Sir Arthur Sullivan, Gilbert, a gifted playwright in such topsy-turvy and slightly cantankerous comedies as *Engaged* (1877), would probably have written some farce to challenge the pre-eminence of *Charley's Aunt* (1892), the one effort likely to be immortal, by Brandon Thomas (1849-1914), a minor actor turned commercial dramatist. *Charley's Aunt* shares with Gilbert's fun a certain sadism, a snobbery, a whimsicality, a gentle satire on safe subjects, and an apologetic air of one who, kicking up his heels, pauses to explain earnestly that laughter is the best and

10. *Quoted by Harley Granville-Barker in "Exit Planché—Enter Gilbert,"* The Eighteen-Sixties, *p. 130.*

cheapest medicine for "this strange disease of modern life." Which is to say, it is typical of Victorian humor. It is virtually unreadable, short on mind, and as painful to study as a student-written skit in a prep school. In performance—and it has been running constantly somewhere since its première in the 1890's—its worst feature, the dialogue, is somehow palatable. We can look forward centuries to that day when the clumsiness and artificiality of the dialogue shall have undergone a seachange into "the quaint and colorful speech of a bygone age." Then it can appear in an anthology with *The Menaechmi.*

Another Victorian play destined for immortality is Oscar Wilde's *The Importance of Being Earnest* (1895), quite the reverse of *Charley's Aunt.* In Wilde's play "the fun depends mainly on what the characters say," said Max Beerbohm, "rather than on what they do." This masterpiece with a message ("That we should treat all the trivial things of life seriously, and all the serious things of life with sincere and studied triviality"), revived for the nineteenth century the great traditions of Congreve and Sheridan in the comedy of manners. Surprisingly, at the same time another Irishman, William Butler Yeats (1865-1939), was sparking the Abbey Theatre movement and creating out of the myths and legends of Old Ireland the viable poetic drama that Coleridge's *Remorse* (1797; first acted 1813), Byron's *Sardanapalus* (1821), Lytton's *Richelieu* (1839), Swinburne's *Chastelard* (1865), and even Shelley's *The Cenci* (1819; first acted 1886) did not achieve.

Tennyson, who in his time enjoyed not only a barony but bardolatry, contributed but little to the theatre. *The Promise of May,* a "realistic drama of modern life," was a complete fiasco at the Globe in November of 1882. But the *Idylls of The King* (published in 1859) had won him the intellectual public and *Enoch Arden* (1864) had won him the common people, so Tennyson's reputation at least gained him a hearing, even when his plays betrayed that unpleasant tinge of Shakespearian imitation that (as Emerson wisely noted) betrays a decadence in the drama. He was the Bard, "And all men looked upon him favorably." Moreover, he wrote with an eye on the theatre, as Browning did not, creating mellifluous items that were amenable to "Arrangement for the stage," and he had Sir Henry Irving and Ellen Terry to speak his lines. Irving opened the Lyceum's season of 1881 with *The Cup* and in *Becket* (1893) gave the most remarkable performance of his whole splendid career. "Modern fame is nothing," Tennyson told William Allingham (a now-forgotten poet). "I'd rather have an acre of land. I shall go down, down! I'm up now. Action and reaction." The reaction even to Tennyson's successful plays has now set in, for his age is distant enough to be quaint and too close to be treated with awe. Today we are more likely to read the prose drama of his period instead of the verse drama of the laureate.

In prose came the society drama, now that the Bancrofts had brought the "swells" to the Prince of Wales' and fashionable society had begun to book seats in the "Dress Circle" to see Irving, Ellen Terry, George Alexander (in Wilde's comedies), and other luminaries. Where Coleridge had failed with remorse, Henry Arthur Jones (1851-1929) succeeded: "Oh, God, put back thy universe and give me yesterday," pleaded the hero of *The Silver King,* a melodrama which gripped the public at the Princess' in 1882. And Jones was neither a Sydney Grundy, fiddling with the symbolism of *A Pair of Spectacles* (1890) nor a James Albery, groping toward naturalness in *Two Roses* (1870). Jones brought the intellectuals (including Matthew Arnold) back to the theatre after a lapse of twenty years, brought them back with appeals in the press, in journals like *The Nineteenth Century* and *New Review,* on public platforms in debate, in serious books (*The Renascence of the English Drama* and *Foundations of a National Drama*), and (the most effective of all) in appealing plays like *Saints and Sinners* (1884), *The Masqueraders* (1894), and *The Case of Rebellious Susan* (1894), among others. With a "wide and clear vision of society," as Shaw said, Jones wrote important drama, even if it was true that his "theories of it have no relation to his observation." The critic William Archer had devastatingly brought his talents to bear in examining the *English Dramatists of To-day* (1882), and such men as Jones were determined that intelligent criticism should find at last "a school of plays of serious intention, plays that implicitly assert the value and dignity of human life, that it has great passions and great aims, and is full of meaning and importance." He aspired to write plays not only worth seeing but worth reading and considering as well. His *Michael and His Lost Angel* (1896) was a commercial failure but epoch-making in the revival of the serious drama.

Less wedded to melodrama and of a more expansive spirit was Sir Arthur Wing Pinero (1855-1934), an actor who aspired to discuss social problems in well-made plays. *The Second Mrs. Tanqueray* (1893) may not have been much more of a criticism of life than *La Dame aux Camélias* (1852), but it established both his reputation and the modern drama. Allardyce Nicoll's standard history of *Late Nineteenth Century Drama* (1962) says:

> It did not face facts so boldly as many imagined. It did not even provide such a fine technical model as some other plays of the same period. To it more than to any other drama of its time, however, the English stage owed its later prevailing tendency towards the naturalism of daily life. The fantasy of Gilbert was forgotten; the artificiality of Wilde was neglected; and the strange poetic quality of Ibsen's work was interpreted in terms of common daily life.

It was to critics, above all, that the New Drama owed its escape from the escapism of melodrama and the fairyland of Sir James Matthew Barrie (1860-1937), who himself had started as a journalist. William Archer (1856-1924) wrote trenchantly about the necessity for a free, new national theatre and, after Ibsen had been writing for forty years, introduced the Norwegian genius in English translations (1889-1890). Ibsen was then produced by the critic J. T. Grein and the Independent Theatre (1890), and the critic George Bernard Shaw (1856-1950) analyzed *The Quintessence of Ibsenism* (1891). Ibsen's influence began to spread. It is seen in Shaw's first play, *Widowers' Houses* (1892), though *Widowers' Houses* was mostly written before Ibsen's influence was felt in England. Shaw thus began a long career of "immoral and heretical plays." These plays seemed witty and paradoxical because they told the truth and dealt with such *outré* subjects as "a married woman in love with her own husband, and without a past" and the Superman. Remembering that the stage was a platform, Shaw strove to make the theatre "a factory of thought, a prompter of conscience, an elucidator of social conduct, an armory against despair and dullness and a temple of the Ascent of Man." Born into a "generation of duffers" when the drama was being written for the theatres rather than the theatres being created to serve the drama, Shaw was a revolutionary: "It is an instinct with me to attack every idea which has been full-grown for ten years, especially if it claims to be the foundation of all society." He saw that Jones and Pinero and the rest were not really a beginning but an end; that they represented a novel conclusion to the nineteenth-century British drama; and that if the twentieth-century drama was to have a harbinger it would have to be Shaw, the Jeremiah who was weary with forebearing and could not stay. He came to propagandize and inspire, to cavil and challenge when Matthew Arnold was characterizing the British theatre as "probably the most contemptible in Europe" and when Henry

James, too American to know the British tradition that foreigners are not supposed to criticize, was writing this:

> When Matthew Arnold speaks of the "contemptible" character of the contemporary English theatre, he points of course not merely at the bad acting which is so largely found there; he alludes also to its perfect literary nudity.

Whatever the depths the drama may have reached at those times when art and audience failed the greatest of man's literary forms, it continued to develop in ways we need to know about. William Archer was not wrong in trying to find "in the history of the drama as a whole any guiding principle of evolution." There was indeed a theatre in England between Sheridan and Shaw, and it included milestones of accomplishment that today can be enjoyed for themselves as well as in connection with the origins of modern theatre.

A NOTE ON STAGE DIRECTIONS

BECAUSE STAGE DIRECTIONS were written for actors before plays ever came to be printed, it has become traditional to write them from the actor's point of view: thus *stage left* means the actor's left as he faces the audience. Stage directions derive from a time when Latin was still used occasionally by those people who could write anything at all: thus *exit* ("he goes out") and other such directions in Latin are still found. The platform on which the actors appeared, rather than the auditorium, was raked for better visibility: thus *upstage* means movement away from the audience (toward the back of the stage) and *downstage* means movement toward the *front* of the stage (toward the audience), toward the *floats* (referring to the wicks floating in the oil lamps that used to light the edge of the stage) or the *footlights*. For the same reason, a stage direction might instruct the actor to move *above* or *below* (rather than "behind" or "in front of") some part of the *set*. An actor, therefore, might have to *move down left* on a certain *line* (single speech), then *cross upstage right,* moving *above* the table, and *exit.* The direction might add *O. P.* to indicate the side of the stage: "Opposite Prompt" is *stage right,* for the prompter in the English-speaking theatre traditionally sits not at the center of the footlights as in the continental theatre but just *offstage left, in the wings.*

Staging in the nineteenth century closely resembled that in the conventional opera houses of today. During this period the *box set* (three walls of a room with an imaginary fourth wall along the footlights) came into use, but older fashions in scenery (for theatre is the most conservative of the arts) persisted side by side with new developments. One traditional system employed *backdrops* or *back scenes* and side walls (called *wings*) placed parallel to the audience in sets, with narrow *entrances* between them. Abbreviated directions in playscripts indicated an entrance at *R. U. E.* (right upper entrance), for example, or an exit at *L. 2 E.* (the second entrance on stage left), etc. Some confusion was created by those who called the spaces between the wings *grooves,* because "grooves" meant something quite different in an earlier system of scenery that was still in use in some places. In it, *scene changes,* or *shifts,* were made by sliding *closes* of scenery that moved in *grooves,* top and bottom, from the wings to meet in the center of the stage.

> We don't expect no grammar,
> But for God's sake join your flats!

These *flats,* meeting in the center, formed a background or *scene* and could be parted quickly to reveal the *scene* behind. Or a pair of them could be *closed in* only part way, forming *wings.* This system dated at least from the time of Sir William D'Avenant, whose *The Siege of Rhodes* (1656) pretty much founded English operatic spectacle. In the nineteenth century "the scene opens" or "the scene closes" still referred to the movement of the scenery. The *first grooves* were nearest the audience and the rest were numbered accordingly.

Later the pieces of scenery flats were *flown,* stored above and behind the *proscenium*—the decorative arch between the stage and the auditorium—rather than in the wings. The word *flat* came to mean any piece of scenery composed of canvas stretched over a wooden frame. With scenery that *opened* and *closed* or was *flown* or *dropped,* of course, it was possible to effect a change of setting much faster than in the latter days of the box set, for that three-sided room had walls composed of flats lashed together, supported by *stage braces* fixed to the floor with *stage screws.* Before the box set it was possible and common to perform a grand *transformation scene,* a complete change of scenery, in full view of the audience with spectacular effect or speedily in a moment of darkness.

The box set had to be *struck,* or taken down, and that took more time, necessitating a *curtain,* or a *drop.* In classical theatre an *act* division occurred whenever the stage was empty, even for a moment, and a new *scene* began whenever a fresh character entered, but the Victorian practice generally equated *scenes* with *sets.* To end an act, an *act drop* (a painted curtain) was *rung* down. The *house curtain* or *front curtain* normally rose before the play began and remained *up* until the play was over. Curtains either rose and fell from the *flies* or were *travelers*—that is, came from the wings to meet in the middle. It was common in the Victorian theatre for an act or scene to end with the characters on stage frozen in some striking pose, a *tableau,* until the curtain was quite down.

The student may wish to consult a dictionary or handbook to discover the meanings of such terms as *practical,* which in theatre parlance means "usable" (a door that opens and closes, for example, rather than one painted on the set), but generally the meaning of terms such as *ground row, batten, spotlight, check* (reduce) *lights, ring* (down), *close in,* and *Right Centre Back* will be clear from the context. After a little practice initials like *L. 3 E., L. U. E., L. C.,* and so on, will cause no trouble, and the student will be able to follow the fashions in stage directions from Shelley (who seems sometimes to have neglected to imagine his characters embodied) through the elaborate acting and pantomime instructions of Robertson, to Shaw, who (admitting that "it is very difficult to induce the English public to buy and read plays" when "there is nothing in them except the bare words") wrote both actable and unactable stage directions for the benefit of the reader. With Barrie we arrive at the playwright who went to see a production of his play, noted minutely what happened, and then wrote those stage directions into the published play, in a sense offering as his own work what the director had contributed.

It is true that until about Pinero's time dramatists did little to make their plays easy to read—they were writing the directions for theatre people who knew the terminology—but they have always relied upon stage movement and setting to do some of their work and have increasingly sought to control or suggest them. A great deal happens in Victorian stage directions; in some plays which relied heavily on spectacle and pantomime they achieve prime importance. They must be read and understood if the reader is to experience the plays properly, if he is to stage the plays in the theatre of his imagination. George Rowell writes:

> Many plays of the period, famous in their day, appear scarcely intelligible on the printed page, so great is their reliance on the

actor's powers of projection and on the machinist's skill, to which a mass of highly technical stage directions testifies. To recreate from the text a performance of a Victorian play calls for imagination strongly disciplined in the theatrical practice of the day, and for the same reason a study of the Victorian drama entails a study of the Victorian theatre.

THE CENCI

The Cenci deals, if ever so meticulously, with incest, a subject inordinately chic during what Mario Praz calls *The Romantic Agony* (1951). Some critics, therefore, have dismissed it as "abnormally revolting in its theme," and the managers of Covent Garden would not even show the script to Eliza O'Neill, whom Shelley had hoped would star as Beatrice Cenci. William Morton Payne hailed *The Cenci* as "the greatest English dramatic poem of the century," and others have contended that it is just that, a dramatic poem, not a play. John Addington Symonds called it "the greatest tragedy composed in English since the death of Shakespeare," and others have derided it as Shakespeare-and-water.

Shelley based *The Cenci* on a somewhat inaccurate account of events which took place in Rome in 1599. Clearly fascinated with the subject matter, aware that John Ford (1586-1640?) and John Webster (1580?-1625?) had fashioned high tragedy out of similar sensational stuff, Shelley tried to leave the lyric for the dramatic mode and to analyze the motivations of the characters with as much "negative capability" and detachment as possible. *The Cenci* does not incorporate any of Shelley's progressive social philosophy, and it is unusual to see him dealing with character rather than with ideas and ideals for (to use Shelley's wife's infelicitous phrase) "to defecate life of its misery and its evil was the ruling passion of his soul." It was composed at the time (1818-1821) of Shelley's maturest works, works which present his romantic rage for revolt and his concepts of social order with a passionate intensity born of conviction and commitment, and yet the play is

> written without any of the peculiar feelings and opinions which characterize my other compositions. I have attended simply to the development of such characters as it is probable the persons really were.

Have we the poet here "Seraphically free/ From taint of personality"? Or have we, as some critics confidently assert, unconscious self-revelation, Shelley as Beatrice? Has Shelley succeeded in baring his soul under the guise of a fiction, or has he anticipated the dramatic monologues of Browning, those marvelous studies in abnormal psychology in which Browning "managed to allow many of his imagined characters to be pretty much themselves" and "say *their* say, not Browning's" (K.L. Knickerbocker)? Indeed, did Browning succeed in doing that?

Whether because of a desire for objectivity or because of a half-grasped reticence that prevented Shelley from the romantic gesture of opening his heart, the play lacks the stirring sublimity and ethereal lyricism of the greatest of Shelley's longer works, *Prometheus Unbound.* It has moments of magnificence but as a whole leaves something unachieved. There is an unhealthy, a decadent smell about the play. Its subject matter is Elizabethan, but it has none of the "hearty, credulous love of straightforward bloodshed, murder and mutilation uncontaminated by sophisticated skill of setting" that Una Ellis-Fermor has recognized in the heaped horrors of *Titus Andronicus,* the sly ironies of *The Jew of Malta,* the almost childish gusto of *The Spanish Tragedy.* Shelley's characters move in the close, dark rooms of Jacobean drama, "moping melancholy mad"—but posturing, speaking the Jacobean disillusion ("With evil hap we are begot alas") with a certain masochistic enjoyment. The plain fact is that they move with declamatory despair in rooms interior-decorated with black velvet, in prefabricated ruins. They are not creatures trapped in life: they are creations escaped from Gothic novels.

We miss the greatness of the Elizabethans and the Jacobeans. We sense the desire to commit literature. We emerge from the play having experienced some moving scenes, particularly those of pathos, but we have not experienced a dramatist fighting his way through a problem to a solution. Ford gives us at last a philosophy, though it be only "Look you, the stars shine still." Shelley gives us a tableau. We have not been involved with "real" people, characters so vital that they can, as they do over and over again in Webster, elevate the human spirit with a simple line ("I am Duchess of Malfi still") or make credible a clever one: "We are meerely the Stars tennys-balls, strooke and banded/ Which way please them." We are never compelled to grant what Shelley's fellow Romantic called "the willing suspension of disbelief" but can, if we wish, sit back and say *that* bit is classical dramaturgy, *that* bit is romantic passion, *that* bit is Gothic claptrap. We miss the thunderous authentic voice of Shelley, and so we note the echoes of Aeschylus and Sophocles, Shakespeare and Webster, Calderón de la Barca and Matthew Gregory ("Monk") Lewis. We notice when the verse is too contrived to be human speech, when the soliloquies hold up the action; when there is more plot than doom, when the actors are declaiming instead of impersonating. Only once does Beatrice, the central figure in this nightmare world, achieve humanity. Then only the most hard-hearted would not weep. But the rest is redolent of ersatz emotionalism and hothouse horror. It is not surprising that Mary Shelley, who wrote *Frankenstein,* should have thought this her husband's masterpiece. In 1869 Swinburne wrote in the *Fortnightly Review:*

> This is evidence enough that if Shelley had lived the 'Cenci' would not now be the one great play written in the great manner of Shakespeare's men that our literature has seen since the time of these.

Modern critics have been a little more acute and less than kind. In 1936 F. R. Leavis had a different view of writing in "the great manner"; in *Revaluation: Tradition and Development in English Poetry* he noted *The Cenci*'s "perverse luxury of insistence, not merely upon horror, but upon malignity" (which Swinburne had called being "able to face the light of hell as well as of heaven, to handle the fires of evil"). Leavis identified Shelley with Beatrice. He insisted that "*vis inertia* . . . the power of conventional valuation to perpetuate itself" should not keep us from seeing that "*The Cenci* is very bad and that its badness is characteristic," that it "confirms all the worst in the account of Shelley." Leavis contrasts Shakespeare with "the vague, generalizing externality" of Shelley's dramatic poetry, and the comparison is justified thus:

> There are, of course, touches of Webster: Beatrice in the trial scene is commonly recognized to have borrowed an effect or two from the White Devil. But the Shakespearian promptings are everywhere, in some places almost ludicrously assorted, obvious and thick. For instance, Act III, Sc. ii starts (stage direction: 'Thunder and the sound of a storm') by being at line two obviously Lear. At line eight Othello comes in and carries on for ten lines; and he reasserts himself at line fifty. At line fifty-five Hamlet speaks. At line seventy-eight we get an effect from *Macbeth,* to be followed by many more in the next act, during which, after much borrowed suspense, the Count's murder is consummated.

What Leavis says about some lines in *The Cenci* that derive from *Othello* ("not from a sharply imagined situation, but from vaguely remembered reading") may in the long run be applied to Shelley's play as a whole and indeed to the poetic dramas of Browning, Tennyson, and the rest:

> They are distasteful because there is strong feeling, and the feeling is false. It is false because it is forced. It does not inhere in a concretely imagined particular situation, but is a general emotion pumped in from outside. . . .

But *The Cenci* has been played. When Thomas Love Peacock offered it for Shelley, anonymously, it was refused. Macready would have returned from retirement to do it, but the censor said no. The Shelley Society production (May 7, 1886) had to be private, for the Lord Chamberlain would not grant a license, but the play had been done in French in Paris two years before (with the poet Paul Fort as Cardinal Camillo). There were several London productions in the 1920's and 1930's, one with Sybil Thorndike, and the Lenox Hill Players gave the first of several American performances on May 19, 1926. I cannot agree with Mary Shelley that it is "the best tragedy of modern times," or with Swinburne that it is "the greatest tragedy that has been written in any language for upward of two centuries," but the eminent English critic James Agate might; for in *At Half-Past Eight* (1923) he wrote that *The Cenci* is

> part of the passionate propaganda of a noble mind, which swells the theatre of its presentation to the scope and dimension of a cathedral. . . . *The Cenci* is written on three planes—a ground floor of normal significance, a middle story of spiritual meaning, and an attic wherein the idea streams out of the window, the emanation of a philosophy.

Beatrice, the absolutely unforgettable scheming and sensual woman, all fire and ice, is therefore

> first . . . an individual victim, then a symbol of maiden virtue rudely strumpeted, and . . . [then] the embodiment of a pure philosophic idea—the idea of Rebellion. That was what Shelley, whose ruling passion was revolt, was after.

DEDICATION TO LEIGH HUNT, Esq.

My Dear Friend—I inscribe with your name, from a distant country, and after an absence whose months have seemed years, this the latest of my literary efforts.

Those writings which I have hitherto published have been little else than visions which impersonate my own apprehensions of the beautiful and the just. I can also perceive in them the literary defects incidental to youth and impatience; they are dreams of what ought to be, or may be. The drama which I now present to you is a sad reality. I lay aside the presumptuous attitude of an instructor, and am content to paint, with such colours as my own heart furnishes, that which has been.

Had I known a person more highly endowed than yourself with all that it becomes a man to possess, I had solicited for this work the ornament of his name. One more gentle, honourable, innocent, and brave; one of more exalted toleration for all who do and think evil, and yet himself more free from evil; one who knows better how to receive, and how to confer a benefit, though he must ever confer far more than he can receive; one of simpler, and, in the highest sense of the word, of purer life and manners I never knew: and I had already been fortunate in friendships when your name was added to the list.

In that patient and irreconcilable enmity with domestic and political tyranny and imposture which the tenor of your life has illustrated, and which, had I health and talents, should illustrate mine, let us, comforting each other in our task, live and die.

All happiness attend you! Your affectionate friend,

Percy B. Shelley.

Rome, May 29, 1819.

PREFACE

A manuscript was communicated to me during my travels in Italy, which was copied from the archives of the Cenci Palace at Rome, and contains a detailed account of the horrors which ended in the extinction of one of the noblest and richest families of that city, during the Pontificate of Clement VIII., in the year 1599. The story is, that an old man, having spent his life in debauchery and wickedness, conceived at length an implacable hatred towards his children; which showed itself towards one daughter under the form of an incestuous passion, aggravated by every circumstance of cruelty and violence. This daughter, after long and vain attempts to escape from what she considered a perpetual contamination both of body and mind, at length plotted with her mother-in-law and brother to murder their common tyrant. The young maiden, who was urged to this tremendous deed by an impulse which overpowered its horror, was evidently a most gentle and amiable being, a creature formed to adorn and be admired, and thus violently thwarted from her nature by the necessity of circumstance and opinion. The deed was quickly discovered, and, in spite of the most earnest prayers made to the Pope by the highest persons in Rome, the criminals were put to death. The old man had during his life repeatedly bought his pardon from the Pope for capital crimes of the most enormous and unspeakable kind, at the price of a hundred thousand crowns: the death therefore of his victims can scarcely be accounted for by the love of justice. The Pope, among other motives for severity, probably felt that whoever killed the Count Cenci deprived his treasury of a certain and copious source of revenue.* Such a story, if told so as to present to the reader all the feelings of those who once acted it, their hopes and fears, their confidences and misgivings, their various interests, passions, and opinions, acting upon and with each other, yet all conspiring to one tremendous end, would be as a light to make apparent some of the most dark and secret caverns of the human heart.

On my arrival at Rome I found that the story of the Cenci was a subject not to be mentioned in Italian society without awakening a deep and breathless interest; and that the feelings of the company never failed to incline to a romantic pity for the wrongs and a passionate exculpation of the horrible deed to which they urged her who has been mingled two centuries with the common dust. All ranks of people knew the outlines of this history, and participated in the overwhelming interest which it seems to have the magic of exciting in the human heart. I had a copy of Guido's picture of Beatrice which is preserved in the Colonna Palace, and my servant instantly recognized it as the portrait of La Cenci.

This national and universal interest which the story produces and has produced for two centuries and among all ranks of people in a great City, where the imagination is kept for ever active and awake, first suggested to me the conception of its fitness for a dramatic purpose. In fact it is a tragedy which has already received, from its capacity of awakening and sustaining the sympathy of men, approbation and success. Nothing remained as I imagined but to clothe it to the apprehensions of my countrymen in such language and action as would bring it home to their hearts. The deepest and the sublimest tragic

* The Papal Government formerly took the most extraordinary precautions against the publicity of facts which offer so tragical a demonstration of its own wickedness and weakness; so that the communication of the MS. had become, until very lately, a matter of some difficulty.

compositions, King Lear *and the two plays in which the tale of Œdipus is told, were stories which already existed in tradition, as matters of popular belief and interest, before Shakespeare and Sophocles made them familiar to the sympathy of all succeeding generations of mankind.*

This story of the Cenci is indeed eminently fearful and monstrous; anything like a dry exhibition of it on the stage would be insupportable. The person who would treat such a subject must increase the ideal and diminish the actual horror of the events, so that the pleasure which arises from the poetry which exists in these tempestuous sufferings and crimes may mitigate the pain of the contemplation of the moral deformity from which they spring. There must also be nothing attempted to make the exhibition subservient to what is vulgarly termed a moral purpose. The highest moral purpose aimed at in the highest species of the drama, is the teaching the human heart, through its sympathies and antipathies, the knowledge of itself; in proportion to the possession of which knowledge, every human being is wise, just, sincere, tolerant and kind. If dogmas can do more, it is well: but a drama is no fit place for the enforcement of them. Undoubtedly, no person can be truly dishonoured by the act of another; and the fit return to make to the most enormous injuries is kindness and forbearance and a resolution to convert the injurer from his dark passions by peace and love. Revenge, retaliation, atonement, are pernicious mistakes. If Beatrice had thought in this manner she would have been wiser and better; but she would never have been a tragic character. The few whom such an exhibition would have interested, could never have been sufficiently interested for a dramatic purpose, from the want of finding sympathy in their interest among the mass who surround them. It is in the restless and anatomizing casuistry with which men seek the justification of Beatrice, yet feel that she has done what needs justification; it is in the superstitious horror with which they contemplate alike her wrongs and their revenge,—that the dramatic character of what she did and suffered, consists.

I have endeavoured as nearly as possible to represent the characters as they probably were, and have sought to avoid the error of making them actuated by my own conceptions of right or wrong, false or true: thus under a thin veil converting names and actions of the sixteenth century into cold impersonations of my own mind. They are represented as Catholics, and as Catholics deeply tinged with religion. To a Protestant apprehension there will appear something unnatural in the earnest and perpetual sentiment of the relations between God and men which pervade the tragedy of the Cenci. It will especially be startled at the combination of an undoubting persuasion of the truth of the popular religion with a cool and determined perseverance in enormous guilt. But religion in Italy is not, as in Protestant countries, a cloak to be worn on particular days; or a passport which those who do not wish to be railed at carry with them to exhibit; or a gloomy passion for penetrating the impenetrable mysteries of our being, which terrifies its possessor at the darkness of the abyss to the brink of which it has conducted him. Religion coexists, as it were, in the mind of an Italian Catholic, with a faith in that of which all men have the most certain knowledge. It is interwoven with the whole fabric of life. It is adoration, faith, submission, penitence, blind admiration; not a rule for moral conduct. It has no necessary connection with any one virtue. The most atrocious villain may be rigidly devout, and without any shock to established faith, confess himself to be so. Religion pervades intensely the whole frame of society, and is, according to the temper of the mind which it inhabits, a passion, a persuasion, an excuse, a refuge; never a check. Cenci himself built a chapel in the Court of his Palace, and dedicated it to St. Thomas the Apostle, and established masses for the peace of his soul. Thus in the first scene of the fourth act Lucretia's design in exposing herself to the consequences of an expostulation with Cenci after having administered the opiate was to induce him by a feigned tale to confess himself before death; this being esteemed by Catholics as essential to salvation: and she only relinquishes her purpose when she perceives that her perseverance would expose Beatrice to new outrages.

*I have avoided with great care in writing this play the introduction of what is commonly called mere poetry, and I imagine there will scarcely be found a detached simile or a single isolated description, unless Beatrice's description of the chasm appointed for her father's murder should be judged to be of that nature.**

In a dramatic composition the imagery and the passion should interpenetrate one another, the former being reserved simply for the full development and illustration of the latter. Imagination is as the immortal God which should assume flesh for the redemption of mortal passion. It is thus that the most remote and the most familiar imagery may alike be fit for dramatic purposes when employed in the illustration of strong feeling, which raises what is low, and levels to the apprehension that which is lofty, casting over all the shadow of its own greatness. In other respects, I have written more carelessly; that is, without an over-fastidious and learned choice of words. In this respect I entirely agree with those modern critics who assert that in order to move men to true sympathy we must use the familiar language of men, and that our great ancestors the ancient English poets are the writers, a study of whom might incite us

---

* *An idea in this speech was suggested by a most sublime passage in* El Purgatorio de San Patricio *of Calderon; the only plagiarism which I have intentionally committed in the whole piece.*

to do that for our own age which they have done for theirs. But it must be the real language of men in general and not that of any particular class to whose society the writer happens to belong. So much for what I have attempted; I need not be assured that success is a very different matter; particularly for one whose attention has but newly been awakened to the study of dramatic literature.

I endeavoured whilst at Rome to observe such monuments of this story as might be accessible to a stranger. The portrait of Beatrice at the Colonna Palace is admirable as a work of art: it was taken by Guido during her confinement in prison. But it is most interesting as a just representation of one of the loveliest specimens of the workmanship of Nature. There is a fixed and pale composure upon the features; she seems sad and stricken down in spirit, yet the despair thus expressed is lightened by the patience of gentleness. Her head is bound with folds of white drapery from which the yellow strings of her golden hair escape and fall about her neck. The moulding of her face is exquisitely delicate; the eyebrows are distinct and arched; the lips have that permanent meaning of imagination and sensibility which suffering has not repressed and which it seems as if death scarcely could extinguish. Her forehead is large and clear; her eyes, which we are told were remarkable for their vivacity, are swollen with weeping and lustreless, but beautifully tender and serene. In the whole mien there is a simplicity and dignity which, united with her exquisite loveliness and deep sorrow, are inexpressibly pathetic. Beatrice Cenci appears to have been one of those rare persons in whom energy and gentleness dwell together without destroying one another: her nature was simple and profound. The crimes and miseries in which she was an actor and a sufferer are as the mask and the mantle in which circumstances clothed her for her impersonation on the scene of the world.

The Cenci Palace is of great extent; and though in part modernized, there yet remains a vast and gloomy pile of feudal architecture in the same state as during the dreadful scenes which are the subject of this tragedy. The Palace is situated in an obscure corner of Rome, near the quarter of the Jews, and from the upper windows you see the immense ruins of Mount Palatine half hidden under their profuse overgrowth of trees. There is a court in one part of the Palace (perhaps that in which Cenci built the Chapel to St. Thomas), supported by granite columns and adorned with antique friezes of fine workmanship, and built up, according to the ancient Italian fashion, with balcony over balcony of open-work. One of the gates of the Palace formed of immense stones and leading through a passage, dark and lofty and opening into gloomy subterranean chambers, struck me particularly.

Of the Castle of Petrella, I could obtain no further information than that which is to be found in the manuscript.

THE CENCI

A TRAGEDY IN FIVE ACTS

by

Percy Bysshe Shelley

First published 1819, this play was first acted by The Shelley Society, on May 7, 1886.

DRAMATIS PERSONÆ

Count FRANCESCO CENCI
GIACOMO, BERNARDO — *his Sons*
Cardinal CAMILLO
Prince COLONNA
ORSINO, *a Prelate*

SAVELLA, *Legate of Pope Clement VIII*
OLIMPIO, MARZIO — *Assassins*
ANDREA, *Servant to Count Cenci*
Nobles, Judges
Guards, Servants

LUCRETIA, *Wife of Count Cenci and Step-Mother of his Children*
BEATRICE, *Daughter of Count Cenci*

Scene:

ACT I
Scene 1: An Apartment in the Cenci Palace, Rome
Scene 2: The Garden of the Cenci Palace
Scene 3: A Magnificent Banquet Hall in the Palace

ACT II
Scene 1: An Apartment in the Cenci Palace
Scene 2: A Chamber in the Vatican, Rome

ACT III
Scene 1: An Apartment in the Cenci Palace
Scene 2: A mean Apartment in Giacomo's House

ACT IV
Scene 1: An Apartment in the Castle of Petrella in the Apulian Apennines
Scene 2: Before the Castle of Petrella
Scene 3: An Apartment in the Castle
Scene 4: Another Apartment in the Castle

Time: During the Pontificate of Clement VIII (1592-1605).

ACT I

SCENE 1: *An Apartment in the Cenci Palace*

(*Enter* COUNT CENCI, *and* CARDINAL CAMILLO.)

CAMILLO. That matter of the murder is hushed up
If you consent to yield his Holiness
Your fief that lies beyond the Pincian gate.
It needed all my interest in the conclave
To bend him to this point; he said that you
Bought perilous impunity with your gold;
That crimes like yours if once or twice compounded
Enriched the Church, and respited from hell
An erring soul which might repent and live;
But that the glory and the interest
Of the high throne he fills little consist
With making it a daily mart of guilt
As manifold and hideous as the deeds
Which you scarce hide from men's revolted eyes.

CENCI. The third of my possessions—let it go!
Ay, I once heard the nephew of the Pope
Had sent his architect to view the ground,
Meaning to build a villa on my vines
The next time I compounded with his uncle.
I little thought he should outwit me so!
Henceforth no witness—not the lamp—shall see
That which the vassal threatened to divulge,
Whose throat is choked with dust for his reward.
The deed he saw could not have rated higher
Than his most worthless life:—it angers me!
Respited me from Hell! So may the Devil

Respite their souls from Heaven! No doubt Pope Clement,
And his most charitable nephews, pray
That the Apostle Peter and the Saints
Will grant for their sake that I long enjoy
Strength, wealth, and pride, and lust, and length of days
Wherein to act the deeds which are the stewards
Of their revenue.—But much yet remains
To which they show no title.

CAMILLO. Oh, Count Cenci!
So much that thou mightst honourably live
And reconcile thyself with thine own heart
And with thy God, and with the offended world.
How hideously look deeds of lust and blood
Through those snow white and venerable hairs!—
Your children should be sitting round you now,
But that you fear to read upon their looks
The shame and misery you have written there.
Where is your wife? Where is your gentle daughter?
Methinks her sweet looks, which make all things else
Beauteous and glad, might kill the fiend within you.
Why is she barred from all society
But her own strange and uncomplaining wrongs?
Talk with me, Count,—you know I mean you well.
I stood beside your dark and fiery youth,
Watching its bold and bad career, as men
Watch meteors, but it vanished not; I marked
Your desperate and remorseless manhood; now
Do I behold you in dishonoured age
Charged with a thousand unrepented crimes.
Yet I have ever hoped you would amend,
And in that hope have saved your life three times.

CENCI. For which Aldobrandino owes you now
My fief beyond the Pincian. Cardinal,
One thing, I pray you, recollect henceforth,
And so we shall converse with less restraint.
A man you knew spoke of my wife and daughter—
He was accustomed to frequent my house;
So the next day *his* wife and daughter came
And asked if I had seen him; and I smiled:
I think they never saw him any more.

CAMILLO. Thou execrable man, beware!—
CENCI. Of thee?
Nay this is idle:—We should know each other.
As to my character for what men call crime
Seeing I please my senses as I list,
And vindicate that right with force or guile,
It is a public matter, and I care not
If I discuss it with you. I may speak
Alike to you and my own conscious heart—
For you give out that you have half reformed me;
Therefore strong vanity will keep you silent,
If fear should not; both will, I do not doubt.
All men delight in sensual luxury;
All men enjoy revenge; and most exult
Over the tortures they can never feel—
Flattering their secret peace with others' pain.
But I delight in nothing else. I love
The sight of agony, and the sense of joy,
When this shall be another's, and that mine.
And I have no remorse and little fear,
Which are, I think, the checks of other men.
This mood has grown upon me, until now
Any design my captious fancy makes
The picture of its wish—and it forms none
But such as men like you would start to know—
Is as my natural food and rest debarred
Until it be accomplished.
CAMILLO. Art thou not
Most miserable?
CENCI. Why, miserable?
No. I am what your theologians call
Hardened; which they must be in impudence,
So to revile a man's peculiar taste.
True, I was happier than I am, while yet
Manhood remained to act the thing I thought;—
While lust was sweeter than revenge; and now
Invention palls:—Ay, we must all grow old—
And but that there remains a deed to act
Whose horror might make sharp an appetite
Duller than mine—I'd do—I know not what.

When I was young I thought of nothing else
But pleasure; and I fed on honey sweets:
Men, by St. Thomas! cannot live like bees,
And I grew tired; yet, till I killed a foe,
And heard his groans, and heard his children's groans,
Knew I not what delight was else on earth,—
Which now delights me little. I the rather
Look on such pangs as terror ill conceals,
The dry, fixed eyeball—the pale, quivering lip,
Which tell me that the spirit weeps within
Tears bitterer than the bloody sweat of Christ.
I rarely kill the body, which preserves,
Like a strong prison, the soul within my power,
Wherein I feed it with the breath of fear
For hourly pain.

CAMILLO. Hell's most abandoned fiend
Did never, in the drunkenness of guilt,
Speak to his heart as now you speak to me;
I thank my God that I believe you not.

(*Enter* ANDREA.)

ANDREA. My Lord, a gentleman from Salamanca
Would speak with you.

CENCI. Bid him attend me in
The grand saloon. (*Exit* ANDREA.)

CAMILLO. Farewell; and I will pray
Almighty God that thy false, impious words
Tempt not his spirit to abandon thee. (*Exit* CAMILLO.)

CENCI. The third of my possessions! I must use
Close husbandry, or gold, the old man's sword,
Falls from my withered hand. But yesterday
There came an order from the Pope to make
Fourfold provision for my cursèd sons,
Whom I had sent from Rome to Salamanca,
Hoping some accident might cut them off,
And meaning, if I could, to starve them there.
I pray thee, God, send some quick death upon them!
Bernardo and my wife could not be worse
If dead and damned. Then, as to Beatrice—

(*Looking around him suspiciously.*)

I think they cannot hear me at that door;

What if they should? And yet I need not speak,
Though the heart triumphs with itself in words.
O, thou most silent air, that shalt not hear
What now I think! Thou pavement which I tread
Towards her chamber,—let your echoes talk
Of my imperious step scorning surprise,
But not of my intent!—Andrea!

(*Enter* ANDREA.)

ANDREA. My Lord?

CENCI. Bid Beatrice attend me in her chamber
This evening:—no, at midnight and alone. (*Exeunt.*)

SCENE 2: *A Garden of the Cenci Palace.*

(*Enter* BEATRICE *and* ORSINO, *as in conversation.*)

BEATRICE. Pervert not truth,
Orsino. You remember where we held
That conversation;—nay, we see the spot
Even from this cypress; two long years are past
Since, on an April midnight, underneath
The moonlight ruins of mount Palatine,
I did confess to you my secret mind.

ORSINO. You said you loved me then.

BEATRICE. You are a Priest,
Speak to me not of love.

ORSINO. I may obtain
The dispensation of the Pope to marry.
Because I am a Priest do you believe
Your image, as the hunter some struck deer,
Follows me not whether I wake or sleep?

BEATRICE. As I have said, speak to me not of love;
Had you a dispensation, I have not;
Nor will I leave this home of misery
Whilst my poor Bernard, and that gentle lady
To whom I owe life, and these virtuous thoughts,
Must suffer what I still have strength to share.
Alas, Orsino! All the love that once
I felt for you, is turned to bitter pain.
Ours was a youthful contract, which you first

Broke, by assuming vows no Pope will loose.
And thus I love you still, but holily,
Even as a sister or a spirit might;
And so I swear a cold fidelity.
And it is well perhaps we shall not marry.
You have a sly, equivocating vein
That suits me not.—Ah, wretched that I am!
Where shall I turn? Even now you look on me
As you were not my friend, and as if you
Discovered that I thought so, with false smiles
Making my true suspicion seem your wrong.
Ah, no! forgive me; sorrow makes me seem
Sterner than else my nature might have been;
I have a weight of melancholy thoughts,
And they forebode,—but what can they forebode
Worse than I now endure?

ORSINO. All will be well.
Is the petition yet prepared? You know
My zeal for all you wish, sweet Beatrice;
Doubt not but I will use my utmost skill
So that the Pope attend to your complaint.

BEATRICE. Your zeal for all I wish;—Ah me, you are cold!
Your utmost skill . . . speak but one word . . . (*Aside.*) Alas!
Weak and deserted creature that I am,
Here I stand bickering with my only friend! (*To* ORSINO.)
This night my father gives a sumptuous feast,
Orsino; he has heard some happy news
From Salamanca, from my brothers there,
And with this outward show of love he mocks
His inward hate. 'Tis bold hypocrisy,
For he would gladlier celebrate their deaths,
Which I have heard him pray for on his knees:
Great God! that such a father should be mine!
But there is mighty preparation made,
And all our kin, the Cenci, will be there,
And all the chief nobility of Rome.
And he has bidden me and my pale Mother
Attire ourselves in festival array.
Poor lady! She expects some happy change
In his dark spirit from this act; I none.

At supper I will give you the petition;
Till when—farewell.

ORSINO. Farewell. (*Exit* BEATRICE.) I know the Pope
Will ne'er absolve me from my priestly vow
But by absolving me from the revenue
Of many a wealthy see; and, Beatrice,
I think to win thee at an easier rate.
Nor shall he read her eloquent petition:
He might bestow her on some poor relation
Of his sixth cousin, as he did her sister,
And I should be debarred from all access.
Then as to what she suffers from her father,
In all this there is much exaggeration:—
Old men are testy, and will have their way;
A man may stab his enemy, or his vassal,
And live a free life as to wine or women,
And with a peevish temper may return
To a dull home, and rate his wife and children;
Daughters and wives call this foul tyranny.
I shall be well content if on my conscience
There rest no heavier sin than what they suffer
From the devices of my love—a net
From which she shall escape not. Yet I fear
Her subtle mind, her awe-inspiring gaze,
Whose beams anatomize me, nerve by nerve,
And lay me bare, and make me blush to see
My hidden thoughts.—Ah, no! A friendless girl
Who clings to me, as to her only hope:—
I were a fool, not less than if a panther
Were panic-stricken by the antelope's eye,
If she escape me. (*Exit.*)

SCENE 3: *A Magnificent Hall in the Cenci Palace. A Banquet.*

(*Enter* CENCI, LUCRETIA, BEATRICE, PRINCE COLONNA, ORSINO, CAMILLO, NOBLES.)

CENCI. Welcome, my friends and kinsmen; welcome ye,
Princes and Cardinals, pillars of the church,
Whose presence honours our festivity.

I have too long lived like an anchorite,
And in my absence from your merry meetings
An evil word is gone abroad of me;
But I do hope that you, my noble friends,
When you have shared the entertainment here,
And heard the pious cause for which 'tis given,
And we have pledged a health or two together,
Will think me flesh and blood as well as you;
Sinful indeed, for Adam made all so,
But tender-hearted, meek and pitiful.

FIRST GUEST. In truth, my Lord, you seem too light of heart,
Too sprightly and companionable a man,
To act the deeds that rumour pins on you.
(*To his Companion.*) I never saw such blithe and open cheer
In any eye!

SECOND GUEST. Some most desired event,
In which we all demand a common joy,
Has brought us hither; let us hear it, Count.

CENCI. It is indeed a most desired event.
If, when a parent from a parent's heart
Lifts from this earth to the great Father of all
A prayer, both when he lays him down to sleep,
And when he rises up from dreaming it;
One supplication, one desire, one hope,
That he would grant a wish for his two sons,
Even all that he demands in their regard—
And suddenly beyond his dearest hope
It is accomplished, he should then rejoice,
And call his friends and kinsmen to a feast,
And task their love to grace his merriment,—
Then honour me thus far—for I am he.

BEATRICE (*to* LUCRETIA). Great God! How horrible! Some dreadful ill
Must have befallen my brothers.

LUCRETIA. Fear not, Child,
He speaks too frankly.

BEATRICE. Ah! My blood runs cold.
I fear that wicked laughter round his eye,
Which wrinkles up the skin even to the hair.

CENCI. Here are the letters brought from Salamanca;
Beatrice, read them to your mother. God!

I thank thee! In one night didst thou perform,
By ways inscrutable, the thing I sought.
My disobedient and rebellious sons
Are dead!—Why, dead!—What means this change of cheer?
You hear me not, I tell you they are dead;
And they will need no food or raiment more;
The tapers that did light them the dark way
Are their last cost. The Pope, I think, will not
Expect I should maintain them in their coffins.
Rejoice with me—my heart is wondrous glad.

(LUCRETIA *sinks, half fainting;* BEATRICE *supports her.*)

BEATRICE. It is not true!—Dear lady, pray look up.
Had it been true—there is a God in heaven—
He would not live to boast of such a boon.
Unnatural man, thou knowest that it is false.

CENCI. Ay, as the word of God; whom here I call
To witness that I speak the sober truth;
And whose most favouring Providence was shown
Even in the manner of their deaths. For Rocco
Was kneeling at the mass, with sixteen others,
When the church fell and crushed him to a mummy;
The rest escaped unhurt. Cristofano
Was stabbed in error by a jealous man,
Whilst she he loved was sleeping with his rival;
All in the self-same hour of the same night;
Which shows that Heaven has special care of me.
I beg those friends who love me, that they mark
The day a feast upon their calendars.
It was the twenty-seventh of December:
Ay, read the letters if you doubt my oath.

(*The Assembly appears confused; several of the Guests rise.*)

FIRST GUEST. Oh, horrible! I will depart—

SECOND GUEST. And I.—

THIRD GUEST. No, stay!
I do believe it is some jest; though, faith!
'Tis mocking us somewhat too solemnly.
I think his son has married the Infanta,
Or found a mine of gold in El Dorado;
'Tis but to season some such news; stay, stay!
I see 'tis only raillery by his smile.

CENCI (*filling a bowl of wine and lifting it up*). Oh, thou bright wine whose purple splendour leaps
And bubbles gaily in this golden bowl
Under the lamplight, as my spirits do,
To hear the death of my accursèd sons!
Could I believe thou wert their mingled blood,
Then would I taste thee like a sacrament,
And pledge with thee the mighty Devil in Hell,
Who, if a father's curses, as men say,
Climb with swift wings after their children's souls,
And drag them from the very throne of Heaven,
Now triumphs in my triumph!—But thou art
Superfluous; I have drunken deep of joy,
And I will taste no other wine to-night.
Here, Andrea! Bear the bowl around.

A GUEST (*rising*). Thou wretch!
Will none among this noble company
Check the abandoned villain?

CAMILLO. For God's sake,
Let me dismiss the guests! You are insane.
Some ill will come of this.

SECOND GUEST. Seize, silence him!

FIRST GUEST. I will!

THIRD GUEST. And I!

CENCI (*addressing those who rise with a threatening gesture*). Who moves? Who speaks? (*turning to the Company*) 'tis nothing,
Enjoy yourselves.—Beware! For my revenge
Is as the sealed commission of a king
That kills, and none dare name the murderer.

(*The Banquet is broken up; several of the Guests are departing.*)

BEATRICE. I do entreat you, go not, noble guests;
What, although tyranny and impious hate
Stand sheltered by a father's hoary hair?
What, if 'tis he who clothed us in these limbs
Who tortures them, and triumphs? What, if we,
The desolate and the dead, were his own flesh,
His children and his wife, whom he is bound
To love and shelter? Shall we therefore find
No refuge in this merciless wide world?
O think what deep wrongs must have blotted out

First love, then reverence, in a child's prone mind,
Till it thus vanquish shame and fear! O think!
I have borne much, and kissed the sacred hand
Which crushed us to the earth, and thought its stroke
Was perhaps some paternal chastisement!
Have excused much, doubted; and when no doubt
Remained, have sought by patience, love and tears
To soften him, and when this could not be
I have knelt down through the long sleepless nights,
And lifted up to God, the Father of all,
Passionate prayers: and when these were not heard
I have still borne,—until I meet you here,
Princes and kinsmen, at this hideous feast
Given at my brothers' deaths. Two yet remain;
His wife remains and I, whom if ye save not,
Ye may soon share such merriment again
As fathers make over their children's graves.
O Prince Colonna, thou art our near kinsman;
Cardinal, thou art the Pope's chamberlain;
Camillo, thou art chief justiciary;
Take us away!

CENCI. (*He has been conversing with* CAMILLO *during the first part of* BEATRICE'S *speech; he hears the conclusion, and now advances.*)
I hope my good friends here
Will think of their own daughters—or perhaps
Of their own throats—before they lend an ear
To this wild girl.

BEATRICE (*not noticing the words of Cenci*). Dare no one look on me?
None answer? Can one tyrant overbear
The sense of many best and wisest men?
Or is it that I sue not in some form
Of scrupulous law, that ye deny my suit?
O God! That I were buried with my brothers!
And that the flowers of this departed spring
Were fading on my grave! And that my father
Were celebrating now one feast for all!

CAMILLO. A bitter wish for one so young and gentle;
Can we do nothing?

COLONNA. Nothing that I see.
Count Cenci were a dangerous enemy;

Yet I would second any one.
A CARDINAL. And I.
CENCI. Retire to your chamber, insolent girl!
BEATRICE. Retire thou, impious man! Ay, hide thyself
Where never eye can look upon thee more!
Wouldst thou have honour and obedience,
Who art a torturer? Father, never dream
Though thou mayst overbear this company,
But ill must come of ill. Frown not on me!
Haste, hide thyself, lest with avenging looks
My brothers' ghosts should hunt thee from thy seat!
Cover thy face from every living eye,
And start if thou but hear a human step;
Seek out some dark and silent corner, there,
Bow thy white head before offended God,
And we will kneel around, and fervently
Pray that he pity both ourselves and thee.
CENCI. My friends, I do lament this insane girl
Has spoilt the mirth of our festivity.
Good night, farewell; I will not make you longer
Spectators of our dull domestic quarrels.
Another time.— (*Exeunt all but* CENCI *and* BEATRICE.)
My brain is swimming round;
Give me a bowl of wine! (*To* BEATRICE.)
Thou painted viper!
Beast that thou art! Fair and yet terrible!
I know a charm shall make thee meek and tame,
Now get thee from my sight! (*Exit* BEATRICE.)
Here, Andrea,
Fill up this goblet with Greek wine. I said
I would not drink this evening; but I must;
For, strange to say, I feel my spirits fail
With thinking what I have decreed to do. (*Drinking the wine.*)
Be thou the resolution of quick youth
Within my veins, and manhood's purpose stern,
And age's firm, cold, subtle villainy;
As if thou wert indeed my children's blood
Which I did thirst to drink! The charm works well;
It must be done; it shall be done, I swear! (*Exit.*)

End of the First Act.

ACT II

SCENE 1: *An Apartment in the Cenci Palace.*

(*Enter* LUCRETIA *and* BERNARDO.)

LUCRETIA. Weep not, my gentle boy; he struck but me
Who have borne deeper wrongs. In truth, if he
Had killed me, he had done a kinder deed.
O God, Almighty, do Thou look upon us,
We have no other friend but only Thee!
Yet weep not; though I love you as my own,
I am not your true mother.

BERNARDO. O more, more,
Than ever mother was to any child,
That have you been to me! Had he not been
My father, do you think that I should weep!

LUCRETIA. Alas! Poor boy, what else couldst thou have done?

(*Enter* BEATRICE.)

BEATRICE (*in a hurried voice*). Did he pass this way? Have you seen him, brother?
Ah, no! that is his step upon the stairs;
'Tis nearer now; his hand is on the door;
Mother, if I to thee have ever been
A duteous child, now save me! Thou, great God,
Whose image upon earth a father is,
Dost Thou indeed abandon me? He comes;
The door is opening now; I see his face
He frowns on others but he smiles on me,
Even as he did after the feast last night.

(*Enter a Servant.*)

Almighty God, how merciful Thou art!
'Tis but Orsino's servant.—Well, what news?

SERVANT. My master bids me say, the Holy Father
Has sent back your petition thus unopened. (*Giving a paper.*)
And he demands at what hour 'twere secure
To visit you again?

LUCRETIA. At the Ave Mary. (*Exit Servant.*)
So, daughter, our last hope has failed. Ah me!
How pale you look; you tremble, and you stand

Wrapped in some fixed and fearful meditation,
As if one thought were over strong for you:
Your eyes have a chill glare; O, dearest child!
Are you gone mad? If not, pray speak to me.
BEATRICE. You see I am not mad; I speak to you.
LUCRETIA. You talked of something that your father did
After that dreadful feast? Could it be worse
Than when he smiled, and cried, "My sons are dead!"
And every one looked in his neighbour's face
To see if others were as white as he?
At the first word he spoke I felt the blood
Rush to my heart, and fell into a trance;
And when it passed I sat all weak and wild;
Whilst you alone stood up, and with strong words
Checked his unnatural pride; and I could see
The devil was rebuked that lives in him.
Until this hour thus have you ever stood
Between us and your father's moody wrath
Like a protecting presence; your firm mind
Has been our only refuge and defence:
What can have thus subdued it? What can now
Have given you that cold melancholy look,
Succeeding to your unaccustomed fear?
BEATRICE. What is that you say? I was just thinking
'Twere better not to struggle any more.
Men, like my father, have been dark and bloody;
Yet never—Oh! Before worse come of it
'Twere wise to die; it ends in that at last.
LUCRETIA. Oh, talk not so, dear child! Tell me at once
What did your father do or say to you?
He stayed not after that accursèd feast
One moment in your chamber.—Speak to me.
BERNARDO. Oh, sister, sister, prithee, speak to us!
BEATRICE (*speaking very slowly with a forced calmness*). It was one word,
Mother, one little word;
One look, one smile. (*Wildly.*) Oh! He has trampled me
Under his feet, and made the blood stream down
My pallid cheeks. And he has given us all
Ditch-water and the fever-stricken flesh
Of buffaloes, and bade us eat or starve,

And we have eaten. He has made me look
On my beloved Bernardo, when the rust
Of heavy chains has gangrened his sweet limbs,
And I have never yet despaired—but now!
What could I say? (*Recovering herself.*)
Ah, no! 'tis nothing new.
The sufferings we all share have made me wild;
He only struck and cursed me as he passed;
He said, he looked, he did,—nothing at all
Beyond his wont, yet it disordered me.
Alas! I am forgetful of my duty;
I should preserve my senses for your sake.
LUCRETIA. Nay, Beatrice; have courage, my sweet girl,
If any one despairs it should be I,
Who loved him once, and now must live with him
Till God in pity call for him or me.
For you may, like your sister, find some husband,
And smile, years hence, with children round your knees;
Whilst I, then dead, and all this hideous coil
Shall be remembered only as a dream.
BEATRICE. Talk not to me, dear lady, of a husband.
Did you not nurse me when my mother died?
Did you not shield me and that dearest boy?
And had we any other friend but you
In infancy, with gentle words and looks,
To win our father not to murder us?
And shall I now desert you? May the ghost
Of my dead Mother plead against my soul
If I abandon her who filled the place
She left, with more, even, than a mother's love!
BERNARDO. And I am of my sister's mind. Indeed
I would not leave you in this wretchedness,
Even though the Pope should make me free to live
In some blithe place, like others of my age,
With sports, and delicate food, and the fresh air.
Oh, never think that I will leave you, Mother!
LUCRETIA. My dear, dear children!
(*Enter* CENCI, *suddenly.*)
CENCI. What, Beatrice here!
Come hither! (*She shrinks back, and covers her face.*)

Nay, hide not your face, 'tis fair;
Look up! Why, yesternight you dared to look
With disobedient insolence upon me,
Bending a stern and an inquiring brow
On what I meant; whilst I then sought to hide
That which I came to tell you—but in vain.

BEATRICE (*wildly staggering towards the door*). O that the earth would gape! Hide me, O God!

CENCI. Then it was I whose inarticulate words
Fell from my lips, and who with tottering steps
Fled from your presence, as you now from mine.
Stay, I command you—from this day and hour
Never again, I think, with fearless eye,
And brow superior, and unaltered cheek,
And that lip made for tenderness or scorn,
Shalt thou strike dumb the meanest of mankind;
Me least of all. Now get thee to thy chamber!
Thou too, loathed image of thy cursèd mother, (*To* BERNARDO.)
Thy milky, meek face makes me sick with hate!

(*Exeunt* BEATRICE *and* BERNARDO.)

(*Aside.*) So much has passed between us as must make
Me bold, her fearful.—'Tis an awful thing
To touch such mischief as I now conceive;
So men sit shivering on the dewy bank,
And try the chill stream with their feet; once in . . .
How the delighted spirit pants for joy!

LUCRETIA (*advancing timidly towards him*). Oh husband! Pray forgive poor Beatrice.
She meant not any ill.

CENCI. Nor you perhaps?
Nor that young imp, whom you have taught by rote
Parricide with his alphabet? Nor Giacomo?
Nor those two most unnatural sons, who stirred
Enmity up against me with the Pope?
Whom in one night merciful God cut off:
Innocent lambs! They thought not any ill.
You were not here conspiring? You said nothing
Of how I might be dungeoned as a madman;
Or be condemned to death for some offence,
And you would be the witnesses?—This failing,

How just it were to hire assassins, or
Put sudden poison in my evening drink?
Or smother me when overcome by wine?
Seeing we had no other judge but God,
And He had sentenced me, and there were none
But you to be the executioners
Of His degree enregistered in Heaven?
Oh, no! You said not this?

LUCRETIA. So help me God,
I never thought the things you charge me with!

CENCI. If you dare speak that wicked lie again
I'll kill you. What! It was not by your counsel
That Beatrice disturbed the feast last night?
You did not hope to stir some enemies
Against me, and escape, and laugh to scorn
What every nerve of you now trembles at?
You judged that men were bolder than they are;
Few dare to stand between their grave and me.

LUCRETIA. Look not so dreadfully! By my salvation
I knew not aught that Beatrice designed;
Nor do I think she designed anything
Until she heard you talk of her dead brothers.

CENCI. Blaspheming liar! You are damned for this!
But I will take you where you may persuade
The stones you tread on to deliver you;
For men shall there be none but those who dare
All things—not question that which I command.
On Wednesday next I shall set out; you know
That savage rock, the Castle of Petrella:
'Tis safely walled, and moated round about:
Its dungeons underground, and its thick towers
Never told tales; though they have heard and seen
What might make dumb things speak. Why do you linger?
Make speediest preparation for the journey! (*Exit* LUCRETIA.)
The all-beholding sun yet shines; I hear
A busy stir of men about the streets;
I see the bright sky through the window panes:
It is a garish, broad, and peering day;
Loud, light, suspicious, full of eyes and ears;
And every little corner, nook, and hole

Is penetrated with the insolent light.
Come darkness! Yet, what is the day to me?
And wherefore should I wish for night, who do
A deed which shall confound both night and day?
'Tis she shall grope through a bewildering mist
Of horror; if there be a sun in heaven
She shall not dare to look upon its beams;
Nor feel its warmth. Let her then wish for night;
The act I think shall soon extinguish all
For me; I bear a darker deadlier gloom
Than the earth's shade, or interlunar air,
Or constellations quenched in murkiest cloud,
In which I walk secure and unbeheld
Towards my purpose.—Would that it were done! (*Exit.*)

SCENE 2: *A Chamber in the Vatican.*

(*Enter* CAMILLO *and* GIACOMO, *in conversation.*)
CAMILLO. There is an obsolete and doubtful law
By which you might obtain a bare provision
Of food and clothing—
GIACOMO. Nothing more? Alas!
Bare must be the provision which strict law
Awards, and agèd, sullen avarice pays.
Why did my father not apprentice me
To some mechanic trade? I should have then
Been trained in no highborn necessities
Which I could meet not by my daily toil.
The eldest son of a rich nobleman
Is heir to all his incapacities;
He has wide wants, and narrow powers. If you,
Cardinal Camillo, were reduced at once
From thrice-driven beds of down, and delicate food,
An hundred servants, and six palaces,
To that which nature doth indeed require?—
CAMILLO. Nay, there is reason in your plea; 'twere hard.
GIACOMO. 'Tis hard for a firm man to bear; but I
Have a dear wife, a lady of high birth,
Whose dowry in ill hour I lent my father,
Without a bond or witness to the deed:

And children, who inherit her fine senses,
The fairest creatures in this breathing world;
And she and they reproach me not. Cardinal,
Do you not think the Pope would interpose
And stretch authority beyond the law?
CAMILLO. Though your peculiar case is hard, I know
The Pope will not divert the course of law.
After that impious feast the other night
I spoke with him, and urged him then to check
Your father's cruel hand; he frowned and said,
"Children are disobedient, and they sting
Their fathers' hearts to madness and despair,
Requiting years of care with contumely.
I pity the Count Cenci from my heart;
His outraged love perhaps awakened hate,
And thus he is exasperated to ill.
In the great war between the old and young
I, who have white hairs and a tottering body,
Will keep at least blameless neutrality."
(*Enter* ORSINO.)
You, my good Lord Orsino, heard those words.
ORSINO. What words?
GIACOMO. Alas, repeat them not again!
There is no redress for me; at least
None but that which I may achieve myself,
Since I am driven to the brink.—But, say,
My innocent sister and my only brother
Are dying underneath my father's eye.
The memorable torturers of this land,
Galeaz Visconti, Borgia, Ezzelin,
Never inflicted on the meanest slave
What these endure; shall they have no protection?
CAMILLO. Why, if they would petition to the Pope
I see not how he could refuse it—yet
He holds it of most dangerous example
In aught to weaken the paternal power,
Being, as 'twere, the shadow of his own.
I pray you now excuse me. I have business
That will not bear delay. (*Exit* CAMILLO.)
GIACOMO. But you, Orsino,

Have the petition; wherefore not present it?
ORSINO. I have presented it, and backed it with
My earnest prayers, and urgent interest;
It was returned unanswered. I doubt not
But that the strange and execrable deeds
Alleged in it—in truth they might well baffle
Any belief—have turned the Pope's displeasure
Upon the accusers from the criminal:
So I should guess from what Camillo said.
GIACOMO. My friend, that palace-walking devil, Gold,
Has whispered silence to his Holiness;
And we are left, as scorpions ringed with fire.
What should we do but strike ourselves to death?
For he who is our murderous persecutor
Is shielded by a father's holy name,
Or I would— (*Stops abruptly.*)
ORSINO. What? Fear not to speak your thought.
Words are but holy as the deeds they cover;
A priest who has forsworn the God he serves;
A judge who makes Truth weep at his decree;
A friend who should weave counsel, as I now,
But as the mantle of some selfish guile;
A father who is all a tyrant seems,—
Were the profaner for his sacred name.
GIACOMO. Ask me not what I think; the unwilling brain
Feigns often what it would not; and we trust
Imagination with such phantasies
As the tongue dares not fashion into words,—
Which have no words, their horror makes them dim
To the mind's eye.—My heart denies itself
To think what you demand.
ORSINO. But a friend's bosom
Is at the inmost cave of our own mind,
Where we sit shut from the wide gaze of day,
And from the all-communicating air.
You look what I suspected—
GIACOMO. Spare me now!
I am as one lost in a midnight wood,
Who dares not ask some harmless passenger
The path across the wilderness, lest he,

As my thoughts are, should be—a murderer.
I know you are my friend, and all I dare
Speak to my soul that will I trust with thee.
But now my heart is heavy, and would take
Lone counsel from a night of sleepless care.
Pardon me, that I say farewell—farewell!
I would that to my own suspected self
I could address a word so full of peace.

ORSINO. Farewell!—Be your thoughts better or more bold.

(*Exit* GIACOMO.)

I had disposed the Cardinal Camillo
To feed his hope with cold encouragement:
It fortunately serves my close designs
That 'tis a trick of this same family
To analyse their own and other minds.
Such self-anatomy shall teach the will
Dangerous secrets; for it tempts our powers,
Knowing what must be thought, and may be done,
Into the depth of darkest purposes:
So Cenci fell into the pit; even I,
Since Beatrice unveiled me to myself,
And made me shrink from what I cannot shun,
Show a poor figure to my own esteem,
To which I grow half reconciled. I'll do
As little mischief as I can; that thought
Shall fee the accuser conscience.

(*After a pause.*) Now what harm
If Cenci should be murdered?—Yet, if murdered,
Wherefore by me? And what if I could take
The profit, yet omit the sin and peril
In such an action? Of all earthly things
I fear a man whose blows outspeed his words;
And such is Cenci: and while Cenci lives,
His daughter's dowry were a secret grave
If a priest wins her.—Oh, fair Beatrice!
Would that I loved thee not, or, loving thee,
Could but despise danger and gold and all
That frowns between my wish and its effect,
Or smiles beyond it! There is no escape . . .
Her bright form kneels beside me at the altar,

And follows me to the resort of men,
And fills my slumber with tumultuous dreams,
So when I wake my blood seems liquid fire;
And if I strike my damp and dizzy head
My hot palm scorches it; her very name,
But spoken by a stranger, makes my heart
Sicken and pant; and thus unprofitably
I clasp the phantom of unfelt delights
Till weak imagination half possesses
The self-created shadow. Yet much longer
Will I not nurse this life of feverous hours:
From the unravelled hopes of Giacomo
I must work out my own dear purposes.
I see, as from a tower, the end of all:
Her father dead; her brother bound to me
By a dark secret, surer than the grave;
Her mother scared and unexpostulating
From the dread manner of her wish achieved:
And she!—Once more take courage, my faint heart;
What dares a friendless maiden matched with thee?
I have such foresight as assures success:
Some unbeheld divinity doth ever,
When dread events are near, stir up men's minds
To black suggestions; and he prospers best,
Not who becomes the instrument of ill,
But who can flatter the dark spirit that makes
Its empire and its prey of other hearts
Till it become his slave—as I will do. (*Exit.*)

End of the Second Act.

ACT III

SCENE 1: *An Apartment in the Cenci Palace.*

(LUCRETIA; *to her enter* BEATRICE.)

BEATRICE. (*She enters staggering and speaks wildly.*) Reach me that handkerchief!—My brain is hurt;

My eyes are full of blood; just wipe them for me...
I see but indistinctly...

LUCRETIA. My sweet child,
You have no wound; 'tis only a cold dew
That starts from your dear brow... Alas! Alas!
What has befallen?

BEATRICE. How comes this hair undone?
Its wandering strings must be what blind me so,
And yet I tied it fast.—O, horrible!
The pavement sinks under my feet! The walls
Spin round! I see a woman weeping there,
And standing calm and motionless, whilst I
Slide giddily as the world reels.... My God!
The beautiful blue heaven is flecked with blood!
The sunshine on the floor is black! The air
Is changed to vapours such as the dead breathe
In charnel pits! Pah! I am choked! There creeps
A clinging, black, contaminating mist
About me... 'tis substantial, heavy, thick,
I cannot pluck it from me, for it glues
My fingers and my limbs to one another,
And eats into my sinews, and dissolves
My flesh to a pollution, poisoning
The subtle, pure, and inmost spirit of life!
My God! I never knew what the mad felt
Before; for I am mad beyond all doubt!
(*More wildly.*) No, I am dead! These putrefying limbs
Shut round and sepulchre the panting soul
Which would burst forth into the wandering air! (*A pause.*)
What hideous thought was that I had even now?
'Tis gone; and yet its burthen remains here
O'er these dull eyes... upon this weary heart!
O world! O life! O day! O misery!

LUCRETIA. What ails thee, my poor child? She answers not.
Her spirit apprehends the sense of pain,
But not its cause; suffering has dried away
The source from which it sprung...

BEATRICE (*franticly*). Like Parricide...
Misery has killed its father: yet its father
Never like mine... O, God! What thing am I?

LUCRETIA. My dearest child, what has your father done?
BEATRICE (*doubtfully*). Who art thou, questioner? I have no father.
(*Aside.*) She is the madhouse nurse who tends on me,
It is a piteous office. (*To* LUCRETIA, *in a slow, subdued voice.*)
Do you know
I thought I was that wretched Beatrice
Men speak of, whom her father sometimes hales
From hall to hall by the entangled hair;
At others, pens up naked in damp cells
Where scaly reptiles crawl, and starves her there,
Till she will eat strange flesh. This woful story
So did I overact in my sick dreams,
That I imagined . . . no, it cannot be!
Horrible things have been in this wide world,
Prodigious mixtures, and confusions strange
Of good and ill; and worse have been conceived
Than ever there was found a heart to do.
But never fancy imaged such a deed
As . . . (*Pauses, suddenly recollecting herself.*)
Who art thou? Swear to me, ere I die
With fearful expectation, that indeed
Thou art not what thou seemest . . . Mother!
LUCRETIA. Oh!
My sweet child, know you . . .
BEATRICE. Yet—speak it not;
For then if this be truth, that other too
Must be a truth, a firm enduring truth,
Linked with each lasting circumstance of life,
Never to change, never to pass away.
Why so it is. This is the Cenci Palace;
Thou art Lucretia; I am Beatrice,
I have talked some wild words, but will no more.
Mother, come near me: from this point of time,
I am . . . (*Her voice dies away faintly.*)
LUCRETIA. Alas! What has befalled thee, child?
What has thy father done?
BEATRICE. What have I done?
Am I not innocent? Is it my crime
That one with white hair, and imperious brow,
Who tortured me from my forgotten years,

As parents only dare, should call himself
My father, yet should be!—Oh, what am I?
What name, what place, what memory shall be mine?
What retrospects, outliving even despair?

LUCRETIA. He is a violent tyrant, surely, child;
We know that death alone can make us free;
His death or ours. But what can he have done
Of deadlier outrage or worse injury?
Thou art unlike thyself; thine eyes shoot forth
A wandering and strange spirit. Speak to me,
Unlock these pallid hands whose fingers twine
With one another.

BEATRICE. 'Tis the restless life
Tortured within them. If I try to speak,
I shall go mad. Ay, something must be done;
What, yet I know not . . . something which shall make
The thing that I have suffered but a shadow
In the dread lightning which avenges it;
Brief, rapid, irreversible, destroying
The consequence of what it cannot cure.
Some such thing is to be endured or done;
When I know what, I shall be still and calm.
And never anything will move me more.
But now!—O blood, which art my father's blood,
Circling through these contaminated veins,
If thou, poured forth on the polluted earth,
Could wash away the crime, and punishment
By which I suffer . . . no, that cannot be!
Many might doubt there were a God above
Who sees and permits evil, and so die;
That faith no agony shall obscure in me.

LUCRETIA. It must indeed have been some bitter wrong;
Yet what, I dare not guess. Oh, my lost child,
Hide not in proud impenetrable grief
Thy sufferings from my fear.

BEATRICE. I hide them not.
What are the words which you would have me speak?
I, who can feign no image in my mind
Of that which has transformed me; I, whose thought
Is like a ghost shrouded and folded up

In its own formless horror: of all words
That minister to mortal intercourse,
Which wouldst thou hear? For there is none to tell
My misery; if another ever knew
Aught like to it, she died as I will die,
And left it, as I must, without a name.
Death! Death! Our law and our religion call thee
A punishment and a reward . . . Oh, which
Have I deserved?

LUCRETIA. The peace of innocence,
Till in your season you be called to heaven.
Whate'er you may have suffered, you have done
No evil. Death must be the punishment
Of crime, or the reward of trampling down
The thorns which God has strewed upon the path
Which leads to immortality.

BEATRICE. Ay, death . . .
The punishment of crime. I pray thee, God,
Let me not be bewildered while I judge.
If I must live day after day, and keep
These limbs, the unworthy temple of Thy spirit,
As a foul den from which what Thou abhorrest
May mock Thee, unavenged . . . it shall not be!
Self-murder . . . no, that might be no escape,
For Thy decree yawns like a Hell between
Our will and it.—O! In this mortal world
There is no vindication and no law
Which can adjudge and execute the doom
Of that through which I suffer.

(*Enter* ORSINO.)

(*She approaches him solemnly.*) Welcome, Friend!
I have to tell you that, since last we met,
I have endured a wrong so great and strange,
That neither life nor death can give me rest.
Ask me not what it is, for there are deeds
Which have no form, sufferings which have no tongue.

ORSINO. And what is he who has thus injured you?

BEATRICE. The man they call my father; a dread name.

ORSINO. It cannot be . . .

BEATRICE. What it can be, or not,

Forbear to think. It is, and it has been;
Advise me how it shall not be again.
I thought to die; but a religious awe
Restrains me, and the dread lest death itself
Might be no refuge from the consciousness
Of what is yet unexpiated. Oh, speak!

ORSINO. Accuse him of the deed, and let the law
Avenge thee.

BEATRICE. Oh, ice-hearted counsellor!
If I could find a word that might make known
The crime of my destroyer; and that done,
My tongue should like a knife tear out the secret
Which cankers my heart's core; ay, lay all bare,
So that my unpolluted fame should be
With vilest gossips a stale mouthèd story;
A mock, a byword, an astonishment:—
If this were done, which never shall be done,
Think of the offender's gold, his dreaded hate,
And the strange horror of the accuser's tale,
Baffling belief, and overpowering speech;
Scarce whispered, unimaginable, wrapped
In hideous hints . . . Oh, most assured redress!

ORSINO. You will endure it then?

BEATRICE. Endure?—Orsino,
It seems your counsel is small profit.

(*Turns from him, and speaks half to herself.*)

Ay,
All must be suddenly resolved and done.
What is this undistinguishable mist
Of thoughts, which rise, like shadow after shadow,
Darkening each other?

ORSINO. Should the offender live?
Triumph in his misdeed? and make, by use,
His crime, whate'er it is, dreadful no doubt,
Thine element; until thou mayst become
Utterly lost; subdued even to the hue
Of that which thou permittest?

BEATRICE (*to herself*). Mighty death!
Thou double-visaged shadow! Only judge!
Rightfullest arbiter! (*She retires absorbed in thought.*)

LUCRETIA. If the lightning
Of God has e'er descended to avenge . . .
ORSINO. Blaspheme not! His high Providence commits
Its glory on this earth, and their own wrongs
Into the hands of men; if they neglect
To punish crime . . .
LUCRETIA. But if one, like this wretch,
Should mock, with gold, opinion, law, and power?
If there be no appeal to that which makes
The guiltiest tremble? If, because our wrongs,
For that they are unnatural, strange, and monstrous,
Exceed all measure of belief? O God!
If, for the very reasons which should make
Redress most swift and sure, our injurer triumphs?
And we, the victims, bear worse punishment
Than that appointed for their torturer?
ORSINO. Think not
But that there is redress where there is wrong,
So we be bold enough to seize it.
LUCRETIA. How?
If there were any way to make all sure,
I know not . . . but I think it might be good
To . . .
ORSINO. Why, his late outrage to Beatrice—
For it is such, as I but faintly guess,
As makes remorse dishonour, and leaves her
Only one duty, how she may avenge;
You, but one refuge from ills ill endured;
Me, but one counsel . . .
LUCRETIA. For we cannot hope
That aid, or retribution, or resource
Will arise thence, where every other one
Might find them with less need. (BEATRICE *advances.*)
ORSINO. Then . . .
BEATRICE. Peace, Orsino!
And, honoured Lady, while I speak, I pray,
That you put off, as garments overworn,
Forbearance and respect, remorse and fear,
And all the fit restraints of daily life,
Which have been borne from childhood, but which now

Would be a mockery to my holier plea.
As I have said, I have endured a wrong,
Which, though it be expressionless, is such
As asks atonement, both for what is past,
And lest I be reserved, day after day,
To load with crimes an overburthened soul,
And be . . . what ye can dream not. I have prayed
To God, and I have talked with my own heart,
And have unravelled my entangled will,
And have at length determined what is right.
Art thou my friend, Orsino? False or true?
Pledge thy salvation ere I speak.

ORSINO. I swear
To dedicate my cunning, and my strength,
My silence, and whatever else is mine,
To thy commands.

LUCRETIA. You think we should devise
His death?

BEATRICE. And execute what is devised,
And suddenly. We must be brief and bold.

ORSINO. And yet most cautious.

LUCRETIA. For the jealous laws
Would punish us with death and infamy
For that which it became themselves to do.

BEATRICE. Be cautious as ye may, but prompt. Orsino.
What are the means?

ORSINO. I know two dull, fierce outlaws,
Who think man's spirit as a worm's, and they
Would trample out, for any slight caprice,
The meanest or the noblest life. This mood
Is marketable here in Rome. They sell
What we now want.

LUCRETIA. To-morrow before dawn,
Cenci will take us to that lonely rock,
Petrella, in the Apulian Apennines.
If he arrive there . . .

BEATRICE. He must not arrive.

ORSINO. Will it be dark before you reach the tower?

LUCRETIA. The sun will scarce be set.

BEATRICE. But I remember

Two miles on this side of the fort, the road
Crosses a deep ravine; 'tis rough and narrow,
And winds with short turns down the precipice;
And in its depth there is a mighty rock,
Which has, from unimaginable years,
Sustained itself with terror and with toil
Over a gulf, and with the agony
With which it clings seems slowly coming down;
Even as a wretched soul hour after hour,
Clings to the mass of life; yet, clinging, leans;
And, leaning, makes more dark the dread abyss
In which it fears to fall; beneath this crag
Huge as despair, as if in weariness,
The melancholy mountain yawns; below,
You hear but see not an impetuous torrent
Raging among the caverns, and a bridge
Crosses the chasm; and high above there grow,
With intersecting trunks, from crag to crag,
Cedars, and yews, and pines; whose tangled hair
Is matted in one solid roof of shade
By the dark ivy's twine. At noonday here
'Tis twilight, and at sunset blackest night.

ORSINO. Before you reach that bridge make some excuse
For spurring on your mules, or loitering
Until . . .

BEATRICE. What sound is that?

LUCRETIA. Hark! No, it cannot be a servant's step;
It must be Cenci, unexpectedly
Returned . . . Make some excuse for being here.

BEATRICE (*to* ORSINO, *as she goes out*). That step we hear approach must never pass
The bridge of which we spoke.

(*Exeunt* LUCRETIA *and* BEATRICE.)

ORSINO. What shall I do?
Cenci must find me here, and I must bear
The imperious inquisition of his looks
As to what brought me hither; let me mask
Mine own in some inane and vacant smile.

(*Enter* GIACOMO, *in a hurried manner.*)

How! Have you ventured hither? Know you then

That Cenci is from home?
GIACOMO. I sought him here;
And now must wait till he returns.
ORSINO. Great God!
Weigh you the danger of this rashness?
GIACOMO. Ay!
Does my destroyer know his danger? We
Are now no more, as once, parent and child,
But man to man; the oppressor to the oppressed;
The slandered to the slanderer; foe to foe.
He has cast Nature off, which was his shield,
And Nature casts him off, who is her shame;
And I spurn both. Is it a father's throat
Which I will shake, and say, I ask not gold;
I ask not happy years; nor memories
Of tranquil childhood; nor home-sheltered love;
Though all these hast thou torn from me, and more;
But only my fair fame; only one hoard
Of peace, which I thought hidden from thy hate
Under the penury heaped on me by thee,
Or I will . . . God can understand and pardon,
Why should I speak with man?
ORSINO. Be calm, dear friend.
GIACOMO. Well, I will calmly tell you what he did.
This old Francesco Cenci, as you know,
Borrowed the dowry of my wife from me,
And then denied the loan; and left me so
In poverty, the which I sought to mend
By holding a poor office in the state.
It had been promised to me, and already
I bought new clothing for my raggèd babes,
And my wife smiled; and my heart knew repose.
When Cenci's intercession, as I found,
Conferred this office on a wretch, whom thus
He paid for vilest service. I returned
With this ill news, and we sate sad together
Solacing our despondency with tears
Of such affection and unbroken faith
As temper life's worst bitterness; when he,
As he is wont, came to upbraid and curse,

Mocking our poverty, and telling us
Such was God's scourge for disobedient sons.
And then, that I might strike him dumb with shame,
I spoke of my wife's dowry; but he coined
A brief yet specious tale, how I had wasted
The sum in secret riot; and he saw
My wife was touched, and he went smiling forth.
And when I knew the impression he had made,
And felt my wife insult with silent scorn
My ardent truth, and look averse and cold,
I went forth too; but soon returned again;
Yet not so soon but that my wife had taught
My children her harsh thoughts, and they all cried,
"Give us clothes, father! Give us better food!
What you in one night squander were enough
For months!" I looked, and saw that home was hell
And to that hell will I return no more
Until mine enemy has rendered up
Atonement, or, as he gave life to me
I will, reversing Nature's law . . .

ORSINO. Trust me,
The compensation which thou seekest here
Will be denied.

GIACOMO. Then . . . Are you not my friend?
Did you not hint at the alternative,
Upon the brink of which you see I stand,
The other day when we conversed together?
My wrongs were then less. That word parricide,
Although I am resolved, haunts me like fear.

ORSINO. It must be fear itself, for the bare word
Is hollow mockery. Mark, how wisest God
Draws to one point the threads of a just doom,
So sanctifying it: what you devise
Is, as it were, accomplished.

GIACOMO. Is he dead?

ORSINO. His grave is ready. Know that since we met
Cenci has done an outrage to his daughter.

GIACOMO. What outrage?

ORSINO. That she speaks not, but you may
Conceive such half conjectures as I do

From her fixed paleness, and the lofty grief
Of her stern brow, bent on the idle air,
And her severe unmodulated voice,
Drowning both tenderness and dread; and last
From this; that whilst her step-mother and I,
Bewildered in our horror, talked together
With obscure hints, both self-misunderstood
And darkly guessing, stumbling, in our talk,
Over the truth, and yet to its revenge,
She interrupted us, and with a look
Which told, before she spoke it, he must die . . .

GIACOMO. It is enough. My doubts are well appeased;
There is a higher reason for the act
Than mine; there is a holier judge than me,
A more unblamed avenger. Beatrice,
Who in the gentleness of thy sweet youth
Hast never trodden on a worm, or bruised
A living flower, but thou hast pitied it
With needless tears! Fair sister, thou in whom
Men wondered how such loveliness and wisdom
Did not destroy each other! Is there made
Ravage of thee? O, heart, I ask no more
Justification! Shall I wait, Orsino,
Till he return, and stab him at the door?

ORSINO. Not so; some accident might interpose
To rescue him from what is now most sure;
And you are unprovided where to fly,
How to excuse or to conceal. Nay, listen:
All is contrived; success is so assured
That . . .

(*Enter* BEATRICE.)

BEATRICE. 'Tis my brother's voice! You know me not?

GIACOMO. My sister, my lost sister!

BEATRICE. Lost indeed!
I see Orsino has talked with you, and
That you conjecture things too horrible
To speak, yet far less than the truth. Now, stay not,
He might return; yet kiss me; I shall know
That then thou hast consented to his death.
Farewell, farewell! Let piety to God,

Brotherly love, justice and clemency,
And all things that make tender hardest hearts,
Make thine hard, brother. Answer not—farewell. (*Exeunt severally.*)

SCENE 2: *A mean Apartment in* GIACOMO'S *House.* GIACOMO *alone.*

GIACOMO. 'Tis midnight, and Orsino comes not yet.
(*Thunder and the sound of a storm.*)
What! can the everlasting elements
Feel with a worm like man? If so, the shaft
Of mercy-wingèd lightning would not fall
On stones and trees. My wife and children sleep:
They are now living in unmeaning dreams;
But I must wake, still doubting if that deed
Be just which is most necessary. Oh,
Thou unreplenished lamp! whose narrow fire
Is shaken by the wind, and on whose edge
Devouring darkness hovers! Thou small flame,
Which, as a dying pulse rises and falls,
Still flickerest up and down, how very soon,
Did I not feed thee, wouldst thou fail and be
As thou hast never been! So wastes and sinks
Even now, perhaps, the life that kindled mine;
But that no power can fill with vital oil
That broken lamp of flesh. Ha! 'tis the blood
Which fed these veins that ebbs till all is cold;
It is the form that moulded mine that sinks
Into the white and yellow spasms of death;
It is the soul by which mine was arrayed
In God's immortal likeness which now stands
Naked before Heaven's judgment seat! (*A bell strikes.*)
One! Two!
The hours crawl on; and, when my hairs are white,
My son will then perhaps be waiting thus,
Tortured between just hate and vain remorse;
Chiding the tardy messenger of news
Like those which I expect. I almost wish
He be not dead, although my wrongs are great;

Yet . . . 'tis Orsino's step.
(*Enter* ORSINO.)
Speak!
ORSINO. I am come
To say he has escaped.
GIACOMO. Escaped!
ORSINO. And safe
Within Petrella. He passed by the spot
Appointed for the deed an hour too soon.
GIACOMO. Are we the fools of such contingencies?
And do we waste in blind misgivings thus
The hours when we should act? Then wind and thunder
Which seemed to howl his knell, is the loud laughter
With which Heaven mocks our weakness! I henceforth
Will ne'er repent of aught designed or done,
But my repentance.
ORSINO. See, the lamp is out.
GIACOMO. If no remorse is ours when the dim air
Has drank this innocent flame, why should we quail
When Cenci's life, that life by which ill spirits
See the worst deeds they prompt, shall sink for ever?
No, I am hardened.
ORSINO. Why, what need of this?
Who feared the pale intrusion of remorse
In a just deed? Although our first plan failed,
Doubt not but he will soon be laid to rest.
But light the lamp; let us not talk i' the dark.
GIACOMO (*lighting the lamp*). And yet once quenched I cannot thus relume
My father's life; do you not think his ghost
Might plead that argument with God?
ORSINO. Once gone
You cannot now recall your sister's peace;
Your own extinguished years of youth and hope;
Nor your wife's bitter words; nor all the taunts
Which, from the prosperous, weak misfortune takes;
Nor your dead mother; nor . . .
GIACOMO. O, speak no more!
I am resolved, although this very hand
Must quench the life that animated it.

ORSINO. There is no need of that. Listen; you know
Olimpio, the castellan of Petrella
In old Colonna's time; him whom your father
Degraded from his post? And Marzio,
That desperate wretch, whom he deprived last year
Of a reward of blood, well earned and due?
GIACOMO. I knew Olimpio; and they say he hated
Old Cenci so, that in his silent rage
His lips grew white only to see him pass.
Of Marzio I know nothing.
ORSINO. Marzio's hate
Matches Olimpio's. I have sent these men,
But in your name, and as at your request,
To talk with Beatrice and Lucretia.
GIACOMO. Only to talk?
ORSINO. The moments which even now
Pass onward to to-morrow's midnight hour
May memorize their flight with death; ere then
They must have talked, and may perhaps have done,
And made an end . . .
GIACOMO. Listen! What sound is that?
ORSINO. The house-dog moans, and the beams crack; nought else.
GIACOMO. It is my wife complaining in her sleep:
I doubt not she is saying bitter things
Of me; and all my children round her dreaming
That I deny them sustenance.
ORSINO. Whilst he
Who truly took it from them, and who fills
Their hungry rest with bitterness, now sleeps
Lapped in bad pleasures, and triumphantly
Mocks thee in visions of successful hate
Too like the truth of day.
GIACOMO. If e'er he wakes
Again, I will not trust to hireling hands . . .
ORSINO. Why, that were well. I must be gone; good-night!
When next we meet—may all be done!
GIACOMO. And all
Forgotten! Oh, that I had never been! (*Exeunt.*)

End of the Third Act.

ACT IV

SCENE 1: *An Apartment in the Castle of Petrella.*

(*Enter* CENCI.)

CENCI. She comes not; yet I left her even now
Vanquished and faint. She knows the penalty
Of her delay; yet what if threats are vain?
Am I not now within Petrella's moat?
Or fear I still the eyes and ears of Rome?
Might I not drag her by the golden hair?
Stamp on her? keep her sleepless till her brain
Be overworn? tame her with chains and famine?
Less would suffice. Yet so to leave undone
What I most seek! No, 'tis her stubborn will
Which, by its own consent, shall stoop as low
As that which drags it down.

(*Enter* LUCRETIA.)

Thou loathèd wretch!
Hide thee from my abhorrence: fly, begone!
Yet stay! Bid Beatrice come hither.

LUCRETIA. Oh,
Husband! I pray, for thine own wretched sake
Heed what thou dost. A man who walks like thee
Through crimes, and through the danger of his crimes,
Each hour may stumble o'er a sudden grave.
And thou are old; thy hairs are hoary gray;
As thou wouldst save thyself from death and hell,
Pity thy daughter; give her to some friend
In marriage; so that she may tempt thee not
To hatred, or worse thoughts, if worse there be.

CENCI. What! like her sister, who has found a home
To mock my hate from with prosperity?
Strange ruin shall destroy both her and thee,
And all that yet remain. My death may be
Rapid, her destiny outspeeds it. Go,
Bid her come hither, and before my mood
Be changed, lest I should drag her by the hair.

LUCRETIA. She sent me to thee, husband. At thy presence

She fell, as thou dost know, into a trance;
And in that trance she heard a voice which said,
"Cenci must die! Let him confess himself!
Even now the accusing Angel waits to hear
If God, to punish his enormous crimes,
Harden his dying heart!"

CENCI. Why—such things are . . .
No doubt divine revealings may be made.
'Tis plain I have been favoured from above,
For when I cursed my sons they died.—Ay . . . so . . .
As to the right or wrong, that's talk . . . repentance?
Repentance is an easy moment's work,
And more depends on God than me. Well . . . well . . .
I must give up the greater point, which was
To poison and corrupt her soul.

(*A pause;* LUCRETIA *approaches anxiously, and then shrinks back as he speaks.*)

One, two;
Ay . . . Rocco and Cristofano my curse
Strangled: and Giacomo, I think, will find
Life a worse Hell than that beyond the grave:
Beatrice shall, if there be skill in hate,
Die in despair, blaspheming; to Bernardo,
He is so innocent, I will bequeath
The memory of these deeds, and make his youth
The sepulchre of hope, where evil thoughts
Shall grow like weeds on a neglected tomb.
When all is done, out in the wide Campagna,
I will pile up my silver and my gold;
My costly robes, paintings, and tapestries;
My parchments, and all records of my wealth;
And make a bonfire in my joy, and leave
Of my possessions nothing but my name;
Which shall be an inheritance to strip
Its wearer bare as infamy. That done,
My soul, which is a scourge, will I resign
Into the hands of him who wielded it;
Be it for its own punishment or theirs,
He will not ask it of me till the lash
Be broken in its last and deepest wound;

Until its hate be all inflicted. Yet,
Lest death outspeed my purpose, let me make
Short work and sure . . . (*Going.*)

LUCRETIA. (*Stops him*). Oh, stay! It was a feint;
She had no vision, and she heard no voice.
I said it but to awe thee.

CENCI. That is well.
Vile palterer with the sacred truth of God,
Be thy soul choked with that blaspheming lie!
For Beatrice worse terrors are in store
To bend her to my will.

LUCRETIA. Oh! to what will?
What cruel sufferings more than she has known
Canst thou inflict?

CENCI. Andrea! Go call my daughter,
And if she comes not tell her that I come. (*To* LUCRETIA.)
What sufferings? I will drag her, step by step,
Through infamies unheard of among men;
She shall stand shelterless in the broad noon
Of public scorn, for acts blazoned abroad,
One among which shall be . . . What? Canst thou guess?
She shall become (for what she most abhors
Shall have a fascination to entrap
Her loathing will) to her own conscious self
All she appears to others; and when dead,
As she shall die unshrived and unforgiven,
A rebel to her father and her God,
Her corpse shall be abandoned to the hounds;
Her name shall be the terror of the earth;
Her spirit shall approach the throne of God
Plague-spotted with my curses. I will make
Body and soul a monstrous lump of ruin.

(*Enter* ANDREA.)

ANDREA. The Lady Beatrice . . .

CENCI. Speak, pale slave! What
Said she?

ANDREA. My Lord, 'twas what she looked; she said:
"Go tell my father that I see the gulf
Of Hell between us two, which he may pass;
I will not." (*Exit* ANDREA.)

CENCI. Go thou quick, Lucretia,
Tell her to come; yet let her understand
Her coming is consent; and say, moreover,
That if she come not I will curse her. (*Exit* LUCRETIA.)
Ha!
With what but with a father's curse doth God
Panic-strike armèd victory, and make pale
Cities in their prosperity? The world's Father
Must grant a parent's prayer against his child,
Be he who asks even what men call me.
Will not the deaths of her rebellious brothers
Awe her before I speak? For I on them
Did imprecate quick ruin, and it came.
(*Enter* LUCRETIA.)
Well; what? Speak, wretch!
LUCRETIA. She said, "I cannot come;
Go tell my father that I see a torrent
Of his own blood raging between us."
CENCI (*kneeling*). God!
Hear me! If this most specious mass of flesh,
Which Thou hast made my daughter; this my blood,
This particle of my divided being;
Or rather, this my bane and my disease,
Whose sight infects and poisons me; this devil
Which sprung from me as from a hell, was meant
To aught good use; if her bright loveliness
Was kindled to illumine this dark world;
If nursed by Thy selectest dew of love
Such virtues blossom in her as should make
The peace of life, I pray Thee for my sake,
As Thou the common God and Father art
Of her, and me, and all; reverse that doom!
Earth, in the name of God, let her food be
Poison, until she be encrusted round
With leprous stains! Heaven, rain upon her head
The blistering drops of the Maremma's dew,
Till she be speckled like a toad; parch up
Those love-enkindled lips, warp those fine limbs
To loathèd lameness! All-beholding sun,
Strike in thine envy those life-darting eyes

With thine own blinding beams!

LUCRETIA. Peace! Peace!
For thine own sake unsay those dreadful words.
When high God grants, He punishes such prayers.

CENCI (*leaping up, and throwing his right hand towards Heaven*). He does His will, I mine! This in addition,
That if she have a child . . .

LUCRETIA. Horrible thought!

CENCI. That if she ever have a child—and thou,
Quick Nature! I adjure thee by thy God,
That thou be fruitful in her, and increase
And multiply, fulfilling his command,
And my deep imprecation!—may it be
A hideous likeness of herself; that as
From a distorting mirror, she may see
Her image mixed with what she most abhors,
Smiling upon her from her nursing breast!
And that the child may from its infancy
Grow, day by day, more wicked and deformed,
Turning her mother's love to misery!
And that both she and it may live until
It shall repay her care and pain with hate,
Or what may else be more unnatural;
So he may hunt her through the clamorous scoffs
Of the loud world to a dishonoured grave!
Shall I revoke this curse? Go, bid her come,
Before my words are chronicled in Heaven. (*Exit* LUCRETIA.)
I do not feel as if I were a man,
But like a fiend appointed to chastise
The offences of some unremembered world.
My blood is running up and down my veins;
A fearful pleasure makes it prick and tingle;
I feel a giddy sickness of strange awe;
My heart is beating with an expectation
Of horrid joy.

(*Enter* LUCRETIA.)

What? Speak!

LUCRETIA. She bids thee curse;
And if thy curses, as they cannot do,
Could kill her soul . . .

CENCI. She would not come. 'Tis well,
I can do both; first take what I demand,
And then extort concession. To thy chamber!
Fly ere I spurn thee; and beware this night
That thou cross not my footsteps. It were safer
To come between the tiger and his prey. (*Exit* LUCRETIA.)
It must be late; mine eyes grow weary dim
With unaccustomed heaviness of sleep.
Conscience! Oh, thou most insolent of lies!
They say that sleep, that healing dew of Heaven,
Sleeps not in balm the foldings of the brain
Which thinks thee an impostor. I will go,
First to belie thee with an hour of rest,
Which will be deep and calm, I feel; and then . . .
O, multitudinous Hell, the fiends will shake
Thine arches with the laughter of their joy!
There shall be lamentation heard in Heaven
As o'er an angel fallen; and upon Earth
All good shall droop and sicken, and ill things
Shall with a spirit of unnatural life
Stir and be quickened . . . even as I am now. (*Exit.*)

SCENE 2: *Before the Castle of Petrella.*

(*Enter* BEATRICE *and* LUCRETIA *above on the Ramparts.*)
BEATRICE. They come not yet.
LUCRETIA. 'Tis scarce midnight.
BEATRICE. How slow
Behind the course of thought, even sick with speed,
Lags leaden-footed time!
LUCRETIA. The minutes pass . . .
If he should wake before the deed is done?
BEATRICE. O, mother! He must never wake again.
What thou hast said persuades me that our act
Will but dislodge a spirit of deep hell
Out of a human form.
LUCRETIA. 'Tis true he spoke
Of death and judgement with strange confidence
For one so wicked; as a man believing
In God, yet recking not of good nor ill,

And yet to die without confession! . . .

BEATRICE. Oh!

Believe that Heaven is merciful and just,
And will not add our dread necessity
To the amount of his offences.

(*Enter* OLIMPIO *and* MARZIO, *below*.)

LUCRETIA. See,

They come.

BEATRICE. All mortal things must hasten thus
To their dark end. Let us go down.

(*Exeunt* LUCRETIA *and* BEATRICE *from above*.)

OLIMPIO. How feel you to this work?

MARZIO. As one who thinks

A thousand crowns excellent market price
For an old murderer's life. Your cheeks are pale.

OLIMPIO. It is the white reflection of your own,
Which you call pale.

MARZIO. Is that their natural hue?

OLIMPIO. Or 'tis my hate, and the deferred desire
To wreak it, which extinguishes their blood.

MARZIO. You are inclined then to this business?

OLIMPIO. Ay.

If one should bribe me with a thousand crowns
To kill a serpent which had stung my child,
I could not be more willing.

(*Enter* BEATRICE *and* LUCRETIA *below*.)

Noble ladies!

BEATRICE. Are ye resolved?

OLIMPIO. Is he asleep?

MARZIO. Is all

Quiet?

LUCRETIA. I mixed an opiate with his drink;
He sleeps so soundly . . .

BEATRICE. That his death will be

But as a change of sin-chastising dreams,
A dark continuance of the Hell within him,
Which God extinguish! But ye are resolved?
Ye know it is a high and holy deed?

OLIMPIO. We are resolved.

MARZIO. As to the how this act

Be warranted, it rests with you.

BEATRICE. Well, follow!

OLIMPIO. Hush! Hark! What noise is that?

MARZIO. Ha! Some one comes!

BEATRICE. Ye conscience-stricken cravens, rock to rest
Your baby hearts. It is the iron gate,
Which ye left open, swinging to the wind,
That enters whistling as in scorn. Come, follow!
And be your steps like mine, light, quick and bold. (*Exeunt.*)

SCENE 3: *An Apartment in the Castle.*

(*Enter* BEATRICE *and* LUCRETIA.)

LUCRETIA. They are about it now.

BEATRICE. Nay, it is done.

LUCRETIA. I have not heard him groan.

BEATRICE. He will not groan.

LUCRETIA. What sound is that?

BEATRICE. List! 'tis the tread of feet
About his bed.

LUCRETIA. My God!
If he be now a cold stiff corpse . . .

BEATRICE. O, fear not
What may be done, but what is left undone;
The act seals all.

(*Enter* OLIMPIO *and* MARZIO.)

Is it accomplished?

MARZIO. What?

OLIMPIO. Did you not call?

BEATRICE. When?

OLIMPIO. Now.

BEATRICE. I ask if all is over?

OLIMPIO. We dare not kill an old and sleeping man;
His thin grey hair, his stern and reverend brow,
His veinèd hands crossed on his heaving breast,
And the calm innocent sleep in which he lay,
Quelled me. Indeed, indeed, I cannot do it.

MARZIO. But I was bolder; for I chid Olimpio,
And bade him bear his wrongs to his own grave,
And leave me the reward. And now my knife

Touched the loose wrinkled throat, when the old man
Stirred in his sleep, and said, "God! hear, O, hear
A father's curse! What, art Thou not our Father?"
And then he laughed. I knew it was the ghost
Of my dead father speaking through his lips,
And could not kill him.

BEATRICE. Miserable slaves!
Where, if ye dare not kill a sleeping man,
Found ye the boldness to return to me
With such a deed undone? Base palterers!
Cowards and traitors! Why, the very conscience
Which ye would sell for gold and for revenge
Is an equivocation; it sleeps over
A thousand daily acts disgracing men;
And when a deed where mercy insults Heaven . . .
Why do I talk? (*Snatching a dagger from one of them, and raising it.*)
Hadst thou a tongue to say,
"She murdered her own father!"—I must do it!
But never dream ye shall outlive him long!

OLIMPIO. Stop, for God's sake!

MARZIO. I will go back and kill him.

OLIMPIO. Give me the weapon, we must do thy will.

BEATRICE. Take it! Depart! Return!

(*Exeunt* OLIMPIO *and* MARZIO.)

How pale thou art!
We do but that which 'twere a deadly crime
To leave undone.

LUCRETIA. Would it were done!

BEATRICE. Even whilst
That doubt is passing through your mind, the world
Is conscious of a change. Darkness and Hell
Have swallowed up the vapour they sent forth
To blacken the sweet light of life. My breath
Comes, methinks, lighter, and the jellied blood
Runs freely through my veins. Hark!

(*Enter* OLIMPIO *and* MARZIO.)

He is . . .

OLIMPIO. Dead!

MARZIO. We strangled him that there might be no blood:
And then we threw his heavy corpse i' the garden

Under the balcony; 'twill seem it fell.

BEATRICE (*giving them a bag of coin*). Here, take this gold, and hasten to your homes.
And, Marzio, because thou wast only awed
By that which made me tremble, wear thou this!

(*Clothes him in a rich mantle.*)

It was the mantle which my grandfather
Wore in his high prosperity, and men
Envied his state; so may they envy thine.
Thou wert a weapon in the hand of God
To a just use. Live long and thrive! And, mark,
If thou hast crimes, repent; this deed is none. (*A horn is sounded.*)

LUCRETIA. Hark, 'tis the castle horn; my God! it sounds
Like the last trump.

BEATRICE. Some tedious guest is coming.

LUCRETIA. The drawbridge is let down; there is a tramp
Of horses in the court; fly, hide yourselves!

(*Exeunt* OLIMPIO *and* MARZIO.)

BEATRICE. Let us retire to counterfeit deep rest;
I scarcely need to counterfeit it now;
The spirit which doth reign within these limbs
Seems strangely undisturbed. I could even sleep
Fearless and calm; all ill is surely past. (*Exeunt.*)

SCENE 4: *Another Apartment in the Castle.*

(*Enter on one side the* LEGATE SAVELLA, *introduced by a Servant, and on the other* LUCRETIA *and* BERNARDO.)

SAVELLA. Lady, my duty to his Holiness
Be my excuse that thus unseasonably
I break upon your rest. I must speak with
Count Cenci; doth he sleep?

LUCRETIA (*in a hurried and confused manner*). I think he sleeps;
Yet wake him not, I pray, spare me awhile,
He is a wicked and a wrathful man;
Should he be roused out of his sleep to-night,
Which is, I know, a hell of angry dreams,
It were not well; indeed it were not well.
Wait till day break . . . (*Aside.*) O, I am deadly sick!

SAVELLA. I grieve thus to distress you, but the Count

Must answer charges of the gravest import,
And suddenly; such my commission is.

LUCRETIA (*with increased agitation*). I dare not rouse him: I know none who dare . . .
'Twere perilous; . . . you might as safely waken
A serpent; or a corpse in which some fiend
Were laid to sleep.

SAVELLA. Lady, my moments here
Are counted. I must rouse him from his sleep,
Since none else dare.

LUCRETIA (*aside*). O, terror! O, despair!
(*To* BERNARDO.) Bernardo, conduct you the Lord Legate to
Your father's chamber. (*Exeunt* SAVELLA *and* BERNARDO.)

(*Enter* BEATRICE.)

BEATRICE. 'Tis a messenger
Come to arrest the culprit who now stands
Before the throne of unappealable God.
Both Earth and Heaven, consenting arbiters,
Acquit our deed.

LUCRETIA. Oh, agony of fear!
Would that he yet might live! Even now I heard
The Legate's followers whisper as they passed
They had a warrant for his instant death.
All was prepared by unforbidden means
Which we must pay so dearly, having done.
Even now they search the tower, and find the body;
Now they suspect the truth; now they consult
Before they come to tax us with the fact;
Oh, horrible, 'tis all discovered!

BEATRICE. Mother,
What is done wisely, is done well. Be bold
As thou are just. 'Tis like a truant child,
To fear that others know what thou hast done,
Even from thine own strong consciousness, and thus
Write on unsteady eyes and altered cheeks
All thou wouldst hide. Be faithful to thyself,
And fear no other witness but thy fear.
For if, as cannot be, some circumstance
Should rise in accusation, we can blind
Suspicion with such cheap astonishment,

Or overbear it with such guiltless pride,
As murderers cannot feign. The deed is done,
And what may follow now regards not me.
I am as universal as the light;
Free as the earth-surrounding air; as firm
As the world's centre. Consequence, to me,
Is as the wind which strikes the solid rock,
But shakes it not. (*A cry within and tumult.*)

VOICES. Murder! Murder! Murder!

(*Enter* BERNARDO *and* SAVELLA.)

SAVELLA (*to his followers*). Go search the castle round; sound the alarm;
Look to the gates, that none escape!

BEATRICE. What now?

BERNARDO. I know not what to say . . . my father's dead.

BEATRICE. How; dead! he only sleeps; you mistake, brother.
His sleep is very calm, very like death;
'Tis wonderful how well a tyrant sleeps.
He is not dead?

BERNARDO. Dead; murdered!

LUCRETIA (*with extreme agitation*). Oh, no, no!
He is not murdered, though he may be dead;
I have alone the keys of those apartments.

SAVELLA. Ha! Is it so?

BEATRICE. My Lord, I pray excuse us;
We will retire; my mother is not well;
She seems quite overcome with this strange horror.

(*Exeunt* LUCRETIA *and* BEATRICE.)

SAVELLA. Can you suspect who may have murdered him?

BERNARDO. I know not what to think.

SAVELLA. Can you name any
Who had an interest in his death?

BERNARDO. Alas!
I can name none who had not, and those most
Who most lament that such a deed is done;
My mother, and my sister, and myself.

SAVELLA. 'Tis strange! There were clear marks of violence.
I found the old man's body in the moonlight
Hanging beneath the window of his chamber,
Among the branches of a pine; he could not

Have fallen there, for all his limbs lay heaped
And effortless; 'tis true there was no blood . . .
Favour me, Sir; it much imports your house
That all should be made clear; to tell the ladies
That I request their presence. (*Exit* BERNARDO.)

(*Enter Guards, bringing in* MARZIO.)

GUARD. We have one.

OFFICER. My Lord, we found this ruffian and another
Lurking among the rocks; there is no doubt
But that they are the murderers of Count Cenci;
Each had a bag of coin; this fellow wore
A gold-inwoven robe, which, shining bright
Under the dark rocks to the glimmering moon,
Betrayed them to our notice; the other fell
Desperately fighting.

SAVELLA. What does he confess?

OFFICER. He keeps firm silence; but these lines found on him
May speak.

SAVELLA. Their language is at least sincere. (*Reads.*)

"To the Lady Beatrice.

"That the atonement of what my nature sickens to conjecture may soon arrive, I send thee, at thy brother's desire, those who will speak and do more than I dare write . . .

"Thy devoted servant, Orsino."

(*Enter* LUCRETIA, BEATRICE, *and* BERNARDO.)

Knowest thou this writing, Lady?

BEATRICE. No.

SAVELLA. Nor thou?

LUCRETIA (*her conduct throughout the scene is marked by extreme agitation*). Where was it found? What is it? It should be
Orsino's hand! It speaks of that strange horror
Which never yet found utterance, but which made
Between that hapless child and her dead father
A gulf of obscure hatred.

SAVELLA. Is it so?
Is it true, Lady, that thy father did
Such outrages as to awaken in thee
Unfilial hate?

BEATRICE. Not hate, 'twas more than hate;
This is most true, yet wherefore question me?

SAVELLA. There is a deed demanding question done;
Thou hast a secret which will answer not.
BEATRICE. What sayest? My Lord, your words are bold and rash.
SAVELLA. I do arrest all present in the name
Of the Pope's Holiness. You must to Rome.
LUCRETIA. O, not to Rome! Indeed we are not guilty.
BEATRICE. Guilty! Who dares talk of guilt? My Lord,
I am more innocent of parricide
Than is a child born fatherless . . . Dear mother,
Your gentleness and patience are no shield
For this keen-judging world, this two-edged lie,
Which seems, but is not. What! will human laws,
Rather will ye who are their ministers,
Bar all access to retribution first,
And then, when Heaven doth interpose to do
What ye neglect, arming familiar things
To the redress of an unwonted crime,
Make ye the victims who demanded it
Culprits? 'Tis ye are culprits! That poor wretch
Who stands so pale, and trembling, and amazed,
If it be true he murdered Cenci, was
A sword in the right hand of justest God.
Wherefore should I have wielded it? Unless
The crimes which mortal tongue dare never name
God therefore scruples to avenge.
SAVELLA. You own
That you desired his death?
BEATRICE. It would have been
A crime no less than his, if for one moment
That fierce desire had faded in my heart.
'Tis true I did believe and hope, and pray,
Ay, I even knew—for God is wise and just—
That some strange sudden death hung over him.
'Tis true that this did happen, and most true
There was no other rest for me on earth,
No other hope in Heaven . . . now what of this?
SAVELLA. Strange thoughts beget strange deeds; and here are both:
I judge thee not.
BEATRICE. And yet, if you arrest me,
You are the judge and executioner

Of that which is the life of life; the breath
Of accusation kills an innocent name,
And leaves for lame acquittal the poor life
Which is a mask without it. 'Tis most false
That I am guilty of foul parricide;
Although I must rejoice, for justest cause,
That other hands have sent my father's soul
To ask the mercy he denied to me.
Now leave us free; stain not a noble house
With vague surmises of rejected crime;
Add to our sufferings and your own neglect
No heavier sum; let them have been enough;
Leave us the wreck we have.

SAVELLA. I dare not, Lady.
I pray that you prepare yourselves for Rome:
There the Pope's further pleasure will be known.

LUCRETIA. O, not to Rome! O, take us not to Rome!

BEATRICE. Why not to Rome, dear mother? There as here
Our innocence is as an armèd heel
To trample accusation. God is there
As here, and with His shadow ever clothes
The innocent, the injured, and the weak;
And such are we. Cheer up, dear Lady, lean
On me; collect your wandering thoughts. My Lord,
As soon as you have taken some refreshment,
And had all such examinations made
Upon the spot, as may be necessary
To the full understanding of this matter,
We shall be ready. Mother; will you come?

LUCRETIA. Ha! they will bind us to the rack, and wrest
Self-accusation from our agony!
Will Giacomo be there? Orsino? Marzio?
All present; all confronted; all demanding
Each from the other's countenance the thing
Which is in every heart! O, misery! (*She faints, and is borne out.*)

SAVELLA. She faints; an ill appearance this.

BEATRICE. My Lord,
She knows not yet the uses of the world.
She fears that power is as a beast which grasps
And loosens not; a snake whose look transmutes

All things to guilt which is its nutriment.
She cannot know how well the supine slaves
Of blind authority read the truth of things
When written on a brow of guilelessness;
She sees not yet triumphant Innocence
Stand at the judgement-seat of mortal man,
A judge and an accuser of the wrong
Which drags it there. Prepare yourself, my Lord;
Our suite will join yours in the court below. (*Exeunt.*)
End of the Fourth Act.

ACT V

SCENE 1: *An Apartment in* ORSINO'S *Palace.*

(*Enter* ORSINO *and* GIACOMO.)
GIACOMO. Do evil deeds thus quickly come to end?
O, that the vain remorse which must chastise
Crimes done, had but as loud a voice to warn
As its keen sting is mortal to avenge!
O, that the hour when present had cast off
The mantle of its mystery, and shown
The ghastly form with which it now returns
When its scared game is roused, cheering the hounds
Of conscience to their prey! Alas! Alas!
It was a wicked thought, a piteous deed,
To kill an old and hoary-headed father.
ORSINO. It has turned out unluckily, in truth.
GIACOMO. To violate the sacred doors of sleep;
To cheat kind Nature of the placid death
Which she prepares for overwearied age;
To drag from Heaven an unrepentant soul,
Which might have quenched in reconciling prayers
A life of burning crimes . . .
ORSINO. You cannot say
I urged you to the deed.
GIACOMO. O, had I never
Found in thy smooth and ready countenance

The mirror of my darkest thoughts; hadst thou
Never with hints and questions made me look
Upon the monster of my thought, until
It grew familiar to desire . . .
ORSINO. 'Tis thus
Men cast the blame of their unprosperous acts
Upon the abettors of their own resolve;
Or anything but their weak, guilty selves.
And yet, confess the truth, it is the peril
In which you stand that gives you this pale sickness
Of penitence; confess 'tis fear disguised
From its own shame that takes the mantle now
Of thin remorse. What if we yet were safe?
GIACOMO. How can that be? Already Beatrice,
Lucretia and the murderer are in prison.
I doubt not officers are, whilst we speak,
Sent to arrest us.
ORSINO. I have all prepared
For instant flight. We can escape even now,
So we take fleet occasion by the hair.
GIACOMO. Rather expire in tortures, as I may.
What! will you cast by self-accusing flight
Assured conviction upon Beatrice?
She, who alone in this unnatural work,
Stands like God's angel ministered upon
By fiends; avenging such a nameless wrong
As turns black parricide to piety;
Whilst we for basest ends . . . I fear, Orsino,
While I consider all your words and looks,
Comparing them with your proposal now,
That you must be a villain. For what end
Could you engage in such a perilous crime,
Training me on with hints, and signs, and smiles,
Even to this gulf? Thou art no liar? No,
Thou art a lie! Traitor and murderer!
Coward and slave! But, no, defend thyself; (*Drawing.*)
Let the sword speak what the indignant tongue
Disdains to brand thee with.
ORSINO. Put up your weapon.
Is it the desperation of your fear

Makes you thus rash and sudden with a friend,
Now ruined for your sake? If honest anger
Have moved you, know, that what I just proposed
Was but to try you. As for me, I think,
Thankless affection led me to this point,
From which, if my firm temper could repent,
I cannot now recede. Even whilst we speak,
The ministers of justice wait below;
They grant me these brief moments. Now, if you
Have any word of melancholy comfort
To speak to your pale wife, 'twere best to pass
Out at the postern, and avoid them so.

GIACOMO. O generous friend! How canst thou pardon me?
Would that my life could purchase thine!

ORSINO. That wish
Now comes a day too late. Haste; fare thee well!
Hear'st thou not steps along the corridor? (*Exit* GIACOMO.)
I'm sorry for it; but the guards are waiting
At his own gate, and such was my contrivance
That I might rid me both of him and them.
I thought to act a solemn comedy
Upon the painted scene of this new world,
And to attain my own peculiar ends
By some such plot of mingled good and ill
As others weave; but there arose a Power
Which grasped and snapped the threads of my device,
And turned it to a net of ruin . . . Ha! (*A shout is heard.*)
Is that my name I hear proclaimed abroad?
But I will pass, wrapped in a vile disguise,
Rags on my back, and a false innocence
Upon my face, through the misdeeming crowd
Which judges by what seems. 'Tis easy then
For a new name and for a country new,
And a new life fashioned on old desires,
To change the honours of abandoned Rome.
And these must be the masks of that within,
Which must remain unaltered . . . Oh, I fear
That what is past will never let me rest!
Why, when none else is conscious, but myself,
Of my misdeeds, should my own heart's contempt

Trouble me? Have I not the power to fly
My own reproaches? Shall I be the slave
Of . . . what? A word? which those of this false world
Employ against each other, not themselves,
As men wear daggers not for self-offence.
But if I am mistaken, where shall I
Find the disguise to hide me from myself,
As now I skulk from every other eye? (*Exit.*)

SCENE 2: *A Hall of Justice.*

(CAMILLO, JUDGES, *&c, are discovered seated;* MARZIO *is led in.*)
FIRST JUDGE. Accused, do you persist in your denial?
I ask you, are you innocent, or guilty?
I demand who were the participators
In your offence? Speak truth, and the whole truth.
MARZIO. My God! I did not kill him; I know nothing;
Olimpio sold the robe to me from which
You would infer my guilt.
SECOND JUDGE. Away with him!
FIRST JUDGE. Dare you, with lips yet white from the rack's kiss,
Speak false? Is it so soft a questioner,
That you would bandy lover's talk with it,
Till it wind out your life and soul? Away!
MARZIO. Spare me! O spare! I will confess.
FIRST JUDGE. Then speak.
MARZIO. I strangled him in his sleep.
FIRST JUDGE. Who urged you to it?
MARZIO. His own son Giacomo and the young prelate
Orsino sent me to Petrella; there
The ladies Beatrice and Lucretia
Tempted me with a thousand crowns, and I
And my companion forthwith murdered him.
Now let me die.
FIRST JUDGE. This sounds as bad as truth. Guards, there,
Lead forth the prisoner!
(*Enter* LUCRETIA, BEATRICE, *and* GIACOMO, *guarded.*)
Look upon this man;

When did you see him last?
BEATRICE. We never saw him.
MARZIO. You know me too well, Lady Beatrice.
BEATRICE. I know thee! How? where? when?
MARZIO. You know 'twas I
Whom you did urge with menaces and bribes
To kill your father. When the thing was done
You clothed me in a robe of woven gold
And bade me thrive; how I have thriven, you see.
You, my Lord Giacomo, Lady Lucretia,
You know that what I speak is true.
(BEATRICE *advances towards him; he covers his face, and shrinks back.*)
Oh, dart
The terrible resentment of those eyes
On the dead earth! Turn them away from me!
They wound; 'twas torture forced the truth. My Lords,
Having said this, let me be led to death.
BEATRICE. Poor wretch, I pity thee; yet stay awhile.
CAMILLO. Guards, lead him not away.
BEATRICE. Cardinal Camillo,
You have a good repute for gentleness
And wisdom; can it be that you sit here
To countenance a wicked farce like this?
When some obscure and trembling slave is dragged
From sufferings which might shake the sternest heart
And bade to answer, not as he believes,
But as those may suspect or do desire
Whose questions thence suggest their own reply;
And that in peril of such hideous torments
As merciful God spares even the damned. Speak now
The thing you surely know, which is, that you,
If your fine frame were stretched upon that wheel,
And you were told: "Confess that you did poison
Your little nephew; that fair blue-eyed child
Who was the lodestar of your life";—and though
All see, since his most swift and piteous death,
That day and night, and heaven and earth, and time,
And all the things hoped for or done therein,
Are changed to you, through your exceeding grief,

Yet you would say, "I confess anything":
And beg from your tormentors, like that slave,
The refuge of dishonourable death.
I pray thee, Cardinal, that thou assert
My innocence.

CAMILLO (*much moved*). What shall we think, my Lords?
Shame on these tears! I thought the heart was frozen
Which is their fountain. I would pledge my soul
That she is guiltless.

JUDGE. Yet she must be tortured.

CAMILLO. I would as soon have tortured mine own nephew
(If he now lived he would be just her age;
His hair, too, was her colour, and his eyes
Like hers in shape, but blue and not so deep)
As that most perfect image of God's love
That ever came sorrowing upon the earth.
She is as pure as speechless infancy!

JUDGE. Well, be her purity on your head, my Lord,
If you forbid the rack. His Holiness
Enjoined us to pursue this monstrous crime
By the severest forms of law; nay, even
To stretch a point against the criminals.
The prisoners stand accused of parricide
Upon such evidence as justifies
Torture.

BEATRICE. What evidence? This man's?

JUDGE. Even so.

BEATRICE (*to* MARZIO). Come near. And who art thou, thus chosen forth
Out of the multitude of living men,
To kill the innocent?

MARZIO. I am Marzio,
Thy father's vassal.

BEATRICE. Fix thine eyes on mine;
Answer to what I ask. (*Turning to the* JUDGES.)
I prithee mark
His countenance: unlike bold calumny,
Which sometimes dares not speak the thing it looks,
He dares not look the thing he speaks, but bends
His gaze on the blind earth.

(*To* MARZIO.) What! wilt thou say
That I did murder my own father?
MARZIO. Oh!
Spare me! My brain swims round . . . I cannot speak . . .
It was that horrid torture forced the truth.
Take me away! Let her not look on me!
I am a guilty miserable wretch;
I have said all I know; now, let me die!
BEATRICE. My Lords, if by my nature I had been
So stern, as to have planned the crime alleged,
Which your suspicions dictate to this slave,
And the rack makes him utter, do you think
I should have left this two-edged instrument
Of my misdeed; this man, this bloody knife
With my own name engraven on the heft,
Lying unsheathed amid a world of foes,
For my own death? That with such horrible need
For deepest silence, I should have neglected
So trivial a precaution, as the making
His tomb the keeper of a secret written
On a thief's memory? What is his poor life?
What are a thousand lives? A parricide
Had trampled them like dust; and, see, he lives!
(*Turning to* MARZIO.) And thou . . .
MARZIO. O, spare me! Speak to me no more!
That stern yet piteous look, those solemn tones,
Wound worse than torture.
(*To the* JUDGES.) I have told it all;
For pity's sake lead me away to death.
CAMILLO. Guards, lead him nearer the Lady Beatrice;
He shrinks from her regard like autumn's leaf
From the keen breath of the serenest north.
BEATRICE. O thou who tremblest on the giddy verge
Of life and death, pause ere thou answerest me,
So mayst thou answer God with less dismay.
What evil have we done thee? I, alas!
Have lived but on this earth a few sad years,
And so my lot was ordered, that a father
First turned the moments of awakening life
To drops, each poisoning youth's sweet hope; and then

Stabbed with one blow my everlasting soul,
And my untainted fame; and even that peace
Which sleeps within the core of the heart's heart;
But the wound was not mortal; so my hate
Became the only worship I could lift
To our great Father, who in pity and love
Armed thee, as thou dost say, to cut him off;
And thus his wrong becomes my accusation;
And art thou the accuser? If thou hopest
Mercy in Heaven, show justice upon earth;
Worse than a bloody hand is a hard heart.
If thou hast done murders, made thy life's path
Over the trampled laws of God and man,
Rush not before thy Judge, and say: "My Maker,
I have done this and more; for there was one
Who was most pure and innocent on earth;
And because she endured what never any
Guilty or innocent endured before;
Because her wrongs could not be told, not thought;
Because Thy hand at length did rescue her;
I with my words killed her and all her kin."
Think, I adjure you, what it is to slay
The reverence living in the minds of men
Towards our ancient house, and stainless fame!
Think what it is to strangle infant pity,
Cradled in the belief of guileless looks,
Till it become a crime to suffer. Think
What 'tis to blot with infamy and blood
All that which shows like innocence, and is—
Hear me, great God!—I swear, most innocent;
So that the world lose all discrimination
Between the sly, fierce, wild regard of guilt,
And that which now compels thee to reply
To what I ask: Am I, or am I not
A parricide?

MARZIO. Thou art not!

JUDGE. What is this?

MARZIO. I here declare those whom I did accuse
Are innocent. 'Tis I alone am guilty.

JUDGE. Drag him away to torments; let them be

Subtle and long drawn out, to tear the folds
Of the heart's inmost cell. Unbind him not
Till he confess.

MARZIO. Torture me as ye will:
A keener pang has wrung a higher truth
From my last breath. She is most innocent!
Bloodhounds, not men, glut yourselves well with me!
I will not give you that fine piece of nature
To rend and ruin. (*Exit* MARZIO, *guarded.*)

CAMILLO. What say ye now, my Lords?

JUDGE. Let tortures strain the truth till it be white
As snow thrice sifted by the frozen wind.

CAMILLO. Yet stained with blood.

JUDGE (*to* BEATRICE). Know you this paper, Lady?

BEATRICE. Entrap me not with questions. Who stands here
As my accuser? Ha! wilt thou be he,
Who art my judge? Accuser, witness, judge,
What, all in one? Here is Orsino's name;
Where is Orsino? Let his eye meet mine.
What means this scrawl? Alas! ye know not what,
And therefore on the chance that it may be
Some evil, will ye kill us?

(*Enter an Officer.*)

OFFICER. Marzio's dead.

JUDGE. What did he say?

OFFICER. Nothing. As soon as we
Had bound him on the wheel, he smiled on us,
As one who baffles a deep adversary;
And holding his breath, died.

JUDGE. There remains nothing
But to apply the question to those prisoners,
Who yet remain stubborn.

CAMILLO. I overrule
Further proceedings, and in the behalf
Of these most innocent and noble persons
Will use my interest with the Holy Father.

JUDGE. Let the Pope's pleasure then be done. Meanwhile
Conduct these culprits each to separate cells;
And be the engines ready: for this night
If the Pope's resolution be as grave,

Pious, and just as once, I'll wring the truth
Out of those nerves and sinews, groan by groan. (*Exeunt.*)

SCENE 3: *The Cell of a Prison.*

(BEATRICE *is discovered asleep on a couch. Enter* BERNARDO.)

BERNARDO. How gently slumber rests upon her face,
Like the last thoughts of some day sweetly spent,
Closing in night and dreams, and so prolonged.
After such torments as she bore last night,
How light and soft her breathing comes. Ay me!
Methinks that I shall never sleep again.
But I must shake the heavenly dew of rest
From this sweet folded flower, thus . . . wake! awake!
What, sister, canst thou sleep?

BEATRICE (*awaking*). I was just dreaming
That we were all in Paradise. Thou knowest
This cell seems like a kind of Paradise
After our father's presence.

BERNARDO. Dear, dear sister,
Would that thy dream were not a dream! O God!
How shall I tell?

BEATRICE. What wouldst thou tell, sweet brother?

BERNARDO. Look not so calm and happy, or even whilst
I stand considering what I have to say,
My heart will break.

BEATRICE. See now, thou mak'st me weep;
How very friendless thou wouldst be, dear child,
If I were dead. Say what thou hast to say.

BERNARDO. They have confessed; they could endure no more
The tortures . . .

BEATRICE. Ha! What was there to confess?
They must have told some weak and wicked lie
To flatter their tormentors. Have they said
That they were guilty? O white innocence,
That thou shouldst wear the mask of guilt to hide
Thine awful and serenest countenance
From those who know thee not!

(*Enter* JUDGE *with* LUCRETIA *and* GIACOMO, *guarded.*)

Ignoble hearts!

For some brief spasms of pain, which are at least
As mortal as the limbs through which they pass,
Are centuries of high splendour laid in dust?
And that eternal honour, which should live
Sunlike, above the reek of mortal fame,
Changed to a mockery and a byword? What!
Will you give up these bodies to be dragged
At horses' heels, so that our hair should sweep
The footsteps of the vain and senseless crowd,
Who, that they may make our calamity
Their worship and their spectacle, will leave
The churches and the theatres as void
As their own hearts? Shall the light multitude
Fling, at their choice, curses or faded pity,
Sad funeral flowers to deck a living corpse,
Upon us as we pass to pass away,
And leave . . . what memory of our having been?
Infamy, blood, terror, despair? O thou,
Who wert a mother to the parentless,
Kill not thy child! Let not her wrongs kill thee!
Brother, lie down with me upon the rack,
And let us each be silent as a corpse;
It soon will be as soft as any grave.
'Tis but the falsehood it can wring from fear
Makes the rack cruel.

GIACOMO. They will tear the truth
Even from thee at last, those cruel pains:
For pity's sake say thou art guilty now.

LUCRETIA. Oh, speak the truth! Let us all quickly die;
And after death, God is our judge, not they;
He will have mercy on us.

BERNARDO. If indeed
It can be true, say so, dear sister mine;
And then the Pope will surely pardon you,
And all be well.

JUDGE. Confess, or I will warp
Your limbs with such keen tortures . . .

BEATRICE. Tortures! Turn
The rack henceforth into a spinning-wheel!
Torture your dog, that he may tell when last

He lapped the blood his master shed . . . not me!
My pangs are of the mind, and of the heart,
And of the soul; ay, of the inmost soul,
Which weeps within tears as of burning gall
To see, in this ill world where none are true,
My kindred false to their deserted selves;
And with considering all the wretched life
Which I have lived, and its now wretched end,
And the small justice shown by Heaven and Earth
To me or mine; and what a tyrant thou art,
And what slaves these; and what a world we make,
The oppressor and oppressed . . . such pangs compel
My answer. What is it thou wouldst with me?

JUDGE. Art thou not guilty of thy father's death?

BEATRICE. Or wilt thou rather tax high-judging God
That He permitted such an act as that
Which I have suffered, and which He beheld;
Made it unutterable, and took from it
All refuge, all revenge, all consequence,
But that which thou hast called my father's death?
Which is or is not what men call a crime,
Which either I have done, or have not done;
Say what ye will. I shall deny no more.
If ye desire it thus, thus let it be,
And so an end of all. Now do your will;
No other pains shall force another word.

JUDGE. She is convicted, but has not confessed.
Be it enough. Until their final sentence
Let none have converse with them. You, young Lord,
Linger not here!

BEATRICE. Oh, tear him not away!

JUDGE. Guards, do your duty.

BERNARDO (*embracing* BEATRICE). Oh! would ye divide
Body from soul?

OFFICER. That is the headsman's business.

(*Exeunt all but* LUCRETIA, BEATRICE, *and* GIACOMO.)

GIACOMO. Have I confessed? Is it all over now?
No hope! No refuge! O weak, wicked tongue
Which hast destroyed me, would that thou hadst been
Cut out and thrown to dogs first! To have killed

My father first, and then betrayed my sister—
Ay, thee! the one thing innocent and pure
In this black guilty world—to that which I
So well deserve! My wife! my little ones!
Destitute, helpless; and I . . . Father! God!
Canst Thou forgive even the unforgiving,
When their full hearts break thus, thus? . . . (*Covers his face and weeps.*)

LUCRETIA. O my child!
To what a dreadful end are we all come!
Why did I yield? Why did I not sustain
Those torments? Oh, that I were all dissolved
Into these fast and unavailing tears,
Which flow and feel not!

BEATRICE. What 'twas weak to do,
'Tis weaker to lament, once being done;
Take cheer! The God who knew my wrong, and made
Our speedy act the angel of His wrath,
Seems, and but seems, to have abandoned us.
Let us not think that we shall die for this.
Brother, sit near me; give me your firm hand,
You had a manly heart. Bear up! Bear up!
O dearest Lady, put your gentle head
Upon my lap, and try to sleep awhile;
Your eyes look pale, hollow and overworn,
With heaviness of watching and slow grief.
Come, I will sing you some low sleepy tune,
Not cheerful, nor yet sad; some dull old thing,
Some outworn and unused monotony,
Such as our country gossips sing and spin,
Till they almost forget they live: lie down!
So, that will do. Have I forgot the words?
Faith! They are sadder than I thought they were.

SONG

False friend, wilt thou smile or weep
When my life is laid asleep?
Little cares for a smile or a tear,
The clay-cold corpse upon the bier!
Farewell! Heigho!

What is this whispers low?
There is a snake in thy smile, my dear;
And bitter poison within thy tear.

Sweet sleep, were death like to thee,
Or if thou couldst mortal be,
I would close these eyes of pain!
When to wake? Never again.
O World! Farewell!
Listen to the passing bell!
It says, thou and I must part,
With a light and a heavy heart. (*The scene closes.*)

SCENE 4: *A Hall of the Prison.*

(*Enter* CAMILLO *and* BERNARDO.)

CAMILLO. The Pope is stern; not to be moved or bent.
He looked as calm and keen as is the engine
Which tortures and which kills, exempt itself
From aught that it inflicts; a marble form,
A rite, a law, a custom; not a man.
He frowned, as if to frown had been the trick
Of his machinery, on the advocates
Presenting the defences, which he tore
And threw behind, muttering with hoarse, harsh voice:
"Which among ye defended their old father
Killed in his sleep?" Then to another: "Thou
Dost this in virtue of thy place; 'tis well."
He turned to me then, looking deprecation,
And said these three words coldly: "They must die."

BERNARDO. And yet you left him not?

CAMILLO. I urged him still;
Pleading, as I could guess, the devilish wrong
Which prompted your unnatural parent's death.
And he replied: "Paolo Santa Croce
Murdered his mother yester evening,
And he is fled. Parricide grows so rife
That soon, for some just cause no doubt, the young
Will strangle us all, dozing in our chairs.
Authority, and power, and hoary hair

Are grown crimes capital. You are my nephew,
You come to ask their pardon; stay a moment;
Here is their sentence; never see me more
Till, to the letter, it be all fulfilled."

BERNARDO. O God, not so! I did believe indeed
That all you said was but sad preparation
For happy news. Oh, there are words and looks
To bend the sternest purpose! Once I knew them,
Now I forget them at my dearest need.
What think you if I seek him out, and bathe
His feet and robe with hot and bitter tears?
Importune him with prayers, vexing his brain
With my perpetual cries, until in rage
He strike me with his pastoral cross, and trample
Upon my prostrate head, so that my blood
May stain the senseless dust on which he treads,
And remorse waken mercy? I will do it!
Oh, wait till I return! (*Rushes out.*)

CAMILLO. Alas! poor boy!
A wreck-devoted seaman thus might pray
To the deaf sea.

(*Enter* LUCRETIA, BEATRICE, *and* GIACOMO, *guarded.*)

BEATRICE. I hardly dare to fear
That thou bring'st other news than a just pardon.

CAMILLO. May God in heaven be less inexorable
To the Pope's prayers, than he has been to mine.
Here is the sentence and the warrant.

BEATRICE (*wildly*). Oh,
My God! Can it be possible I have
To die so suddenly? So young to go
Under the obscure, cold, rotting, wormy ground!
To be nailed down into a narrow place;
To see no more sweet sunshine; hear no more
Blithe voice of living thing; muse not again
Upon familiar thoughts, sad, yet thus lost—
How fearful! to be nothing! Or to be . . .
What? Oh, where am I? Let me not go mad!
Sweet Heaven, forgive weak thoughts! If there should be
No God, no Heaven, no Earth in the void world;—
The wide, grey, lampless, deep, unpeopled world!

If all things then should be . . . my father's spirit,
His eye, his voice, his touch surrounding me;
The atmosphere and breath of my dead life!
If sometimes, as a shape more like himself,
Even the form which tortured me on earth,
Masked in grey hairs and wrinkles, he should come,
And wind me in his hellish arms, and fix
His eyes on mine, and drag me down, down, down!
For was he not alone omnipotent
On Earth, and ever present? Even though dead,
Does not his spirit live in all that breathe,
And work for me and mine still the same ruin,
Scorn, pain, despair? Who ever yet returned
To teach the laws of Death's untrodden realm?
Unjust perhaps as those which drive us now,
Oh, whither, whither?

LUCRETIA. Trust in God's sweet love,
The tender promises of Christ; ere night,
Think, we shall be in Paradise.

BEATRICE. 'Tis past!
Whatever comes my heart shall sink no more.
And yet, I know not why, your words strike chill;
How tedious, false, and cold seem all things. I
Have met with much injustice in this world;
No difference has been made by God or man,
Or any power moulding my wretched lot,
'Twixt good or evil, as regarded me.
I am cut off from the only world I know,
From light, and life, and love, in youth's sweet prime.
You do well telling me to trust in God,
I hope I do trust in Him. In whom else
Can any trust? And yet my heart is cold.

(*During the latter speeches* GIACOMO *has retired conversing with* CAMILLO, *who now goes out;* GIACOMO *advances.*)

GIACOMO. Know you not, Mother . . . Sister, know you not?
Bernardo even now is gone to implore
The Pope to grant our pardon.

LUCRETIA. Child, perhaps
It will be granted. We may all then live
To make these woes a tale for distant years:

Oh, what a thought! It gushes to my heart
Like the warm blood.
BEATRICE. Yet both will soon be cold.
Oh, trample out that thought! Worse than despair,
Worse than the bitterness of death, is hope:
It is the only ill which can find place
Upon the giddy, sharp, and narrow hour
Tottering beneath us. Plead with the swift frost
That it should spare the eldest flower of spring;
Plead with awakening earthquake, o'er whose couch
Even now a city stands, strong, fair, and free;
Now stench and blackness yawn, like death. Oh, plead
With famine, or wind-walking Pestilence,
Blind lightning, or the deaf sea, not with man!
Cruel, cold, formal man; righteous in words,
In deeds a Cain. No, Mother, we must die:
Since such is the reward of innocent lives,
Such the alleviation of worst wrongs.
And whilst our murderers live, and hard, cold men,
Smiling and slow, walk through a world of tears
To death as to life's sleep; 'twere just the grave
Were some strange joy for us. Come, obscure Death,
And wind me in thine all embracing arms!
Like a fond mother hide me in thy bosom,
And rock me to the sleep from which none wake.
Live ye, who live, subject to one another
As we were once, who now . . .
(BERNARDO *rushes in.*)
BERNARDO. Oh, horrible!
That tears, that looks, that hope poured forth in prayer,
Even till the heart is vacant and despairs,
Should all be vain! The ministers of death
Are waiting round the doors. I thought I saw
Blood on the face of one . . . What if 'twere fancy?
Soon the heart's blood of all I love on earth
Will sprinkle him, and he will wipe it off
As if 'twere only rain. O life! O world!
Cover me! let me be no more! To see
That perfect mirror of pure innocence
Wherein I gazed, and grew happy and good,

Shivered to dust! To see thee, Beatrice,
Who made all lovely thou didst look upon . . .
Thee, light of life . . . dead, dark! while I say, sister,
To hear I have no sister; and thou, Mother,
Whose love was as a bond to all our loves . . .
Dead! The sweet bond broken!
(*Enter* CAMILLO *and Guards.*)
They come! Let me
Kiss those warm lips before their crimson leaves
Are blighted . . . white . . . cold. Say farewell, before
Death chokes that gentle voice! Oh, let me hear
You speak!
BEATRICE. Farewell, my tender brother. Think
Of our sad fate with gentleness, as now;
And let mild, pitying thoughts lighten for thee
Thy sorrow's load. Err not in harsh despair,
But tears and patience. One thing more, my child;
For thine own sake be constant to the love
Thou bearest us; and to the faith that I,
Though wrapped in a strange cloud of crime and shame,
Lived ever holy and unstained. And though
Ill tongues shall wound me, and our common name
Be as a mark stamped on thine innocent brow
For men to point at as they pass, do thou
Forbear, and never think a thought unkind
Of those, who perhaps love thee in their graves.
So mayest thou die as I do: fear and pain
Being subdued. Farewell! Farewell! Farewell!
BERNARDO. I cannot say, farewell!
CAMILLO. Oh, Lady Beatrice!
BEATRICE. Give yourself no unnecessary pain,
My dear Lord Cardinal. Here, Mother, tie
My girdle for me, and bind up this hair
In any simple knot; ay, that does well.
And yours I see is coming down. How often
Have we done this for one another; now
We shall not do it any more. My Lord,
We are quite ready. Well, 'tis very well.
The End

BLACK-EY'D SUSAN

Black-Ey'd Susan, a milestone in the English drama, opened at the Royal Surrey Theatre in the Blackfriars Road, one of the most important and most fashionably attended of the illegitimate or minor theatres in the first half of the century. It was a house famous for grandiose spectacle, broad melodrama (Thomas Porter Cooke as the monster Goyoneche in *The War Woolf of Tlascala,* Cooke as *The Vampire*), and nautical varieties. These ranged from naval spectacles spawned by Nelson's victories and staged by the sons of that Charles Dibdin (1745-1814) who had introduced the Jolly Jack Tar to the stage in his comic operas, to Fitzball's version of James Fenimore Cooper's *The Pilot.* All the elements were at hand, therefore, when the house dramatist Douglas Jerrold decided to take John Gay's charming ballad of "Sweet William"

> Though battle call me from thy arms,
> Let not my pretty Susan mourn.
> Though Cannons roar, yet free from harms,
> William shall to his dear return

and create a nautical melodrama called *Black-Ey'd Susan; or, All in the Downs.*

Perhaps Jerrold's greatest asset was T. P. Cooke who, born in

1786, had gone to sea at the age of ten aboard H.M.S. *Raven**. When he turned to the stage he was well prepared to represent the pig-tailed and straw-hatted, swashbuckling and shiver-my-timbers "soaring soul" of a British tar. Jerrold himself had become a "first-class volunteer" midshipman at age ten aboard H.M.S. *Namur* and served until peace was declared and the ship's company disbanded after Waterloo. He knew the Navy and servitude (printer's devil, compositor for the *Sunday Monitor,* hack dramatist at the poor-paying Coburg Theatre) and was determined to write about both. His *Fifteen Years of a Drunkard's Life* (1828) and a new play, *Sweet Poll of Plymouth; or, All in the Downs,* got the young man a job at the Royal Surrey. Maurice Willson Disher in *Blood and Thunder* tells what happened:

> Six songs had to be introduced to make it ['Sweet Poll'] pass muster as a burletta [the minor theatres were theoretically not permitted to present anything but musical entertainments], and among these was Gay's ballad which caused the first part of the title to change into *Black-Ey'd Susan.* No drama was ever more nautical; no other seamen so redolent of tar, so virtuous compared with landsmen, so full of sea-faring oaths, exclamations, similes and metaphors—salt water is rarely out of their mouths and often fills their eyes.

A whole new kind of play had appeared, one so firmly established that Gilbert could parody it fifty years later, and Jerrold and Cooke were famous. *The Athenaeum* reported:

---

*[*Cooke*] *was a sharer in the Earl St. Vincent's victory* [*defeat of the Spanish fleet off Cape St. Vincent, 1797*], *was wrecked off Cuxhaven, and afterwards joined the* [*H.M.S.*] Prince of Wales. *He left the Navy after the Peace of Amiens* [*1802*], *and joined the dramatic profession in January, 1804, at the Royalty Theatre, and subsequently was a member of Astley's* [*equestrian melodrama and spectacle*], *the Lyceum* (*under Laurent the clown*), *and then went to Dublin.*

In 1809 he was at the Surrey, and made his first appearance at Drury Lane, October 19th, 1816, as Diego in "The Watchword; or, the Quito Gate." Went to Covent Garden, October, 1822. He first played Long Tom Coffin in "The Pilot" at the Adelphi, October 25th, and William in "Black-Eyed Susan" June 6th, 1829. His last appearance was on March 29th, 1860, as William, at Covent Garden, for the Dramatic College Benefit. His most celebrated characters he acted the following number of times: William, 785; Long Tom Coffin, 562; the Monster in "Frankenstein" and the Vampire (*this character he also played in 1826 at the Porte St. Martin, Paris*), *365; Roderick Dhu, 250; Aubrey ("Dog of Montargis"), 250; Vanderdecken, 165; "My Poll and My Partner Joe," 269. He was the best representative of the British sailor ever seen on the stage. . . . "* (*Clement Scott,* The Drama of Yesterday and Today)

> All London went over the water [the theatre was across the Thames], and Cooke became a personage in society, as Garrick had been in the days of Goodman's Fields [where he made his name as Richard III, 1741]. Covent Garden borrowed the play and engaged the actor, [to present it there] for an after-piece. A hackney cab carried the triumphant William in his blue jacket and white trousers from the Obelisk to Bow Street, and Mayfair maidens wept over the stirring situations and laughed over the searching dialogue, which had moved, an hour before [at the Royal Surrey], the laughter and tears of the Borough. On the three hundredth night of representation the [outside] walls of the theatre were illuminated, and vast multitudes filled the thoroughfare . . . testimonials were got up for [R. W.] Elliston [manager] and Cooke on the glory of its success, but Jerrold's share of the gain was slight—about seventy pounds of the many thousands realized for the management. With unapproachable meanness, Elliston abstained from presenting the youthful writer with the value of a toothpick.

"Before I was out of my teens it was my misfortune," said Jerrold in later life, "to write for the Minor theatres." But it was there that his sense of the dramatic, his clear-cut ideas of right and wrong, his simple morality, and his crude but vivid effects earned him a lasting fame. He attempted to write literary drama, but he is remembered for *Black-Ey'd Susan, The Mutiny at the Nore* (1830, which showed things were not all ship-shape in the Navy), *The Rent Day* (1832), and other melodramas. "If you'd pass for somebody," he said after he had become the editor of one of the most influential weeklies in the history of British journalism, "you must sneer at a play, but idolize *Punch*." His contributions to that periodical, witty as they were, have gathered dust, but *Black-Ey'd Susan* remains, and reading it, we are tempted to echo what Jerrold's close friend Charles Dickens wrote to him after that historic opening night: "It was so fresh and vigorous, so manly and gallant, that I felt as if it splashed against my theatre-heated face along with the spray of the breezy sea."

BLACK-EY'D SUSAN

OR,

"ALL IN THE DOWNS"

A Nautical and Domestic Drama in Two Acts

by

Douglas Jerrold

First presented in England on June 8, 1829, and in America in 1838 with the following casts:

	The Royal Surrey (London)	*The Tremont (Boston)*
WILLIAM	Mr. T. P. Cooke	Mr. T. Cline
Captain CROSSTREE	Mr. Forrester	Mr. J. E. Murdock
RAKER	Mr. Warwick	Mr. P. C. Cunningham
HATCHET	Mr. Yardley	Mr. W. H. Curtis
DOGGRASS	Mr. Dibdin Pitt	Mr. W. F. Johnson
ADMIRAL	Mr. Gough	Mr. J. G. Gilbert
JACOB TWIG	Mr. Rogers	Mr. D. Whiting
GNATBRAIN	Mr. Buckstone	Mr. G. H. Andrews
BLUE PETER	Mr. Williamson	——
SEAWEED	Mr. Asbury	Mr. B. L. Benson
QUID	Mr. Lee	Mr. Powell
Lieutenant PIKE	Mr. Hicks	Mr. Seaver
YARN	Mr. Dowsing	——
PLOUGHSHARE	Mr. Webb	——
BLACK-EY'D SUSAN	Miss Scott	Mrs. G. H. Barrett
DOLLY MAYFLOWER	Mrs. Vale	Miss A. Fisher

Sailors, Marines, Midshipmen, Officers, etc.

The music throughout this piece is chiefly selections from Charles Dibdin's Naval Airs.

ACT I

SCENE FIRST: *A View of the Country.*

(*Enter* DOGGRASS *and* GNATBRAIN.)

DOGGRASS. Tut! if you are inclined to preach, here is a mile-stone—I'll leave you in its company.

GNATBRAIN. Ay, it's all very well—very well; but you have broken poor Susan's heart, and as for William—

DOGGRASS. What of him?

GNATBRAIN. The sharks of him, for what you care. Didn't you make him turn a sailor, and leave his young wife, the little, delicate black-ey'd Susan, that pretty piece of soft-speaking womanhood, your niece? Now say, haven't you qualms? On a winter's night, now, when the snow is drifting at your door, what do you do?

DOGGRASS. Shut it.

GNATBRAIN. And what, when you hear the wind blowing at your chimney corner?

DOGGRASS. Get closer to it.

GNATBRAIN. What, when in your bed, you turn up one side at the thunder?

DOGGRASS. Turn round on the other. Will you go on with your catechism?

GNATBRAIN. No, I'd rather go and talk to the echoes. A fair day to you, Master Doggrass! If your conscience—

DOGGRASS. Conscience! Phoo! my conscience sleeps well enough.

GNATBRAIN. Sleeps! Don't wake it then—it might alarm you.

DOGGRASS. One word with you,—no more of your advice: I go about like a surly bull, and you a gadfly buzzing around me. From this moment throw off the part of counsellor.

GNATBRAIN. But don't you see?—

DOGGRASS. Don't you see these trees growing about us?

GNATBRAIN. Very well.

DOGGRASS. If a cudgel was cut from them for every knave who busies himself in the business of others—don't you think it would mightily open the prospect?

GNATBRAIN. Perhaps it might: and don't you think that if every hard-hearted, selfish rascal that destroys the happiness of others, were strung up to the boughs before they were cut for cudgels, don't you think that instead of opening the prospect, it would mightily darken it?

DOGGRASS. I have given you warning—take heed! take heed! and with this counsel, I give you a good day. (*Exit.*)

GNATBRAIN. Ay, it's the only thing good you can give; and that only good, because it's not your own. That rascal has no more heart than a bagpipe! One could sooner make Dover Cliffs dance a reel to a penny whistle, than move him with words of pity or distress. No matter, let the old dog bark; his teeth will not last forever—and I yet hope to see the day when poor black-ey'd Susan, and the jovial sailor, William, may defy the surly cur that now divides them. (*Exit.*)

(*Enter* RAKER *and* HATCHET.)

RAKER. A plague on him!—if I thought he meant us foul play,—

HATCHET. Not he—'twas a mistake.

RAKER. Aye, a mistake that nearly threw us into the hands of the Philistines. But I know why you have ever a good word for this same Doggrass.

HATCHET. Know! you know as much as the weathercock that answers every wind, yet cannot tell the point from which it blows. And what do you know?

RAKER. I know that Mrs. Susan, Doggrass's niece, has two black eyes.

HATCHET. Umph! your knowledge proves that, though a fool, you are not yet blind.

RAKER. Civil words, Master Hatchet.

HATCHET. What! be you as dumb as the figure-head of the *Starling;* as soft and as yielding as teazed oakum—let my little finger be your helm, and see you answer it. Who am I?

RAKER. Tom Hatchet, the smuggler of Deal; Captain of the *Redbreast,* and trading partner with old Doggrass.

HATCHET. Thank'ee: now I'll tell you what you are—Bill Raker, first mate of the *Redbreast,* as great a rogue as ever died at the foreyard, and consequently—

RAKER. The best person to go on your errands.

HATCHET. Just so; see you do them well. Now, bear up, whilst I pour a broadside of intelligence into you. I'm going to be married.

RAKER. You generally are at every port you put into.

HATCHET. Belay your jokes. To whom do you think?—you can't guess?

RAKER. No. It isn't to the last port-admiral's widow? Perhaps to big Betsy, the bumboat woman.

HATCHET. No, you albatross,—to Susan—black-ey'd Susan.

RAKER. Steady there—steady!—I'm no younker. The lass is married already.

HATCHET. Aye, she had a husband. (*Significantly.*)

RAKER. What!—why no!

HATCHET. How blows the wind now—what do you stare at? He's dead.

RAKER. William dead! Then there's not so fine, so noble, so taut-rigged a fellow in His Majesty's navy. Poor lad—poor lad!

HATCHET. Turning whimperer?

RAKER. Why not? Such news would make a mermaid cry in the middle of her singing.

HATCHET. Avast with your salt water! William is not dead: what think you now?

RAKER. That there is one more brave fellow in the world and one more liar.

HATCHET. Ha!—

RAKER. Slack your fore-sheet, Captain Hatchet; if you must spin such galley yarns, let it be to the marines, or the landlady of the Ship; but see that you don't again bring tears into an old sailor's eyes, and laugh at him for hoisting and answering pendant to signals of distress. You marry Susan? Now belay, belay the joke.

HATCHET. Listen to my story: it shall be short—short as a marlin-spike. I must marry Susan: she knows not you—you must swear that you were her husband's shipmate—that you saw him drowned. Susan now lives with old Dame Hatley—she has no other home; and if she refuse, Doggrass will seize for long arrears of rent, on the old woman's goods, and turn Susan adrift; then the girl has no chance left but to marry. Is it not a good scheme?

RAKER. Had the devil been purser, he could not have made a better.

HATCHET. I'm going now to Doggrass, to see further about it; mean-time, do you think of the part you are to play, and I'll think how I can best reward you. (*Exit.*)

RAKER. I must certainly look a scoundrel. There must be an invitation in my figure-head to all sorts of wickedness, else Captain Hatchet could never have offered such dirty work to an old sailor. I must look a villain, and that's the truth. Well, there is no help for an ugly countenance; but if my face be ill-favoured, I'll take care to keep my heart of the right colour: like the Dolphin tap, if I hang out a badly-painted sign-post, I'll see and keep good cheer within. (*Exit.*)

SCENE SECOND: DAME HATLEY'S *Cottage.* SUSAN *is heard without, singing a verse of "Black-ey'd Susan."*

(*Enter* SUSAN.)

SUSAN. Twelve long, tedious months have passed, and no, no tidings of William. Shame upon the unkind hearts that parted us—that sent my dear husband to dare the perils of the ocean, and made me a pining, miserable creature! Oh, the pangs, the dreadful pangs that tear the sailor's wife, as, wakeful on her tear-wet pillow, she lists and trembles at the roaring sea!

(*Enter* GNATBRAIN, *at the cottage door.*)

GNATBRAIN. There she is, like a caged nightingale, singing her heart out against her prison-bars—for this cottage is little better than a gaol to her. Susan!

SUSAN. Gnatbrain!

GNATBRAIN. In faith, Susan, if sorrow makes such sweet music, may I never turn skylark, but always remain a goose.

SUSAN. Have you seen my uncle?

GNATBRAIN. Oh, yes!

SUSAN. Will he show any kindness?

GNATBRAIN. I cannot tell. Did you ever see gooseberries grow upon a cabbage-stump? You have flowers from an aloe-tree, if you wait a hundred years.

SUSAN. He has threatened to distress the good dame.

GNATBRAIN. Ay, for the rent. Oh, Susan, I would I were your landlord! I should think myself well paid if you would allow me every quarter-day to put my ear to the key-hole, and listen to one of your prettiest ditties. Why, for such payment, were I your landlord, I'd find you in board, washing, and lodging, and the use of a gig on Sundays. I wish I—But la! what's the use of my wishing? I'm nobody but half gardener, half waterman—a kind of alligator, that gets his breakfast from the shore, and his dinner from the sea—a—(DOGGRASS *passes window.*)

SUSAN. Oh, begone! I see Mr. Doggrass; if he find you here—

GNATBRAIN. He must not; here's a cupboard—I'm afraid there's plenty of room in it.

SUSAN. No, no, I would not for the world—there is no occasion—meet him.

GNATBRAIN. Not I, for quiet's sake. We never meet but, like gunpowder and fire, there is an explosion. This will do. (*Goes into the closet.*)

(*Enter* DOGGRASS.)

DOGGRASS. Now, Susan, you know my business—I say, you know my business. I come for money.

SUSAN. I have none, sir.

DOGGRASS. A pretty answer, truly. Are people to let their houses to beggars?

SUSAN. Beggars! Sir, I am your brother's orphan child.

DOGGRASS. I am sorry for it. I wish he were alive to pay for you. And where is your husband?

SUSAN. Do you ask where he is? I am poor, sir—poor and unprotected; do not, as you have children of your own, do not insult me. (*Weeps.*)

DOGGRASS. Ay, this is to let houses to women; if the tax-gatherers were to be paid with crying, why, nobody would roar more lustily than myself: let a man ask for his rent, and you pull out your pocket-handkerchief. Where's Dame Hatley?

SUSAN. In the next room—ill, very ill.

DOGGRASS. An excuse to avoid me; she shall not. (*Going.*)

SUSAN. You will not enter!

DOGGRASS. Who shall stop me?

SUSAN. If heaven give me power, I! Uncle, the old woman is sick—I fear dangerously. Her spirit, weakened by late misfortune, flickers, like a dying light. Your sudden appearance might make all dark. Uncle—landlord! would you have murder on your soul?

DOGGRASS. Murder?

SUSAN. Yes; though such may not be the common word, hearts are daily crushed, spirits broken—whilst he who slays, destroys in safety.

DOGGRASS. Can Dame Hatley pay me the money?

SUSAN. No.

DOGGRASS. Then she shall to prison.

SUSAN. She will die there.

DOGGRASS. Well?

SUSAN. Would you make the old woman close her eyes in a gaol?

DOGGRASS. I have no time to hear sentiment. Mrs. Hatley has no money—you have none. Well, though she doesn't merit lenity of me, I'll not be harsh with her.

SUSAN. I thought you could not.

DOGGRASS. I'll just take whatever may be in the house, and put up with the rest of the loss.

(*Enter* DOLLY MAYFLOWER.)

DOLLY. So, Mr. Doggrass, this is how you behave to unfortunate folks—coming and selling them up, and turning them out. Is this your feeling for the poor?

DOGGRASS. Feeling! I pay the rates. What business have you here? Go to your spinning.

DOLLY. Spinning! if it were to spin a certain wicked old man a halter, I'd never work faster. Ugh! I always thought you very ugly, but now you look hideous.

SUSAN. Peace, good Dolly.

DOLLY. Peace! Oh, you are too quiet—too gentle! Take example by me: I only wish he'd come to sell me up, that's all. (DOGGRASS *goes to door.*) Oh, I know who you are looking after—your man, Jacob Twig; he hops after you on your dirty work, like a tomtit after a jackdaw—I saw him leering in at the door. I wish my dear Gnatbrain was here. Oh, Susan, I wish he was here; he's one of the best, most constant of lovers—he'd befriend you for my sake.

DOGGRASS (*goes to the door*). Jacob! (*Enter* JACOB TWIG. *He has a memorandum book in his hand, a pen in his ear, and an ink-bottle in the buttonhole of his coat.*) You know your business.

JACOB. What, here, master? What, at old Dame Hatley's?

DOLLY. To be sure, good Jacob; if your master had a tree, and but one squirrel lived in it, he'd take its nuts, sooner than allow it lodging gratis.

SUSAN. Uncle, have compassion—wait but another week—a day.

DOGGRASS. Not an hour—a minute. Jacob, do your duty. Now begin; put down everything you see in the cottage.

JACOB. Master, hadn't you better wait a little? Perhaps the Dame can find friends. (DOGGRASS *is imperative.*) Well, here goes: I'll first begin with the cupboard.

SUSAN (*stopping him*). No, let me entreat you do not. Come this way, if you are still determined.

DOGGRASS. Eh! why that way? why not with the cupboard? I suspect—

JACOB. And now, so do I.

DOLLY. You suspect! I dare say, suspicion is all your brain can manage. What should you suspect—a thing that never had a thought deeper than a mug of ale? You suspect Susan! Why, we shall have the crows suspecting the lilies.

JACOB. You say so, do you? Now, I'll show you my consequence. I'll put everything down, master, and begin with the cupboard. Ah! it's fast: I'll have it open—and I'll put the first thing down. (*Pulls open the door, when* GNATBRAIN *knocks* JACOB *down with rolling-pin, and stands in attitude.*—SUSAN *in corner.*—DOLLY *in surprise.*—DOGGRASS *exulting.*)

GNATBRAIN. No, I'll put the first thing down.

DOLLY. Gnatbrain! Oh, Susan, Susan!

DOGGRASS. Oh, oh! we shall have the crows suspecting the lilies! Pretty flower! how it hangs its head! Go on with your duty, Jacob; put down everything in the house.

GNATBRAIN. Do, Jacob; begin with "one broken head"—then, one stony-hearted landlord—one innocent young woman—ditto, jealous—one man tolerably honest—and one somewhat damaged.

JACOB. I'll have you up before justices—you have broken my crown.

GNATBRAIN. Broken your crown! Jacob, Jacob, it was cracked before!

JACOB. How do you know that?

GNATBRAIN. By the ring of it, Jacob—by the ring: I never heard such a bit of Brummagem in my life.

DOGGRASS (*to* SUSAN). Well, Susan, it is sometimes convenient, is it not, for a husband to be at sea?

SUSAN. Sir, scorn has no word,—contempt no voice to speak my loathing of your insinuations. Take, sir, all that is here; satisfy your avarice; but dare not indulge your malice at the cost of one who has now nothing left her in her misery but the sweet consciousness of virtue. (*Exit.*)

DOGGRASS. The way with all women when they are found out, is it not, Mrs. Dolly?

DOLLY. I can't tell, sir; I never was found out.

DOGGRASS. Ay, you are lucky.

DOLLY. Yes—we don't meet often. But as for you, Mr. Gnatbrain—

GNATBRAIN. Now, no insinuations. I wish I could remember what Susan said about virtue: it would apply to my case admirably. Nothing like a sentiment to stop accusation—one may apply it to a bleeding reputation, as barbers do cobwebs to a wound.

DOGGRASS. Jacob, do you stay here—see that nothing of the least value leaves the house.

GNATBRAIN. In that case, Jacob, you may let your master go out.

DOGGRASS. Some day, my friend, I shall be a match for you. (*Exit.*)

GNATBRAIN. Perhaps so, but one of us must change greatly to make us pairs. (GNATBRAIN *then pursues* JACOB *into corner.*) Jacob, I never look upon your little carcase, but it puts me in mind of a pocket edition of the Newgate Calendar—a neat Old Bailey duodecimo. You are a most villainous-looking rascal—an epitome of a noted highwayman.

JACOB. What!

GNATBRAIN. True as the light. You have a most Tyburnlike physiognomy: there's Turpin in the curl of your upper lip—Jack Sheppard in the under one—your nose is Jerry Abershaw himself—Duval and Barrington are your eyes—and as for your chin, why Sixteen-String Jack lives again in it. (GNATBRAIN *goes to window, affecting to see what is passing outside.*) Eh! well done—excellent! there's all the neighbours getting the furniture out the garden window.

JACOB. Is there? It's against the law. I'm his Majesty's officer, and I'll be among them in a whistle. (JACOB *rushes off;* GNATBRAIN *instantly bolts door.*)

GNATBRAIN. A bailiff, like a snowstorm, is always best on the outside. Now Dolly, sweet Dolly Mayflower, won't you look at me? Won't you be the summer cabbage of my heart, and let me cultivate you?

DOLLY. Don't talk to me, sir!—the cupboard, sir—the cupboard.

GNATBRAIN. Hear my defence. On my word, I had not the least idea that you would have found me, or the cupboard is the last place I should have gone into.

DOLLY. It's no matter; there's Mr. James Rattlin, boatswain's mate of the *Bellerophon*—

GNATBRAIN. What! you wouldn't marry a sailor?

DOLLY. And why not?

GNATBRAIN. Your natural timidity wouldn't allow you.

DOLLY. My timidity?

GNATBRAIN. Yes; you wouldn't like to be left alone o'nights. Your husband would be at sea for six months out of the twelve; there would be a wintry prospect for you.

DOLLY. But he would be at home the other six months—and there's summer, sir.

GNATBRAIN. True, but when you can have summer all the year round, don't you think it more to your advantage?

DOLLY. No—for, if it always shone, we should never really enjoy fine weather.

GNATBRAIN. Oh, my dear, when we are married, we'll get up a thunderstorm or two, depend upon it. But come, Dolly, your heart is too good, your head too clear, to nourish idle suspicion. Let us go and see poor Susan. There is real calamity enough in our every-day paths; we need not add to it by our idle follies. (*Exeunt.*)

SCENE THIRD: *A View of the Country.*

(*Enter* HATCHET.)

HATCHET. Doggrass has made the seizure by this time. Now I'll step in, pay the money, and thus buy the gratitude of Susan, before I tell her the story of her husband's death. (*Enter* JACOB, *running*.) Bring up there, my young skiff. Whither bound?

JACOB. I'm in a hurry.

HATCHET. Bring up, I say, or I'll spoil your figurehead. (*Lifting his cudgel.*)

JACOB. Do you know who I am?

HATCHET. No; what are you, my young flying-fish?

JACOB. I'm a bailiff—aren't you frightened? I serve Mr. Doggrass.

HATCHET. The very craft I was sailing after. You have been to Susan's—Black-ey'd Susan's, as she's called?

JACOB. How do you know that?

HATCHET. You have made a seizure there?

JACOB. Right again.

HATCHET. Have secured everything?

JACOB. Wrong. I had made as pretty a piece of business of it as any of my craft—a very pretty stroke of handiwork; but somehow or the other—

HATCHET. You frighten me. Nobody paid the money, I hope?

JACOB. Oh, don't be alarmed at that; no, but somehow or the other, quite by a mistake, when I thought I was in possession, I found myself on the wrong side of the house. And, here comes Susan.

(*Enter* SUSAN.)

JACOB. Aren't you ashamed of yourself, Mrs. Susan, to make one to cozen so innocent a little bailiff as myself—aren't you ashamed of yourself?

HATCHET (*throwing Jacob over to left*). Stand o' one side! What, in trouble, my pretty Susan? What, have the land-sharks got aboard of the cottage? Come, cheer up.

SUSAN. What, do you indeed pity me? This is kind, and, from a stranger, unexpected.

HATCHET. Not such a stranger as you may think.

SUSAN. No.

HATCHET. No, I know your husband—sailed with him.

SUSAN. You did! Oh, tell me everything!

HATCHET. All in good time. (*To* JACOB.) What do you want here—sticking like a barnacle to a ship's copper? (*Strikes* JACOB *with cudgel.*)

JACOB. Want! Oh, here comes my master—he'll tell you what I want. I'll leave you with him—he'll answer all questions. (*Exit, but returns, and strikes* HATCHET *with book, and runs off.*)

(*Enter* DOGGRASS.)

DOGGRASS. So, madam, you must show contempt to a king's officer—put a servant of the law out of doors!

HATCHET. Steady there! none of your overhauling. What do you want with the young woman?

DOGGRASS. What's that to you?

SUSAN. Oh, pray don't quarrel on my account—do not, I entreat you!

HATCHET (*aside*). I'll swagger a little. Quarrel, my dear—I'd fight yard-arm to yard-arm for you—go on a boarding party, cut out, row under a battery, or fight in a rocket-boat; anything for the pretty black-ey'd Susan.

DOGGRASS. Well, as you'll do all this, perhaps you'll pay the money she owes.

HATCHET. That will I, though it were the last shot in my locker.

SUSAN. No, no, there is no occasion; I would not have it for the world.

DOGGRASS. You wouldn't? I would—but don't be afraid—he'll talk, but he'll be long ere he pays twelve pounds seventeen and sixpence for you, black-ey'd and pretty as you are.

HATCHET. See how little you know of a sailor; there's thirteen pounds—I'm not much of an accountant, but it strikes me that that will pay your little bill, and just leave a dirty two-and-sixpence for young Jibboom, the bailiff.

SUSAN. Oh, my good, kind friend—this generosity—my thanks, my prayers!

HATCHET. Not a word, not a word—good-bye.

SUSAN. Yet, do not leave me; you said you knew my husband—had a tale to tell of him.

HATCHET. Yes, but not now; to-morrow. If I have done anything to oblige you, let me ask the delay. Besides, then I will bring one with me who can tell you more of William than myself; meantime, farewell. (*Aside.*) She's softened. A woman is like sealing-wax—only melt her, and she will take what form you please. I've bought her heart with the chink, and to-morrow will secure it. (*Exit.*)

SUSAN. Wait till to-morrow! Alas! there is no remedy but patience; yet, spite of myself, I feel forebodings which I know 'tis weakness to indulge.

DOGGRASS. I suppose, Mrs. Susan, as the case at present stands, neither you nor the old dame will now think of leaving the cottage?

SUSAN. Indeed, landlord, we shall.

DOGGRASS. Landlord! why not uncle? it is a much better word.

SUSAN. It might have been, but your unkindness has taught me to forget it.

DOGGRASS. Now, hear reason. (*She turns from him.*) Well, to be sure, a plain-spoken man can't expect it from one of your sex, so I'll leave you. You'll think again about the cottage? it has a pretty situation, and as for the rent, why, as one may say, it's a mere nothing. (*Exit.*)

SUSAN. Cruel man! Oh, William! when, when will you return to your almost heartbroken Susan? Winds, blow prosperously, be tranquil, seas, and bring my husband to my longing eyes. (*Exit.*)

SCENE FOURTH: *A View of the Downs.—The fleet at anchor.*

(*Enter* JACOB TWIG.)

JACOB. After all, I don't much like this trade of bailiff. I've a great mind to give it up, go back to my native Dover again, and turn ploughman. (*Three cheers.*) Holloa! the boats are putting off from the ships. Deal will be crowded again; there will be no getting a sweetheart for these six months. (*Music.—Three cheers.*)

(*Enter* SEAWEED, BLUE PETER, SAILORS, *and* WILLIAM.)

WILLIAM. Huzza! huzza! my noble fellows, my heart jumps like a dolphin—my head turns round like a capstern; I feel as if I were driving before the gale of pleasure for the haven of joy.

SEAWEED. But I say, William, there's nobody here to meet us.

WILLIAM. Why, no! that is, you see, because we dropped anchor afore the poor things had turned out of their hammocks. Ah! if my Susan knew who was here, she'd soon lash and carry, roused up by the whistle of that young boatswain's mate, Cupid, piping in her heart. Holloa! what craft is this? Cutter, ahoy!—what ship?

JACOB (*taking off his hat*). My name is Jacob Twig.

WILLIAM. You needn't bring to, under bare poles—cover your truck, and up with your answering pendant. Come, clear your signal halyards, and hoist away. What service?

JACOB. I'm in the law.

WILLIAM. Umph! belongs to the rocket boats. May my pockets be scuttled, if I didn't think so! 'Tis Beelzebub's ship, the Law! she's neither privateer, bomb-ship, nor letter-o-mark; she's built of green timber, manned with lob-lolly boys and marines; provisioned with mouldy biscuit and bilge-water, and fires nothing but red-hot shot: there's no grappling with or boarding her. She always sails best in a storm, and founders in fair weather. I'd sooner be sent adrift in the North Sea, in a butter cask, with a 'bacco-box for my store-room, than sail in that devil's craft, the Law. My young grampus, I should like to have the mast-heading of you in a stiff north-wester. (*Threatening him.*)

SEAWEED. Avast there, messmate! don't rake the cock-boat fore and aft.

JACOB (*corner*). Don't cock the rake-boat fore and aft. (*Frightened.*)

WILLIAM. Why, yes, I know it's throwing away powder and shot to sink cockle-shells with forty-two-pounders. But warn't it the lawyers that turned me and Susan out of our stowage? Why, I'd as soon had met one of Mother Carey's Chickens, as—eh! (*Looking out.*) There's a fleet bearing down.

PETER. A fleet?—Ay, and as smart as a seventy-four on the King's birthday.

WILLIAM. A little more to larboard, messmate. (WILLIAM *throws* JACOB *to his right, the sailors pass him from one to the other till he is off.*) There's my Susan! Now pipe all hands for a royal salute; there she is, schooner-rigged. I'd swear to her canvas from a whole fleet. Now she makes more sail!—outs with her studding-booms—mounts her royals, moon-rakers and skyscrapers; now she lies to it!—now!—now!—eh? May I be put on six-water grog for a lubber.

PETER. What's the matter?

WILLIAM. 'Tisn't she—'tisn't my craft. (*Music.—Enter women, who welcome all the sailors.—Every one, except* WILLIAM, *is met by a female.—He looks anxiously at every one.—All go off except* WILLIAM.) What! and am I left alone in the doctor's list, whilst all the crew are engaging! I know I look as lubberly as a Chinese junk under a jewry mast. I'm afraid to throw out a signal—my heart knocks against my timbers, like a jolly-boat in a breeze, alongside a seventy-four. Damn it, I feel as if half of me was wintering in the Baltic, and the other half stationed in Jamaica. (*Enter* PLOUGHSHARE.—*Music.*) It's no use, I must ask for despatches. Damn it, there can be no black seal to them! Messmate!

PLOUGHSHARE. Now, friend. (*Comes down.*)

WILLIAM. Give us your grappling-iron! Mayhap you don't know me!

PLOUGHSHARE. No.

WILLIAM. Well, that's hard to a sailor, come to his native place. We have ploughed many an acre together in Farmer Sparrow's ground.

PLOUGHSHARE. What—William! William that married Susan!

WILLIAM. Avast there! hang it—that name, spoke by another, has brought the salt water up; I can feel one tear standing in either eye like a marine at each gangway: but come, let's send them below. (*Wipes his eyes.*) Now, don't pay away your line till I pipe. I have been three years at sea; all that time I have heard but once from Susan—she has been to me a main-stay in all weathers. I have been piped up,—roused from my hammock, dreaming of her,—for the cold, black middle watch; I have walked the deck, the surf beating in my face, but Susan was at my side, and I did not feel it. I have been reefing on the yards, in cold and darkness, when I could hardly see the hand of my next messmate; —but Susan's eyes were on me, and there was light. I have heard the boatswain pipe to quarters;—a voice in my heart whispered "Susan", and I strode like a lion. The first broadside was given;—shipmates, whose words were hardly off their lips, lay torn and mangled about me; —their groans were in my ears, and their blood hot on my face;— I whispered "Susan!" it was a word that seemed to turn the balls aside, and keep me safe. When land was cried from the mast-head, I seized the glass—my shipmates saw the cliffs of England—I, I could see but Susan! I leap upon the beach; my shipmates find hands to grasp and lips to press—I find not Susan's.

PLOUGHSHARE. Believe me—

WILLIAM. Avast there! if you must hoist the black flag—gently. Is she yet in commission?—Does she live?

PLOUGHSHARE. She does.

WILLIAM. Thank heaven! I'll go to church next Sunday, and you shall have a can of grog—eh! but your figurehead changes like a dying dolphin; she lives, but perhaps hove down in the port of sickness. No? what then, eh?—avast! not dead—not sick—yet—why, there's a galley-fire lighted up in my heart—there's not an R in her name?

PLOUGHSHARE. What do you mean?

WILLIAM. Mean! grape and canister! She's not run,—not shown false colours?

PLOUGHSHARE. No, no.

WILLIAM. I deserve a round dozen for the question. Damn it, none of your small arms; but open all your ports and give fire.

PLOUGHSHARE. Susan is well—is constant; but has been made to feel that poverty is too often punished for crime.

WILLIAM. What, short of ammunition to keep off the land-sharks? But her uncle?

PLOUGHSHARE. He has treated her very unkindly.

WILLIAM. I see it! damn it, I'll overhaul him—I'll bring him on his beam-ends. Heave a-head, shipmate!—Now for my dear Susan, and no quarters for her uncle. (*Music.—Exeunt* PLOUGHSHARE *and* WILLIAM.)

(*Enter* CAPTAIN CROSSTREE.)

CROSSTREE. In faith that's the prettiest little vessel I ever saw in a long cruise. I threw out signals to her, but she wouldn't answer. Here comes the fellow that passed me whilst I was talking to her. (*Enter* GNATBRAIN.) Shipmate, there is a dollar for you.

GNATBRAIN. Truly, sir, I would we had been messmates, you might then have made it ten shillings.

CROSSTREE. You passed me a few minutes since, when I was in company with a petticoat.

GNATBRAIN. Ay; it's no use, Captain; she's a tight little craft, and as faithful to all that is good as your ship to her helm.

CROSSTREE. What is her name?—Who is she?

GNATBRAIN. We simply call her Susan—Black-ey'd Susan. She is the wife of a sailor.

CROSSTREE. Ay, what, fond of the blue-jackets?

GNATBRAIN. Yes, so fond of the jacket, that she'll never look at your long coat. Good-day, Captain. (*Exit.*)

CROSSTREE. The wife of a sailor! wife of a common seaman! why, she's fit for an admiral. I know it's wrong, but I will see her—and come what may, I must, and will possess her. (*Exit.*)

SCENE FIFTH: *Interior of* SUSAN'S *Cottage.—Same as Scene Second.*

(*Enter* WILLIAM *at door.*)

WILLIAM. Well, here I am at last! I've come fifteen knots an hour, yet I felt as if I were driving astern all the time. So, this is poor Susan's berth—not aboard—out on liberty, and not come to the beach?

SUSAN (*without*). Oh, say not so, for mercy's sake!

WILLIAM. Eh! that's she;—ha! and with two strange-rigged craft in convoy; I'll tack a bit, and—damn it, if there's foul play! chain-shot and bar-shot! I'll rake 'em fore and aft. (*Retires.*)

(*Enter* SUSAN, HATCHET, *and* RAKER.—*Slow music.*)
(*Aside.*) What, hanging out signals of distress?

SUSAN. Oh, these are heavy tidings indeed!

HATCHET. Don't take on so, pretty Susan! If William is dead, there are husbands enough for so pretty a face as yours.

WILLIAM. Dead! may I never splice the mainbrace, if that swab don't want to get into my hammock. (HATCHET *approaches nearer to* SUSAN.) Now, he's rowing alongside her with muffled oars, to cut her cable!—I'll tomahawk his rigging for him.

SUSAN. But is there no hope?

HATCHET. Hope! none. I tell you, Susan, this honest fellow was William's messmate; he saw him go down;—you didn't rightly hear him when he first told the story—tell it again, Tom. (RAKER *suddenly indicates his unwillingness.*) Poor fellow! he was William's friend, and the story hurts him. I'll tell it you. You see, the ship had got upon the rocks, and it came on to blow great guns; her timbers opened, and she broke her back;—all her masts were overboard, and orders were given to take to the boats. William was in the jolly-boat:—well, she hadn't got the length of a boarding-pike from the wreck, when she shipped a sea, and down she went. William, and twelve other brave fellows, were in the water;—his shipmate here threw out a rope;—it was too late; William sunk, and was never seen more. His shipmate turned round and saw—(*during his speech,* RAKER *has moved into the corner of the stage, his back to* HATCHET, *as if unwilling to hear the story,*—WILLIAM, *by the conclusion of this speech, has placed himself between* HATCHET *and* SUSAN) Damnation!

SUSAN (*shrieking and throwing herself into* WILLIAM'S *arms*). William!

WILLIAM. Damn it, I'm running over at the scuppers, or, you lubbers, I'd been aboard of you before this. What! hang out false signals to the petticoat?—May you both have the yellow flag over you, and go up in the smoke of the fore-castle. Bring-to a minute, and I'll be yard-arm and yard-arm with you. What, Susan, Susan! See, you swabs, how you've brought the white flag into her pretty figurehead. (SUSAN *revives; he relinquishes his hold of her.*) Now, then, I'll make junk of one of you.

SUSAN. William! William! for heaven's sake!—

WILLIAM. Just one little bout, Susan, to see how I'd make small biscuit of 'em. You won't fight? Then take *that* to the paymaster, and ask him for the change. (*Strikes* HATCHET.)

HATCHET. Struck! then here's one of us for old Davy! (*Music.*—*Runs at* WILLIAM *with a drawn cutlass, who catches his right arm; they struggle round.* WILLIAM *throws him off, and stands over him.* HATCHET *on his knee; same time* LIEUTENANT PIKE *appears inside of door.*—TWO MARINES *appear at window.*—*Tableau.*)

PIKE. Smugglers, surrender! or you have not a moment's life. (HATCHET *and* RAKER, *startled by the appearance of* PIKE'S *party, recoil.*)

WILLIAM. *Smugglers!* I thought they were not man-of-war's-men; true blue never piloted a woman on a quicksand.

PIKE (*takes belt from* HATCHET). Here, William, wear this as a trophy of your victory.

WILLIAM. Thank ye, your honour, I'll ship it.

PIKE. Come, my lads, as you have cheated the King long enough, you shall now serve him—the fleet wants hands, and you shall aboard.

WILLIAM. If they are drafted aboard of us, all I wish is that I was boatswain's mate, for their sake! Oh, wouldn't I start 'em! (*Music.*—*Exeunt* PIKE, HATCHET, RAKER.—*The* MARINES *follow.*) Now, Susan (*embraces her*), may I be lashed here until death gives the last whistle.

SUSAN. Oh, William! I never thought we should meet again.

WILLIAM. Not meet! Why, we shall never part again. The Captain has promised to write to the Admiralty for my discharge. I saved his life in the Basque Roads. But I say, Sue, why wasn't you on the beach?

SUSAN. I knew not of your arrival.

WILLIAM. Why, a sailor's wife, Susan, ought to know her husband's craft, if he sailed in a washing-tub, from a whole fleet. But how is this, Sue?—how is this? Poverty aboard?—and then your uncle—

(*Enter* DOGGRASS.)

DOGGRASS (*advances*). Now, Mrs. Susan, I am determined—(*Sees* WILLIAM.)

WILLIAM. The very griffin I was talking of. Now, what are you staring at? What are you opening your mouth for like the main hold of a seventy-four? I should like to send you to sea in a leaky gun-boat, and keep you at the pumps for a six months' cruise.

DOGGRASS. What! William! (*In a fawning tone, offering his hand.*)

WILLIAM. Avast, there! don't think to come under my lee in that fashion. Aren't you a neat gorgon of an uncle now, to cut the painter of a pretty pinnace like this, and send her drifting down the tide of poverty, without ballast, provisions, or compass? May you live a life of ban-yan days, and be put six upon four for't!

DOGGRASS. But you mistake, William—

WILLIAM. No palaver! tell it to the marines. What, tacking and double tacking! Come to what you want to say at once. If you want to get into the top, go up the futtock shrouds like a man—don't creep through lubber's hole. What have you got to say?

DOGGRASS. Don't—you have put my heart into my mouth.

WILLIAM. Have I? I couldn't put a blacker morsel there! Just come alongside here. (*Pulls him by neckcloth.*) I am not much of a scholar, and don't understand fine words. Your heart is as hard as a ring-bolt—to coil it up at once, you are a d——d rascal! If you come here after your friends, you'll find 'em in the cock-pit of one of the fleet. You have missed the rattlin this time, but brought yourself up by the shrouds. Now, take my advice,—strike your false colours, or I wouldn't give a dead marine for the chance of your neck. (DOGGRASS *hurries off.*) That fellow would sit still at his grog, at the cry of "A man overboard!" Oh, Susan, when I look at your eyes, you put me in mind of a frigate, with marines firing from the tops! Come along, Sue: first to fire a salute to old Dame Hatley, then to my shipmates. To-day we'll pitch care overboard, without putting a buoy over him—call for the fiddles—start the rum cask—tipple the grog—and pipe all hands to mischief. (*Exeunt.*)

SCENE SIXTH: *A View near Deal.—Public House.—Table with bottles and cups at back,—forms and stools for sailors, &c.—Loud laughing as scene opens.*—PETER, SEAWEED, GNATBRAIN, DOLLY, SAILORS, RUSTICS, MEN, *and* WOMEN *discovered drinking.*

SEAWEED. Belay that galley yarn, Peter, belay!

GNATBRAIN. Oh, let him go on—he lies like a purser at reckoning day.

SEAWEED. Where's William, I wonder? He promised to meet us. I suppose he's with his Susan now.

PETER. And where can he be better, do you think? But suppose, just to pass the time away, I give you the song that was made by Tom Splinter, upon Susan's parting with William in the Downs?

ALL. Ay, the song—the song!

SEAWEED. Come, pipe up, my boy! Poor Tom Splinter! he was cut in half by a bar-shot from the Frenchman. Well, every ball's commissioned. The song—the song!

PETER. Here goes; but I know I can't sing it now.

SEAWEED. Can't sing! bless you, whenever we want to catch a mermaid, we only make him chant a stave, and we've twenty round the ship in the letting go of an anchor.

SONG—BLUE PETER

All in the Downs the fleet was moor'd,
  The streamers waving on the wind,
When black-ey'd Susan came on board—
  Oh! where shall I my true love find?
Tell me, ye jovial sailors, tell me true,
Does my sweet William sail among your crew?

William, who high upon the yard,
  Rock'd with the billows to and fro;
Soon as her well-known voice he heard,
  He sigh'd and cast his eyes below.
The cord slides swiftly through his glowing hands,
And quick as lightning on the deck he stands.

The boatswain gave the dreadful word,
  The sails their swelling bosom spread;
No longer must she stay on board;
  They kiss'd; she sighed; he hung his head.
Her less'ning boat unwilling rows to land;
Adieu! she cries, and waves her lily hand.

PETER. Halloo! who have we here? Man the yards, my boys—here comes the Captain.

(*Enter* CAPTAIN CROSSTREE.—SAILORS *take off their hats.*—LASSES *curtsy.*)

CROSSTREE. I am sorry, my fine fellows, to interrupt your festivities, but you must aboard to-night.

ALL. To-night, your honour?

CROSSTREE. Yes! it is yet uncertain, that we may not be ordered to set sail to-morrow.

PETER. Set sail to-morrow! why the lords of the Admiralty will break the women's hearts, your honour.

CROSSTREE. Where is William?

PETER. He's with Susan, your honour; pretty black-ey'd Susan, as she is called.

CROSSTREE. With black-ey'd Susan! How is that?

PETER. How, your honour? why they are spliced together for life.

CROSSTREE. Married! I never heard of this!

PETER. No? why your honour, I thought it was as well known as the union-jack. They were spliced before we went upon the last station. Not know it, your honour? why, many a time has the middle-watch sung the parting of William and Susan.

CROSSTREE (*aside*). Married! I had rather forfeited all chance of being an admiral. Well, my lads, you hear my advice; so make the best of your time, for to-morrow you may be sailing for blue water again. (SAILORS *bow, go up*—CROSSTREE *exits in house.*)

PETER. Them lords of the Admiralty know no more about pleasures of liberty, plenty of grog, and dancing with the lasses, than I knows about 'stronomy. Here comes William.

(*Music.—Enter* WILLIAM *and* SUSAN.—*They cheer him.*)

WILLIAM. Here's my shipmates, Susan! Look at her, my hearties—I wouldn't give up the command of this craft, no—not to be made Lord High Admiral.

GNATBRAIN (*brings* DOLLY *down*). Here's my craft. I wouldn't give up the command of this 'ere craft to be made Lord High Gardener on.

WILLIAM. What, honest Gnatbrain,—Susan has told me about you—give us a grapple! (*Shakes hands very forcibly.*—GNATBRAIN *writhes under it.*) What are you looking for?

GNATBRAIN. Looking for my fingers.

WILLIAM (*takes out box*). Here, take a bit from St. Domingo Billy.

GNATBRAIN. From what? (SAILORS *gather round* WILLIAM.)

WILLIAM. From St. Domingo Billy! I see you are taken back—steering in a fog; well, I'll just put on my top-lights to direct your course.

GNATBRAIN. Now, I'm a bit of a sailor—but none of your hard words.

WILLIAM. Hard words! no, I always speak good English. You don't think I'm like Lieutenant Lavender, of the lily-white schooner.

GNATBRAIN. But about St. Domingo Billy.

WILLIAM. It's lucky for you, that you've been good to Susan, or I shouldn't spin you these yarns. You see it was when the fleet was lying off St. Domingo, in the West Indies, the crew liked new rum and dancing with the niggers. Well, the Admiral (a good old fellow, and one as didn't like flogging) wouldn't give the men liberty; some of 'em, howsomever, would swim ashore at night, and come off in the morning. Now, you see, to hinder this, the Admiral and the Captains put St. Domingo Billy on the ship's books, and served him out his mess every morning.

GNATBRAIN. Who was St. Domingo Billy?

WILLIAM. Why, a shark, as long as the Captain's gig. This shark, or Billy—for that's what the sailors called him—used to swim round the fleet, and go from ship to ship, for his biscuit and raw junk, just like a Christian.

GNATBRAIN. Well, but your 'bacco-box, what about that?

WILLIAM. Steady!—I'm coming to it. Well, one morning, about eight bells, there was a black bumboat woman aboard, with a little piccaninny, not much longer than my hand. Well, she sat just in the gangway,—and there was Billy alongside, with his three decks of grinders, ready for what might come. Well, afore you could say about-ship, the little black baby jumped out of its mother's grappling, and fell into Billy's jaws. The black woman gave a shriek that would have split the boatswain's whistle! Tom Gunnell saw how the wind was: he was as fine a seaman as ever stept—stood six feet two, and could sit upon his pig-tail. Well, he snatched up a knife, overboard, he jumps, and dives under Billy, and in a minute the sea was as red as a marine; all the crew hung like a swarm of bees upon the shrouds, and when Tom came up, all over blood with the little baby in his hand, and the shark turned over dead upon its side—my eyes! such a cheer—it might have been heard at Greenwich.

DOLLY. Oh, no, William, not quite so far!

GNATBRAIN. Oh, yes, you might; that is, if the wind had blown that way very strong.

WILLIAM. We had 'em aboard, cut up Billy, and what do you think we found in him? all the watches and 'bacco-boxes as had been lost for the last ten years—an Admiral's cocked hat, and three pilot's telescopes. This is one on 'em! (*Showing box.*)

GNATBRAIN. What! one of the telescopes?

WILLIAM. No, of the boxes, you lubber!

GNATBRAIN. Well, friend William, that's a tolerable yarn.

WILLIAM. True, true as the Nore Light. But come, my hearties, we are not by the galley fire—let's have a dance.

OMNES. Ay, a dance!—a dance!

(*Dance—end of which,* QUID *enters.*)

QUID. Now, lads, all hands on board.

WILLIAM. On board, Master Quid! why, you are not in earnest?

QUID. Indeed, but I am: there's the first lieutenant waiting on the beach for all the liberty men. (SAILORS *and* LASSES *retire and converse together, bidding each other farewell.*)

SUSAN. Oh, William, must you leave me so early?

WILLIAM. Why, duty, you know, Susan, must be obeyed. (*Aside.*) Cruise about here a little while—I'll down to the lieutenant and ax him for leave till to-morrow. Well, come along, shipmates; if so be that blue Peter must fly at the fore, why it's no use putting a black face on the matter. (*Music.*—WILLIAM, SAILORS, *and* GIRLS, *exeunt.*)

GNATBRAIN. This it is, you see, pretty Susan, to be married to a sailor. Now, don't you think it would be much better if William had a little cot, with six feet square for the cultivation of potatoes, than the forecastle for the rearing of laurels? To be obliged to leave you now!

SUSAN. Yes, but I trust he will be enabled to return; nay, there are hopes that he will gain his discharge; and then, with his prize-money,—

GNATBRAIN. Ay, I see, go into the mercantile line—take a shop for marine stores. But, come along, Susan, the evening is closing in—I'll see you to your cottage.

SUSAN. I thank you, good Gnatbrain, but I would, for a time, be alone.

GNATBRAIN. Ah, I see, melancholy and fond of moonlight. Well, poor thing, it's not to be wondered at. I was melancholy when I was first in love, but now I contrive to keep a light heart, though it is struck with an arrow. (*Exit.*)

SUSAN. I hope he will return—surely, his officer will not be so unkind as to refuse him.

(*Enter* CAPTAIN CROSSTREE, *from Inn, intoxicated.*)

CROSSTREE (*singing*). "Cease, rude Boreas."—Confound that fellow's wine!—or mischief on that little rogue's black eyes, for one or the other of them has made sad havoc here.

SUSAN (*aside*). The stranger officer that accosted me.

CROSSTREE. Well, now for the boat. (*Sees* SUSAN.) May I never see salt water again, if this is not the very wench. My dear! my love! come here!

SUSAN. Intoxicated, too! I will hence. (*Going.*)

CROSSTREE (*staying her*). Stop! why, what are you fluttering about? Don't you know I've found out a secret?—ha, ha! I'm your husband's Captain.

SUSAN. I'm glad of it, sir.

CROSSTREE. Are you so? well, that sounds well.

SUSAN. For I think you will give my husband leave of absence, or, if that is impossible, allow me to go on board his ship.

CROSSTREE. Go on board—that you shall! You shall go in the Captain's gig—you shall live in the Captain's cabin.

SUSAN. Sir!

CROSSTREE. Would it not be a shame for such a beautiful, black-ey'd, tender little angel as yourself to visit between decks? Come, think of it. As for William, he's a fine fellow, certainly, but you can forget him.

SUSAN. Sir, let me go!

CROSSTREE. Forget him and live for me. By heavens, I love you, and must have you!

SUSAN. If you are a gentleman, if you are a sailor, you will not insult a defenceless woman.

CROSSTREE. My dear, I have visited too many seaports not to understand all this. I know I may be wrong, but passion hurries me—the wine fires me—your eyes dart lightning into me, and you shall be mine! (*Seizes* SUSAN.)

SUSAN. Let me go! in mercy!—William, William!

CROSSTREE. Your cries are vain! resistance useless!

SUSAN. Monster! William, William! (*Music.—She breaks away from him, and runs off; he follows and drags her back, and, as he throws her round, she shrieks.*)

(*Enter* WILLIAM, *with drawn cutlass,* SAILORS *and* GIRLS.)

WILLIAM. Susan! and attacked by the buccaneers! Die! (*Strikes* CROSSTREE *with cutlass, who staggers and is caught by* SEAWEED.—SUSAN *rushes up to* WILLIAM.)

OMNES. The Captain!

Slow music.—Tableau, and
End of Act First

ACT II

SCENE FIRST: *A Street in Deal.*

(*Enter* GNATBRAIN.—*Distant gun heard without.*)

GNATBRAIN. Oh, dear! the Court Martial is ordered: the Captains, with the Admiral at their head, are assembling on board the ship, and there goes the signal gun for the commencement of the proceedings. Poor William!

(*Enter* DOGGRASS.)

DOGGRASS. Poor William! aye, if pity would save him, his neck would be insured. Didn't he attempt to kill his Captain?

GNATBRAIN. True; he deserves hanging for that. You would have doubtless gone a different way to work. William cut down his officer in defence of his wife—now you, like a good, prudent man, would have thrust your hands into your pockets, and looked on.

DOGGRASS. None of your sneering, sirrah. William—hanging is too good for him!

GNATBRAIN. You know best what hanging is good for—but I know this,—if all the rascals who, under the semblance of a snug respectability, sow the world with dissensions and deceit, were fitted with a halter, rope would double its price, and the executioner set up his carriage.

DOGGRASS. Have you any meaning in this?

GNATBRAIN. No—none: you can couple my meaning with your honesty.

DOGGRASS. When will your tongue change its pertness?

GNATBRAIN. When your heart changes its colour.

DOGGRASS. My heart! I have nothing to reproach myself with; I feel strong in—

GNATBRAIN. Yes, you must be strong, there's no doubting that—else you'd never be able to carry that lump of marble in your bosom—that's a load would break the back of any porter.

DOGGRASS. I tell you what, my friend, I had some thoughts—

GNATBRAIN. Stop! I'll tell you what I had only just now—a dream.

DOGGRASS. A dream?

GNATBRAIN. Aye; I dreamt that a young lamb was set upon by a wolf, when, strange to say, a lion leapt upon it, and tore it piecemeal; at this moment a band of hunters came up, and secured the noble brute: they were about to kill the lion, their guns were pointed, their swords drawn, when a thing, at first no bigger than my hand, appeared in the sky—it came closer, and I saw it was a huge vulture; it went wheeling round and round the victim lion, and appeared to anticipate the feast of blood—and with a red and glaring eye, and grasping talons, seemed to demand the carcass, ere the lion yet was dead.

DOGGRASS. And this was a dream?

GNATBRAIN. Yes, a day-dream.

DOGGRASS. And what, since you will talk, say you to the vulture?

GNATBRAIN. Nothing; but I looked at it—and with a loathing, left it. (*Exit, looking significantly at* DOGGRASS.)

DOGGRASS. I shall never sleep quietly until I lay that rascal by the heels. Confusion take him! I'm ashamed to say I am almost afraid of him.

(*Enter* JACOB TWIG.)

Now, Jacob, how fares Captain Crosstree?

JACOB. Better; it is thought he will recover.

DOGGRASS. Another disappointment; yet, by the rules of the service, William must die. Here, Jacob, I've something for you to—

JACOB. I've something for you, sir. (*Gives him money.*)

DOGGRASS. Why, what's this?

JACOB. Three guineas, two shillings, and sixpence half-penny! That's just, sir, what I've received of you since I've been in your employ.

DOGGRASS. Well, and what of that?

JACOB. I don't feel comfortable with it, sir; I'd thank you to take it.

DOGGRASS. Take it! Are you mad?

JACOB. No, sir—I have been; I have been wicked, and I now think—and I wish you would think so too—that all wickedness is madness.

DOGGRASS. How is all this brought about?

JACOB. A short tale, sir; it's all with the Captain.

DOGGRASS. The Captain!

JACOB. Yes; I was in the public-house when the Captain was brought in with that gash in his shoulder; I stood beside his bed; it was steeped in blood—the doctor shook his head—the parson came and prayed; and when I looked on the Captain's blue lips and pale face, I thought what poor creatures we are; then something whispered in my heart, "Jacob, thou hast been a mischief-making, wicked lad—and suppose, Jacob, thou wert, at a moment's notice, to take the Captain's place!" I heard this—heard it as plain as my own voice—and my hair moved, and I felt as if I'd been dipped in a river, and I fell like a stone on my knees—when I got up again, I was quite another lad.

DOGGRASS. Ha, ha!

JACOB. That's not a laugh; don't deceive yourself, it sounds to my ears like the croak of a frog, or the hoot of an owl.

DOGGRASS. Fool!

JACOB. I ran as hard as I could run to Farmer Arable—told him what a rascal I was, and begged he'd hire me—he did, and gave me half-a-year's wages in advance, that I might return the money you had paid me—there it is.

DOGGRASS. Idiot! take the money.

JACOB. Every coin of it is a cockatrice's egg—it can bring forth nought but mischief.

DOGGRASS. Take it, or I'll throw it into the sea.

JACOB. Don't, for coming from your hand, it would poison all the fishes.

DOGGRASS. You will be a fool, then?

JACOB. Yes; one of your fools, Master Doggrass—I will be honest. (*Exit.*)

DOGGRASS. All falling from me; no matter. I'll wait to see William disposed of; then, since the people here seem leagued against me, sell off my stock, and travel. The postman brought this packet (*producing one*) to my house, directed to Captain Crosstree. What can it contain? No matter—it is a virtue on the right side to be over-cautious; so go you into my pocket, until William is settled for. (*Distant gun heard without.*) The Court is opened—now to watch its progress. (*Exit.*)

SCENE SECOND: *The State Cabin.—The Court Martial.—Three guns on each side of the cabin.—Music.*

(*The* ADMIRAL *sits at the head of the table, a union-jack flying over his chair; six* CAPTAINS *sit on each side of the table.* WILLIAM, *the* MASTER-AT-ARMS, *and* MARINE OFFICER. *A* MARINE *at each side, and one behind. A* MIDSHIPMAN *is in attendance.*)

ADMIRAL. Prisoner, as your ship is ordered for instant service, and it has been thought expedient that your shipmates should be witnesses of whatever punishment the Court may award you, if found guilty of the crime wherewith you are charged, it will be sufficient to receive the depositions of the witnesses, without calling for the attendance of Captain Crosstree, whom it is yet impossible to remove from shore. One of the witnesses, I am sorry to say, is your wife; however, out of mercy to your peculiar situation, we have not summoned her to attend.

WILLIAM. Bless you, your honours, bless you! My wife, Susan, standing here before me, speaking words that would send me to the fore-yard—it had been too much for an old sailor. I thank your honours! If I must work for the dead reckoning, I wouldn't have it in sight of my wife.

ADMIRAL. Prisoner, you are charged with an attempt to slay Robert Crosstree, Captain of his Majesty's Navy, and your superior officer. Answer, are you guilty, or not guilty?

WILLIAM. I want, your honour, to steer well between the questions. If it be asked, whether I wished to kill the Captain, I could, if I'd a mind to brag, show that I loved him—loved him next to my own Susan! All's one for that. I am not guilty of an attempt to kill the Captain; but, if it be guilt to strike in defence of a sailor's own sheet-anchor, his wife, why I say guilty, your honour; I say it, and think I've no cause to hang out the red at my fore.

ADMIRAL. You plead guilty—let me, as one of your judges, advise you to reconsider the plea. At least take the chances which the hearing of your case may allow.

WILLIAM. I leave that chance to your own hearts, your honours; if they have not a good word for poor Will, why, it is below the honesty of a sailor to go upon the half tack of a lawyer.

ADMIRAL. You will not retract the plea?

WILLIAM. I'm fixed; anchored to it, fore an' aft, with chain cable.

ADMIRAL. Does no one of your shipmates attend to speak to your character? Have you no one?

WILLIAM. No one, your honour? I didn't think to ask them—but let the word be passed, and may I never go aloft, if, from the boatswain to the black cook, there's one that could spin a yarn to condemn me.

ADMIRAL. Pass the word forward for witnesses.

MIDSHIPMAN. Witnesses for the prisoner.

(*Enter* QUID.—*Bows to Court.*)

ADMIRAL. What are you?

QUID. Boatswain, your honour.

ADMIRAL. What know you of the prisoner?

QUID. Know, your honour?—the trimmest sailor as ever handled rope; the first on his watch, the last to leave the deck; one as never belonged to the after-guard. He has the cleanest top, and the whitest hammock. From reefing a main-topsail to stowing a netting, give me taut Will afore any able seaman in his Majesty's fleet.

ADMIRAL. But what know you of his moral character?

QUID. His moral character, your honour? Why, he plays upon the fiddle like an angel!

ADMIRAL. Are there any other witnesses? (*Exit* QUID.)

(*Enter* SEAWEED.)

What do you know of the prisoner?

SEAWEED. Nothing but good, your honour.

ADMIRAL. He was never known to disobey command?

SEAWEED. Never but once, your honours, and that was when he gave me half of his grog when I was upon the black list.

ADMIRAL. What else do you know?

SEAWEED. Why this. I know, your honour, if William goes aloft, there's sartin promotion for him.

ADMIRAL. Have you nothing else to show? Did he ever do any great benevolent action?

SEAWEED. Yes, he twice saved the Captain's life, and once ducked a Jew slopseller. (ADMIRAL *motions witnesses to retire. Exit* SEAWEED.)

ADMIRAL. Are there any more witnesses?

WILLIAM. Your honours, I feel as if I were in irons, or seized to the grating, to stand here and listen,—like the landlord's daughter of the Nelson,—to nothing but yarns about service and character. My actions, your honours, are kept in the log-book aloft. If, when that's overhauled, I'm not found a trim seaman, why it's only throwing salt to the fishes to patter here.

ADMIRAL. Remove the prisoner. (*Exeunt* MASTER-AT-ARMS, *with* WILLIAM, MARINES, *and* MIDSHIPMAN.) Gentlemen, nothing more remains for us than to consider the justice of our verdict. Although the case of the unfortunate man admits of many palliatives, still, for the upholding of a necessary discipline, any commiseration would afford a dangerous precedent, and I fear, cannot be indulged. Gentlemen, are you all determined on your verdict? Guilty, or not guilty?—Guilty? (*After a pause, the* CAPTAINS *bow assent.*) It remains then for me to pass the sentence of the law? (CAPTAINS *bow.*) Bring back the prisoner.

(*Reënter* WILLIAM *and* MASTER-AT-ARMS.)

ADMIRAL. Prisoner—after a patient and impartial investigation of your case, this Court has unanimously pronounced you—*Guilty.* (*Pause.*) If you have anything to say in arrest of judgment,—now is your time to speak.

WILLIAM. In a moment, your honours.—Damn it, my top-lights are rather misty! Your honours, I had been three years at sea, and had never looked upon or heard from my wife—as sweet a little craft as was ever launched. I had come ashore, and I was as lively as a petrel in a storm. I found Susan—that's my wife, your honours—all her gilt taken by the land-sharks; but yet all taut, with a face as red and rosy as the King's head on the side of a fire-bucket. Well, your honours, when we were as merry as a ship's crew on a pay-day, there comes an order to go aboard. I left Susan, and went with the rest of the liberty-men to ax leave of the first-lieutenant. I hadn't been gone the turning of an hour-glass, when I heard Susan giving signals of distress; I out with my cutlass, made all sail, and came up to my craft. I found her battling with a pirate. I never looked at his figure-head, never stopped

—would any of your honours? Long live you and your wives, say I! Would any of your honours have rowed alongside as if you'd been going aboard a royal yacht? No, you wouldn't; for the gilt swabs on the shoulders can't alter the heart that swells beneath; you would have done as I did; and what did I? why, I cut him down like a piece of old junk. Had he been the first lord of the Admiralty, I had done it! (*Overcome with emotion.*)

ADMIRAL. Prisoner, we keenly feel for your situation; yet you, as a good sailor, must know that the course of justice cannot be evaded.

WILLIAM. Your honours, let me be no bar to it; I do not talk for my life. Death! why, if I 'scaped it here,—the next capful of wind might blow me from the yard-arm. All I would strive for, is to show I had no malice; all I wish whilst you pass sentence, is your pity; that, your honours, whilst it is your duty to condemn the sailor, may, as having wives you honour and children you love, respect the husband.

ADMIRAL. Have you anything further to advance?

WILLIAM. All my cable is run out. I'm brought to.

ADMIRAL (*all the* CAPTAINS *rise*). Prisoner! it is now my most painful duty to pass the sentence of the Court upon you. The Court commiserates your situation; and, in consideration of your services, will see that every care is taken of your wife when deprived of your protection.

WILLIAM. Poor Susan!

ADMIRAL. Prisoner! your case falls under the twenty-second Article of War. (*Reads.*) "If any man in, or belonging to the Fleet, shall draw, or offer to draw, or lift up his hand against his superior officer, he shall suffer death." (*Putting on his hat.*) The sentence of the Court is, that you be hanged at the fore-yard-arm of this, his Majesty's ship, at the hour of ten o'clock. Heaven pardon your sins, and have mercy on your soul! This Court is now dissolved. (*Music.*—ADMIRAL *and* CAPTAINS *come forward.*—ADMIRAL *shakes hands with* WILLIAM, *who, overcome, kneels.* —*After a momentary struggle, he rises, collects himself, and is escorted from the cabin in the same way that he entered.*—*The scene closes.*—*Gun fires.*)

SCENE THIRD: *The Gun-room of* WILLIAM'S *Ship. Tomahawks crossed, and fire-buckets in a row.*—*Music.*

(*Enter* LIEUTENANT PIKE, *two* MARINES, WILLIAM, MASTER-AT-ARMS, *followed by* QUID *and* SEAWEED.)

PIKE. Now, William, what cheer?

WILLIAM. Water-logged, your honour—my heart's sprung a leak—I'm three feet water in the hold.

PIKE. Come, summon all your firmness.

WILLIAM. I will, your honour; but just then I couldn't help thinking that when I used to keep the middle watch with you, I never thought it would come to this.

PIKE. But you are a brave fellow, William, and fear not death.

WILLIAM. Death! No—since I first trod the King's oak, he has been about me. I have slept near him, watched near him—he has looked upon my face, and saw I shrunk not. In a storm I have heeded him not—in the fury of the battle I thought not of him. Had I been mowed down by ball or cutlass, my shipmates, as they had thrown me to the sharks, would have given me a parting look of friendship, and over their grog have said I did my duty. This, your honour, would not have been death, but lying-up in ordinary. But to be swayed up like a wet jib, to dry—the whole fleet—nay, the folks of Deal, people that knew me, used to pat me on the head when a boy,—all these looking at me! Oh, thank heaven, my mother's dead!

PIKE. Come, William. (*Shakes his head.*) There, think no more after that fashion. Are there any of your shipmates, on whom you would wish to bestow something?

WILLIAM. Thankee, your honour. Lieutenant—I know you won't despise the gift because it comes from one who walked the forecastle—here's my box—keep it for poor Will's sake—you and I, your honour, have laid yard-arm and yard-arm with many a foe—let us hope we shall come gunwale to gunwale in another climate. (*Gives him box.—To* MARINE OFFICER.) Your honour's hand—blue Peter's flying—the vessel of life has her anchor a-trip, and must soon get under way for the ocean of eternity. Your honour will have to march me to the launching place. You won't give a ship a bad name because she went awkwardly off the stocks. Take this, your honour. (*Opens watch.*) This paper was cut by Susan's fingers before we left the Downs; take it, your honour, I can't look at it. Master Quid, take this for my sake. (*Gives chain and seals, among which is a bullet.*) You see that bullet—preserve that more than the gold. That ball was received by Harry Trunnion in defence of me. I was disarmed, and the enemy was about to fire, when Harry threw himself before me, and received that bullet in his breast. I took it flattened from his dead body—have worn it about me—it has served to remind me that Harry suffered for my sake, and that it was my duty, when chance might serve, to do the like for another.

PIKE. And now, William, have you any request to make?

WILLIAM. Lieutenant, you see this locket. (*Points to locket at his neck.*) It is Susan's hair. When I'm in dock, don't let it be touched: I know you won't. You have been most kind to me, Lieutenant, and if those who go aloft may know what passes on the high sea, I shall yet look down upon you in the middle-watch, and bless you. Now, one word more. How fares the Captain?

PIKE. Very ill. So ill that he has been removed from the command, and the first lieutenant acts until the new Captain arrives.

WILLIAM. His case, then, is desperate. Well, if he goes out of commission, I can't tremble to meet him. I bear no malice, your honour—I loved the Captain.

PIKE. You have nothing to ask?

WILLIAM. Nothing, your honour. Susan and some friends will shortly be on board. All I want is, that I may ask for strength to see my wife—my poor, young, heart-broken wife, for the last time, and then die like a seaman and a man. (*Music.*—LIEUTENANT PIKE, QUID, SEAWEED, *and* MARINES, *exeunt.*) I am soon to see poor Susan! I should like, first, to beat all my feelings to quarters, that they may stand well to their guns, in this their last engagement. I'll try and sing that song, which I have many a time sung in the mid-watch—that song which has often placed my heart, though a thousand miles at sea, at my once happy home. (WILLIAM *sings a verse of "Black-Ey'd Susan".*) My heart is splitting! (SUSAN *shrieks without—rushes in, and throws herself into* WILLIAM'S *arms.*)

Oh, Susan! Well, my poor wench, how fares it?

SUSAN. Oh, William! and I have watched, prayed for your return—smiled in the face of poverty, stopped my ears to the reproaches of the selfish, the worse pity of the thoughtless—and all, all for this!

WILLIAM. Ay, Sue, it's hard! but that's all over—to grieve is useless. Susan, I might have died disgraced—have left you the widow of a bad, black-hearted man. I know 'twill not be so—and in this, whilst you remain behind me, there is at least some comfort. I died in a good cause; I died in defence of the virtue of a wife—her tears will fall like spring rain on the grass that covers me.

SUSAN. Talk not so—your grave! I feel it is a place where my heart must throw down its heavy load of life.

WILLIAM. Come, Susan, shake off your tears. There, now, smile a bit—we'll not talk again of graves. Think, Susan, that I am a-going on a long foreign station—think so. Now, what would you ask?—have you nothing, nothing to say?

SUSAN. Nothing! Oh, when at home, hoping, yet trembling for this meeting, thoughts crowded on me; I felt as if I could have talked to you for days—stopping for want of power, not words. Now, the terrible time is come—now I am almost tongue-tied—my heart swells to my throat—I can but look and weep. (*Gun fires.*) That gun! Oh, William! husband! is it so near? You speak not—tremble!

WILLIAM. Susan, be calm. If you love your husband, do not send him on the deck a white-faced coward. Be still, my poor girl, I have something to say—until you are calm, I will not utter it; now, Susan—

SUSAN. I am cold, motionless as ice.

WILLIAM. Susan! you know the old aspen that grows near to the church porch. You and I, when children, almost before we could speak plainly, have sat and watched and wondered at its shaking leaves. I grew up, and that tree seemed to me a friend that loved me, yet had not the tongue to tell me so. Beneath its boughs our little arms have been locked together—beneath its boughs I took the last kiss of your white lips, when hard fortune made me turn sailor. I cut from that tree this branch. (*Produces it.*) Many a summer's day aboard, I've lain in the top and looked at these few leaves, until I saw green meadows in the salt sea, and heard the bleating of the sheep. When I am dead, Susan, let me be laid under that tree—let me—(*Gun fires.*—SUSAN *falls.* —*Slow Music.*—LIEUTENANT PIKE *and* SEAWEED *enter.*—WILLIAM *gives* SUSAN *in charge of* SEAWEED, *takes his handkerchief off, ties it around her neck, kisses her, and she is carried off.*—LIEUTENANT PIKE *and* WILLIAM *exeunt.*)

SCENE FOURTH: *The Forecastle of the Ship.—Procession along the starboard gangway.*—MASTER-AT-ARMS, *with a drawn sword under his arm, point next to the prisoner.*—WILLIAM, *without his neckcloth.*— MARINES, OFFICER OF MARINES, ADMIRAL, CAPTAIN, LIEUTENANTS, *and* MIDSHIPMEN.—*A* SAILOR *standing at one of the forecastle guns, with the lock-string in his hand.—A platform extends from the cat-head to the fore rigging.—Music.*

MASTER-AT-ARMS. Prisoner, are you prepared?

WILLIAM. Bless you! bless you all—(*Mounts the platform.* CAPTAIN CROSSTREE *rushes on from gangway.*)

CROSSTREE. Hold! hold!

ADMIRAL. Captain Crosstree—retire, sir, retire.

CROSSTREE. Never! If the prisoner be executed, he is a murdered man. I alone am the culprit—'twas I who would have dishonoured him.

ADMIRAL. This cannot plead here—he struck a superior officer.

CROSSTREE. No.

OMNES. No?

CROSSTREE. He saved my life; I had written for his discharge—villainy has kept back the document—'tis here, dated back. When William struck me he was not the King's sailor—I was not his officer.

ADMIRAL (*taking the paper.—Music*). He is free! (*The* SEAMEN *give three cheers.*—WILLIAM *leaps from the platform.*—SUSAN *is brought on by* CAPTAIN CROSSTREE.)

Curtain

THE LADY OF LYONS

Coleridge and Byron and Talfourd, Sheridan Knowles and Browning and Tennyson—many were the poets who attempted to write for the stage in the nineteenth century, beneath their dignity though some thought it to be. But they were

> Seldom insulted with a *three-days run,*
> And complimented often with—*not one.*

Yet a novelist who undertook to raise the *ton* of the stage and palmed off bombast for poetry, gusto for grandeur, and sentimentalism for sentiment, succeeded in writing a hit. Pauline in *The Lady of Lyons,* whatever we think today of the characterization, was dazzling as played by Helen Faucit and was to bring plaudits to Ellen Terry, Mary Anderson, Mrs. Lily Langtry, and dozens of lesser stars.

What made *The Lady of Lyons* a standard of the nineteenth-century repertory? Thomas H. Dickinson in 1925 offered this explanation:

> *The Lady of Lyons* has the one indispensable merit of the romantic play. It has in it the free plunge of life. Against this merit all its faults, its sentimentality, its mock revolutionary spirit, its tawdry imagery, bad verse, and tricky intrigue count for nothing. The play has succeeded because the author has caught the one trick of

> the Elizabethans that most imitators miss. . . . Bulwer-Lytton rendered no service to the stage save to find the weak point in the romantic tradition and stab it through the heart.

He went about this task aided and abetted by Charles Macready, and *The Lady of Lyons* was the actor's play as well as the author's, quite as much as *The Bells* was Sir Henry Irving's or *The Only Way* was Sir John Martin-Harvey's. Macready took over the management of Covent Garden in 1837 (to restore its "legitimacy" by a series of classics) and within a few months was £1000 in debt. About the middle of November, 1837, his friend Bulwer-Lytton, novelist and statesman, wrote to the actor-manager offering assistance: "I have been considering deeply the elements of Dramatic art, and I think I see the secret." He offered to write a play—"tell me which you prefer, Comedy or Tragedy"—in which Macready could star.

Macready expressed interest and within a month Bulwer-Lytton sent word of his having begun a play and of his confidence in its success. It was, like John Tobin's *The Honey Moon* (1805), in which Macready had played the lead to great applause, a comedy in five acts about "a vain and ambitious woman shorn of her pride of place." Macready's part was to be "part comic—part tragic": "The Honey Moon hero, with more, I think, of lightness and ease on one hand, and sentiment and high passion on the other." Also, "My heroine (who by the by is charming tho' I say it)—ought to be played by a Lady light in hand—something like [Madame] Vestris only with more feeling." Bulwer-Lytton had completed Acts III and IV, "the 2 Acts of more sentiment and passion." Eight days later Macready had in hand four acts of *The Fraudulent Marriage,* as Bulwer-Lytton was then calling his drama, and *"devoured"* it. Encouraged, the dramatist went on with his "attempt . . . to give you a popular and taking play." By January 4, 1838, he was writing: "I send you Act 5 in its rough copy. . . . I have thrown into it more passion and interest than I had dared to hope for and cannot but trust it will tell and sustain the others." He mentioned that he was thinking of calling the play *Nobility* (Macready's suggestion) or *How It Will End* or *Lost and Won* or *Love and Pride.* Macready made some suggestions about Act V and Bulwer-Lytton rewrote it overnight. "I now send you the play completed. I have done my part. I now confess I like Act 5 much." The author complained of fatigue. "I cannot wonder at your fatigue," wrote Macready. "My astonishment is, that you keep your health and mind under the labours you impose upon yourself." For his part, the actor would guarantee a good production: "Believe me, I shall be more tender of it, than if it were my own." Whose it was, was to be a secret, for Bulwer-Lytton wanted to remain out of the limelight and have it announced as "the work of a young man called Calvert—I fancy some relation to Sir Harry Calvert [1763-1826], formerly Adjutant General."

The Lady of Lyons; or, Love and Pride (for Bulwer-Lytton had finally decided to put his two favorite titles together) opened on February 15, 1838, and the author managed to get away from the House of Commons in time to catch the last act. Meeting Sir Thomas Noon Talfourd (to whom he later dedicated the play), who was leaving the theatre, Bulwer-Lytton asked, as casually as he could, how the piece was going. "Oh," he was told, "very well, for that sort of thing." (A little later Talfourd announced that he had been "disgusted" by the play.) The reaction of the pompous author of *Ion,* however, was atypical. It was a long evening; in those days audiences spent many hours at a performance and in addition to the main feature got the Christmas pantomime *Harlequin and Peeping Tom of Coventry* and another full-length presentation such as *King Lear* or a comic opera. But at the end the crowds rose and cheered lustily: "It was a scene to raise, to revive, to give a new zest to play-going," said the *Examiner* of their delight. Macready, generally pessimistic, was pleased: "[I] Acted Claude Melnotte in Bulwer's play pretty well; the audience felt it very much, and were carried away by it; the play in the acting was completely successful."

The Lady of Lyons ran through ten editions in a year, and its brass, polished to gleam like gold, was still bright when Irving revived it forty years later. Not George Croly's earlier version of the theme in *Pride Shall Have a Fall* (1824) nor the later *Beauty of Lyons* (1842) by William Charles Moncrieff (who also adapted Bulwer-Lytton's novel *Eugene Aram* for the stage) could displace it, any more than the burlesques which followed, including Henry James Byron's *The Lady of Lyons; or, Twopenny Pride and Pennytence* (1858), Herman Charles Merivale's ("Felix Dale") *The Lady of Lyons Married and Settled* (1878), Robert Reece's ("E. G. Lankester") *The Lady of Lyons Married and Claude Unsettled*)1884), or the St. John Hankin "dramatic sequel," printed on page 666.

The Lady of Lyons may be as theatrical as Bulwer-Lytton's *Richelieu* (1839). It is as full of exaggerated French romanticism. But it reads better because it reveals less of what its author called "my dependence on the stage . . . my reliance on the acting of *Richelieu* himself, the embodiment of the portraiture, the look, the gesture, the personation, which reading cannot give." *The Lady of Lyons* is just as sentimental as *Money* (1840) but not nearly as forward-looking. It was in plays such as *Money* and Boucicault's *London Assurance* that the old ideas of conventional comedy gave way to the new, but *The Lady of Lyons* is in the long run the play by which Bulwer-Lytton and all the dramatists of his period and calibre are best represented, and we have Justin McCarthy's judgment that *The Lady of Lyons* was "probably the most successful acting drama produced in England since the days of Shakespeare."

As to its quality, it seems only fair to allow Charles H. Shattuck, to whose scholarly editing in *Bulwer and Macready* (1958) we owe the texts of the letters we have been quoting, to have the final say:

> *The Lady of Lyons* is a charming and durable fable ruined by superficial writing. . . . If the author could have supplanted the dialogue verbiage with true verse or firm prose, and the banality with wit, we might still enjoy it today.

TO

THE AUTHOR OF "ION"

[Sir Thomas Noon Talfourd],

Whose genius and example have alike contributed
towards the regeneration
of
The National Drama,
THIS PLAY IS INSCRIBED.

PREFACE

An indistinct recollection of the very pretty little tale,—called "Perouse, or the Bellows-Mender," suggested the plot of this Drama. The incidents are, however, greatly altered from those in Perouse, and the characters entirely re-cast. In the selection of the time in which the Play has been laid, I was guided, naturally and solely, by the wish to take that period in which the incidents might be rendered most probable, and in which the probationary career of the hero, in the Fifth Act,—upon which the dénouement, *and, indeed, the* design, *depends,—might be sufficiently rapid for dramatic effect, and (on account of that very rapidity) in accordance with the ordinary character and events of the age. The early years of the first and most brilliant successes of the French Republic appeared to constitute the only epoch in which these objects could be attained. It was a period when, in the general ferment of society, and the brief equalization of ranks, Claude's high-placed love, his ardent feelings, his unsettled principles,—the struggle between which makes the passion of this drama, —his ambition, and his career, were phenomena that characterised the time itself, and in which the spirit of the nation went along with the extravagance of the individual. In some respects, Claude Melnotte is a type of that restless, brilliant, and evanescent generation that sprung up from the ashes of the terrible Revolution,—men, born to be agents of the genius of Napoleon, to accomplish the most marvellous exploits, and to leave but little of permanent triumph and solid advantage to the succeeding race.*

In selecting this period as one best suited to the development of a story which seemed to me rich in materials of dramatic interest, I can honestly say that I endeavoured, as much as possible, to avoid every political allusion applicable to our own time and land,—our own party prejudices and passions. How difficult a task this was, a reference to any Drama, in which the characters are supposed to live under Republican institutions, will prove! There is scarcely a single play, the scene of which is laid in Rome, in Greece, in Switzerland, wherein political allusions and political declamations are not carefully elaborated as the most striking and telling parts of the performance.[1]

The principal fault of this Play, as characteristic of the time, is, perhaps, indeed, the too cautious avoidance of all those references to Liberty and Equality in which, no doubt, every man living at that day would have hourly indulged. The old and classical sentiment, that virtue is nobility (virtus est sola nobilitas), *contains the pith of all the political creed announced by Claude Melnotte; and that sentiment is the founder, and often the motto, of Aristocracy itself. It is a sentiment that never will, I trust, be considered revolutionary in a country which boasts, among its proudest names, the Wellesleys and the Russells—the Stanleys and the Howards.—It is one which the scribblers, sprung from a dunghill, may be assured that there are few men of blood and birth who will disavow. In fact, the enthusiasm of Claude is far more that of a soldier than a citizen,*[2] *and it is not the reasoner nor the politician,—but the man, with his feelings and his struggles,—with whom the audience sympathise, when he glories in the redemption of his name. It is perfectly clear that neither the English author nor the English audience can recognise much in harmony with their own sentiments, when Claude declares that the gold he has won in the campaign in Italy* "is hallowed in the cause of nations!" *The question for us to consider is, not whether an Englishman or a philosopher would think that there was any sanctity in the principles of that brilliant war, but whether an enthusiastic soldier under Napoleon would not have believed it. Our national prepossessions and prejudices,—our closeness to an age, the false glitter of which we can so well detect—alike, I hope, guard us against all political infection from a play cast in a time when the coming shadow of a military despotism was already darkening the prospects of an unwise and weak Republic: and if there be anywhere the antipodes to the French Jacobin of the*

---

[1] *The noble Tragedy of "Ion" has for its very plot, its very catastrophe, almost its very moral, the abolition of Royalty and the establishment of a Republic;—yet no one would suspect Serjeant Talfourd of designing the overthrow of the British Constitution.*

[2] *The allusion to the rapidity of promotion in the French army was absolutely necessary to the conduct of the story; and, after all, it is expressed in language borrowed and adapted from that very jacobinical authority Horatio Viscount Nelson. Nor is it easy to conceive how the sentiment—that merit, not money, should purchase promotion in the army—can be called a* Republican *doctrine; since, though it certainly did pervade the French Republican Army, it inculcates a principle far more common in Despotic Countries than under Free Institutions. We must look to the annals of the East for the most frequent examples of the rise of fortunate soldiers.*

last century, it is the English Reformer of the present. For my own part, I never met with any one, however warm a lover of abstract liberty, who had a sympathy with the principles of the Directory and the Government of M. Barras. But enough in contradiction of a charge which the whole English public have ridiculed and scouted, and which has sought to introduce into the free domains of art, all the miserable calumnies and wretched spleen of party hostilities.

The faults of the Play itself I do not seek to defend: such faults are the fair and just materials for criticism and cavil. I am perfectly aware that it is a very slight and trivial performance, and, being written solely for the Stage, may possess but a feeble interest in the closet. It was composed with a twofold object. In the first place, sympathising with the enterprise of Mr. Macready, as Manager of Covent Garden, and believing that many of the higher interests of the Drama were involved in the success or failure of an enterprise equally hazardous and disinterested, I felt, if I may so presume to express myself, something of the Brotherhood of Art; and it was only for Mr. Macready to think it possible that I might serve him, to induce me to make the attempt.

Secondly, in that attempt I was mainly anxious to see whether or not certain critics had truly declared that it was not in my power to attain the art of dramatic construction and theatrical effect. I felt, indeed, that it was in this that a writer, accustomed to the narrative class of composition, would have the most both to learn and to unlearn. Accordingly, it was to the development of the plot and the arrangement of the incidents that I directed my chief attention;—and I sought to throw whatever belongs to poetry less into the diction and the 'felicity of words' than into the construction of the story, the creation of the characters, and the spirit of the pervading sentiment. With this acknowledgment, may I hazard a doubt whether any more ornate or more elevated style of language would be so appropriate to the rank of the characters introduced, or would leave so clear and uninterrupted an effect to the strength and progress of that domestic interest, which (since I do not arrogate the entire credit of its invention) I may, perhaps, be allowed to call the chief attraction of the Play.

Having, on presenting this drama to the Theatre, confided the secret of its authorship to the Manager alone;—having, therefore, induced no party—no single friend or favourer of my own,—to attend the early performances which decided its success,—I hope that on my side "The Lady of Lyons" has been fairly left to the verdict of the Public,—let me now also hope an equal fairness from those who wish to condemn the Politician in the Author. I have no intention of writing again for the Stage; and, therefore, so far as my own experiment is concerned, I have but little to hope or fear. Do not let those who love the literature of the Drama discourage other men, immeasurably more *fitted to adorn it, solely because in a free country they may, like the Author of this Play, have ventured elsewhere to express political opinions.*

I cannot conclude without expressing my high sense of the care with which the "Lady of Lyons" was introduced on the Stage,—of its obligations to Mr. Macready, not less as a Manager who neglected no detail that could conduce to the effect of the representation, than as an Actor who realised and exalted every design of the Author. The power and pathos which Miss Faucit's acting infused into language that will seem comparatively tame and cold to the reader, —the easy skill with which Mr. Bartley threw his own racy and vigorous humour into the character of Colonel Damas,—the zeal and ability which, in Mr. Elton's Beauseant, relieved and elevated a part necessarily unpleasing to an actor of his station; and the performances, so accurate and spirited, of the characters less prominent in the development of the story, especially of Mrs. Clifford and Mr. Meadows,—have already received a far higher reward than the acknowledgment of the Author, in the cordial applauses of the Audience.

E. L. B.

London, February 26, 1838

THE LADY OF LYONS

OR

LOVE AND PRIDE

by

Edward George Earle Lytton Bulwer-Lytton, Lord Lytton

First presented at the Theatre Royal, Covent Garden, on Thursday, February 15, 1838, starring Charles Macready, with the following cast:

BEAUSEANT, *a rich gentleman of Lyons, in love with, and refused by, Pauline Deschappelles*	Mr. Elton
GLAVIS, *his friend, also a rejected suitor of Pauline*	Mr. Meadows
Colonel (afterwards General) DAMAS, *cousin to Mde. Deschappelles*	Mr. Bartley
Monsieur DESCHAPPELLES, *a merchant of Lyons, father to Pauline*	Mr. Strickland
Landlord of the Golden Lion [an Inn]	Mr. Yarnold
GASPAR	Mr. Diddear
CLAUDE MELNOTTE	Mr. Macready
First Officer	Mr. Howe
Second Officer	Mr. Pritchard
Third Officer	Mr. Roberts
Servants, A Notary, etc.	
Madame DESCHAPPELLES	Mrs. Clifford
PAULINE, *her daughter*	Miss Helen Faucit
The Widow MELNOTTE, *mother to Claude*	Mrs. Griffith
JANET, *the inn-keeper's daughter*	Mrs. East
MARIAN, *maid to Pauline*	Miss Garrick

Time: 1795–1798

Scene: Lyons and the neighborhood

ACT I

SCENE 1: *A room in the house of* M. DESCHAPPELLES, *at Lyons.* PAULINE *reclining on a sofa;* MARIAN, *her Maid, fanning her.* —*Flowers and notes on a table beside the sofa.*—MADAME DESCHAPPELLES *seated.*—*The Gardens are seen from the open window.*

MME. DESCHAP. Marian, put that rose a little more to the left.— (MARIAN *alters the position of a rose in* PAULINE'S *hair.*) Ah, so!—that improves the air,—the *tournure,*—the *je ne sais quoi!*—You are certainly very handsome, child!—quite my style!—I don't wonder that you make such a sensation!—Old, young, rich, and poor, do homage to the Beauty of Lyons!—Ah, we live again in our children,—especially when they have our eyes and complexion!

PAULINE (*languidly*). Dear mother, you spoil your Pauline!——(*Aside.*) I wish I knew who sent me these flowers!

MME. DESCHAP. No, child!—If I praise you, it is only to inspire you with a proper ambition.—You are born to make a great marriage.— Beauty is valuable or worthless according as you invest the property to the best advantage.—Marian, go and order the carriage! (*Exit* MARIAN.)

PAULINE. Who *can* it be that sends me, every day, these beautiful flowers?—how sweet they are!

(*Enter* SERVANT.)

SERVANT. Monsieur Beauseant, madam.

MME. DESCHAP. Let him enter. Pauline, this is another offer!—I know it is!—Your father should engage an additional clerk to keep the account-book of your conquests.

(*Enter* BEAUSEANT.)

BEAU. Ah, ladies, how fortunate I am to find you at home!— (*Aside.*) How lovely she looks!—It is a great sacrifice I make in marrying into a family in trade!—they will be eternally grateful!——(*Aloud.*) Madame, you will permit me a word with your charming daughter.— (*Approaches* PAULINE, *who rises disdainfully.*)—Mademoiselle, I have ventured to wait upon you, in a hope that you must long since have divined. Last night, when you outshone all the beauty of Lyons, you completed your conquest over me! You know that my fortune is not exceeded by any estate in the Province,—you know that, but for the

Revolution, which has defrauded me of my titles, I should be noble. May I, then, trust that you will not reject my alliance? I offer you my hand and heart.

PAULINE (*aside*). He has the air of a man who confers a favour!—(*Aloud.*) Sir, you are very condescending—I thank you humbly; but, being duly sensible of my own demerits, you must allow me to decline the honour you propose. (*Curtsies, and turns away.*)

BEAU. Decline! impossible!—you are not serious!—Madame, suffer me to appeal to *you.* I am a suitor for your daughter's hand—the settlements shall be worthy her beauty and my station. May I wait on M. Deschappelles?

MME. DESCHAP. M. Deschappelles never interferes in the domestic arrangements,—you are very obliging. If you were still a Marquis, or if my daughter were intended to marry a commoner,—why, perhaps, we might give you the preference.

BEAU. A commoner!—we are all commoners in France now.

MME. DESCHAP. In France, yes; but there is a nobility still left in the other countries in Europe. We are quite aware of your good qualities, and don't doubt that you will find some lady more suitable to your pretensions. We shall be always happy to see you as an acquaintance, M. Beauseant!—My dear child, the carriage will be here presently.

BEAU. Say no more, Madame!—say no more!—(*Aside.*) Refused! and by a merchant's daughter!—refused! It will be all over Lyons before sunset!—I will go and bury myself in my chateau, study philosophy, and turn woman-hater. Refused! they ought to be sent to a madhouse!—Ladies, I have the honour to wish you a very good morning. (*Exit* BEAUSEANT.)

MME. DESCHAP. How forward these men are!—I think, child, we kept up our dignity. Any girl, however inexperienced, knows how to accept an offer, but it requires a vast deal of address to refuse one with proper condescension and disdain. I used to practise it at school with the dancing-master!

(*Enter* DAMAS.)

DAMAS. Good morning, cousin Deschappelles.—Well, Pauline, are you recovered from last night's ball?—So many triumphs must be very fatiguing. Even M. Glavis sighed most piteously when you departed; but that might be the effect of the supper.

PAULINE. M. Glavis, indeed!

MME. DESCHAP. M. Glavis!—as if my daughter would think of M. Glavis!

DAMAS. Hey-day!—why not?—His father left him a very pretty fortune, and his birth is higher than yours, cousin Deschappelles. But perhaps you are looking to M. Beauseant,—his father was a Marquis before the Revolution.

PAULINE. M. Beauseant!—Cousin, you delight in tormenting me!

MME. DESCHAP. Don't mind him, Pauline!—Cousin Damas, you have no susceptibility of feeling,—there is a certain indelicacy in all your ideas.—M. Beauseant knows already that he is no match for my daughter!

DAMAS. Pooh! pooh! one would think you intended your daughter to marry a prince!

MME. DESCHAP. Well, and if I did?—what then?—Many a foreign prince—

DAMAS (*interrupting her*). Foreign prince!—foreign fiddlestick!—you ought to be ashamed of such nonsense at your time of life.

MME. DESCHAP. My time of life!—That is an expression never applied to any lady till she is sixty-nine and three-quarters;—and only then by the clergyman of the parish.

(*Enter* SERVANT.)

SERVANT. Madame, the carriage is at the door. (*Exit* SERVANT.)

MME. DESCHAP. Come, child, put on your bonnet—you really have a very thorough-bred air—not at all like your poor father.—(*Fondly.*) Ah, you little coquette! when a young lady is always making mischief, it is a sure sign that she takes after her mother!

PAULINE. Good day, cousin Damas—and a better humour to you—(*going back to the table and taking the flowers*). Who *could* have sent me these flowers? (*Exeunt* PAULINE *and* MADAME DESCHAPPELLES.)

DAMAS. That would be an excellent girl if her head had not been turned. I fear she is now become incorrigible! Zounds, what a lucky fellow I am to be still a bachelor! They may talk of the devotion of the sex—but the most faithful attachment in life is that of a woman in love—with herself! (*Exit.*)

SCENE 2: *The exterior of a small Village Inn—Sign the Golden Lion—a few leagues from Lyons, which is seen at a distance.*

BEAU. (*behind the scenes*). Yes, you may bait the horses, we shall rest here an hour.

(*Enter* BEAUSEANT *and* GLAVIS.)

GLA. Really, my dear Beauseant, consider that I have promised to spend a day or two with you at your chateau—that I am quite at your mercy for my entertainment—and yet you are as silent and as gloomy as a mute at a funeral, or an Englishman at a party of pleasure.

BEAU. Bear with me!—the fact is that I am miserable.

GLA. You—the richest and gayest bachelor in Lyons?

BEAU. It is because I am a bachelor that I am miserable.—Thou knowest Pauline—the only daughter of the rich merchant, Mons. Deschappelles?

GLA. Know her! who does not?—as pretty as Venus, and as proud as Juno.

BEAU. Her taste is worse than her pride—(*drawing himself up*). Know, Glavis, she has actually refused *me*!

GLA. (*aside*). So she has me!—very consoling! In all cases of heart-ache, the application of another man's disappointment draws out the pain, and allays the irritation.—(*Aloud.*) Refused you! and wherefore?

BEAU. I know not, unless it be because the Revolution swept away my father's title of Marquis—and she will not marry a commoner. Now, as we have no noblemen left in France, as we are all citizens and equals, she can only hope that, in spite of the war, some English Milord or German Count will risk his life, by coming to Lyons and making her my Lady. Refused me, and with scorn!—By heaven, I'll not submit to it tamely—I'm in a perfect fever of mortification and rage.—Refuse me, indeed!

GLA. Be comforted, my dear fellow—I will tell you a secret. For the same reason she refused me!

BEAU. You!—that's a very different matter! But give me your hand, Glavis—we'll think of some plan to humble her. By Jove, I should like to see her married to a strolling player!

(*Enter* LANDLORD *and his* DAUGHTER, *from the Inn.*)

LAND. Your servant, citizen Beauseant—servant, Sir. Perhaps you will take dinner before you proceed to your chateau; our larder is most plentifully supplied.

BEAU. I have no appetite.

GLA. Nor I. Still it is bad travelling on an empty stomach. What have you got? (*Takes and looks over the bill of fare.*)

(*Shout without*)—"Long live the Prince!—Long live the Prince!"

BEAU. The Prince!—what Prince is that! I thought we had no princes left in France.

LAND. Ha, ha! the lads always call him Prince. He has just won the prize in the shooting-match, and they are taking him home in triumph.

BEAU. Him! and who's Mr. Him?

LAND. Who should he be, but the pride of the village, Claude Melnotte?—Of course you have heard of Claude Melnotte?

GLA. (*giving back the bill of fare*). Never had that honour. Soup—ragout of hare—roast chicken, and, in short, all you have!

BEAU. The son of old Melnotte, the gardener?

LAND. Exactly so—a wonderful young man.

BEAU. How wonderful?—are his cabbages better than other people's?

LAND. Nay, he don't garden any more; his father left him well off. He's only a genus.

GLA. A what?

LAND. A genus! a man who can do everything in life, except anything that's useful;—that's a genus.

BEAU. You raise my curiosity—proceed.

LAND. Well, then, about four years ago, old Melnotte died and left his son well to do in the world. We then all observed that a great change came over young Claude: he took to reading and Latin, and hired a professor from Lyons, who had so much in his head that he was forced to wear a great, full-bottom wig to cover it. Then he took a fencing-master, and a dancing-master, and a music-master; and then he learned to paint; and at last it was said that young Claude was to go to Paris, and set up for a painter. The lads laughed at him at first; but he is a stout fellow, is Claude, and as brave as a lion, and soon taught them to laugh the wrong side of their mouths; and now all the boys swear by him, and all the girls pray for him.

BEAU. A promising youth, certainly! And why do they call him Prince?

LAND. Partly because he is at the head of them all, and partly because he has such a proud way with him, and wears such fine clothes—and, in short—looks like a prince.

BEAU. And what could have turned the foolish fellow's brain? The Revolution, I suppose?

LAND. Yes—the Revolution that turns us all topsy-turvy—the revolution of Love.

BEAU. Romantic young Corydon! And with whom is he in love?

LAND. Why—but it is a secret, gentlemen.

BEAU. Oh! certainly.

LAND. Why, then, I hear from his mother, good soul! that it is no less a person than the Beauty of Lyons, Pauline Deschappelles.

BEAU. *and* GLA. Ha! ha! Capital!

LAND. You may laugh, but it is as true as I stand here.

BEAU. And what does the Beauty of Lyons say to his suit?

LAND. Lord, Sir, she never even condescended to look at him, though when he was a boy he worked in her father's garden.

BEAU. Are you sure of that!

LAND. His mother says that Mademoiselle does not know him by sight.

BEAU. (*taking Glavis aside*). I have hit it,—I have it;—here is our revenge! Here is a prince for our haughty damsel. Do you take me?

GLA. Deuce take me if I do!

BEAU. Blockhead!—it's as clear as a map. What if we could make this elegant clown pass himself off as a foreign prince?—lend him money, clothes, equipage for the purpose?—make him propose to Pauline?—marry Pauline? Would it not be delicious?

GLA. Ha! ha!—Excellent! But how shall we support the necessary expenses of his highness?

BEAU. Pshaw! Revenge is worth a much larger sacrifice than a few hundred louis;—as for details, my valet is the trustiest fellow in the world, and shall have the appointment of his highness's establishment. Let's go to him at once, and see if he be really this Admirable Crichton.

GLA. With all my heart;—but the dinner?

BEAU. Always thinking of dinner! Hark ye, Landlord, how far is it to young Melnotte's cottage? I should like to see such a prodigy.

LAND. Turn down the lane,—then strike across the common,—and you will see his mother's cottage.

BEAU. True, he lives with his mother.—(*Aside.*) We will not trust to an old woman's discretion; better send for him hither. I'll just step in and write him a note. Come, Glavis.

GLA. Yes,—Beauseant, Glavis, and Co., manufacturers of princes, wholesale and retail,—an uncommonly genteel line of business. But why so grave?

BEAU. You think only of the sport,—I of the revenge. (*Exeunt within the Inn.*)

SCENE 3: *The Interior of* MELNOTTE'S *Cottage; flowers placed here and there; a guitar on an oaken table, with a portfolio, &c.; a picture on an easel, covered by a curtain; fencing-foils crossed over the mantelpiece; an attempt at refinement in spite of the homeliness of the furniture, &c.; a staircase to the right conducts to the upper story.*

(*Shout without*)—"Long live Claude Melnotte!" "Long live the Prince!"

THE WIDOW MEL. Hark!—there's my dear son;—carried off the prize, I'm sure: and now he'll want to treat them all.

CLAUDE MEL. (*opening the door*). What! you won't come in, my friends! Well, well,—there's a trifle to make merry elsewhere. Good day to you all,—good day!

(*Shout*)—"Hurrah! Long live Prince Claude!"

(*Enter* CLAUDE MELNOTTE, *with a rifle in his hand.*)

MEL. Give me joy, dear mother! I've won the prize!—never missed one shot! Is it not handsome, this gun?

WIDOW. Humph! Well, what is it worth, Claude?

MEL. Worth! What is a ribbon worth to a soldier? Worth!—everything! Glory is priceless!

WIDOW. Leave glory to great folks. Ah! Claude, Claude, castles in the air cost a vast deal to keep up! How is all this to end? What good does it do thee to learn Latin, and sing songs, and play on the guitar, and fence, and dance, and paint pictures? All very fine; but what does it bring in?

MEL. Wealth! wealth, my mother!—Wealth to the mind—wealth to the heart—high thoughts—bright dreams—the hope of fame—the ambition to be worthier to love Pauline.

WIDOW. My poor son!—The young lady will never think of thee.

MEL. Do the stars think of us? Yet if the prisoner see them shine into his dungeon, would'st thou bid him turn away from *their* lustre? Even so from this low cell, poverty,—I lift my eyes to Pauline and forget my chains. (*Goes to the picture and draws aside the curtain.*) See, this is her image—painted from memory.—Oh, how the canvas wrongs her! (*Takes up the brush and throws it aside.*) I shall never be a painter. I can paint no likeness but one, and that is above all art. I would turn soldier—France needs soldiers! But to leave the air that Pauline breathes! What is the hour?—so late? I will tell thee a secret, mother. Thou knowest that for the last six weeks I have sent every day the rarest flowers to Pauline;—she wears them. I have seen them on her breast. Ah, and then the whole universe seemed filled with odours! I have now grown more bold—I have poured my worship into poetry—I have sent the verses to Pauline—I have signed them with my own name. My messenger ought to be back by this time; I bade him wait for the answer.

WIDOW. And what answer do you expect, Claude?

MEL. That which the Queen of Navarre sent to the poor troubadour:—"Let me see the Oracle that can tell nations I am beautiful!" She will admit me. I shall hear her speak—I shall meet her eyes—I shall read upon her cheek the sweet thoughts that translate themselves into blushes. Then—then, oh, then,—she may forget that I am the peasant's son!

WIDOW. Nay, if she will but hear thee talk, Claude!

MEL. I foresee it all. She will tell me that desert is the true rank. She will give me a badge—a flower—a glove! Oh rapture! I shall join the armies of the Republic—I shall rise—I shall win a name that beauty will not blush to hear. I shall return with the right to say to her—"See, how love does not level the proud, but raise the humble!" Oh, how my heart swells within me!—Oh, what glorious Prophets of the Future are Youth and Hope! (*Knock at the door.*)

WIDOW. Come in.

(*Enter* GASPAR.)

MEL. Welcome, Gaspar, welcome. Where is the letter? Why do you turn away, man? where is the letter?—(GASPAR *gives him one.*) This!—This is mine, the one I entrusted to thee. Didst thou not leave it?

GASPAR. Yes, I left it.

MEL. My own verses returned to me. Nothing else?

GASPAR. Thou wilt be proud to hear how thy messenger was honoured. For thy sake, Melnotte,—I have borne that which no Frenchman can bear without disgrace.

MEL. Disgrace, Gaspar! Disgrace?

GASPAR. I gave thy letter to the porter, who passed it from lackey to lackey till it reached the lady it was meant for.

MEL. It reached her, then;—you are sure of that? It reached her,—well, well!

GASPAR. It reached her, and was returned to me with blows. Dost hear, Melnotte? with blows! Death! are we slaves still, that we are to be thus dealt with, we peasants?

MEL. With blows? No, Gaspar, no; not blows!

GASPAR. I could show thee the marks if it were not so deep a shame to bear them. The lackey who tossed thy letter into the mire swore that his lady and her mother never were so insulted. What could thy letter contain, Claude?

MEL. (*looking over the letter*). Not a line that a serf might not have written to an empress. No, not one.

GASPAR. They promise thee the same greeting they gave me, if thou wilt pass that way. Shall we endure this, Claude?

MEL. (*wringing* GASPAR'S *hand*). Forgive me, the fault was mine, I have brought this on thee; I will not forget it; thou shalt be avenged! The heartless insolence!

GASPAR. Thou art moved, Melnotte; think not of me; I would go through fire and water to serve thee; but,—a blow! It is not the *bruise* that galls,—it is the *blush,* Melnotte.

MEL. Say, what message?—How insulted?—Wherefore?—What the offence?

GASPAR. Did you not write to Pauline Deschappelles, the daughter of the rich merchant?

MEL. Well?—

GASPAR. And are you not a peasant—a gardener's son?—that was the offence. Sleep on it, Melnotte. Blows to a French citizen, blows! (*Exit.*)

WIDOW. Now you are cured, Claude!

MEL. (*tearing the letter*). So do I scatter her image to the winds—I will stop her in the open streets—I will insult her—I will beat her menial ruffians—I will——(*Turns suddenly to* WIDOW.) Mother, am I hump-backed—deformed—hideous?

WIDOW. You!

MEL. A coward—a thief—a liar?

WIDOW. You!

MEL. Or a dull fool—a vain, drivelling, brainless idiot?

WIDOW. No, no.

MEL. What am I then—worse than all these? Why, I am a peasant! What has a peasant to do with love? Vain Revolutions, why lavish your cruelty on the great? Oh that we—we, the hewers of wood and drawers of water, had been swept away, so that the proud might learn what the world would be without us!— (*Knock at the door.*)

(*Enter* SERVANT *from the Inn.*)

SERVANT. A letter for Citizen Melnotte.

MEL. A letter! from her perhaps—who sent thee?

SERVANT. Why, Monsieur—I mean Citizen—Beauseant, who stops to dine at the Golden Lion, on his way to his chateau.

MEL. Beauseant!—(*Reads.*)

"Young man, I know thy secret—thou lovest above thy station: if thou hast wit, courage, and discretion, I can secure to thee the realization of thy most sanguine hopes; and the sole condition I ask in return is, that thou shalt be steadfast to thine own ends. I shall demand from thee a solemn oath to marry her whom thou lovest; to bear her to thine home on thy wedding night. I am serious—if thou would'st learn more, lose not a moment, but follow the bearer of this letter to thy friend and patron,

"CHARLES BEAUSEANT."

MEL. Can I believe my eyes? Are our own passions the sorcerers that raise up for us spirits of good or evil? I will go instantly.

WIDOW. What is this, Claude?

MEL. "Marry her whom thou lovest"—"bear her to thine own home" —O, revenge and love! which of you is the strongest?—(*Gazing on the picture.*) Sweet face, thou smilest on me from the canvas: weak fool that I am, do I then love her still? No, it is the vision of my own romance that I have worshipped: it is the reality, to which I bring scorn for scorn.—Adieu, mother; I will return anon. My brain reels—the earth swims before me.—(*Looks again at the letter.*) No it is *not* a mockery; I do *not* dream! (*Exit.*)

End of Act I

ACT II

SCENE 1: *The Gardens of* M. DESCHAPPELLES' *House, at Lyons —The House seen at the back of the Stage.*

(*Enter* BEAUSEANT *and* GLAVIS.)

BEAU. Well, what think you of my plot? Has it not succeeded to a miracle? The instant that I introduced His Highness the Prince of Como to the pompous mother and the scornful daughter, it was all over with them: he came—he saw—he conquered: and, though it is not many days since he arrived, they have already promised him the hand of Pauline.

GLA. It is lucky, though, that you told them his Highness travelled incognito, for fear the Directory (who are not very fond of princes) should lay him by the heels; for he has a wonderful wish to keep up his rank, and scatters our gold about with as much coolness as if he were watering his own flower-pots.

BEAU. True, he is damnably extravagant; I think the sly dog does it out of malice. However, it must be owned that he reflects credit on his loyal subjects, and makes a very pretty figure in his fine clothes, with my diamond snuff-box—

GLA. And my diamond ring! But do you think he will be firm to the last? I fancy I see symptoms of relenting: he will never keep up his rank, if he once let out his conscience.

BEAU. His oath binds him; he cannot retract without being forsworn, and those low fellows are always superstitious! But, as it is, I tremble lest he be discovered: that bluff Colonel Damas (Madame Deschappelles' cousin) evidently suspects him: we must make haste and conclude the farce: I have thought of a plan to end it this very day.

GLA. This very day! Poor Pauline! her dream will be soon over.

BEAU. Yes, this day they shall be married; this evening according to his oath, he shall carry his bride to the Golden Lion, and then pomp, equipage, retinue, and title, all shall vanish at once; and her Highness the Princess shall find that she has refused the son of a Marquis, to marry the son of a Gardener.—Oh, Pauline! once loved, now hated, yet still not relinquished, thou shalt drain the cup to the dregs,—thou shalt know what it is to be humbled!

(*Enter, from the House,* MELNOTTE *as the Prince of Como, leading in* PAULINE; MADAME DESCHAPPELLES *fanning herself; and* COLONEL DAMAS. BEAUSEANT *and* GLAVIS *bow respectfully.* PAULINE *and* MELNOTTE *walk apart.*)

MME. DESCHAP. Good morning, gentlemen; really I am so fatigued with laughter; the dear Prince is so entertaining. What wit he has! Any one may see that he has spent his whole life in courts.

DAMAS. And what the deuce do you know about courts, cousin Deschappelles? You women regard men just as you buy books—you never care what is in them, but how they are bound and lettered. S'death, I don't think you would even look at your Bible if it had not a title to it.

MME. DESCHAP. How coarse you are, cousin Damas!—quite the manners of a barrack—you don't deserve to be one of our family; really we must drop your acquaintance when Pauline marries. I cannot patronise any relations that would discredit my future son-in-law the Prince of Como.

MEL. (*advancing*). These are beautiful gardens, Madame, (BEAUSEANT *and* GLAVIS *retire*)—who planned them?

MME. DESCHAP. A gardener named Melnotte, your Highness—an honest man who knew his station. I can't say as much for his son—a presuming fellow, who—ha! ha!—actually wrote verses—such doggrel! —to my daughter.

PAULINE. Yes—how you would have laughed at them, Prince!—*you* who write such beautiful verses!

MEL. This Melnotte must be a monstrous impudent person!

DAMAS. Is he good-looking?

MME. DESCHAP. I never notice such *canaille*—an ugly, mean-looking clown, if I remember right.

DAMAS. Yet I heard your porter say he was wonderfully like his Highness.

MEL. (*taking snuff*). You are complimentary.

MME. DESCHAP. For shame, cousin Damas!—like the Prince, indeed!

PAULINE. Like you! Ah, mother, like our beautiful Prince! I'll never speak to you again, cousin Damas.

MEL. (*aside*). Humph!—rank is a great beautifier! I never passed for an Apollo while I was a peasant; if I am so handsome as a prince, what should I be as an emperor?—(*Aloud.*) Monsieur Beauseant, will you honour me? (*Offers snuff.*)

BEAU. No, your Highness; I have no small vices.

MEL. Nay, if it were a vice you'd be sure to have it, Monsieur Beauseant.

MME. DESCHAP. Ha! ha!—how very severe!—what wit!

BEAU. (*in a rage and aside*). Curse his impertinence!

MME. DESCHAP. What a superb snuff-box!

PAULINE. And what a beautiful ring!

MEL. You like the box—a trifle—interesting perhaps from associations—a present from Louis XIV to my great-great-grandmother. Honour me by accepting it.

BEAU. (*plucking him by the sleeve*). How!—what the devil! My box—are you mad? It is worth five hundred louis.

MEL. (*unheeding him, and turning to* PAULINE). And you like this ring? Ah, it has, indeed, a lustre since your eyes have shone on it (*placing it on her finger*). Henceforth hold me, sweet enchantress, the Slave of the Ring.

GLA. (*pulling him*). Stay, stay—what are you about? My maiden aunt's legacy—a diamond of the first water. You shall be hanged for swindling, Sir.

MEL. (*pretending not to hear*). It is curious, this ring; it is the one with which my grandfather, the Doge of Venice, married the Adriatic! (MADAME *and* PAULINE *examine the ring.*)

MEL. (*to* BEAUSEANT *and* GLAVIS). Fie, gentlemen, princes must be generous!—(*Turns to* DAMAS, *who watches them closely.*) These kind friends have my interest so much at heart, that they are as careful of my property as if it were their own!

BEAU. *and* GLA. (*confusedly*). Ha! ha!—very good joke that! (*Appear to remonstrate with* MELNOTTE *in dumb show.*)

DAMAS. What's all that whispering? I am sure there is some juggle here: hang me, if I think he is an Italian, after all. Gad! I'll try him. Servitore umilissimo, Eccellenza.[1]

MEL. Hum—what does he mean, I wonder?

DAMAS. Godo di vedervi in buona salute.[2]

MEL. Hem—hem!

DAMAS. Fa bel tempo—che si dice di nuovo.[3]

MEL. Well, Sir, what's all that gibberish?

DAMAS. Oh, oh!—only Italian, your Highness!—The Prince of Como does not understand his own language.

MEL. Not as you pronounce it,—who the deuce could?

MME. DESCHAP. Ha! ha! cousin Damas, never pretend to what you don't know.

PAULINE. Ha! ha! cousin Damas; *you* speak Italian, indeed! (*Makes a mocking gesture at him.*)

BEAU. (*to* GLAVIS). Clever dog!—how ready!

GLA. Ready, yes; with my diamond ring!—Damn his readiness!

DAMAS. Laugh at me!—laugh at a Colonel in the French army!—The fellow's an impostor; I know he is. I'll see if he understands fighting as well as he does Italian—(*Goes up to him, and aside.*) Sir, you are a jackanapes!—Can you construe that?

MEL. No, Sir; I never construe affronts in the presence of ladies; by-and-by I shall be happy to take a lesson—or give one.

DAMAS. I'll find the occasion, never fear!

MME. DESCHAP. Where are you going, cousin?

DAMAS. To correct my Italian. (*Exit.*)

BEAU. (*to* GLAVIS). Let us after, and pacify him; he evidently suspects something.

GLA. Yes!—but my diamond ring!

BEAU. And my box!—We are over-taxed, fellow-subject!—we must stop the supplies, and dethrone the Prince!

GLA. Prince!—he ought to be heir-apparent to King Stork! (*Exeunt.*)

MME. DESCHAP. Dare I ask your Highness to forgive my cousin's insufferable vulgarity?

PAULINE. Oh, yes!—you will forgive his manner for the sake of his heart.

---

[1] *"Your most humble servant, Excellency."*

[2] *"I am glad to see you well."*

[3] *"Fine weather!—What's the news?"*

MEL. And the sake of his cousin.—Ah, Madame, there is one comfort in rank,—we are so sure of our position that we are not easily affronted. Besides, M. Damas has bought the right of indulgence from his friends, by never showing it to his enemies.

PAULINE. Ah! he is, indeed, as brave in action as he is rude in speech. He rose from the ranks to his present grade,—and in two years!

MEL. In two years!—two years, did you say?

MME. DESCHAP. (*aside*). I don't like leaving girls alone with their lovers; but, with a prince, it would be so ill-bred to be prudish. (*Exit.*)

MEL. You can be proud of your connexion with one who owes his position to merit,—not birth.

PAULINE. Why, yes; but still—

MEL. Still what, Pauline?

PAULINE. There is something glorious in the Heritage of Command. A man who has ancestors is like a Representative of the Past.

MEL. True; but, like other representatives, nine times out of ten he is a silent member. Ah, Pauline! not to the Past, but to the Future, looks true nobility, and finds its blazon in posterity.

PAULINE. You say this to please me, who have no ancestors; but you, Prince, must be proud of so illustrious a race!

MEL. No, no! I would not, were I fifty times a prince, be a pensioner on the Dead! I honour birth and ancestry when they are regarded as the incentives to exertion, not the title-deeds to sloth! I honour the laurels that overshadow the graves of our fathers;—it is our fathers I emulate, when I desire that beneath the evergreen I myself have planted my own ashes may repose! Dearest! could'st thou but see with my eyes!

PAULINE. I cannot forego pride when I look on thee, and think that thou lovest me. Sweet Prince, tell me again of thy palace by the Lake of Como; it is so pleasant to hear of thy splendours since thou didst swear to me that they would be desolate without Pauline; and when thou describest them, it is with a mocking lip and a noble scorn, as if custom had made thee disdain greatness.

MEL. Nay, dearest, nay, if thou would'st have me paint
The home to which, could Love fulfil its prayers,
This hand would lead thee, listen!—a deep vale
Shut out by Alpine hills from the rude world;
Near a clear lake, margined by fruits of gold
And whispering myrtles; glassing softest skies

As cloudless, save with rare and roseate shadows,
As I would have thy fate!

PAULINE. My own dear love!

MEL. A palace lifting to eternal summer
Its marble walls, from out a glossy bower
Of coolest foliage musical with birds,
Whose songs should syllable thy name! At noon
We'd sit beneath the arching vines, and wonder
Why Earth could be unhappy, while the Heavens
Still left us youth and love! We'd have no friends
That were not lovers; no ambition, save
To excel them all in love; we'd read no books
That were not tales of love—that we might smile
To think how poorly eloquence of words
Translates the poetry of hearts like ours!
And when night came, amidst the breathless Heavens
We'd guess what star should be our home when love
Becomes immortal; while the perfumed light
Stole through the mists of alabaster lamps,
And every air was heavy with the sighs
Of orange groves and music from sweet lutes,
And murmurs of low fountains that gush forth
I' the midst of roses!—Dost thou like the picture?

PAULINE. Oh! as the bee upon the flower, I hang
Upon the honey of thy eloquent tongue!
Am I not blest? And if I love too wildly,
Who would not love thee like Pauline?

MEL. (*bitterly*). Oh, false one!
It is the *prince* thou lovest, not the *man;*
If in the stead of luxury, pomp, and power,
I had painted poverty, and toil, and care,
Thou hadst found no honey on my tongue;—Pauline,
That is not love!

PAULINE. Thou wrong'st me, cruel Prince!
'Tis true I might not at the first been won,
Save through the weakness of a flattered pride;
But *now,*—Oh! trust me,—could'st thou fall from power,
And sink—

MEL. As low as that poor gardener's son

Who dared to lift his eyes to thee.

PAULINE. Even then,
Methinks thou would'st be only made more dear
By the sweet thought that I could prove how deep
Is woman's love! We are like the insects, caught
By the poor glittering of a garish flame;
But, oh, the wings once scorched,—the brightest star
Lures us no more; and by the fatal light
We cling till death!

MEL. Angel! (*Aside.*) O conscience! conscience!
It must not be;—her love hath grown a torture
Worse than her hate. I will at once to Beauseant,
And——ha! he comes.——Sweet love, one moment leave me.
I have business with these gentlemen—I—I
Will forthwith join you.

PAULINE. Do not tarry long! (*Exit.*)

(*Enter* BEAUSEANT *and* GLAVIS.)

MEL. Release me from my oath,—I will not marry her!

BEAU. Then thou art perjured.

MEL. No, I was not in my senses when I swore to thee to marry her! I was blind to all but her scorn!—deaf to all but my passion and my rage! Give me back my poverty and my honour!

BEAU. It is too late,—you must marry her! and this day. I have a story already coined,—and sure to pass current. This Damas suspects thee,—he will set the police to work;—thou wilt be detected—Pauline will despise and execrate thee. Thou wilt be sent to the common gaol as a swindler.

MEL. Fiend!

BEAU. And in the heat of the girl's resentment (you know of what resentment is capable) and the parent's shame, she will be induced to marry the first that offers—even perhaps your humble servant.

MEL. You! No; that were worse—for thou hast no mercy! I will marry her—I will keep my oath. Quick, then, with the damnable invention thou art hatching;—quick, if thou would'st not have me strangle thee or myself.

GLA. What a tiger! Too fierce for a Prince; he ought to have been the Grand Turk.

BEAU. Enough—I will despatch; be prepared. (*Exeunt* BEAUSEANT *and* GLAVIS.)

(*Enter* DAMAS *with two swords.*)

DAMAS. Now, then, Sir, the ladies are no longer your excuse. I have brought you a couple of dictionaries; let us see if your Highness can find out the Latin for *bilbo.*

MEL. Away, Sir!—I am in no humour for jesting.

DAMAS. I see you understand something of the grammar; you decline the noun substantive "small sword" with great ease; but that won't do —you must take a lesson in *parsing.*

MEL. Fool!

DAMAS. Sir,—a man who calls me a fool insults the lady who bore me; there's no escape for you—fight you shall, or——

MEL. Oh, enough! enough!—take your ground. (*They fight;* DAMAS *is disarmed.*—MELNOTTE *takes up the sword and returns it to* DAMAS *respectfully.*) A just punishment to the brave soldier who robs the State of its best property—the sole right to his valour and his life.

DAMAS. Sir, you fence exceedingly well; you must be a man of honour—I don't care a jot whether you are a prince; but a man who has carte and tierce at his fingers' ends must be a gentleman.

MEL. (*aside*). Gentleman! Ay, I was a gentleman before I turned conspirator; for honest men are the gentlemen of Nature! Colonel, they tell me you rose from the ranks.

DAMAS. I did.

MEL. And in two years?

DAMAS. It is true; that's no wonder in our army at present. Why, the oldest general in the service is scarcely thirty, and we have some of two-and-twenty.

MEL. Two-and-twenty!

DAMAS. Yes; in the French army, now-a-days, promotion is not a matter of purchase. We are all heroes because we may be all generals. We have no fear of the cypress because we may all hope for the laurel.

MEL. A general at two-and-twenty (*turning away*).—Sir, I may ask you a favour one of these days.

DAMAS. Sir, I shall be proud to grant it.—It is astonishing how much I like a man after I've fought with him.—(*Hides the swords.*)

(*Enter* MADAME *and* BEAUSEANT.)

MME. DESCHAP. Oh, Prince!—Prince!—What do I hear? You must fly,—you must quit us!

MEL. I!—

BEAU. Yes, Prince; read this letter, just received from my friend at Paris, one of the Directory; they suspect you of designs against the Republic; they are very suspicious of princes, and your family take part with the Austrians. Knowing that I introduced your Highness at Lyons, my friend writes to me to say that you must quit the town immediately or you will be arrested,—thrown into prison,—perhaps guillotined! Fly!—I will order horses to your carriage instantly. Fly to Marseilles; there you can take ship to Leghorn.

MME. DESCHAP. And what's to become of Pauline? Am I not to be mother to a princess, after all?

(*Enter* PAULINE *and* M. DESCHAPPELLES.)

PAULINE (*throwing herself into* MELNOTTE'S *arms*). You must leave us! —Leave Pauline!

BEAU. Not a moment is to be wasted.

MONS. DESCHAP. I will go to the magistrates and inquire——

BEAU. Then he is lost; the magistrates, hearing he is suspected, will order his arrest.

MME. DESCHAP. And I shall not be Princess Dowager!

BEAU. Why not? There is only one thing to be done:—send for the priest—let the marriage take place at once, and the Prince carry home a bride!

MEL. Impossible!—(*Aside.*) Villain!—I know not what to say.

MME. DESCHAP. What, lose my child?

BEAU. And gain a Princess!

MME. DESCHAP. Oh, Monsieur Beauseant, you are so very kind,—it must be so,—we ought not to be selfish,—my daughter's happiness is at stake. She will go away, too, in a carriage and six!

PAULINE. Thou art here still,—I cannot part from thee,—my heart will break.

MEL. But thou wilt not consent to this hasty union,—thou wilt not wed an outcast—a fugitive.

PAULINE. Ah! If thou art in danger, who should share it but Pauline?

MEL. (*aside*). Distraction!—If the earth could swallow me!

MONS. DESCHAP. Gently!—gently! The settlements—the contracts—my daughter's dowry!

MEL. The dowry!—I am not base enough for that; no, not one farthing!

BEAU. (*to* MADAME). Noble fellow! Really your good husband is too mercantile in these matters. Monsieur Deschappelles, you hear his Highness: we can arrange the settlements by proxy,—tis the way with people of quality.

MONS. DESCHAP. But——

MME. DESCHAP. Hold your tongue!—Don't expose yourself!

BEAU. I will bring the priest in a trice. Go in all of you and prepare; —the carriage shall be at the door before the ceremony is over.

MME. DESCHAP. Be sure there are six horses, Beauseant! You are very good to have forgiven us for refusing you; but, you see—a prince!

BEAU. And such a prince! Madame, I cannot blush at the success of so illustrious a rival.—(*Aside.*) Now will I follow them to the village—enjoy my triumph, and to-morrow—in the hour of thy shame and grief, I think, proud girl, thou wilt prefer even these arms to those of the gardener's son. (*Exit* BEAUSEANT.)

MME. DESCHAP. Come, Monsieur Deschappelles—give your arm to her Highness that is to be.

MONS. DESCHAP. I don't like doing business in such a hurry—'tis not the way with the house of Deschappelles and Co.

MME. DESCHAP. There, now—you fancy you are in the counting-house—don't you? (*Pushes him to* PAULINE.)

MEL. Stay,—stay, Pauline—one word. Have you no scruple—no fear? Speak—it is not yet too late.

PAULINE. When I loved thee, thy fate became mine. Triumph or danger—joy or sorrow—I am by thy side.

DAMAS. Well, well, Prince, thou art a lucky man to be so loved. She is a good little girl in spite of her foibles—make her as happy as if she were not to be a princess (*slapping him on the shoulder*). Come, Sir, I wish you joy—young—tender—lovely; zounds I envy you!

MEL. (*who has stood apart in gloomy abstraction*).
Do you? Wise judges are we of each other.
"Woo, wed, and bear her home!" So runs the bond
To which I sold myself—and then—what then?
Away!—I will not look beyond the Hour.
Like children in the dark, I dare not face
The shades that gather round me in the distance.
You envy me—I thank you—you may read
My joy upon my brow—I thank you, Sir!
If hearts had audible language, you would hear
How mine would answer when you talk of *envy*![4]

End of Act II

---

[4] *Printed versions omitted everything after "Do you?" in this scene.*

ACT III

SCENE 1: *The Exterior of the Golden Lion—time, twilight. The moon rises during the Scene.*

(*Enter* LANDLORD *and his* DAUGHTER *from the inn.*)

LAND. Ha—ha—ha! Well, I never shall get over it. Our Claude is a prince with a vengeance now. His carriage breaks down at my inn—ha—ha!

JANET. And what airs the young lady gives herself! "Is this the best room you have, young woman?" with such a toss of her head!

LAND. Well, get in, Janet; get in and see to the supper: the servants must sup before they go back. (*Exeunt* LANDLORD *and* JANET.)

(*Enter* BEAUSEANT *and* GLAVIS.)

BEAU. You see our Princess is lodged at last—one stage more, and she'll be at her journey's end—the beautiful palace at the foot of the Alps!—ha—ha!

GLA. Faith, I pity the poor Pauline—especially if she's going to sup at the Golden Lion (*makes a wry face*). I shall never forget that cursed ragout.

(*Enter* MELNOTTE *from the Inn.*)

BEAU. Your servant, my Prince; you reigned most worthily. I condole with you on your abdication. I am afraid that your Highness's retinue are not very faithful servants. I think they will quit you in the moment of your fall—'tis the fate of greatness. But you are welcome to your fine clothes—also the diamond snuff-box, which Louis XIV gave to your great-great-grandmother.

GLA. And the ring, with which your grandfather the Doge of Venice married the Adriatic.

MEL. I have kept my oath, gentlemen, say—have I kept my oath?

BEAU. Most religiously.

MEL. Then you have done with me and mine—away with you!

BEAU. How, knave?

MEL. Look you, our bond is over. Proud conquerors that we are, we have won the victory over a simple girl—compromised her honour—embittered her life—blasted, in their very blossoms, all the flowers of her youth. This is your triumph,—it is my shame! (*Turns to* BEAUSEANT.) Enjoy that triumph, but not in my sight. I *was* her betrayer—I *am* her protector! Cross but her path—one word of scorn, one look of insult—nay, but one quiver of that mocking lip, and I will teach thee that bitter word thou hast graven eternally in this heart—*Repentance!*

BEAU. His Highness is most grandiloquent.

MEL. Highness me no more. Beware! Remorse has made me a new being. Away with you! There is danger in me. Away!

GLA. (*aside*). He's an awkward fellow to deal with: come away, Beauseant.

BEAU. I know the respect due to rank. Adieu, my Prince. Any commands at Lyons? Yet hold—I promised you 200 louis on your wedding-day; here they are.

MEL. (*dashing the purse to the ground*). I gave you revenge, I did not sell it. Take up your silver, Judas; take it. Ay, it is fit you should learn to stoop.

BEAU. You will beg my pardon for this some day. (*Aside to* GLAVIS.) Come to my chateau—I shall return hither to-morrow, to learn how Pauline likes her new dignity.

MEL. Are you not gone yet?

BEAU. Your Highness's most obedient, most faithful—

GLA. And most humble servants. Ha! ha! (*Exeunt* BEAUSEANT *and* GLAVIS.)

MEL. Thank Heaven, I had no weapon, or I should have slain them. Wretch! what can I say? Where turn? On all sides mockery—the very boors within—(*Laughter from the inn.*)—'Sdeath, if even in this short absence the exposure should have chanced. I will call her. We will go hence. I have already sent one I can trust to my mother's house. There at least none can insult her agony—gloat upon her shame! There alone must she learn what a villain she has sworn to love.

(*As he turns to the door, enter* PAULINE *from the Inn.*)

PAULINE. Ah, my Lord, what a place! I never saw such rude people. They stare and wink so. I think the very sight of a prince, though he travels incognito, turns their honest heads. What a pity the carriage should break down in such a spot! You are not well—the drops stand on your brow—your hand is feverish.

MEL. Nay, it is but a passing spasm; the air—

PAULINE. Is not the soft air of your native south.
How pale he is!—indeed thou art not well.
Where are our people? I will call them.

MEL. Hold!
I—I am well.

PAULINE. Thou art!—Ah! now I know it.
Thou fanciest, my kind Lord—I know thou dost—
Thou fanciest these rude walls, these rustic gossips,
Brick'd floors, sour wine, coarse viands, vex Pauline;
And so they might, but thou art by my side,
And I forget all else!
(*Enter* LANDLORD, *the servants peeping and laughing over his shoulder.*)
LAND. My Lord—your Highness—
Will your most noble Excellency choose—
MEL. Begone, Sir! (*Exit* LANDLORD, *laughing.*)
PAULINE. How could they have learn'd thy rank?
One's servants are so vain!—nay, let it not
Chafe thee, sweet Prince!—a few short days, and we
Shall see thy palace by its lake of silver,
And—nay, nay, Spendthrift, is thy wealth of smiles
Already drained, or dost thou play the miser?
MEL. Thine eyes would call up smiles in deserts, fair one.
Let us escape these rustics. Close at hand
There is a cot, where I have bid prepare
Our evening lodgment—a rude, homely roof,
But honest, where our welcome will not be
Made torture by the vulgar eyes and tongues
That are as death to Love! A heavenly night!
The wooing air and the soft moon invite us.
Wilt walk? I pray thee, now,—I know the path,
Ay, every inch of it!
PAULINE. What, *thou!* methought
Thou wert a stranger in these parts. Ah! truant,
Some village beauty lured thee;—thou art now
Grown constant.
MEL. Trust me.
PAULINE. Princes are so changeful!
MEL. Come, dearest, come.
PAULINE. Shall I not call our people
To light us?
MEL. Heaven will lend its stars for torches!
It is not far.
PAULINE. The night breeze chills me.
MEL. Nay,
Let me thus mantle thee;—it is not cold.

PAULINE. Never beneath thy smile!
MEL. (*aside*). Oh, Heaven! forgive me! (*Exeunt.*)

SCENE 2: MELNOTTE'S *cottage—Widow bustling about—A table spread for supper.*

WIDOW. So, I think that looks very neat. He sent me a line, so blotted that I can scarcely read it, to say he would be here almost immediately. She must have loved him well, indeed, to have forgotten his birth; for though he was introduced to her in disguise, he is too honourable not to have revealed to her the artifice which her love only could forgive. Well, I do not wonder at it; for though my son is not a prince, he ought to be one, and that's almost as good. (*Knock at the door.*) Ah! here they are.

(*Enter* MELNOTTE *and* PAULINE.)

WIDOW. Oh, my boy—the pride of my heart!—welcome, welcome! I beg pardon, Ma'am, but I do love him so!

PAULINE. Good woman, I really—why, Prince, what is this?—does the old lady know you? Oh, I guess, you have done her some service: another proof of your kind heart, is it not?

MEL. Of my kind heart, ay!

PAULINE. So you know the Prince?

WIDOW. Know him, Madam?—ah, I begin to fear it is you who know him not!

PAULINE. Do you think she is mad? Can we stay here, my Lord? I think there's something very wild about her.

MEL. Madam, I—no I can not tell her, my knees knock together: what a coward is a man who has lost his honour! Speak to her—speak to her (*to his Mother*)—tell her that—Oh, Heaven, that I were dead!

PAULINE. How confused he looks!—this strange place—this woman—what can it mean?—I half suspect—Who are you, Madam?—who are you? can't you speak? are you struck dumb?

WIDOW. Claude, you have not deceived her?—Ah, shame upon you! I thought that, before you went to the altar, she was to have known all.

PAULINE. All! what? My blood freezes in my veins!

WIDOW. Poor lady!—dare I tell her, Claude? (MELNOTTE *makes a sign of assent.*) Know you not then, Madam, that this young man is of poor though honest parents? Know you not that you are wedded to my son, Claude Melnotte?

PAULINE. Your son! hold—hold! do not speak to me—(*Approaches* MELNOTTE, *and lays her hand on his arm.*) Is this a jest? is it? I know it is, only speak—one word—one look—one smile. I cannot believe —I who loved thee so—I cannot believe that thou art such a——No, I will not wrong thee by a harsh word—speak!

MEL. Leave us—have pity on her, on me: leave us.

WIDOW. Oh, Claude, that I should live to see thee bowed by shame! thee of whom I was so proud! (*Exit* WIDOW *by the staircase.*)

PAULINE. Her son—her son—

MEL. Now, lady, hear me.

PAULINE. Hear thee!
Ay, speak—her son! have fiends a parent? speak,
That thou may'st silence curses—speak!

MEL. No, curse me:
Thy curse would blast me less than thy forgiveness.

PAULINE (*laughing wildly*). "This is thy palace, where the perfumed light
"Steals through the mist of alabaster lamps,
"And every air is heavy with the sighs
"Of orange groves, and music from sweet lutes,
"And murmurs of low fountains, that gush forth
"I' the midst of roses! Dost thou like the picture?"
This is my bridal home, and *thou* my bridegroom!
O fool—O dupe—O wretch!—I see it all—
The bye-word and the jeer of every tongue
In Lyons. Hast thou in thy heart one touch
Of human kindness? if thou hast, why, kill me,
And save thy wife from madness. No, it cannot—
It cannot be: this is some horrid dream:
I shall wake soon.—(*Touching him.*) Art flesh? art man? or but
The shadows seen in sleep?—It is too real.
What have I done to thee? how sinn'd against thee,
That thou should'st crush me thus?

MEL. Pauline, by pride
Angels have fallen ere thy time: by pride—
That sole alloy of thy most lovely mould—
The evil spirit of a bitter love,
And a revengeful heart, had power upon thee.—
From my first years, my soul was fill'd with thee:
I saw thee midst the flow'rs the lowly boy

Tended, unmark'd by thee—a spirit of bloom,
And joy, and freshness, as if Spring itself
Were made a living thing, and wore thy shape!
I saw thee, and the passionate heart of man
Enter'd the breast of the wild-dreaming boy;
And from that hour I grew—what to the last
I shall be—thine adorer! Well; this love,
Vain, frantic, guilty, if thou wilt, became
A fountain of ambition and bright hope;
I thought of tales that by the winter hearth
Old gossips tell—how maidens sprung from Kings
Have stoop'd from their high sphere; how Love, like Death,
Levels all ranks, and lays the shepherd's crook
Beside the sceptre. Thus I made my home
In the soft palace of a fairy Future!
My father died; and I, the peasant-born,
Was my own lord. Then did I seek to rise
Out of the prison of my mean estate;
And, with such jewels as the exploring Mind
Brings from the caves of Knowledge, buy my ransom
From those twin gaolers of the daring heart—
Low Birth and iron Fortune. Thy bright image,
Glass'd in my soul, took all the hues of glory,
And lured me on to those inspiring toils
By which man masters men! For thee I grew
A midnight student o'er the dreams of sages!
For thee I sought to borrow from each Grace,
And every Muse, such attributes as lend
Ideal charms to Love. I thought of thee,
And Passion taught me poesy—of thee,
And on the painter's canvas grew the life
Of beauty!—Art became the shadow
Of the dear starlight of thy haunting eyes!
Men call'd me vain—some mad—I heeded not;
But still toiled on—hoped on—for it was sweet,
If not to win, to feel more worthy thee!

PAULINE. Has he a magic to exorcise hate?

MEL. At last, in one mad hour, I dared to pour
The thoughts that burst their channels into song,
And sent them to thee—such a tribute, lady,

As beauty rarely scorns, even from the meanest.
The name—appended by the burning heart
That long'd to show its idol what bright things
It had created—yea, the enthusiast's name,
That should have been thy triumph, was thy scorn!
That very hour—when passion, turned to wrath,
Resembled hatred most—when thy disdain
Made my whole soul a chaos—in that hour
The tempters found me a revengeful tool
For their revenge! Thou hadst trampled on the worm—
It turn'd and stung thee!

PAULINE. Love, Sir, hath no sting.
What was the slight of a poor powerless girl
To the deep wrong of this most vile revenge?
Oh, how I loved this man!—a serf!—a slave!

MEL. Hold, lady!—No, not slave! Despair is free!
I will not tell thee of the throes—the struggles—
The anguish—the remorse: No—let it pass!
And let me come to such most poor atonement
Yet in my power. Pauline!—

(*Approaching her with great emotion, and about to take her hand.*)

PAULINE. No, touch me not!
I know my fate. You are, by law, my tyrant;
And I—oh Heaven!—a peasant's wife! I'll work—
Toil—drudge—do what thou wilt—but touch me not;
Let my wrongs make me sacred!

MEL. Do not fear me.
Thou dost not know me, Madam: at the altar
My vengeance ceased—my guilty oath expired!
Henceforth, no image of some marble saint,
Nich'd in cathedral aisles, is hallow'd more
From the rude hand of sacrilegious wrong.
I am thy husband—nay, thou need'st not shudder;—
Here, at thy feet, I lay a husband's rights.
A marriage thus unholy—unfulfilled—
A bond of fraud—is, by the laws of France,
Made void and null. To-night sleep—sleep in peace.
To-morrow, pure and virgin as this morn
I bore thee, bathed in blushes, from the shrine,

Thy father's arms shall take thee to thy home.
The law shall do thee justice, and restore
Thy right to bless another with thy love.
And when thou art happy, and hast half forgot
Him who so loved—so wrong'd thee, think at least
Heaven left some remnant of the angel still
In that poor peasant's nature!
Ho! my mother!

(*Enter* WIDOW.)

Conduct this lady—(she is not my wife;
She is our guest,—our honour'd guest, my mother!)—
To the poor chamber, where the sleep of virtue,
Never, beneath my father's honest roof,
Ev'n villains dared to mar! Now, lady, now,
I think thou wilt believe me.—Go, my mother!

WIDOW. She is not thy wife!—

MEL. Hush! hush! for mercy's sake!
Speak not, but go.

(WIDOW *ascends the stairs;* PAULINE *follows, weeping—turns to look back.*)

MEL. (*sinking down*). All angels bless and guard her!

End of Act III

ACT IV

SCENE 1: *The Cottage as before*—MELNOTTE *seated before a table—writing implements, &c.*—(*Day breaking.*)

MEL. Hush, hush!—she sleeps at last!—thank Heaven, for awhile, she forgets even that I live! Her sobs, which have gone to my heart the whole, long, desolate night, have ceased!—all calm—all still! I will go now; I will send this letter to Pauline's father—when he arrives, I will place in his hands my own consent to the divorce, and then, O France! my country! accept among thy protectors, thy defenders—the Peasant's Son! Our country is less proud than Custom, and does not refuse the blood, the heart, the right hand of the poor man!

(*Enter* WIDOW.)

WIDOW. My son, thou hast acted ill, but sin brings its own punishment. In the hour of thy remorse, it is not for a mother to reproach thee!

MEL. What is past is past. There is a future left to all men, who have the virtue to repent and the energy to atone. Thou shalt be proud of thy son, yet. Meanwhile, remember this poor lady has been grievously injured. For the sake of thy son's conscience, respect, honour, bear with her. If she weep, console—if she chide, be silent! 'Tis but a little while more—I shall send an express fast as horse can speed to her father. Farewell!—I shall return shortly.

WIDOW. It is the only course left to thee—thou wert led astray, but thou art not hardened. Thy heart is right still, as ever it was, when in thy most ambitious hopes, thou wert never ashamed of thy poor mother!

MEL. Ashamed of thee!—No, if I yet endure, yet live, yet hope—it is only because I would not die till I have redeemed the noble heritage I have lost—the heritage I took unstained from thee and my dead father—a proud conscience and an honest name. I shall win them back yet—Heaven bless you! (*Exit.*)

WIDOW. My dear Claude!—How my heart bleeds for him!

(PAULINE *looks down from above, and after a pause descends.*)

PAULINE. Not here!—he spares me that pain at least: so far he is considerate—yet the place seems still more desolate without him. Oh, that I could hate him—the gardener's son!—and yet how nobly he—no—no—no I will not be so mean a thing as to forgive him!

WIDOW. Good morning, Madam; I would have waited on you if I had known you were stirring.

PAULINE. It is no matter, Ma'am—your son's wife ought to wait on herself.

WIDOW. My son's wife—let not that thought vex you, Madam—he tells me that you will have your divorce. And I hope I shall live to see him smile again. There are maidens in this village, young and fair, Madam, who may yet console him.

PAULINE. I dare say—they are very welcome—and when the divorce is got, he will marry again. I am sure I hope so (*weeps*).

WIDOW. He could have married the richest girl in the province, if he had pleased it; but his head was turned, poor child!—he could think of nothing but you (*weeps*).

PAULINE. Don't weep, *mother*!

WIDOW. Ah, he has behaved very ill, I know—but love is so headstrong in the young. Don't weep, Madam.

PAULINE. So, as you were saying—go on.

WIDOW. Oh, I cannot excuse him, Ma'am—he was not in his right senses.

PAULINE. But he always—always (*sobbing*) loved—loved me then.

WIDOW. He thought of nothing else—see here—he learnt to paint that he might take your likeness (*uncovers the picture*). But that's all over now—I trust you have cured him of his folly—but, dear heart, you have had no breakfast!

PAULINE. I can't take anything—don't trouble yourself.

WIDOW. Nay, Madam, be persuaded; a little coffee will refresh you. Our milk and eggs are excellent. I will get out Claude's coffee-cup—it is of real Sèvre; he saved up all his money to buy it three years ago, because the name of *Pauline* was inscribed on it.

PAULINE. Three years ago! Poor Claude! Thank you. I think I will have some coffee. Oh! if he were but a poor gentleman, even a merchant: but a gardener's son—and what a home!—Oh no, it is too dreadful! (*They seat themselves at the table—*BEAUSEANT *opens the lattice and looks in.*)

BEAU. So—so—the coast is clear! I saw Claude in the lane—I shall have an excellent opportunity. (*Shuts the lattice, and knocks at the door.*)

PAULINE (*starting*). Can it be my father?—he has not sent for him yet? No, he cannot be in such a hurry to get rid of me.

WIDOW. It is not time for your father to arrive yet; it must be some neighbour.

PAULINE. Don't admit any one.

(WIDOW *opens the door—*BEAUSEANT *pushes her aside, and enters.*)

Ah! Heavens! that hateful Beauseant! This is indeed bitter!

BEAU. Good morning, Madam! Oh, Widow, your son begs you will have the goodness to go to him in the village—he wants to speak to you on particular business; you'll find him at the inn, or the grocer's shop, or the baker's, or at some other friend's of your family—make haste!

PAULINE. Don't leave me, mother!—don't leave me!

BEAU. (*with great respect*). Be not alarmed, Madam. Believe me your friend—your servant.

PAULINE. Sir, I have no fear of you, even in this house! Go, Madam, if your son wishes it; I will not contradict his commands whilst, at least, he has still the right to be obeyed.

WIDOW. I don't understand this; however, I shan't be long gone. (*Exit.*)

PAULINE. Sir, I divine the object of your visit—you wish to exult in the humiliation of one who humbled you. Be it so; I am prepared to endure all—even your presence!

BEAU. You mistake me, Madam—Pauline, you mistake me! I come to lay my fortune at your feet. You must already be disenchanted with this impostor; these walls are not worthy to be hallowed by your beauty! Shall that form be clasped in the arms of a base-born peasant? Beloved, beautiful Pauline! fly with me—my carriage waits without—I will bear you to a home more meet for your reception. Wealth, luxury, station —all shall yet be yours. I forget your past disdain—I remember only your beauty, and my unconquerable love!

PAULINE. Sir! leave this house—it is humble: but a husband's roof, however lowly, is, in the eyes of God and Man, the temple of a wife's honour! Know that I would rather starve—yes!—with him who has betrayed me, than accept your lawful hand, even were you the Prince whose name he bore!—Go!

BEAU. What, is not your pride humbled yet?

PAULINE. Sir, what was pride in prosperity, in affliction becomes virtue.

BEAU. Look round: these rugged floors—these homely walls—this wretched struggle of poverty for comfort—think of this! and contrast with such a picture the refinement, the luxury, the pomp that the wealthiest gentleman of Lyons offers to the loveliest lady. Ah, hear me!

PAULINE. Oh! my father!—why did I leave you?—why am I thus friendless? Sir, you see before you a betrayed, injured, miserable woman! —respect her anguish!

(MELNOTTE *opens the door silently, and pauses at the threshold.*)

BEAU. No! let me rather thus console it;—let me snatch from those lips one breath of that fragrance which never should be wasted on the low churl thy husband.

PAULINE. Help! Claude!—Claude! Have I no protector?

BEAU. Be silent! (*Showing a pistol.*) See, I do not come unprepared even for violence. I will brave all things—thy husband and all his race —for thy sake. Thus, then, I clasp thee!

MEL. (*dashing him to the other end of the stage*). Pauline—look up, Pauline! thou art safe.

BEAU. (*levelling his pistol*). Dare you thus insult a man of my birth, ruffian?

PAULINE. Oh spare him—spare my husband!—Beauseant—Claude— no—no—(*faints*).

MEL. Miserable trickster! Shame upon you! brave devices to terrify a woman! coward—you tremble—you have outraged the laws—you know that your weapon is harmless—you have the courage of the mountebank, not the bravo!—Pauline, there is no danger.

BEAU. I wish thou wert a gentleman—as it is thou art beneath me. —Good day, and a happy honeymoon. (*Aside.*) I will not die till I am avenged. (*Exit* BEAUSEANT.)

MEL. I hold her in these arms—the last embrace!
Never, ah never more, shall this dear head
Be pillow'd on the heart that should have shelter'd
And has betray'd! Soft—soft! one kiss—poor wretch!
No scorn on that pale lip forbids me now!
One kiss—so ends all record of my crime!
It is the seal upon the tomb of Hope,
By which, like some lost, sorrowing angel, sits
Sad Memory evermore;—she breathes—she moves—
She wakes to scorn, to hate, but not to shudder
Beneath the touch of my abhorred love. (*Places her on a seat.*)
There—we are strangers now!

PAULINE. All gone—all calm—
Is *every* thing a dream? thou art safe, unhurt—
I do not love thee; but—but I am woman,
And—and—no blood is spilt?

MEL. No, lady, no;
My guilt hath not deserved so rich a blessing
As even danger in thy cause.

(*Enter* WIDOW.)

WIDOW. My son, I have been everywhere in search of you; why did you send for me?

MEL. I did not send for you.

WIDOW. No! but I must tell you your express has returned.

MEL. So soon! impossible!

WIDOW. Yes, he met the lady's father and mother on the road; they were going into the country on a visit. Your messenger says that Monsieur Deschappelles turned almost white with anger, when he read your letter. They will be here almost immediately. Oh, Claude, Claude! what will they do to you? How I tremble!—Ah, Madam! do not let them injure him—if you knew how he doted on you!

PAULINE. Injure him! no, Ma'am, be not afraid;—my father! how shall I meet him? how go back to Lyons? the scoff of the whole city!—cruel, cruel, Claude—(*in great agitation*)—Sir, you have acted most treacherously.

MEL. I know it, Madam.

PAULINE (*aside*). If he would but ask me to forgive him!—I never can forgive you, Sir!

MEL. I never dared to hope it.

PAULINE. But you are my husband now, and I have sworn to—to love you, Sir.

MEL. That was under a false belief, Madam; Heaven and the laws will release you from your vow.

PAULINE. He will drive me mad! if he were but less proud—if he would but ask me to remain—hark, hark—I hear the wheels of the carriage—Sir—Claude, they are coming; have you no word to say ere it is too late? quick—speak!

MEL. I can only congratulate you on your release. Behold your parents!

(*Enter* MONSIEUR *and* MADAME DESCHAPPELLES *and* COLONEL DAMAS.)

MONS. DESCHAP. My child!—my child!

MME. DESCHAP. Oh my poor Pauline!—what a villainous hovel this is! Old woman, get me a chair—I shall faint—I certainly shall. What will the world say?—Child, you have been a fool. A mother's heart is easily broken.

DAMAS. Ha, ha!—most noble Prince—I am sorry to see a man of your quality in such a condition; I am afraid your Highness will go to the House of Correction.

MEL. Taunt on, Sir—I spared *you* when you were unarmed—I am unarmed now. A man who has no excuse for crime is indeed defenceless!

DAMAS. There's something fine in the rascal, after all!

MONS. DESCHAP. Where is the impostor?—Are you thus shameless, traitor? Can you brave the presence of that girl's father?

MEL. Strike me, if it please you—you *are* her father!

PAULINE. Sir—sir, for my sake;—whatever his guilt, he has acted nobly in atonement.

MME. DESCHAP. Nobly! Are you mad, girl? I have no patience with you—to disgrace all your family thus! Nobly! Oh you abominable, hardened, pitiful, mean, ugly villain!

DAMAS. Ugly! Why he was beautiful yesterday!

PAULINE. Madam, this is his roof, and he is my husband. Respect your daughter, and let blame fall alone on her.

MME. DESCHAP. You—you—Oh, I'm choking.

MONS. DESCHAP. Sir, it were idle to waste reproach upon a conscience like yours—you renounce all pretensions to the person of this lady?

MEL. I do.—(*Gives a paper.*) Here is my consent to a divorce—my full confession of the fraud, which annuls the marriage. Your daughter has been foully wronged—I grant it, Sir; but her own lips will tell you, that from the hour in which she crossed this threshold, I returned to my own station, and respected hers. Pure and inviolate, as when yestermorn you laid your hand upon her head and blessed her, I yield her back to you. For myself—I deliver you for ever from my presence. An outcast and a criminal, I seek some distant land, where I may mourn my sin and pray for your daughter's peace. Farewell—farewell to you all, for ever!

WIDOW. Claude, Claude, you will not leave your poor old mother? *She* does not disown you in your sorrow—no, not even in your guilt. No divorce can separate a mother from her son.

PAULINE. This poor widow teaches me my duty. No, mother—no, for you are now *my* mother also!—nor should any law, human or divine, separate the wife from her husband's sorrows. Claude—Claude—all is forgotten—forgiven—I am thine for ever!

MME. DESCHAP. What do I hear?—Come away, or never see my face again.

MONS. DESCHAP. Pauline, *we* never betrayed you!—do you forsake us for him?

PAULINE (*going back to her father*). Oh, no—but you will forgive him too; we will live together—he shall be your son.

MONS. DESCHAP. Never! Cling to him and forsake your parents! His home shall be yours—his fortune yours—his fate yours: the wealth I have acquired by honest industry shall never enrich the dishonest man.

PAULINE. And you would have a wife enjoy luxury while a husband toils! Claude, take me; thou canst not give me wealth, titles, station—but thou canst give me a true heart. I will work for thee, tend thee, bear with thee, and never, never shall these lips reproach thee for the past.

DAMAS. I'll be hanged if I am not going to blubber!

MEL. This is the heaviest blow of all!—What a heart I have wronged! —Do not fear me, Sir; I am not all hardened—I will not rob her of a holier love than mine. Pauline!—angel of love and mercy!—your memory shall lead me back to virtue!—The husband of a being so beautiful in her noble and sublime tenderness may be poor—may be low-born;—(there is no guilt in the decrees of Providence!)—but he should be one who can look thee in the face without a blush,—to whom thy love does not bring remorse,—who can fold thee to his heart, and say,—"*Here* there is no deceit!"—I am not that man!

DAMAS (*aside to* MELNOTTE). Thou art a noble fellow, notwithstanding; and would'st make an excellent soldier. Serve in my regiment. I have had a letter from the Directory—our young General takes the command of the army in Italy,—I am to join him at Marseilles,—I will depart this day, if thou wilt go with me.

MEL. It is the favour I would have asked thee, if I dared. Place me wherever a foe is most dreaded,—wherever France most needs a life!

DAMAS. There shall not be a forlorn hope without thee!

MEL. There is my hand!—Mother! your blessing. I shall see you again, —a better man than a prince,—a man who has bought the right to high thoughts by brave deeds. And thou!—thou! so wildly worshipped, so guiltily betrayed,—all is not yet lost!—for thy memory, at least, must be mine till death! If I live, the name of him thou hast once loved shall not rest dishonoured;—if I fall, amidst the carnage and the roar of battle, my soul will fly back to thee, and Love shall share with Death my last sigh!—More—more would I speak to thee!—to pray! —to bless! But, no!—when I am less unworthy I will utter it to Heaven! —I cannot trust myself to—(*turning to* DESCHAPPELLES) Your pardon, Sir;—they are my last words—Farewell! (*Exit.*)

DAMAS. I will go after him.—France will thank me for this. (*Exit.*)

PAULINE (*starting from her father's arms*). Claude!—Claude!—my husband!

MONS. DESCHAP. You have a father still!

End of Act IV

ACT V

SCENE 1: (*Two years and a half from the date of Act IV.*) *The Streets of Lyons.*

(*Enter* FIRST, SECOND, *and* THIRD OFFICER.)

FIRST OFFICER. Well, here we are at Lyons, with gallant old Damas: it is his native place.

SECOND OFFICER. Yes; he has gained a step in the army since he was here last. The Lyonnese ought to be very proud of stout General Damas.

THIRD OFFICER. Promotion is quick in the French army. This mysterious Morier,—the hero of Lodi, and the favourite of the Commander-in-Chief,—has risen to a colonel's rank in two years and a half.

(*Enter* DAMAS, *as a General.*)

DAMAS. Good morrow, gentlemen; I hope you will amuse yourselves during our short stay at Lyons. It is a fine city; improved since I left it. Ah! it is a pleasure to grow old,—when the years that bring decay to ourselves do but ripen the prosperity of our country. You have not met with Morier?

FIRST OFFICER. No: we were just speaking of him.

SECOND OFFICER. Pray, General, can you tell us who this Morier really is?

DAMAS. Is!—why a Colonel in the French army.

THIRD OFFICER. True. But what was he at first?

DAMAS. At first?—Why, a baby in long clothes, I suppose.

FIRST OFFICER. Ha!—ha!—Ever facetious, General.

SECOND OFFICER (*to Third*). The General is sore upon this point; you will only chafe him.—Any commands, General?

DAMAS. None.—Good day to you! (*Exeunt* SECOND *and* THIRD OFFICERS.)

DAMAS. Our comrades are very inquisitive. Poor Morier is the subject of a vast deal of curiosity.

FIRST OFFICER. Say interest, rather, General. His constant melancholy, —the loneliness of his habits,—his daring valour,—his brilliant rise in the profession,—your friendship, and the favours of the Commander-in-Chief,—all tend to make him as much the matter of gossip as of admiration. But where is he, General? I have missed him all the morning.

DAMAS. Why, Captain, I'll let you into a secret. My young friend has come with me to Lyons in hopes of finding a miracle.

FIRST OFFICER. A miracle!—

DAMAS. Yes, a miracle! In other words,—a constant woman.

FIRST OFFICER. Oh!—an affair of love!

DAMAS. Exactly so. No sooner did he enter Lyons than he waved his hand to me, threw himself from his horse, and is now, I warrant, asking every one, who can know anything about the matter, whether a certain lady is still true to a certain gentleman!

FIRST OFFICER. Success to him!—and of that success there can be no doubt. The gallant Colonel Morier, the hero of Lodi, might make his choice out of the proudest families in France.

DAMAS. Oh, if pride be a recommendation, the lady and her mother are most handsomely endowed. By the way, Captain, if you should chance to meet with Morier, tell him he will find me at the hotel.

FIRST OFFICER. I will, General. (*Exit.*)

DAMAS. Now will I go to the Deschappelles, and make a report to my young Colonel. Ha! by Mars, Bacchus, Apollo, Virorum,—here comes Monsieur Beauseant!

(*Enter* BEAUSEANT.)

Good morrow, Monsieur Beauseant! How fares it with you?

BEAU. (*aside*). Damas! that is unfortunate;—if the Italian campaign should have filled his pockets, he may seek to baffle me in the moment of my victory. (*Aloud.*) Your servant, General,—for such, I think, is your new distinction! Just arrived in Lyons?

DAMAS. Not an hour ago. Well, how go on the Deschappelles? Have they forgiven you in that affair of young Melnotte? You had some hand in that notable device,—eh?

BEAU. Why, less than you think for! The fellow imposed upon me. I have set it all right now. What has become of him? He could not have joined the army, after all. There is no such name in the books.

DAMAS. I know nothing about Melnotte. As you say, I never heard the name in the Grand Army.

BEAU. Hem!—You are not married, General?

DAMAS. Do I look like a married man, Sir?—No, thank Heaven! My profession is to make widows, not wives.

BEAU. You must have gained much booty in Italy! Pauline will be your heiress—eh?

DAMAS. Booty! Not I! Heiress to what? Two trunks and a portmanteau,—four horses,—three swords,—two suits of regimentals, and six pair of white leather inexpressibles! A pretty fortune for a young lady!

BEAU. (*aside*). Then all is safe! (*Aloud.*) Ha! ha! Is that really all your capital, General Damas? Why, I thought Italy had been a second Mexico to you soldiers.

DAMAS. All a toss up, Sir. I was not one of the lucky ones! My friend Morier, indeed, saved something handsome. But our Commander-in-Chief took care of him, and Morier is a thrifty, economical dog,—not like the rest of us soldiers, who spend our money as carelessly as if it were our blood.

BEAU. Well, it is no matter! I do not want fortune with Pauline. And you must know, General Damas, that your fair cousin has at length consented to reward my long and ardent attachment.

DAMAS. You!—the devil! Why, she is already married! There is no divorce!

BEAU. True; but this very day she is formally to authorise the necessary proceedings,—this very day she is to sign the contract that is to make her mine within one week from the day on which her present illegal marriage is annulled.

DAMAS. You tell me wonders!—Wonders! No; I believe anything of women!

BEAU. I must wish you good morning.

(*As he is going, enter* DESCHAPPELLES.)

MONS. DESCHAP. Oh, Beauseant! well met. Let us come to the notary at once.

DAMAS (*to Deschappelles*). Why, cousin!

MONS. DESCHAP. Damas, welcome to Lyons. Pray call on us; my wife will be delighted to see you.

DAMAS. Your wife be——blessed for her condescension! But (*taking him aside*), what do I hear? Is it possible that your daughter has consented to a divorce?—that she will marry Monsieur Beauseant?

MONS. DESCHAP. Certainly! What have you to say against it? A gentleman of birth, fortune, character. We are not so proud as we were; even my wife has had enough of nobility and princes!

DAMAS. But Pauline loved that young man so tenderly!

MONS. DESCHAP. (*taking snuff*). That was two years and a half ago!

DAMAS. Very true. Poor Melnotte!

MONS. DESCHAP. But do not talk of that impostor; I hope he is dead or has left the country. Nay, even were he in Lyons at this moment, he ought to rejoice that, in an honourable and suitable alliance, my daughter may forget her sufferings and his crime.

DAMAS. Nay, if it be all settled, I have no more to say. Monsieur Beauseant informs me that the contract is to be signed this very day.

MONS. DESCHAP. It is; at one o'clock precisely. Will you be one of the witnesses?

DAMAS. I?—No; that is to say—yes, certainly!—at one o'clock I will wait on you.

MONS. DESCHAP. Till then, adieu—come, Beauseant. (*Exeunt* BEAUSEANT *and* DESCHAPPELLES.)

DAMAS. The man who sets his heart upon a woman
Is a chameleon, and doth feed on air;
From air he takes his colours,—holds his life,—
Changes with every wind,—grows lean or fat;
Rosy with hope, or green with jealousy,
Or pallid with despair—just as the gale
Varies from north to south—from heat to cold!
Oh, woman! woman! thou should'st have few sins

Of thine own to answer for! Thou art the author
Of such a book of follies in a man,
That it would need the tears of all the angels
To blot the record out!
(*Enter* MELNOTTE, *pale and agitated.*)
I need not tell thee! Thou hast heard—
MEL. The worst!
I have!
DAMAS. Be cheer'd; others are as fair as she is!
MEL. Others!—The world is crumbled at my feet!
She *was* my world; fill'd up the whole of being—
Smiled in the sunshine—walk'd the glorious earth—
Sate in my heart—was the sweet life of life.
The Past was hers: I dreamt not of a Future
That did not wear her shape! Mem'ry and Hope
Alike are gone. Pauline is faithless! Henceforth
The universal space is desolate!
DAMAS. Hope yet.
MEL. Hope, yes!—one hope is left me still—
A soldier's grave! Glory has died with Love;
I look into my heart, and, where I saw
Pauline, see Death!
(*After a pause.*)—But am I not deceived?
I went but by the rumour of the town;
Rumour is false,—I was too hasty! Damas,
Whom hast thou seen?
DAMAS. Thy rival and her father.
Arm thyself for the truth! He heeds not—
MEL. She
Will never know how deeply she was loved!
The charitable night, that was wont to bring
Comfort to day, in bright and eloquent dreams,
Is henceforth leagued with misery! Sleep, farewell,
Or else become eternal! Oh, the waking
From false oblivion, and to see the sun,
And know she is another's!—
DAMAS. Be a man;
MEL. I am a man!—it is the sting of woe,
Like mine, that tells us we are men!

DAMAS. The false one
Did not deserve thee.
MEL. Hush!—No word against her!
Why should she keep, thro' years and silent absence,
The holy tablets of her virgin faith
True to a traitor's name? Oh, blame her not,
It were a sharper grief to think her worthless
Than to be what I am! To-day,—to-day!
They said 'to-day!' This day, so wildly welcomed—
This day, my soul had singled out of time
And mark'd for bliss! This day! oh, could I see her,
See her once more, unknown; but hear her voice,
So that one echo of its music might
Make ruin less appalling in its silence.
DAMAS. Easily done! Come with me to her house;
Your dress—your cloak—moustache—the bronzed hues
Of time and toil—the name you bear—belief
In your absence, all will ward away suspicion.
Keep in the shade. Ay, I would have you come.
There may be hope! Pauline is yet so young,
They may have forced her to these second bridals
Out of mistaken love.
MEL. No, bid me hope not!
Bid me not hope! I could not bear again
To fall from such a heaven! One gleam of sunshine,
And the ice breaks and I am lost! Oh, Damas,
There's no such thing as courage in a man;
The veriest slave that ever crawl'd from danger
Might spurn me now. When first I lost her, Damas,
I bore it, did I not? I still had hope,
And now I—I— (*Bursts into an agony of grief.*)
DAMAS. What, comrade! all the women
That ever smiled destruction on brave hearts
Were not worth tears like these!
MEL. 'Tis past—forget it.
I am prepared; life has no farther ills!
The cloud has broken in that stormy rain,
And on the waste I stand, alone with Heaven!
DAMAS. His very face is changed; a breaking heart

Does its work soon!—Come, Melnotte, rouse thyself:
One effort more. Again thou'lt see her.

MEL. See her!
There is a passion in that simple sentence
That shivers all the pride and power of reason
Into a chaos!

DAMAS. Time wanes;—come, ere yet
It be too late.

MEL. Terrible words—"*Too late!*"
Lead on. One last look more, and then——

DAMAS. Forget her!

MEL. Forget her, yes!—For death remembers not. (*Exeunt.*)

SCENE 2: *A room in the house of* MONSIEUR DESCHAPPELLES; PAULINE *seated in great dejection.*

PAULINE. It is so then, I must be false to Love,
Or sacrifice a father! Oh, my Claude,
My lover, and my husband! have I lived
To pray that thou may'st find some fairer boon
Than the deep faith of this devoted heart,—
Nourish'd till now—now broken?

(*Enter* MONSIEUR DESCHAPPELLES.)

MONS. DESCHAP. My dear child,
How shall I thank—how bless thee? Thou hast saved
I will not say my fortune—I could bear
Reverse, and shrink not—but that prouder wealth
Which merchants value most—my name, my credit—
The hard-won honours of a toilsome life—
These thou hast saved, my child!

PAULINE. Is there no hope?
No hope but this?

MONS. DESCHAP. None. If, without the sum
Which Beauseant offers for thy hand, this day
Sinks to the west—to-morrow brings our ruin!
And hundreds, mingled in that ruin, curse
The bankrupt merchant! and the insolent herd
We feasted and made merry cry in scorn
"How pride has fallen!—Lo, the bankrupt merchant!"—
My daughter, thou hast saved us!

PAULINE. And am lost!

MONS. DESCHAP. Come, let me hope that Beauseant's love—

PAULINE. His love!
Talk not of love—Love has no thought of self!
Love buys not with the ruthless usurer's gold
The loathsome prostitution of a hand
Without a heart! Love sacrifices all things
To bless the thing it loves! *He* knows not love.
Father, his love is hate—his hope revenge!
My tears, my anguish, my remorse for falsehood—
These are the joys he wrings from our despair!

MONS. DESCHAP. If thou deem'st thus, reject him! Shame and ruin
Were better than thy misery;—think no more on't.
My sand is well-nigh run—what boots it when
The glass is broken? We'll annul the contract.
And if to-morrow in the prisoner's cell
These aged limbs are laid, why still, my child,
I'll think thou art spared; and wait the Liberal Hour
That lays the beggar by the side of kings!

PAULINE. No—no—forgive me! You, my honour'd father,—
You, who so loved, so cherish'd me, whose lips
Never knew one harsh word! I'm not ungrateful,
I am but human!—hush! *Now*, call the bridegroom—
You see I am prepared—no tears—all calm;
But, father, *talk no more of love!*

MONS. DESCHAP. My child,
'Tis but one struggle; he is young, rich, noble;
Thy state will rank first 'mid the dames of Lyons;
And when this heart can shelter thee no more,
Thy youth will not be guardianless.

PAULINE. I have set
My foot upon the ploughshare—I will pass
The fiery ordeal. (*Aside.*) Merciful Heaven, support me!
And on the absent wanderer shed the light
Of happier stars—lost evermore to me!

(*Enter* MADAME DESCHAPPELLES, BEAUSEANT, GLAVIS, *and* NOTARY.)

MME. DESCHAP. Why, Pauline, you are quite in *déshabillé*—you ought to be more alive to the importance of this joyful occasion. We had once looked higher, it is true; but you see, after all, Monsieur Beauseant's father *was* a Marquis, and that's a great comfort! Pedigree and jointure!

—you have them both in Monsieur Beauseant. A young lady decorously brought up should only have two considerations in her choice of a husband:—first, is his birth honorable,—secondly, will his death be advantageous? All other trifling details should be left to parental anxiety!

BEAU. (*approaching, and waving aside Madame*). Ah, Pauline! let me hope that you are reconciled to an event which confers such rapture upon me.

PAULINE. I am reconciled to my doom.

BEAU. Doom is a harsh word, sweet lady.

PAULINE (*aside*). This man must have some mercy—his heart cannot be marble. (*Aloud.*) Oh, Sir, be just—be generous!—Seize a noble triumph—a great revenge!—Save the father, and spare the child!

BEAU. (*aside*). Joy—joy alike to my hatred and my passion! The haughty Pauline is at last my suppliant. (*Aloud.*) You ask from me what I have not the sublime virtue to grant—a virtue reserved only for the gardener's son! I cannot forego my hopes in the moment of their fulfilment!—I adhere to the contract—your father's ruin, or your hand!

PAULINE. Then all is over. Sir, I have decided. (*The Clock strikes One.*)

(*Enter* DAMAS *and* MELNOTTE.)

DAMAS. Your servant, cousin Deschappelles—Let me introduce Colonel Morier.

MME. DESCHAP. (*curtsying very low*). What, the celebrated hero? This is indeed an honour! (MELNOTTE *bows and remains in the background.*)

DAMAS (*to* PAULINE). My little cousin, I congratulate you! What, no smile—no blush? You are going to be divorced from poor Melnotte, and marry this rich gentleman. You ought to be excessively happy!

PAULINE. Happy!

DAMAS. Why, how pale you are, child!—Poor Pauline! Hist—confide in me! Do they force you to this?

PAULINE. No!

DAMAS. You act with your own free consent?

PAULINE. My own consent—yes.

DAMAS. Then you are the most—I will not say what you are.

PAULINE. You think ill of me—be it so—yet if you knew all—

DAMAS. There is some mystery—speak out, Pauline.

PAULINE (*suddenly*). Oh! perhaps you can save me! you are our relation—our friend. My father is on the verge of bankruptcy—this day he requires a large sum to meet demands that cannot be denied; that sum Beauseant will advance—this hand the condition of the barter. Save me if you have the means—save me! You will be repaid above!

DAMAS (*aside*). I recant—Women are not so bad after all!—(*Aloud.*) Humph, child! I cannot help you—I am too poor!

PAULINE. The last plank to which I clung is shivered!

DAMAS. Hold—you see my friend Morier: Melnotte is his most intimate friend—fought in the same fields—slept in the same tent. Have you any message to send to Melnotte?—any word to soften this blow?

PAULINE. He knows Melnotte—he will see him—he will bear to him my last farewell—(*approaches* MELNOTTE)—He has a stern air—he turns away from me—he despises me! Sir, one word I beseech you.

MEL. Her voice again! How the old time comes o'er me!

DAMAS (*to* MADAME). Don't interrupt them. He is going to tell her what a rascal young Melnotte is; he knows him well, I promise you.

MME. DESCHAP. So considerate in you, cousin Damas! (DAMAS *approaches* DESCHAPPELLES; *converses apart with him in dumb show.*—DESCHAPPELLES *shows him a paper, which he inspects, and takes.*)

PAULINE. Thrice have I sought to speak; my courage fails me.
Sir, is it true that you have known—nay, are
The friend of—Melnotte?

MEL. Lady, yes!—Myself
And Misery know the man!

PAULINE. And you will see him.
And you will bear to him—ay—word for word,
All that this heart, which breaks in parting from him,
Would send, ere still for ever.

MEL. He hath told me
You have the right to choose from out the world
A worthier bridegroom;—he foregoes all claim
Even to murmur at his doom. Speak on!

PAULINE. Tell him, for years I never nursed a thought
That was not his;—that on his wandering way,
Daily and nightly, poured a mourner's prayers.
Tell him ev'n now that I would rather share
His lowliest lot,—walk by his side, an outcast;—
Work for him, beg with him,—live upon the light
Of one kind smile from him, than wear the crown
The Bourbon lost!

MEL. (*aside*). Am I already mad?

And does Delirium utter such sweet words
Into a Dreamer's ear? (*Aloud.*) You love him thus,
And yet desert him?

PAULINE. Say, that, if his eye
Could read this heart,—its struggles, its temptations—
His love itself would pardon that desertion!
Look on that poor old man—he is my father;
He stands upon the verge of an abyss;—
He calls his child to save him! Shall I shrink
From him who gave me birth?—withhold my hand,
And see a parent perish? Tell him this,
And say—that we shall meet again in Heaven!

MEL. (*aside*). The night is past—joy cometh with the morrow.
(*Aloud.*) Lady—I—I—what is this riddle?—what
The nature of this sacrifice?

PAULINE (*pointing to* DAMAS). Go, ask him!

BEAU. (*from the table*). The papers are prepared—we only need
Your hand and seal.

MEL. Stay, lady—one word more.
Were but your duty with your faith united,
Would you still share the low-born peasant's lot?

PAULINE. Would I? Ah, better death with him I love
Than all the pomp—which is but as the flowers
That crown the victim!—(*turning away*) I am ready.

(MELNOTTE *rushes to* DAMAS.)

DAMAS. There—
This is the schedule—this the total.

BEAU. (*to* DESCHAPPELLES, *showing notes*). These
Are yours the instant she has signed; you are
Still the great House of Lyons!

(*The* NOTARY *is about to hand the Contract to* PAULINE, *when* MELNOTTE *seizes and tears it.*)

BEAU. Are you mad?

MONS. DESCHAP. How, Sir! What means this insult?

MEL. Peace, old man!
I have a prior claim. Before the face
Of man and Heaven I urge it! I outbid
Yon sordid huckster for your priceless jewel.

(*Giving a pocket-book.*)

There is the sum twice told! Blush not to take it:

There's not a coin that is not bought and hallow'd
In the cause of nations with a soldier's blood!

BEAU. Torments and death!

PAULINE. That voice! Thou art—

MEL. Thy husband!

(PAULINE *rushes into his arms.*)

MEL. Look up! Look up, Pauline!—for I can bear
Thine eyes! The stain is blotted from my name.
I have redeem'd mine honour. I can call
On France to sanction thy divine forgiveness!
Oh, joy!—Oh, rapture! By the midnight watch-fires
Thus have I seen thee!—thus foretold this hour!
And, 'midst the roar of battle, thus have heard
The beating of thy heart against my own!

BEAU. Fool'd, duped, and triumph'd over in the hour
Of mine own victory! Curses on ye both!
May thorns be planted in the marriage bed!
And love grow sour'd and blacken'd into hate,
Such as the hate that gnaws me!

DAMAS. Curse away!
And let me tell thee, Beauseant, a wise proverb
The Arabs have,—"Curses are like young chickens, (*Solemnly.*)
And still come home to roost!"

BEAU. Their happiness
Maddens my soul! I am powerless and revengeless! (*To* MADAME.)
I wish you joy! Ha, ha! The gardener's son! (*Exit.*)

DAMAS (*to* GLAVIS). Your friend intends to hang himself! Methinks
You ought to be his travelling companion!

GLA. Sir, you are exceedingly obliging! (*Exit.*)

PAULINE. Oh!
My father, you are saved,—and by my husband!
Ah! blessed hour!

MEL. Yet you weep still, Pauline!

PAULINE. But on thy breast!—these tears are sweet and holy!

MONS. DESCHAP. You have won love and honour nobly, Sir!
Take her;—be happy both!

MME. DESCHAP. I'm all astonish'd!
Who, then, is Colonel Morier?

DAMAS. You behold him!

MEL. Morier no more after this happy day!

I would not bear again my father's name
Till I could deem it spotless! The hour's come!
Heaven smiled on Conscience! As the soldier rose
From rank to rank, how sacred was the fame
That cancell'd crime, and raised him nearer thee!
MME. DESCHAP. A colonel and a hero! Well, that's something!
He's wondrously improved! I wish you joy, Sir!
MEL. Ah! the same love that tempts us into sin,
If it be true love, works out its redemption;
And he who seeks repentance for the Past
Should woo the Angel Virtue in the Future!

The End

LONDON ASSURANCE

On March 14, 1841, the theatre at Covent Garden was barely half full. A new play called *London Assurance* was to be presented, but its author "Mr. Lee Moreton" was quite unknown. He was a boy of nineteen who had been seen on stage at Brighton as Sir Giles Overreach and Rory O'More but who was a stranger to London.

His anonymity enabled the young Dion Boucicault to eavesdrop unnoticed on the playwrights Mark Lemon, Douglas Jerrold, and Gilbert à Beckett, all of whom were sitting together in a box. At the end of the first act the audience applauded loudly. Jerrold said: "That is fatal. He has reached his climax too early in the play. Nothing will go after that." But Boucicault had more to come. "We are glutted with farces," Charles Matthews had told him when Boucicault came out of obscurity with "Fire in each eye, and papers in each hand." "What we want nowadays is a good five-act comedy," said the actor-manager. That is what, a month later, he was given. A clever, light, modern comedy with a good part (Dazzle) for Matthews and a stupendous part for a boisterous broad with an infectious laugh. That was the ace Boucicault had yet to play: Mrs. Nesbitt as Lady Gay Spanker, "A devilish fine woman!" When she described the hunt, it is reported, the three playwright-critics rose in their seats and cheered.

Lester Wallack, of the famous family of actors, tells us that the idea for the play originally came from John Brougham (1814-1880), who intended to write it up and play the part of Dazzle, but (says Wallack in his *Memories of Fifty Years*) "for a certain sum of money, [Brougham] conceded to Mr. Boucicault his entire rights in the comedy . . . [and] the success of the whole thing was due to Mr. Boucicault, to his tact and cleverness, and to the brilliancy of his dialogue." Whatever he paid Brougham, Boucicault had made a good investment. *London Assurance* brought him the princely sum of £300 (as much as Bulwer-Lytton had received for *The Lady of Lyons*) and, to start him auspiciously on a long and very busy career in both England and America, brought him the adulation of all London.

Well, not quite. There was a rather obscure young journalist (writing in *Fraser's Magazine* under such names as "C. J. Yellowplush," "Major Goliath Gahagan," and "Ikey Solomons") who had his own opinion and who in his *Sketches* (under his real name of William Makepeace Thackeray) produced this parody of *London Assurance*:

> It was one of Mr. Boyster's comedies of English life. Frank Nightrake and his friend, Bob Fitzoffley, appeared in the first scene, having a conversation with that impossible valet of English Comedy, whom many gentlemen would turn out of doors before he could get through half a length of the dialogue assigned. And as your true English Comedy is the representation of nature, I could not but think how like these figures on the stage and the dialogue which they used were to the appearance and talk of the English gentlemen of the present day.

The dialogue went on somewhat in the following fashion:

BOB FITZOFFLEY (*Entering whistling.*)—The top of the morning to thee, Frank! What, at breakfast already? At chocolate and the morning toast, like a dowager of sixty? Slang! (*He pokes the servant with his cane.*) What has come to thy master, thou Prince of Valets! Thou pattern of Slaveys! Thou swiftest of Mercuries! Has the Honorable Francis Nightrake lost his heart or his head or his health?

FRANK (*Laying down the paper.*)—Bob, Bob, I have lost all three. I have lost my health, Bob, with thee and thy like over the Burgundy at the Club; I have lost my head, Bob, with thinking how I shall pay my debts; and I have lost my heart, Bob—oh, to such a creature!

BOB—A Venus, of course?

SLANG—With the presence of Juno.

Bob—And the modesty of Minerva.

Frank—And the coldness of Diana.

Bob—Pish! What a sigh is that about a woman! Thou shalt be Endymion, the Nightrake of old, and conquer this shy goddess—hey, Slang?

> Here Slang takes the lead of the conversation, and propounds a plot for running away with the heiress; and I could not help remarking how the comedy was like to life—how the gentlemen always say "thou" and "prythee", and "go to", and talk about heathen goddesses to each other; how their servants are always their particular intimates; how, when there is serious love-making between a gentleman and a lady, a comic attachment invariably springs up between the valet and the waiting-maid of each; how Lady Grace Gadabout, when she calls upon Rose Ringdove to pay a morning visit, appears in a low satin dress with jewels in her hair; how Saucebox, her attendant, wears diamond brooches and rings on all her fingers; while Mrs. Tallyho, on the other hand, transacts all the business of life in a riding-habit, and always points her jokes by a cut of the whip.

Had Mr. Thackeray known as much about plays as he did about Mrs. Nesbitt (whom he lost to a Sir William Boothby, Bart., of Ashbourne Hall, Derbyshire, and no other distinction), he would not so have missed the point. We cannot expect him to have known of Henry Medwall, who introduced the convention which required that "a comic attachment invariably springs up between the valet and the waiting-maid" of the principals, for Medwall's *Fulgens and Lucrece* (printed sometime around 1512 or 1516) did not turn up until a unique copy was found in 1919. But surely Thackeray had heard of some of Medwall's followers—say, Shakespeare? Perhaps he did not approve of the artificial language of English comedy, at least as old as Lyly's *Endymion* (1588), but Thackeray should have been aware that characters in English plays did indeed "talk about heathen goddesses to each other." Any comedy from Plautus and Terence to his own day could have taught Thackeray the effectiveness of the clever servant and the other stock characters of "English Comedy," which never was and never will be "the representation of nature"—it will at most be naturalistic (not natural), that is, a dramatic distortion of reality, a lie about the truth.

There is a point to be made in connection with *London Assurance,* even though Thackeray missed it completely. The fact is that *London Assurance* represented a radical development, the beginning of a new and much closer relationship between English Comedy and nature. However much was derived from Shakespeare and his predecessors, from Jonson and his followers, from the comedies of Sheridan and the melodramas of Holcroft, Boucicault brought to the British stage (and later to the American stage) a fresh light touch in comedy, an admirable straightforwardness in plot development, and, if no profundity in his subject matter, deftness and modernity in handling it.

LONDON ASSURANCE

A COMEDY IN FIVE ACTS

by

Dion Boucicault

First produced at the Theatre Royal, Covent Garden, on March 4, 1841, and at the Park Theatre, New York, on October 11, 1841, with the following casts:

	Covent Garden (London)	*Park (New York)*
Sir HARCOURT COURTLY	Mr. W. Farren	Mr. Placide
MAX HARKAWAY	Mr. Bartley	Mr. Fisher
CHARLES COURTLY	Mr. Anderson	Mr. Wheatley
Mr. SPANKER	Mr. Keeley	Mr. Williams
DAZZLE	Mr. Charles Matthews	Mr. Browne
MARK MEDDLE	Mr. Harley	Mr. Latham
COOL, *a Valet*	Mr. Brindal	Mr. Andrews
SIMPSON, *a Butler*	Mr. Honner	Mr. King
MARTIN	Mr. Ayliffe	Mr. Howard
Lady GAY SPANKER	Mrs. Nesbitt	Miss Cushman
GRACE HARKAWAY	Madame Vestris	Miss Clarendon
PERT	Mrs. Humby	Mrs. Vernon

Time: The Present [1841]. Three Days.

Scene: London and Gloucestershire.

TO
CHARLES KEMBLE
this comedy
(*with his kind permission*)
is dedicated
by his fervent admirer and humble servant
DION. L. BOUCICAULT

ACT I

SCENE FIRST: *An Ante-Room in* SIR HARCOURT COURTLY'S *House in Belgrave Square.*

(*Enter* COOL.)

COOL. Half-past nine, and Mr. Charles has not yet returned. I am in a fever of dread. If his father happen to rise earlier than usual on any morning, he is sure to ask first for Mr. Charles. Poor deluded old gentleman—he little thinks how he is deceived. (*Enter* MARTIN, *lazily.*) Well, Martin, he has not come home yet!

MARTIN. No; and I have not had a wink of sleep all night—I cannot stand this any longer; I shall give warning. This is the fifth night Mr. Courtly has remained out, and I'm obliged to stand at the hall window to watch for him.

COOL. You know, if Sir Harcourt was aware that we connived at his son's irregularities, we should all be discharged.

MARTIN. I have used up all my common excuses on his duns.—"Call again", "Not at home", and "Send it down to you", won't serve any more; and Mr. Crust, the wine merchant, swears he will be paid.

COOL. So they all say. Why, he has arrests out against him already. I've seen the fellows watching the door—(*loud knock and ring heard*)—There he is, just in time—quick, Martin, for I expect Sir William's bell every moment—(*bell rings*)—and there it is. (*Exit* MARTIN, *slowly.*) Thank heaven! he will return to college to-morrow, and this heavy responsibility will be taken off my shoulders. A valet is as difficult a post to fill properly as that of prime minister. (*Exit.*)

YOUNG COURTLY (*without*). Hollo!

DAZZLE (*without*). Steady!

(*Enter* YOUNG COURTLY *and* DAZZLE.)

YOUNG COURTLY. Hollo-o-o!

DAZZLE. Hush! what are you about, howling like a Hottentot. Sit down there, and thank heaven you are in Belgrave Square, instead of Bow Street.

YOUNG COURTLY. D—n — damn Bow Street.

DAZZLE. Oh, with all my heart!—you have not seen as much of it as I have.

YOUNG COURTLY. I say—let me see—what was I going to say?—oh, look here—(*Pulls out a large assortment of bell-pulls, knockers, etc., from his pocket.*) There! dam'me! I'll puzzle the two-penny postmen,—I'll deprive them of their right of disturbing the neighbourhood. That black lion's head did belong to old Vampire, the money-lender; this bell-pull to Miss Stitch, the milliner.

DAZZLE. And this brass griffin—

YOUNG COURTLY. That! oh, let me see—I think—I twisted that off our own hall-door as I came in, while you were paying the cab.

DAZZLE. What shall I do with them?

YOUNG COURTLY. Pack 'em in a small hamper, and send 'em to the sitting magistrate with my father's compliments; in the mean time, come into my room, and I'll astonish you with some Burgundy.

(*Re-enter* COOL.)

COOL. Mr. Charles—

YOUNG COURTLY. Out! out! not at home to any one.

COOL. And drunk—

YOUNG COURTLY. As a lord.

COOL. If Sir Harcourt knew this, he would go mad, he would discharge me.

YOUNG COURTLY. You flatter yourself: that would be no proof of his insanity.—(*To* DAZZLE.) This is Cool, sir, Mr. Cool; he is the best liar in London—there is a pungency about his invention, and an originality in his equivocation, that is perfectly refreshing.

COOL (*aside*). Why, Mr. Charles, where did you pick him up?

YOUNG COURTLY. You mistake, he picked *me* up. (*Bell rings.*)

COOL. Here comes Sir Harcourt—pray do not let him see you in this state.

YOUNG COURTLY. State! what do you mean? I am in a beautiful state.

COOL. I should lose my character.

YOUNG COURTLY. That would be a fortunate epoch in your life, Cool.

COOL. Your father would discharge me.

YOUNG COURTLY. Cool, my dad is an old ass.

COOL. Retire to your own room, for heaven's sake, Mr. Charles.

YOUNG COURTLY. I'll do so for my own sake. (*To* DAZZLE.) I say, old fellow, (*staggering*) just hold the door steady while I go in.

DAZZLE. This way. Now, then!—take care! (*Helps him into the room.*)

(*Enter* SIR HARCOURT COURTLY *in an elegant dressing-gown, and Greek scull-cap and tassels, etc.*)

SIR HARCOURT. Cool, is breakfast ready?

COOL. Quite ready, Sir Harcourt.

SIR HARCOURT. Apropos. I omitted to mention that I expect Squire Harkaway to join us this morning, and you must prepare for my departure to Oak Hall immediately.

COOL. Leave town in the middle of the season, Sir Harcourt? So unprecedented a proceeding!

SIR HARCOURT. It is! I confess it: there is but one power could effect such a miracle—that is divinity.

COOL. How!

SIR HARCOURT. In female form, of course. Cool, I am about to present society with a second Lady Courtly; young—blushing eighteen;—lovely! I have her portrait; rich! I have her banker's account;—an heiress, and a Venus!

COOL. Lady Courtly could be none other.

SIR HARCOURT. Ha! ha! Cool, your manners are above your station. —Apropos, I shall find no further use for my brocade dressing-gown.

COOL. I thank you, Sir Harcourt; might I ask who the fortunate lady is?

SIR HARCOURT. Certainly: Miss Grace Harkaway, the niece of my old friend, Max.

COOL. Have you never seen the lady, sir?

SIR HARCOURT. Never—that is, yes—eight years ago. Having been, as you know, on the continent for the last seven years, I have not had the opportunity of paying my devoirs. Our connexion and betrothal was a very extraordinary one. Her father's estates were contiguous to mine;—being a penurious, miserly, *ugly* old scoundrel, he made a market of my indiscretion, and supplied my extravagance with large sums of money on mortgages, his great desire being to unite the two properties. About seven years ago, he died—leaving Grace, a girl, to the guardianship of her uncle, with this will:—if, on attaining the age of nineteen, she would consent to marry me, I should receive those deeds, and all his property, as her dowry. If she refused to comply with this condition, they should revert to my heir-presumptive or apparent. —She consents.

COOL. Who would not?

SIR HARCOURT. I consent to receive her 15,000*l.* a year.

COOL (*aside*). Who would not?

SIR HARCOURT. So prepare, Cool, prepare;—but where is my boy, where is Charles?

COOL. Why—oh, he is gone out, Sir Harcourt; yes, gone out to take a walk.

SIR HARCOURT. Poor child! A perfect child in heart—a sober, placid mind—the simplicity and verdure of boyhood, kept fresh and unsullied by any contact with society. Tell me, Cool, at what time was he in bed last night?

COOL. Half-past nine, Sir Harcourt.

SIR HARCOURT. Half-past nine! Beautiful! What an original idea! Reposing in cherub slumbers, while all around him teems with drinking and debauchery! Primitive sweetness of nature! No pilot-coated, bear-skinned brawling!

COOL. Oh, Sir Harcourt!

SIR HARCOURT. No cigar-smoking—

COOL. Faints at the smell of one.

SIR HARCOURT. No brandy and water bibbing.

COOL. Doesn't know the taste of anything stronger than barley-water.

SIR HARCOURT. No night parading—

COOL. Never heard the clock strike twelve, except at noon.

SIR HARCOURT. In fact, he is my son, and became a gentleman by right of paternity. He inherited my manners.

(*Enter* MARTIN.)

MARTIN. Mr. Harkaway!

(*Enter* MAX HARKAWAY.)

MAX. Squire Harkaway, fellow, or Max Harkaway, another time. (MARTIN *bows, and exit.*) Ah! Ha! Sir Harcourt, I'm devilish glad to see you! Gi' me your fist. Dang it, but I'm glad to see ye! Let me see: six—seven years, or more, since we have met. How quickly they have flown!

SIR HARCOURT (*throwing off his studied manner*). Max, Max! Give me your hand, old boy.—(*Aside.*) Ah! he *is* glad to see me: there is no fawning pretence about that squeeze. Cool, you may retire. (*Exit* COOL.)

MAX. Why, you are looking quite rosy.

SIR HARCOURT. Ah! ah! rosy! Am I too florid?

MAX. Not a bit; not a bit.

SIR HARCOURT. I thought so.—(*Aside.*) Cool said I had put too much on.

MAX. How comes it, Courtly, that you manage to retain your youth? See, I'm as grey as an old badger, or a wild rabbit; while you are—are as black as a young rook. I say, whose head grew your hair, eh?

SIR HARCOURT. Permit me to remark that all the beauties of my person are of home manufacture. Why should you be surprised at my youth? I have scarcely thrown off the giddiness of a very boy—elasticity of limb—buoyancy of soul! Remark this position—(*Throws himself into an attitude.*) I held that attitude for ten minutes at Lady Acid's last *reunion,* at the express desire of one of our first sculptors, while he was making a sketch of me for the Apollo.

MAX (*aside*). Making a butt of thee for their gibes.

SIR HARCOURT. Lady Sarah Sarcasm started up, and, pointing to my face, ejaculated, "Good gracious! Does not Sir Harcourt remind you of the countenance of Ajax, in the Pompeian portrait?"

MAX. Ajax!—humbug.

SIR HARCOURT. You are complimentary.

MAX. I'm a plain man, and always speak my mind. What's in a face or figure? Does a Grecian nose entail a good temper? Does a waspish waist indicate a good heart? Or, do oily perfumed locks necessarily thatch a well-furnished brain?

SIR HARCOURT. It's an undeniable fact,—*plain* people always praise the beauties of the *mind.*

MAX. Excuse the insinuation; I had thought the first Lady Courtly had surfeited you with beauty.

SIR HARCOURT. No; she lived fourteen months with me, and then eloped with an intimate friend. Etiquette compelled me to challenge the seducer; so I received satisfaction—and a bullet in my shoulder at the same time. However, I had the consolation of knowing that he was the handsomest man of the age. She did not insult me, by running away with a d—d ill-looking scoundrel.

MAX. That, certainly, was flattering.

SIR HARCOURT. I felt so, as I pocketed the ten thousand pounds damages.

MAX. That must have been a great balm to your sore honour.

SIR HARCOURT. It was—Max, my honour would have died without it; for on that year the wrong horse won the Derby—by some mistake. It was one of the luckiest chances—a thing that does not happen twice in a man's life—the opportunity of getting rid of his wife and his debts at the same time.

MAX. Tell the truth, Courtly! Did you not feel a little frayed in your delicacy—your honour, now? Eh?

SIR HARCOURT. Not a whit. Why should I? I married *money*, and I received it—virgin gold! My delicacy and honour had nothing to do with hers. The world pities the bereaved husband, when it should congratulate. No: the affair made a sensation, and I was the object. Besides, it is vulgar to make a parade of one's feelings, however acute they may be: impenetrability of countenance is the sure sign of your highly-bred man of fashion.

MAX. So, a man must, therefore, lose his wife and his money with a smile,—in fact, every thing he possesses but his temper.

SIR HARCOURT. Exactly,—and greet ruin with *vive la bagatelle!* For example,—your modish beauty never discomposes the shape of her features with convulsive laughter. A smile rewards the *bon mot*, and also shows the whiteness of her teeth. She never weeps impromptu—tears might destroy the economy of her cheek. Scenes are vulgar,—hysterics obsolete; she exhibits a calm, placid, impenetrable lake, whose surface is reflexion, but of unfathomable depth,—a statue, whose life is hypothetical, and not a *prima facie* fact.

MAX. Well, give me the girl that will fly at your eyes in an argument, and stick to her point like a fox to his own tail.

SIR HARCOURT. But etiquette! Max,—remember etiquette!

MAX. Damn etiquette! I have seen a man who thought it sacrilege to eat fish with a knife, that would not scruple to rise up and rob his brother of his birthright in a gambling-house. Your thorough-bred, well-blooded heart will seldom kick over the traces of good feeling. That's my opinion, and I don't care who knows it.

SIR HARCOURT. Pardon me,—etiquette is the pulse of society, by regulating which the body politic is retained in health. I consider myself one of the faculty in the art.

MAX. Well, well; you are a living libel upon common sense, for you are old enough to know better.

SIR HARCOURT. Old enough! What do you mean? Old! I still retain all my little juvenile indiscretions, which your niece's beauties must teach me to discard. I have not sown my wild oats yet.

MAX. Time you did, at sixty-three.

SIR HARCOURT. Sixty-three! Good God!—forty, 'pon my life! forty, next March.

MAX. Why, you are older than I am.

SIR HARCOURT. Oh! you are old enough to be my father.

MAX. Well, if I am, I am; that's etiquette, I suppose. Poor Grace how often I have pitied her fate! That a young and beautiful creature should be driven into wretched splendour, or miserable poverty!

SIR HARCOURT. Wretched! wherefore? Lady Courtly wretched! Impossible!

MAX. Will she not be compelled to marry you, whether she likes you or not?—a choice between you and poverty. (*Aside.*) And hang me if it isn't a tie! But why do you not introduce your son Charles to me? I have not seen him since he was a child. You would never permit him to accept any of my invitations to spend his vacation at Oak Hall,—of course, we shall have the pleasure of his company now.

SIR HARCOURT. He is not fit to enter society yet. He is a studious, sober boy.

MAX. Boy! Why, he's five-and-twenty.

SIR HARCOURT. Good gracious! Max,—you will permit me to know my own son's age,—he is not twenty.

MAX. I'm dumb.

SIR HARCOURT. You will excuse me while I indulge in the process of dressing.—Cool! (*Enter* COOL.) Prepare my toilet. (*Exit* COOL.) That is a ceremony, which, with me, supersedes all others. I consider it a duty which every gentleman owes to society—to render himself as agreeable an object as possible: and the least compliment a mortal can pay to nature, when she honours him by bestowing extra care in the manufacture of his person, is to display her taste to the best possible advantage; and so, *au revoir.* (*Exit.*)

MAX. That's a good soul—he has his faults, and who has not? Forty years of age! Oh, monstrous!—but he does look uncommonly young for sixty, spite of his foreign locks and complexion.

(*Enter* DAZZLE.)

DAZZLE. Who's my friend, with the stick and gaiters, I wonder—one of the family—the governor, may be?

MAX. Who's this? Oh, Charles—is that you, my boy? How are you? (*Aside.*) This is the *boy.*

DAZZLE. He knows me—he is too respectable for a bailiff. (*Aloud.*) How are you?

MAX. Your father has just left me.

DAZZLE (*aside*). The devil he has! He has been dead these ten years. Oh! I see, he thinks I'm young Courtly. (*Aloud.*) The honour you would confer upon me, I must unwillingly disclaim,—I am not Mr. Courtly.

MAX. I beg your pardon—a friend, I suppose?

DAZZLE. Oh, a most intimate friend—a friend of years—distantly related to the family—one of my ancestors married one of his. (*Aside.*) Adam and Eve.

MAX. Are you on a visit here?

DAZZLE. Yes. Oh! yes. (*Aside.*) Rather a short one, I'm afraid.

MAX (*aside*). This appears a dashing kind of fellow—as he is a friend of Sir Harcourt's, I'll invite him to the wedding. (*Aloud.*) Sir, if you are not otherwise engaged, I shall feel honoured by your company at my house, Oak Hall, Gloucestershire.

DAZZLE. Your name is—

MAX. Harkaway—Max Harkaway.

DAZZLE. Harkaway—let me see—I ought to be related to the Harkaways, somehow.

MAX. A wedding is about to come off—will you take a part on the occasion?

DAZZLE. With pleasure! any part, but that of the husband.

MAX. Have you any previous engagement?

DAZZLE. I was thinking—eh! why, let me see. (*Aside.*) Promised to meet my tailor and his account to-morrow; however, I'll postpone that. (*Aloud.*) Have you good shooting?

MAX. Shooting! Why, there's no shooting at this time of the year.

DAZZLE. Oh! I'm in no hurry—I can wait till the season, of course. I was only speaking precautionally—you have good shooting?

MAX. The best in the country.

DAZZLE. Make yourself comfortable!—Say no more—I'm your man—wait till you see how I'll murder your preserves.

MAX. Do you hunt?

DAZZLE. Pardon me—but will you repeat that? (*Aside.*) Delicious and expensive idea!

MAX. You ride?

DAZZLE. Anything! Everything! From a blood to a broomstick. Only catch me a flash of lightning, and let me get on the back of it, and dam'me if I wouldn't astonish the elements.

MAX. Ha! ha!

DAZZLE. I'd put a girdle round about the earth, in very considerably less than forty minutes.

MAX. Ah! ha! We'll show old Fiddlestrings how to spend the day.

He imagines that Nature, at the earnest request of Fashion, made summer days long for him to saunter in the Park, and winter nights, that he might have good time to get cleared out at hazard or at whist. Give me the yelping of a pack of hounds, before the shuffling of a pack of cards. What state can match the chase in full cry, each vying with his fellow which shall be most happy? A thousand deaths fly by unheeded in that one hour's life of ecstasy. Time is outrun, and Nature seems to grudge our bliss by making the day so short.

DAZZLE. No, for then rises up the idol of my great adoration.

MAX. Who's that?

DAZZLE. The bottle—that lends a lustre to the soul!—When the world puts on its night-cap, and extinguishes the sun—then comes the bottle! Oh, mighty wine! Don't ask me to apostrophise. Wine and love are the only two indescribable things in nature; but I prefer the wine, because its consequences are not entailed, and are more easily got rid of.

MAX. How so?

DAZZLE. Love ends in matrimony, wine in soda water.

MAX. Well, I can promise you as fine a bottle as ever was cracked.

DAZZLE. Never mind the bottle, give me the wine. Say no more; but, when I arrive, just shake one of my hands, and put the key to the cellar into the other, and, if I don't make myself intimately acquainted with its internal organization—well, I say nothing—time will show.

MAX. I foresee some happy days.

DAZZLE. And I some glorious nights.

MAX. It mustn't be a flying visit.

DAZZLE. I despise the word—I'll stop a month with you.

MAX. Or a year or two.

DAZZLE. I'll live and die with you!

MAX. Ha! ha! Remember Max Harkaway, Oak Hall, Gloucestershire.

DAZZLE. I'll remember—fare ye well. (MAX *is going*.) I say, holloa!—Tallyho-o-o-o!

MAX. Yoicks!—Tallyho-o-o-o! (*Exit*.)

DAZZLE. There I am—quartered for a couple of years, at the least. The old boy wants somebody to ride his horses, shoot his game, and keep a restraint on the morals of the parish; I'm eligible. What a lucky accident to meet young Courtly last night! Who could have thought it?—Yesterday, I could not make certain of a dinner, except at my own proper peril; to-day, I would flirt with a banquet.

(*Enter* YOUNG COURTLY.)

YOUNG COURTLY. What infernal row was that? Why, (*seeing* DAZZLE) are you here still?

DAZZLE. Yes. Ain't you delighted? I'll ring, and send the servant for my luggage.

YOUNG COURTLY. The devil you will! Why, you don't mean to say you seriously intend to take up a permanent residence here? (*He rings the bell.*)

DAZZLE. Now, that's a most inhospitable insinuation.

YOUNG COURTLY. Might I ask your name?

DAZZLE. With a deal of pleasure—Richard Dazzle, late of the Unattached Volunteers, vulgarly entitled the Dirty Buffs.

(*Enter* MARTIN.)

YOUNG COURTLY. Then, Mr. Richard Dazzle, I have the honour of wishing you a very good morning. Martin, show this gentleman the door.

DAZZLE. If he does, I'll kick Martin out of it.—No offence. (*Exit* MARTIN.) Now, sir, permit me to place a dioramic view of your conduct before you. After bringing you safely home this morning—after indulgently waiting, whenever you took a passing fancy to a knocker or bell-pull—after conducting a retreat that would have reflected honour on Napoleon—you would kick me into the street, like a mangy cur; and that's what you call gratitude. Now, to show you how superior I am to petty malice, I give you an unlimited invitation to my house—my country house—to remain as long as you please.

YOUNG COURTLY. Your house!

DAZZLE. Oak Hall, Gloucestershire,—fine old place!—for further particulars see roadbook—that is, it *nominally* belongs to my old friend and relation, Max Harkaway; but I'm privileged. Capital old fellow—say, shall we be honoured?

YOUNG COURTLY. Sir, permit me to hesitate a moment. (*Aside.*) Let me see: I go back to college to-morrow, so I shall not be missing; tradesmen begin to dun—(*Enter* COOL.) I hear thunder; here is shelter ready for me.

COOL. Oh, Mr. Charles, Mr. Solomon Isaacs is in the hall, and swears he will remain till he has arrested you!

YOUNG COURTLY. Does he!—sorry he is so obstinate—take him my compliments, and I will bet him five to one he will not.

DAZZLE. Double or quits, with my kind regards.

COOL. But, sir, he has discovered the house in Curzon Street; he says he is aware the furniture, at least, belongs to you, and he will put a man in immediately.

YOUNG COURTLY. That's awkward—what's to be done?

DAZZLE. Ask him whether he couldn't make it a woman.

YOUNG COURTLY. I must trust that to fate.

DAZZLE. I will give you my acceptance, if it will be of any use to you—it is of none to me.

YOUNG COURTLY. No, sir; but in reply to your most generous and kind invitation, if you be in earnest, I shall feel delighted to accept it.

DAZZLE. Certainly.

YOUNG COURTLY. Then off we go—through the stables—down the Mews, and so slip through my friend's fingers.

DAZZLE. But, stay, you must do the polite; say farewell to him before you part. Damn it, don't cut him!

YOUNG COURTLY. You jest!

DAZZLE. Here, lend me a card. (COURTLY *gives him one.*) Now, then, (*Writes.*) "Our respects to Mr. Isaacs—sorry to have been prevented from seeing him."—Ha! ha!

YOUNG COURTLY. Ha! ha!

DAZZLE. We'll send him up some game.

YOUNG COURTLY. (*To* COOL.) Don't let my father see him. (*Exeunt* YOUNG COURTLY *and* DAZZLE.)

COOL. What's this?—"Mr. Charles Courtly, P.P.C., returns thanks for obliging inquiries." (*Exit.*)

End of Act I

ACT II

SCENE FIRST: *The Lawn before Oak Hall, a fine Elizabethan mansion; a Drawing-Room is seen through large French windows at the back. Statues, urns, and garden chairs about the stage.*

(*Enter* PERT *and* JAMES.)

PERT. James, Miss Grace desires me to request that you will watch at the avenue, and let her know when the squire's carriage is seen on the London road.

JAMES. I will go to the lodge. (*Exit.*)

PERT. How I do long to see what kind of a man Sir Harcourt Courtly is! They say he is sixty; so he must be old, and consequently ugly. If I was Miss Grace, I would rather give up all my fortune and marry the man I liked, than go to church with a stuffed eel-skin. But taste is everything,—she doesn't seem to care whether he is sixty or sixteen; jokes at love; prepares for matrimony as she would for dinner; says it is a necessary evil, and what can't be cured must be endured. Now, I say this is against all nature; and she is either no woman, or a deeper one than I am, if she prefers an old man to a young one. Here she comes! looking as cheerfully as if she was going to marry Mr. Jenks! my Mr. Jenks! whom nobody won't lead to the halter till I have that honour.

(*Enter* GRACE *from the Drawing-Room.*)

GRACE. Well, Pert? any signs of the squire yet?

PERT. No, Miss Grace; but James has gone to watch the road.

GRACE. In my uncle's letter, he mentions a Mr. Dazzle, whom he has invited; so you must prepare a room for him. He is some friend of my husband that is to be, and my uncle seems to have taken an extraordinary predilection for him. Apropos! I must not forget to have a bouquet for the dear old man when he arrives.

PERT. The dear old man! Do you mean Sir Harcourt?

GRACE. Law, no! my uncle, of course. (*Plucking flowers.*) What do I care for Sir Harcourt Courtly?

PERT. Isn't it odd, Miss, you have never seen your intended, though it has been so long since you were betrothed?

GRACE. Not at all; marriage matters are conducted now-a-days in a most mercantile manner; consequently, a previous acquaintance is by no means indispensable. Besides, my *prescribed* husband has been upon the continent for the benefit of his—property! They say a southern climate is a great restorer of consumptive estates.

PERT. Well, Miss, for my own part, I should like to have a good look at my bargain before I paid for it; 'specially when one's life is the price of the article. But why, ma'am, do you consent to marry in this blind-man's-buff sort of manner? What would you think if he were not quite so old?

GRACE. I should think he was a little younger.

PERT. I should like him all the better.

GRACE. That wouldn't I. A young husband might expect affection and nonsense, which 'twould be deceit in me to render; nor would he permit me to remain with my uncle.—Sir Harcourt takes me with the incumbrances on his estate, and I shall beg to be left among the rest of the live stock.

PERT. Ah, Miss! but some day you might chance to stumble over *the* man,—what could you do then?

GRACE. Do! beg *the* man's pardon, and request *the* man to pick me up again.

PERT. Ah! you were never in love, Miss?

GRACE. I never was, nor will be, till I am tired of myself and common sense. Love is a pleasant scape-goat for a little epidemic madness. I must have been inoculated in my infancy, for the infection passes over poor me in contempt.

(*Enter* JAMES.)

JAMES. Two gentlemen, Miss Grace, have just alighted.

GRACE. Very well, James. (*Exit* JAMES.) Love is pictured as a boy; in another century they will be wiser, and paint him as a fool, with cap and bells, without a thought above the jingling of his own folly. Now, Pert, remember this as a maxim,—A woman is always in love with one of two things.

PERT. What are they, Miss?

GRACE. A man, or herself—and I know which is the most profitable. (*Exit.*)

PERT. I wonder what my Jenks would say, if I was to ask him. Law! here comes Mr. Meddle, his rival contemporary solicitor, as he calls him,—a nasty, prying, ugly wretch—what brings him here? He comes puffed with some news. (*Retires.*)

(*Enter* MEDDLE, *with a newspaper.*)

MEDDLE. I have secured the only newspaper in the village—my character, as an attorney-at-law, depended on the monopoly of its information.—I took it up by chance, when this paragraph met my astonished view: (*Reads.*) "We understand that the contract of marriage so long in abeyance on account of the lady's minority, is about to be celebrated, at Oak Hall, Gloucestershire, the well-known and magnificent mansion of Maximilian Harkaway, Esq., between Sir Harcourt Courtly, Baronet, of fashionable celebrity, and Miss Grace Harkaway, niece of the said Mr. Harkaway. The preparations are proceeding in the good old English style." Is it possible! I seldom swear, except in a witness box, but, damme, had it been known in the village, my reputation would have been lost; my voice in the parlour of the Red Lion mute, and Jenks, a fellow who calls himself a lawyer, without more capability than a broomstick, and as much impudence as a young barrister after getting a verdict by mistake; why, he would actually have taken the Reverend Mr. Spout by the button, which is now my sole privilege. Ah! here is Mrs. Pert: couldn't have hit upon a better person. I'll cross-examine her—Lady's maid to Miss Grace,—confidential purloiner of second-hand silk—a *nisi prius* of her mistress—Ah! sits on the woolsack in the pantry, and dictates the laws of kitchen etiquette.—Ah! Mrs. Pert, good morning; permit me to say,—and my word as a legal character is not unduly considered—I venture to affirm, that you look a—quite like the—a—

PERT. Law! Mr. Meddle.

MEDDLE. Exactly like the law.

PERT. Ha! indeed; complimentary, I confess; like the law; tedious, prosy, made up of musty paper. You sha'n't have a long suit of me. Good morning. (*Going.*)

MEDDLE. Stay, Mrs. Pert; don't calumniate my calling, or dissimulate vulgar prejudices.

PERT. Vulgar! you talk of vulgarity to me! you, whose sole employment is to sneak about like a pig, snouting out the dust-hole of society, and feeding upon the bad ends of vice! you, who live upon the world's iniquity; you miserable specimen of a bad six-and-eightpence!

MEDDLE. But, Mrs. Pert—

PERT. Don't but me, sir; I won't be butted by any such low fellow.

MEDDLE. This is slander; an action will lie.

PERT. Let it lie; lying is your trade. I'll tell you what, Mr. Meddle; if I had my will, I would soon put a check on your prying propensities. I'd treat you as the farmers do the inquisitive hogs.

MEDDLE. How?

PERT. I would ring your nose. (*Exit.*)

MEDDLE. Not much information elicited from that witness. Jenks is at the bottom of this. I have very little hesitation in saying, Jenks is a libellous rascal; I heard reports that he was undermining my character here, through Mrs. Pert. Now I'm certain of it. Assault is expensive; but, I certainly will put by a small weekly stipendium, until I can afford to kick Jenks.

DAZZLE (*outside*). Come along; this way!

MEDDLE. Ah! whom have we here? Visitors; I'll address them.

(*Enter* DAZZLE.)

DAZZLE. Who's this, I wonder; one of the family? I must know him. (*To* MEDDLE.) Ah! how are ye?

MEDDLE. Quite well. Just arrived?—ah!—um!—Might I request the honour of knowing whom I address?

DAZZLE. Richard Dazzle, Esquire; and you—

MEDDLE. Mark Meddle, attorney-at-law.

(*Enter* YOUNG COURTLY.)

DAZZLE. What detained you?

YOUNG COURTLY. My dear fellow, I have just seen such a woman!

DAZZLE (*aside*). Hush! (*Aloud.*) Permit me to introduce you to my very old friend, Meddle. He's a capital fellow; know him.

MEDDLE. I feel honoured. Who is your friend?

DAZZLE. Oh, he? What, my friend? Oh! Augustus Hamilton.

YOUNG COURTLY. How d'ye do? (*Looking off.*) There she is again!

MEDDLE (*looking off*). Why, that is Miss Grace.

DAZZLE. Of course, Grace.

YOUNG COURTLY. I'll go and introduce myself. (DAZZLE *stops him.*)

DAZZLE (*aside*). What are you about? would you insult my old friend, Puddle, by running away? (*Aloud.*) I say, Puddle, just show my friend the lions, while I say how d'ye do to my young friend, Grace. (*Aside.*) Cultivate his acquaintance. (*Exit.*—YOUNG COURTLY *looks after him.*)

MEDDLE. Mr. Hamilton, might I take the liberty?

YOUNG COURTLY (*looking off*). Confound the fellow!

MEDDLE. Sir, what did you remark?

YOUNG COURTLY. She's gone! Oh, are you here still, Mr. Thingomerry? Puddle?

MEDDLE. Meddle, sir, Meddle, in the list of attorneys.

YOUNG COURTLY. Well, Muddle, or Puddle, or whoever you are, you are a bore.

MEDDLE (*aside*). How excessively odd! Mrs. Pert said I was a pig; now I'm a boar! I wonder what they'll make of me next.

YOUNG COURTLY. Mr. Thingamy, will you take a word of advice?

MEDDLE. Feel honoured.

YOUNG COURTLY. Get out.

MEDDLE. Do you mean to—I don't understand.

YOUNG COURTLY. Delighted to quicken your apprehension. You are an ass, Puddle.

MEDDLE. Ha! ha! another quadruped! Yes; beautiful—(*Aside.*) I wish he'd call me something libellous: but that would be too much to expect. —(*Aloud.*) Anything else?

YOUNG COURTLY. Some miserable, pettifogging scoundrel!

MEDDLE. Good! ha! ha!

YOUNG COURTLY. What do you mean by laughing at me?

MEDDLE. Ha! ha! ha! excellent! delicious!

YOUNG COURTLY. Mr.——are you ambitious of a kicking?

MEDDLE. Very, very—Go on—kick—go on.

YOUNG COURTLY (*looking off*). Here she comes! I'll speak to her.

MEDDLE. But, sir—sir—

YOUNG COURTLY. Oh, go to the devil! (*He runs off*.)

MEDDLE. There, there's a chance lost—gone! I have no hesitation in saying that, in another minute, I should have been kicked; literally kicked—a legal luxury. Costs, damages, and actions rose up like sky-rockets in my aspiring soul, with golden tails reaching to the infinity of my hopes. (*Looking*.) They are coming this way; Mr. Hamilton in close conversation with Lady Courtly that is to be. Crim. Con.—Courtly versus Hamilton—damages problematical—Meddle, chief witness for plaintiff—guinea a day—professional man! I'll take down their conversation verbatim. (*He retires behind a bush*.)

(*Enter* GRACE, *followed by* YOUNG COURTLY.)

GRACE. Perhaps you would follow your friend into the dining-room; refreshment after your long journey must be requisite.

YOUNG COURTLY. Pardon me, madam; but the lovely garden and the loveliness before me is better refreshment than I could procure in any dining-room.

GRACE. Ha! Your company and compliments arrive together.

YOUNG COURTLY. I trust that a passing remark will not spoil so welcome an introduction as this by offending you.

GRACE. I am not certain that anything you could say would offend me.

YOUNG COURTLY. I never meant—

GRACE. I thought not. In turn, pardon me, when I request you will commence your visit with this piece of information:—I consider compliments impertinent, and sweetmeat language fulsome.

YOUNG COURTLY. I would condemn my tongue to a Pythagorean silence if I thought it could attempt to flatter.

GRACE. It strikes me, sir, that you are a stray bee from the hive of fashion; if so, reserve your honey for its proper cell. A truce to compliments.—You have just arrived *from town*, I apprehend.

YOUNG COURTLY. This moment I left mighty London, under the fever of a full season, groaning with the noisy pulse of wealth and the giddy whirling brain of fashion. Enchanting, busy London! how have I prevailed on myself to desert you! Next week the new ballet comes out, —the week after comes Ascot.—Oh!

GRACE. How agonizing must be the reflection.

YOUNG COURTLY. Torture! Can you inform me how you manage to avoid suicide here? If there was but an opera, even, within twenty miles! We couldn't get up a rustic ballet among the village girls? No? —ah!

GRACE. I am afraid you would find that difficult. How I contrive to support life I don't know—it is wonderful—but I have not precisely contemplated suicide yet, nor do I miss the opera.

YOUNG COURTLY. How can you manage to kill time?

GRACE. I can't. Men talk of killing time, while time quietly kills them. I have many employments—this week I devote to study and various amusements—next week to being married—the following week to repentance, perhaps.

YOUNG COURTLY. Married!

GRACE. You seem surprised; I believe it is of frequent occurrence in the metropolis.—Is it not?

YOUNG COURTLY. Might I ask to whom?

GRACE. A gentleman who has been strongly recommended to me for the situation of husband.

YOUNG COURTLY. What an extraordinary match! Would you not consider it advisable to see him, previous to incurring the consequences of such an act?

GRACE. You must be aware that fashion says otherwise. The gentleman swears eternal devotion to the lady's fortune, and the lady swears she will outvie him still. My lord's horses and my lady's diamonds shine through a few seasons, until a seat in Parliament, or the continent, stares them in the face; then, when thrown upon each other for resources of comfort, they begin to quarrel about the original conditions of the sale.

YOUNG COURTLY. Sale! No! that would be degrading civilization into Turkish barbarity.

GRACE. Worse, sir, a great deal worse; for there at least they do not attempt concealment of the barter; but here, every London ball-room is a marriage mart—young ladies are trotted out, while the mother, father, or chaperone plays auctioneer, and knocks them down to the highest bidder—young men are ticketed up with their fortunes on their backs,—and Love, turned into a dapper shopman, descants on the excellent qualities of the material.

YOUNG COURTLY. Oh! that such a custom could have ever emanated from the healthy soil of an English heart!

GRACE. No. It never did—like most of our literary dandyisms and dandy literature, it was borrowed from the French.

YOUNG COURTLY. You seem to laugh at love.

GRACE. Love! why, the very word is a breathing satire upon man's reason—a mania, indigenous to humanity—nature's jester, who plays off tricks upon the world, and trips up common sense. When I'm in love, I'll write an almanac, for very lack of wit—prognosticate the sighing season—when to beware of tears—about this time, expect matrimony to be prevalent! Ha! ha! Why should I lay out my life in love's bonds upon the bare security of a man's word?

(*Enter* JAMES.)

JAMES. The Squire, madam, has just arrived, and another gentleman with him.

GRACE (*aside*). My intended, I suppose. (*Exit* JAMES.)

YOUNG COURTLY. I perceive you are one of the railers against what is termed the follies of high life.

GRACE. No, not particularly; I deprecate all folly. By what prerogative can the west-end mint issue absurdity, which, if coined in the east, would be voted vulgar?

YOUNG COURTLY. By a sovereign right—because it has Fashion's head upon its side, and that stamps it current.

GRACE. Poor Fashion, for how many sins hast thou to answer! The gambler pawns his birth-right for fashion—the *roué* steals his friend's wife for fashion—each abandons himself to the storm of impulse, calling it the breeze of fashion.

YOUNG COURTLY. Is this idol of the world so radically vicious?

GRACE. No; the root is well enough, as the body was, until it had outgrown its native soil; but now, like a mighty giant lying over Europe, it pillows its head in Italy, its heart in France, leaving the heels alone its sole support for England.

YOUNG COURTLY. Pardon me, madam, you wrong yourself to rail against your own inheritance—the kingdom to which loveliness and wit attest your title.

GRACE. A mighty realm, forsooth,—with milliners for ministers, a cabinet of coxcombs, envy for my homage, ruin for my revenue—my right of rule depending on the shape of a bonnet or the sit of a pelisse, with the next grand noodle as my heir-apparent. Mr. Hamilton, when I am crowned, I shall feel happy to abdicate in your favour. (*Curtseys and exit.*)

YOUNG COURTLY. What did she mean by that? Hang me if I can

understand her—she is evidently not used to society. Ha!—takes every word I say for infallible truth—requires the solution of a compliment, as if it were a problem in Euclid. She said she was about to marry, but I rather imagine she was in jest. 'Pon my life, I feel very queer at the contemplation of such an idea—I'll follow her. (MEDDLE *comes down.*) Oh! perhaps this booby can inform me something about her. (MEDDLE *makes signs at him.*) What the devil is he at!

MEDDLE. It won't do—no—ah! um—it's not to be done.

YOUNG COURTLY. What do you mean?

MEDDLE (*points after* GRACE). Counsel retained—cause to come off!

YOUNG COURTLY. Cause to come off!

MEDDLE. Miss Grace is about to be married.

YOUNG COURTLY. Is it possible?

MEDDLE. Certainly. If *I* have the drawing out of the deeds—

YOUNG COURTLY. To whom?

MEDDLE. Ha! hem! Oh, yes! I dare say—Information being scarce in the market, I hope to make mine valuable.

YOUNG COURTLY. Married! married!

MEDDLE. Now I shall have another chance.

YOUNG COURTLY. I'll run and ascertain the truth of this from Dazzle. (*Exit.*)

MEDDLE. It's of no use: he either dare not kick me, or he can't afford it—in either case, he is beneath my notice. Ah! who comes here?—can it be Sir Harcourt Courtly himself? It can be no other. (*Enter* COOL.) Sir, I have the honour to bid you welcome to Oak Hall and the village of Oldborough.

COOL (*aside*). Excessively polite. (*Aloud.*)—Sir, thank you.

MEDDLE. The township contains two thousand inhabitants.

COOL. Does it! I am delighted to hear it.

MEDDLE (*aside*). I can charge him for that—ahem—six and eightpence is not much—but it is a beginning. (*Aloud.*) If you will permit me, I can inform you of the different commodities for which it is famous.

COOL. Much obliged—but here comes Sir Harcourt Courtly, my master, and Mr. Harkaway—any other time I shall feel delighted.

MEDDLE. Oh! (*Aside.*) Mistook the man for the master. (*He retires up.*)

(*Enter* MAX *and* SIR HARCOURT.)

MAX. Here we are at last. Now give ye welcome to Oak Hall, Sir Harcourt, heartily!

SIR HARCOURT (*languidly*). Cool, assist me. (COOL *takes off his furred cloak and gloves; gives him white gloves and a handkerchief.*)

MAX. Why, you require unpacking as carefully as my best bin of port. Well, now you are decanted, tell me what did you think of my park as we came along.

SIR HARCOURT. That it would never come to an end. You said it was only a stone's throw from your infernal lodge to the house; why, it's ten miles, at least.

MAX. I'll do it in ten minutes any day.

SIR HARCOURT. Yes, in a steam carriage. Cool, perfume my handkerchief.

MAX. Don't do it. Don't! perfume in the country! why, it's high treason in the very face of Nature; 'tis introducing the robbed to the robber. Here are the sweets from which your fulsome essences are pilfered, and libelled with their names;—don't insult them, too.

SIR HARCOURT (*to* MEDDLE). Oh! cull me a bouquet, my man!

MAX (*turning*). Ah, Meddle! how are you? This is Lawyer Meddle.

SIR HARCOURT. Oh! I took him for one of your people.

MEDDLE. Ah! naturally—um—Sir Harcourt Courtly, I have the honour to congratulate—happy occasion approaches. Ahem! I have no hesitation in saying this *very* happy occasion approaches.

SIR HARCOURT. Cool, is the conversation addressed towards me?

COOL. I believe so, Sir Harcourt.

MEDDLE. Oh, certainly! I was complimenting you.

SIR HARCOURT. Sir, you are very good; the honour is undeserved; but I am only in the habit of receiving compliments from the fair sex. Men's admiration is so damnably insipid.

MEDDLE. I had hoped to make a unit on that occasion.

SIR HARCOURT. Yes, and you hoped to put an infernal number of cyphers after your unit on that and any other occasion.

MEDDLE. Ha! ha! very good. Why, I did hope to have the honour of drawing out the deeds; for, whatever Jenks may say to the contrary, I have no hesitation in saying—

SIR HARCOURT (*putting him aside*). (*To* MAX.) If the future Lady Courtly be visible at so unfashionable an hour as this, I shall beg to be introduced.

MAX. Visible! Ever since six this morning, I'll warrant ye. Two to one she is at dinner.

SIR HARCOURT. Dinner! Is it possible? Lady Courtly dine at half-past one P.M.!

MEDDLE. I rather prefer that hour to peck a little my—

SIR HARCOURT. Dear me! who was addressing you?

MEDDLE. Oh! I beg pardon.

MAX (*calling*). Here, James! (*Enter* JAMES.) Tell Miss Grace to come here directly. (*Exit* JAMES.) Now prepare, Courtly, for, though I say it, she *is*—with the exception of my bay mare, Kitty—the handsomest thing in the country. Considering she is a biped, she is a wonder! Full of blood, sound wind and limb, plenty of bone, sweet coat, in fine condition, with a thorough-bred step, as dainty as a pet greyhound.

SIR HARCOURT. Damme, don't compare her to a horse!

MAX. Well, I wouldn't, but she's almost as fine a creature,—close similarities.

MEDDLE. Oh, very fine creature! Close similarity, amounting to identity.

SIR HARCOURT. Good gracious, sir! What can a lawyer know about women!

MEDDLE. Everything. The consistorial court is fine study of the character, and I have no hesitation in saying that I have examined more women than Jenks, or—

SIR HARCOURT. Oh, damn Jenks!

MEDDLE. Sir, thank you. Damn him again, sir, damn him again!

(*Enter* GRACE.)

GRACE. My dear uncle!

MAX. Ah, Grace, you little jade, come here.

SIR HARCOURT (*eyeing her through his glass*). Oh, dear! she is a rural Venus! I'm astonished and delighted.

MAX. Won't you kiss your old uncle? (*He kisses her.*)

SIR HARCOURT (*draws an agonizing face*). Oh!—ah—um!—*N'importe!*—my privilege in embryo—hem! It's very tantalizing, though.

MAX. You are not glad to see me, you are not. (*Kissing her.*)

SIR HARCOURT. Oh; no, no! (*aside*) that is too much. I shall do something horrible presently, if this goes on. (*Aloud.*) I should be sorry to curtail any little ebullition of affection; but—ahem! May I be permitted?

MAX. Of course you may. There, Grace, is Sir Harcourt, your husband that will be. Go to him, girl.

SIR HARCOURT. Permit me to do homage to the charms, the presence of which have placed me in sight of Paradise. (SIR HARCOURT *and* GRACE *retire.*)

(*Enter* DAZZLE.)

DAZZLE. Ah! old fellow, how are you?

MAX. I'm glad to see you! Are you comfortably quartered, yet, eh?

DAZZLE. Splendidly quartered! What a place you've got here! Here, Hamilton. (*Enter* YOUNG COURTLY.) Permit me to introduce my friend,

Augustus Hamilton. Capital fellow! drinks like a sieve, and rides like a thunder-storm.

MAX. Sir, I'm devilish glad to see you. Here, Sir Harcourt, permit me to introduce to you—

YOUNG COURTLY. The devil!

DAZZLE (*aside*). What's the matter?

YOUNG COURTLY (*aside*). Why, that is my governor, by Jupiter!

DAZZLE (*aside*). What, old Whiskers? you don't say that!

YOUNG COURTLY (*aside*). It is: what's to be done now?

MAX. Mr. Hamilton, Sir Harcourt Courtly—Sir Harcourt Courtly, Mr. Hamilton.

SIR HARCOURT. Hamilton! Good gracious! God bless me!—why, Charles, is it possible?—why, Max, that's my son!

YOUNG COURTLY (*aside*). What shall I do!

MAX. Your son!

GRACE. Your son, Sir Harcourt! have you a son as old as that gentleman!

SIR HARCOURT. No—that is—a—yes,—not by twenty years—a—Charles, why don't you answer me, sir?

YOUNG COURTLY (*aside to* DAZZLE). What shall I say?

DAZZLE (*aside*). Deny your identity.

YOUNG COURTLY (*aside*). Capital! (*Aloud.*) What's the matter, sir?

SIR HARCOURT. How came you down here, sir?

YOUNG COURTLY. By one of Newman's—best fours—in twelve hours and a quarter.

SIR HARCOURT. Isn't your name Charles Courtly?

YOUNG COURTLY. Not to my knowledge.

SIR HARCOURT. Do you mean to say that you are usually called Augustus Hamilton?

YOUNG COURTLY. Lamentable fact—and quite correct.

SIR HARCOURT. Cool, is that my son?

COOL. No, sir—it is not Mr. Charles—but is very like him.

MAX. I cannot understand all this.

GRACE (*aside*). I think I can.

DAZZLE (*aside to* YOUNG COURTLY). Give him a touch of the indignant.

YOUNG COURTLY. Allow me to say, Sir What-d'ye-call-'em Hartly—

SIR HARCOURT. Hartly, sir! Courtly, sir! Courtly!

YOUNG COURTLY. Well, Hartly, or Court-heart, or whatever your name may be, I say your conduct is—a—a—, and were it not for the presence of this lady, I should feel inclined—to—to—

SIR HARCOURT. No, no, that can't be my son,—he never would address me in that way.

MAX (*coming down*). What is all this?

SIR HARCOURT. Sir, your likeness to my son Charles is so astonishing, that it, for a moment—the equilibrium of my etiquette—'pon my life, I—permit me to request your pardon.

MEDDLE (*to* SIR HARCOURT). Sir Harcourt, don't apologize, don't—bring an action. I'm witness.

SIR HARCOURT. Some one take this man away.

(*Enter* JAMES.)

JAMES. Luncheon is on the table, sir.

SIR HARCOURT. Miss Harkaway, I never swore before a lady in my life—except when I promised to love and cherish the late Lady Courtly, which I took care to preface with an apology,—I was compelled to the ceremony, and consequently not answerable for the language—but to that gentleman's identity I would have pledged—my hair.

GRACE (*aside*). If that security were called for, I suspect the answer would be—no effects. (*Exeunt* SIR HARCOURT *and* GRACE.)

MEDDLE (*to* MAX). I have something very particular to communicate.

MAX. Can't listen at present. (*Exit.*)

MEDDLE (*to* DAZZLE *and* YOUNG COURTLY). I can afford you information, which I—

DAZZLE. Oh, don't bother!

YOUNG COURTLY. Go to the devil! (*Exeunt.*)

MEDDLE. Now, I have no hesitation in saying that is the height of ingratitude.—Oh—Mr. Cool—can you oblige me? (*Presents his account.*)

COOL. Why, what is all this?

MEDDLE. Small account *versus* you—to giving information concerning the last census of the population of Oldborough and vicinity, six and eightpence.

COOL. Oh, you mean to make me pay for this, do you?

MEDDLE. Unconditionally.

COOL. Well, I have no objection—the charge is fair—but remember, I am a servant on board wages,—will you throw in a little advice gratis—if I give you the money?

MEDDLE. Ahem!—I will.

COOL. A fellow has insulted me. I want to abuse him—what terms are actionable?

MEDDLE. You may call him anything you please, providing there are no witnesses.

COOL. Oh, may I? (*looks round*)—then you rascally, pettifogging scoundrel!

MEDDLE. Hallo!

COOL. You mean—dirty—disgrace to your profession.

MEDDLE. Libel—slander—

COOL. Aye, but where are your witnesses?

MEDDLE. Give me the costs—six and eightpence.

COOL. I deny that you gave me information at all.

MEDDLE. You do!

COOL. Yes, where are your witnesses? (*Exit.*)

MEDDLE. Ah—damme! (*Exit.*)

End of Act II

ACT III

SCENE FIRST: *A Morning-Room in Oak Hall, French windows opening to the Lawn.*

(MAX *and* SIR HARCOURT *seated on one side,* DAZZLE *on the other;* GRACE *and* YOUNG COURTLY *are playing chess at back. All dressed for dinner.*)

MAX (*aside to* SIR HARCOURT). What can I do?

SIR HARCOURT. Get rid of them civilly.

MAX. What, turn them out, after I particularly invited them to stay a month or two?

SIR HARCOURT. Why, they are disreputable characters; as for that young fellow, in whom my Lady Courtly appears so particularly absorbed, —I am bewildered—I have written to town for my Charles, my boy—it certainly is the most extraordinary likeness—

DAZZLE. Sir Harcourt, I have an idea—

SIR HARCOURT. Sir, I am delighted to hear it.—(*Aside.*) That fellow is a swindler.

MAX. I met him at your house.

SIR HARCOURT. Never saw him before in all my life.

DAZZLE (*crossing to* SIR HARCOURT). I will bet you five to one that I can beat you three out of four games at billiards, with one hand.

SIR HARCOURT. No, sir.

DAZZLE. I don't mind giving you ten points in fifty.

SIR HARCOURT. Sir, I never gamble.

DAZZLE. You don't! Well, I'll teach you—easiest thing in life—you have every requisite—good temper.

SIR HARCOURT. I have not, sir.

DAZZLE. A long-headed, knowing old buck.

SIR HARCOURT. Sir! (*They go up conversing with* MAX.)

GRACE. Really, Mr. Hamilton, you improve.—A young man pays us a visit, as you half intimate, to escape inconvenient friends—that is complimentary to us, his hosts.

YOUNG COURTLY. Nay, that is too severe.

GRACE. After an acquaintanceship of two days, you sit down to teach me chess, and domestic economy at the same time.—Might I ask where you graduated in that science—where you learned all that store of matrimonial advice which you have obliged me with?

YOUNG COURTLY. I imbibed it, madam, from the moment I beheld you, and having studied my subject *con amore*, took my degrees from your eyes.

GRACE. Oh, I see you are a Master of Arts already.

YOUNG COURTLY. Unfortunately, no—I shall remain a bachelor—till you can assist me to that honour. (SIR HARCOURT *comes down—aside to* DAZZLE.) Keep the old boy away.

DAZZLE (*aside*). How do you get on?

YOUNG COURTLY (*aside*). Splendidly!

SIR HARCOURT. Is the conversation strictly confidential?—or might I join?

DAZZLE (*taking his arm*). Oh, not in the least, my dear sir—we were remarking that rifle shooting was an excellent diversion during the summer months.

SIR HARCOURT (*drawing himself up*). Sir, I was addressing—

DAZZLE. And I was saying what a pity it was I couldn't find any one reasonable enough to back his opinion with long odds—come out on the lawn, and pitch up your hat, and I will hold you ten to one I put a bullet into it every time, at forty paces.

SIR HARCOURT. No, sir—I consider you—

MAX. Here, all of you—look, here is Lady Gay Spanker coming across the lawn at a hand gallop!

SIR HARCOURT (*running to the window*). Bless me, the horse is running away!

MAX. Look how she takes that fence! there's a seat.

SIR HARCOURT. Lady Gay Spanker—who may she be?

GRACE. Gay Spanker, Sir Harcourt? My cousin and dearest friend—you *must* like her.

SIR HARCOURT. It will be my devoir, since it is your wish—though it will be a hard task in your presence.

GRACE. I am sure she will like you.

SIR HARCOURT. Ha! ha! I flatter myself.

YOUNG COURTLY. Who, and what is she?

GRACE. Glee, glee made a living thing—Nature, in some frolic mood, shut up a merry devil in her eye, and, spiting Art, stole joy's brightest harmony to thrill her laugh, which peals out sorrow's knell. Her cry rings loudest in the field—the very echo loves it best, and, as each hill attempts to ape her voice, earth seems to laugh that it made a thing so glad.

MAX. Ay, the merriest minx I ever kissed. (LADY GAY *laughs without.*)

LADY GAY (*without*). Max!

MAX. Come in, you mischievous puss.

(*Enter* JAMES.)

JAMES. Mr. Adolphus and Lady Gay Spanker.

(*Enter* LADY GAY, *fully equipped in riding habit, etc.*)

LADY GAY. Ha! ha! Well, Governor, how are ye? I have been down five times, climbing up your stairs in my long clothes. How are you, Grace, dear? (*Kisses her.*) There, don't fidget, Max. And there—(*kisses him*) there's one for you.

SIR HARCOURT. Ahem!

LADY GAY. Oh, gracious, I didn't see you had visitors.

MAX. Permit me to introduce—Sir Harcourt Courtly, Lady Gay Spanker. Mr. Dazzle, Mr. Hamilton—Lady Gay Spanker.

SIR HARCOURT (*aside*). A devilish fine woman!

DAZZLE (*aside to* SIR HARCOURT). She's a devilish fine woman.

LADY GAY. You mustn't think anything of the liberties I take with my old papa here—bless him!

SIR HARCOURT. Oh, no! (*Aside.*) I only thought I should like to be in his place.

LADY GAY. I am so glad you have come, Sir Harcourt. Now we shall be able to make a decent figure at the heels of a hunt.

SIR HARCOURT. Does your ladyship hunt?

LADY GAY. Ha! I say, Governor, does my ladyship hunt? I rather flatter myself that I do hunt! Why, Sir Harcourt, one might as well live without laughing as without hunting. Man was fashioned expressly to fit a horse. Are not hedges and ditches created for leaps? Of course!

And I look upon foxes to be one of the most blessed dispensations of a benign Providence.

SIR HARCOURT. Yes, it is all very well in the abstract: I tried it once.

LADY GAY. Once! Only once?

SIR HARCOURT. Once, only once. And then the animal ran away with me.

LADY GAY. Why, you would not have him walk?

SIR HARCOURT. Finding my society disagreeable, he instituted a series of kicks, with a view to removing the annoyance; but aided by the united stays of the mane and tail, I frustrated his intentions. His next resource, however, was more effectual, for he succeeded in rubbing me off against a tree.

MAX AND LADY GAY. Ha! ha! ha!

DAZZLE. How absurd you must have looked with your legs and arms in the air, like a shipwrecked tea-table.

SIR HARCOURT. Sir, I never looked absurd in my life. Ah, it may be very amusing in relation, I dare say, but very unpleasant in effect.

LADY GAY. I pity you, Sir Harcourt; it was criminal in your parents to neglect your education so shamefully.

SIR HARCOURT. Possibly; but be assured I shall never break my neck awkwardly from a horse, when it might be accomplished with less trouble from a bed-room window.

YOUNG COURTLY (*aside*). My dad will be caught by this she-Bucephalus tamer.

MAX. Ah! Sir Harcourt, had you been here a month ago, you would have witnessed the most glorious run that ever swept over merry England's green cheek—a steeple-chase, sir, which I intended to win, but my horse broke down the day before. I had a chance, notwithstanding, and but for Gay here, I should have won. How I regretted my absence from it! How did my filly behave herself, Gay?

LADY GAY. Gloriously, Max! gloriously! There were sixty horses in the field, all mettle to the bone: the start was a picture—away we went in a cloud—pell-mell—helter-skelter—the fools first, as usual, using themselves up—we soon passed them—first your Kitty, then my Blueskin, and Craven's colt last. Then came the tug—Kitty skimmed the walls—Blueskin flew over the fences—the Colt neck and neck, and half a mile to run—at last the Colt baulked a leap and went wild. Kitty and I had it all to ourselves—she was three lengths ahead as we breasted the last wall, six feet, if an inch, and a ditch on the other side. Now, for the first time, I gave Blueskin his head—ha! ha!—Away he flew like a thunderbolt—over went the filly—I over the same spot, leaving Kitty in the ditch—walked the steeple, eight miles in thirty minutes, and scarcely turned a hair.

ALL. Bravo! Bravo!

LADY GAY. Do you hunt?

DAZZLE. Hunt! I belong to a hunting family. I was born on horse-back and cradled in a kennel! Aye, and I hope I may die with a whoo-whoop!

MAX (*to* SIR HARCOURT). You must leave your town habits in the smoke of London: here we rise with the lark.

SIR HARCOURT. Haven't the remotest conception when that period is.

GRACE. The man that misses sunrise loses the sweetest part of his existence.

SIR HARCOURT. Oh, pardon me; I have seen sunrise frequently after a ball, or from the windows of my travelling carriage, and I always considered it disagreeable.

GRACE. I love to watch the first tear that glistens in the opening eye of morning, the silent song the flowers breathe, the thrilling choir of the woodland minstrels, to which the modest brook trickles applause: —these swelling out the sweetest chord of sweet creation's matins, seem to pour some soft and merry tale into the daylight's ear, as if the waking world had dreamed a happy thing, and now smiled o'er the telling of it.

SIR HARCOURT. The effect of a rustic education! Who could ever discover music in a damp foggy morning, except those confounded waifs, who never play in tune, and a miserable wretch who makes a point of crying coffee under my window just as I am persuading myself to sleep; in fact, I never heard any music worth listening to, except in Italy.

LADY GAY. No? then you never heard a well-trained English pack, full cry?

SIR HARCOURT. Full cry!

LADY GAY. Aye! there is harmony, if you will. Give me the trumpet-neigh; the spotted pack just catching scent. What a chorus is their yelp! The viewhallo, blent with a peal of free and fearless mirth! That's our old English music,—match it where you can.

SIR HARCOURT (*aside*). I must see about Lady Gay Spanker.

DAZZLE (*aside to* SIR HARCOURT). Ah, would you—

LADY GAY. Time then appears as young as love, and plumes as swift a wing. Away we go! The earth flies back to aid our course! Horse, man, hound, earth, heaven!—all—all—one piece of glowing ecstasy! Then I love the world, myself, and every living thing,—my jocund soul cries out for very glee, as it could wish that all creation had but one mouth that I might kiss it!

SIR HARCOURT (*aside*). I wish I were the mouth!

MAX. Why, we will regenerate you, Baronet! But Gay, where is your husband?—Where is Adolphus!

LADY GAY. Bless me, where is my Dolly?

SIR HARCOURT. You are married, then?

LADY GAY. I have a husband somewhere, though I can't find him just now. Dolly, dear! (*Aside to* MAX.) Governor, at home I always whistle when I want him.

(*Enter* SPANKER.)

SPANKER. Here I am,—did you call me, Gay?

SIR HARCOURT (*eyeing him*). Is that your husband?

LADY GAY (*aside*). Yes, bless his stupid face, that's my Dolly.

MAX. Permit me to introduce you to Sir Harcourt Courtly.

SPANKER. How d'ye do? I—ah!—um! (*Appears frightened.*)

LADY GAY. Delighted to have the honour of making the acquaintance of a gentleman so highly celebrated in the world of fashion.

SPANKER. Oh, yes, delighted, I'm sure—quite—very, so delighted—delighted! (*Gets quite confused, draws on his glove, and tears it.*)

LADY GAY. Where have you been, Dolly?

SPANKER. Oh, ah, I was just outside.

MAX. Why did you not come in?

SPANKER. I'm sure I didn't—I don't exactly know, but I thought as—perhaps—I can't remember.

DAZZLE. Shall we have the pleasure of your company to dinner?

SPANKER. I always dine—usually—that is, unless Gay remains.

LADY GAY. Stay to dinner, of course; we came on purpose to stop three or four days with you.

GRACE. Will you excuse my absence, Gay?

MAX. What! what! Where are you going? What takes you away?

GRACE. We must postpone the dinner till Gay is dressed.

MAX. Oh, never mind,—stay where you are.

GRACE. No, I must go.

MAX. I say you sha'n't! I will be king in my own house.

GRACE. Do, my dear uncle;—you shall be king, and I'll be your prime minister,—that is, I will rule, and you shall have the honour of taking the consequences. (*Exit.*)

LADY GAY. Well said, Grace; have your own way; it is the only thing we women ought to be allowed.

MAX. Come, Gay, dress for dinner.

SIR HARCOURT. Permit me, Lady Gay Spanker.

LADY GAY. With pleasure,—what do you want?

SIR HARCOURT. To escort you.

LADY GAY. Oh, never mind, I can escort myself, thank you, and Dolly too;—come, dear! (*Exit.*)

SIR HARCOURT. Au revoir!

SPANKER. Ah, thank you! (*Exit awkwardly.*)

SIR HARCOURT. What an ill-assorted pair!

MAX. Not a bit! She married him for freedom, and she has it; he married her for protection, and he has it.

SIR HARCOURT. How he ever summoned courage to propose to her, I can't guess.

MAX. Bless you, he never did. She proposed to him! She says he would, if he could; but as he couldn't, she did it for him. (*Exeunt, laughing.*)

(*Enter* COOL *with a letter.*)

COOL. Mr. Charles, I have been watching to find you alone. Sir Harcourt has written to town for you.

YOUNG COURTLY. The devil he has!

COOL. He expects you down to-morrow evening.

DAZZLE. Oh! he'll be punctual. A thought strikes me.

YOUNG COURTLY. Pooh! Confound your thoughts! I can think of nothing but the idea of leaving Grace, at the very moment when I had established the most—

DAZZLE. What if I can prevent her marriage with your Governor?

YOUNG COURTLY. Impossible!

DAZZLE. He's pluming himself for the conquest of Lady Gay Spanker. It will not be difficult to make him believe she accedes to his suit. And if she would but join in the plan—

YOUNG COURTLY. I see it all. And do you think she would?

DAZZLE. I mistake my game if she would not.

COOL. Here comes Sir Harcourt!

DAZZLE. I'll begin with him. Retire, and watch how I'll open the campaign for you. (YOUNG COURTLY *and* COOL *retire.*)

(*Enter* SIR HARCOURT.)

SIR HARCOURT. Here is that cursed fellow again.

DAZZLE. Ah, my dear old friend!

SIR HARCOURT. Mr. Dazzle!

DAZZLE. I have a secret of importance to disclose to you. Are you a man of honour? Hush! don't speak; you are. It is with the greatest pain I am compelled to request you, as a gentleman, that you will shun studiously the society of Lady Gay Spanker!

SIR HARCOURT. Good gracious! Wherefore, and by what right do you make such a demand?

DAZZLE. Why, I am distantly related to the Spankers.

SIR HARCOURT. Why, damme, sir, if you don't appear to be related to every family in Great Britain!

DAZZLE. A good many of the nobility claim me as a connexion. But, to return—she is much struck with your address; evidently, she laid herself out for display.

SIR HARCOURT. Ha! you surprise me!

DAZZLE. To entangle you.

SIR HARCOURT. Ha! ha! why, it did appear like it.

DAZZLE. You will spare her for my sake; give her no encouragement; if disgrace come upon my relatives, the Spankers, I should never hold up my head again.

SIR HARCOURT (*aside*). I shall achieve an easy conquest, and a glorious. Ha! ha! I never remarked it before; but this is a gentleman.

DAZZLE. May I rely on your generosity?

SIR HARCOURT. Faithfully. (*Shakes his hand.*) Sir, I honour and esteem you; but, might I ask, how came you to meet our friend, Max Harkaway, in my house in Belgrave Square?

(*Re-enter* YOUNG COURTLY. *Sits on sofa at back.*)

DAZZLE. Certainly. I had an acceptance of your son's for one hundred pounds.

SIR HARCOURT (*astonished*). Of my son's? Impossible!

DAZZLE. Ah, sir, fact! he paid a debt for a poor, unfortunate man—fifteen children—half-a-dozen wives—the devil knows what all.

SIR HARCOURT. Simple boy!

DAZZLE. Innocent youth, I have no doubt; when you have the hundred convenient, I shall feel delighted.

SIR HARCOURT. Oh! follow me to my room, and if you have the document, it will be happiness to me to pay it. Poor Charles! good heart!

DAZZLE. Oh, a splendid heart! I dare say. (*Exit* SIR HARCOURT.) Come here; write me the bill.

YOUNG COURTLY. What for?

DAZZLE. What for? why, to release the unfortunate man and his family, to be sure, from jail.

YOUNG COURTLY. Who is he?

DAZZLE. Yourself.

YOUNG COURTLY. But I haven't fifteen children!

DAZZLE. Will you take your oath of that?

YOUNG COURTLY. Nor four wives.

DAZZLE. More shame for you, with all that family. Come, don't be obstinate; write and date it back.

YOUNG COURTLY. Ay, but where is the stamp?

DAZZLE. Here they are, of all patterns. (*Pulls out a pocketbook.*) I keep them ready drawn in case of necessity, all but the date and acceptance. Now, if you are in an autographic humour, you can try how your signature will look across half a dozen of them;—there—write—exactly—you know the place—across—good—and thank your lucky stars that you have found a friend at last, that gives you money and advice. (*Takes paper and exit.*)

YOUNG COURTLY. Things are approaching to a climax; I must appear *in propriâ personâ*—and immediately—but I must first ascertain what are the real sentiments of this riddle of a woman. Does she love me? I flatter myself—By Jove, here she comes—I shall never have such an opportunity again!

(*Enter* GRACE.)

GRACE. I wish I had never seen Mr. Hamilton. Why does every object appear robbed of the charm it once presented to me? Why do I shudder at the contemplation of this marriage, which, till now, was to me a subject of indifference? Am I in love? In love! if I am, my past life has been the work of raising up a pedestal to place my own folly on—I—the infidel—the railer!

YOUNG COURTLY. Meditating upon matrimony, madam?

GRACE (*aside*). He little thinks he was the subject of my meditations! (*Aloud.*) No.

YOUNG COURTLY (*aside*). I must unmask my battery now.

GRACE (*aside*). How foolish I am—he will perceive that I tremble—I must appear at ease. (*A pause.*)

YOUNG COURTLY. Eh? ah! um!

GRACE. Ah! (*They sink into silence again. Aside.*) How very awkward!

YOUNG COURTLY (*aside*). It is a very difficult subject to begin. (*Aloud.*) Madam—ahem—there was—is—I mean—I was about to remark—a—

(*Aside.*) Hang me if it is not a very slippery subject. I must brush up my faculties; attack her in her own way. (*Aloud.*) Sing! oh, muse! (*Aside.*) Why, I have made love before to a hundred women!

GRACE (*aside*). I wish I had something to do, for I have nothing to say.

YOUNG COURTLY. Madam—there is—a subject so fraught with fate to my future life, that you must pardon my lack of delicacy, should a too hasty expression mar the fervent courtesy of its intent. To you, I feel aware, I must appear in the light of a comparative stranger.

GRACE (*aside*). I know what's coming.

YOUNG COURTLY. Of you—I know perhaps too much for my own peace.

GRACE (*aside*). He *is* in love.

YOUNG COURTLY. I forget all that befell before I saw your beauteous self; I seem born into another world—my nature changed—the beams of that bright face falling on my soul, have, from its chaos, warmed into life the flowrets of affection, whose maiden odours now float toward the sun, pouring forth on their pure tongue a mite of adoration, midst the voices of a universe. (*Aside.*) That's something in her own style.

GRACE. Mr. Hamilton!

YOUNG COURTLY. You cannot feel surprised—

GRACE. I am more than surprised. (*Aside.*) I am delighted.

YOUNG COURTLY. Do not speak so coldly.

GRACE. You have offended me.

YOUNG COURTLY. No, madam; no woman, whatever her state, can be offended by the adoration even of the meanest; it is myself whom I have offended and deceived—but still I ask your pardon.

GRACE (*aside*). Oh! he thinks I am refusing him. (*Aloud.*) I am not exactly offended, but—

YOUNG COURTLY. Consider my position—a few days—and an insurmountable barrier would have placed you beyond my wildest hopes—you would have been my mother.

GRACE. I should have been your mother! (*Aside.*) I thought so.

YOUNG COURTLY. No—that is, I meant Sir Harcourt Courtly's bride.

GRACE (*with great emphasis*). Never!

YOUNG COURTLY. How! never! may I then hope?—you turn away—you would not lacerate me by a refusal?

GRACE (*aside*). How stupid he is!

YOUNG COURTLY. Still silent! I thank you, Miss Grace—I ought to have expected this—fool that I have been—one course alone remains—farewell!

GRACE (*aside*). Now he's going.

YOUNG COURTLY. Farewell forever! (*Sits.*) Will you not speak one word? I shall leave this house immediately—I shall not see you again.

GRACE. Unhand me, sir, I insist.

YOUNG COURTLY (*aside*). Oh! what an ass I've been! (*Rushes up to her, and seizes her hand.*) Release this hand? Never! never! (*Kissing it.*) Never will I quit this hand! it shall be my companion in misery—in solitude—when you are far away.

GRACE. Oh! should any one come! (*Drops her handkerchief; he stoops to pick it up.*) For heaven's sake do not kneel.

YOUNG COURTLY (*kneels*). Forever thus prostrate, before my soul's saint, I will lead a pious life of eternal adoration.

GRACE. Should we be discovered thus—pray, Mr. Hamilton—pray—pray.

YOUNG COURTLY. Pray! I am praying; what more can I do?

GRACE. Your conduct is shameful.

YOUNG COURTLY. It is. (*Rises.*)

GRACE. And if I do not scream, it is not for your sake—that—but it might alarm the family.

YOUNG COURTLY. It might—it would. Say, am I wholly indifferent to you? I entreat one word—I implore you—do not withdraw your hand—(*She snatches it away—he puts his round her waist.*) You smile.

GRACE. Leave me, dear Mr. Hamilton!

YOUNG COURTLY. Dear! Then I am dear to you; that word once more; say—say you love me!

GRACE. Is this fair? (*He catches her in his arms, and kisses her.*)

(*Enter* LADY GAY SPANKER.)

LADY GAY. Ha! oh!

GRACE. Gay! destruction! (*Exit.*)

YOUNG COURTLY. Fizgig! The devil!

LADY GAY. Don't mind me—pray, don't let me be any interruption!

YOUNG COURTLY. I was just—

LADY GAY. Yes, I see you were.

YOUNG COURTLY. Oh! madam, how could you mar my bliss, in the very ecstasy of its fulfilment?

LADY GAY. I always like to be in at the death. Never drop your ears; bless you, she is only a little fresh—give her her head, and she will outrun herself.

YOUNG COURTLY. Possibly; but what am I to do?

LADY GAY. Keep your seat.

YOUNG COURTLY. But in a few days she will take a leap that must throw me—she marries Sir Harcourt Courtly.

LADY GAY. Why, that is awkward, certainly; but you can challenge him, and shoot him.

YOUNG COURTLY. Unfortunately, that is out of the question.

LADY GAY. How so?

YOUNG COURTLY. You will not betray a secret, if I inform you?

LADY GAY. All right—what is it?

YOUNG COURTLY. I am his son.

LADY GAY. What—his son? But he does not know you?

YOUNG COURTLY. No. I met him here, by chance, and faced it out. I never saw him before in my life.

LADY GAY. Beautiful!—I see it all—you're in love with your mother, that should be—your wife, that will be.

YOUNG COURTLY. Now, I think I could distance the old gentleman, if you will but lend us your assistance.

LADY GAY. I will, in anything.

YOUNG COURTLY. You must know, then, that my father, Sir Harcourt, has fallen desperately in love with you.

LADY GAY. With me!—(*Utters a scream of delight.*)—That is delicious!

YOUNG COURTLY. Now, if you only could—

LADY GAY. Could!—I will. Ha! ha! I see my cue. I'll cross his scent—I'll draw him after me. Ho! ho! won't I make love to him? Ha!

YOUNG COURTLY. The only objection might be Mr. Spanker, who might—

LADY GAY. No, he mightn't,—he's no objection. Bless him, he's an inestimable little character—you don't know him as well as I do. I dare say—ha! ha! (*Dinner-bell rings.*) Here they come to dinner. I'll commence my operations on your Governor immediately. Ha! ha! how I shall enjoy it.

YOUNG COURTLY. Be guarded!

(*Enter* MAX HARKAWAY, SIR HARCOURT, DAZZLE, GRACE, *and* SPANKER.)

MAX. Now, gentlemen—Sir Harcourt, do you lead Grace.

LADY GAY. I believe Sir Harcourt is engaged to me. (*Takes his arm.*)

MAX. Well, please yourselves. (*They file out,* MAX *first,* YOUNG COURTLY *and* GRACE, SIR HARCOURT *coquetting with* LADY GAY, *leaving* DAZZLE, *who offers his arm to* SPANKER.)

End of Act III

ACT IV

SCENE FIRST: *A handsome Drawing-Room in Oak Hall, chandeliers, tables with books, drawings, etc.* GRACE *and* LADY GAY *discovered.* SERVANT *handing Coffee.*

GRACE. If there be one habit more abominable than another, it is that of the gentlemen sitting over their wine: it is a selfish, unfeeling fashion, and a gross insult to our sex.

LADY GAY. We are turned out just when the fun begins. How happy the poor wretches look at the contemplation of being rid of us.

GRACE. The conventional signal for the ladies to withdraw is anxiously and deliberately waited for.

LADY GAY. Then I begin to wish I were a man.

GRACE. The instant the door is closed upon us, there rises a roar!

LADY GAY. In celebration of their short-lived liberty, my love; rejoicing over their emancipation.

GRACE. I think it very insulting, whatever it may be.

LADY GAY. Ah! my dear, philosophers say that man is the creature of an hour—it is the dinner hour, I suppose. (*Loud noise. Cries of* "A song, a song.")

GRACE. I am afraid they are getting too pleasant to be agreeable.

LADY GAY. I hope the squire will restrict himself; after his third bottle, he becomes rather voluminous. (*Cries of* "Silence.") Some one is going to sing. (*Jumps up.*) Let us hear! (SPANKER *is heard to sing.*)

GRACE. Oh, no, Gay, for heaven's sake!

LADY GAY. Oho! ha! ha! why, that is my Dolly. (*At the conclusion of the verse.*) Well, I never heard my Dolly sing before! Happy wretches, how I envy them!

(*Enter* JAMES, *with a note.*)

JAMES. Mr. Hamilton has just left the house for London.

GRACE. Impossible!—that is, without seeing—that is—

LADY GAY. Ha! ha!

GRACE. He never—speak, sir!

JAMES. He left, Miss Grace, in a desperate hurry, and this note, I believe, for you. (*Presenting a note on a salver.*)

GRACE. For me! (*She is about to snatch it, but restraining herself, takes it coolly. Exit* JAMES.)

(*Reads.*) "Your manner during dinner has left me no alternative but instant departure; my absence will release you from the oppression which my society must necessarily inflict on your sensitive mind. It may tend also to smother, though it can never extinguish, that indomitable passion, of which I am the passive victim. Dare I supplicate pardon and oblivion for the past? It is the last request of the self-deceived, but still loving

"AUGUSTUS HAMILTON."

(*Puts her hand to her forehead and appears giddy.*)

LADY GAY. Hallo, Grace! what's the matter?

GRACE (*recovering herself*). Nothing—the heat of the room.

LADY GAY. Oh! what excuse does he make? particular unforeseen business, I suppose?

GRACE. Why, yes—a mere formula—a—a—you may put it in the fire. (*She puts it in her bosom.*)

LADY GAY (*aside*). It is near enough to the fire where it is.

GRACE. I'm glad he's gone.

LADY GAY. So am I.

GRACE. He was a disagreeable, ignorant person.

LADY GAY. Yes; and so vulgar!

GRACE. No, he was not at all vulgar.

LADY GAY. I mean in appearance.

GRACE. Oh! how can you say so; he was very *distingué.*

LADY GAY. Well, I might have been mistaken, but I took him for a forward, intrusive—

GRACE. Good gracious, Gay! he was very retiring—even shy.

LADY GAY (*aside*). It's all right. *She* is in love,—blows hot and cold in the same breath.

GRACE. How can you be a competent judge? Why, you have not known him more than a few hours,—while I—I—

LADY GAY. Have known him two days and a quarter! I yield—I confess, I never was, or will be so intimate with him as you appeared to be! Ha! ha! (*Loud noise of argument. The folding-doors are thrown open.*)

(*Enter the whole party of gentlemen apparently engaged in warm discussion. They assemble in knots, while the* SERVANTS *hand Coffee, etc.,* MAX, SIR HARCOURT, DAZZLE, *and* SPANKER, *together.*)

DAZZLE. But, my dear sir, consider the position of the two countries under such a constitution.

SIR HARCOURT. The two countries! What have they to do with the subject?

MAX. Everything. Look at their two legislative bodies.

SPANKER. Ay, look at their two legislative bodies.

SIR HARCOURT. Why, it would inevitably establish universal anarchy and confusion.

GRACE. I think they are pretty well established already.

SPANKER. Well, suppose it did, what has anarchy and confusion to do with the subject?

LADY GAY. Do look at my Dolly: he is arguing—talking politics—'pon my life he is. (*Calling.*) Mr. Spanker, my dear!

SPANKER. Excuse me, love, I am discussing a point of importance.

LADY GAY. Oh, that is delicious; he must discuss that to me.—(*She goes up and leads him down; he appears to have shaken off his gaucherie; she shakes her head.*) Dolly! Dolly!

SPANKER. Pardon me, Lady Gay Spanker, I conceive your mutilation of my sponsorial appellation derogatory to my *amour propre.*

LADY GAY. Your what? Ho! ho!

SPANKER. And I particularly request that, for the future, I may not be treated with that cavalier spirit which does not become your sex, nor your station, your ladyship.

LADY GAY. You have been indulging till you have lost the little wit nature dribbled into your unfortunate little head—your brains want the whipperin—you are not yourself.

SPANKER. Madam, I am doubly myself; and permit me to inform you, that unless you voluntarily pay obedience to my commands, I shall enforce them.

LADY GAY. Your commands!

SPANKER. Yes, madam; I mean to put a full stop to your hunting.

LADY GAY. You do! ah! (*Aside.*) I can scarcely speak from delight. (*Aloud.*) Who put such an idea into your head, for I am sure it is not an original emanation of your genius?

SPANKER. Sir Harcourt Courtly, my friend; and now, mark me! I request, for your own sake, that I may not be compelled to assert my a—my authority, as your husband. I shall say no more than this—if you persist in this absurd rebellion—

LADY GAY. Well!

SPANKER. Contemplate a separation. (*He looks at her haughtily, and retires.*)

LADY GAY. Now I'm happy! My own little darling, inestimable Dolly, has tumbled into a spirit, somehow. Sir Harcourt, too! Ha! ha! he's trying to make him ill-treat me, so that his own suit may thrive.

SIR HARCOURT (*advances*). Lady Gay!

LADY GAY. Now for it.

SIR HARCOURT. What hours of misery were those I passed, when, by your secession, the room suffered a total eclipse.

LADY GAY. Ah! you flatter.

SIR HARCOURT. No, pardon me, that were impossible. No, believe me, I tried to join in the boisterous mirth, but my thoughts would desert to the drawing-room. Ah! how I envied the careless levity and cool indifference with which Mr. Spanker enjoyed your absence.

DAZZLE (*who is lounging in a chair*). Max, that Madeira is worth its weight in gold; I hope you have more of it.

MAX. A pipe, I think.

DAZZLE. I consider a magnum of that nectar, and a meerschaum of kanaster, to consummate the ultimatum of all mundane bliss. To drown myself in liquid ecstasy, and then blow a cloud on which the enfranchised soul could soar above Olympus.—Oh!

(*Enter* JAMES.)

JAMES. Mr. Charles Courtly!

SIR HARCOURT. Ah, now, Max, you must see a living apology for my conduct.

(*Enter* YOUNG COURTLY, *dressed very plainly.*)

Well, Charles, how are you? Don't be afraid. There, Max, what do you say now?

MAX. Well, this is the most extraordinary likeness.

GRACE (*aside*). Yes—considering it is the original. I am not so easily deceived!

MAX. Sir, I am delighted to see you.

YOUNG COURTLY. Thank you, sir.

DAZZLE. Will you be kind enough to introduce me, Sir Harcourt?

SIR HARCOURT. This is Mr. Dazzle, Charles.

YOUNG COURTLY. Which? (*Looking from* MR. SPANKER *to* DAZZLE.)

SIR HARCOURT (*to* LADY GAY). Is not that refreshing? Miss Harkaway—Charles, this is your mother, or rather will be.

YOUNG COURTLY. Madam, I shall love, honour, and obey you punctually. (*Takes out a book, sighs, and goes up reading.*)

(*Enter* JAMES.)

SIR HARCOURT. You perceive? Quite unused to society—perfectly ignorant of every conventional rule of life.

JAMES. The Doctor and the young ladies have arrived. (*Exit.*)

MAX. The young ladies—now we must to the ball—I make it a rule always to commence the festivities with a good old country dance—a rattling Sir Roger de Coverly; come, Sir Harcourt.

SIR HARCOURT. Does this antiquity require a war-whoop in it?

MAX. Nothing but a nimble foot and a light heart.

SIR HARCOURT. Very antediluvian indispensables! Lady Gay Spanker, will you honour me by becoming my preceptor?

LADY GAY. Why, I am engaged—but (*aloud*) on such a plea as Sir Harcourt's, I must waive all obstacles.

MAX. Now, Grace, girl—give your hand to Mr. Courtly.

GRACE. Pray, excuse me, uncle—I have a headache.

SIR HARCOURT (*aside*). Jealousy! by the gods.—Jealous of my devotions at another's fane! (*Aloud.*) Charles, my boy! amuse Miss Grace during our absence. (*Exit with* LADY GAY.)

MAX. But don't you dance, Mr. Courtly!

YOUNG COURTLY. Dance, sir!—I never dance—I can procure exercise in a much more rational manner—and music disturbs my meditations.

MAX. Well, do the gallant. (*Exit.*)

YOUNG COURTLY. I never studied that Art—but I have a Prize Essay on a Hydrostatic subject, which would delight her—for it enchanted the Reverend Doctor Pump, of Corpus Christi.

GRACE (*aside*). What on earth could have induced him to disguise himself in that frightful way!—I rather suspect some plot to entrap me into a confession.

YOUNG COURTLY (*aside*). Dare I confess this trick to her? No! Not until I have proved her affection indisputably.—Let me see—I must concoct. (*He takes a chair, and, forgetting his assumed character, is about to take his natural free manner.*—GRACE *looks surprised.—He turns abashed.*) Madam, I have been desired to amuse you.

GRACE. Thank you.

YOUNG COURTLY. "The labour we delight in, physics pain." I will draw you a moral, ahem! Subject, the effects of inebriety!—which, according to Ben Jonson—means perplexion of the intellects, caused by imbibing spirituous liquors.—About an hour before my arrival, I passed an appalling evidence of the effects of this state—a carriage was overthrown—horses killed—gentleman in a helpless state, with his neck broken—all occasioned by the intoxication of the post-boy.

GRACE. That is very amusing.

YOUNG COURTLY. I found it edifying—nutritious food for reflection—the expiring man desired his best compliments to you.

GRACE. To me?

YOUNG COURTLY. Yes.

GRACE. His name was—

YOUNG COURTLY. Mr. Augustus Hamilton.

GRACE. Augustus! Oh! (*Affects to faint.*)

YOUNG COURTLY (*aside*). Huzza!

GRACE. But where, sir, did this happen?

YOUNG COURTLY. About four miles down the road.

GRACE. He must be conveyed here.

(*Enter* SERVANT.)

SERVANT. Mr. Meddle, madam.

(*Enter* MEDDLE.)

MEDDLE. On very particular business.

GRACE. The very person. My dear sir!

MEDDLE. My dear madam!

GRACE. You must execute a very particular commission for me immediately. Mr. Hamilton has met with a frightful accident on the London road, and is in a dying state.

MEDDLE. Well! I have no hesitation in saying, he takes it uncommonly easy—he looks as if he was used to it.

GRACE. You mistake: that is not Mr. Hamilton, but Mr. Courtly, who will explain everything, and conduct you to the spot.

YOUNG COURTLY (*aside*). Oh! I must put a stop to all this, or I shall be found out.— (*Aloud.*) Madam, that were useless; for I omitted to mention a small fact which occurred before I left Mr. Hamilton—he died.

GRACE. Dear me! Oh, then we needn't trouble you, Mr. Meddle. (*Music heard.*) Hark! I hear they are commencing a waltz—if you will ask me—perhaps your society and conversation may tend to dispel the dreadful sensation you have aroused.

YOUNG COURTLY (*aside*). Hears of my death—screams out—and then asks me to waltz! I am bewildered! Can she suspect me? I wonder which she likes best—me or my double? Confound this disguise—I must retain it—I have gone too far with my dad to pull up now.—At your service, madam.

GRACE (*aside*). I will pay him well for this trick! (*Exeunt, all but* MEDDLE.)

MEDDLE. Well, if that is not Mr. Hamilton, scratch me out with a big blade, for I am a blot—a mistake upon the rolls. There is an error in the pleadings somewhere, and I will discover it. I would swear to his identity before the most discriminating jury. By the bye, this accident will form a capital excuse for my presence here. I just stepped in to see how matters worked, and—stay—here comes the bridegroom elect—and, oh! in his very arms, Lady Gay Spanker! (*Looks round.*) Where are my witnesses? Oh, that some one else were here! However, I can retire and get some information, eh—Spanker versus Courtly—damages—witness. (*Gets into an arm-chair, which he turns round.*)

(*Enter* SIR HARCOURT, *supporting* LADY GAY.)

SIR HARCOURT. This cool room will recover you.

LADY GAY. Excuse my trusting to you for support.

SIR HARCOURT. I am transported! Allow me thus ever to support this lovely burden, and I shall conceive that Paradise is regained. (*They sit.*)

LADY GAY. Oh! Sir Harcourt, I feel very faint.

SIR HARCOURT. The waltz made you giddy.

LADY GAY. And I have left my salts in the other room.

SIR HARCOURT. I always carry a flacon, for the express accommodation of the fair sex. (*Producing a smelling-bottle.*)

LADY GAY. Thank you—ah! (*She sighs.*)

SIR HARCOURT. What a sigh was there!

LADY GAY. The vapour of consuming grief.

SIR HARCOURT. Grief? Is it possible! Have you a grief? Are you unhappy? Dear me!

LADY GAY. Am I not married?

SIR HARCOURT. What a horrible state of existence!

LADY GAY. I am never contradicted, so there are none of those enlivening, interesting little differences, which so pleasingly diversify the monotony of conjugal life, like spots of verdure—no quarrels, like oases in the desert of matrimony—no rows.

SIR HARCOURT. How vulgar! what a brute!

LADY GAY. I never have anything but my own way; and he won't permit me to spend more than I like.

SIR HARCOURT. Mean-spirited wretch!

LADY GAY. How can I help being miserable?

SIR HARCOURT. Miserable! I wonder you are not in a lunatic asylum, with such unheard-of barbarity!

LADY GAY. But worse than all that!

SIR HARCOURT. Can it be outheroded?

LADY GAY. Yes, I could forgive that—I do—it is my duty. But only imagine—picture to yourself, my dear Sir Harcourt, though I, the third daughter of an Earl, married him out of pity for his destitute and helpless situation as a bachelor with ten thousand a year—conceive, if you can —he actually permits me, with the most placid indifference, to flirt with any old fool I may meet.

SIR HARCOURT. Good gracious! miserable idiot!

LADY GAY. I fear there is an incompatibility of temper, which renders a separation inevitable.

SIR HARCOURT. Indispensable, my dear madam! Ah! had I been the happy possessor of such a realm of bliss—what a beatific eternity unfolds itself to my extending imagination! Had another man but looked at you, I should have annihilated him at once; and if he had the temerity to speak, his life alone could have expiated his crime.

LADY GAY. Oh, an existence of such a nature is too bright for the eye of thought—too sweet to bear reflection.

SIR HARCOURT. My devotion, eternal, deep—

LADY GAY. Oh, Sir Harcourt!

SIR HARCOURT (*more fervently*). Your every thought should be a separate study,—each wish forestalled by the quick apprehension of a kindred soul.

LADY GAY. Alas! how can I avoid my fate?

SIR HARCOURT. If a life—a heart—were offered to your astonished view by one who is considered the index of fashion—the vane of the *beau monde*,—if you saw him at your feet, begging, beseeching your acceptance of all, and more than this, what would your answer—

LADY GAY. Ah! I know of none so devoted!

SIR HARCOURT. You do! (*Throwing himself upon his knees.*) Behold Sir Harcourt Courtly! (MEDDLE *jumps up in the chair.*)

LADY GAY (*aside*). Ha! ha! Yoicks! Puss has broken cover.

SIR HARCOURT. Speak, adored, dearest Lady Gay!—speak—will you fly from the tyranny, the wretched misery of such a monster's roof, and accept the soul which lives but in your presence!

LADY GAY. Do not press me. Oh, spare a weak, yielding woman, —be contented to know that you are, alas! too dear to me. But the world—the world would say—

SIR HARCOURT. Let us be a precedent, to open a more extended and liberal view of matrimonial advantages to society.

LADY GAY. How irresistible is your argument! Oh! pause!

SIR HARCOURT. I have ascertained for a fact, that every tradesman of mine lives with his wife, and thus you see it has become a vulgar and plebeian custom.

LADY GAY. Leave me; I feel I cannot withstand your powers of persuasion. Swear that you will never forsake me.

SIR HARCOURT. Dictate the oath. May I grow wrinkled,—may two inches be added to the circumference of my waist,—may I lose the fall in my back,—may I be old and ugly the instant I forego one tithe of adoration!

LADY GAY. I must believe you.

SIR HARCOURT. Shall we leave this detestable spot—this horrible vicinity?

LADY GAY. The sooner the better: to-morrow evening let it be. Now let me return; my absence will be remarked. (*He kisses her hand.*) Do I appear confused? Has my agitation rendered me unfit to enter the room?

SIR HARCOURT. More angelic by a lovely tinge of heightened colour.

LADY GAY. To-morrow, in this room, which opens on the lawn.

SIR HARCOURT. At eleven o'clock.

LADY GAY. Have your carriage in waiting, and four horses. Remember, please be particular to have four; don't let the affair come off shabbily. Adieu, dear Sir Harcourt! (*Exit.*)

SIR HARCOURT. Veni, vidi, vici! Hannibal, Cæsar, Napoleon, Alexander never completed so fair a conquest in so short a time. She dropped fascinated. This is an unprecedented example of the irresistible force of personal appearance combined with polished address. Poor creature! how she loves me! I pity so prostrating a passion, and ought to return it. I will: it is a duty I owe to society and fashion. (*Exit.*)

MEDDLE (*turns the chair round*). "There is a tide in the affairs of men, which, taken at the flood, leads on to fortune." This is my tide—I am the only witness. "Virtue is sure to find its own reward." But I've no time to contemplate what I shall be—something huge. Let me see—Spanker *versus* Courtly—Crim. Con.—Damages placed at 150,000*l.*, at least, for juries always decimate your hopes.

(*Enter* MR. SPANKER.)

SPANKER. I cannot find Gay anywhere.

MEDDLE. The plaintiff himself—I must commence the action. Mr. Spanker, as I have information of deep, vital importance to impart, will you take a seat? (*They sit solemnly.* MEDDLE *takes out a note-book and pencil.*) Ahem! You have a wife?

(*Re-enter* LADY GAY *behind.*)

SPANKER. Yes, I believe I—

MEDDLE. Will you be kind enough, without any prevarication, to answer my questions?

SPANKER. You alarm—I—

MEDDLE. Compose yourself and reserve your feelings; take time to consider. You have a wife?

SPANKER. Yes—

MEDDLE. He has a wife—good—a *bona-fide* wife—bound morally and legally to be your wife, and nobody else's in effect, except on your written permission—

SPANKER. But what has this—

MEDDLE. Hush! allow me, my dear sir, to congratulate you. (*Shakes his hand.*)

SPANKER. What for?

MEDDLE. Lady Gay Spanker is about to dishonour the bond of wedlock by eloping from you.

SPANKER (*starting*). What?

MEDDLE. Be patient—I thought you would be overjoyed. Will you place the affair in my hands, and I will venture to promise the largest damages on record.

SPANKER. Damn the damages!—I want my wife. Oh, I'll go and ask her not to run away. She may run away with me—she may hunt—she may ride—anything she likes. Oh, sir, let us put a stop to this affair.

MEDDLE. Put a stop to it! do not alarm me, sir. Sir, you will spoil the most exquisite brief that was ever penned. It must proceed—it shall proceed. It is illegal to prevent it, and I will bring an action against you for wilful intent to injure the profession.

SPANKER. Oh, what an ass I am! Oh, I have driven her to this. It was all that damned brandy punch on the top of Burgundy. What a fool I was!

MEDDLE. It was the happiest moment of your life.

SPANKER. So I thought at the time; but we live to grow wiser. Tell me, who is the vile seducer?

MEDDLE. Sir Harcourt Courtly.

SPANKER. Ha! he is my best friend.

MEDDLE. I should think he is. If you will accompany me—here is a verbatim copy of the whole transaction in short-hand—sworn to by me.

SPANKER. Only let me have Gay back again.

MEDDLE. Even that may be arranged:—this way.

SPANKER. That ever I should live to see my wife run away. Oh, I will do any thing—keep two packs of hounds—buy up every horse and ass in England—myself included—oh! (*Exit with* MEDDLE.)

LADY GAY. Ha! ha! ha! Poor Dolly! I'm sorry I must continue to deceive him. If he would kindle up a little—So, that fellow overheard all—well, so much the better.

(*Enter* YOUNG COURTLY.)

YOUNG COURTLY. My dear madam, how fares the plot? does my Governor nibble?

LADY GAY. Nibble! he is caught, and in the basket. I have just left him with a hook in his gills, panting for very lack of element. But how goes on your encounter?

YOUNG COURTLY. Bravely. By a simple ruse, I have discovered that she loves me. I see but one chance against the best termination I could hope.

LADY GAY. What is that?

YOUNG COURTLY. My father has told me that I return to town again to-morrow afternoon.

LADY GAY. Well, I insist you stop and dine—keep out of the way.

YOUNG COURTLY. Oh, but what excuse shall I offer for disobedience? What can I say when he sees me before dinner?

LADY GAY. Say—say Grace.

(*Enter* GRACE, *who gets behind the window curtains.*)

YOUNG COURTLY. Ha! ha!

LADY GAY. I have arranged to elope with Sir Harcourt myself to-morrow night.

YOUNG COURTLY. The deuce you have!

LADY GAY. Now, if you could persuade Grace to follow that example—his carriage will be waiting at the Park—be there a little before eleven, and it will just prevent our escape. Can you make her agree to that?

YOUNG COURTLY. Oh, without the slightest difficulty, if Mr. Augustus Hamilton supplicates.

LADY GAY. Success attend you. (*Going.*)

YOUNG COURTLY. I will bend the haughty Grace. (*Going.*)

LADY GAY. Do. (*Exeunt severally.*)

GRACE. Will you?

End of Act IV

ACT V

SCENE FIRST: *A Drawing-Room in Oak Hall*

(*Enter* COOL.)

COOL. This is the most serious affair Sir Harcourt has ever been engaged in. I took the liberty of considering him a fool when he told me he was going to marry: but voluntarily to incur another man's incumbrance is very little short of madness. If he continues to conduct himself in this absurd manner, I shall be compelled to dismiss him.

(*Enter* SIR HARCOURT, *equipped for travelling.*)

SIR HARCOURT. Cool!

COOL. Sir Harcourt.

SIR HARCOURT. Is my chariot in waiting?

COOL. For the last half hour at the park wicket. But, pardon the insinuation, sir; would it not be more advisable to hesitate a little for a short reflection before you undertake the heavy responsibility of a woman?

SIR HARCOURT. No: hesitation destroys the romance of a *faux pas,* and reduces it to the level of a mere mercantile calculation.

COOL. What is to be done with Mr. Charles?

SIR HARCOURT. Ay, much against my will, Lady Gay prevailed on me to permit him to remain. You, Cool, must return him to college. Pass through London, and deliver these papers: here is a small notice of the coming elopement for the *Morning Post;* this, by an eye-witness, for the *Herald;* this, with all the particulars, for the *Chronicle;* and the full and circumstantial account for the evening journals—after which, meet us at Boulogne.

COOL. Very good, Sir Harcourt. (*Going.*)

SIR HARCOURT. Lose no time. Remember—Hotel Anglais, Boulogne-sur-Mer. And, Cool, bring a few copies with you, and don't forget to distribute some amongst very particular friends.

COOL. It shall be done. (*Exit* COOL.)

SIR HARCOURT. With what indifference does a man of the world view the approach of the most perilous catastrophe! My position, hazardous as it is, entails none of that nervous excitement which a neophyte in the school of fashion would feel. I am as cool and steady as possible. Habit, habit! Oh! how many roses will fade upon the cheek of beauty, when the defalcation of Sir Harcourt Courtly is whispered—then hinted—at last, confirmed and bruited. I think I see them. Then, on my return, they will not dare to eject me—I am their sovereign! Whoever attempts to think of treason, I'll banish him from the West End—I'll cut him—I'll put him out of fashion!

(*Enter* LADY GAY.)

LADY GAY. Sir Harcourt!

SIR HARCOURT. At your feet.

LADY GAY. I had hoped you would have repented.

SIR HARCOURT. Repented!

LADY GAY. Have you not come to say it was a jest?—say you have!

SIR HARCOURT. Love is too sacred a subject to be trifled with. Come, let us fly! See, I have procured disguises—

LADY GAY. My courage begins to fail me. Let me return.

SIR HARCOURT. Impossible!

LADY GAY. Where do you intend to take me?

SIR HARCOURT. You shall be my guide. The carriage waits.

LADY GAY. You will never desert me?

SIR HARCOURT. Desert! Oh, heavens! Nay, do not hesitate—flight, now, alone is left to your desperate situation! Come, every moment is laden with danger. (*They are going.*)

LADY GAY. Oh! gracious!

SIR HARCOURT. Hush! what is it?

LADY GAY. I have forgotten—I must return.

SIR HARCOURT. Impossible!

LADY GAY. I must! I must! I have left Max—a pet staghound, in his basket—without whom, life would be unendurable—I could not exist!

SIR HARCOURT. No, no. Let him be sent after us in a hamper.

LADY GAY. In a hamper! Remorseless man! Go—you love me not. How would you like to be sent after me—in a hamper? Let me fetch him. Hark! I hear him squeal! Oh! Max—Max!

SIR HARCOURT. Hush! for heaven's sake. They'll imagine you're calling the Squire. I hear footsteps; where can I retire?

(*Enter* MEDDLE, SPANKER, DAZZLE, *and* MAX. LADY GAY *screams.*)

MEDDLE. Spanker *versus* Courtly!—I subpoena every one of you as witnesses!—I have 'em ready—here they are—shilling a-piece. (*Giving them round.*)

LADY GAY. Where is Sir Harcourt?

MEDDLE. There!—bear witness!—call on the vile delinquent for protection!

SPANKER. Oh! his protection!

LADY GAY. What? ha!

MEDDLE. I'll swear I overheard the whole elopement planned—before any jury!—where's the book?

SPANKER. Do you hear, you profligate?

LADY GAY. Ha! ha! ha! ha!

DAZZLE. But where is this wretched Lothario?

MEDDLE. Ay, where is the defendant?

SPANKER. Where lies the hoary villain?

LADY GAY. What villain?

SPANKER. That will not serve you!—I'll not be blinded that way!

MEDDLE. We won't be blinded any way!

MAX. I must seek Sir Harcourt, and demand an explanation! Such a thing never occurred in Oak Hall before!—It must be cleared up! (*Exit.*)

MEDDLE (*aside to* SPANKER). Now, take my advice; remember your gender. Mind the notes I have given you.

SPANKER (*aside*). All right! Here they are! Now, madam, I have procured the highest legal opinion on this point.

MEDDLE. Hear! hear!

SPANKER. And the question resolves itself into a—into—What's this? (*Looks at notes.*)

MEDDLE. A nutshell!

SPANKER. Yes, we are in a nutshell. Will you, in every respect, subscribe to my requests—desires—commands—(*looks at notes*)—orders—imperative—indicative—injunctive—or otherwise?

LADY GAY (*aside*). 'Pon my life, he's actually going to assume the ribbons, and take the box-seat. I must put a stop to this. I will! It will all end in smoke. I know Sir Harcourt would rather run than fight!

DAZZLE. Oh! I smell powder!—command my services. My dear madam, can I be of any use?

SPANKER. Oh! a challenge!—I must consult my legal adviser.

MEDDLE. No! Impossible!

DAZZLE. Pooh! the easiest thing in life! Leave it to me: What has an attorney to do with affairs of honour?—they are out of his element.

MEDDLE. Compromise the question! Pull his nose!—we have no objection to that.

DAZZLE (*turning to* LADY GAY). Well, we have no objection either—have we?

LADY GAY. No!—pull his nose—that will be something.

MEDDLE. And, moreover, it is not exactly actionable!

DAZZLE. Isn't it!—thank you—I'll note down that piece of information—it may be useful.

MEDDLE. How! cheated out of my legal knowledge.

LADY GAY. Mr. Spanker, I am determined!—I insist upon a challenge being sent to Sir Harcourt Courtly!—and—mark me—if you refuse to fight him—I will.

MEDDLE. Don't. Take my advice—you'll incapacit—

LADY GAY. Look you, Mr. Meddle, unless you wish me to horsewhip you, hold your tongue.

MEDDLE. What a she-tiger—I shall retire and collect my costs. (*Exit.*)

LADY GAY. Mr. Spanker, oblige me by writing as I dictate.

SPANKER. He's gone—and now I am defenceless! Is this the fate of husbands?—A duel!—Is this the result of becoming master of my own family?

LADY GAY. "Sir, the situation in which you were discovered with my wife, admits neither of explanation nor apology."

SPANKER. Oh, yes! but it does—I don't believe you really intended to run quite away.

LADY GAY. You do not; but I know better, I say I did! and if it had not been for your unfortunate interruption, I do not know where I might have been by this time. Go on.

SPANKER. "Nor apology." I'm writing my own death-warrant,—committing suicide on compulsion.

LADY GAY. "The bearer will arrange all preliminary matters, for another day must see this sacrilege expiated by your life, or that of

"Yours very sincerely,

"Dolly Spanker."

Now, Mr. Dazzle. (*Gives it over his head.*)

DAZZLE. The document is as sacred as if it were a hundred-pound bill.

LADY GAY. We trust to your discretion.

SPANKER. His discretion! Oh, put your head in a tiger's mouth, and trust to his discretion!

DAZZLE (*sealing letter, etc., with* SPANKER'S *seal*). My dear Lady Gay, matters of this kind are indigenous to my nature, independently of their pervading fascination to all humanity; but this is more especially delightful, as you may perceive I shall be the intimate and bosom friend of both parties.

LADY GAY. Is it not the only alternative in such a case?

DAZZLE. It is a beautiful panacea in any, in every case. (*Going—returns.*) By the way, where would you like this party of pleasure to come off? Open air shooting is pleasant enough, but if I might venture to advise, we could order half a dozen of that Madeira and a box of cigars into the billiard-room, so make a night of it; take up the irons every now and then; string for first shot, and blaze away at one another in an amicable and gentlemanlike way; so conclude the matter before the potency of the liquor could disturb the individuality of the object, or the smoke of the cigars render the outline dubious. Does such an arrangement coincide with your views?

LADY GAY. Perfectly.

DAZZLE. I trust shortly to be the harbinger of happy tidings. (*Exit.*)

SPANKER (*coming forward*). Lady Gay Spanker, are you ambitious of becoming a widow?

LADY GAY. Why, Dolly, woman is at best but weak, and weeds become me.

SPANKER. Female! am I to be immolated on the altar of your vanity?

LADY GAY. If you become pathetic, I shall laugh.

SPANKER. Farewell—base, heartless, unfeeling woman! (*Exit.*)

LADY GAY. Ha! well, so I am. I am heartless, for he is a dear, good little fellow, and I ought not to play upon his feelings: but 'pon my life he sounds so well up at concert pitch, that I feel disinclined to untune him. Poor Dolly, I didn't think he cared so much about me. I will put him out of pain. (*Exit.* SIR HARCOURT *comes down.*)

SIR HARCOURT. I have been a fool! a dupe to my own vanity. I shall be pointed at as a ridiculous old coxcomb—and so I am. The hour of conviction is *arrived.* Have I deceived myself?—Have I turned all my senses inward—looking towards self—always self?—and has the world been ever laughing at me? Well, if they have, I will revert the joke; —they may say I am an old ass; but I will prove that I am neither too old to repent my folly, nor such an ass as to flinch from confessing it. A blow half met is but half felt.

(*Enter* DAZZLE.)

DAZZLE. Sir Harcourt, may I be permitted the honour of a few minutes' conversation with you?

SIR HARCOURT. With pleasure.

DAZZLE. Have the kindness to throw your eye over that. (*Gives the letter.*)

SIR HARCOURT (*reads*). "Situation—my wife—apology—expiate—my life." Why, this is intended for a challenge.

DAZZLE. Why, indeed, I am perfectly aware that it is not quite *en regle* in the couching, for with that I had nothing to do; but I trust that the irregularity of the composition will be confounded in the beauty of the subject.

SIR HARCOURT. Mr. Dazzle, are you in earnest?

DAZZLE. Sir Harcourt Courtly, upon my honour I am, and I hope that no previous engagement will interfere with an immediate reply *in propriâ personâ.* We have fixed upon the billiard-room as the scene of action, which I have just seen properly illuminated in honour of the occasion; and, by-the-bye, if your implements are not handy, I can oblige you with a pair of the sweetest things you ever handled—hair-triggered

—saw grip; heir-looms in my family. I regard them almost in the light of relations.

SIR HARCOURT. Sir, I shall avail myself of one of your relatives. (*Aside.*) One of the hereditaments of my folly—I must accept it. (*Aloud.*) Sir, I shall be happy to meet Mr. Spanker at any time or place he may appoint.

DAZZLE. The sooner the better, sir. Allow me to offer you my arm. I see you understand these matters;—my friend Spanker is wofully ignorant—miserably uneducated. (*Exeunt.*)

(*Re-enter* MAX, *with* GRACE.)

MAX. Give ye joy, girl, give ye joy. Sir Harcourt Courtly must consent to waive all title to your hand in favour of his son Charles.

GRACE. Oh, indeed! Is that the pith of your congratulation—humph! the exchange of an old fool for a young one? Pardon me if I am not able to distinguish the advantage.

MAX. Advantage!

GRACE. Moreover, by what right am I a transferable cipher in the family of Courtly? So, then, my fate is reduced to this, to sacrifice my fortune, or unite myself with a worm-eaten edition of the Classics!

MAX. Why, he certainly is not such a fellow as I could have chosen for my little Grace; but consider, to retain fifteen thousand ayear! Now, tell me honestly—but why should I say *honestly?* Speak, girl, would you rather not have the lad?

GRACE. Why do you ask me?

MAX. Why, look ye, I'm an old fellow; another hunting season or two, and I shall be in at my own death—I can't leave you this house and land, because they are entailed, nor can I say I'm sorry for it, for it is a good law; but I have a little box with my Grace's name upon it, where, since your father's death and miserly will, I have yearly placed a certain sum to be yours, should you refuse to fulfil the conditions prescribed.

GRACE. My own dear uncle! (*Clasping him round the neck.*)

MAX. Pooh! pooh! what's to do now? Why, it was only a trifle—why, you little rogue, what are you crying about?

GRACE. Nothing, but—

MAX. But what? Come, out with it: Will you have young Courtly? (*Re-enter* LADY GAY.)

LADY GAY. Oh! Max, Max!

MAX. Why, what's amiss with you?

LADY GAY. I'm a wicked woman!

MAX. What have you done?

LADY GAY. Everything—oh, I thought Sir Harcourt was a coward, but now I find a man may be a coxcomb without being a poltroon. Just to show my husband how inconvenient it is to hold the ribands sometimes, I made him send a challenge to the old fellow, and he, to my surprise, accepted it, and is going to blow my Dolly's brains out in the billiard-room.

MAX. The devil!

LADY GAY. Just when I imagined I had got my whip hand of him again, out comes my linch-pin—and over I go—oh!

MAX. I will soon put a stop to that—a duel under my roof! Murder in Oak Hall! I'll shoot them both! (*Exit.*)

GRACE. Are you really in earnest?

LADY GAY. Do you think it looks like a joke? Oh! Dolly, if you allow yourself to be shot, I will never forgive you—never! Ah, he is a great fool, Grace! but I can't tell why, but I would sooner lose my bridle hand than he should be hurt on my account. (*Enter* SIR HARCOURT COURTLY.) Tell me—tell me—have you shot him—is he dead—my dear Sir Harcourt? You horrid old brute—have you killed him? I shall never forgive myself. (*Exit.*)

GRACE. Oh! Sir Harcourt, what has happened?

SIR HARCOURT. Don't be alarmed, I beg—your uncle interrupted us—discharged the weapons—locked the challenger up in the billiard-room to cool his rage.

GRACE. Thank heaven!

SIR HARCOURT. Miss Grace, to apologise for my conduct were useless, more especially as I am confident that no feelings of indignation or sorrow for my late acts are cherished by you; but still, reparation is in my power, and I not only waive all title, right, or claim to your person or your fortune, but freely admit your power to bestow them on a more worthy object.

GRACE. This generosity, Sir Harcourt, is most unexpected.

SIR HARCOURT. No, not generosity, but simply justice, justice!

GRACE. May I still beg a favour?

SIR HARCOURT. Claim anything that is mine to grant.

GRACE. You have been duped by Lady Gay Spanker, I have also been cheated and played upon by her and Mr. Hamilton—may I beg that the contract between us may, to all appearances, be still held good?

SIR HARCOURT. Certainly, although I confess I cannot see the point of your purpose.

(*Enter* MAX, *with* YOUNG COURTLY.)

MAX. Now, Grace, I have brought the lad.

GRACE. Thank you, uncle, but the trouble was quite unnecessary—Sir Harcourt holds to his original contract.

MAX. The deuce he does!

GRACE. And I am willing—nay, eager, to become Lady Courtly.

YOUNG COURTLY (*aside*). The deuce you are!

MAX. But, Sir Harcourt—

SIR HARCOURT. One word, Max, for an instant. (*They retire.*)

YOUNG COURTLY (*aside*). What can this mean? Can it be possible that I have been mistaken—that she is not in love with Augustus Hamilton?

GRACE. Now we shall find how he intends to bend the haughty Grace.

YOUNG COURTLY. Madam—Miss, I mean,—are you really in love with my father?

GRACE. No, indeed I am not.

YOUNG COURTLY. Are you in love with any one else?

GRACE. No, or I should not marry him.

YOUNG COURTLY. Then you actually accept him as your real husband?

GRACE. In the common acceptation of the word.

YOUNG COURTLY (*aside*). Hang me if I have not been a pretty fool! (*Aloud.*) Why do you marry him, if you don't care about him?

GRACE. To save my fortune.

YOUNG COURTLY (*aside*). Mercenary, cold-hearted girl! (*Aloud.*) But if there be any one you love in the least—marry him;—were you never in love?

GRACE. Never!

YOUNG COURTLY (*aside*). Oh! what an ass I've been! (*Aloud.*) I heard Lady Gay mention something about a Mr. Hamilton.

GRACE. Ah, yes, a person who, after an acquaintanceship of two days, had the assurance to make love to me, and I—

YOUNG COURTLY. Yes,—you—Well?

GRACE. I pretended to receive his attentions.

YOUNG COURTLY (*aside*). It was the best pretence I ever saw.

GRACE. An absurd, vain, conceited coxcomb, who appeared to imagine that I was so struck with his fulsome speech, that he could turn me round his finger.

YOUNG COURTLY (*aside*). My very thoughts!

GRACE. But he was mistaken.

YOUNG COURTLY (*aside*). Confoundedly! (*Aloud.*) Yet you seemed rather concerned about the news of his death?

GRACE. His accident! No, but—

YOUNG COURTLY. But what?

GRACE (*aside*). What can I say? (*Aloud.*) Ah! but my maid Pert's brother is a post-boy, and I thought he might have sustained an injury, poor boy.

YOUNG COURTLY (*aside*). Damn the post-boy! (*Aloud.*) Madam, if the retention of your fortune be the plea on which you are about to bestow your hand on one you do not love, and whose very actions speak his carelessness for that inestimable jewel he is incapable of appreciating—Know that I am devotedly, madly attached to you.

GRACE. You, sir? Impossible!

YOUNG COURTLY. Not at all,—but inevitable,—I have been so for a long time.

GRACE. Why, you never saw me till last night.

YOUNG COURTLY. I have seen you in imagination—you are the ideal I have worshipped.

GRACE. Since you press me into a confession,—which nothing but this could bring me to speak,—know, I did love poor Augustus Hamilton—(*Re-enter* MAX *and* SIR HARCOURT.) but he—he is—no—more! Pray, spare me, sir.

YOUNG COURTLY (*aside*). She loves me! And, oh! what a situation I am in!—if I own I am the man, my Governor will overhear, and ruin me—if I do not, she'll marry him.—What is to be done?

(*Enter* LADY GAY.)

LADY GAY. Where have you put my Dolly? I have been racing all round the house—tell me, is he quite dead!

MAX. I'll have him brought in. (*Exit.*)

SIR HARCOURT. My dear madam, you must perceive this unfortunate occurrence was no fault of mine. I was compelled to act as I have done—I was willing to offer any apology, but that resource was excluded, as unacceptable.

LADY GAY. I know—I know—'twas I made with him that letter—there was no apology required—'twas I that apparently seduced you from the paths of propriety,—'twas all a joke, and here is the end of it. (*Enter* MAX, MR. SPANKER, *and* DAZZLE.) Oh! if he had but lived to say, "I forgive you, Gay!"

SPANKER. So I do!

LADY GAY (*seeing him*). Ah! he is alive!

SPANKER. Of course I am!

LADY GAY. Ha! ha! ha! (*Embraces him.*) I will never hunt again—unless you wish it. Sell your stable—

SPANKER. No, no—do what you like—say what you like for the future! I find the head of a family has less ease and more responsibility than I, as a member, could have anticipated. I abdicate!

(*Enter* COOL.)

SIR HARCOURT. Ah! Cool, here! (*Aside to* COOL.) You may destroy those papers—I have altered my mind,—and I do not intend to elope at present. Where are they?

COOL. As you seemed particular, Sir Harcourt, I sent them off by mail to London.

SIR HARCOURT. Why, then, a full description of the whole affair will be published to-morrow.

COOL. Most irretrievably!

SIR HARCOURT. You must post to town immediately, and stop the press.

COOL. Beg pardon—they would see me hanged first, Sir Harcourt; they don't frequently meet with such a profitable lie.

SERVANT (*without*). No, sir! no, sir!

(*Enter* SIMPSON.)

SIMPSON. Sir, there is a gentleman, who calls himself Mr. Solomon Isaacs, insists upon following me up.

(*Enter* MR. SOLOMON ISAACS.)

ISAACS. Mr. Courtly, you will excuse my performance of a most disagreeable duty at any time, but more especially in such a manner. I must beg the honour of your company to town.

SIR HARCOURT. What!—how!—what for?

ISAACS. For debt, Sir Harcourt.

SIR HARCOURT. Arrested?—impossible! Here must be some mistake.

ISAACS. Not the slightest, sir. Judgment has been given in five cases, for the last three months; but Mr. Courtly is an eel rather too nimble for my men.—We have been on his track, and traced him down to this village, with Mr. Dazzle.

DAZZLE. Ah! Isaacs! how are you?

ISAACS. Thank you, sir. (*Speaks to* SIR HARCOURT.)

MAX. Do you know him?

DAZZLE. Oh, intimately! Distantly related to his family—same arms on our escutcheon—empty purse falling through a hole in a—pocket: motto, "Requiescat in pace"—which means, "Let virtue be its own reward."

SIR HARCOURT (*to* ISAACS). Oh, I thought there was a mistake! Know, to your misfortune, that Mr. Hamilton was the person you dogged to Oak Hall, between whom and my son a most remarkable likeness exists.

ISAACS. Ha! ha! Know, to your misfortune, Sir Harcourt, that Mr. Hamilton and Mr. Courtly are one and the same person!

SIR HARCOURT. Charles!

YOUNG COURTLY. Concealment is in vain—I am Augustus Hamilton.

SIR HARCOURT. Hang me, if I didn't think it all along! Oh, you infernal, cozening dog!

ISAACS. Now, then, Mr. Hamilton—

GRACE. Stay, sir—Mr. Charles Courtly is under age—ask his father.

SIR HARCOURT. Ahem!—I won't—I won't pay a shilling of the rascal's debts—not a sixpence!

GRACE. Then, I will—you may retire. (*Exit* ISAACS.)

YOUNG COURTLY. I can now perceive the generous point of your conduct towards me; and, believe me, I appreciate, and will endeavour to deserve it.

MAX. Ha! ha! Come, Sir Harcourt, you have been fairly beaten—you must forgive him—say you will.

SIR HARCOURT. So, sir, it appears you have been leading, covertly, an infernal town life?

YOUNG COURTLY. Yes, please, father. (*Imitating* MASTER CHARLES.)

SIR HARCOURT. None of your humbug sir! (*Aside.*) He is my own son—how could I expect him to keep out of the fire? (*Aloud.*) And you, Mr. Cool!—have you been deceiving me?

COOL. Oh! Sir Harcourt, if your perception was played upon, how could I be expected to see?

SIR HARCOURT. Well, it would be useless to withhold my hand. There, boy! (*He gives his hand to* YOUNG COURTLY. GRACE *comes down on the other side, and offers her hand; he takes it.*) What is all this? What do you want?

YOUNG COURTLY. Your blessing, father.

GRACE. If you please, father.

SIR HARCOURT. Oho! the mystery is being solved. So, so, you young scoundrel, you have been making love—under the rose.

LADY GAY. He learnt that from you, Sir Harcourt.

SIR HARCOURT. Ahem! What would you do now, if I were to withhold my consent?

GRACE. *Do* without it.

MAX. The will says, if Grace marries any one but you,—her property reverts to your heir-apparent—and there he stands.

LADY GAY. Make virtue of necessity.

SPANKER. I married from inclination; and see how happy I am. And if ever I have a son—

LADY GAY. Hush! Dolly, dear!

SIR HARCOURT. Well! take her, boy! Although you are too young to marry. (*They retire with* MAX.)

LADY GAY. Am I forgiven, Sir Harcourt?

SIR HARCOURT. Ahem! Why—a—(*Aside.*) Have you really deceived me?

LADY GAY. Can you not see through this?

SIR HARCOURT. And you still love me?

LADY GAY. As much as I ever did.

SIR HARCOURT (*is about to kiss her hand, when* SPANKER *interposes between*). A very handsome ring, indeed.

SPANKER. Very. (*Puts her arm in his, and they go up.*)

SIR HARCOURT. Poor little Spanker!

MAX (*coming down, aside to* SIR HARCOURT). One point I wish to have settled. Who is Mr. Dazzle?

SIR HARCOURT. A relative of the Spankers, he told me.

MAX. Oh, no, a near connexion of yours.

SIR HARCOURT. Never saw him before I came down here, in all my life. (*To* YOUNG COURTLY.) Charles, who is Mr. Dazzle?

YOUNG COURTLY. Dazzle, Dazzle,—will you excuse an impertinent question?—but who the deuce are you?

DAZZLE. Certainly. I have not the remotest idea.

ALL. How, sir?

DAZZLE. Simple question as you may think it, it would puzzle half the world to answer. One thing I can vouch—Nature made me a gentleman—that is, I live on the best that can be procured for credit. I never spend my own money when I can oblige a friend. I'm always thick on the winning horse. I'm an epidemic on the trade of a tailor. For further particulars, inquire of any sitting magistrate.

SIR HARCOURT. And these are the deeds which attest your title to the name of gentleman? I perceive that you have caught the infection of the present age. Charles, permit me, as your father, and you, sir, as his friend, to correct you on one point. Barefaced assurance is the vulgar substitute for gentlemanly ease; and there are many who, by aping the *vices* of the great, imagine that they elevate themselves to the rank of those, whose faults alone they copy. No, sir! The title of gentleman is the only one *out* of any monarch's gift, yet within the reach of every peasant. It should be engrossed by *Truth*—stamped with *Honour*—sealed with *good-feeling*—signed *Man*—and enrolled in every true young English heart.

The End

CASTE

T. W. Robertson came into a theatre of spectacular scenery and hokum and insisted on a modicum of truth in the presentation of

> the merest everyday stories—stories of the joys and sorrows of ordinary, unromantic people, stories of youth and age, love, parting, and reunion, of quarrels and reconciliation, of modest acts of chivalry and self-sacrifice, the whole stippled with a thousand humorous and pathetic touches, yet narrated in language devoid of ornament and set in surroundings of the most commonplace description.

There you have the tribute of Sir Arthur Wing Pinero to the "vision and courage" of his predecessor, some explanation of why *Caste* (1867) was as important to the development of the drama as was *The Second Mrs. Tanqueray* (1893). Robertson did not cope with the real and important social problems of his time any more than did Pinero; the Indian Mutiny is a "painted" and not a "practical" part of *Caste,* and the clash of classes is wholly a theatrical confrontation. But in telling the story of the Honorable George D'Alroy's uppity friends and his wife Esther's frowzy relations, Robertson succeeded in creating at least the illusion of reality.

Like all pioneers, even Ibsen, Robertson was quickly left behind. Today he seems dated. The *New Statesman* (August 8, 1925) voiced its objections when the reaction against Robertson was at its height:

> *Caste* has no body to it. It has neither psychology or wit, the humour is crude, the sentiment is obvious, the language is stilted and platitudinous.

And then the critic was compelled to add, "Yet Robertson was the best English playwright of his age."

What was there about Robertson in his time that drew the public to the Prince of Wales' Theatre to see his rapid succession of comedies, that inspired the young Bernard Shaw, that outraged the old school of actors, and that gave birth to a whole new style in the theatre? In half a dozen years Robertson moved from his early *The Half-Caste, or, The Poison'd Pearl* (1856) to *Caste,* from the melodrama to the modern drama. His intellectual content may have been slight—"Caste is a good thing if it's not carried too far," Robertson said—but his sympathy for his characters, his knowledge of them and his power to bring them to life on the stage speaking a reasonable facsimile of human speech, were not only remarkable but for too long unique. The effect that he produced on his contemporaries was immense, as the critic Clement Scott testified in 1896:

> I do not wish obstinately to pose as a "laudator temporis acti" when I say that I shall never see "Caste" played again as I did on the night of the 6th of April, 1867. . . .
>
> You must never forget that in nearly all these cases Robertson drew from the life . . . [and] gave the exact manner of the man. And the scene with the baby, as played by Fred Younge [George D'Alroy], was the most touching, natural, and pathetic thing, I have ever seen on the modern stage. Picture it! A great, hulking, handsome, well-bred officer, who becomes a "great baby" again, lisping inarticulate sentences over the infant that he could have crushed to death in his great, strong, manly arms. The modern generation will doubtless say, "What rot!" But I said then, and repeat now, "How true!"

Scott goes on to praise the play for its "change from mock heroics to truth," for the part of Esther Eccles ("one of the most sympathetic parts ever written for a woman"), for its honest humanity so out-of-fashion "because the age is artificial and supposed to be unsentimental." Robertson's constant subject, the one that impressed not only critics of his day but the public itself, is the truth of the representation.

Today Robertson is best known for the realism he introduced into the staging rather than the writing of plays, for the "cup-and-saucer" drama, for chairs placed on the stage and not painted on the backdrop, for doors and windows that opened and closed, for bric-a-brac in the living room and real Staffordshire dogs on the mantlepiece, even for a certain realism that he demanded of the actors (whom he ruled with an iron hand). This attention to detail seems unimpressive to us now, but it was important; it led to attention to every detail of the production. Read Robertson's elaborate stage directions with care, and you will see that the man was not far wrong who claimed that *Caste,* given good actors, could be played entirely in pantomime, with no dialogue at all.

CASTE

An Original Comedy in Three Acts

by

T. W. Robertson

First produced, by the Bancrofts, at the Prince of Wales's Theatre, April 6, 1867, with the following cast:

Hon. GEORGE D'ALROY	Mr. Frederick Younge
Captain HAWTREE	Mr. Squire Bancroft
ECCLES	Mr. George Honey
SAM GERRIDGE	Mr. John Hare
DIXON	Mr. Hill
Marquise de ST. MAUR	Miss Larkin
ESTHER ECCLES	Miss Lydia Foote
POLLY ECCLES	Miss Marie Wilton

ACT I *The Little House in Stangate*—COURTSHIP

Eight months pass

ACT II *The Lodgings in Mayfair*—MATRIMONY

A year passes

ACT III *The Little House in Stangate*—WIDOWHOOD

ACT I

SCENE: *A plain set chamber, paper soiled. A window,* C., *with practicable blind; street backing and iron railings. Door practicable,* R. 3 E.; *when opened showing street door (practicable). Fire-place,* L.; *two-hinged gas-burners on each side of mantelpiece. Sideboard cupboard in recess,* L. *3* E.; *tea-things, teapot, tea-caddy, tea-tray, &c., on it. Long table,* L.C., *before fire; old piece of carpet and rug down; plain chairs; book-shelf back* L.; *a small table under it with ballet-shoe and skirt on it; bunch of benefit bills hanging under book-shelf. Theatrical printed portraits, framed, hanging about; chimney glass clock; box of lucifers and ornaments on mantelshelf; kettle on hob, and fire laid; door-mats on the outside of door. Bureau,* R.

(*Rapping heard at door* R., *the handle is then shaken as curtain rises. The door is unlocked. Enter* GEORGE D'ALROY.)

GEORGE. Told you so; the key was left under the mat in case I came. They're not back from rehearsal. (*Hangs up hat on peg near door as* HAWTREE *enters.*) Confound rehearsal! (*Crosses to fire-place.*)

HAWTREE (C. *of stage, back to audience, looking round*). And this is the fairy's bower!

GEORGE. Yes! And this is the fairy's fire-place; the fire is laid. I'll light it. (*Lights fire with lucifer from mantelpiece.*)

HAWTREE (*turning to* GEORGE). And this is the abode rendered blessed by her abiding. It is here that she dwells, walks, talks—eats and drinks. Does she eat and drink?

GEORGE. Yes, heartily. I've seen her.

HAWTREE. And you are really spoons!—case of true love—hit—dead.

GEORGE. Right through. Can't live away from her. (*With elbow on end of mantelpiece down stage.*)

HAWTREE. Poor old Dal! and you've brought me over the water to—

GEORGE. Stangate.

HAWTREE. Stangate—to see her for the same sort of reason that when a patient is in a dangerous state one doctor calls in another—for a consultation.

GEORGE. Yes. Then the patient dies.

HAWTREE. Tell us all about it—you know I've been away. (*Sits* R. *of table, leg on a chair.*)

GEORGE. Well, then, eighteen months ago——

HAWTREE. Oh, cut that; you told me all about that. You went to a theatre, and saw a girl in a ballet, and you fell in love.

GEORGE. Yes. I found out that she was an amiable, good girl.

HAWTREE. Of course; cut that. We'll credit her with all the virtues and accomplishments.

GEORGE. Who worked hard to support a drunken father.

HAWTREE. Oh! the father's a drunkard, is he? The father does not inherit the daughter's virtues?

GEORGE. No. I hate him.

HAWTREE. Naturally. Quite so! quite so!

GEORGE. And she—that is, Esther—is very good to her younger sister.

HAWTREE. Younger sister also angelic, amiable, accomplished, &c., &c.

GEORGE. Um—good enough, but got a temper—large temper. Well, with some difficulty I got to speak to her. I mean to Esther. Then I was allowed to see her to her door here.

HAWTREE. I know—pastry-cooks—Richmond dinner—and all that.

GEORGE. You're too fast. Pastry-cooks—yes. Richmond—no. Your knowledge of the world, fifty yards round barracks, misleads you. I saw her nearly every day, and I kept on falling in love—falling and falling, till I thought I should never reach the bottom; then I met you.

HAWTREE. I remember the night when you told me; but I thought it was only an amourette. However, if the fire is a conflagration, subdue it; try dissipation.

GEORGE. I have.

HAWTREE. What success?

GEORGE. None; dissipation brought me bad health and self-contempt, a sick head and a sore heart.

HAWTREE. Foreign travel; absence makes the heart grow (*slight pause*) —stronger. Get leave and cut away.

GEORGE. I did get leave, and I did cut away; and while away, I was miserable and a gone-er coon than ever.

HAWTREE. What's to be done? (*Sits cross-legged on chair, facing* GEORGE.)

GEORGE. Don't know. That's the reason I asked you to come over and see.

HAWTREE. Of course, Dal, you're not such a sort as to think of marriage. You know what your mother is. Either you are going to behave properly, with a proper regard for the world, and all that, you know; or you're going to do the other thing. Now, the question is, what do you mean to do? The girl is a nice girl, no doubt; but as to your making her Mrs. D'Alroy, the thing is out of the question.

GEORGE. Why? What should prevent me?

HAWTREE. Caste!—the inexorable law of caste! The social law, so becoming and so good, that commands like to mate with like, and forbids a giraffe to fall in love with a squirrel.

GEORGE. But my dear Bark——

HAWTREE. My dear Dal, all those marriages of people with common people are all very well in novels and in plays on the stage, because the real people don't exist, and have no relatives who exist, and no connections, and so no harm's done, and it's rather interesting to look at; but in real life with real relations, and real mothers, and so forth, it's absolute bosh. It's worse—it's utter social and personal annihilation and damnation.

GEORGE. As to my mother, I haven't thought about her. (*Sits corner of table* L.)

HAWTREE. Of course not. Lovers are so damned selfish; they never think of anybody but themselves.

GEORGE. My father died when I was three years old, and she married again before I was six, and married a Frenchman.

HAWTREE. A nobleman of the most ancient families in France, of equal blood to her own. She obeyed the duties imposed on her by her station and by caste.

GEORGE. Still, it caused a separation and a division between us, and I never see my brother, because he lives abroad. Of course the Marquise de St. Maur is my mother, and I look upon her with a sort of superstitious awe. (*Moves chair with which he has been twisting about during speech from* R. *of table, to corner* L.)

HAWTREE. She's a grand Brahmin priestess.

GEORGE. Just so; and I know I'm a fool. Now you're clever, Bark—a little too clever, I think. You're paying your *devoirs*—that's the correct word, isn't it?—to Lady Florence Carberry, the daughter of a countess. She's above you—you've no title. Is she to forget *her* caste?

HAWTREE. That argument doesn't apply. A man can be no more than a gentleman.

GEORGE. 'True hearts are more than coronets,
And simple faith than Norman blood.'

HAWTREE. Now, George, if you're going to consider this question from the point of view of poetry, you're off to No Man's Land, where I won't follow you.

GEORGE. No gentleman can be ashamed of the woman he loves. No matter what her original station, once his wife, he raises her to his rank.

HAWTREE. Yes, he raises her—*her*; but her connections—her relatives. How about them?

(ECCLES *enters, door* R.)

ECCLES (*outside*). Polly! Polly! (*Enters.*) Why the devil——(GEORGE *crosses to* HAWTREE, *who rises.* ECCLES *sees them, and assumes a deferential manner.*)

ECCLES. Oh, Mr. De-Alroy! I didn't see you, sir. Good afternoon; the same to you, sir, and many on 'em. (*Puts hat on bureau and comes down* R.)

HAWTREE. Who is this?

GEORGE. This is papa.

HAWTREE. Ah! (*Turns up to book-shelf, scanning* ECCLES *through eye-glass.*)

GEORGE. Miss Eccles and her sister not returned from rehearsal yet?

ECCLES. No, sir, they have not. I expect 'em in directly. I hope you've been quite well since I seen you last, sir?

GEORGE. Quite, thank you; and how have you been, Mr. Eccles?

ECCLES. Well, sir, I have not been the thing at all. My 'elth, sir, and my spirits is both broke. I'm not the man I used to be. I am not accustomed to this sort of thing. I've seen better days, but they are gone—most like for ever. It is a melancholy thing, sir, for a man of my time of life to look back on better days that are gone most like for ever.

GEORGE. I dare say.

ECCLES. Once proud and prosperous, now poor and lowly. Once master of a shop, I am now, by the pressure of circumstances over which I have no control, driven to seek work and not to find it. Poverty is a dreadful thing, sir, for a man as has once been well off.

GEORGE. I dare say.

ECCLES (*sighing*). Ah, sir, the poor and lowly is often 'ardly used. What chance has the working man?

HAWTREE. None when he don't work.

ECCLES. We are all equal in mind and feeling.

GEORGE (*aside*). I hope not.

ECCLES. I am sorry, gentlemen, that I cannot offer you any refreshment; but luxury and me has long been strangers.

GEORGE. I am very sorry for your misfortunes, Mr. Eccles. (*Looking round at* HAWTREE, *who turns away.*) May I hope that you will allow me to offer you this trifling loan? (*Giving him a half-sovereign.*)

ECCLES. Sir, you're a gentleman. One can tell a real gentleman with half a sov—I mean with half a eye—a real gentleman understands the natural emotions of the working man. Pride, sir, is a thing as should be put down by the strong 'and of pecuniary necessity. There's a friend of mine round the corner as I promised to meet on a little matter of business; so, if you will excuse me, sir——

GEORGE. With pleasure.

ECCLES (*going up* R.). Sorry to leave you, gentlemen, but——

GEORGE. Don't stay on my account.
HAWTREE. Don't mention it.

ECCLES. Business is business. (*Goes up to door* R.) The girls will be in directly. Good afternoon, gentlemen—good afternoon—(*going out*)—good afternoon! (*Exit, door* R. GEORGE *sits in chair, corner of table* R.)

HAWTREE (*coming down* L. *of table*). Papa is not nice, but (*sitting on corner of table, down stage*)——

'True hearts are more than coronets,
And simple faith than Norman blood.'

Poor George! I wonder what your mamma—the Most Noble the Marquise de St. Maur—would think of Papa Eccles. Come, Dal, allow that there *is something* in caste. Conceive that dirty ruffian—that rinsing of stale beer—that walking tap-room, for a father-in-law. Take a spin to Central America. Forget her.

GEORGE. Can't.

HAWTREE. You'll be wretched and miserable with her.

GEORGE. I'd rather be wretched with her, than miserable without her. (HAWTREE *takes out cigar case.*) Don't smoke here!

HAWTREE. Why not?

GEORGE. She'll be coming in directly.

HAWTREE. I don't think she'd mind.

GEORGE. I should. Do you smoke before Lady Florence Carberry?

HAWTREE (*closing case*). Ha! You're suffering from a fit of the morals.

GEORGE. What's that?

HAWTREE. The morals is a disease like the measles, that attacks the young and innocent.

GEORGE (*with temper*). You talk like Mephistopheles, without the cleverness. (*Goes up to window, and looks at watch.*)

HAWTREE (*arranging cravat at glass*). I don't pretend to be a particularly good sort of fellow, nor a particularly bad sort of fellow. I suppose I'm about the average standard sort of thing, and I don't like to see a friend go down hill to the devil while I can put the drag on. (*Turning, with back to fire.*) Here is a girl of very humble station—poor, and all that, with a drunken father, who evidently doesn't care how he gets money so long as he don't work for it. Marriage! Pah! Couldn't the thing be arranged?

GEORGE. Hawtree, cut that! (*At window.*) She's here! (*Goes to door and opens it.*)

(*Enter* ESTHER, *door* R.)

GEORGE (*flurried at sight of her*). Good morning. I got here before you, you see.

ESTHER. Good morning. (*Sees* HAWTREE—*slight pause, in which* HAWTREE *has removed his hat.*)

GEORGE. I've taken the liberty—I hope you won't be angry—of asking you to let me present a friend of mine to you: Miss Eccles—Captain Hawtree. (HAWTREE *bows.* GEORGE *assists* ESTHER *in taking off bonnet and shawl.*)

HAWTREE (*back* L., *aside*). Pretty.

ESTHER (*aside*). Thinks too much of himself.

GEORGE (*hangs up bonnet and shawl on pegs*). You've had a late rehearsal. Where's Polly?

ESTHER. She stayed behind to buy something.

(*Enter* POLLY, *door* R.)

POLLY. Hallo! (*Head through door.*) How de do, Mr. D'Alroy? Oh! I'm tired to death. Kept at rehearsal by an old fool of a stage manager. But stage managers are always old fools—except when they are young. We shan't have time for any dinner, so I've brought something for tea.

ESTHER. What is it?

POLLY. Ham. (*Showing ham in paper.* ESTHER *sits* R. *at window. Crossing* R.C. *Seeing* HAWTREE.) Oh! I beg your pardon, sir. I didn't see you.

GEORGE. A friend of mine, Mary. Captain Hawtree—Miss Mary Eccles. (GEORGE *sits* L., *at window.*)

(POLLY *bows very low, 1* R., *2* L., *3* C., *half burlesquely, to* HAWTREE.)

HAWTREE. Charmed.

POLLY (*aside*). What a swell! Got nice teeth, and he knows it. How quiet we all are; let's talk about something. (*Hangs up her hat. She crosses to fire* L., *round table-front.* HAWTREE *crosses and places hat on bureau.*)

ESTHER. What can we talk about?

POLLY. Anything. Ham. Mr. D'Alroy, do you like ham?

GEORGE. I adore her—(POLLY *titters*)—I mean I adore it.

POLLY (*to* HAWTREE, *who has crossed to table* R., *watching* POLLY *undo paper containing the ham. She turns the plate on top of the ham still in the paper, then throws the paper aside and triumphantly brings the plate under* HAWTREE'*s nose,* HAWTREE *giving a little start back*). Do you like ham, sir? (*Very tragically.*)

HAWTREE. Yes.

POLLY. Now that is very strange. I should have thought you'd have been above ham. (*Getting tea-tray.*)

HAWTREE. May one ask why?

POLLY. You look above it. You look quite equal to tongue—glazed. (*Laughing.*) Mr. D'Alroy is here so often that he knows our ways. (*Getting tea-things from sideboard and placing them on table.*)

HAWTREE. I like everything that is piquante and fresh, and pretty and agreeable.

POLLY (*laying table all the time for tea*). Ah! you mean that for me. (*Curtseying.*) Oh! (*Sings.*) Tra, la, lal, la, la, la. (*Flourishes cup in his face; he retreats a step.*) Now I must put the kettle on. (GEORGE *and* ESTHER *are at window.*) Esther never does any work when Mr. D'Alroy is here. They're spooning; ugly word spooning, isn't it?—reminds one of red-currant jam. By the by, love *is* very like red-currant jam—at the first taste sweet, and afterwards shuddery. Do you ever spoon?

HAWTREE (*leaning across table*). I should like to do so at this moment.

POLLY. I dare say you would. No, you're too grand for me. You want taking down a peg—I mean a foot. Let's see—what are you—a corporal?

HAWTREE. Captain.

POLLY. I prefer a corporal. See here. Let's change about. You be corporal—it'll do you good, and I'll be 'my lady'.

HAWTREE. Pleasure.

POLLY. You must call me 'my lady', though, or you shan't have any ham.

HAWTREE. Certainly, 'my lady'; but I cannot accept your hospitality, for I'm engaged to dine.

POLLY. At what time?

HAWTREE. Seven.

POLLY. Seven! Why, that's half-past tea-time. Now corporal, you must wait on me.

HAWTREE. As the pages did of old.

POLLY. My lady.

HAWTREE. My lady.

POLLY. Here's the kettle, corporal. (*Holding out kettle at arm's length.* HAWTREE *looks at it through eye-glass.*)

HAWTREE. Very nice kettle!

POLLY. Take it into the back kitchen.

HAWTREE. Eh!

POLLY. Oh! I'm coming too.

HAWTREE. Ah! that alters the case. (*He takes out handkerchief and then takes hold of kettle—crosses to* R. *as* GEORGE *rises and comes down, slapping* HAWTREE *on back.* HAWTREE *immediately places kettle on the floor.* POLLY *throws herself into chair by fire-side up stage, and roars with laughter.* GEORGE *and* ESTHER *laugh.*)

GEORGE. What are you about?

HAWTREE. I'm about to fill the kettle.

ESTHER (*going to* POLLY). Mind what you are doing, Polly! What will Sam say?

POLLY. Whatever Sam chooses. What the sweetheart don't see the husband can't grieve at. Now then—Corporal!

HAWTREE. 'My lady!' (*Takes up kettle.*)

POLLY. Attention! Forward! March! and mind the soot don't drop upon your trousers. (*Exeunt* POLLY *and* HAWTREE, *door* R., HAWTREE *first.*)

ESTHER. What a girl it is—all spirits! The worst is that it is so easy to mistake her.

GEORGE. And so easy to find out your mistake. (*They cross to* L., *down stage,* ESTHER *first.*) But why won't you let me present you with a piano? (*Following* ESTHER.)

ESTHER. I don't want one.

GEORGE. You said you were fond of playing.

ESTHER. We may be fond of many things without having them. (*Leaning against end of table. Taking out letter.*) Now here is a gentleman says that he is attached to me.

GEORGE (*jealous*). May I know his name?

ESTHER. What for? It would be useless, as his solicitations—— (*Throws letter into fire.*)

GEORGE. I lit that fire.

ESTHER. Then burn these too. (GEORGE *crosses to fire.*) No, not that. (*Taking one back.*) I must keep that; burn the others. (GEORGE *throws letters on fire, crosses back of table quickly—takes hat from peg and goes to door as if leaving hurriedly.* ESTHER *takes chair* R. *of table and goes* C. *with it, noticing* GEORGE'*s manner.* GEORGE *hesitates at door. Shuts it quickly, hangs his hat up again and comes down to back of chair in which* ESTHER *has seated herself.*)

GEORGE. Who is that from?

ESTHER. Why do you wish to know?

GEORGE. Because I love you, and I don't think you love me, and I fear a rival.

ESTHER. You have none.

GEORGE. I know you have so many admirers.

ESTHER. They're nothing to me.

GEORGE. Not one?

ESTHER. No. They're admirers, but there's not a husband among them.

GEORGE. Not the writer of that letter?

ESTHER. Oh, I like him very much. (*Coquettishly.*)

GEORGE. Ah! (*Sighing.*)

ESTHER. And I'm very fond of this letter.

GEORGE. Then, Esther, you don't care for me.

ESTHER. Don't I! How do you know?

GEORGE. Because you won't let me read that letter.

ESTHER. It won't please you if you see it.

GEORGE. I dare say not. That's just the reason that I want to. You won't?

ESTHER (*hesitates*). I will. There! (*Giving it to him.*)

GEORGE (*reads*). 'Dear Madam.'

ESTHER. That's tender, isn't it?

GEORGE. 'The terms are four pounds—your dresses to be found. For eight weeks certain, and longer if you should suit. (GEORGE L., *in astonishment.*) I cannot close the engagement until the return of my partner. I expect him back today, and will write you as soon as I have seen him.—Yours very,' &c. Four pounds—find dresses. What does this mean?

ESTHER. It means that they want a Columbine for the pantomime at Manchester, and I think I shall get the engagement.

GEORGE. Manchester; then you'll leave London!

ESTHER. I must. (*Pathetically.*) You see this little house is on my shoulders. Polly only earns eighteen shillings a week, and father has been out of work a long, long time. I make the bread here, and it's hard to make sometimes. I've been mistress of this place, and forced to think ever since my mother died, and I was eight years old. Four pounds a week is a large sum, and I can save out of it. (*This speech is not to be spoken in a tone implying hardship.*)

GEORGE. But you'll go away, and I shan't see you.

ESTHER. P'raps it will be for the best. (*Rises and crosses* L.) What future is there for us? You're a man of rank, and I am a poor girl who gets her living by dancing. It would have been better that we had never met.

GEORGE. No.

ESTHER. Yes, it would, for I'm afraid that——

GEORGE. You love me?

ESTHER. I don't know. I'm not sure; but I think I do. (*Stops* L., *and turns half-face to* GEORGE.)

GEORGE (*trying to seize her hand*). Esther!

ESTHER. No. Think of the difference of our stations.

GEORGE. That's what Hawtree says. Caste! caste! curse caste! (*Goes up* C.)

ESTHER. If I go to Manchester it will be for the best. We must both try to forget each other.

GEORGE (*comes down* L., *and* L. *of table*). Forget you! no, Esther; let me——(*Seizing her hand.*)

POLLY (*without*). Mind what you're about. Oh dear! oh dear! (GEORGE *and* ESTHER *sit in window seat.*)

(*Enter* POLLY *and* HAWTREE, *door* R.)

POLLY. You nasty, great, clumsy, corporal, you've spilt the water all over my frock. Oh dear! (*Coming down* R.C., HAWTREE *puts kettle on ham on table.*) Take it off the ham! (HAWTREE *then places it on the mantelpiece.*)

POLLY. No, no; put it in the fire-place. (HAWTREE *does so.*) You've spoilt my frock. (*Sitting* C.)

HAWTREE. Allow me to offer you a new one. (*Crossing to* L.C.)

POLLY. No, I won't. You'll be calling to see how it looks when it's on. Haven't you got a handkerchief?

HAWTREE. Yes!

POLLY. Then wipe it dry. (HAWTREE *bends almost on one knee, and wipes dress, on her* L. *Enter* SAM, *whistling, door* R. *Throws cap into* HAWTREE'*s hat on drawers.*)

SAM (*sulkily*). Arternoon—yer didn't hear me knock!—the door was open. I'm afraid I intrude.

POLLY. No, you don't. We're glad to see you if you've got a handkerchief. Help to wipe this dry. (SAM *pulls out handkerchief from slop, and dropping on one knee snatches skirt of dress from* HAWTREE, *who looks up surprised.*)

HAWTREE. I'm very sorry. (*Rising.*) I beg your pardon. (*Business;* SAM *stares* HAWTREE *out.*)

POLLY. It won't spoil it.

SAM. The stain won't come out. (*Rising.*)

POLLY. It's only water!

SAM. Arternoon, Miss Eccles! (*To* ESTHER.) Arternoon, sir! (*To* GEORGE. POLLY *rises.*) Who's the other swell? (*To* POLLY.)

POLLY. I'll introduce you. (SAM R., POLLY C., HAWTREE L.) Captain Hawtree—Mr. Samuel Gerridge.

HAWTREE. Charmed, I'm sure. (*Staring at* SAM *through eye-glass.* SAM *acknowledges* HAWTREE'*s recognition by a 'chuck' of the head over left shoulder; going up to* GEORGE.) Who's this?

GEORGE. Polly's sweetheart.

HAWTREE. Oh! Now if I can be of no further assistance, I'll go. (*Comes back down* R. *to drawers.*)

POLLY. Going, corporal?

HAWTREE. Yaas! (*Business; taking up hat and stick from bureau he sees* SAM'*s cap. He picks it out carefully, and coming down stage* R., *examines it as a curiosity, drops it on the floor and pushes it away with his stick, at the same time moving backwards, causing him to bump against* SAM, *who turns round savagely.*) I beg your pardon! (*Crossing up stage.*) George, will you—(GEORGE *takes no notice.*) Will you—

GEORGE. What?

HAWTREE. Go with me?

GEORGE. Go? No!

HAWTREE (*coming down* C. *to* POLLY L.). Then, Miss Eccles—I mean 'my lady'. (*Shaking hands and going; as he backs away bumps against* SAM, *and business repeated.* HAWTREE *close to door* R., *keeping his eye on* SAM, *who has shown signs of anger.*)

POLLY. Good-bye, corporal!

HAWTREE (*at door*). Good-bye! Good afternoon, Mr.—Mr.—er—Pardon me.

SAM (*with constrained rage*). Gerridge, sir, Gerridge!

HAWTREE (*as if remembering name*). Ah! Gerridge. Good day. (*Exit, door* R.)

SAM (*turning to* POLLY *in awful rage*). Who's that fool? Who's that long idiot?

POLLY. I told you; Captain Hawtree.

SAM. What's 'e want 'ere?

POLLY. He's a friend of Mr. D'Alroy's.

SAM. Ugh! Isn't one of 'em enough?

POLLY. What do you mean?

SAM. For the neighbours to talk about. Who's he after?

POLLY. What do you mean by after? You're forgetting yourself, I think.

SAM. No, I'm not forgetting myself—I'm remembering you. What can a long fool of a swell dressed up to the nines within an inch of his life want with two girls of your class? Look at the difference of your stations! 'E don't come 'ere after any good. (*During the speech,* ESTHER *crosses to fire and sits before it in a low chair.* GEORGE *follows her, and sits on her* L.)

POLLY. Samuel!

SAM. I mean what I say. People should stick to their own class. Life's a railway journey, and Mankind's a passenger—first class, second class, third class. Any person found riding in a superior class to that for which he has taken his ticket will be removed at the first station stopped at, according to the bye-laws of the company.

POLLY. You're giving yourself nice airs! What business is it of yours who comes here? Who are you?

SAM. I'm a mechanic.

POLLY. That's evident.

SAM. I ain't ashamed of it. I'm not ashamed of my paper cap.

POLLY. Why should you be? I dare say Captain Hawtree isn't ashamed of his fourteen-and-sixpenny gossamer.

SAM. You think a deal of him 'cos he's a captain. Why did he call you my lady?

POLLY. Because he treated me as one. I wish you'd make the same mistake!

SAM. Ugh! (SAM *goes angrily to bureau,* POLLY *bounces up stage, and sits in window seat.*)

ESTHER (*sitting with* GEORGE, *tête-à-tête, by fire*). But we must listen to reason.

GEORGE. I hate reason!

ESTHER. I wonder what it means?

GEORGE. Everything disagreeable! When people talk unpleasantly, they always say listen to reason.

SAM (*turning round*). What will the neighbours say?

POLLY. I don't care! (*Coming down* C.)

SAM. What will the neighbours *think*?

POLLY. They can't think. They're like you, they've not been educated up to it.

SAM. It all comes of your being on the stage. (*Going to* POLLY.)

POLLY. It all comes of your not understanding the stage or anything else—but putty. Now, if you were a gentleman——

SAM. Why then, of course, I should make up to a lady!

POLLY. Ugh! (POLLY *flings herself into chair* R. *of table.* SAM *down* R.)

GEORGE. Reason's an idiot! Two and two are four, and twelve are fifteen, and eight are twenty. That's reason!

SAM (*turning to* POLLY). Painting your cheeks!

POLLY (*rising*). Better paint our *cheeks* than paint *nasty old doors* as you do. How can you understand art? You're only a mechanic! you're not a professional. You're in trade. You are not of the same station that we are. When the manager speaks to you, you touch your hat, and say, 'Yes, sir,' because he's your superior. (*Snaps fingers under* SAM'*s nose.*)

GEORGE. When people love there's no such thing as money—it don't exist.

ESTHER. Yes, it does.

GEORGE. Then it oughtn't to.

SAM. The manager employs me same as he does you. Payment is good everywhere and anywhere. Whatever's commercial, is right.

POLLY. Actors are not like mechanics. They wear cloth coats, and not fustian jackets.

SAM. I despise play actors. (*Sneeringly, in* POLLY'*s face.*)

POLLY. And I despise mechanics. (POLLY *slaps his face.*)

GEORGE. I never think of anything else but you.

ESTHER. Really?

SAM (*goes to bureau, misses cap, looks around, sees it on floor, picks it up angrily and comes to* POLLY, *who is sitting in chair* R. *of table*). I won't stay here to be insulted. (*Putting on cap.*)

POLLY. Nobody wants you to stay. Go! Go! Go˙

SAM. I will go. Good-bye, Miss Mary Eccles. (*Goes off and returns quickly.*) I shan't come here again! (*At door half-open.*)

POLLY. Don't! Good riddance to bad rubbish.

SAM (*rushing down stage to* POLLY). You can go to your *captain!*

POLLY. And you to your *putty.* (*Throws his cap down and kicks it—*

then goes up stage and picks it up. POLLY *turns and rises, leaning against table, facing him, crosses to door, and locks it.* SAM, *hearing the click of the lock, turns quickly.*)

ESTHER. And shall you always love me as you do now?

GEORGE. More.

POLLY. Now you *shan't* go. (*Locking door, taking out key, which she pockets and placing her back against door.*) Nyer! Now I'll just show you my power. Nyer!

SAM. *Miss Mary* Eccles, let me out! (*Advancing to door.*)

POLLY. *Mr.* Samuel Gerridge, I shan't. (SAM *turns away.*)

ESTHER. Now you two. (*Postman's knock.*) The postman!

SAM. Now you must let me out. You must unlock the door.

POLLY. No, I needn't. (*Opens window, looking out.*) Here—postman. (*Takes letter from postman, at window.*) Thank you. (*Business; flicks* SAM *in the face with letter.*) For you, Esther!

ESTHER (*rising*). For me?

POLLY. Yes. (*Gives it to her, and closes window, and returns to door triumphantly.* SAM *goes to window.*)

ESTHER (*going down* R.C.). From Manchester!

GEORGE. Manchester? (*Coming down* L., *back of* ESTHER.)

ESTHER (*reading*). I've got the engagement—four pounds a week.

GEORGE (*placing his arm around her*). You shan't go. Esther—stay—be my wife!

ESTHER. But the world—your world?

GEORGE. Hang the world! You're my world. Stay with your husband, *Mrs. George D'Alroy.* (*During this* POLLY *has been dancing up and down in front of door.*)

SAM. I *will* go out! (*Turning with sudden determination.*)

POLLY. You can't, and you shan't!

SAM. I can—I will! (*Opens window, and jumps out.*)

POLLY (*frightened*). He's hurt himself. Sam—Sam, dear Sam! (*Running to window.* SAM *appears at window.* POLLY *slaps his face and shuts window down violently.*)

POLLY. Nyer! (*During this* GEORGE *has kissed* ESTHER.)

GEORGE. *My wife!* (*The handle of the door is heard to rattle, then the door is shaken violently.* ESTHER *crosses to door; finding it locked turns to* POLLY, *sitting in window seat, who gives her the key.* ESTHER *then opens the door.* ECCLES *reels in, very drunk, and clings to the corner of bureau* R., *for support.* GEORGE *stands* L.C., *pulling his moustache.* ESTHER, *a little way up*

R.C., *looking with shame first at her father, then at* GEORGE. POLLY *sitting in window recess* C.)

ACT DROP

*For Call—*GEORGE, *hat in hand, bidding* ESTHER *good bye,* R. ECCLES *sitting in chair, nodding before fire.* SAM *again looks in at window.* POLLY *pulls the blind down violently.*

ACT II

SCENE: D'ALROY'*s lodgings in Mayfair. A set chamber. Folding-doors opening on to drawing-room,* L. *in flat. Door,* R. *in flat. Two windows, with muslin curtains,* R. *Loo-table,* L.C. *Sofa above piano. Two easy chairs,* R. *and* L. *of table. Dessert—Claret in jug; two wineglasses half full. Box of cigarettes, vase of flowers, embroidered slipper on canvas, and small basket of coloured wools, all on table. Footstool,* L. *of* L. *easy chair. Ornamental gilt work-basket on stand in window,* R. 1 E. *Easy chair,* R. 2 E. *Piano,* L. *Mahogany-stained easel with oil-painting of* D'ALROY *in full Dragoon regimentals. Davenport, with vase of flowers on it,* R.C.; *a chair on each side; a water-colour drawing over it, and on each side of room. Half moon-light through window.*

(ESTHER *and* GEORGE *discovered.* ESTHER *at window* R.; *when curtain has risen she comes down slowly to chair* R. *of table, and* GEORGE *sitting in easy chair* L. *of table.* GEORGE *has his uniform trousers and spurs on.*)

ESTHER. George, dear, you seem out of spirits.

GEORGE (*smoking cigarette*). Not at all, dear, not at all. (*Rallying.*)

ESTHER. Then why don't you talk?

GEORGE. I've nothing to say.

ESTHER. That's no reason.

GEORGE. I can't talk about nothing.

ESTHER. Yes, you can; you often do. (*Crossing round to back of table and caressing him.*) You used to do before we were married.

GEORGE. No, I didn't. I talked about you, and my love for you. D'ye call that nothing?

ESTHER (*sitting on stool* L. *of* GEORGE). How long have we been married, dear? Let me see; six months yesterday. (*Dreamily.*) It hardly seems a week; it almost seems a dream.

GEORGE (*putting his arm around her*). Awfully jolly dream. Don't let us wake up. (*Aside and recovering himself.*) How ever shall I tell her?

ESTHER. And when I married you I was twenty-two; wasn't I?

GEORGE. Yes, dear; but then, you know, you must have been some age or other.

ESTHER. No; but to think that I lived two-and-twenty years without knowing you!

GEORGE. What of it, dear?

ESTHER. It seems such a dreadful waste of time.

GEORGE. So it was—awful!

ESTHER. Do you remember our first meeting? Then I was in the ballet.

GEORGE. Yes; now you're in the heavies.

ESTHER. Then I was in the front rank—now I am of high rank—the Honourable Mrs. George D'Alroy. You promoted me to be your wife.

GEORGE. No, dear, you promoted me to be your husband.

ESTHER. And now I'm one of the aristocracy; ain't I?

GEORGE. Yes, dear; I suppose that we may consider ourselves——

ESTHER. Tell me, George; are you quite sure that you are proud of your poor little humble wife?

GEORGE. Proud of you! Proud as the winner of the Derby.

ESTHER. Wouldn't you have loved me better if I'd been a lady?

GEORGE. You *are* a lady—you're my wife.

ESTHER. What will your mamma say when she knows of our marriage? I quite tremble at the thought of meeting her.

GEORGE. So do I. Luckily, she's in Rome.

ESTHER. Do you know, George, I should like to be married all over again.

GEORGE. Not to anybody else, I hope.

ESTHER. My darling!

GEORGE. But why over again? Why?

ESTHER. Our courtship was so beautiful. It was like in a novel from the library, only better. You, a fine, rich, high-born gentleman, coming to our humble little house to court poor me. Do you remember the ballet you first saw me in? That was at Covent Garden. 'Jeanne la Folle; or, the Return of the Soldier.' (*Goes to piano.*) Don't you remember the dance? (*Plays a quick movement.*)

GEORGE. Esther, how came you to learn to play the piano? Did you teach yourself?

ESTHER. Yes. (*Turning on music-stool.*) So did Polly. We can only just touch the notes to amuse ourselves.

GEORGE. How was it?

ESTHER. I've told you so often. (*Rises and sits on stool at* GEORGE'*s feet.*)

GEORGE. Tell me again. I'm like the children—I like to hear what I know already.

ESTHER. Well, then, mother died when I was quite young. I can only just remember her. Polly was an infant; so I had to be Polly's mother. Father—who is a very eccentric man (GEORGE *sighs deeply*—ESTHER *notices it and goes on rapidly—all to be simultaneous in action*) but a very good one when you know him—did not take much notice of us, and we got on as we could. We used to let the first floor, and a lodger took it—Herr Griffenhaagen. He was a ballet master at the Opera. He took a fancy to me, and asked me if I should like to learn to dance, and I told him father couldn't afford to pay for my tuition; and he said that (*imitation*) he did not vant bayment, but dat he would teach me for noding, for he had taken a fancy to me, because I was like a leetle lady he had known long years ago in de far off land he came from. Then he got us an engagement at the theatre. That was how we first were in the ballet.

GEORGE (*slapping his leg*). That fellow was a great brick; I should like to ask him to dinner. What became of him?

ESTHER. I don't know. He left England. (GEORGE *fidgets and looks at watch.*) You are very restless, George. What's the matter?

GEORGE. Nothing.

ESTHER. Are you going out?

GEORGE. Yes. (*Looking at his boots and spurs.*) That's the reason I dined in——

ESTHER. To the barracks?

GEORGE. Yes.

ESTHER. On duty?

GEORGE (*hesitatingly*). On duty. (*Rising.*) And, of course, when a man is a soldier, he must go on duty when he's ordered, and where he's ordered, and—and—(*aside*)—why did I ever enter the service! (*Crosses to* R.)

ESTHER (*rises—crosses to* GEORGE—*and twining her arm round him*). George, if you must go out to your club, go; don't mind leaving me. Somehow or other, George, these last few days everything seems to have changed with me—I don't know why. Sometimes my eyes fill with tears, for no reason, and sometimes I feel so happy, for no reason. I don't mind being left by myself as I used to do. When you are a few minutes behind time I don't run to the window and watch for you, and turn irritable. Not that I love you less—no, for I love you more; but often when you are away I don't feel that I am by myself. (*Dropping her head on his breast.*) I never feel alone. (*Goes to piano and turns over music.*)

GEORGE (*watching* ESTHER). What angels women are! At least, this one is. I forget all about the others. (*Carriage-wheels heard off* R.) If I'd known I could have been so happy, I'd have sold out when I married. (*Knock at street door.*)

ESTHER (*standing at table*). That for us, dear?

GEORGE (*at first window*). Hawtree in a hansom. He's come for—(*aside*) me. I *must* tell her sooner or later. (*At door.*) Come in, Hawtree.

(*Enter* HAWTREE, *in regimentals, door* R.)

HAWTREE. How do? Hope you're well, Mrs. D'Alroy? (*Coming down* R.) George, are you coming to——

GEORGE (*coming down* L. *of* HAWTREE). No, I've dined (*gives a significant look*)——we dined early. (ESTHER *plays scraps of music at piano.*)

HAWTREE (*sotto voce*). Haven't you told her?

GEORGE. No, I daren't.

HAWTREE. But you must.

GEORGE. You know what an awful coward I am. You do it for me.

HAWTREE. Not for worlds. I've just had my own adieux to make.

GEORGE. Ah, yes—to Florence Carberry. How did she take it?

HAWTREE. Oh, (*slight pause*) very well.

GEORGE. Did she cry? (*Earnestly.*)

HAWTREE. No.

GEORGE. Nor exhibit any emotion whatever?

HAWTREE. No, not particularly.

GEORGE. Didn't you kiss her? (*Surprisedly.*)

HAWTREE. No; Lady Clardonax was in the room.

GEORGE. Didn't she squeeze your hand? (*Wonderingly.*)

HAWTREE. No.

GEORGE. Didn't she say anything? (*Impressively.*)

HAWTREE. No, except that she hoped to see me back again soon, and that India was a bad climate.

GEORGE. Umph! It seems to have been a tragic parting (*serio-comically*)—almost as tragic as parting—your back hair.

HAWTREE. Lady Florence is not the sort of person to make a scene.

GEORGE. To be sure, she's not your wife. I wish Esther would be as cool and comfortable. (*After a pause.*) No, I don't—no, I don't. (*A rap at door.*)

(*Enter* DIXON, *door* R.)

GEORGE (*goes up to* DIXON). Oh, Dixon, lay out my—

DIXON. I have laid them out, sir; everything is ready.

GEORGE (*coming down to* HAWTREE—*after a pause, irresolutely*). I must tell her—mustn't I?

HAWTREE. Better send for her sister. Let Dixon go for her in a cab.

GEORGE. Just so. I'll send him at once. Dixon! (*Goes up and talks to* DIXON.)

ESTHER (*rising and going to back of chair* L. *of table*). Do you want to have a talk with my husband? Shall I go into the dining-room?

HAWTREE. No, Mrs. D'Alroy. (*Going to* R. *of table and placing cap on it.*)

GEORGE. No, dear. At once, Dixon. Tell the cabman to drive like—(*exit* DIXON, *door* R.)—like a—cornet just joined.

ESTHER (*to* HAWTREE). Are you going to take him anywhere?

HAWTREE (L. GEORGE *comes down* R. *of* HAWTREE *and touches him quickly on the shoulder before he can speak*). No. (*Aside.*) Yes—to India. (*Crossing to* R. *to* GEORGE.) Tell her now.

GEORGE. No, no. I'll wait till I put on my uniform. (*Going up* R.)

(*Door* R. *opens, and* POLLY *peeps in.*)

POLLY. How d'ye do, good people—quite well? (POLLY *gets* C., *back of table—kisses* ESTHER.)

GEORGE. Eh? Didn't you meet Dixon?

POLLY. Who?

GEORGE. Dixon—my man.

POLLY. No.

GEORGE. Confound it! he'll have his ride for nothing. How d'ye do, Polly? (*Shakes hands.*)

POLLY. How d'ye do, George? (ESTHER *takes* POLLY'*s things and places them up* L. POLLY *places parasol on table* C. ESTHER *returns,* L. *of* POLLY.)

POLLY (*back* C.). Bless you my turtles. (*Blessing them, ballet-fashion.*) George, kiss your mother. (*Back* C.; *he kisses her.*) That's what I call an honourable brother-in-law's kiss. I'm not in the way, am I?

GEORGE (*behind easy chair* R. *of table*). Not at all. I'm very glad you've come. (ESTHER *shows* POLLY *the new music.* POLLY *sits at piano and plays comic tune.*)

HAWTREE (*back to audience, and elbow on easy chair* R.; *aside to* GEORGE). Under ordinary circumstances she's not a very eligible visitor.

GEORGE. Caste again. (*Going up* R.) I'll be back directly. (*Exit* GEORGE, *door* R.)

HAWTREE (*looking at watch, and crossing* L.). Mrs. D'Alroy, I—

ESTHER (*who is standing over* POLLY *at piano*). Going?

POLLY (*rising*). Do I drive you away, captain? (*Taking her parasol from table.* ESTHER *gets to back of chair* L. *of table.*)

HAWTREE. No.

POLLY. Yes, I do. I frighten you, I'm so ugly. I know I do. You frighten me.

HAWTREE. How so?

POLLY. You're so handsome. (*Coming down* L.) Particularly in those clothes, for all the world like an inspector of police.

ESTHER (L., *half aside*). Polly!

POLLY. I will! I like to take him down a bit.

HAWTREE (R.C., *aside*). This is rather a wild sort of thing in sisters-in-law.

POLLY. Any news, captain?

HAWTREE (*in a drawling tone*). No. Is there any news with you?

POLLY. Yaas; (*imitating him*) we've got a new piece coming out at our theatre.

HAWTREE (*interested*). What's it about?

POLLY (*drawling*). I don't know. (*To* ESTHER.) Had him there! (HAWTREE *drops his sword from his arm;* POLLY *turns round quickly, hearing the noise, and pretends to be frightened.*) Going to kill anybody today, that you've got your sword on?

HAWTREE. No.

POLLY. I thought not. (*Sings.*)

'With a sabre on his brow,
And a helmet by his side,
The soldier sweethearts servant-maids,
And eats cold meat besides.'

(*Laughs and walks about waving her parasol.*)

(*Enter* GEORGE, *door* R., *in uniform, carrying in his hand his sword, sword belt, and cap.* ESTHER *takes them from him, and places them on sofa* L.; *then comes half down* L. GEORGE *goes down* R.C. *by* HAWTREE.)

POLLY (*clapping her hands*). Oh! here's a beautiful brother-in-law. Why didn't you come in on horseback, as they do at Astley's?—gallop in and say (*imitating soldier on horseback and prancing up and down stage during the piece*), Soldiers of France! the eyes of Europe are a-looking at you! The Empire has confidence in you, and France expects that every man this day will do his—little utmost! The foe is before you—

more's the pity—and you are before them—worse luck for you! Forward! Go and get killed; and to those who escape the Emperor will give a little bit of ribbon! Nineteens, about! Forward! Gallop! Charge! (*Galloping to* R., *imitating bugle, and giving a point with parasol. She nearly spears* HAWTREE's *nose.* HAWTREE *claps his hand upon his sword-hilt. She throws herself into chair, laughing, and clapping* HAWTREE's *cap* [*from table*] *upon her head. All laugh and applaud. Carriage-wheels heard without.*)

POLLY. Oh, what a funny little cap, it's got no peak. (*A peal of knocks heard at street-door.*) What's that?

GEORGE (*who has hastened to window* R.). A carriage! Good heavens—my mother!

HAWTREE (*at window* R. 1 E.) The Marchioness!

ESTHER (*crossing to* GEORGE, *back* C.). Oh, George!

POLLY (*crossing to window*). A Marchioness! A real, live Marchioness! Let me look! I never saw a real live Marchioness in all my life.

GEORGE (*forcing her from window*). No, no, no. She doesn't know I'm married. I must break it to her by degrees. What shall I do? (*By this time* HAWTREE *is at door* R., ESTHER *at door* L.)

ESTHER. Let me go into the bedroom until—

HAWTREE. Too late! She's on the stairs.

ESTHER. Here then! (*At* C. *doors, opens them.*)

POLLY. I want to see a real, live March—

(GEORGE *lifts her in his arms and places her within folding-doors with* ESTHER—*then shutting doors quickly, turns and faces* HAWTREE, *who, gathering up his sword, faces* GEORGE. *They then exchange places much in the fashion of soldiers 'mounting guard'. As* GEORGE *opens door* R., *and admits* MARCHIONESS, HAWTREE *drops down* L.)

GEORGE (*with great ceremony*). My dear mother, I saw you getting out of the carriage.

MARCHIONESS. My dear boy (*kissing his forehead*), I'm so glad I got to London before you embarked. (GEORGE *nervous.* HAWTREE *coming down* L.) Captain Hawtree, I think. How do you do?

HAWTREE (*coming forward a little*). Quite well, I thank your ladyship. I trust you are—

MARCHIONESS (*sitting in easy chair*). Oh, quite, thanks. (*Slight pause.*) Do you still see the Countess and Lady Florence? (*Looking at him through her glasses.*)

HAWTREE. Yes.

MARCHIONESS. Please remember me to them—(HAWTREE *takes cap from table, and places sword under his arm.*) Are you going?

HAWTREE. Ya-a-s. Compelled. (*Bows, crossing round back of table. To* GEORGE, *who meets him* C.) I'll be at the door for you at seven. We must be at barracks by the quarter. (GEORGE *crosses* L., *back of table.*) Poor devil! This comes of a man marrying beneath him! (*Exit* HAWTREE, *door* R. GEORGE *comes down* L. *of table.*)

MARCHIONESS. I'm not sorry that he's gone, for I wanted to talk to you alone. Strange that a woman of such good birth as the Countess should encourage the attentions of Captain Hawtree for her daughter Florence. (*During these lines* D'ALROY *conceals* POLLY'*s hat and umbrella under table.*) Lady Clardonax was one of the old Carberrys of Hampshire —not the Norfolk Carberrys, but the direct line. And Mr. Hawtree's grandfather was in trade—something in the City—soap, I think—Stool, George! (*Points to stool.* GEORGE *brings it to her. She motions that he is to sit at her feet;* GEORGE *does so with a sigh.*) He's a very nice person, but *parvenu*, as one may see by his languor and his swagger. My boy (*kissing his forehead*), I am sure, will never make a *mésalliance.* He is a D'Alroy, and by his mother's side *Planta-genista.* The source of our life stream is royal.

GEORGE. How is the Marquis?

MARCHIONESS. Paralysed. I left him at Spa with three physicians. He always is paralysed at this time of the year; it is in the family. The paralysis is not personal, but hereditary. I came over to see my steward; got to town last night.

GEORGE. How did you find me out here?

MARCHIONESS. I sent the footman to the barracks, and he saw your man Dixon in the street, and Dixon gave him this address. It's so long since I've seen you. (*Leans back in chair.*) You're looking very well, and I dare say when mounted are quite a 'beau cavalier'. And so, my boy (*playing with his hair*), you are going abroad for the first time on active service.

GEORGE (*aside*). Every word can be heard in the next room. If they've only gone upstairs.

MARCHIONESS. And now, my dear boy, before you go I want to give you some advice; and you mustn't despise it because I'm an old woman. We old women know a great deal more than people give us credit for. You are a soldier—so was your father—so was his father—so was mine—so was our royal founder; we were born to lead! The common people expect it from us. It is our duty. Do you not remember in the Chronicles of Froissart? (*With great enjoyment.*) I think I can quote it word for word; I've a wonderful memory for my age. (*With closed eyes.*)

It was in the fifty-ninth chapter—'How Godefroy D'Alroy helde the towne of St. Amande duryng the siege before Tournay. It said the towne was not closed but with pales, and captayne there was Sir Amory of Pauy—the Seneschall of Carcassoune—who had said it was not able to hold agaynste an hooste, when one Godefroy D'Alroy sayd that rather than he woulde depart, he woulde keep it to the best of his power. Whereat the souldiers cheered and sayd, "Lead us on, Sir Godefroy." And then began a fierce assault; and they within were chased, and sought for shelter from street to street. But Godefroy stood at the gate so valyantly that the souldiers helde the towne until the commyng of the Earl of Haynault with twelve thousande men.'

GEORGE (*aside*). I wish she'd go. If she once gets on to Froissart, she'll never know when to stop.

MARCHIONESS. When my boy fights—and you will fight—he is sure to distinguish himself. It is his nature to—(*toys with his hair*)—he cannot forget his birth. And when you meet these Asiatic ruffians, who have dared to revolt, and to outrage humanity, you will strike as your ancestor Sir Galtier of Chevrault struck at Poictiers. (*Changing tone of voice as if remembering.*) Froissart mentions it thus—'Sir Galtier, with his four squires, was in the front of that battell, and there did marvels in arms. And Sir Galtier rode up to the Prince, and sayd to him—"Sir, take your horse and ryde forth, this journey is yours. God is this day in your hands. Gette us to the French Kynge's batayle. I think verily by his valyantesse he woll not fly. Advance banner in the name of God and of Saynt George!" And Sir Galtier galloped forward to see his Kynge's victory, and meet his own death.'

GEORGE (*aside*). If Esther hears all this!

MARCHIONESS. There is another subject about which I should have spoken to you before this; but an absurd prudery forbade me. I may never see you more. I am old—and you—are going into battle—(*kissing his forehead with emotion*)—and this may be our last meeting. (*A noise heard within folding-doors*). What's that?

GEORGE. Nothing—my man Dixon is there.

MARCHIONESS. We may not meet again on this earth. I do not fear your conduct, my George, with men; but I know the temptations that beset a youth who is well born. But a true soldier, a true gentleman, should not only be without fear, but without reproach. It is easier to fight a furious man than to forego the conquest of a love-sick girl. A thousand Sepoys slain in battle cannot redeem the honour of a man who has betrayed the confidence of a trusting woman. Think, George, what dishonour—what stain upon your manhood—to hurl a girl to shame and degradation! And what excuse for it? That she is plebeian? A man of real honour will spare the woman who has confessed her love for him, as he would give quarter to any enemy he had disarmed. (*Taking his hands.*) Let my boy avoid the snares so artfully spread; and when he asks his mother to welcome the woman he has chosen for his wife, let me take her to my arms and plant a motherly kiss upon the white brow of a lady. (*Noise of a fall heard within folding-doors; rising.*) What's that?

GEORGE. Nothing. (*Rising.*)

MARCHIONESS. I heard a cry. (*Folding-doors open, discovering* ESTHER *with* POLLY, *staggering in, fainting.*)

POLLY. George! George! (GEORGE *goes up and* ESTHER *falls in his arms.* POLLY *stands* R.C. GEORGE *places* ESTHER *on sofa.* GEORGE *on her* R., POLLY *on her* L.)

MARCHIONESS (*coming down* R.). Who are these *women*?

POLLY. Women!

MARCHIONESS. George D'Alroy, these persons should have been sent away. How could you dare to risk your mother meeting women of their stamp?

POLLY (*violently*). What does she mean? How dare she call me a woman? What's she, I'd like to know?

GEORGE (R. *of sofa*). Silence, Polly! You mustn't insult my mother.

MARCHIONESS. The insult is from you. I leave you, and I hope that time may induce me to forget this scene of degradation. (*Turning to go.*)

GEORGE. Stay, mother. (MARCHIONESS *turns slightly away.*) Before you go (GEORGE *has raised* ESTHER *from sofa in both arms*) let me present to you Mrs. George D'Alroy, *my wife!*

MARCHIONESS. Married!

GEORGE. Married.

(*The* MARCHIONESS *sinks into easy chair* R. GEORGE *replaces* ESTHER *on sofa, up* L., *but still retains her hand. Three hesitating taps at door heard.* GEORGE *crosses to door* R., *opens it, discovers* ECCLES, *who enters.* GEORGE *drops down back of* MARCHIONESS'*s chair.*)

ECCLES. They told us to come up. When your man came Polly was out; so I thought I should do instead. (*Calling at door.*) Come up, Sam.

(*Enter* SAM *in his Sunday clothes, with short cane and smoking a cheroot. He nods and grins*—POLLY *points to* MARCHIONESS—SAM *takes cheroot from his mouth and quickly removes his hat.*)

ECCLES. Sam had just called; so we three—Sam and I, and your man, all came in the 'ansom cab together. Didn't we, Sam? (ECCLES *and* SAM *go over to the girls* L., *and* ECCLES *drops down to front of table—smilingly.*)

MARCHIONESS (*with glasses up, to* GEORGE). Who is this?

GEORGE (*coming* L. *of* MARCHIONESS). My wife's father.

MARCHIONESS. What is he?

GEORGE. A—nothing.

ECCLES. I am one of nature's noblemen. Happy to see you, my lady —(*turning to her*)—now, my daughters have told me who you are— (GEORGE *turns his back in an agony as* ECCLES *crosses to* MARCHIONESS) —we old folks, fathers and mothers of the young couples, ought to make friends. (*Holding out his dirty hand.*)

MARCHIONESS (*shrinking back*). Go away! (ECCLES *goes back to table again, disgusted,* L.) What's his name?

GEORGE. Eccles.

MARCHIONESS. Eccles! Eccles! There never was an Eccles. He don't exist.

ECCLES. Don't he, though! What d'ye call this? (*Goes up again* L., *to back of table as* SAM *drops down. He is just going to take a decanter when* SAM *stops him.*)

MARCHIONESS. No Eccles was ever born!

GEORGE. He takes the liberty of breathing notwithstanding. (*Aside.*) And I wish he wouldn't!

MARCHIONESS. And who is the little man? Is he also Eccles? (SAM *looks round.* POLLY *gets close up to him, and looks with defiant glance at the* MARCHIONESS.)

GEORGE. No.

MARCHIONESS. Thank goodness! What then?

GEORGE. His name is Gerridge.

MARCHIONESS. *Gerridge!* It breaks one's teeth. Why is he here?

GEORGE. He is making love to Polly, my wife's sister.

MARCHIONESS. And what is he?

GEORGE. A gasman.

MARCHIONESS. He looks it. (GEORGE *goes up to* ESTHER L.) And what is she—the—the—the sister? (ECCLES, *who has been casting longing eyes at the decanter on table, edges towards it, and when he thinks no one is noticing, fills wineglass.*)

POLLY (*asserting herself indignantly*). I'm in the ballet at the Theatre Royal, Lambeth. So was Esther. We're not ashamed of what we are! We have no cause to be.

SAM (*back* L.C.). That's right, Polly! pitch into them swells!—who are they?

(ECCLES *by this time has seized wineglass, and, turning his back, is about to drink, when* HAWTREE *enters, door* R. *flat.* ECCLES *hides glass under his coat, and pretends to be looking up at picture.*)

HAWTREE (*entering*). George! (*Stops suddenly, looking round.*) So, all's known!

MARCHIONESS (*rising*). Captain Hawtree, see me to my carriage; I am broken-hearted! (*Takes* HAWTREE'*s arm, and is going up.*)

ECCLES (*who has tasted the claret, spits it out with a grimace, exclaiming*) —Rot! (POLLY *goes to piano, sits on stool*—SAM *back to audience, leaning on piano*—ECCLES *exits through folding-doors.*)

GEORGE (L.; *to* MARCHIONESS). Don't go in anger. You may not see me again. (ESTHER *rises in nervous excitement, clutching* GEORGE'*s hand.* MARCHIONESS *stops* R. ESTHER *brings* GEORGE *down* C.)

ESTHER (L.C.; *with arm round his neck*). Oh, George! must you go? (*They come* L. *to front of table.*)

GEORGE. Yes.

ESTHER. I can't leave you! I'll go with you!

GEORGE. Impossible! The country is too unsettled.

ESTHER. May I come after you?

GEORGE. Yes.

ESTHER (*with her head on his shoulder*). I may.

MARCHIONESS (*coming down* R. HAWTREE *at door* R.). It is his duty to go. His honour calls him. The honour of his family—*our* honour!

ESTHER. But I love him so! Pray don't be angry with me!

HAWTREE (*looking at watch, and coming down* C.). George!

GEORGE. I must go, love! (HAWTREE *goes up to door again.*)

MARCHIONESS (*advancing*). Let me arm you, George—let your mother, as in the days of old. There is blood—and blood, my son. See, your wife cries when she should be proud of you!

GEORGE. My Esther is all that is good and noble. No lady born to a coronet could be gentler or more true. Esther, my wife, fetch me my sword, and buckle my belt around me.

ESTHER (*clinging to him*). No, no; I can't!

GEORGE. Try. (*Whispers to* ESTHER.) To please my mother. (*To* MARCHIONESS.) You shall see. (ESTHER *totters up stage,* POLLY *assisting her* L., *and brings down his sword. As* ESTHER *is trying to buckle his belt, he whispers.*) I've left money for you, my darling. My lawyer will call on you tomorrow. Forgive me! I tried hard to tell you we were ordered for

India; but when the time came, my heart failed me, and I—(ESTHER, *before she can succeed in fastening his sword-belt, reels, and falls fainting in his arms.* POLLY *hurries to her.* SAM, *standing at piano, looking frightened;* HAWTREE *with hand upon handle of door* R.; MARCHIONESS *looking on,* R. *of* GEORGE.)

ACT DROP

*For Call—*GEORGE *and* HAWTREE *gone.* ESTHER *in chair* C., *fainting;* POLLY *and* SAM *each side of her,* POLLY *holding her hands and* SAM *fanning her with his red handkerchief. The folding-doors* L.C. *thrown open, and* ECCLES *standing at back of table offering glass of claret.*

ACT III

SCENE: *The room in Stangate (as in Act I). Same furniture as in Act I with exception of piano, with roll of music tied up on it in place of bureau,* R. *Map of India over mantelpiece. Sword with crape knot, spurs, and cap, craped, hanging over chimney-piece. Portrait of* D'ALROY *(large) on mantelpiece. Berceaunette, and child, with coral, in it.* POLLY'*s bonnet and shawl hanging on peg,* R. *flat. Small tin saucepan in fender, fire alight, and kettle on it. Two candles (tallow) in sticks, one of which is broken about three inches from the top and hangs over. Slate and pencil on table. Jug on table, bandbox and ballet skirt on table.*

(*At rise of curtain* POLLY *discovered at table, back of stage. Comes down and places skirt in bandbox. She is dressed in black.*)

POLLY (*placing skirt in box, and leaning her chin upon her hand*). There—there's the dress for poor Esther in case she gets the engagement, which I don't suppose she will. It's too good luck, and good luck never comes to her, poor thing. (*Goes up to back of cradle.*) Baby's asleep still. How good he looks—as good as if he were dead, like his poor father; and alive too, at the same time, like his dear self. Ah! dear me; it's a strange world. (*Sits in chair* R. *of table, feeling in pocket for money.*) Four and elevenpence. That must do for today and tomorrow. Esther is going to bring in the rusks for Georgy. (*Takes up slate.*) Three, five—eight, and four—twelve, one shilling—father can only have twopence (*this all to be said in one breath*), he must make do with that till Saturday, when I get my salary. If Esther gets the engagement, I shan't have many more salaries to take; I shall leave the stage and retire into private life. I wonder if I shall like private life, and if private life will like me. It will seem so strange being no longer Miss Mary Eccles—but Mrs. Samuel Gerridge. (*Writes it on slate.*) 'Mrs. Samuel Gerridge.' (*Laughs bashfully.*) La! to think of my being Mrs. Anybody. How annoyed Susan Smith will be! (*Writing on slate.*) 'Mrs. Samuel Gerridge presents her compliments to Miss Susan Smith, and Mrs. Samuel Gerridge requests the favour of Miss Susan Smith's company to tea, on Tuesday evening next, at Mrs. Samuel Gerridge's house.' (*Pause.*) Poor Susan! (*Beginning again.*) 'P.S.—Mrs. Samuel Gerridge——' (*Knock heard at room door;* POLLY *starts.*)

SAM (*without*). Polly, open the door.

POLLY. Sam! Come in.

SAM (*without*). I can't.

POLLY. Why not?

SAM. I've got somethin' on my 'ead.

(POLLY *rises and opens door* R., SAM *enters, carrying two rolls of wall-paper, one in each hand, and a small table on his head, which he deposits, down stage* R., *then puts rolls of paper on piano, as also his cap.* SAM *has a rule-pocket in corduroys.*)

POLLY (*shuts door*). What's that? (*Coming* R.C.)

SAM (*pointing to table with pride*). Furniture. How are you, my Polly? (*Kissing her.*) You look handsomer than ever this morning. (*Dances and sings.*) 'Tid-dle-di-tum-ti-di-do.'

POLLY. What's the matter, Sam?—are you mad?

SAM. No, 'appy—much the same thing.

POLLY. Where have you been these two days?

SAM (*all excitement*). That's just what I'm goin' to tell yer. Polly, my pet, my brightest batswing and most brilliant burner, what do yer think?

POLLY. Oh, do go on, Sam, or I'll slap your face.

SAM. Well, then, you've 'eard me speak of old Binks, the plumber, glazier, and gasfitter, who died six months ago?

POLLY. Yes.

SAM (*sternly and deliberately*). I've bought 'is business.

POLLY. No!

SAM (*excitedly*). Yes, of 'is widow, old Mrs. Binks—so much down, and so much more at the end of the year.
(*Dances and sings, up* R.)

'Ri-ti-toodle
Roodle-oodle
Ri-ti-tooral-lay.'

POLLY. La, Sam!

SAM (*pacing stage up and down*). Yes; I've bought the goodwill, fixtures, fittin's, stock, rolls of gas-pipe, and sheets of lead. (*Jumps on table* R., *quickly facing* POLLY.) Yes, Polly, I'm a tradesman with a shop—a master tradesman. (*Coming to* POLLY *seriously.*) All I want to complete the premises is a missus. (*Tries to kiss her. She pushes him away.*)

POLLY. Sam, don't be foolish!

SAM (*arm round her waist*). Come and be Mrs. Sam Gerridge, Polly, my patent-safety-day-and-night-light. You'll furnish me completely. (POLLY *goes up* L., SAM *watching her admiringly. He then sees slate, snatches it up and looks at it. She snatches it from him with a shriek, and rubs out writing, looking daggers at him, both* L.C., SAM *laughing.*)

SAM. Only to think now. (*Putting arm round her waist,* POLLY *pouting.*)

POLLY. Don't be a goose.

SAM (*going towards table* R.) I spent the whole of yesterday lookin' up furniture. Now I bought that a bargain, and I brought it 'ere to show you for your approval. I've bought lots of other things, and I'll bring 'em all here to show yer for your approval.

POLLY. I couldn't think what had become of you. (*Seated* R. *of table.*)

SAM. Couldn't yer? Oh, I say, I want yer to choose the new paper for the little back parlour just behind the shop, you know. Now what d'yer think o' this? (*Fetching a pattern from piano and unrolling it* C.)

POLLY (*standing* L.C.). No. I don't like that. (SAM *fetches the other, a flaming pattern.*) Ah! that's neat.

SAM. Yes, that's neat and quiet. I'll new-paper it, and new-furnish it, and it shall all be bran-new. (*Puts paper on top of piano.*)

POLLY. But won't that cost a lot of money?

SAM (*bravely*). I can work for it. With customers in the shop, and you in the back-parlour, I can work like fifty men. (*Sits on table* R., *beckons* POLLY *to him. She comes* L. *of table.* SAM *puts his arm round* POLLY, *sentimentally.*) Only fancy, at night, when the shop's closed, and the shutters are up, counting out the till together! (*Changing his manner.*) Besides, that isn't all I've been doin'. I've been writin', and what I've written I've got printed.

POLLY. No!

SAM. True.

POLLY. You've been writing—about me? (*Delighted.*)

SAM. No—about the shop. (POLLY *disgusted.*) Here it is. (*Takes roll of circulars from pocket of his canvas slop.*) Yer mustn't laugh—you know —it's my first attempt. I wrote it the night before last; and when I thought of you the words seemed to flow like—red-hot solder. (*Reads.*) Hem! 'Samuel Gerridge takes this opportunity of informin' the nobility, gentry, and inhabitants of the Borough-road—'

POLLY. The Borough-road?

SAM. Well, there ain't many of the nobility and gentry as lives in the Borough-road, but it pleases the inhabitants to make 'em believe yer think so (*resuming*)—'of informin' the nobility, gentry, and inhabitants of the Borough-road, and its vicinity,' and 'its vicinity'. (*Looking at her.*) Now I think that's rather good, eh?

POLLY. Yes. (*Doubtfully.*) I've heard worse.

SAM. I first thought of saying neighbour'ood; but then vicinity sounds so much more genteel (*resuming*)—'*and* its vicinity, that 'e has entered upon the business of the late Mr. Binks, 'is relict, the present Mrs. B., 'avin' disposed to 'im of the same'—now listen, Polly, because it gets interestin'—'S. G.—'

POLLY. S. G. Who's he?

SAM (*looking at* POLLY *with surprise*). Why me. S. G.—Samuel Gerridge—me, us. We're S. G. Now don't interrupt me, or you'll cool my metal, and then I can't work. 'S. G. 'opes that, by a constant attention to business, and'—mark this—'by supplyin' the best articles at the most reasonable prices, to merit a continuance of those favours which it will ever be 'is constant study to deserve.' There! (*Turning on table to* R., *triumphantly.*) Stop a bit—there's a little bit more yet. 'Bell-'angin', gas-fittin', plumbin', and glazin', as usual.' There!—it's all my own. (*Puts circular on mantelpiece, and crosses* R., *contemplates it.*)

POLLY. Beautiful Sam. It looks very attractive from here, don't it?

SAM (*postman's knock*). There's the postman. I'll go. I shall send some of these out by post. (*Goes off, door* R., *and returns with letter.*)

POLLY (C., *taking it*). Oh, for Esther. I know who it's from. (*Places letter on mantelpiece. At chair,* L. *of table* L. SAM *sits, corner of table* R., *reading circular. Seriously.*) Sam, who do you think was here last night?

SAM. Who?

POLLY. Captain Hawtree.

SAM (*deprecatingly*). Oh, 'im!—come back from India, I suppose.

POLLY. Yes; luckily, Esther was out.

SAM. I never liked that long swell. He was a 'uppish, conceited—

POLLY (*sitting* L., *at end of table* L.). Oh, he's better than he used to be—he's a major now. He's only been in England a fortnight.

SAM. Did he tell yer anything about poor De Alroy?

POLLY (*leaning against table end*). Yes; he said he was riding out not far from the cantonment, and was surrounded by a troop of Sepoy cavalry, which took him prisoner, and galloped off with him.

SAM. But about 'is death?

POLLY. Oh! (*hiding her face*)—that he said was believed to be too terrible to mention.

SAM (*crossing to* POLLY, R. *of table* L.). Did 'e tell yer anything else?

POLLY. No; he asked a lot of questions, and I told him everything. How poor Esther had taken her widowhood and what a dear, good baby the baby was, and what a comfort to us all, and how Esther had come back to live with us again.

SAM (*sharply*). And the reason for it?

POLLY. (*looking down*). Yes.

SAM. How your father got all the money that 'e'd left for Esther.

POLLY (*sharply*). Don't say any more about that, Sam.

SAM. Oh! I only think Captain 'awtree ought to know where the money *did* go to, and you shouldn't try and screen your father, and let 'im suppose that you and Esther spent it all.

POLLY. I told him—I told him—I told him. (*Angrily.*)

SAM. Did you tell 'im that your father was always at 'armonic meetin's at taverns, and 'ad arf cracked 'isself with drink, and was always singin' the songs and makin' the speeches 'e 'eard there, and was always goin' on about 'is wrongs as one of the workin' classes? 'E's a pretty one for one of the workin' classes, 'e is! 'Asn't done a stroke o' work these twenty year. Now, I *am* one of the workin' classes, but I *don't* 'owl about it. I work, I don't spout.

POLLY. Hold your tongue, Sam. I won't have you say any more against poor father. He has his faults, but he's a very clever man. (*Sighing.*)

SAM. Ah! What else did Captain Hawtree say?

POLLY. He advised us to apply to Mr. D'Alroy's mother.

SAM. What! the Marquissy? And what did you say to that?

POLLY. I said that Esther wouldn't hear of it. And so the Major said that he'd write to Esther, and I suppose this is the letter.

SAM. Now, Polly, come along and choose the paper for the little back parlour. (*Going towards table* R., *and takes it up to wall, behind door* R.)

POLLY (*rising*). Can't! Who's to mind baby?

SAM. The baby? Oh, I forgot all about 'im. (*Goes to cradle.*) I see yer! (*Goes to window casually.*) There's your father comin' down the street. Won't 'e mind 'im?

POLLY (*going up* C.). I dare say he will. If I promise him an extra sixpence on Saturday. (SAM *opens window.*) Hi! Father! (POLLY *goes to cradle.*)

SAM (*aside*). 'E looks down in the mouth, 'e does. I suppose 'e's 'ad no drink this mornin'. (*Goes to* POLLY.)

(*Enter* ECCLES *in shabby black. Pauses on entering, looks at* SAM, *turns away in disgust, takes off hat, places it on piano, and shambles across to* L. *Taking chair,* L. *of table* L., *places it and sits before fire.*)

POLLY (*goes to* ECCLES, *down* L. *of table* L.). Come in to stop a bit, father?

ECCLES. No; not for long. (SAM *comes down* C.) Good morning, Samuel. Going back to work? that's right, my boy—stick to it. (*Pokes fire.*) Stick to it—nothing like it.

SAM (*down* R.C.; *aside*). Now, isn't that too bad! No, Mr. Eccles. I've knocked off for the day.

ECCLES (*waving poker*). That's bad! That's very bad! Nothing like work—for the young. I don't work so much as I used to, myself, but I like to (POLLY *sitting on corner of table up* L.) see the young 'uns at it. It does me good, and it does them good too. What does the poet say? (*Rising, impressively, and leaning on table.*)

> 'A Carpenter said tho' that was well spoke,
> It was better by far to defend it with hoak.
> A currier, wiser than both put together,
> Said say what you will, there is nothing like *labour*.
> For a' that, an' a' that,
> Your ribbon, gown, an' a' that,
> The rank is but the guinea stamp,
> The working man's the gold for a' that.'

(*Sits again, triumphantly wagging his head.*)

SAM (*aside*). This is one of the public-house loafers, that wants all the wages and none of the work, an idle old——(*Goes in disgust to piano, puts on cap, and takes rolls of paper under his arm.*)

POLLY (*to* ECCLES, L.). Esther will be in by and by. (*Persuasive.*) Do, father!

ECCLES. No, no. I tell you I won't!

POLLY (*whispering, arm round his neck*). And I'll give you sixpence extra on Saturday. (ECCLES's *face relaxes into a broad grin.* POLLY *gets hat and cloak, peg up* R.)

ECCLES. Ah! you sly little puss, you know how to get over your poor old father.

SAM (*aside*). Yes, with sixpence.

POLLY (*putting on bonnet and cloak at door*). Give the cradle a rock if baby cries.

SAM (*crossing to* ECCLES). If you should 'appen to want employment or amusement, Mr. Eccles, just cast your eye over this. (*Puts circular on table* L., *then joins* POLLY *at door.*) Stop a bit, I've forgot to give the baby one. (*Throws circular into cradle. Exeunt,* POLLY *first.* ECCLES *takes out pipe from pocket, looks into it, then blows through it making a squeaking noise and finishes by tenderly placing it on the table. He then hunts all his pockets for tobacco, finally finding a little paper packet containing a screw of tobacco in his* R. *waistcoat pocket, which he also places on table after turning up the corner of the table-cloth for the purpose of emptying the contents of his* R. *pocket of the few remnants of past screws of tobacco on to the bare table and mixing a little out of the packet with it and filling pipe. He then brushes all that remains on the table into the paper packet, pinches it up, and carefully replaces it in* R. *waistcoat pocket. Having put the pipe into his mouth, he looks about for a light, across his shoulder and under table, though never rising from the chair; seeing nothing his face assumes an expression of comic anguish. Turning to table he angrily replaces table-cloth and then notices* SAM'*s circular. His face relazes into a smile, and picking it up tears the circular in half, makes a spill of it, and lighting it at fire, stands with his back to fire-place and smokes vigorously.*)

ECCLES. Poor Esther! Nice market she's brought her pigs to—ugh! Mind the baby indeed! What good is he to me? That fool of a girl to throw away all her chances!—a *honourable-hess*—and her father not to have on him the price of a pint of early beer or a quartern of cool, refreshing gin! Stopping in here to rock a young honourable! Cuss him! (*Business, puffs smoke in baby's face* L. *of cradle, rocking it.*) Are we slaves, we working men? (*Sings savagely.*)

'Britons never, never, never shall be——'

(*Nodding his head sagaciously, sits* R. *of table* L.) I won't stand this, I've writ to the old cat—I mean to the Marquissy—to tell her that her daughter-in-law and her grandson is almost starving. That fool Esther's too proud to write to her for money. I hate pride—it's *beastly!* (*Rising.*) There's no beastly pride about me. (*Goes up* L. *of table, smacking his lips.*) I'm as dry as a lime-kiln. (*Takes up jug.*) Milk!—(*with disgust*)—for this young aristocratic pauper. Everybody in the house is sacrificed for him! (*At foot of cradle* R.C., *with arms on chair back.*) And to think that a *working man,* and a member of the Committee of the Banded Brothers for the Regeneration of Human Kind, by means of equal diffusion of intelligence and equal division of property, should be thusty, while this cub—(*Draws aside curtain, and looks at child. After a pause.*) That there coral he's got round his neck is *gold,* real *gold!* (*With hand on knob at end of cradle* R.C.) Oh, Society! Oh, Governments! Oh, Class Legislation!—*is this right?* Shall this mindless wretch enjoy himself, while sleeping, with a jewelled gawd, and his poor old grandfather want the price of half a pint? *No!* it shall not be! Rather than see it, I will myself resent this outrage on the rights of man! and in this holy crusade of class against class, of the weak and lowly against the *powerful and strong* —(*pointing to child*)—I will strike one blow for freedom! (*Goes to back of cradle.*) He's asleep. It will fetch ten bob round the corner; and if the Marquissy gives us anything it can be got out with some o' that. (*Steals coral.*) Lie still, my darling!—it's grandfather's a-watching over you—

'Who ran to catch me when I fell,
And kicked the place to make it well?
My grandfather!'

(*Rocking cradle with one hand; leaves it quickly, and as he takes hat off piano* ESTHER *enters. She is dressed as a widow, her face pale, and her manner quick and imperious. She carries a parcel and paper bag of rusks in her hand; she puts parcel on table, goes to cradle, kneels down and kisses child.*) My lovey had a nice walk? You should wrap yourself up well—you're so liable to catch cold!

ESTHER. My Georgy?—Where's his coral? (ECCLES *going, door* R.; *fumbles with the lock nervously, and is going out as* ESTHER *speaks.*) Gone! —Father!—(*Rising*—ECCLES *stops.*)—The child's coral—where is it?

ECCLES (*confused*). Where's what, ducky?

ESTHER. The coral! You've got it—I know it! Give it me!—(*Quickly and imperiously.*)—*Give it me!* (ECCLES *takes coral from his pocket and gives it back.*) If you *dare* to touch *my* child—(*Goes to cradle.*)

ECCLES. Esther! (*Going quickly to piano and banging his hat on it.*) Am I not your father?——(ESTHER *gets round to front of cradle.*)

ESTHER. And I am his mother!

ECCLES (*coming to her*). Do you bandy words with me, you pauper! you pauper! ! you pauper! ! ! to whom I have given shelter—shelter to you and your brat! I've a good mind——(*Raising his clenched fist.*)

ESTHER (*confronting him*). If you dare! I am no longer your little drudge—your frightened servant. When mother died—(ECCLES *changes countenance and cowers beneath her glance*)—and I was so high, I tended you, and worked for you—and you beat me. That time is past. I am a woman—I am a wife—a widow—a *mother!* Do you think I will let you outrage *him?* (*Pointing to cradle.*) *Touch me if you dare!* (*Advancing a step.*)

ECCLES (*bursting into tears and coming down* R.C.). And this is my own child, which I nussed when a babby, and sung 'Cootsicum Coo' to afore she could speak. (*Gets hat from piano, and returns a step or two.*) Hon. Mrs. De Alroy (ESTHER *drops down behind chair,* R. *of table* L.), I forgive you for all that you have said. I forgive you for all that you have done. In everything that I have done I have acted with the best intentions. May the babe in that cradle never treat you as you have this day *tret* a grey 'aired father. May he never cease to love and *h*onour you, as you have ceased to love and *h*onour me, after all that I have done for you, and the position to which I 'ave raised you by my own *industry*. (*Goes to door* R.) May he never behave to you like the bad daughters of King Lear; and may he never live to feel how much more sharper than a serpent's (*slight pause as if remembering quotation*) scale it is to have a thankless child! (*Exit, door* R.)

ESTHER (*kneeling back of cradle*). My darling! (*Arranging bed and placing coral to the baby's lips, and then to her own.*) Mamma's come back to her own. Did she stay away from him so long? (*Rises, and looks at the sabre, &c.*) My George! to think that you can never look upon his face or hear his voice. My brave, gallant, handsome husband! My lion and my love! (*Comes down* C., *pacing the stage.*) Oh! to be a soldier, and to fight the wretches who destroyed him—who took my darling from me! (*Action of cutting with sabre.*) To gallop miles upon their upturned faces. (*Crossing* L., *with action—breaks down sobbing at mantelpiece—sees letter.*) What's this?—Captain Hawtree's hand. (*Sitting in chair, reads, at left hand of table.*) 'My dear Mrs. D'Alroy—I returned to England less than a fortnight ago. I have some papers and effects of my poor friend's, which I am anxious to deliver to you, and I beg of you to name a day when I can call with them and see you; at the same time let me express my deepest sympathy with your affliction. Your husband's loss was mourned by every man in the regiment. (ESTHER *lays the letter on her heart, and then resumes reading.*) I have heard with great pain of the pecuniary embarrassments into which accident and the imprudence of others have placed you. I trust you will not consider me, one of poor George's oldest comrades and friends, either intrusive or impertinent in sending the enclosed (*she takes out a cheque*), and in hoping that, should any further difficulties arise, you will inform me of them, and remember that I am, dear Mrs. D'Alroy, now, and always, your faithful and sincere friend, Arthur Hawtree.' (ESTHER *goes to cradle, and bends over it.*) Oh, *his* boy, if you could read it! (*Sobs, with head on head of cradle.*)

(*Enter* POLLY, *door* R.)

POLLY. Father gone!

ESTHER. Polly, you look quite flurried. (*Goes.*)

(POLLY *laughs, and whispers to* ESTHER.)

ESTHER (*near head of table. Taking* POLLY *in her arms and kissing her*). So soon? Well—my darling, I hope you may be happy.

POLLY. Yes. Sam's going to speak to father about it this afternoon. (*Crosses* L., *round table, and putting rusks in saucepan.*) Did you see the agent, dear?

ESTHER (*sits* R. *of table*). Yes; the manager didn't come—he broke his appointment again.

POLLY (*sits* L. *of table*). Nasty, rude fellow!

ESTHER. The agent said it didn't matter, he thought I should get the engagement. He'll only give me thirty shillings a week, though.

POLLY. But you said that two pounds was the regular salary.

ESTHER. Yes, but they know I'm poor, and want the engagement, and so take advantage of me.

POLLY. Never mind, Esther. I put the dress in that bandbox. It looks almost as good as new.

ESTHER. I've had a letter from Captain Hawtree.

POLLY. I know, dear; he came here last night.

ESTHER. A dear, good letter—speaking of George, and enclosing me a cheque for thirty pounds.

POLLY. Oh, how kind! Don't you tell father. (*Noise of carriage-wheels without.*)

ESTHER. I shan't.

(ECCLES *enters, breathless.* ESTHER *and* POLLY *rise.*)

ECCLES. It's the Marquissy in her coach. (ESTHER *puts on the lid of bandbox.*) Now, girls, do be civil to her, and she may do something for us. (*Places hat on piano.*) I see the coach as I was coming out of the 'Rainbow'. (*Hastily pulls an old comb out of his pocket, and puts his hair in order.*)

ESTHER. The Marquise! (ESTHER *comes down to end of table* R., POLLY *holding her hand.*)

ECCLES (*at door*). This way, my lady—up them steps. They're rather awkward for the likes o' you; but them as is poor and lowly must do as best they can with steps and circumstances. (ESTHER *and* POLLY L., *at end of table.*)

(*Enter* MARCHIONESS, *door* R. *She surveys the place with aggressive astonishment.*)

MARCHIONESS (*going down* R.; *half aside*). What a hole! And to think that my grandson should breathe such an atmosphere, and be contaminated by such associations! (*To* ECCLES, *who is a little up* R.C.) Which is the young woman who married my son?

ESTHER. I am Mrs. George D'Alroy, widow of George D'Alroy. Who are you?

MARCHIONESS. I am his mother, the Marquise de Saint Maur.

ESTHER (*with the grand air*). Be seated, I beg. (ECCLES *takes chair from* R.C., *which* ESTHER *immediately seizes as* SAM *enters with an easy chair on his head, which he puts down* L., *not seeing* MARCHIONESS, *who instantly sits down in it, concealing it completely.*)

SAM (*astonished,* L. *of* MARCHIONESS). It's the Marquissy! (*Looking at her.*) My eye! These aristocrats are fine women—plenty of 'em—(*describing circle*) quality and quantity!

POLLY (L. *of table end*). Go away, Sam; you'd better come back. (ECCLES *nudges him, and bustles him towards door. Exit* SAM. ECCLES *shuts door on him.*)

ECCLES (*coming down* R. *of* MARCHIONESS, *rubbing his hands*). If we'd a know'd your ladyship had bin a-coming we'd a had the place cleaned up a bit. (*With hands on chair-back,* R. *corner, down. He gets round to* R. *behind* MARCHIONESS, *who turns the chair slightly from him.*)

POLLY. Hold your tongue, father! (ECCLES *crushed.*)

MARCHIONESS (*to* ESTHER). You remember me, do you not?

ESTHER. Perfectly, though I only saw you once. (*Seating herself en grande dame,* L.C.) May I ask what has procured me the honour of this visit?

MARCHIONESS. I was informed that you were in want, and I came to offer you assistance.

ESTHER. I thank you for your offer, and the delicate consideration for my feelings with which it is made. I need no assistance. (ECCLES *groans and leans on piano.*)

MARCHIONESS. A letter I received last night informed me that you did.

ESTHER. May I ask if that letter came from Captain Hawtree?

MARCHIONESS. No—from this person—your father, I think.

ESTHER (*to* ECCLES). How dare you interfere in my affairs?

ECCLES. My lovey, I did it with the best intentions.

MARCHIONESS. Then you will not accept assistance from me?

ESTHER. No.

POLLY (*aside to* ESTHER, *holding her hand*). Bless you, my darling! (POLLY *is standing beside her.*)

MARCHIONESS. But you have a child—a son—my grandson. (*With emotion.*)

ESTHER. Master D'Alroy wants for nothing.

POLLY (*aside*). And never shall. (ECCLES *groans and turns up to piano.*)

MARCHIONESS. I came here to propose that my grandson should go back with me. (POLLY *rushes up to cradle.*)

ESTHER (*rising defiantly*). What! part with my boy! I'd sooner die!

MARCHIONESS. You can see him when you wish. As for money, I—

ESTHER. Not for ten thousand million worlds—not for ten thousand million marchionesses!

ECCLES (R. *corner*). Better do what the good lady asks you, my dear; she's advising you for your own good, and for the child's likewise.

MARCHIONESS. Surely you cannot intend to bring up my son's son in a place like this?

ESTHER. I do. (*Goes up to cradle.*)

ECCLES. It *is* a poor place, and we are poor people, sure enough. We ought not to fly in the faces of our pastors and masters—our pastresses and mistresses.

POLLY (*aside*). Oh, hold your tongue, do! (*Up at cradle.*)

ESTHER (*before cradle*). Master George D'Alroy will remain with his mother. The offer to take him from her is an insult to his dead father and to him.

ECCLES (*aside*). He don't seem to feel it, stuck-up little beast!

MARCHIONESS. But you have no money—how can you rear him?—how can you educate him?—how can you live?

ESTHER (*tearing dress from bandbox*). Turn columbine—go on the stage again and dance!

MARCHIONESS (*rising*). You are insolent—you forget that I am a lady.

ESTHER. You forget that I am a mother. Do you dare to offer to buy my child—*his* breathing image, *his* living memory—with money? (*Crosses to door* R., *and throws it open.*) There is the door—go! (*Picture.*)

ECCLES (*to* MARCHIONESS, *who has risen, aside*). Very sorry, my lady, as you should be tret in this way, which was not my wishes.

MARCHIONESS. Silence! (ECCLES *retreats, putting back chair,* MARCHIONESS *goes up to door* R.) Mrs. D'Alroy, if anything could have increased my sorrow for the wretched marriage my poor son was *decoyed* into, it would be your conduct this day to his mother. (*Exit, door* R.)

ESTHER (*falling in* POLLY'*s arms*). Oh, Polly! Polly!

ECCLES (*looking after her*). To go away, and not to leave a sov. behind her! (*Running up to open door.*) Cat! Cat! Stingy old cat! (*Almost runs to fire* L., *sits, and pokes it violently; carriage-wheels heard without.*)

ESTHER. I'll go to my room and lie down. Let me have the baby, or that old woman may come back and steal him. (*Exit* ESTHER, POLLY *follows with the baby, door* R.)

ECCLES. Well, women is the obstinatest devils as never wore horse-shoes. Children? Beasts! Beasts!

(*Enter* SAM *and* POLLY, *door* R.)

SAM. Come along, Polly, and let's get it over at once. (SAM *places cap on piano and goes to* R. *of table* L. POLLY *takes bandbox from table, and places it up* L. *corner.*) Now, Mr. Eccles (ECCLES *turns suddenly, facing* SAM), since you've been talkin' on family matters, I'd like to 'ave a word with yer, so take this opportunity to—

ECCLES (*waving his hand grandly*). Take what you like, and then order more (*rising, and leaning over table*), Samuel Gerridge. That hand is a hand that never turned its back on a friend, or a bottle to give him. (*Sings front of table.*)

I'll stand by my friend,
I'll stand by my friend,
I'll stand by my friend,
If he'll stand to me—me, genelmen!

SAM. Well, Mr. Eccles, sir, it's this—

POLLY (*aside, coming down* R. *of* SAM). Don't tell him too sudden, Sam—it might shock his feelings.

SAM. It's this: Yer know that for the last four years I've been keepin' company with Mary—Polly. (*Turning to her and smiling.* ECCLES *drops into chair* R.C., *as if shot.*)

ECCLES. Go it! go it! strike home, young man! Strike on this grey head! (*Sings.*) 'Britons, strike home!' Here (*tapping his chest*), to my heart! Don't spare me. Have a go at my grey hairs. Pull 'em—pull 'em out! A long pull, and a strong pull, and a pull all together! (*Cries, and drops his face on arm, upon table.*)

POLLY (L. *of table*). Oh, father! I wouldn't hurt your feelings for the world. (*Patting his head.*)

SAM. No; Mr. Eccles, I don't want to 'urt your feelin's, but I'm a-goin' to enter upon a business. Here's a circ'lar. (*Offering one.*)

ECCLES (*indignantly*). Circ'lars. What are circ'lars compared to a father's feelings?

SAM. And I want Polly to name the day, sir, and so I ask you—

ECCLES. This is 'ard, this is 'ard. One of my daughters marries a soger. The other goes a-gasfitting.

SAM (*annoyed*). The business which will enable me to maintain a wife is that of the late Mr. Binks, plumber, glazier, &c.

ECCLES (*rising, sings. Air, 'Lost Rosabelle'*).

'They have given thee to a plumber,
They have broken every vow,
They have given thee to a plumber,
And my heart, my heart is breaking now.'

(*Drops into chair again.*) Now, genelmen! (SAM *thrusts circulars into his pocket, and turns away angrily.*)

POLLY. You know, father, you can come and see me. (*Leans over him* L.)

SAM (*sotto voce*). No, no. (*Motions to* POLLY.)

ECCLES (*looking up*). So I can, and that's a comfort. (*Shaking her hand.*) And you can come and see me, and that's a comfort. I'll come and see you often—very often—every day (SAM *turns up stage in horror*), and crack a fatherly bottle (*rising*) and shed a friendly tear. (*Wipes eyes with dirty pocket-handkerchief, which he pulls from breast pocket.*)

POLLY. Do, father, do. (*Goes up and gets tea-tray.*)

SAM (*with a gulp*). Yes, Mr. Eccles, do. (*Goes to* POLLY *and gesticulates behind tray.*)

ECCLES. I will. (*Goes* C.) And this it is to be a father. I would part with any of my children for their own good, readily—if I was paid for it. (*Goes to* R. *corner; sings.*) 'For I know that the angels are whispering to me'—me, genelmen! (POLLY *gets tea-things.*)

SAM (L. *of* ECCLES). I'll try and make Polly a good husband, and anything that I can do to prove it (*lowering his voice*), in the way of spirituous liquors and tobacco (*slipping coin into his hand, unseen by* POLLY) shall be done.

ECCLES (*lightening up and placing his* L. *hand on* SAM'*s head*).

'Be kind to thy father,
Wherever you be,
For he is a blessing
And credit to thee—thee, genelmen.'

(*Gets* C.) Well, my children—bless you, take the blessing of a grey 'air'd father. (POLLY *looking from one to the other,* ECCLES C., *to* SAM R.) Samuel Gerridge, she shall be thine. (*Mock heroically, looking at money.*) You shall be his wife (*looking at* POLLY), and you (*looking at* SAM), shall be her husband—for a husband I know no fitter—no 'gas-fitter' man. (*Runs to piano and takes hat; goes to door* R., *looks comically pathetic at* SAM R. *and* POLLY L., *puts on hat and comes towards* C.) I've a friend waiting for me round the corner, which I want to have a word with; and may you never know how much more sharper than a serpent's tooth it is to have a marriageable daughter. (*Sings.*)

'When I heard she was married
I breathed not a tone,
The h'eyes of all round me
Was fixed on my h'own;
I flew to my chamber
To hide my despair,
I tore the bright circlet
Of gems from my hair.
When I heard she was married,
When I heard she was married—'

(*Breaks down. Exit, door* R.)

POLLY (*drying her eyes*). There, Sam. I always told you that though father had his faults, his heart was in the right place.

SAM. Poor Polly. (*Crosses to fire-place,* L. *corner. Knock at* R. *door.*)

POLLY (*top of table*). Come in!

(*Enter* HAWTREE.)

POLLY. Major Hawtree! (SAM *turns away as they shake hands,* C. *of stage.*)

HAWTREE. I met the Marquise's carriage on the bridge. Has she been here? (SAM *at fire, with back to it.*)

POLLY. Yes.

HAWTREE. What happened?

POLLY. Oh, she wanted to take away the child. (*At head of table.*)

SAM. In the coach. (POLLY *sets tea-things.*)

HAWTREE. And what did Mrs. D'Alroy say to that?

SAM. Mrs. D'Alroy said that she'd see her blow'd first! (POLLY *pushes* SAM)—or words to that effect.

HAWTREE. I'm sorry to hear this; I had hoped—however, that's over.

POLLY (*sitting* L. *of table*). Yes, it's over; and I hope we shall hear no more about it. Want to take away the child, indeed—like her impudence! What next! (*Getting ready tea-things.*) Esther's gone to lie down. I shan't wake her up for tea, though she's had nothing to eat all day.

SAM (*head of table*). Shall I fetch some shrimps?

POLLY (L. *of table*). No. What made you think of shrimps?

SAM. They're a relish, and consolin'—at least I always found 'em so. (*Check lights, gradually.*)

POLLY. I won't ask you to take tea with us, major—you're too grand. (SAM *motions approbation to* POLLY, *not wanting* HAWTREE *to remain.*)

HAWTREE (*placing hat on piano*). Not at all. I shall be most happy. (*Aside.*) 'Pon my word, these are very good sort of people. I'd no idea——

SAM (*points to* HAWTREE, *who is* R.). He's a-going to stop to tea—well, I ain't. (*Goes up to window and sits.* HAWTREE *crosses and sits* R. *of table.*)

POLLY. Sam! Sam! (*Pause—he says* Eh?) Pull down the blind and light the gas.

SAM (L. *of table*). No, don't light up; I like this sort of dusk. It's unbusiness-like, but pleasant. (SAM *cuts enormous slice of bread, and hands it on point of knife to* HAWTREE. *Cuts small lump of butter, and hands it on point of knife to* HAWTREE, *who looks at it through eye-glass, then takes it.* SAM *then helps himself.* POLLY *meantime has poured out tea in two cups, and one saucer for* SAM, *sugars them, and then hands cup and saucer to* HAWTREE, *who has both hands full. He takes it awkwardly, and places it on table.* POLLY, *having only one spoon, tastes* SAM'*s tea, then stirs* HAWTREE'*s, attracting his attention by so doing. He looks into his tea-cup.* POLLY *stirs her own tea, and drops spoon into* HAWTREE'*s cup, causing it to spurt in his eye. He drops eye-glass and wipes his eyes.*)

POLLY (*making tea*). Sugar, Sam! (SAM *takes tea and sits facing fire.*) Oh, there isn't any milk—it'll be here directly—it's just his time.

VOICE (*outside; rattle of milk-pails*). Mia-oow!

POLLY. There he is. (*Knock at door* R.) Oh, I know; I owe him fourpence. (*Feeling her pockets.*) Sam, have you got fourpence? (*Knock again, louder.*)

SAM. No (*his mouth full*)—I ain't got no fourpence.

POLLY. He's very impatient. Come in!

(*Enter* GEORGE, *his face bronzed, and in full health. He carries a milk-can in his hand, which, after putting his hat on piano, he places on table.*)

GEORGE. A fellow hung this on the railings, so I brought it in. (POLLY *sees him, and gradually sinks down under the table* R. *Then* SAM, *with his mouth full, and bread and butter in hand, does the same* L. HAWTREE *pushes himself back a space, in chair, remains motionless.* GEORGE *astonished. Picture.*)

GEORGE. What's the matter with you?

HAWTREE (*rising*). George!

GEORGE. Hawtree! You here?

POLLY (*under table*). O-o-o-o-oh! the ghost!—the ghost!

SAM. It shan't hurt you, Polly. Perhaps it's only indigestion.

HAWTREE. Then you are not dead?

GEORGE. Dead, no. Where's my wife?

HAWTREE. You were reported killed.

GEORGE. It wasn't true.

HAWTREE. Alive! My old friend alive!

GEORGE. And well. (*Shakes hands.*) Landed this morning. Where's my wife?

SAM (*who has popped his head from under table-cloth*). He ain't dead, Poll—he's alive! (POLLY *rises from under table slowly.*)

POLLY (*pause; approaches him, touches him, retreats*). George! (*He nods.*) George! George!

GEORGE. Yes! Yes!

POLLY. Alive!—My dear George!—Oh, my dear brother!—(*looking at him intensely*)—Alive!—(*going to him*). Oh, my dear, dear, brother!—(*in his arms*)—how could you go and do so? (*Laughs hysterically.*)

(GEORGE L.C.; HAWTREE R.C.; SAM *down* L.; GEORGE *places* POLLY *in his arms.* SAM *goes to* POLLY. SAM *kisses* POLLY'*s hand violently.* HAWTREE *comes up, stares—business.* SAM *goes* L. *with a stamp of his foot;* HAWTREE R.)

GEORGE. Where's Esther?

HAWTREE. Here—in this house.

GEORGE. Here!—doesn't she know I'm back?

POLLY. No; how could she?

GEORGE (*to* HAWTREE). Didn't you get my telegram?

HAWTREE. No; where from?

GEORGE. Southampton! I sent it to the Club.

HAWTREE. I haven't been there these three days.

POLLY (*hysterically*). Oh, my dear, dear, dear dead-and-gone!—come back all alive, oh, brother George! (GEORGE *passes her down to* R.C.)

SAM. Glad to see yer, sir.

GEORGE. Thank you, Gerridge. (*Shakes hands.*) Same to you—but Esther?

POLLY (*back to audience, and 'kerchief to her eyes*). She's asleep in her room. (GEORGE *is going to door* R.; POLLY *stops him.*)

POLLY. You mustn't see her!

GEORGE. Not see her!—after this long absence?—why not?

HAWTREE. She's ill today. She has been greatly excited. The news of your death, which we all mourned, has shaken her terribly.

GEORGE. Poor girl! poor girl!

POLLY (*down* R.C.). Oh, we all cried so when you died!—(*crying*)—and now you're alive again, I want to cry ever so much more! (*Crying.*)

HAWTREE. We must break the news to her gently and by degrees. (*Crosses behind, to fire, taking his tea with him.*)

SAM. Yes. If you turn the tap on to full pressure, she'll explode! (SAM *turns to* HAWTREE, *who is just raising cup to his lips and brings it down on saucer with a bang; both annoyed.*)

GEORGE. To return, and not to be able to see her—to love her—to kiss her! (*Stamps.*)

POLLY. Hush!

GEORGE. I forgot! I shall wake her!

POLLY. More than that—you'll wake the baby!

GEORGE. Baby!—what baby?

POLLY. Yours.

GEORGE. Mine?—mine?

POLLY. Yes—yours and Esther's! Why, didn't you know there was a baby?

GEORGE. No!

POLLY. La! the ignorance of these men!

HAWTREE. Yes, George, you're a father. (*At fire-place.*)

GEORGE. Why wasn't I told of this? Why didn't you write?

POLLY. How could we when you were dead?

SAM. And 'adn't left your address. (*Looks at* HAWTREE, *who turns away quickly.*)

GEORGE. If I can't see Esther, I will see the child. The sight of me won't be too much for its nerves. Where is it?

POLLY. Sleeping in its mother's arms. (GEORGE *goes to door* R.; *she intercepts him.*) Please not! Please not!

GEORGE. I must. I will.

POLLY. It might kill her, and you wouldn't like to do that. I'll fetch the baby; but oh, please don't make a noise. (*Going up* R.) You won't make a noise—you'll be as quiet as you can, won't you? Oh! I can't believe it. (*Exit* POLLY, *door* R.)

(SAM *dances break-down and finishes up looking at* HAWTREE, *who turns away astonished.* SAM *disconcerted; sits on chair,* R. *of table;* GEORGE *at door.*)

GEORGE. My baby; my ba—It's a dream! You've seen it. (*To* SAM.) What's it like?

SAM. Oh! it's like a—like a sort of—infant—white and—milky, and all that.

(*Enter* POLLY, *with baby wrapped in shawls.* GEORGE *shuts door and meets her* C.)

POLLY. Gently, gently—take care! Esther will hardly have it touched. (SAM *rises and gets near to* GEORGE.)

GEORGE. But I'm its father!

POLLY. That don't matter. She's very particular.

GEORGE. Boy or girl?

POLLY. Guess.

GEORGE. Boy! (POLLY *nods.* GEORGE *proud.*) What's his name?

POLLY. Guess.

GEORGE. George? (POLLY *nods.*) Eustace? (POLLY *nods.*) Fairfax? Algernon? (POLLY *nods; pause.*) My names!

SAM (*to* GEORGE). You'd 'ardly think there was room enough in 'im to 'old so many names, would yer? (HAWTREE *looks at him—turns to fire.* SAM *disconcerted again; sits* R.C.)

GEORGE. To come back all the way from India to find that I'm dead, and that you're alive. To find my wife a widow with a new love aged —How old are you? I'll buy you a pony tomorrow, my brave little boy! What's his weight? I should say two pound nothing. My—baby—my—boy! (*Bends over him and kisses him.*) Take him away, Polly, for fear I should break him. (POLLY *takes child, and places it in cradle.*)

HAWTREE (*crosses to piano. Passes* SAM *front—stares—business.* SAM *goes round to fire-place, flings down bread and butter in a rage and drinks his tea out of saucer*). But tell us how it is you're back?—how you escaped? (*Leaning up against piano.*)

GEORGE (R.C., *coming down*). By and by. Too long a story just now. Tell *me* all about it. (POLLY *gives him chair* R.C.) How is it Esther's living here? (POLLY L. *of* GEORGE.)

POLLY. She came back after the baby was born, and the furniture was sold up.

GEORGE. Sold up? What furniture?

POLLY. That you bought for her.

HAWTREE. It couldn't be helped, George—Mrs. D'Alroy was so poor.

GEORGE. Poor! but I left her £600 to put in the bank!

HAWTREE. We '*must*' tell you. She gave it to her father, who banked it in his own name.

SAM. And lost it in bettin'—every copper.

GEORGE. Then she's been in want?

POLLY. No—not in want. Friends lent her money.

GEORGE (*seated* R.C.). What friends? (*Pause; he looks at* POLLY, *who indicates* HAWTREE.) You?

POLLY. Yes.

GEORGE (*rising, and shaking* HAWTREE'*s hand*). Thank you, old fella. (HAWTREE *droops his head.*)

SAM (*aside*). Now who'd ha' thought that long swell 'ad it in 'im? 'e never mentioned it.

GEORGE. So Papa Eccles had the money? (*Sitting* R.C. *again.*)

SAM. And blued it! (*Sits on* L. *corner of table.*)

POLLY (*pleadingly*). You see, father was very unlucky on the racecourse. He told us that if it hadn't been that all his calculations were upset by a horse winning who had no business to, he should have made our fortunes. Father's been unlucky, and he gets tipsy at times, but he's a very clever man, if you only give him scope enough.

SAM. I'd give 'im scope enough!

GEORGE. Where is he now?

SAM. Public-house.

GEORGE. And how is he?

SAM. Drunk! (POLLY *pushes him off table,* SAM *sits at fire-place up stage.*)

GEORGE (*to* HAWTREE). You were right. There is *'something'* in caste. (*Aloud.*) But tell us all about it. (*Sits.*)

POLLY. Well, you know, you went away; and then the baby was born. Oh! he was such a sweet little thing, just like—your eyes—your hair. (*Standing* L. *of* GEORGE *who is sitting* R.C.)

GEORGE. Cut that!

POLLY. Well, baby came; and when baby was six days old, your letter came, Major (*to* HAWTREE). I saw that it was from India, and that it wasn't in your hand (*to* GEORGE); I guessed what was inside it, so I opened it unknown to her, and I read there of your capture and death. I daren't tell her. I went to father to ask his advice, but he was too tipsy to understand me. Sam fetched the doctor. He told us that the news would kill her. When she woke up, she said she had dreamt there was a letter from you. I told her, No; and day after day she asked for a letter. So the doctor advised us to write one as if it came from you. So we did. Sam and I and the doctor told her—told Esther, I mean, that her eyes were bad, and she mustn't read, and we read our letter to her; didn't we Sam? But, bless you! she always knew it hadn't come from you! At last, when she was stronger, we told her all.

GEORGE (*after a pause*). How did she take it?

POLLY. She pressed the baby in her arms, and turned her face to the wall. (*A pause.*) Well, to make a long story short, when she got up, she found that father had lost all the money you left her. There was a dreadful scene between them. She told him he'd robbed her and her child, and father left the house, and swore he'd never come back again.

SAM. Don't be alarmed—'e did come back. (*Sitting by fire* L.)

POLLY. Oh, yes; he was too good-hearted to stop long from his children. He has his faults, but his good points, when you find 'em, are wonderful!

SAM. Yes, when you find 'em! (*Rises, gets bread and butter from table, and sits* L. *corner of table.*)

POLLY. So she had to come back here to us; and that's all.

GEORGE. Why didn't she write to my mother?

POLLY. Father wanted her; but she was too proud—she said she'd die first.

GEORGE (*rising, to* HAWTREE). There's a woman! Caste's all humbug. (*Sees sword over mantelpiece.*) That's my sword (*crossing round* L.), and a map of India, and that's the piano I bought her—I'll swear to the silk!

POLLY. Yes; that was bought in at the sale.

GEORGE (*to* HAWTREE). Thank ye, old fella!

HAWTREE. Not by me;—I was in India at the time.

GEORGE. By whom then? (GEORGE C.)

POLLY. By Sam. (SAM *winks to her to discontinue.*) I shall! He knew Esther was breaking her heart about any one else having it, so he took the money he'd saved up for our wedding, and we're going to be married now—ain't we, Sam?

SAM (*rushing to* GEORGE *and pulling out circulars from pocket*). And hope by constant attention to business to merit——(POLLY *pushes him away to* L.)

POLLY. Since you died it hasn't been opened, but if I don't play it tonight, may I die an old maid! (*Goes up.* GEORGE *crosses to* SAM, *and shakes his hand, then goes up stage, pulls up blind, and looks into street.* SAM *turns up and meets* POLLY *top of table.*)

HAWTREE (*aside*). Now who'd have thought that little cad had it in him? He never mentioned it. (*Aloud.*) *Apropos,* George, your mother—I'll go to the square, and tell her of——(*Takes hat from piano.*)

GEORGE. Is she in town? (*At cradle.*)

HAWTREE. Yes. Will you come with me?

GEORGE. And leave my wife?—and such a wife!

HAWTREE. I'll go at once. I shall catch her before dinner. Good-bye, old fellow. Seeing you back again, alive and well, makes me feel quite —that I quite feel——(*Shakes* GEORGE'*s hand. Goes to door, then crosses to* SAM, *who has turned* POLLY'*s tea into his saucer, and is just about to drink; seeing* HAWTREE, *he puts it down quickly, and turns his back.*) Mr. Gerridge, I fear I have often made myself very offensive to you.

SAM. Well, sir, yer 'ave!

HAWTREE (*at bottom of table*). I feared so. I didn't know you then. I beg your pardon. Let me ask you to shake hands—to forgive me, and forget it. (*Offering his hand.*)

SAM (*taking it*). Say no more, sir; and if ever I've made myself offensive to you, I ask your pardon; forget it, and forgive me. (*They shake hands warmly; as* HAWTREE *crosses to door, recovering from* SAM'*s hearty shake of the hand,* SAM *runs to him.*) Hi, sir! When yer marry that young lady as I know you're engaged to, if you should furnish a house, and require anything in my way——(*Bringing out circular; begins to read it.* POLLY *comes down* L., *and pushes* SAM *away, against* HAWTREE. SAM *goes and sits in low chair by fire-place, down stage, disconcerted, cramming circulars into his pocket.*)

HAWTREE. Good-bye, George, for the present. (*At door.*) Bye, Polly. (*Resumes his Pall Mall manner as he goes out.*) I'm off to the square. (*Exit* HAWTREE, *door* R.)

GEORGE (*at cradle*). But Esther?

POLLY (*meets* GEORGE *in* C.). Oh, I forgot all about Esther. I'll tell her all about it. (*She goes up* R.C.)

GEORGE. How? (*By door.*)

POLLY. I don't know; but it will come. Providence will send it to me, as it has sent you, my dear brother. (*Embracing him.*) You don't know how glad I am to see you back again! You must go. (*Pushing him.* GEORGE *takes hat off piano.*) Esther will be getting up directly. (*At door with* GEORGE, *who looks through keyhole.*) It's no use looking there; it's dark.

GEORGE (*at door*). It isn't often a man can see his own widow.

POLLY. And it isn't often that he wants to! Now, you must go. (*Pushing him off.*)

GEORGE. I shall stop outside.

SAM. And I'll whistle for you when you may come in.

POLLY. Now—hush!

GEORGE (*opening door wide*). Oh, my Esther, when you know I'm alive! I'll marry you all over again, and we'll have a second honeymoon, my darling. (*Exit.*)

POLLY. Oh, Sam! Sam! (*Commences to sing and dance.* SAM *also dances; they meet in* C. *of stage, join hands, and dance around two or three times, leaving* SAM L. *of* POLLY, *near table.* POLLY *going down* R.) Oh, Sam, I'm so excited, I don't know what to do. What shall I do—what shall I do?

SAM (*taking up* HAWTREE'*s bread and butter*). 'ave a bit of bread and butter, Polly.

POLLY. Now, Sam, light the gas; I'm going to wake her up. (*Opening door* R.) Oh, my darling, if I dare tell you! (*Whispering.*) He's come back! He's come back! He's come back! Alive! Alive! Alive! Sam, kiss me! (SAM *rushes to* POLLY, *kisses her, and she jumps off,* SAM *shutting the door.*)

SAM (*dances shutter dance*). I'm glad the swells are gone; now I can open my safety valve and let my feelin's escape. To think of 'is comin' back alive from India, just as I am goin' to open my shop. Perhaps he'll get me the patronage of the Royal Family. It would look stunnin' over the door, a lion and a unicorn a-standin' on their 'ind legs, doin' nothin' furiously, with a lozenge between 'em—thus. (*Seizes plate on table, puts his left foot on chair* R. *of table, and imitates the picture of the Royal arms.*) Polly said I was to light up, and whatever Polly says must be done. (*Lights brackets over mantelpiece, then candles; as he lights the broken one, says.*) Why this one is for all the world like old Eccles! (*Places candles on piano, and sits on music-stool.*) Poor Esther! to think of my knowin' 'er when she was in the ballet line—then in the 'onourable line; then a mother—no, *h*onourables is 'mammas'—then a widow, and then in the ballet line again!—and 'im to come back (*growing affected*) —and find a baby, with all 'is furniture and fittin's ready for immediate use (*crossing back of table during last few lines, sits in chair* L. *of table*)— and she, poor thing, lyin' asleep, with 'er eye-lids 'ot and swollen, not knowin' that that great, big, 'eavy, 'ulking, overgrown dragoon is prowlin' outside, ready to fly at 'er lips, and strangle 'er in 'is strong, lovin' arms—it—it—it—(*Breaks down and sobs with his head upon the table.*)

(*Enter* POLLY.)

POLLY. Why, Sam! What's the matter?

SAM (*rises and crosses* R.). I dunno. The water's got into my meter.

POLLY. Hush! here's Esther.

(*Enter* ESTHER, *door* L. *They stop suddenly.* POLLY *down stage.*)

SAM (R., *singing and dancing*). 'Tiddy-ti-tum,' &c.

ESTHER (*sitting near fire,* L. *of head of table, taking up costume and beginning to work*). Sam, you seem in high spirits tonight?

SAM. Yes; yer see Polly and I are goin' to be married—and—and 'opes by bestowing a merit—to continue the favour—

POLLY (*who has kissed* ESTHER *two or three times*). What are you talking about?

SAM. I don't know—I'm off my burner. (*Brings music-stool* R.C. POLLY *goes round to chair,* L. *corner, facing* ESTHER.)

ESTHER. What's the matter with you tonight, dear? (*To* POLLY.) I can see something in your eyes.

SAM. P'r'aps it's the new furniture! (*Sits on music-stool* R.)

ESTHER. Will you help me with the dress, Polly? (*They sit,* ESTHER *upper end, back of table,* POLLY *facing her, at lower end.*)

POLLY (*seated* L. *of table*). It was a pretty dress when it was new—not unlike the one Mademoiselle Delphine used to wear. (*Suddenly clapping her hands.*) Oh!

ESTHER. What's the matter?

POLLY. A needle! (*Crosses to* SAM, *who examines finger.*) I've got it!

SAM. What—the needle—in your finger?

POLLY. No; an idea in my head!

SAM (*still looking at finger*). Does it 'urt?

POLLY. Stupid! (SAM *still sitting on stool. Aloud.*) Do you recollect Mademoiselle Delphine, Esther?

ESTHER. Yes.

POLLY. Do you recollect her in that ballet that old Herr Griffenhaagen arranged?—'Jeanne la Folle, or, the Return of the Soldier'?

ESTHER. Yes; will you do the fresh hem?

POLLY. What's the use? Let me see—how did it go? How well I remember the scene!—the cottage was on that side, the bridge at the back—then ballet of villagers, and the entrance of Delphine as Jeanne, the bride—tra-lal-lala-lala-la-la (*sings and pantomimes,* SAM *imitating her*). Then the entrance of Claude, the bridegroom—(*To* SAM, *imitating swell.*) How-de-do, how-de-do?

SAM (*rising*). 'ow are yer? (*Imitating* POLLY, *then sitting again.*)

POLLY. Then there was the procession to church—the march of the soldiers over the bridge—(*sings and pantomimes*)—arrest of Claude, who is drawn for the conscription (*business;* ESTHER *looks dreamily*), and is torn from the arms of his bride, at the church porch. *Omnes* broken-hearted. This is *Omnes* broken-hearted. (*Pantomimes.*)

ESTHER. Polly, I don't like this; it brings back memories.

POLLY (*going to table, and leaning her hands on it, looks over at* ESTHER). Oh, fuss about memories!—one can't mourn for ever. (ESTHER *surprised.*) Everything in this world isn't sad. There's bad news, and—and there's good news sometimes—when we least expect it.

ESTHER. Ah! not for me.

POLLY. Why not?

ESTHER (*anxiously*). Polly!

POLLY. Second Act! (*This to be said quickly, startling* SAM, *who has been looking on the ground during last four or five lines.*) Winter—the Village Pump. This is the village pump. (*Pointing to* SAM, *seated by piano, on music-stool.* SAM *turns round on music-stool, disgusted.*) Entrance of Jeanne—now called Jeanne la Folle, because she has gone mad on account of the supposed loss of her husband.

SAM. The supposed loss?

POLLY. The supposed loss!

ESTHER (*dropping costume*). Polly!

SAM. Mind! (*Aside to* POLLY).

POLLY. Can't stop now! Entrance of Claude, *who isn't dead,* in a captain's uniform—a cloak thrown over his shoulders.

ESTHER. Not dead?

POLLY. Don't you remember the ballet? Jeanne is mad, and can't recognize her husband; and don't, till he shows her the ribbon she gave him when they were betrothed! A bit of ribbon! Sam, have you got a bit of ribbon? Oh, that crape sword-knot, that will do! (*Crosses down* R.C. SAM *astonished.*)

ESTHER. Touch that! (*Rising, and coming down* L.C.)

POLLY. Why not?—it's no use *now!*

ESTHER (*slowly, looking into* POLLY'*s eyes*). You have heard of George—I know you have—I see it in your eyes. You may tell me—I can bear it—I can indeed—indeed I can. Tell me—he is not dead? (*Violently agitated.*)

POLLY. No!

ESTHER. No?

POLLY. No!

ESTHER (*whispers*). Thank Heaven! (SAM *turns on stool, back to audience.*) You've seen him—I see you have!—I know it!—I feel it! I had a bright and happy dream—I saw him as I slept! Oh, let me know if he is near! Give me some sign—some sound—(POLLY *opens piano*)—some token of his life and presence! (SAM *touches* POLLY *on the shoulder, opens piano, takes hat and exits, door* R. *All to be done very quickly.* POLLY *sits immediately at piano and plays air softly—the same air played by* ESTHER *Act II, on the treble only.*)

ESTHER (*in an ecstasy*). Oh, my husband! come to me! for I know that you are near! Let me feel your arms clasp round me!—Do not fear for me!—I can bear the sight of you!—(*door opens showing* SAM *keeping* GEORGE *back*)—it will not kill me!——George—love—husband—come, oh, come to me! (GEORGE *breaks away from* SAM, *and coming down behind* ESTHER *places his hands over her eyes; she gives a faint scream, and turning, falls in his arms.* POLLY *plays the bass as well as treble of the air, forte, then fortissimo. She then plays at random, endeavouring to hide her tears. At last strikes piano wildly, and goes off into a fit of hysterical laughter, to the alarm of* SAM, *who, rushing down as* POLLY *cries 'Sam! Sam!' falls on his knees in front of her. They embrace,* POLLY *pushing him contemptuously away afterwards.* GEORGE *gets chair* R.C., *sits, and* ESTHER *kneels at his feet—he snatches off* ESTHER'*s cap, and throws it up stage.* POLLY *goes* L. *of* GEORGE. SAM *brings music-stool, and she sits.*)

ESTHER. To see you here again—to feel your warm breath upon my cheek—is it real, or am I dreaming?

SAM (R., *rubbing his head*). No; it's real.

ESTHER (*embracing* GEORGE). My darling!

SAM. My darling! (POLLY *on music-stool, which* SAM *has placed for her.* SAM, *kneeling by her, imitates* ESTHER—POLLY *scornfully pushes him away.*) But tell us—tell us how you escaped.

GEORGE. It's a long story; but I'll condense it. I was riding out, and suddenly found myself surrounded and taken prisoner. One of the troop that took me was a fella who had been my servant, and to whom I had done some little kindness. He helped me to escape, and hid me in a sort of cave, and for a long time used to bring me food. Unfortunately, he was ordered away; so he brought another Sepoy to look after me. I felt from the first this man meant to betray me, and I watched him like a lynx during the one day he was with me. As evening drew on, a Sepoy picket was passing. I could tell by the look in the fella's eyes, he meant to call out as soon as they were near enough; so I seized him by the throat, and shook the life out of him.

ESTHER. You strangled him?

GEORGE. Yes.

ESTHER. Killed him—dead?

GEORGE. He didn't get up again. (*Embraces* ESTHER.)

POLLY (*to* SAM). You never go and kill Sepoys. (*Pushes him over.*)

SAM. No! I pay rates and taxes.

GEORGE. The day after, Havelock and his Scotchmen marched through the village, and I turned out to meet them. I was too done up to join, so I was sent straight on to Calcutta. I got leave, took a berth on the P. and O. boat; the passage restored me. I landed this morning, came on here, and brought in the milk.

(*Enter the* MARCHIONESS, *door* R.; *she rushes to embrace* GEORGE C. *All rise,* SAM *putting piano stool back* R. POLLY *and* SAM R. *corner,* ESTHER *in front of table* L.)

MARCHIONESS. My dear boy!—my dear, dear boy!

POLLY. Why, see, she's crying! She's glad to see him alive, and back again.

SAM (*profoundly*). Well! There's always some good in women, even when they're ladies. (*Goes up to window.*)

(POLLY *puts dress in box, and goes to cradle, then beside* SAM.)

MARCHIONESS (*crossing to* ESTHER L.C.). My dear daughter, we must forget our little differences. (*Kissing her.*) Won't you? How history repeats itself! You will find a similar and as unexpected a return mentioned by Froissart in the chapter that treats of Philip Dartnell——

GEORGE. Yes, mother—I remember. (*Kisses her.*)

MARCHIONESS (*to* GEORGE, *aside*). We must take her abroad, and make a lady of her.

GEORGE. Can't, mamma—she's ready-made. Nature has done it to our hands.

MARCHIONESS (L.C.; *aside, to* GEORGE). But I won't have the man who smells of putty (SAM *business at back. He is listening, and at the word 'putty' throws his cap irritably on table* R. *of him.* POLLY *pacifies him, and makes him sit down beside her on window*) nor the man who smells of beer. (*Goes to* ESTHER, *who offers her chair, and sits in chair opposite to her.* MARCHIONESS *back to audience.* ESTHER *facing audience.*)

(*Enter* HAWTREE, *pale.*)

HAWTREE. George! Oh, the Marchioness is here.

GEORGE. What's the matter?

HAWTREE (R.). Oh, nothing. Yes, there is. I don't mind telling you. I've been thrown. I called at my chambers as I came along and found this. (*Gives* GEORGE *a note; sits on music-stool.*)

GEORGE. From the Countess, Lady Florence's mother. (*Reads.*) 'Dear Major Hawtree—I hasten to inform you that my daughter Florence is about to enter into an alliance with Lord Saxeby, the eldest son of the Marquis of Loamshire. Under these circumstances, should you think fit to call here again, I feel assured—' Well, perhaps it's for the best. (*Returning letter.*) Caste! you know. Caste! And a marquis is a bigger swell than a major.

HAWTREE. Yes, best to marry in your own rank of life.

GEORGE. If you can find *the* girl. But if ever you find *the* girl, marry her. As to her station—

'True hearts are more than coronets,
And simple faith than Norman blood.'

HAWTREE. Ya-as. But a gentleman should hardly ally himself to a nobody.

GEORGE. My dear fella, Nobody's a mistake—he don't exist. Nobody's nobody! Everybody's somebody.

HAWTREE. Yes. But still—Caste.

GEORGE. Oh, Caste's all right. Caste is a good thing if it's not carried too far. It shuts the door on the pretentious and the vulgar; but it should open the door very wide for exceptional merit. Let brains break through its barriers, and what brains can break through love may leap over.

HAWTREE. Yes. Why George, you're quite inspired—quite an orator. What makes you so brilliant? Your captivity? The voyage? What then?

GEORGE. I'm in love with my wife!

(*Enter* ECCLES, *drunk, a bottle of gin in his hand.*)

ECCLES (*crossing to* C.). Bless this 'appy company. May we 'ave in our arms what we love in our 'earts. (*Goes to head of table.* ESTHER *goes to cradle, back to audience.* POLLY *and* SAM *half amused, half angry.* MARCHIONESS *still sitting in chair, back to audience.* HAWTREE *facing* ECCLES. GEORGE *up stage leaning on piano in disgust.*) Polly, fetch wineglasses—a tumbler will do for me. Let us drink a toast. Mr. Chairman (*to* MARCHIONESS), ladies, and gentlemen—I beg to propose the 'elth of our newly returned warrior, *my son-in-law.* (MARCHIONESS *shivers.*) The Right Honourable George De Alroy. Get glasses, Polly, and send for a bottle of sherry wine for my ladyship. *My* ladyship! My ladyship! M'lad'ship. (*She half turns to him.*) You and me'll have a drain together on the quiet. So delighted to see you under these altered circum—circum—circum—stangate. (POLLY, *who has shaken her head at him to desist, in vain, very distressed.*)

SAM. Shove 'is 'ead in a bucket! (*Exit, in disgust, door* R.)

HAWTREE (*aside to* GEORGE). I think I can abate this nuisance—at least, I can remove it. (*Rises and crosses* C. *to* ECCLES, *who has got round to* R. *side of table, leaning on it. He taps* ECCLES *with his stick, first on* R.

shoulder, then on L., *and finally sharply on* R. ECCLES *turns round and falls on point of stick*—HAWTREE *steadying him.* GEORGE *crosses behind, to* MARCHIONESS, *who has gone to cradle—puts his arm round* ESTHER *and takes her to mantelpiece.*)

HAWTREE. Mr. Eccles, don't you think that, with your talent for liquor, if you had an allowance of about two pounds a week, and went to Jersey, where spirits are cheap, that you could drink yourself to death in a year?

ECCLES. I think I could—I'm sure I'll try. (*Goes up* L. *of table, steadying himself by it, and sits in chair by fire, with the bottle of gin.* HAWTREE *standing by fire.* ESTHER *and* POLLY *stand embracing* C. *As they turn away from each other*——)

GEORGE (*coming across with* ESTHER). Come and play me that air that used to ring in my ears as I lay awake, night after night, captive in the cave—you know. (*He hands* ESTHER *to piano. She plays the air.*)

MARCHIONESS (*bending over the cradle, at end,* R.). My grandson! (ECCLES *falls off the chair in the last stage of drunkenness, bottle in hand.* HAWTREE, *leaning one foot on chair from which* ECCLES *has fallen, looks at him through eye-glass.* SAM *enters and goes to* POLLY, *back* C., *behind cradle, and, producing wedding-ring from several papers, holds it up before her eyes.* ESTHER *plays until curtain drops.*)

THE END

THE BELLS

The story is told, illustrative of the abysmal ignorance of playgoers in the city of Bristol in the last century, of one of Sir Henry Irving's early appearances there in the role of Hamlet. As he took his curtain call after the first act (that being then a custom), Irving heard a man turn to his neighbor in the orchestra seats and ask, "Can you tell me, sir, does that young man appear much in this play?" Upon being assured that Hamlet does indeed figure largely in the tragedy, the inquirer said, "Oh! Then I'm off"—and he left.

The public reaction to Leopold David Lewis' *The Bells* was altogether different. The play had been tailored to the measurement of Sir Henry. Two eminent scene designers had been hired to lavish money on decoration, some dazzling new machinery was employed for special effects, and the music director of the Théâtre Cluny had been especially brought over from Paris for the occasion, but essentially it was Sir Henry Irving as Sir Henry Irving in *The Bells* that firmly established both Irving and the Lyceum. A. E. Wilson, writing the history of that theatre (1952), said of *The Bells:*

> When it opened on November 25, 1871, it revealed in Irving an actor of great and remarkable powers and gave him a part as the conscience-stricken burgomaster Mathias, with which his name will always be inseparably linked.

Wilson gives us, in connection with "the magic" of Irving's acting, the review that appeared in *The Times* after the first performance:

> It will be obvious to every reader that the efficiency of this singular play depends almost wholly upon the actor who represents Mathias. Mr. Irving has thrown the whole force of his mind into the character and works out bit by bit the concluding hours of a life passed in a constant effort to preserve a cheerful exterior, with a conscience tortured until it has become a monomania. It is a marked peculiarity of the moral position of Mathias that he has no confidence, that he is not subject to the extortions of some mercenary wretch who would profit by his knowledge. He is at once in two worlds between which there is no link—an outer world that is ever smiling, and an inner world which is a purgatory. Hence a dreaminess in his manner which Mr. Irving accurately represents in his frequent transitions from a display of the domestic affections to the fearful work of self-communion. The outer world is gone, and conscience is all triumphant, assisted by an imagination which violently brings together the anticipated terrors of a criminal court and the mesmeric feats he has recently witnessed. The struggles of the miserable culprit, convinced that all is lost, but desperately fighting against hope, rebelling against the judges, protesting against the clairvoyant who wrings his secret from him, are depicted by Mr. Irving with a degree of energy that, fully realizing the horror of the situation, seems to hold the audience in suspense. It was not until the curtain fell, and they summoned the actor before it with a storm of acclamation, that they seemed to recover their self-expression.

And it was not until they experienced the play as literature rather than as theatre, reading it in their easy chairs instead of seeing it enacted before them, that those audiences would recover their sense of proportion, seeing its faults as well as its thrills, for as acted it had such intensity that, as Keats said of *King Lear,* all the disagreeables evaporated. This does not really condemn the play, for after all *drama* means *doing* and there is something seriously wrong with any play that is not better seen than studied. *The Bells* may seem old-fashioned now, but it was stunning then. It may read badly, but (whether at the Lyceum or a command performance at Sandringham) it played well; its characters may seem as synthetic as those in George Du Maurier's *Trilby* (1894), but Mathias, once experienced, is as unforgettable as Svengali. Those who read *The Bells* with imagination and perspicuity will not fail to understand why it was one of the greatest hits of the Victorian theatre and how a skillful actor-manager could himself supply (when the author did not) the "elaboration," of which Bernard Shaw spoke, that could turn a melodrama into a masterpiece. Francis Cowley Burnand (1836-1917), one of the busiest of all Victorian hacks, also wrote a version of this French melodrama *Le Juif polonais* (1869; *The Polish Jew*) by Emile Erckmann and Alexandre Chatrian, and Burnand's play opened in London only a matter of days before *The Bells.* However, the Irving-Lewis collaboration succeeded and Burnand did not; for Irving played the story to the hilt as a melodrama, as a plot to thrill, not to teach. James William Wallack played *The Bells* in New York (1872-1873) in precisely the same way, as a shocker, hoking up the eve of the wedding and the ghostly trial and transfixing the audience with terror. That is the sole secret of this astoundingly successful play, and it is such a performance that you must re-create as you read. "On your imaginary forces work."

THE BELLS

A DRAMA IN THREE ACTS

(Adapted from 'The Polish Jew',
a Dramatic Study by MM. ERCKMANN and CHATRIAN)

by

Leopold Lewis

First produced at the Royal Lyceum Theatre, London,
November 25, 1871, with the following cast:

MATHIAS, *the Burgomaster*	Mr. Henry Irving
Father WALTER	Mr. Frank Hall
HANS, *a Forester*	Mr. F. W. Irish
CHRISTIAN	Mr. H. Crellin
Mesmerist	Mr. A. Tapping
Doctor ZIMMER, *a Physician*	Mr. Dyas
Notary	Mr. Collett
TONY, *a Villager*	Mr. Fredericks
FRITZ, *a Gendarme*	Mr. Fotheringham
President of the Court	Mr. Gaston Murray
Clerk of the Court	Mr. Branscombe
CATHERINE, *Wife of the Burgomaster*	Miss G. Pauncefort
ANNETTE, *their Daughter*	Miss Fanny Heywood
SOZEL, *a Maid*	Miss Ellen Mayne

Place—*A Village in Alsace*
Time—*December 24th & 26th, 1833*

ACT I

SCENE: *Interior of a Village Inn in Alsace. Table and chairs,* R. *1* E.; L. *1* E., *an old-fashioned sideboard, with curious china upon it, and glasses; door,* R.; *door,* L.; *large window at back, cut in scene,* R.; *large door at back, cut in scene,* L.; *a candle or lamp burns upon the table; a stove at back,* R., *with kettle on it; the pipe of stove going off through the wing at* R. *The country covered with snow is seen through the window; snow is falling; a large clock in* L. *corner, at back—hands to work. The Inn is the residence of the Burgomaster. It is Christmas Eve.*

(CATHERINE, *the Burgomaster's wife, discovered seated at a spinning-wheel,* L. *1* E. *Music upon rising of curtain.* HANS *passes window; he carries a gun, and a large game-bag is slung across his shoulders.*)

HANS (*taking off his hat and shaking away the snow*). More snow, Madame Mathias, more snow! (*He places his gun by the stove.*)

CATHERINE. Still in the village, Hans?

HANS. Yes, on Christmas Eve one may be forgiven some small indulgence.

CATHERINE. You know your sack of flour is ready for you at the mill?

HANS. Oh, yes; but I am not in a hurry. Father Walter will take charge of it for me in his cart. Now one glass of wine, madame, and then I'm off. (*He sits at table,* R., *laughing.*)

CATHERINE. Father Walter still here? I thought he had left long ago.

HANS. No, no. He is still at the Golden Fleece emptying his bottle. As I came along, I saw his cart standing outside the grocer's, with the coffee, the cinnamon, and the sugar, all covered with snow, he, he, he! He is a jolly old fellow. Fond of good wine, and I don't blame him, you may be sure. We shall leave together.

CATHERINE. And you have no fear of being upset?

HANS. What does it matter? As I said before, on Christmas Eve one may be forgiven some small indulgence.

CATHERINE. I will lend you a lanthorn when you go. (*Calling without moving from her wheel.*) Sozel!

SOZEL (*from within,* L.). Madame!

CATHERINE. Some wine for Hans!

SOZEL (*the same*). Yes, madame.

HANS. That's the sort. Considering the festive character of weather like this, one really must take something.

CATHERINE. Yes, but take care, our white wine is very strong.

HANS. Oh, never fear, madame! But, where is our Burgomaster? How is it he is not to be seen? Is he ill?

CATHERINE. He went to Ribeauville five days ago.

(*Enter* SOZEL, *carrying a decanter of white wine and glass; she places it on table,* R.; *she enters, door,* L.U.E.) Here is the wine, Master Hans. (*Exit* SOZEL, L.)

HANS. Good, good! (*He pours out a glass, and drinks with gusto.*) I wager, now, that the Burgomaster has gone to buy the wine for the wedding.

CATHERINE (*laughing*). Not at all improbable.

HANS. Only, just now, when I was at the Golden Fleece, it was talked about publicly, that the pretty Annette, the daughter of the Burgomaster, and Christian, the Quarter-master of Gendarmes, were going to be married! I could scarcely believe my ears. Christian is certainly a brave man, and an honest man, and a handsome man! I do not wish to maintain anything to the contrary. Our village is rather distinguished in that respect. (*Pulls up his shirt collar.*) But he has nothing but his pay to live upon, whilst Annette is the richest match in the village.

CATHERINE. Do you believe, then, Hans, that money ought always to be the one consideration?

HANS. No, no, certainly not—on the contrary. Only, I thought that the Burgomaster—

CATHERINE. Well, you have been mistaken; Mathias did not even ask, 'What have you?' He said at once, 'Let Annette give her free consent, and I give mine!'

HANS. And did she give her free consent?

CATHERINE. Yes; she loves Christian, and as we have no other thought but the happiness of our child, we do not look for wealth!

HANS. Oh, if the Burgomaster consents and you consent, and Annette consents, why, I suppose I cannot refuse my consent either. Only, I may make this observation, I think Christian a very lucky dog, and I wish I was in his place!

(*Music. Enter* ANNETTE, L., *she crosses and looks through window, then turns to* HANS.)

ANNETTE. Good evening, Hans! (*Music ceases.*)

HANS (*rising from table and turning round*). Ah, it is you. Good evening! Good evening! We were just talking about you!

ANNETTE. About me!

HANS. Yes! (*He takes off his game-bag and hangs on back of chair, then looking at* ANNETTE *with admiration.*) Oh, oh! How smiling you look, and how prettily dressed; one would almost think that you were going to a wedding.

ANNETTE. Ah, you are always joking.

HANS. No, no, I am not joking! I say what I think, that's all! That pretty cap, and that pretty dress, and those pretty shoes were not put on for the pleasure of a tough middle-aged forest-keeper like myself. It has been all arranged for another—for another I say, and I know who that particular 'another' happens to be—he, he, he!

ANNETTE (*blushing*). How can you talk such nonsense!

HANS. Oh, yes, it is nonsense to say that you are fascinating, merry, good and pretty, no doubt and it is nonsense to say that the particular another I refer to—you know the one I mean—the tall one with the handsome moustaches, is a fellow to be envied. Yes, it is nonsense to say it, for I for one do not envy him at all—no, not at all! (FATHER WALTER *has passed the window, now opens door at back and puts his head in.* ANNETTE *turns to look at him.*)

WALTER (*laughing and coming in—he is covered with snow*). Ah, she turned her head! It's not he you expect!

ANNETTE. Who, Father Walter?

WALTER. Ha, ha, ha! That's right. Up to the last minute she will pretend that she knows nothing. (*Crosses to* R.)

ANNETTE (*simply*). I do not understand what you mean. (WALTER *and* HANS *both laugh.*)

CATHERINE. You are a couple of old fools!

WALTER (*still laughing*). You're not such an old fool as you look, are you, Hans?

HANS. No; and you don't look such an old fool as you are, do you, Walter?

(*Enter* SOZEL, L., *with a lighted lanthorn, which she places upon the sideboard.* L., *then exits.*)

WALTER. No. What is the meaning of that lanthorn?

HANS. Why, to act as a light for the cart.

ANNETTE. You can go by moonlight! (*She opens the lanthorn and blows out the candle.*)

WALTER. Yes, yes certainly we will go by the light of the moon! Let us empty a glass in honour of the young couple. (*They fill glasses.*) Here's to the health of Christian and Annette! (*They drink—*HANS *taking a long time in drinking the contents of his glass, and then heaving a deep sigh, and Music commences.*)

WALTER (*seriously*). And now listen, Annette; as I entered I saw Christian returning with two gendarmes, and I am sure that in a quarter of an hour—

ANNETTE. Listen! (*Wind, off.*)

CATHERINE. The wind is rising. I hope that Mathias is not now on the road!

ANNETTE. No, no, it is Christian! (*Music, forte.* CHRISTIAN *passes the window, enters the door at back, covered with snow.*)

ALL. Christian! (*Music ceases.*)

CHRISTIAN. Good evening, all. (ANNETTE *runs to him.*) Good evening, Annette.

ANNETTE. Where have you come from, Christian?

CHRISTIAN. From the Hôvald! From the Hôvald! What a snow-storm! I have seen many in Auvergne or the Pyrenees, but never anything like this. (*He sits by the stove, and warms his hands. After hanging up his hat,* ANNETTE *goes out and returns with a jug of wine, which she places upon the stove.*)

WALTER (*lighting his pipe and smoking, to* HANS, *who is also smoking*). There, look at that! What care she takes of him! It would not be for us that she would fetch the sugar and the cinnamon and warm the wine.

CHRISTIAN (*to* ANNETTE, *laughing*). Do not allow me, Annette, to be crushed by the satire of Father, who knows how to defy the wind and the snow by the side of a good fire. I should like to see the figure he would present, if he had been five hours on duty as I have been in the snow, on the Hôvald.

CATHERINE. You have been five hours in the snow, Christian! Your duties must be terribly severe.

CHRISTIAN. How can it be helped? At two o'clock we received information that smugglers had passed the river the previous night with tobacco and gunpowder; so we were bound to be off at once. (*Music.* ANNETTE *pours out hot wine into glass and hands it to* CHRISTIAN, C.)

ANNETTE. Drink this, Christian, it will warm you.

CHRISTIAN (*standing,* C.). Thank you, Annette. (*Takes glass—looks at her tenderly, and drinks.*) Ah! that's good!

WALTER. The Quarter-master is not difficult to please. (*Music ceases.*)

CATHERINE (*to* CHRISTIAN). Never mind. Christian, you are fortunate to have arrived this early! (*Wind heard off.*) Listen to the wind! I hope that Mathias will have the prudence to stop for shelter somewhere on the road. (*To* HANS *and* WALTER.) I was right, you see, in advising you to go; you would now have been safely at home!

HANS (*laughing*). Annette was the cause of our stopping. Why did she blow out the lanthorn?

ANNETTE. Oh, you were glad enough to stop!

CHRISTIAN. Your winters are very severe here.

WALTER. Oh, not every year, Quarter-master! For fifteen years we have not had a winter so severe as this.

HANS. No—I do not remember to have seen so much snow since what is called 'The Polish Jew's Winter'. In that year the Schnieberg was covered in the first days of November, and the frost lasted till the end of March.

CHRISTIAN. And for that reason it is called 'The Polish Jew's Winter'?

WALTER. No—it is for another and terrible reason, which none of us will ever forget. Madame Mathias remembers it well, I am sure.

CATHERINE (*solemnly*). You are right, Walter, you are right.

HANS. Had you been here at that time, Quarter-master, you might have won your cross.

CHRISTIAN. How? (ANNETTE *at work in* C., *on stool*—CATHERINE *at spinning-wheel, and* HANS *at table,* R., *smoking.*)

WALTER (*at last, to* CHRISTIAN, *in* C., *seated*). I can tell you all about this affair from the beginning to the end, since I saw it nearly all myself. Curiously enough, it was this very day, just fifteen years ago, that I was seated at this very table. There was Mathias, who sat there, and who had only bought his mill just six months before; there was old John Roebec, who sat there—they used to call him 'the Little Shoemaker'; and several others, who are now sleeping under the turf—we shall all go there some day! Happy are those who have nothing upon their conscience! We were just beginning a game of cards, when, just as the old clock struck ten, the sound of horse-bells was heard; a sledge stopped before the door, and almost immediately afterwards a Polish Jew entered. He was a well-made, vigorous man, between forty and fifty years of age. I fancy I can see him even now entering at that door with his green cloak and his fur cap, his large black beard and his great boots covered with hare skin. He was a seed merchant. He said as he came in, 'Peace be with you!' Everybody turned to look at him, and thought, 'Where has he come from? What does he want?' Because you must know that the Polish Jews who come to dispose of seed do not arrive in this province till the month of February. Mathias said to him, 'What can I do for you?' But the Jew, without replying, first opened his cloak, and then unbuckled a girdle which he wore round his waist. This he threw upon the table, and we all heard the ringing sound of the gold it contained. Then he said, 'The snow is deep; the road difficult; put my horse in the stable. In one hour I shall continue my journey.' After that he drank his wine without speaking to anyone, and sat like a man depressed, and who is anxious about his affairs. At eleven o'clock the Night Watchman came in. Everyone went his way, and the Jew was left alone! (*Chord of Music—loud gust of wind—crash of glass off at* L.—*hurried music.* ALL *start to their feet. Music continued.*)

CATHERINE. What has happened? I must go and see.

ANNETTE. Oh! no, you must not go!

CATHERINE. I will return immediately. Don't be alarmed. (*Exit* CATHERINE, *at* L. *During the following,* ANNETTE *takes up the spinning-wheel, and listens at the door for her mother.*)

CHRISTIAN. But I do not yet see how I could have gained the cross in this affair—

WALTER. Stop a minute. The next morning they found the Jew's horse dead under the Bridge of Vechem, and a hundred yards further on, the green cloak and the fur cap, deeply stained with blood. As to what became of the Jew himself that has never to this day been discovered. (*Music ceases.*)

HANS. Everything that Walter has stated is strictly true. The gendarmes came here the next morning, notwithstanding the snow; and, in fact, it is since that dreadful time that the brigade has been established here.

CHRISTIAN. But was no inquiry instituted?

HANS. Inquiry! I should think there was. It was the former Quartermaster, Kelz, who undertook the case. How he travelled about! What witnesses he badgered! What clues he discovered! What information and reports were written! and how the coat and the cap were analysed, and examined by magistrates and doctors!—but it all came to nothing!

CHRISTIAN. But, surely, suspicion fell on someone.

HANS. Oh, of course, the gendarmes are never at a loss for suspicions in such cases. But proofs are required. About that time, you see, there were two brothers living in the village who had an old bear, with his ears all torn, two big dogs, and a donkey, that they took about with them to the fairs, and made the dogs bait the bear. This brought them a great deal of money; and they lived a rollicking dissipated life. When the Jew disappeared, they happened to be at Vechem; suspicions fastened upon them, and the report was that they had caused the Jew to be eaten by the dogs and the bear, and that they only refrained from swallowing the cloak and cap, because they had had enough. They were arrested, and it would have gone hard with the poor devils, but Mathias interested himself in their case, and they were discharged, after being in prison fifteen months. That was the specimen of suspicion of the case.

CHRISTIAN. What you have told me greatly astonished me. I never heard a word of this before.

(*Re-enter* CATHERINE, L.)

CATHERINE. I was sure that Sozel had left the windows in the kitchen open. Now every pane of glass in them is broken. (*To* CHRISTIAN.) Fritz is outside. He wishes to speak with you.

CHRISTIAN. Fritz, the gendarme!

CATHERINE. Yes, I asked him to come in, but he would not. It is upon some matter of duty.

CHRISTIAN. Ah! good, I know what it is! (*He rises, takes down his hat, and is going to the door.*)

ANNETTE. You will return, Christian?

CHRISTIAN. In a few minutes. (*Music to take him off. Exit, door,* C.)

WALTER. Ah! there goes a brave young fellow—gentle in character, I will admit, but not a man to trifle with rogues.

HANS. Yes, Mathias is fortunate in finding so good a son-in-law; but everything has succeeded with Mathias for the last fifteen years. (*Music commences.*) He was comparatively poor then, and now he is one of the richest men in the village, and the Burgomaster. He was born under a lucky star.

WALTER. Well, and he deserves all the success he has achieved.

CATHERINE. Hark!

ANNETTE. It is, perhaps, Christian returning as he promised. (*Hurried music.* MATHIAS *passes the window, then enters at* C. *door; he wears a long cloak covered with snow, large cap made of otter's skin, gaiters and spurs, and carries a large riding-whip in his hand—chord—tableau.*)

MATHIAS. It is I—It is I! (*Music ceases.*)

CATHERINE (*rising*). Mathias!

HANS / WALTER } (*starting up*). The Burgomaster!

ANNETTE (*running and embracing him*). At last you have come.

MATHIAS. Yes, yes! Heaven be praised! What a snow-storm. I was obliged to leave the carriage at Vechem. It will be brought over to-morrow.

CATHERINE (*embracing him and taking off his coat*). Let me take this off for you. It was very kind of you not to stop away. We were becoming so anxious about you.

MATHIAS. So I thought, Catherine; and that was the reason I determined to reach home tonight. (*Looking round.*) Ha, ha! Father Walter and Hans, you will have nice weather in which to go home (*He takes off his hat, &c., and gives them to his wife and daughter.*) There! You will have to get all those things dried.

CATHERINE (*at door,* L.). Sozel, get ready your master's supper at once, and tell Nickel to take the horse to the stable!

SOZEL (*within*). Yes madame. (MATHIAS *sits* R., *by table.*)

ANNETTE. We thought perhaps that your cousin Bôth would have detained you.

MATHIAS (*unbuttoning his gaiters*). Oh, I had finished all my business yesterday morning, and I wished to come away; but Bôth made me stop to see a performance in the town.

ANNETTE. A performance! Is Punchinello at Ribeauville?

MATHIAS. No, it was not Punchinello. It was a Parisian who did extraordinary tricks. He sent people to sleep.

ANNETTE. Sent people to sleep!

MATHIAS. Yes.

CATHERINE. He gave them something to drink, no doubt.

MATHIAS. No; he simply looked at them and made signs, and they went fast asleep.—It certainly was an astonishing performance. If I had not myself seen it I should never have believed it.

HANS. Ah! the Brigadier Stenger was telling me about it the other day. He had seen the same thing at Saverne. This Parisian sends people to sleep, and when they are asleep he makes them tell him everything that weighs upon their consciences.

MATHIAS. Exactly. (*To* ANNETTE.) Annette?

ANNETTE. What, father?

MATHIAS. Look in the big pocket of my cloak.

(*Enter* SOZEL.)

Sozel! take these gaiters and spurs; hang them in the stable, with the harness.

SOZEL. Yes, Burgomaster. (*Exit.*)

(ANNETTE, *who has taken a small box out of the pocket of the cloak, approaches her father,* C. *Music.*)

ANNETTE. What is it, father?

MATHIAS (*rising*). Open the box. (*She opens the box, and takes out a handsome Alsatian hat, with gold and silver stars upon it—the others approach to look at it.*)

ANNETTE. Oh, how pretty! Is it for me?

MATHIAS. For whom else could it be? Not for Sozel, I fancy. (ANNETTE *puts on the hat after taking off her ribbon, and looks at herself in glass on sideboard—all express admiration.*)

ANNETTE. Oh! what will Christian say?

MATHIAS. He will say you are the prettiest girl in the province.

ANNETTE (*kissing her father*). Thank you, dear father. How good you are!

MATHIAS. It is my wedding present, Annette. The day of your marriage I wish you to wear it, and to preserve it for ever. In fifteen or twenty years hence, will you remember your father gave it you?

ANNETTE (*with emotion*). Yes, dear father!

MATHIAS. All that I wish is to see you happy with Christian. (*Music ceases.*) And now for supper and some wine. (*To* WALTER *and* HANS.) You will stop and take a glass of wine with me?

WALTER. With pleasure, Burgomaster.

HANS. For you, Burgomaster, we will try and make that little effort. (SOZEL *has entered,* L., *with tray of supper and wine which she has placed upon table.* MATHIAS *now sits at table, helps wine, and then commences to eat with a good appetite.* SOZEL *draws the curtains across window at back, and exits,* L.)

MATHIAS. There is one advantage about the cold. It gives you a good appetite. Here's to your health! (*He drinks.*)

WALTER AND HANS. Here's yours, Burgomaster! (*They touch glasses and drink.*)

MATHIAS. Christian has not been here this evening?

ANNETTE. Yes; they came to fetch him, but he will return presently.

MATHIAS. Ah! Good! good!

CATHERINE. He came late today, in consequence of some duty he had to perform in the Hôvald, in the capture of smugglers.

MATHIAS (*eating*). Nice weather for such a business. By the side of the river, I found the snow five feet deep.

WALTER. Yes; we were talking about that. We were telling the Quarter-master, that since the 'Polish Jew's Winter' we had never seen weather like this. (MATHIAS, *who was raising the glass to his lips—places it on the table again without drinking.*)

MATHIAS. Ah! you were talking of that? (*Distant sound of Bells heard. To himself—*'Bells! Bells!' *His whole aspect changes, and he leaves off eating, and sits listening. The Bells continue louder.*)

HANS. That winter, you remember, Burgomaster, the whole valley was covered several feet deep with snow, and it was a long time before the horse of the Polish Jew could be dug out.

MATHIAS (*with indifference*). Very possibly; but that tale is too old! It is like an old woman's story now, and is thought about no more. (*Watching them and starting up.*) Do you not hear the sound of Bells upon the road? (*The Bells still go on.*)

WALTER }
HANS } (*listening*). Bells? No!

CATHERINE. What is the matter, Mathias? you appear ill. You are cold; some warm wine will restore you. The fire in the stove is low; come, Annette, we will warm your father his wine in the kitchen. (*Exeunt* CATHERINE *and* ANNETTE, *door* L.)

MATHIAS. Thank you; it is nothing.

WALTER. Come, Hans, let us go and see to the horse. At the same time, it is very strange that it was never discovered who did the deed.

MATHIAS. The rogues have escaped, more's the pity. Here's your health! (*Music.*)

WALTER AND HANS. Thank you!

HANS. It is just upon the stroke of ten! (*They drink, and go out together at door* R.)

MATHIAS (*alone—comes forward and listens with terror. Music with frequent chords*). Bells! Bells! (*He runs to the window and slightly drawing the curtains, looks out.*) No one on the road. (*Comes forward.*) What is this jangling in my ears? What is tonight? Ah, it is the very night—the very hour! (*Clock strikes ten.*) I feel a darkness coming over me. (*Stage darkens.*) A sensation of giddiness seizes me. (*He staggers to chair.*) Shall I call for help? No, no, Mathias. Have courage! The Jew is dead! (*Sinks on chair, the Bells come closer, then the back of the Scene rises and sinks, disclosing the Bridge of Vechem, with the snow-covered country and frozen rivulet; lime-kiln burning in the distance; the* JEW *is discovered seated in sledge dressed as described in speech in Act I; the horse carrying Bells; the* JEW's *face is turned away; the snow is falling fast; the scene is seen through a gauze; limelight;* L., *vision of a man dressed in a brown blouse and hood over his head, carrying an axe, stands in an attitude of following the sledge; when the picture is fully disclosed the Bells cease.*)

MATHIAS (*his back to scene*). Oh, it is nothing. It is the wine and cold that have overcome me! (*He rises and turns, goes up stage; starts violently upon seeing the vision before him; at the same time the* JEW *in the sledge suddenly turns his face, which is ashy pale, and fixes his eyes sternly upon him;* MATHIAS *utters a prolonged cry of terror, and falls senseless. Hurried Music.*)

End of the First Act

ACT II

SCENE: *Best room in the Burgomaster's house. Door,* L.; *door* R.; *three large windows at back, looking out upon a street of the village, the church and the buildings covered with snow; large stove in the centre of room, practicable door to stove, tongs in grate; arm-chair near the stove; at* L. (*1st grooves*), *an old escritoire; near* L., *a table and arm-chair; chairs about room. It is morning; the room and street bright with sunlight.*

(*As the Curtain rises to Music,* MATHIAS *is discovered seated in arm-chair at table;* CATHERINE *and* DOCTOR ZIMMER *standing at back by stove contemplating him. They advance.*)

DOCTOR. You feel better, Burgomaster?

MATHIAS. Yes, I am quite well.

DOCTOR. No more pains in the head?

MATHIAS. No.

DOCTOR. No more strange noises in the ears?

MATHIAS. When I tell you that I am quite well—that I never was better—that is surely enough.

CATHERINE. For a long time he has had bad dreams. He talks in his sleep, and his thirst at night is constant, and feverish.

MATHIAS. Is there anything extraordinary in being thirsty during the night?

DOCTOR. Certainly not: but you must take more care of yourself. You drink too much white wine, Burgomaster. Your attack of the night before last arose from this cause. You had taken too much wine at your cousin's and then the severe cold having seized you, the blood had flown to the head.

MATHIAS. I *was* cold, but that stupid gossip about the Polish Jew was the cause of all.

DOCTOR. How was that?

MATHIAS. Well, you must know, when the Jew disappeared, they brought me the cloak and cap that had belonged to the poor devil, and the sight of them quite upset me, remembering he had, the night before, stopped at our house. Since that time I had thought no more of the matter until the night before last, when some gossip brought the affair again to my mind. It was as if I had seen the ghost of the

Jew. We all know that there are no such things, but—(*suddenly to his wife*). Have you sent for the Notary?

CATHERINE. Yes; but you must be calm.

MATHIAS. I am calm. But Annette's marriage must take place at once. When a man in robust health and strength is liable to such an attack as I have had, nothing should be postponed till the morrow. What occurred to me the night before last might again occur tonight. I might not survive the second blow, and then I should not have seen my dear children happy. And now leave me. Whether it was the wine, or the cold, or the gossip about the Polish Jew, it comes to the same thing. It is all past and over now.

DOCTOR. But, perhaps, Burgomaster, it would be better to adjourn the signing of the marriage contract for a few days. It is an affair of so much interest and importance that the agitation might—

MATHIAS (*angrily*). Good heavens, why will not people attend to their own business! I was ill, you bled me—I am well again—so much the better. Let the Notary be sent for at once. Let Father Walter and Hans be summoned as witnesses, and let the whole affair be finished without further delay.

DOCTOR (*to* CATHERINE, *aside*). His nerves are still very much shaken. Perhaps it will be better to let him have his own way. (*To* MATHIAS.) Well, well, we'll say no more about it. Only don't forget what I have said—be careful of the white wine.

MATHIAS (*angrily striking the table, turning his back*). Good! Good! Ah! (*The* DOCTOR *looks with pity towards him, bows to* CATHERINE, *and exits, door* L. *The church bell commences to ring. Music.*)

CATHERINE (*at door* R., *calling*). Annette! Annette!

ANNETTE (*off* R.). I am coming.

CATHERINE (*impatiently*). Be quick. Be quick.

ANNETTE (*off*). Directly—directly!

MATHIAS. Don't hurry the poor child. You know that she is dressing.

CATHERINE. But I don't take two hours to dress.

MATHIAS. You; oh! that is different. She expects Christian. He was to have been here this morning. Something has detained him.

(*Enter* ANNETTE, *door* R., *she is in gala dress, and wears the golden heart upon her breast, and the hat given her by* MATHIAS *in the First Act.*)

CATHERINE. At last, you are ready!

ANNETTE. Yes, I am ready.

MATHIAS (*with affection*). How beautiful you look Annette.

ANNETTE. You see, dear father, I have put on the hat.

MATHIAS. You did right—you did right.

CATHERINE (*impatiently*). Are you not coming, Annette? The service will have commenced. (*Takes book off table.*) Come, come.

ANNETTE. Christian has not yet been here.

MATHIAS. No, you may be sure some business detains him.

CATHERINE. Do come, Annette; you will see Christian by and by. (*Exit,* R., ANNETTE *is following.*)

MATHIAS. Annette, Annette! Have you nothing to say to me? (ANNETTE *runs to him, and kisses him—he embraces her with affection.*)

ANNETTE. You know, dear father, how much I love you.

MATHIAS. Yes, yes. There, go now, dear child! your mother is impatient. (*Exit* ANNETTE, *door* R.)

(*The villagers, men and women in Sunday clothes, pass the window in couples.* MATHIAS *goes up and looks through the window,* ANNETTE *and* CATHERINE *pass and kiss hands to him—a woman in the group says* 'Good morning, Burgomaster.' *Church bell ceases. Music ceases.*)

MATHIAS (*coming forward to* R. *of stage, taking pinch of snuff*). All goes well! Luckily all is over. But what a lesson, Mathias,—what a lesson! Would anyone believe that the mere talk about the Jew could bring on such a fit? Fortunately the people about here are such idiots they suspect nothing. (*Seats himself in chair by table.*) But it was that Parisian fellow at the fair who was the real cause of all. The rascal had really made me nervous. I said to myself, 'Stop, stop, Mathias—this sending you to sleep may be an invention of the devil, you might relate certain incidents in your past life! You must be cleverer than that, Mathias; you mustn't run your neck into a halter; you must be cleverer than that—ah! you must be cleverer than that.' (*Starting up and crossing to* R.) You will die an old man yet, Mathias, and the most respected in the Province—(*takes snuff*)—only this, since you dream and are apt to talk in your dreams, for the future you will sleep alone in the room above, the door locked, and the key safe in your pocket. They say walls have ears—let them hear me as much as they please. (*Music. Takes bunch of keys out of his pocket.*) And now to count the dowry of Annette, to be given to our dear son-in-law, in order that our dear son-in-law may love us. (*He crosses to* L., *unlocks the escritoire, takes out a large leather bag, unties it and empties the contents, consisting of gold pieces and rouleaux, upon the table.*) Thirty thousand francs—a fine dowry for Annette. Ah! it is pleasant to hear the sound of gold! A fine dowry for the husband of Annette. He's a clever fellow, is Christian. He's not a Kelz—half deaf and half blind; no, no—he's a clever fellow is Christian, and quite capable of getting on a right track. (*A pause.*) The first time I saw him I said to myself. 'You shall be my son-in-law, and if anything should be discovered, you will defend me.' (*Continues to count, weighing each piece upon his finger—takes up a piece and examines it.*) A piece of old gold! (*Looks at it more closely—starts.*) Ah! that came from the girdle; not for them, for me. (*Places the piece of gold in his waistcoat pocket—he goes to the escritoire, opens a drawer, takes out another piece of gold and throws it upon the table in substitution.*) That girdle did us a good turn—without it—without it we were ruined. If Catherine only knew—poor, poor Catherine. (*He sobs—his head sinks on his breast. Music ceases—the Bells heard off* L., *he starts.*) The Bells! the Bells again! They must come from the mill. (*Rushes across to door* R., *calling.*) Sozel! Sozel, I say, Sozel!

(*Enter* SOZEL, *door* R., *holding an open book, she is in her Sunday dress.*)

MATHIAS. Is there anyone at the mill?

SOZEL. No, Burgomaster. They have all gone to church, and the wheel is stopped.

MATHIAS. Don't you hear the sound of Bells?

SOZEL. No, Burgomaster, I hear nothing. (*The Bells cease.*)

MATHIAS (*aside*). Strange—strange. (*Rudely.*) What were you doing?

SOZEL. I was reading, Burgomaster.

MATHIAS. Reading—what? Ghost stories, no doubt.

SOZEL. Oh, no, Burgomaster! I was reading such a curious story, about a band of robbers being discovered after twenty-three years had passed, and all through the blade of an old knife having been found in a blacksmith's shop, hidden under some rusty iron. They captured the whole of them, consisting of the mother, two sons, and the grandfather, and they hanged them all in a row. Look, Burgomaster, there's a picture. (*Shows book—he strikes it violently out of her hand.*)

MATHIAS. Enough, enough! It's a pity you have nothing better to do. There, go—go! (*Exit* SOZEL, *door* R. *Seats himself at the table and puts remaining money into the bag.*) The fools!—not to destroy all evidence against them. To be hanged through the blade of an old knife. Not like that—not like that am I to be caught! (*Music—a sprightly military air.* CHRISTIAN *passes at back, stops at centre window and taps upon it.* MATHIAS *looks round, with start, is reassured upon seeing who it is, and says.* 'Ah, it is Christian!'—*he ties up the bag and places it in the escritoire.* CHRISTIAN *enters at door* R. MATHIAS *meets him half way—they shake hands. Music ceases.* CHRISTIAN *is in the full dress of a Quarter-master of Gendarmes.*)

CHRISTIAN. Good morning, Burgomaster, I hope you are better.

MATHIAS. Oh, yes, I am well, Christian. I have just been counting

Annette's dowry, in good sounding gold. It was a pleasure to me to do so, as it recalled to me the days gone by, when by industry and good fortune I had been enabled to gain it; and I thought that in the future my children would enjoy and profit by all that I had so acquired.

CHRISTIAN. You are right, Burgomaster. Money gained by honest labour is the only profitable wealth. It is the good seed which in time is sure to bring a rich harvest.

MATHIAS. Yes, yes; especially when the good seed is sown in good ground. The contract must be signed today.

CHRISTIAN. Today?

MATHIAS. Yes, the sooner the better. I hate postponements. Once decided, why adjourn the business? It shows a great want of character.

CHRISTIAN. Well, Burgomaster, nothing to me could be more agreeable.

MATHIAS. Annette loves you.

CHRISTIAN. Ah, she does.

MATHIAS. And the dowry is ready—then why should not the affair be settled at once? I hope, my boy, you will be satisfied.

CHRISTIAN. You know, Burgomaster, I do not bring much.

MATHIAS. You bring courage and good conduct—I will take care of the rest; and now let us talk of other matters. You are late today. I suppose you were busy. Annette waited for you, and was obliged to go without you. (*He goes up and sits by stove in arm-chair, opens stove door, takes up tongs and arranges fire.*)

CHRISTIAN (*Unbuckling his sword and sitting in chair*). Ah, it was a very curious business that detained me. Would you believe it, Burgomaster, I was reading old depositions from five o'clock till ten? The hours flew by, but the more I read the more I wished to read.

MATHIAS. And what was the subject of the depositions?

CHRISTIAN. They were about the case of the Polish Jew who was murdered on the Bridge of Vechem fifteen years ago.

MATHIAS (*dropping the tongs*). Ah!

CHRISTIAN. Father Walter told me the story the night before last. It seems to me very remarkable that nothing was ever discovered.

MATHIAS. No doubt—no doubt.

CHRISTIAN. The man who committed that murder must have been a clever fellow.

MATHIAS. Yes, he was not a fool.

CHRISTIAN. A fool! He would have made one of the cleverest gendarmes in the department.

MATHIAS (*with a smile*). Do you really think so?

CHRISTIAN. I am sure of it. There are so many ways of detecting criminals, and so few escape, that to have committed a crime like this, and yet to remain undiscovered, showed the possession of extraordinary address.

MATHIAS. I quite agree with you, Christian; and what you say shows your good sense. When a man has committed a crime, and by it gained money, he becomes like a gambler, and tries his second and his third throw. I should think it requires a great amount of courage to resist the first success in crime.

CHRISTIAN. You are right, but what is most remarkable to me in the case is this, that no trace of the murdered man was ever found. Now do you know what my idea is?

MATHIAS (*rising*). No, no! What is your idea? (*They come forward.*)

CHRISTIAN. Well, I find at that time there were a great many lime-kilns in the neighbourhood of Vechem. Now it is my idea that the murderer, to destroy all traces of his crime, threw the body of the Jew into one of these kilns. Old Kelz, my predecessor, evidently never thought of that.

MATHIAS. Very likely—very likely. Do you know that idea never occurred to me. You are the first who ever suggested it.

CHRISTIAN. And this idea leads to many others. Now suppose—suppose inquiry had been instituted as to those persons who were burning lime at the time.

MATHIAS. Take care, Christian—take care. Why, I, myself, had a lime-kiln burning at the time the crime was committed.

CHRISTIAN (*laughing*). Oh, you, burgomaster! (MATHIAS *laughs heartily —they go up together.* ANNETTE *and* CATHERINE *pass the window.*)

ANNETTE (*as she passes the window before entering*). He is there!

(*Enter* ANNETTE *and* CATHERINE, *door* R.)

MATHIAS (*to* CATHERINE). Is the Notary here?

CATHERINE. Yes, he is in the next room with Father Walter and Hans, and the others. He is reading the contract to them now.

MATHIAS. Good—good!

CHRISTIAN (*to* ANNETTE). Oh, Annette, how that pretty hat becomes you!

ANNETTE. Yes; it was dear father who gave it to me. (*Music.*)

CHRISTIAN. It is today, Annette.

ANNETTE. Yes, Christian, it is today.

MATHIAS (*coming between them*). Well; you know what is customary when father, mother, and all consent.

CHRISTIAN. What, Burgomaster?

MATHIAS (*smiling*). You embrace your intended wife.

CHRISTIAN. Is that so, Annette?

ANNETTE. I don't know, Christian. (*He kisses her forehead, and leads her up to stove, talking.*)

MATHIAS (*to* CATHERINE, *who is seated in arm-chair* L., *by table*). Look at our children, Catherine; how happy they are! When I think that we were once as happy! It's true; yes, it's true, we were once as happy as they are now! Why are you crying, Catherine? Are you sorry to see our children happy?

CATHERINE. No, no, Mathias; these are tears of joy, and I can't help them. (*Throws herself upon* MATHIAS'*s shoulder. Music ceases.*)

MATHIAS. And now to sign the contract! (*Crosses to* R. *door and throws it open.*) Walter, Hans, come in! Let everyone present come in! The most important acts in life should always take place in the presence of all. It is an old and honest custom of Alsace. (*Music—'The Lauterbach', played forte.*)

(*Enter at door* R., HANS *with two girls on his arm—*FATHER WALTER *with two girls—men and women villagers arm-in-arm—they wear ribbons in their button-holes—the* NOTARY *with papers—*SOZEL. *The men wear their hats through the whole scene.* MATHIAS *advances and shakes hands with the* NOTARY *and conducts him to table on which is spread out the contract—pen and ink on table. The company fill the stage in groups.*)

NOTARY. Gentlemen and witnesses—You have just heard read the marriage contract between Christian Bême, Quarter-master of Gendarmes, and Annette Mathias. Has anyone any observations to make?

SEVERAL VOICES. No, no.

NOTARY. Then we can at once proceed to take the signatures. (MATHIAS *goes to the escritoire and takes out the bag of gold which he places on the table before the* NOTARY.) There is the dowry. It is not in promises made on paper, but in gold. Thirty thousand francs in good French gold.

ALL. Thirty thousand francs!

CHRISTIAN. It is too much, Burgomaster.

MATHIAS. Not at all, not at all. When Catherine and myself are gone there will be more. And now, Christian—(*Music commences*)—I wish you to make me one promise.

CHRISTIAN. What promise?

MATHIAS. Young men are ambitious. It is natural they should be.

You must promise me that you will remain in this village while both of us live. (*Takes* CATHERINE'*s hand.*) You know Annette is our only child; we love her dearly, and to lose her altogether would break our hearts. Do you promise?

CHRISTIAN (*looks to* ANNETTE; *she returns a glance of approval*). I do promise.

MATHIAS. Your word of honour, given before all?

CHRISTIAN. My word of honour, given before all. (*They shake hands. Music ceases.*)

MATHIAS (*crossing to* L. *corner, and taking pinch of snuff—aside*). It was necessary. And now to sign the contract. (*He goes to table; the* NOTARY *hands him the pen, and points to the place where he is to sign his name.* MATHIAS *is about to write. The Bells heard off.* MATHIAS *stops, listens with terror—his face to the audience, and away from the persons upon the stage—aside.*) Bells! Courage, Mathias! (*After an effort he signs rapidly—the Bells cease—he throws the pen down.*) Come, Christian, sign! (CHRISTIAN *approaches the table to sign—as he is about to do so* WALTER *taps him on the shoulder.* MATHIAS *starts at the interruption.*)

WALTER. It is not every day you sign a contract like that. (ALL *laugh.* MATHIAS *heaves a sigh and is reassured.* CHRISTIAN *signs—the* NOTARY *hands the pen to* CATHERINE, *who makes her cross—she then takes* ANNETTE *to table, who signs her name.* CATHERINE *kisses her affectionately and gives her to* CHRISTIAN.)

MATHIAS (*aside*). And now should the Jew return to this world, Christian must drive him back again. (*Aloud.*) Come, come, just one waltz and then dinner.

WALTER. Stop! stop! Before we go we must have the song of the betrothal.

ALL. Yes, yes, Annette! Annette! the song of the betrothal.

(*Song,* ANNETTE, *Air—'The Lauterbach'.*)
Suitors of wealth and high degree,
In style superbly grand,
Tendered their love on bended knee
And sought to win my hand. (*Tyrolienne by all, and waltz.*)

But a soldier brave came to woo,
No maid such love could spurn—
Proving his heart was fond and true,
Won my love in return.

(*Tyrolienne as before by all, and waltz.* MATHIAS *is seated—in the midst of the waltz Bells are heard off.* MATHIAS *starts up and rushes into the midst of the waltzers.*)

MATHIAS. The Bells! The Bells!

CATHERINE. Are you mad? (MATHIAS *seizes her by the waist and waltzes wildly with her.*)

MATHIAS. Ring on! Ring on! Houp! Houp! (*Music, forte—while the waltz is at its height the Act Drop falls.*)

End of the Second Act

ACT III

SCENE: *Bedroom in the Burgomaster's house. The whole back of scene painted on a gauze; alcove on left; door,* R.; *two windows at back; small table by bed; chair,* L. *Night.*

(*Music—Enter at door* R., MATHIAS, FATHER WALTER, HANS, CHRISTIAN, ANNETTE, *and* CATHERINE; SOZEL *carrying a lighted candle, bottle of water and glass, which she places on table; they enter suddenly, the men appear to be slightly excited by wine; lights down at rising of curtain; lights turned up upon entrance of* SOZEL.)

HANS (*laughing*). Ha, ha! Everything has gone off admirably. We only wanted something to wind up with, and I may say that we are all as capitally wound up as the great clock at Strasbourg.

WALTER. Yes, and what wine we have consumed! For many a day we shall remember the signing of Annette's marriage contract. I should like to witness such a contract every second day.

HANS. There, I object to your argument. Every day, I say!

CHRISTIAN (*to* MATHIAS). And so you are determined, Mathias, to sleep here tonight?

MATHIAS. Yes, I am decided. I wish for air. I know what is necessary for my condition. The heat was the cause of my accident. This room is cooler, and will prevent its recurrence. (*Laughter heard outside.*)

HANS. Listen, how they are still reveling! Come, Father Walter, let us rejoin the revels!

WALTER. But Mathias already deserts us, just at the moment when we were beginning to thoroughly enjoy ourselves.

MATHIAS. What more do you wish me to do? From noon till midnight is surely enough!

WALTER. Enough, it may be, but not too much; never too much of such wine.

HANS. There, again, I object to your argument—never enough, I say.

CATHERINE. Mathias is right. You remember that Doctor Zimmer told him to be careful of the wine he took, or it would one day play him false. He has already taken too much since this morning.

MATHIAS. One glass of water before I go to rest is all I require. It will calm me—it will calm me.

(KARL, FRITZ, *and* TONY, *three of the guests of the previous Act, enter suddenly, slightly merry, pushing each other.*)

GUESTS. Good night, Burgomaster. Good night.

TONY. I say Hans! don't you know that the Night Watchman is below?

HANS. The Night Watchman! What in the name of all that is political, does he want?

KARL. He requires us all to leave, and the house to be closed. It is past hours.

MATHIAS. Give him a bumper of wine, and then good night all!

WALTER. Past hours! For a Burgomaster no regulations ought to exist.

HANS AND OTHERS. Certainly not.

MATHIAS (*with fierceness*). Regulations made for all must be obeyed by all.

WALTER (*timidly*). Well, then, shall we go?

MATHIAS. Yes, yes, go! Leave me to myself.

CATHERINE (*to* WALTER). Don't thwart his wish. Follow his directions.

WALTER (*shaking hands with* MATHIAS). Good night, Mathias. I wish you calm repose, and no unpleasant dreams.

MATHIAS (*fiercely*). I never dream. (*Mildly.*) Good night, all. Go, friends, go. (*Music. Exeunt* WALTER, HANS, *and the three guests, saying* 'Good night, Burgomaster.' CATHERINE, ANNETTE, *and* CHRISTIAN *remain.*)

MATHIAS. Good night, Catherine. (*Embracing her.*). I shall be better here. The wine, the riot, those songs have quite dazed my brain. I shall sleep better here, I shall sleep better.

CHRISTIAN. Yes, this room is fresh and cool. Good night.

MATHIAS. The same to you, Christian; the same to you. (*They shake hands.*)

ANNETTE (*running to her father and kissing him*). Good night, dear father; may you sleep well!

MATHIAS (*kissing her with affection*). Good night, dear child; do not fear for me—do not fear. (*Music. Exeunt all but* MATHIAS. *Music ceases. He goes up cautiously, locks the door* R., *and puts the key in his pocket.*) At last I am alone! Everything goes well. Christian the gendarme is caught! Tonight I shall sleep without a fear haunting me! If any new danger should threaten the father-in-law of the Quarter-master, it would soon be averted. Ah! What a power it is to know how to guide your destiny in life. You must hold good cards in your hands. Good cards! as I have done, and if you play them well you may defy ill fortune.

CHORUS OF REVELLERS (*outside* [*without accompaniment*]).
Now, since we must part, let's drain a last glass:
Let's drink!
Let us first drink to this gentle young lass;
Let's drink!
From drinking this toast, we'll none of us shrink:
Others shall follow, when we've time to think.
Our burden shall be, let us drink!
The burden to bear is good drink! (*Loud laughter heard outside.*)

MATHIAS (*taking off his coat*). Ha, ha, ha! Those jolly topers have got all they want. What holes in the snow they will make before they reach their homes! Drink! Drink! Is it not strange? To drink and drown every remorse! Yes, everything goes well! (*He drinks a glass of water.*) Mathias, you can at least boast of having well managed your affairs—the contract signed—rich—prosperous—respected—happy! (*Takes off waistcoat.*) No one now will hear you, if you dream. No one! No more folly!—no more Bells! Tonight, I triumph; for conscience is at rest! (*He enters the alcove. The* CHORUS OF REVELLERS *heard again, in the distance. A hand is extended from alcove and extinguishes the candle—stage dark. Curtain at back of gauze rises, disclosing an extensive set of a Court of Justice, arched, brilliantly lighted—at back, three* JUDGES *on the bench, dressed in black caps and red robes—at* R. *and* L., *the public, in Alsatian costumes—in front of the* JUDGES, *but beneath them, a table, on which lies the* JEW'S *cloak and cap—on* R., *the* PUBLIC PROSECUTOR *and* BARRISTERS*—on* L., *the* CLERK *or* REGISTRAR OF THE COURT, *and* BARRISTERS*—a gendarme at each corner of the Court.* MATHIAS *is discovered seated on a stool in* C. *of Court—he is dressed in the brown blouse and hood worn by the man in the vision in Act I—he has his back to the audience, face to* JUDGES.)

THE CLERK OF THE COURT (L., *standing, reading the Act of Accusation*). Therefore, the prisoner, Mathias, is accused of having, on the night of the 24th December, 1818, between midnight and one o'clock, assassinated the Jew Koveski, upon the Bridge of Vechem, to rob him of his gold.

PRESIDENT. Prisoner, you have heard the Act of Accusation read; you have already heard the depositions of the witnesses. What have you to say in answer?

MATHIAS (*violently—throws back hood, and starting up*). Witnesses! People who saw nothing; people who live miles from the place where the crime was committed; at night, and in the winter time! You call such people witnesses!

PRESIDENT. Answer with calmness; these gestures—this violence will avail you nothing. You are a man full of cunning.

MATHIAS (*with humility*). No, I am a man of simplicity.

PRESIDENT. You knew well the time to select; you knew well how to evade all suspicion; you knew well how to destroy all direct evidence. You are a dangerous man!

MATHIAS (*derisively*). Because nothing can be proved against me I am dangerous! Every honest man then is dangerous when nothing can be proved against him! A rare encouragement for honesty!

PRESIDENT. The public voice accuses you. Answer me this: How is it that you hear the noise of Bells?

MATHIAS (*passionately*). I do not hear the noise of Bells! (*Music. Bells heard off as before.* MATHIAS *trembles.*)

PRESIDENT. Prisoner, you speak falsely. At this moment you hear that noise. Tell us why is this?

MATHIAS. It is nothing. It is simply a jangling in my ears.

PRESIDENT. Unless you acknowledge the true cause of this noise you hear, we shall summon the Mesmerist to explain the matter to us.

MATHIAS (*with defiance*). It is true then that I hear this noise. (*Bells cease.*)

PRESIDENT (*to the* CLERK OF THE COURT). It is well; write that down.

MATHIAS. Yes; but I hear it in a dream.

PRESIDENT. Write, that he hears it in a dream.

MATHIAS (*furiously*). Is it a crime to dream?

THE CROWD (*murmur very softly among themselves, and move simultaneously, each person performing exactly the same movement of negation*). N—N—N—o!

MATHIAS (*with confidence*). Listen, friends! Don't fear for me! All this is but a dream—I am in a dream. If it were not a dream should I be clothed in these rags? Should I have before me such judges as these? Judges who, simply acting upon their own empty ideas, would hang a fellow creature. Ha, ha, ha! It is a dream—a dream! (*He bursts into a loud derisive laugh.*)

PRESIDENT. Silence, prisoner—silence! (*Turning to his companion* JUDGES.) Gentlemen—this noise of Bells arises in the prisoner's mind from the remembrance of what is past. The prisoner hears this noise because there rankles in his heart the memory of that he would conceal from us. The Jew's horse carried Bells.

MATHIAS. It is false, I have no memories.

PRESIDENT. Be silent!

MATHIAS (*with rage*). A man cannot be condemned upon such suppositions. You must have proofs. I do not hear the noise of Bells.

PRESIDENT. You see, gentlemen, the prisoner contradicts himself. He has already made the avowal—now he retracts it.

MATHIAS. No! I hear nothing. (*The Bells heard.*) It is the blood rushing to my brain—this jangling in my ears. (*The Bells increase in sound.*) I ask for Christian. Why is not Christian here?

PRESIDENT. Prisoner! do you persist in your denial?

MATHIAS (*with force*). Yes. There is nothing proved against me. It is a gross injustice to keep an honest man in prison. I suffer in the cause of justice. (*The Bells cease.*)

PRESIDENT. You persist. Well! Considering that since this affair took place fifteen years have passed, and that it is impossible to throw light upon the circumstances by ordinary means—first, through the cunning and audacity of the prisoner, and second, through the deaths of witnesses who could have given evidence—for these reasons we decree that the Court hear the Mesmerist. Officer, summon the Mesmerist.

MATHIAS (*in a terrible voice*). I oppose it! I oppose it! Dreams prove nothing.

PRESIDENT. Summon the Mesmerist! (*Exit* GENDARME, R.)

MATHIAS (*striking the table*). It is abominable! It is in defiance of all justice!

PRESIDENT. If you are innocent, why should you fear the Mesmerist, because he can read the inmost secrets of your heart? Be calm, or, believe me, your own indiscretion will prove that you are guilty.

MATHIAS. I demand an advocate. I wish to instruct the advocate Linder of Saverne. In a case like this, I do not care for cost. I am calm—as calm as any man who has no reproach against himself. I fear nothing; but dreams are dreams. (*Loudly.*) Why is Christian not here? My honour is his honour. Let him be sent for. He is an honest man. (*With exultation.*) Christian, I have made you rich. Come, and defend me! (*Music. The* GENDARME *who had gone out, returns with the* MESMERIST.)

MESMERIST (*bending to the Court respectfully*). Your honours, the President and Judges of the Court, it is your decree that has brought me before your tribunal; without such direction, terror alone would have kept me far from here.

MATHIAS. Who can believe in the follies of the Mesmerist? They deceive the public for the purpose of gaining money! They merely perform the tricks of conjurers. I have seen this fellow already at my cousin Bôth's at Ribeauville.

PRESIDENT (*to the* MESMERIST). Can you send this man to sleep?

MESMERIST (*looking full at* MATHIAS, *who sinks upon chair, unable to endure the* MESMERIST'*s gaze*). I can!

MATHIAS (*starting up*). I will not be made the subject of this conjurer's experiments.

PRESIDENT. I command it!

MATHIAS. Christian—where is Christian? He will prove that I am an honest man.

PRESIDENT. Your resistance betrays you.

MATHIAS (*with defiance*). I have no fear. (*Sits*).

(*The* MESMERIST *goes up stage to back of* MATHIAS, *makes some passes. Music.*)

MATHIAS (*to himself*). Mathias, if you sleep you are lost. (*His eyes are fixed as if struck with horror—in a hollow voice.*) No—no—I will not sleep —I—will—(*in a hesitating voice*) I will—not—no——(*Falls asleep. Music ceases.*)

MESMERIST (*to the* PRESIDENT). He sleeps. What shall I ask him?

PRESIDENT. Ask him what he did on the night of the 24th of December, fifteen years ago.

MESMERIST (*to* MATHIAS, *in a firm voice*). You are at the night of the 24th of December, 1818?

MATHIAS (*in a low voice*). Yes.

MESMERIST. What time is it?

MATHIAS. Half-past eleven.

MESMERIST. Speak on, I command you!

MATHIAS (*still in the same attitude, speaking as if he were describing a vision presented to his sight*). The people are leaving the inn—Catherine and little Annette have gone to rest. Our man Kasper comes in. He tells me the lime-kiln is lighted. I answer him, it is well; go to bed, I will see to the kiln. He leaves me; I am alone with the Jew, who warms himself at the stove. Outside, everything sleeps. Nothing is heard, except from time to time the Jew's horse under the shed, when he shakes his bells.

MESMERIST. Of what are you thinking?

MATHIAS. I am thinking that I must have money—that if I have not three thousand francs by the 31st, the inn will be taken from me. I am thinking that no one is stirring; that it is night; that there are two feet of snow upon the ground, and that the Jew will follow the high road quite alone!

MESMERIST. Have you already decided to attack him?

MATHIAS (*after a short silence*). That man is strong. He has broad shoulders. I am thinking that he would defend himself well, should any one attack him. (*He makes a movement.*)

MESMERIST. What ails you?

MATHIAS (*in a low voice*). He looks at me. He has grey eyes. (*As if speaking to himself.*) I must strike the blow!

MESMERIST. You are decided?

MATHIAS. Yes—yes; I will strike the blow! I will risk it!

MESMERIST. Go on!

MATHIAS (*continuing*). I must, however, look round. I go out; all is dark! It still snows; no one will trace my footsteps in the snow. (*He raises his hand as if feeling for something.*)

MESMERIST. What are you doing?

MATHIAS. I am feeling in the sledge—should he carry pistols! There is nothing—I will strike the blow! (*He listens.*) All is silent in the village! Little Annette is crying; a goat bleats in the stable; the Jew is walking in his room!

MESMERIST. You re-enter?

MATHIAS. Yes. The Jew has placed six francs upon the table; I return him his money; he fixes his eyes steadily upon me!

MESMERIST. He speaks to you?

MATHIAS. He asks me how far it is to Mutzig? Four leagues. I wish him well on his journey! He answers—'God bless you!' He goes out—He is gone! (MATHIAS, *with body bent, takes several steps forward as if following and watching his victim, he extends his hands.*) The axe! Where is the axe? Ah, here, behind the door! How cold it is! (*He trembles.*) The snow falls—not a star! Courage, Mathias, you shall possess the girdle—courage!

MESMERIST. You follow him?

MATHIAS. Yes, yes. I have crossed the fields! (*Pointing.*) Here is the old bridge, and there below, the frozen rivulet! How the dogs howl at Daniel's farm—how they howl! And old Finck's forge, how brightly it glows upon the hillock. (*Low, as if speaking to himself.*) Kill a man!

—kill a man! You will not do that, Mathias—you will not do that! Heaven forbids it. (*Proceeding to walk with measured steps and bent body.*) You are a fool! Listen, you will be rich, your wife and child will no longer want for anything! The Jew came; so much the worse—so much the worse. He ought not to have come! You will pay all you owe; you will no more be in debt. (*Loud, in a broken tone.*) It must be, Mathias, that you kill him! (*He listens*). No one on the road—no one! (*With an expression of terror.*) What dreadful silence! (*He wipes his forehead with his hand.*) One o'clock strikes, and the moon shines. Ah! The Jew has already passed! Thank God! thank God! (*He kneels—a pause—he listens—the Bells heard without as before.*) No! The Bells! The Bells! He comes! (*He bends down in a watching attitude, and remains still—a pause—in a low voice.*) You will be rich—you will be rich—you will be rich! (*The noise of the Bells increase—the* CROWD *express alarm simultaneously—all at once* MATHIAS *springs forward, and with a species of savage roar, strikes a terrible blow with his right hand.*) Ah! ah! I have you now, Jew! (*He strikes again—the* CROWD *simultaneously express horror.* MATHIAS *leans forward and gazes anxiously on the ground—he extends his hand as if to touch something, but draws it back in horror.*) He does not move! (*He raises himself, utters deep sigh of relief and looks round.*) The horse has fled with the sledge! (*The Bells cease—kneeling down.*) Quick, quick! The girdle! I have it. Ha! (*He performs the action in saying this of taking it from the Jew's body and buckling it round his own.*) It is full of gold, quite full. Be quick, Mathias, be quick! Carry him away. (*He bends low down and appears to lift the body upon his back; then he walks across stage, his body bent, his step slow as a man who carries a heavy load.*)

MESMERIST. Where are you going?

MATHIAS (*stopping*). To the lime-kiln. I am there. (*He appears to throw the body upon the kiln.*) How heavy he was! (*He breathes with force, then he again bends down to take up a pole—in a hoarse voice.*) Go into the fire, Jew, go into the fire! (*He appears to push the body with the pole, using his whole force, suddenly he utters a cry of horror and staggers away, his face covered with his hands.*) Those eyes, oh, those eyes! How he glares at me. (*He sinks on to stool, and takes the same attitude as when first thrown into sleep.*)

PRESIDENT (*with a sign to the* MESMERIST). It is well. (*To the* CLERK OF THE COURT.) You have written all?

CLERK. All!

PRESIDENT (*to* MESMERIST). It is well—awake him now, and let him read himself.

MESMERIST. Awake! I command you!

MATHIAS (*awakes gradually—he appears bewildered*). Where am I? (*He looks round.*) Ah! Yes; what is going on?

CLERK (*handing him paper*). Here is your deposition—read it.

MATHIAS (*takes it and, before reading it, aside*). Wretched, wretched fool! I have told all; I am lost! (*With rage, after reading the paper.*) It is false! (*Tears the paper into pieces.*) You are a set of rogues! Christian—where is Christian? It is a crime against justice! They will not let my only witness speak. Christian! They would kill the father of your wife! Help me—help me!

PRESIDENT. You force me to speak of an event of which I had wished to remain silent. Your son-in-law Christian, upon hearing of the crimes with which you are charged, by his own hand sought his death. He is no more.

MATHIAS. Ah! (*He appears stupefied with dismay.*)

PRESIDENT (*after consulting the other* JUDGES, *rises, speaks in a solemn tone of voice*). Considering that on the night of the 24th December, 1818, between midnight and one o'clock, Mathias committed the crime of assassination upon the person of one Koveski, and considering that this crime was committed under circumstances which aggravates its enormity—such as premeditation, and for the purpose of highway robbery; the Court condemns the said Mathias to be hanged by the neck until he is dead! (MATHIAS *staggers and falls on his knees. The* CROWD *make a movement of terror—the death-bell tolls—lights lowered gradually—then curtain at back of gauze descends, disclosing the scene as at commencement—lights up. Music—a peal of joyous bells heard ringing.*)

CROWD (*without*). Annette! Annette! The bride! (*Hurried steps are heard upon the stairs outside, and then a loud knocking at the door of the room.*)

CATHERINE (*without*). Mathias! Mathias! get up at once. It is late in the morning, and all our guests are below. (*More knocking.*)

CHRISTIAN (*without*). Mathias! Mathias! (*Silence*). How soundly he sleeps!

WALTER (*without*). Ho! Mathias, the wedding has commenced—Houp, houp! (*More knocking.*)

CROWD (*outside*). Burgomaster! Burgomaster! (*Loud knocking.*)

CATHERINE (*in an anxious voice*). He does not answer. It is strange. Mathias! (*A discussion among many voices is heard without.*)

CHRISTIAN. No—it is useless. Leave it to me!

(*At the same moment several violent blows are struck upon the door, which *falls into the room from its hinges. Enter* CHRISTIAN, *hurriedly—he runs to the alcove. Hurried music.*)

CHRISTIAN. Mathias! (*Looks into alcove and staggers back into room.*) Ah! (*Enter* CATHERINE *and* ANNETTE, *followed by* WALTER, HANS, *and the* CROWD, *all dressed for the wedding.*)

CATHERINE. What has happened, Christian, what has happened? (*She is rushing to alcove.*)

CHRISTIAN (*stopping her*). Don't come near—don't come near.

CATHERINE (*endeavouring to pass*). I will see what it is. Let me pass; do not fear for me. (MATHIAS *appears from the alcove—he is dressed in the same clothes as when he retired into the alcove at the commencement of the scene, but his face is haggard, and ghastly pale—he comes out, his eyes fixed, his arms extended—as he rushes forward with uncertain steps, the* CROWD *fall back with horror, and form groups of consternation, with a general exclamation of terror.*)

MATHIAS (*in a voice of strangulation*). The rope! the rope! Take the rope from my neck! (*He falls suddenly, and is caught in the arms of* HANS *and* WALTER, *who carry him to the chair in centre of stage. The Bells heard off. Music, the melody played in the Second Act when promise given. His hands clutch at his throat as if to remove something that strangles him—he looks pitifully round as if trying to recognize those about him, and then his head falls on his breast.* CATHERINE, *kneeling, places her hand on* MATHIAS'S *heart.*

CATHERINE. Dead! (*The Bells cease.*) (ANNETTE *bursts into tears. The women in the crowd kneel, the men remove their hats and bend their heads upon their breasts—tableau.*)

Curtain.

EAST LYNNE

Thomas Holcroft's *A Tale of Mystery* (1802) started an avalanche of crude but electrifying melodramas of sensation and spectacle, all related to the Gothic novels of Horace Walpole, Ann Radcliffe, and "Monk" Lewis, and heralded by Lewis' play *The Castle Spectre* (1797). Edward Stirling, for instance, typical of the time, wrote about two hundred plays like *The Orphan of the Frozen Sea* (1856) and served as actor and stage-manager as well as house dramatist at the Adelphi under Frederick Henry Yates, Daniel Terry, and Charles Matthews. They constantly attempted to outdo the other "minor" theatres in popular melodrama.

The appeal of melodrama (so named by Jean-Jacques Rousseau, who accompanied and intensified the effect of his dialogue with music) was simple and direct. Watson (in *Sheridan to Robertson*) explains:

> The freshness of this new art form as observed by the audience was due to clear-cut characters, embodying simple vices and virtues; tense and economical dialogue [in comparison with contemporaneous literary tragedy] which, although inflated, never allowed itself to wander from the action for merely literary purposes; startling contrasts both in character and action; and, above all, thrilling situations in which the physical played the major part, heightened to an appalling degree by the palpitations of the orchestra.

> The frank directness with which it produced its effects made its utter unreality seem real for the time being and its excessive artificiality seem simple.

One would have to have the leisure of Sardanapalus to read many melodramas today, but they played well. There was an undeniable attraction in burning buildings; erupting volcanoes; equestrian, nautical, supernatural effects; grand transformation scenes of incredible ingenuity, no expense spared. Sometimes plays (such as those of Boucicault) turned upon a "sensation scene"; sometimes they were merely excuses for such scenes, as historical plays were excuses for costuming. The melodrama was the wide-screen, color-drenched, cast of thousands (count them!), cinematographic supercolossal stupendemonium of its period.

The spectacle aside—and that is hardly fair, since these plays require more than any others to be read with vivid imagination—the simple morality of the melodrama spoke to the complacent, earnest, self-satisfied, class-conscious, and profoundly sentimental Victorians who had declined (says G. M. Young) from being "once so alert, so masculine, and so responsible." In melodramas the good are rewarded and the bad are punished, which, as Oscar Wilde noted, is the definition of fiction. Of these rules of art James Baldwin Buckstone (1802-1879), author of *Luke the Laborer; or, The Lost Son* (1826), *The Wreck Ashore* (1830), *Rural Felicity* (1834), *Jack Sheppard* (1839), and uncounted other "Adelphi melodramas," was the chief inventor and proprietor, aided and abetted by Edward Fitzball, Douglas Jerrold, and a thousand others. Their heroes were good as gold, their villains deep-dyed, their heroines always in distress. Most of all, they touched the heart. Their message was that

> Kind hearts are more than coronets
> And simple faith than Norman blood,

and they did not trouble to point out to their predominantly middle-class audiences that neither kind hearts nor coronets are satisfactory substitutes for heads. The problems they dealt with called for sympathy, not analysis. Consequently they were extravagantly popular for, to quote again from Wilde (whose *The Importance of Being Earnest* is both a standard melodrama and a parody of melodramatic machinery): "It is easy for people to have sympathy with suffering. It is so difficult for them to have sympathy with thought."

In *Nicholas Nickleby* the melodramatic novelist Charles Dickens has his hero fall in with one Vincent Crummles, the manager of a traveling troupe of actors who presented as their stock in trade the kind of melodrama we have been discussing. Mr. Crummles himself is a remarkable man of artful dodges and long experience ("I played the heavy children when I was eighteen months old") who specializes in "bricks and mortar" (ponderous) tragedy. His wife, "a stout, portly female, apparently between forty and fifty," with a sepulchral voice and an iron grip, also acts, as do the children, including Miss Ninetta, "The Infant Phenomenon," who "must be seen, sir—seen—to be ever so faintly appreciated."

> "I am in the theatrical profession myself [said Mr. Crummles], my wife is in the theatrical profession, my children are in the theatrical profession. I had a dog that lived and died in it from a puppy, and my chaise pony goes on, in Timour the Tartar."

The pony's dam was on the stage: "She ate apple-pie at a circus for upwards of fourteen years . . . fired pistols, and went to bed in a night-cap; and, in short, took the low comedy entirely." His sire "was a dancer . . . clever in melodrama too, but too broad—too broad." He drank "port wine with the clown . . . but he was too greedy, and one night bit off the bowl of the glass, and choked himself, so his vulgarity was the death of him at last." The rest of the company (and this was a touring group; a London house would have employed literally hundreds) consisted of Mr. Folair (the pantomimist), Mr. Lenville ("who does our first tragedy"), "a slim young gentleman with weak eyes, who played the low-spirited lovers and sang tenor songs," the comic countryman, "an inebriated elderly gentleman in the last depths of shabbiness, who played the calm and virtuous old men," and "another elderly gentleman, a shade more respectable, who played the irascible old men—those funny fellows who have nephews in the army, and perpetually run about with thick sticks to compel them to marry heiresses," a man with "an air of exaggerated gentility about him, which bespoke the hero of swaggering comedy," and some extras, "a little group of three or four young men, with lantern jaws and thick eyebrows." And then there were the ladies of the ensemble:

> There was Miss Snevellicci—who could do anything, from a medley dance to Lady Macbeth. . . . There was Miss Belvawney—who seldom aspired to speaking parts, and usually went on as a page in white silk hose . . . [and] the beautiful Miss Bravassa. . . . There

> was Mrs. Lenville, in a very limp bonnet and veil . . . [and] Miss Gazingi, with an imitation ermine boa. . . . Lastly, there was Mrs. Grudden . . . who assisted Mrs. Crummles in her domestic affairs, and took money at the doors, and dressed the ladies, and swept the house, and held the prompt book when everybody else was on for the last scene, and acted any kind of part in any emergency without ever learning it, and was put down in the bills under any name or names whatsoever, that occurred to Mr. Crummles as looking well in print.

This brave band trooped through the Provinces bringing the standard plots and stock characters of the time to as few as "five people and a baby in the pit, and two boys in the gallery." Nicholas is dragooned into writing a "new piece" for them:

> "But really, I can't," returned Nicholas; "my invention is not accustomed to these demands, or possibly I might produce—"
>
> "Invention! what the devil's that got to do with it!" cried the manager, hastily.
>
> "Everything, my dear sir."
>
> "Nothing, my dear sir," retorted the manager, with evident impatience. "Do you understand French?"
>
> "Perfectly well."
>
> "Very good," said the manager, opening the table-drawer, and giving a roll of paper from it to Nicholas. "There! Just turn that into English, and put your name on the title-page. . . ."

The rough translation is made overnight and the script tailored to the talents of the stock company, including the Infant Prodigy (who has been the same age for five years or more and is fed on gin and water to keep her small). In such circumstances, when comedies were mostly plays on words, not plays, and the rest was stolen from French dramas and English novels, Mr. Curdle was obliged to remark:

> "As an exquisite embodiment of the poet's visions, and a realization of human intellectuality, gilding with refulgent light our dreary moments, and laying open a new and magic world before the mental eye, the drama is gone, perfectly gone. . . ."

To an eager, scrambling audience, transfixed with wonder, moved to tears and thrilled with anxious fears, Nicholas' potboiler, accompanied by such dazzling effects as might be hastily achieved, went on:

> At last the orchestra left off, and the curtain rose upon the new piece. The first scene, in which there was nobody particular, passed off calmly enough, but when Miss Snevellicci went on in the second, accompanied by the [infant] phenomenon as child, what a roar of applause broke out! . . . [And] when Nicholas came on for his crack scene with Mrs. Crummles, what a clapping of hands there was! When Mrs. Crummles (who was his unworthy mother) sneered, and called him "presumptuous boy," and he defied her, what a tumult of applause came on! When he quarreled with the other gentleman about the young lady, and producing a case of pistols, said, that if *he* was a gentleman he would fight him in that drawing-room, until the furniture was sprinkled with the blood of one, if not of two—how boxes, pit, and gallery, joined in one most vigorous cheer! When he called his mother names, because she wouldn't give up the young lady's property, and she relenting, caused him to relent likewise, and fall down on one knee and ask her blessing, how the ladies in the audience sobbed! When he was hid behind the curtain in the dark, and the wicked relation poked a sharp sword in every direction, save where his legs were plainly visible, what a thrill of anxious fear ran through the house! His air, his figure, his walk, his look, everything he said or did was the subject of commendation. There was a round of applause every time he spoke. And when, at last, in the pump-and-tub scene [Nicholas had been instructed to include them: "We'll have a new show-piece out directly," said the manager. "Let me see—peculiar resources of this establishment—new and splendid scenery—you must manage to introduce a real pump and two washing-tubs . . . I bought 'em cheap . . . and they'll come in admirably. That's the London plan. They look up some dresses, and properties, and have a piece written to fit 'em. Most of the theatres keep an author on purpose"] Mrs. Grudden lighted the blue fire, and all the unemployed members of the company came in, and tumbled down in various directions—not because that had anything to do with the plot, but in order to finish off with a tableau—the audience (who had by this time increased considerably) [it being possible to buy cheaper tickets for admission late

> in the program] gave vent to such a shout of enthusiasm, as had not been heard in these walls for many and many a day.

It is in such an atmosphere as that that the adapter of *East Lynne* for the stage undertook to deal with a social problem adumbrated in Mrs. Henry Wood's important novel of 252,091 words. Says G. M. Young in *Victorian England: Portrait of an Age* (1964):

> The domestic system involved the employment of untrained gentlewomen as teachers, and the figure of the governess, snubbed, bullied, loving, and usually quite incompetent, is a standby of Victorian pathos. Lady Blessington [Marguerite, Countess of Blessington, journalist and authoress, died 1849] first introduced it into literature, it reached its apotheosis in *East Lynne.*

East Lynne is played for pathos in a wholly unrealistic way, surrounded by all the devices of the melodramatist's art. This was a period in which strong men wept publicly, when orators in Parliament dissolved in tears, when the British and American publics sorrowfully joined to lament the demise of Little Nell. No one bothered about the stilted language, the clumsy characterizations, the unmotivated exits and entrances, the artificial asides, the creaking and manipulated plot. They simply rejoiced when the bills—sometimes nine inches wide and three feet long—proclaimed "Next Week! EAST LYNNE!!!" and made a mental note to bring an extra handkerchief. Enter into the spirit of the play and, if you have tears, prepare to shed them now.

EAST LYNNE

A Domestic Drama in a Prologue and Four Acts

Adapted from Mrs. Wood's Novel
by
T. A. Palmer

First produced at Nottingham, November 19, 1874,
with the following cast:

Lord Mount Severn, *of Castle Marling*	Mr. T. A. Palmer
Captain Levison, *later* Sir Francis Levison, *Bart.*	E. Concanon
Archibald Carlyle	W. H. Kendal James Elmore
Mr. Hare, *Justice of the Peace*	Alfred Leslie
Richard Hare	Franks
Mr. Dill, *a Law Clerk*	A. Beaky
George Hallijohn	E. Silburn[e]
Colonel Otway Bethell	H. Towers
Locksley, *a Poacher*	Carvill
Cornelia Carlyle	Miss Ewell
Barbara Hare	Miss Morton
Lady Isabel	Miss Madge Robertson Miss Maude Brennan
Afy Hallijohn	Miss Kate Lawler
Wilson, *a Maid*	Miss Chalgrove
Joyce, *a Maid*	Mrs. [T. A.] Palmer
Susanne, *a Maid*	———
Willie Carlyle, *Archibald's son*	Miss Silburne

PROLOGUE[1]

SCENE I: *Library at Castle Marling. 2nd grooves, long window,* R. C. *door* L. H., LORD MOUNT SEVERN *discovered at table* R. H., *looking over papers.*

LORD M. Well, well; there's no help for it, I must go to town at once and see Warburton about these mortgages. I would my unfortunate cousin had not died in the prime of life, leaving that poor girl Isabel penniless, through his reckless extravagance, and burdening me with the accession to title and estates so hopelessly involved that I hardly know what is mine and what belongs to his numerous creditors. (*Rings bell. Enter* SERVANT, L. H.) Tell Barton to put the horses to directly, I wish to catch the express to London. (*Exit* SERVANT. LORD M. *goes to window, looks off to* L. H.) Ah! there's Isabel with Levison again. I hope she will not lose her heart to him, he's a bad man, vain, idle, and unprincipled, and were he not my wife's cousin, should not be suffered here, to trifle with Isabel. I wish my lady could be made to see his faults and behave more kindly to that gentle girl, fatherless as she is, with no home but ours.

(Servant *enters* L. H.)

1. *Mrs. Henry Wood* (née *Ellen Price*) *published her sensational and melodramatic romance* East Lynne *first as a serial in* The New Monthly Magazine *and then as a book* (*1861*). *Lucille Western, an American actress, hired Clifton W. Tayleure to adapt the novel for the stage so that she could star as Lady Isabel.* East Lynne *was first seen in America at the Academy of Music in Brooklyn* (*1862*), *and later Miss Western's company played the Winter Garden, New York City* (*1863*). *In 1864 one W. Archer adapted the novel as* The Marriage Bells; or, The Cottage on the Cliff *for performances in London. Mrs. Wood's story first appeared in England on stage under its original title in John Oxenford's* East Lynne *at the Surrey* (*1866*) *and after that versions were both plentiful* (*Allardyce Nicoll lists nine anonymous ones, among others*) *and popular* (*in 1879 the Olympic, Astley's, and the Standard theatres were all running* East Lynne *in London*). *This text is an acting version of T. A. Palmer's famous adaptation, a standard since its premiere with the Palmers and the Kendals* (*Tom Robertson's sister and brother-in-law*) *in the cast* (*1874*). *We have silently corrected some obvious misprints, principally punctuation, but we leave the words basically untouched, for the student will be interested to see the sort of book from which actors worked in those days. Throughout, this acting version of the play takes problems of scenery, etc., into consideration and, though the punctuation and such details are poorly indicated, the "blocking" is carefully worked out. For a collection of the British drama, Palmer's version seems more logical than any of the American adaptations of* East Lynne. *It is preferable to the version, advertised as "A Spirited and Powerful Mellow Drammer in Three Acts," by Ned Albert* (*1941*).

SER. The carriage, sir. (*Exit* Servant.)

LORD M. (*gathers letters on table*). I very much fear that my wife's dislike to Isabel arises from jealousy of the poor girl's youth and beauty; however, I shall insist on her showing more kindness and consideration for one who has every claim to our care and affection. (*Exit* L. H. D.)

(LEVISON *and* ISABEL VANE *enter from garden by window.* R. C.)

LEV. (*on her* R. H.). No, Isabel, I can never forget those happy hours —happy at least to me when first we met at East Lynne. *I had hopes then*—hopes that to cherish now would be folly, broken down and fettered with debts, surrounded by difficulties as I am. Ah, Isabel, if I had a home to offer you, a home worthy of your grace and bounty.

ISA. Love and contentment can make the humblest home happy.

LEV. (*aside*). Humph! Love in a cottage frame of mind. I am beyond the pale of such happiness myself and dare not think of entering the happy state; like other men I *have* sometimes indulged in dreams, but a poor gentleman, with no property, no prospects can only play the butterfly to his life's end.

ISA. (*aside*). He does not love me, or he—

SER. (*enters* L. H. D. *with card*). A gentleman wished to see you, my lady.

ISA. (*looking at card*). Mr. Carlyle! oh, how that name recalls the sad days at Lynne. (*Aside.*)

LEV. (R. C., *looks at watch*). Umph! time I started on my ten mile ride to West Lynne, poor little Afy Hallijohn will be anxiously awaiting me. (*Aside.*)

ISA. (*abstractedly, aside*). When I was so overwhelmed with grief how generous and noble he was in his—(*Suddenly recollecting the* Servant *is waiting, turns to* Servant.) Show him in. (*Exit* Servant L.)

LEV. (R. C.). Au revoir, dear Isabel, Mr. Carlyle may wish to see you alone on business. (*Exit through window to* R. H.)

ISA. (*goes to window, looks after him*). When *he* leaves me, it seems as though the sunshine had faded from my life.

(Servant *shows in* MR. CARLYLE L. H.)

CAR. Lady Isabel, having some business in the neighbourhood, I could not resist the impulse which prompted me to call and see you, but how is this, you look pale, sad, and there are tears in your eyes. I claim the privilege of one, whom you honour by calling friend, to ask why you are so distressed; I hope this a happy home to you?

ISA. No, Mr. Carlyle, it is not, it is a miserable home, and I cannot remain here, I have lain awake night after night thinking of what is to become of me, I have no friend in the world (CARLYLE *looks surprised*), but you, *you* have indeed been a true friend; but I cannot stay here with Lady Mount Severn, she insults me daily, taunts me with my helplessness and poverty, my dependence on her bounty, she hates me (I know not why), I have never given her any cause; Lord Mount Severn is most kind, but she, she would break my heart, as she has already wellnigh broken my spirit.

CAR. Indeed, I am grieved to hear that, what can I do to serve you?

ISA. Nothing—what can *any* one do to serve me—oh Carlyle, if I could but awake and find that the last few years had been past only in a hideous dream—awake, to see dear papa alive again; ah! were *he* alive East Lynne (with all the trouble we had to encounter there) would be a very Eden to me now.

CAR. There is but one way by which you could return to East Lynne; may I be permitted to point out that way? If my words should offend you Lady Isabel, check them, as my presumption deserves. May I dare to offer you a welcome to your old home, as—as—its mistress.

ISA. As its mistress?

CAR. As my wife.

ISA. Mr. Carlyle! (*Surprised.*)

CAR. I know how presumptuous it must seem to you that *I,* a mere lawyer, in an obscure country town, should venture on such a proposal to the daughter of the late Earl Mount Severn, but my excuse is, that your father was good enough to call me friend, to confide in me when trouble was hastening him to an early grave. (ISABEL *affected.*) Forgive me for awakening memories which must be so full of pain; my dearest hope is to soften the anguish of those recollections in a future of such tenderness and care on my part, that you might, in time, feel less keenly the loss of that love which died with him to whom you were so dear, my life-long study would be your happiness.

ISA. Mr. Carlyle, I esteem and respect you very, very much knowing your noble nature as I do from past experience of your kindness, but I do not feel that I could love you yet, as *you should* be loved.

CAR. I do not dare to hope so, but will you let me try to be deserving of that priceless treasure, *your love.*

ISA. You are more than *"deserving"* of the truest love which the best of women could bestow, but I—(*She rises and goes to window. Looking off through window.*) (*Aside.*) His wife, and I fear that I love, or almost love another, ah! if *he* would ask me to be his wife, or that I had never seen him. (*Abstracted.*)

CAR. (*after pause*). You do not answer me, you turn from me! Oh, say that I have not offended you by—

ISA. (*recovering herself*). Oh, no—no! But will you give me a few days for consideration, your—your proposal is so sudden!

CAR. I am only too happy to find that you are willing to give my proposal your consideration, for that emboldens me to hope!

Close in.

SCENE II: *Room in* HARE'S *house, 1st grooves* (*or long window*) L. C.

BAR. (*comes to window* C., *looks off* L. H.). East Lynne is tenantless. Lady Isabel is no longer there to act as a magnet [for] Archibald Carlyle. She has gone, and he will be free from the memory of her beauty!

(MR. HARE *through window,* C. F.)

HAR. Well, that cobs all. I can hardly believe it.

BAR. Believe what, papa?

HAR. Why, the report that Carlyle has bought East Lynne!

BAR. Can it be true?

HAR. As likely as not; he's rich enough. His father, Mr. Carlyle, had the finest practice in the three counties. I have just been over to see him, but he's away; gone over to Castle Marling!

BAR. (*aside*). To Castle Marling! *She* is there!

HAR. I put the question to old Dill, his clerk; but he's close—very close. However, he didn't deny it, so you may depend there's some truth in the rumour.

BAR. He has lost no time in making the purchase!

HAR. Let lawyers alone for despatching business when they are their own clients, and their friends are as embarrassed as that prodigal spendthrift, the late Lord Mount Severn.

BAR. I heard there was not enough money left, even for Lady Isabel to buy her mourning with. The Smiths told the Herberts, and the Herberts told me!

HAR. Ah, gossips all. "Mrs. Grundy" has as many relatives in the Lynnes as everywhere else. Where's Dick?

BAR. He took his gun and said he was going over to the woods this evening.

HAR. What business has he there—in the evening? Is the young scamp going to poach? A pretty thing it would be if he were had up for dropping some of Carlyle's game. (HARE *goes off* R. H.)

BAR. Castle Marling—has he gone there to—to—see *her?* Oh, Archibald, if you did but know that a heart nearer home was aching for your love. But it must come some day—I feel it must, and when I am your wife you will know how dear you are to me. (*Exit* R. *through gate.*)

SCENE III: *Lynne wood. Cottage* R. H. 2 E. *Door, centre wood, 2nd grooves. Sets trees* R. *and* L.*, *to back of stage. Moonlight.*

(RICHARD HARE, *with gun enters* L. H., *goes to door of cottage: knocks.*)

RIC. Afy, Afy! Afy, Afy! (*Softly.*)

(AFY *comes to door* R. H., *which she closes.*)

AFY. Oh, Richard, why have you come? What are you doing with your gun?

RIC. I promised to lend your father one, while his own is being repaired. Why do you hold the door fast behind you?

AFY. You must not stay now, I'm busy!

RIC. Yes, with that fellow Thorne! he is there. It is not the first time you have made excuses for sending me away after you have appointed to meet me; I know the reason—that man is there!

AFY. No, no, he is not, indeed!

RIC. Then you expect him. Afy, he means you no good! Why does he always come at dusk, and take by-roads, so that no one shall see him as he comes here to dazzle you with his glittering diamond rings? Ah, I don't believe his name is Thorne; none of the Swainson Thornes are like him. Oh, Afy, why do you deceive me in this way?

AFY. I am not deceiving you; but do go, now!

RIC. Why do you wish me to "go—now?"

AFY. Because my father has heard the gossips of West Lynne talking about you and me in a bad way. He says you must not come here any more, for when gentlemen come after poor girls in secret they have'nt marriage in their thoughts.

RIC. But *you* know mine is as honourable a love as I could feel for any woman in my own station of life. I cannot marry you in opposition to my father's will; but if you are content to wait, and believe me true, I—

AFY. Well, dear Richard, I do believe that; but I expect father home every minute, so do—do go!

---

*NOTE: *The set trees in this scene need not be struck as they serve (from behind 4 to back of stage) for the avenue backing of chamber sets in Acts 1 and 4 if placed obliquely from* L. 3 E. *to extreme back* R. H.

RIC. Then you will not let me come in and wait for him?

AFY. I dare not.

RIC. Then come out with me for a stroll!

AFY. No, no! Father would be so angry if he comes home and finds me out, he'll be sure I'm with you.

RIC. Oh, very well, give him the gun, but mind how you handle it, for it's loaded. (*Gives her the gun, she goes in.*) I know that man is there. I'll watch and confound her with the proofs of her treachery! (*Goes off* L. 2 E.)

(OTWAY BETHELL *from wood at back.*)

BET. Ha, ha, Miss Hallijohn, mind you don't come to grief between your two lovers. Young Hare is suspicious, and is watching the cottage from yonder trees; a young fool, to be hoodwinked by that cunning young Circé. Ah! (*Turns as though at the sound of some movement of game in the wood* C. L.; *goes off cautiously* C. L.)

(LEVISON *and* AFY *come from cottage.*)

AFY. And must you go so soon?

LEV. My dear Afy, I must be back at Swainson by ten, I have an appointment.

AFY. Oh, yes, to meet some other lady, I suppose?

LEV. Now, Afy, have you so little trust in me as to harbour such suspicions. Now don't pout, my pretty one, but walk with me to the hollow, where I have tethered my horse and as we walk along I hope I shall convince you that you have no rival in my affections! (*They stroll up* C. *and through wood at back, as* OLD HALLIJOHN *comes from* L. 2 E., *and goes into cottage.*)

HAL. (*inside* R. H.). Afy, Afy, where are you? (*Comes to door, looks out.*) Umph, out again with young Hare I s'pose, his gun is here.

LEV. (*at back*). I've left something in the cottage, I'll not be a moment my dear Afy.

HAL. Ah! who is this stranger with my girl? (*Retires into cottage as* LEVISON *comes from wood towards door* R. H.)

LEV. That riding whip has my name on it, and mustn't be left there. (*Goes into cottage.*)

HAL. (*in house*). Who are you, why is my girl with you—

LEV. (*in house*). Take your hands from me.

HAL. You mean no good to her, or why have you come here, like a thief in the night.

LEV. Let go your hold, let go man, or—

HAL. No, not till you have—

(*Shot fired in house*—LEVISON, *the gun in his hand, rushes out, pale and excited,* HALLIJOHN *staggers to door as though to detain* LEVISON *who throws down gun.* R. C., *and rushing to* L. 2 E., *is met by* OTWAY BETHELL, *who catches his arm as he tries to pass.*)

BET. What have you been doing, that you look so wild, and horrified —was it you fired that shot *Captain Levison?*

LEV. Hush! for heaven's sake, since you know me.

BET. I know *Thorne* of *Swainson,* and I know *you are* not he. (*Not seeing* HALLIJOHN'S *body, which is masked by* LEVISON.)

LEV. It was an accident, done in the heat of passion, what right had the fellow to strike me, I will make it worth your while to keep silent, your saying you saw me here can do no good, shall it be silence? Though a *gentleman* you are a *needy man*—under a cloud—here are two notes for £50, all I have about me at present—shall it be silence?

BET. Yes, yes! (LEVISON *gives notes and rushes off* L. 2 E.) I know him, and may bleed him again, when he becomes *Sir* Francis Levison, *Baronet.* (*Exit to back.*)

(RICHARD HARE *from* L. 2 E. *looking off.*)

RIC. The deceitful coquette, he *was* with her. That was Thorne who passed me, looking so pale and terrified. (*Going* R. *sees* HAL.) Good heavens! what is this—Hallijohn (*kneeling by body*) bleeding! dead! (*placing his hand on the heart of* HALLIJOHN)—my gun by his side (*takes gun*) and discharged.

(*Is going* L. H., *with gun,* LOCKSLEY *a poacher, emerges from wood.* L.U.E., RICHARD *retreats* R. H., *throws down gun, surprised and alarmed, rushes off* R. 2 E.)

LOC. Why, that's young Hare. (*Looking after* RICHARD; *following to* R. H., *sees body of* HALLIJOHN.) Ah, Hallijohn, bleeding, "dead," did young Dick Hare fire the shot I heard! (*As he is stooping over body* AFY *returns.*)

AFY. What can detain him so long? (*Sees* LOCKSLEY.) Locksley, what are you doing here? (*He points.*) Ah! my father senseless, who has done this?

LOC. I don't know for sure, but I heard a shot and came up just in time to see Dick Hare fling away the gun, and fly from the place like mad, but I must go for help, there may yet be life in him. (*Exit* L. 2 E.)

RIC. (*comes from* R. 2 E.). I must not leave my gun by his body or they may suspect that I—(*Turns and sees* AFY.) Ah, Afy!

AFY. Murderer! what had my poor father done to you that you should take his life.

RIC. I! Afy, do you imagine *me* capable of such a foul deed?

AFY. *Yes,* who else could have done it, here is your gun—discharged—still warm. 'Twas your wicked hand that killed him.

RIC. I swear that I am innocent, I was not here—till—

AFY. 'Twas *you* Richard Hare, do not think I'll spare you, no *I* will avenge my poor father's death by *yours*—I swear it over the corpse of him—*you* have slain—oh—my poor kind dear—dear father.

RIC. If *she* can think me guilty, who will believe in my innocence! (*Voices* L. 2 E.) *No one*—I dare not stay to be accused by her in the face of all—(*voices* L. 2 E.)—nearer, and nearer yet. (*Bewildered he looks around, and rushes into wood at back.*)

(LOCKSLEY, JUSTICE HARE, *and* Villagers *enter* L. 2 E.)

HAR. Hallijohn murdered! by whom?

AFY. By your son Richard.

HAR. No, do not say by him, by—by—my son.

AFY. *Yes,* he was here by the body not a moment since, but you see he has fled guilt stricken; he dared not wait to answer for his crime.

LOC. And, this is his gun, sir. (*Murmurs.*)

VILLAGERS. Poor Hallijohn, &c., shame on the murderous villain, &c.

HAR. Hark ye all! if it can be *proved* that his hand is red with the blood of this poor man, justice shall be done, son of mine though he be—I—I will *myself* assist to bring him to the punishment his foul crime should meet—aye, as though he were a stranger to my blood and name. Till his innocence is made clear *my* doors shall not shelter him, nor shall his name be spoken in the house he has disgraced. This I swear before ye all.

Ring.

TABLEAU AND CURTAIN.

[House] Villagers. Villagers.
Hallijohn, Afy, Mr. Hare, Locksley.

ACT I

SCENE I: *Garden in* CARLYLE'S *Estate at East Lynne* (*1st grooves*).

(LEVISON *and* CARLYLE *from* L. H.)

LEV. 'Pon my soul, Carlyle, this game of hide and seek is infernally boring. I'm sick of Boulogne and all other places of refuge for the impecunious.

CAR. Then stay here till I can see your uncle, Sir Peter, and arrange with him about your affairs. I may prevail on him to relieve you once more from your embarrassments, and make you a free man again.

LEV. Really now, that is very kind of you, I dread going abroad, away from all my friends; but I dread the bailiffs still more.

CAR. You will be safe enough here. No one will think of looking for you in my house; you are my Isabel's cousin, and for *her* sake you are welcome, so keep close, don't show yourself beyond the grounds till—

(*Enter* BARBARA HARE, R. H.)

BAR. Oh, Archibald! (*Seeing* LEVISON.) Mr. Carlyle, can I speak to—to you for one moment.

CAR. Excuse, Mr. Levison, I will join you presently.

BAR. I am so glad to have met you; I've actually been to your office, and not finding you—

LEV. (*aside*). Umph! his wife's bête noir; Isabel is jealous of her now, and if she should by chance walk this way and see them—(*Exit* L. 1 E.)

CAR. But why does Richard venture here? a warrant for his arrest still—

BAR. But *you* do not believe him guilty of Hallijohn's murder? (*They cross to* L. H.)

CAR. No, *I do* not! but as the jury at the coroner's inquest returned a verdict of wilful murder against him, and the warrant for his arrest is still out: it is most perilous for him to venture here where he's so well known. (*Crosses back to* R.)

BAR. He is not *here,* but at an obscure place, four miles away, disguised as a farm labourer! (*Walking* R. *to* L. *and back as they talk.*)

CAR. Why did he not come forward and state all he knew, instead of absconding, and for four years hiding away?

BAR. (*crosses to* L. H.). He said that he felt the proofs were so strong against him, and as even Afy Hallijohn denounced him he feared no one would believe in his innocence, and now poor mamma is dying to see him; she has never seen him since his flight; he dare not venture near the house while papa is at home; for you know the oath he took, and you also know his obdurate, unforgiving nature. Now I thought if you would kindly make an appointment with him to meet you at your office to-night on some justice business, you might detain him while poor Richard stole a meeting with mamma. (*Crosses to* R. H.)

CAR. Certainly, I was going with my wife to a dinner party at the

Jeffersons, but for your mother's and Dick's sake, I will forgo the engagement.

BAR. Oh, that is kind of you.

CAR. Dill shall go to your father and ask him to meet me, &c., &c., &c. (*By this time they have strolled back from* L. *to* R., *and go off* R. H. *as* ISABEL *enters* L. H. *on* LEVISON'S *arm.*)

ISA. "Doubt him"! never! how *could* I doubt one so good and affectionate, as my dear husband, no! I am too happy in his love, to wrong him by suspicion.

LEV. Then he is indeed to be congratulated; few men are blessed with such blindly confiding wives. (*They have walked over to* R. H., LEVISON *starts and turns quickly.*) Ah!

ISA. Why did you start, and turn so quickly?

LEV. We might disturb a pleasant tête-a-tête, if we go that way. (*Points* R., ISABEL *looks* L. H.)

ISA. Ah! again with her, what does this mean? (*Half aside.*)

LEV. You seem surprised, you would be less so, if *you* had seen them together as often as *I* have, when I am strolling about in the evening (the only time I'm safe from my infernal creditors) I frequently see—(ISABEL *turns on him sharply.*)

ISA. And if you do, by what right dare you impugn Mr. Carlyle's proceedings, if you have not quite forgotten your duty as a gentleman, you would scorn to play the part of a spy and informer, or even attempt to raise doubts in the mind of a wife who loves and honors the husband to whom she owes so much. (*Exit* L. 1 E.)

LEV. (*lights cigar*). Ha! a splendid spasm of conjugal confidence, but you *have* your doubts, and the jealous fire that is now smouldering could easily be fanned into a flame that would consume you, ma bella. (*Exit* L. H.)

SCENE II: *Apartment at East Lynne, long window,* C. *avenue at back, set trees, oblique from* L. *to* R., *folding doors* L. H., *fireplace* R., *door,* L. H. ISABEL *coming up avenue.*

(WILSON *and* JOYCE *discovered.*)

WIL. Ah,—yes; she does look ill indeed, (ISABEL. C. *is coming in, but hearing* BARBARA HARE'S *name, stops*) I shouldn't wonder if she dies young. Oh, wouldn't Barbara Hare's hopes be up again then, if anything should happen she'd snap him up to a certainty, she wouldn't let him escape her a second time. Why *now* she's as much in love with him as ever.

JOY. Oh, nonsense. (ISABEL *listening* C., *concealed by foliage.*)

WIL. Oh, you may say "nonsense," but if *you'd* lived in the Hare family as *I* did for seven years before I came here, and seen *and* heard what *I* have. Why *he* gave her that locket and chain she wears, with a lock of *his hair* in it, too.

JOY. What of that? they were children together and playfellows.

WIL. Um—yes; "playfellows." *She* didn't regard him *only* as a playfellow. Why, even now she'll watch at the gate for his passing, and take every chance of speaking to him.

JOY. Well, well: I don't want to hear anything about her. She must be a great fool to think so much of a man who didn't care for her.

WIL. You don't know that he *didn't* care for [her] then, we don't know how it was between 'em, and if anything *should* happen to Lady Isabel——

JOY. Nothing is going to happen to her I hope, for the sake of the dear children.

WIL. I'm sure *I* hope so, too. Barbara Hare wouldn't make a very kind stepmother, hating the *mother* as she does, the *children* wouldn't be loved much.

JOY. If you wish to remain in your place here you'd better put a curb on your tongue, Miss Cornelia says yours is the longest in Lynne, and if my lady heard you——

WIL. Well, I only say what, &c., &c. (*Exeunt* L. H., *talking.*)

ISA. (*comes forward*). I begin to understand all now. There *is* a calmness almost amounting to indifference compared to the passionate ardour of his love in the early days of our married life. What if she *were* the companion of his youth, he is *mine* now; but is his *heart* all—*all*—mine. Or does she still cast a spell over him, good, kind, tender, as he is. I cannot help the feeling that there is a change. (*In chair,* R. C.)

(*Enter* CARLYLE C.)

CAR. Isabel dearest! how's this—in tears. (ISABEL *rises and speaks with great emotion.*)

ISA. Oh, Archy, Archy, you will never marry her, if anything should happen to me—never let *her* usurp my place—she would be unkind to my children, draw your love from them, and from *my* memory.

CAR. Of whom are you speaking dearest, what is troubling you so sorely?

ISA. Did you love no one, before you—you married me—oh Archy—even now, perhaps you love her still.

CAR. Her! of whom do you speak Isabel?

ISA. Barbara Hare.

CAR. I *never* loved Barbara Hare but as a brother, never loved any woman but you; and to you I have never been false in word, deed, or thought; what proof of true and earnest love can man give, that have *I* not given to *you?*

ISA. None, none. Oh do not be angry with me, I think sometimes that I must be dreaming; wild, strange, feverish dreams; I mistrust myself, *you,* all the world; I feel how much I owe you, and knowing how little I have to repay you with, I grow sad, suspicious, miserable.

CAR. Indulge no more in such wild fancies, they are mere illusions, as unfair to me, as they are distressing to you.

ISA. I will try—to—to—

CAR. You will not be yourself my darling, nor recover your spirits till you have had change of air, the sea breezes will soon bring the roses to your cheeks again—and—

(*Enter* CORNELIA L. H. *with* LEVISON.)

COR. Sea breezes indeed, and change of air! what do people want with them, a parcel of new fangled notions that doctors put in people's heads—ugh! they'll recommend change of air for a scratched finger next, I never want change of air. (LEVISON *saunters up* C. *and over to* R. C.)

CAR. (*not heeding* CORNELIA). Some quiet watering place on the French or Belgian coast—Trouville, for instance.

COR. You'd better sit down and calculate the cost of gallivanting over the water, &c.

CAR. Two or three months there will set you up.

COR. (*aside*). Set her up indeed! (L. C.) She wants setting down.

CAR. And make you blooming as ever.

ISA. (R. C.). But cannot you stay there with me? I shall be so lonely without you.

CAR. (C.). I shall run over as often as business will allow; I must not neglect business even for *you,* darling.

COR. (L.). I think you are neglecting it! What are you doing now, away from your office? (ISABEL *joins* LEVISON *up* R. C.)

CAR. (C.). There's Dill to represent me, and a staff of clerks under him.

COR. Ah! you never used to neglect your business *before* you were *married.*

LEV. (R. C.—*to* ISABEL *aside*). Your husband will miss you very much when you go to Trouville; he will have only his sister and Miss Hare to console him in your absence. (*Pointedly.*—HARE *and* CORNELIA *talking aside,* L. C.)

COR. (*aloud*). And pray what did Barbara Hare want with you this morning? (ISABEL *starts, hearing* BARBARA'S *name.*)

CAR. She came to see me on business.

COR. She seems to be always wanting to see you. What is the business? (*Aside.*) Ah! surely that old affair is not being revived again? (*Aloud.*)

CAR. (*crosses* L. C.). I may trust to you, sister. Richard Hare is— (*Aside* L. H.)

COR. Richard Hare!

CAR. Hush! (*Hurries her off* L. H.)

(LEVISON, *talking earnestly to* ISABEL *up* R. C.)

LEV. (*leaning on mantel*). But you will believe me some day when the truth is forced upon you, *you* saw them in the garden—in earnest conversation.

ISA. Why remind me of that again? you make a poor return for Mr. Carlyle's hospitality, in maligning him, to *me, his wife.* (ISABEL *comes* C. *sits.*)

LEV. (*leaning over her chair*). His wife, ah, Isabel, there is the bitterness in reflection, that you *are his;* had we listened to our hearts in those days we might have been happier now, you and I were created to love each other, and (ISABEL *rises*) I would have declared the love that was consuming me, but—

ISA. I will not, dare not, listen to you. (LEVISON *takes her hand and presses her into chair.*)

LEV. You must for a few moments. What I say now can do no harm; the time has gone by, the gulf between us is impassable; I know the fault was mine, I might then have won you and been happy.

ISA. You are talking to me—as—as you have no right to talk. (*Rises and crosses* L.)

LEV. Only the right of my deep, my undying love. (*Following her to* L. H.)

ISA. Must I again remind you that you are here as the guest of *him* whose wife you insult by such language, the roof *which* shelters *you, should* be *my* protection—(*Turns from him up* C.)

LEV. (*in a low tone*). Isabel, there are moments, when the sweet remembrances of earlier, happier, more *hopeful* years, make us forget reason, duty, even our *honor,* when our hearts beat wildly, and our feelings cry louder than our judgment or the voice of conscience, but say that you forgive me. (*Goes to her up* C. *on her* R. H.)

ISA. (R. C.). I forgive you Captain Levison, but you must leave this house, you have lost all right to the name of friend. (*They come down* R. C.)

LEV. (R.). Oh, my dear Isabel, do not say that you banish me for a few rash words spoken in the inconsiderate warmth of a disappointed spirit, that is now dead to hope for evermore. (*Very earnestly.*)

ISA. Leave me now. I would be alone.

LEV. I obey. (*Crosses to* C.) The poison works; that (*aside*) last touch of emotion, combined with her growing jealousy, must have its effect in the end. (*Exit* C. *to* L. H.)

ISA. How can I succeed in my endeavors to forget him while he remains at East Lynne, and I am thrown daily, hourly, into his dangerous companionship. Dangerous! where should be the danger to *me?* (*Pacing the room.*) The wife of such a man as Archibald Carlyle, the mother of his children, and yet these sinful throbbings of my heart when Levison is by me, speak only too plainly of the peril there is to my peace in his insidious sophistries. (*Goes up, looks off* C., *comes down* R. C.) Oh, if I had but courage to tell my husband all—tell him that I once had a girl's passing fancy for my Cousin Francis, and that now *he* is here, my thoughts, in spite of myself, my duty, and my conscience will stray back to that time, when I was free to love, when there was no sin in—(CARLYLE *speaks off* L. H.) I *will* confide in him as a wife should. I will beg him to send Francis away, and—yes—Archibald shall tell me what is the secret between him and Barbara Hare. (ISABEL *goes to* L. H.)

(CARLYLE *enters* L. H. D.)

ISA. Archy, my dear Archy, I want you to listen to me so patiently and calmly. (CARLYLE, C., ISABEL, R. C.) I have a—a—secret to confide—a secret that has long—

(LEVISON *strolls on* C.)

LEV. Oh, by the bye, Carlyle, you are going to dine with the Jeffersons to-night, are you not? (ISABEL *goes down* R. H.)

CAR. Yes! (*Speaks aside to* LEVISON *up* C.)

ISA. What strange fatality thwarts me every time I resolve to confide my fears to him who *should* know how cruelly I am beset by them?

(WILSON *enters* L., CARLYLE *crosses to her.*)

WIL. Mr. Hare's servant brought this note, Sir! (*Exit* WILSON L.)

(LEVISON *up* R. C. ISABEL *starts.*)

LEV. Umph, Hare's servant. (*Aside.*)

CAR. (*reads down* L. C.). "I fear that Richard is no longer safe where he has *hitherto been concealed,* he is now hiding in the fir copse behind your *garden,* and *will steal* out *after dark* to *see* mamma WHEN PAPA HAS LEFT HOME *if you* can persuade him to *come out.*—Yours, Barbara." Dear, dear, how incautious to venture here! (*He crosses* R. *to* ISABEL, *the note in his hand. Throws note on fire, and brings her forward* R. C. LEVISON *comes down and snatches it off fire, throws it in fender. Goes up again.*)

CAR. (*his back to* LEVISON). Oh, Isabel, my dear, I forgot to tell you that I shall not be able to go with you to the Jeffersons! (*Down* R. H.)

ISA. (*down* R. C.). Not go too Archibald! Why not?

CAR. I have an appointment on important business that may detain me till late. (*Crosses* L.) (*Aside.*) Foolish boy, foolish boy! (*As he goes off* L. H.)

ISA. Ah, that note! (*Aloud.*)

LEV. (*up* R. C.). The note cannot be of the same importance as the "business" or he would (*points to fender*) not have thrown it *there,* and as *Hare's servant* brought it—(ISABEL *looks at him sharply. He goes up* C.) (*Aside.*) She'll never resist the temptation to read it! (*Goes out on verandah, watching her from behind foliage.*)

ISA. Hare's servant! (*Pause.*) (*Then goes* R. *and snatches note from fender.*) Some of the words are obliterated by fire, but there may be enough to give me a clue to the purport. (*Reads.*) "*I fear* (*the note is partially burnt*) —*no* longer safe—*hitherto been concealed* in copse—garden—will—after dusk—see—you—when—has—left home.—Barb—" Yes, the word half calcined was "Barbara"—(*looking at note*)—has left home—"Has left home"! When *she* has left home, that is the word—missing. Yes, when *I* have left (*passionately*) home! Oh, shameless woman! and *he, my husband!* The words scarce spoken that my grief had wrung from me—can leave me to be by *her* side! False friend, false love—all false alike—all! (*Sinks in chair* C. *sobbing.*)

(LEVISON *comes down quickly.*)

LEV. But *me* dear Isabel.

Close in quickly.

SCENE III: *Chamber* (*in* 1) *door in flat*

CAR. (*dragging* RICHARD HARE, *who is disguised in smock-frock, false beard, &c., &c.*). Come in here till I can think what shall be done, no one will come here. My dear lad what folly—to—to—why have you come here to Lynne?

RIC. (*takes off hat and beard*). What could I do, I fear the officers are on my track—I've been followed by *one* I know. I met that villain Thorne in London, and from that hour I have been dogged: I came here because I felt I was not safe in my old hiding place at Dale's-end, a stranger has followed me even there. Oh, Mr. Carlyle, the life I have led has been dreadful—many and many a time I have thought that if I had lain down in the snow on some door step, and have been found dead in the morning it would—(CORNELIA *outside.*)

COR. Archibald, who's with you now?

RIC. Don't let her come in. (*Alarmed.*)

CAR. You remember what she *was,* and she's not a bit altered, if she has a *mind* to come in *I* cannot keep her out—you need not fear, *she* will be as anxious as I am to shield you. (*Opens door in flat to* CORNELIA.)

COR. Powers of mercy, what brought *you* here, you must be mad? (*To* RICHARD.)

RIC. I am, almost, leading such a life as I have, I don't mind toil (though that's hard enough, after being brought up like a gentleman), but to be banned, hunted, afraid to show my face among my fellow-men, in dread every hour that the law may doom me to——

COR. Well, you've only yourself to thank, you would go dangling after that brazen hussy, Afy Hallijohn—its all through your—

RIC. No! it is all through that villain, Thorne, who killed her father, that I am hunted down like this.

COR. Well, it seems to me a most extraordinary thing that the real truth can't be brought to light. You tell a cock and bull story about some man, some Thorne, whom nobody ever saw, or heard of.

CAR. Dick has seen him again, lately, and says that it is he who has set the officers on his track.

COR. Then why didn't you turn the tables on him, and *set* the *officers* on *him?*

RIC. I have no proof that he was the murderer, my bare word would not be taken, and he might swear my life away. He saw me in the wood that night.

COR. Ugh! you always were the biggest noodle that was ever let out of leading strings, and always will be.

CAR. Well, well, Cornelia. (*Expostulating.*)

COR. Ugh! I've no patience, and if he wasn't so miserably woe-begone, I'd treat him to a bit of my mind, you may depend on that.

CAR. We must think of some way to dispose of him. After he has crept home to-night to see his mother he must return here, for *here* he must stop for the present.

COR. I'm sure I don't know how he's to get to a bedroom, without servants knowing he's here, the only safe room is the one beyond mine.

CAR. How is he to get to that?

COR. How! why, through *mine,* to be sure.

CAR. Well, if *you* don't mind.

COR. I! Do you suppose I mind young Dick Hare, whom I've so often spanked when a child, and I wish he was young enough to spank now; he richly deserves it, if ever any body did. I shall be in bed, and his passing through won't alarm me. I shan't be frightened if *he* isn't. Stand on ceremony with young Dick Hare, indeed! What next, I wonder? Archy, you go and see that the coast is clear. (*Exit* CARLYLE D. F.) (*Turns to* DICK, *kindly.*) Poor hunted boy, I'll bring you some food up, you look as though you wanted it. Though you deserve a good thrashing before you get anything else. (*Looks out* D. F.) (*Kindly.*) There, there! we won't talk of that now, but if ever you do get clear of this trouble I'll let you have a bit of mind, I promise you! (*Exeunt* D. F.)

SCENE IV: *Same as Scene II*

LEV. (*discovered by fireplace*). I think that partially calcined note has added fuel to the flame, jealousy will develop into resentment; then will arise a desire for revenge, next to love a woman's pet passion. I may venture to take a stroll beyond the sanctuary of East Lynne; I shall surely be safe for this evening from those infernal pests of society—the sheriff's officers. (*Exit* C. *to* R. *down avenue.*)

(*Enter* CARLYLE *and* ISABEL, R. H., ISABEL *dressed as for a party, crosses to table* R. *for fan or handkerchief.*)

CAR. I really am very sorry, my dear; you must make my excuses to Mrs. Jefferson.

ISA. You never before have had business, so mysterious and important as to demand your attendance at your office at this hour.

CAR. I regret that it should have so happened now, but it is too momentous to be neglected; and it must be done by myself alone.

ISA. Shall you join us later in the evening. (*Coldly.*)

CAR. I much fear that I shall be unable to do so; I will put you in the carriage, Isabel. (*She sweeps past him to* L. H.) (*Exeunt* L. D.)

(LEVISON *enters hurriedly* C. R.)

LEV. (*agitated, putting his hair off his brow*). What is Dick Hare doing about here, is he dogging me, lucky that he was so much astonished at my sudden appearance, that I had time to make off and double back here, before he was able to decide on any course of action. What is his errand here? Is it to denounce me as the soi disant Thorne? If so I must become a fugitive once more, but, *not alone,* I will have a fair partner in my exile. (*Down* R.)

(*Enter* CARLYLE, *his hat on,* L. H.)

CAR. Why, Levison, you look as agitated as though you had seen a bailiff.

(LEVISON *having started on hearing his footsteps turns quickly.* BARBARA *comes from* R. *up avenue to window* C.)

BAR. Oh Archibald. (*Seeing* LEVISON.) Mr. Carlyle, will you. (*Retiring from window,* CARLYLE *goes to her.*)

LEV. Do not let me drive you away Miss Hare. (*Crosses to* L. H.) Umph! Isabel's back hardly turned before her hated rival appears; the carriage cannot have gone far on the road; by the fields I may overtake the injured wife. (*Exit* L. H. D.)

BAR. Yes, he was emerging from the clump of trees in Bean-lane, and came upon Thorne face to face. (*They come forward.*)

CAR. Dick must have been mistaken.

BAR. He says he can swear to him. Thorne was walking fast with his hat in one hand, while with the other he pushed back the hair from his brow. Dick knew him by that action alone, as he was always doing so in the old days. There was the hand adorned with the flashing diamond ring.

CAR. Why did your brother allow him to escape?

BAR. He was so surprised, he had not the presence of mind to spring on him and accuse him of the murder. When he had recovered from his astonishment Thorne was making off rapidly in the direction of East Lynne.

CAR. Where is Dick now.

BAR. Hiding in the fir copse till he sees my signal that all is safe in doors, for papa is still at home, and he says, with his usual contrariety, that if you want to see him to-night you must come to him (to use his own words) he is not going over to your office to sit with Dill and you among dusty deed boxes and mouldy old parchments.

CAR. Oh, indeed Mr. Justice Hare, then we must bring you up here out of the way.

BAR. Will you come over with me now and entice him away on some pretence; poor mamma is waiting so anxiously to see her boy. I am sorry to give you all this trouble.

CAR. (*takes up his hat from chair*). My dear Barbara, it is no trouble to me if I can make any one happy, if only for an hour. I'll coax your obstinate dad up here, and Cornelia shall find him a long pipe and some strong October, such as he delights in at the "Buck's Head," and we'll talk parochial politics while Dick—(*Going* C.)

BAR. But papa must not know that I've been up here, or he'll think it a plan.

CAR. O, no, we'll, &c., &c.

(*Talking as they go off* C., *down avenue to* R. LEVISON *and* ISABEL *enter* L. H. D., *he goes up, points off* C.)

LEV. There, dear Isabel, will you believe your own eyes. (ISABEL *goes into verandah.*)

ISA. With *her?* Then my fears were *not* unfounded.

LEV. You see now why he could not accompany you—you see now why he is so anxious for your retirement at Trouville, that with the seas between you he may have the opportunity daily, *hourly,* of enjoying her dear society.

ISA. Oh! you torture me.

LEV. You whom I have loved so constantly through all, through coldness and disdain on your part, through the helpless, hopeless misery I have endured in seeing you the wife of one who loves you as you see. (*Points off* C. R.)

ISA. Oh! why have you shown me this? (*Fiercely.*)

LEV. To prove how grossly you are deceived. Be avenged on him. Leave this life of doubts and fears; come to happiness with one whose love for you will never change.

ISA. Tempt me not, leave me, I am almost mad! (*Comes into room.*)

LEV. (*points*). Look there again. Even from here you may see how he whispers in her ear, how close his lips are to hers. (*She goes to window again.*) Can you not in imagination hear the loving words that he should speak to none *but you.*

ISA. It is too plain he loves her, and I am—

LEV. Deceived. Can you endure the sight of that, and yet seek no revenge? Will you still spurn my true love? Will you—oh, say, dear Isabel—will you fly with me—fly from him who insults you thus? (*Pointing off* R. C.)

ISA. Yes, come weal, come woe, I will—I will be avenged on him for so cruelly wronging me. (*Music p.p.*)

LEV. Come then, swift horses shall be in readiness, and we—

ISA. Go, I will rejoin you in a few minutes. (*He goes off* C. L., *she sits at table* R. C., *and writes, reading as she writes.*) "When years have passed and my—my—children ask where is their mother and why she left her home, then tell them that you, their father, goaded her to the rash act. Tell them that you deceived, outraged her feelings and her pride, until driven to the verge of madness, she—she—quitted them for ever." (*Rises from table.*) Now, Francis Levison, I trust my future in your hands, and may heaven forgive me.

(*As she is looking despairingly around the room* JOYCE *enters* L. D.)

JOY. Oh, my lady, are you ill?

ISA. Aye! ill and wretched! (*Crosses to* JOYCE.) Joyce once before, when I was near death, you promised me to stay with my children, whatever might happen; promise me that again, promise, that when I am gone, you will not leave them.

JOY. Never! my dear lady—never! but do, my dear mistress, tell me, are you ill? What is the matter? What can I do?

ISA. Nothing that can avail me now, I am beyond mortal aid. Remember your promise, dear Joyce! Leave me now! Remember your promise, as you hope for mercy! (*Puts* JOYCE *to door,* L. H., *and rushes off* C. *to* L. H.)

JOY. (*goes up* C.). What can she mean?—"when I am gone"—"once before near death." Ah! I know what her wild looks, her sad, pale face, and broken-acted tones meant. Merciful heavens! where is Mr. Carlyle? (CARLYLE *and* HARE *come up* R. H. *avenue.*) Oh, sir! have you seen my lady?

CAR. She has gone to Mrs. Jeffersons! (C.)

JOY. She has returned, and gone—gone—to take the life that is not hers; to take—

CAR. Joyce, what do you mean?

JOY. (*sobbing*). My lady made me promise to—to—

(CORNELIA *enters* L.)

JOY. (*to* CORNELIA). Ah, when my dear lady is laid before us dead, what will be your feeling for having driven her to it!

CAR. Joyce, I am at a loss to understand your meaning.

JOY. I know, sir you have done your duty to her in love and kindness, but Miss Cornelia has made her life a misery; yes ma'am you have; I've seen her with tears in her eyes after enduring your reproach a gentle high-born lady like her to be—eh! you've driven her to desperation! I know it!

CAR. Oh, Cornelia! if Joyce's fears are well founded, heaven forgive you! She may be in the grounds. (HARE *and* CORNELIA *go off to grounds* C.; *going up* R. C., *sees note on desk* R. C., *hesitates to read it.*) Ah! writing in her hand! Why do I fear to read? (*Reads note.*)

JOY. What does it say, sir; does it say—that—she—is dead? (*Music p.p. to Curtain.*)

CAR. Worse, far worse than death. Had she died, I could still have worshipped, honoured her memory while I mourned her loss, but now —(*A little boy and girl run on from* L. H.)

CHILD. Where's mamma? They are saying that mamma has gone. Where is she?

JOY. Oh! my dear Miss Isabel, you must not—

CAR. Joyce! that name no more—no more—My children motherless—my home dishonoured—oh! God! give me strength to bear this blow (*sinks in chair*) my children—you will see her no—no more. In this world you will have but me and your little brother to love you—my darlings, we must be all in all to each other now. I have only you—only you—(*Embracing the children.*)

RING.

ACT II

SCENE I: *Chamber at* JUSTICE HARE'S—*1st Grooves—Window* L. F., *same as second scene of Prologue.*

(BARBARA *and* CARLYLE *discovered.*)

CAR. And what do they say of me, Barbara?

BAR. That you go over to Lynboro' so often, not to see Sir John Dobede, but his daughter Louisa.

CAR. And do *you* believe that?

BAR. Well, I don't know, why should it not be true.

CAR. Because I shall never marry again. How can I? *she* who *was* my wife still lives.

BAR. But the law has—(*Stops suddenly.*)

CAR. I know what you would say: *the law* has now pronounced me free; *I* cannot accept that decree as a dissolution of so sacred a compact, *I* cannot forget those solemn words "Till *death* do us part." (CARLYLE *has gone up to window* L. F., *looking out* L. H.)

BAR. His heart still clings to *her,* how he must have loved her, how could she have forsaken such a man. *I* would have died for him, happy to give my life for his love.

(*Enter* MR. HARE *hastily,* L. 1 E.)

CAR. What's the matter, Justice, you seem excited.

HAR. (*wiping his brow*). Excited! yes, and so would you be *excited* if you were worried out of your senses as I am; why, there's Barbara, as if we were not scandalised enough by her scamp of a brother, *she* must give folks reason to say that no one will have her because of his misdeeds.

CAR. More shame on those who say so. (BARBARA *crosses to* L. *as though to go.*)

HAR. (*stopping her*). No, no, you shan't escape that way; that's how you always try to evade me when I'm telling you of your conduct, any one would think that rather than be under such a stigma and allow the parish to say that of her she would marry the first man who offered, even if it was the parish beadle, just to stop their chattering tongues.

CAR. I should hardly think you'd like to have a parish beadle for your son-in-law.

HAR. But she's had bushels of *good* offers, and says no to all of them. There's Tom Herbert, he was the last one whom she refused, point blank.

CAR. Indeed! and why, eh Barbara? I'm sure he's a very nice fellow.

BAR. Oh yes, he *is* a very "pleasant fellow," to *some* people. (*Exit* L. H.)

HAR. Ugh, she's one of the obstinate, contrary, self-willed ones.

CAR. She may have an excuse for that.

HAR. Excuse! what excuse?

CAR. She is your child.

HAR. Of course she is, whose should she be? and as she is *my child,* she ought to do as I bid her, and now, to add to my vexations, here's this infernal report about the place.

CAR. What report?

HAR. What report! why, that *he* has been here, disguised as a labourer, has dared to show himself here, *here* where he may yet come to the gibbet.

CAR. Of *whom* are you speaking?

HAR. Of *whom* should I be *speaking,* but of that scoundrel. Dick (*spluttering*), *who else* is likely to come to a felon's death? If he has dared to come near Lynne, I'll put the police on his track, oh! I was in such a passion that I was nearly knocking down the man who told me; however, I'll have no more of this worry.

CAR. I'm inclined to think you bring all this worry on yourself.

HAR. Now, that cobs all! Bring it on myself; did *I* shoot Hallijohn? Did *I* fly from justice and hide the devil knows where? Did *I* come back to my native parish disguised as a—a—dirty labourer, to worry my *own father,* eh? Bring it on myself, ugh.

CAR. It was just the same when you received that anonymous letter some days ago, you were in a passion then.

HAR. And enough to make any man in a passion, here, this says (*takes a letter from his pocket*) he may come down, and warns me to put him on his guard, and hush it up, as if I would put him on his guard—If I drop on him, I'll—

CAR. I daresay some one has circulated this report, and written anonymous letters, merely for the purpose of vexing you.

HAR. I'd like to find out who had.

CAR. I daresay you would—now, you follow my advice, take no notice of *rumours*, and put all anonymous letters in the fire—a pretty laugh they'd have at you if they thought you'd been hoaxed by——

HAR. Laugh at *me*,—would they? If they dared to do that, I'd have the whole parish of Lynne up before me, and I'd—I'd—(*Spluttering, in a rage.*)

CAR. *What* would you do, eh?

HAR. Do? why commit them all for trial.

CAR. You couldn't do that.

HAR. Couldn't I? But I would—I would.

CAR. No you would not. Even "great unpaids" cannot commit or fine people for laughing at them, or they would have to sign commitments every hour in the day.

HAR. What do you mean by that? However, I'll call at the police-station and tell them to keep a sharp look-out for the young villain.

CAR. You'll do nothing of the kind.

HAR. Y—yes I—will. (*Blustering.*)

CAR. I say you will *not.* Every man would cry shame on you, and justly so, if you did such a monstrous act. Oh, you may look angry, but if others shrink from telling you the truth, I do not; your unnatural harshness, your blind obstinacy have become a bye word.

HAR. *My* obstinacy! (*As though astonished.*)

CAR. Yes! give your own son up to justice. You will never do so cruel an act. Or if you *do,* you may take leave of your friends, for you'll not find any man willing to own *you* for one.

HAR. (*awed by* CARLYLE'S *tone*). But I took an oath to do it.

CAR. But you did not "take an oath" to go open mouthed to the police-station on the strength of some paltry anonymous letter or lying rumour, and say "my son will be in Lynne to-day or to-morrow, look out for him." You let the police look after their own business, don't *you* set them on.

HAR. Then you think this rumour——

CAR. Not worth listening to.

HAR. And this letter? (*Showing it.*)

CAR. Put it in the fire.

HAR. Eh?

CAR. That's what *I* should do.

HAR. Would you—eh? would you? (*More calmly.*)

CAR. I certainly would.

HAR. Umph—ha! Well I think I will. I don't know how it is Carlyle, but you've got a way of talking people over that's—that's damned annoying. (*Takes out handkerchief.*) You talk, and you gammon and palaver, and twist them round your finger as easily—as easily as—as I——(*Flourishing his pockethandkerchief as though at a loss for a word, blows his nose, and exits* R. H. CARLYLE *follows. Four bars of music before change.*)

SCENE II: *Chamber* (*in* 3)—*Fireplace* R. H., *table* R. C.—*Door* L. 2. E.—LADY ISABEL *discovered by fire.*

ISA. He comes too late now, too late to save the poor child from the life-long reproach that must rest on him.

(LEVISON *enters* L. H. D., *sits* L. *of table.*)

LEV. I'm sorry I could not get away from town before.

ISA. Why did you come now?

LEV. Why did I come! I thought you at least would have been glad to welcome me.

ISA. When you left me in May last, you gave me a sacred promise to come back in time for our marriage, you know what I mean when I say "in time" but—

LEV. Of course I meant to be back—but business—

ISA. You cannot deceive me now, you *did not* mean to be back in time, or you would have arranged our marriage before you went away.

LEV. What fancies have you taken up now Isabel?

ISA. No fancies, but bitter truths. On the morning of your departure you received two letters—one announcing the death of your uncle, and your accession to the title and estates, the other contained the information that the divorce was decreed—thus enabling you to make the only reparation in your power.

LEV. Well, you know—

ISA. You left those letters on your table. It would have been better to have undeceived me before you left, better to have told me that the hopes I was cherishing (for the sake of the poor unborn child) were worse than vain.

LEV. The excited state you were then in would have precluded your listening to any sort of reason.

ISA. You think it would not be in reason, that I should aspire to be made the wife of Sir Francis Levison.

LEV. Well, Isabel, you must be aware that it would be an awful sacrifice for a man in my position to marry a divorced woman. I am now the representative of an ancient and honorable baronetcy, and to make you my wife would—

ISA. I understand you, you need not be at any trouble to invent or seek for excuses. The injury to the child can never be repaired now; and for myself, I cannot imagine any worse fate in life than being obliged to pass it with *you.* You have made me what I am, but all the reparation in your power to make now, cannot undo my sin—that —and its effect must lie upon me forever more.

LEV. The sin! ha, ha! you women should think of that beforehand.

ISA. Ah, yes. May heaven help all to think of it when you're tempted as I was.

LEV. If you mean that as a reproach to me it is rather out of place. The temptation to *sin* (as you call it) did not lie so much in *my* persuasion as in *your own* jealous anger towards your husband.

ISA. Alas! too true—too true.

LEV. And I believe you were so outrageously jealous of him without any cause; their secret meetings were on some business matters in which Mrs. Hare was much interested.

ISA. You told a different tale to me then.

LEV. All stratagems are fair in love and war. (ISABEL *takes banknotes from desk on table,* R. C.)

ISA. I received these from you by post a month ago—I return them.

LEV. Return them!—why?

ISA. I have no more to do with you; all is over between us. (*Haughtily.*)

LEV. Oh, very well; if it be your wish that all relations between us should end, be it so. I must confess I think it better so, for the cat and dog [life] we should, as it seems to me, henceforth lead, would be far from agreeable. (*Waiting for her to make some reply.*) Remember, it is your doing, not mine. A sum (we will fix the amount) shall be placed to your account, and—(ISABEL *turns vehemently.*)

ISA. Not one farthing will I receive from *you* Sir Francis Levison.

LEV. You have no fortune of your own, you must have assistance from some one.

ISA. Not from *you*! If all the world denied me help, and I could find none from strangers, I would *die* rather than touch one coin of *your* money.

LEV. In time you may wish to recall your words, in that case a line to my bankers—

ISA. Put away those notes if you please. And now I have said all, we part; henceforth we are strangers.

LEV. As you please; good-bye. Will you not give me your hand? (ISABEL *stands with her back towards him.*)

ISA. I would prefer not.

LEV. Very well. (*Crosses* L.) An encumbrance well got rid of, and by her own wish, so my conscience is clear on that score. (*Exit* L. D.)

ISA. What am I now—an outcast, whom men pity, and from whom all good women will shrink. I have abandoned my husband, children, my home, cast away my good name, wrecked my happiness for evermore, and deliberately offended heaven, for him—for *him*—oh! my punishment is hard to bear—but I have deserved it, all my future life spent in repentant expiation can never atone for the past, never, never.

SUSANNE (*enter* L. D.). An English nobleman to see my lady.

ISA. Who can wish to see me, it cannot be my hus—— Mr. Carlyle.

SUS. Not a young gentleman—he is 50 if an hour—and his hair a fine grey.

(LORD MOUNT SEVERN L. H. *Exit* SUSANNE L. D.)

LORD M. Isabel, I have sought you, that I might afford you aid in your time of trouble. (ISABEL *covers her face with her hands.*)

ISA. How did you find me?

LORD M. I sought Levison when he was in London, and demanded what he had done with *you,* as I heard he was going to marry Blanche Challoner.

ISA. Poor Blanche (*aside*) poor Blanche. (*In chair* C.)

LORD M. (*with intense feelings*). Had this occurred in my young days, when gentlemen wiped out dishonour in blood, he would have had a bullet in his black heart ere now. (*Vehemently.*) The coward! the heartless villain! may all good men shun him from henceforth, and may every *pure* woman look on him with scorn and loathing—oh! Isabel my poor girl, what demon tempted you to sacrifice yourself to that bad, heartless man.

ISA. He *is* heartless.

LORD M. I warned you at the commencement of your married life, not to admit him to your home.

ISA. His coming to East Lynne was not my doing—Mr. Carlyle invited him.

LORD M. Invited him in unsuspecting confidence, believing his wife to be a true woman, to whom honour was dear as life, a woman whom he trusted, as he loved.

ISA. I believed that his love was no longer mine, that he had deserted me for another.

LORD M. Deserted you, why he was never from—

ISA. There is desertion of the heart.

LORD M. Tut, tut! I read the note you left, and I put the question to him as between man and man, whether he had ever given you cause to write such words, and he answered me (as with heaven above us) that he had always been faithful to you in thought and deed; but that is beside the question now, and foreign to the purpose of my visit here. Your father is gone and there is no one to stand in his place but *me.* (*In a kind tone.*)

ISA. My father! oh, my father! (*Weeping.*)

LORD M. You have no means of your own, no fortune, how will you live?

ISA. I have some money yet.

LORD M. That man's money? (*Sharply.*)

ISA. No; I have sold my trinkets, and I shall try to earn my living by teaching.

LORD M. You earn! Tut, tut, my dear child; as much as you need I will supply.

ISA. No, no! I do not deserve such kindness, I have forfeited all claim to assistance.

LORD M. Not to *mine*; I am acting as for your dead father. Do you suppose that he would have abandoned you to work or starve. I never willfully neglect a duty, and I look upon it as an imperative duty to settle on you an income sufficient for a modest competency, and these notes will, I hope, meet your present demands Isabel. (*Tenderly.*)

ISA. No, no; you are too good to me, I do not deserve this kindness.

LORD M. I am resolved not to leave you to the mercy of the harsh world without some protection against its trials and temptations. Adieu for the present, I shall see you again before I return to England, and we will talk of your future. (*Going to door,* L. H.)

ISA. My future? ah! what do they say of me at East Lynne? (*Following him,* L. C.)

LORD M. Your name is never mentioned there; you are thought of as one, who was once dearly loved, but now dead, no stop. To your husband and your children: you are mourned with gentle pity, but the name of Isabel is never heard in that deserted home, the happiness of which you have for ever blighted. Adieu. (*Moved by her look of despairing anguish he kisses her on the brow and exits slowly* L. H. D.)

ISA. (*music p.p. plaintive to drop*). My name is never mentioned, I am mourned as one dead. Oh, would that I had died when I might have heard kind loving voices as my spirit passed away from earth to heaven! My husband, my children!—Oh, never again to hear *him* say "Isabel, my wife!" Never again to hear *their* infant tongues murmur the holy name of *"mother!"* Lost, degraded, friendless, abandoned, and alone! Alone—utterly alone—for evermore!

Sinks on her knees despairingly as

THE CURTAIN FALLS: *Music, "Home, sweet home."*

ACT III

SCENE I: *Same as Act I, Scene II, but instead of fireplace folding doors* R. H., *long window* C.*

(LORD MOUNT SEVERN *and* CORNELIA *discovered.*)

COR. (*seated* L. *of table* L. H.). No! I reside now in my house at West Lynne; when my brother was such a simpleton as to get married again, he was good enough to say that two mistresses in one house would not answer; so, after being like a mother to him ever since he was a boy, I have to turn out—ugh! what did he want to get married for? I never did! Why couldn't he remain single as I have done?

LORD M. (C *of table*). Well, ma'am, why should he? Marriage is a happy state—happy, honourable, and—

COR. (*bitterly*). Very happy, very honourable; his first marriage brought him all that; did it not?—oh, I beg your pardon, I forgot you were a relative of—of—by-the-bye, was it positively ascertained as a fact, that Lady Isabel did die after that dreadful railway accident at Canmeres, in France?

*NOTE: *In a theatre where the chamber scenes are limited, this set may be the same as Scene II of Act I. With that arrangement the piano will be off stage* L. H., *and the sides reversed for business and entrances.*

LORD M. She certainly did die, poor child! Did not Carlyle tell you of the letter she wrote to me on her death-bed?

COR. No! I never heard of any letter; may I ask the nature of it?

LORD M. The letter was to the effect that she was dying from injuries she had received; she said that she was glad to die, and so deliver all who had ever loved her from the shame she had brought on them. I cannot remember the exact words now, but I recollect the last few lines, for they were written in characters such as might be scrawled by some poor sufferer who had signed a confession, forced by the tortures of the rack; they were: "Go to Mr. Carlyle, say that I humbly beg him to forgive me; tell him that I repent, bitterly repent; (I have no words to express how bitterly) the wrong I have done him; I can write no more, my bodily pain is so great, but no greater than my mental agony and remorse—farewell—forgive—Isabel—"

COR. Poor, erring creature; heaven be merciful to her! (*Rises.*)

LORD M. When I received that letter I made every possible inquiry as to its truth in all the details, and was told at Canmeres that she died the night following the day of the—the accident; but why do you ask; have you any doubts?

COR. A thought came over me to-day as to whether she really *was* dead!

LORD M. Alas, poor child, she has gone, beyond all doubt.

(*Enter* BARBARA R. H. LORD MOUNT SEVERN *goes to her* C.)

BAR. What can detain Archibald so long? (*Rings.*)

COR. (*aside*). Ugh, I've no patience with him, letting that Barbara Hare catch him at last, after angling for him so long. I'd have gone into the church and have forbidden the banns if it would have been any use!

(L. D. JOYCE *enters, goes to* BARBARA.)

LORD M. (*looking off* C *to* L.). Your new governess, Madame Vine, seems very fond of the children, especially that delicate little fellow, Willie.

BAR. (JOYCE *going* L.). Yes, she is all we could wish. Our friend, Mrs. Latimer, met her in Germany, and recommended her to us. (*Exeunt by window* C. *to* H. *talking.*)

COR. Joyce, of whom does the governess remind you! (*As* JOYCE *is going* L. H.)

JOY. The governess? Do you mean Madame Vine?

COR. Do I mean *you* or *myself*? Are *we* governesses? Have you seen her without her glasses?

JOY. No, ma'am, never!

COR. Well, I have, to-day, and was astounded by the wonderful likeness, one would have thought it was the ghost of—of Lady Isabel!

JOY. Oh, ma'am, pray don't joke on such a subject please!

COR. Joyce! did you ever know *me* guilty of *joking*?

JOY. N—no ma'am.

COR. No, and I hope you never will! (*Exit* L. D. H.)

JOY. (*aside*). Ah, there are times when, in voice and manner, she puts *me* in mind of poor dear Lady Isabel! (*Music p.p.*)

(*Enter* BARBARA *and* MADAME VINE, *with* WILLIE C. *from* L. H.)

BAR. I must protest, Madame Vine, against your thus fatiguing yourself, you are not strong. It is very, *very* kind of you, but—Come, William, Joyce will take you to your room with Archie.

MME. V. I will take him, if you please. He is not well, and I—I— (*Clinging to* WILLIE.)

BAR. No, no, madame, You have quite enough trouble with them in school hours. If you will not think for yourself we must think for you.

(CARLYLE *and* HARE *and* LORD M., *front garden* C. *the two latter talk on verandah, while* CARLYLE *greets* BARBARA. *Down* C.)

WIL. Ah! here's papa. (*Runs to* CARLYLE C.)

CAR. Well, my darling, I was detained by a deputation. (*To* BARBARA, *up* C.) ·

MME. V. Oh! to witness his loving tenderness for *her!* (*Down* L. C.) It is part of the cross I have undertaken to bear, and I *must* endure the penance.

JOY. Ah! poor little Willie, he's going to his grave fast. (L. H. *Half aside.*)

MME. V. Oh! Joyce, Joyce, don't say that.

JOY. Why, ma'am, I wonder *you* can't see it. Ah! it's plain that he has got *no mother,* poor boy, or there would have been an outcry over him long ago. Of course, Mrs. Carlyle can't be expected to have the feelings of one for him—(MME. V. *talks to* JOYCE, L. H.)

WIL. Papa, I want to ask you something. (*Dragging* CARLYLE *down* C.)

CAR. Well, my dear, what is it?

WIL. Why should Madame Vine cry so often?

CAR. Cry, my boy, does she?

WIL. Oh, yes, papa, often, she wipes her eyes under her spectacles, and thinks I don't see her. I know I'm very ill, but why should *she* cry for that?

BAR. Nonsense, William, who told you that, you are ill? (R. C.)

WIL. I heard the doctor tell Madame Vine and papa so; now why should she cry about that? If Lucy or Joyce cried there'd be some reason, for they have known me all my life.

BAR. There, there, Joyce, take him away, and don't let him worry Madame Vine. (JOYCE *takes* WILLIE *off* L. H. D.)

CAR. (*coming* L *to* ISABEL). You seem naturally fond of children, Madame, and I am very grateful to you for your great kindness to mine. (*He holds out his hand. She puts her shaking hand in his.*)

MME. V. I am but discharging a duty, and we cannot help loving those, whom we—(*Attracted by her voice, he looks at her earnestly. She avoids his gaze.*)

CAR. The tones of her voice remind me of—ah! (*Sighs heavily and goes up* C.)

MME. V. Oh, how the pressure of that hand thrilled me to my heart—(BARBARA *crosses, talks to* MADAME V. L. C., *and takes her over to* R. H.)

CAR. (*comes down* C.). Barbara, my love, your papa, Mr. Herbert, and the rest of the squirearchy have been worrying me to be put in nomination for our borough member.

HAR. (*down* C.). Yes, and you must stand, who else is there fit to send to parliament, there's *Pinner,* would he do? his head's full of mangold wurzel patent manure, and all such rubbish.

CAR. Complimentary to Squire Pinner.

HAR. Well, who else is there?

CAR. Colonel Bethell. (*Exit* BARBARA *and* MADAME V. R. 2 E. *conversing.*)

HAR. Oh, he's got no money to throw away on the free and incorruptible electors of Lynne.

CAR. Pobjoy, or Swindon.

HAR. Pretty fellows they'd be to send to parliament, one's always drunk and the other is never sober.

CAR. Well there's Richard Hare, Esq., J.P.

HAR. Me! no, no, thank you, I should want my own way too much for my constituents, and I should lose my temper listening to the damned nonsense which crotchetty members inflict on the house, to the interruption of important business.

LORD M. No, no, the only fit and proper person as member of parliament for East Lynne is Archibald Carlyle.

(*Enter* CORNELIA L. H.)

COR. Archibald Carlyle in parliament! what next?

LORD M. In the House of Peers, I hope.

HAR. We're going to nominate him.

COR. You'd better nominate him for admission to the county lunatic asylum. The idea of his entering that idle do-nothing House of Commons, have you thought of the cost pray? (*Crosses to* CARLYLE.)

CAR. Oh, that's a mere nothing, the expense is not worth naming, if there is no opposition.

COR. Not worth naming! oh, that ever I should live to hear money talked of as not worth naming, and your business going to rack and ruin while you are kicking up your heels in that wicked Babylon, London, night after night; where's my bonnet and umbrella? (*Going* L. H.) Let me get out of this; parliament indeed.

CAR. You are not going Cornelia? Do—nay, you *must* stay [to] dinner. (*Piano played in room* R. H.)

COR. Ugh! this is dinner enough for one day. My brother, a chattering, humbugging, stuck-up parliament man. (*Exit* L. H. D., LORD M. *listening to piano by door,* R. 2 E.)

LORD M. How charmingly that Madame Vine plays.

CAR. Yes she does. Come in, and Barbara shall sing for us. Come Justice, I know you'll be—

HAR. Not I, I'm thankful to say I've no ear for music, and all that rubbish. Barb used to drive me nearly mad with her howling when she was at home. I'll leave you and my lord to the enjoyment of it while I go and commence to canvass the electors.

(*Exit* HARE, C. *to* L., CARLYLE *and* LORD M., R. 2 E. *to room.* BARBARA *sings one verse of song, and during the symphony that follows,* MME. VINE *comes on from* R. 2 E.)

MME. V. I cannot stay by them to be reminded of the happiness that I have lost. (*Piano in room* R., *and laughter.*) Laugh on, Barbara Hare, laugh on; you've won him, I have sealed the forfeit of his esteem and love by my own mad act. (*The little boy* ARCHIE *runs in,* MME. V. *catches him in her arms and sits in a low chair, or on a stool, and caresses him fondly.*) You will learn to love me I hope. I am very fond of—(WILSON *enters* L. H.) Ah! (*Confused.*) You are surprised no doubt to see me so overcome. But I once had a dear boy so like him—oh! so like him! and this dear child made me think of my—my irreparable loss.

WIL. You naughty young monkey, how dare you run away in this manner?

MME. V. Oh, pray do not scold him.

WIL. Oh, ma'am, you've no idea what he is; he's getting too audacious and rumbustical for the nursery. Come here sir, I'll speak to your mamma about you. (*Shakes boy away from* MME. V.)

(BARBARA *sings "Then you'll remember me."*)

MME. V. Oh! do not beat him, I cannot bear to see him beaten.

WIL. Beaten! If he did get a good sound one it's no more than he deserves. You come along, sir, do. (*Jerks him out of the room.* MME. V. *with difficulty restraining her emotion.*)

MME. V. My own child! and I dare not say to a servant, you shall not beat him.

(BARBARA *sings one verse of "You'll remember me" during the foregoing, so that the last three lines are heard after* MADAME V. *has said "You shall not beat him."*)

BAR. "Some recollection be
Of days that have as happy been.
Then you'll remember me," &c., &c.

MME. V. Does he remember me? Does he give one thought to me as those words fall on his ear? Does he think of the time when *I* sat *there* and sang them to him? Oh, to love him as I do now, to yearn for his affection with such jealous, passionate longing, and to know that we are separated for ever and for ever! To see that I am nothing—worse than nothing—to him now! (*During this speech* BARBARA *has sung the second verse, and the final symphony is played as the scene closes in on* ISABEL, *leaning by door.*)

SCENE II: *Garden, same as Scene I., Act I.*
(*Enter* HARE *and* LORD M. L. H., *and* DILL.)

HAR. Carlyle must know of this at once, *at once.* The—the beast must be mad to dare—to *da-are*—to—to come down here to oppose the man he has injured—(*Very excitedly.*)

LORD M. I heard the rumour in town, and I hurried down here to find if it were true.

HAR. Oh, it's true enough. I saw the men placarding the walls with bills, *"Vote for Levison,"* as I'm a living sinner. I was so enraged that I was a great mind to knock the dirty wretches down with their own paste cans. It's scandalous! Phew!

(*Enter* CARLYLE R.)

CAR. (R. C.). What's scandalous? What has put you in such a heat, Justice?

HAR. Heat, I don't believe I shall ever be cool again. There's an opposition—another man in the field!

CAR. Very well, the more the merrier!

DIL. You don't know who it is.

HAR. I'll buy up every egg in the place and have him pelted till—

CAR. Really gentlemen, this violence toward a candidate who has a right to oppose me if—

HAR. A right! do you know who the blackguard is—you tell him, you're a relation. (*Aside to* M.)

LORD M. (*Aside to* HARE). No really, Mr. Hare, I hardly like to soil my lips with his name—you tell him.

CAR. Well, and who is the opponent?

(*Enter* CORNELIA, *bonnet and umbrella,* L. H.)

COR. Sir Francis Levison indeed! the sneaking, crawling, worm. (*Crosses* C.) Archibald, when I left you half an hour ago I was averse to your going into parliament, now I insist on your going on with the election; you'll be no brother of mine if you abandon the field to that sneaking reptile, Levison.

CAR. Has he dared?

DIL. He has done this on purpose to insult Mr. Carlyle.

HAR. Aye, and to insult you, me, *all* of us—oh! he shall have a bath in the horse pond.

LORD M. The hound ought to be gibbetted.

COR. And I'd turn him off with pleasure. I'll canvass for you brother. I'll spend £1000 on ale for electors.

DIL. Take care Miss Cornelia, you may cause him to be unseated for bribery and corruption, you'd better keep your money.

HAR. Leave it to me, I know how to work an election, patriotic speeches and promises, beer for the blackguards, blankets for the old women. Tell 'em they shall have no taxes, no laws, no masters, no work, no—no—anything.

LORD M. Do nothing every day in the week.

DIL. And have double wages for that!

LORD M. All be masters and nobody servants.

HAR. Yes, down with everybody and up with somebody else.

COR. Down with Levison and up with Carlyle.

HAR. Some of the free and independent electors are my tenants, I'll put the screw on, and bring them all to the poll in a body.

DIL. You forget, *that* will be intimidation.

HAR. I'll go and promise all my men 5s. a head to put that hound Levison in the horse pond.

COR. And I'll give them another 5s. a head to keep him there. (*Exeunt* DILL, CORNELIA, *and* HARE, L. H.)

(CARLYLE *stands* L. C., *absorbed and heedless of their conversation.* LORD M. *goes to him, takes his hand kindly.*)

LORD M. Carlyle, you will not be driven from the field by—by—him; You'll face him—and—

CAR. Face him! yes—yes—

LORD M. That's right, I'll bring all my influence to bear—ugh! the treacherous scoundrel, if duelling had been legal I would have shot him like a dog! (*Exit* L. H.)

CAR. Levison here! Oh, how the bitter memory of my irreparable wrong makes heart and brain burn with a mad, wicked desire for vengeance on the head of that man, who brought shame and death on her whom I loved. And you O Isabel, when I think of your untimely fate, I feel that his life would be a just sacrifice to your dear shade, but I dare not break a holier law than any made by man. I dare not disobey the voice of the Omnipotent, who hath said, "Vengeance is mine alone, I will repay." To his eternal Justice I leave the punishment of the wretched man, who dishonoured my name, and betrayed my poor lost Isabel. (*Exit* R. H.)

Change Scene. Eight bars of plaintive music before change. (*Exit slowly* L. H.)

SCENE III: *Bed-chamber, in* 3, *bed* C., *window* R. (*lime-light*) *Moonlight streaming through window on to bed. Music p.p. "Fading away."*

(WILLIE *on bed,* JOYCE *by side.*)

WIL. Joyce, where is papa?

JOY. He will soon be here; he has gone out with grandpapa Hare.

(MADAME VINE *at door* L.)

MME. V. (*comes* L. C.). Is—is—he worse, Joyce?

JOY. I'm afraid he is, and will not last long. Ah! well, he'll be better off, poor child.

MME. V. Yes—yes; though it is a sore trial to see those we love fading away; there are worse—more bitter partings on earth than death. I think he is dropping off to sleep again, poor dear. You need not wait, Joyce, I will stay with him, and ring if he requires anything.

JOY. Very well, Madam. (*Exit* L. D. H.)

MME. V. And have I come back but to see him die?—my own bright, beautiful Willie!

WIL. Are you there, Joyce?

MME. V. No, my darling; but one who loves you more than Joyce, or any one can love you!

WIL. It will not be very long to wait, will it, Madame Vine?

MME. V. Wait for what, my own darling?

WIL. Before they all come—papa, and Lucy, and Archie, and we all meet, where papa says there is no more pain.

MME. V. Not long, my darling; oh, not long!

WIL. Do you think we shall know everybody there, or only our own relations?

MME. V. My child, we cannot tell that, we must trust to our Father in heaven, who knows what is best for us.

WIL. Do you think my mama will be there? I mean my own, my very own mama; she who is gone away.

MME. V. I hope so—if—if she is forgiven!

WIL. And shall I know her, I have quite forgotten what she was like; shall I know her?

MME. V. I hope so, I do hope so; but there—there, my darling, do not talk any more now, try and sleep. (*Pause.*)

WIL. Where are you, Madame Vine?

MME. V. Here, my sweet boy—here!

WIL. I cannot see you, I can only see a bright shining light like the sun on the waters, and beyond that, oh! such a beautiful garden full of flowers, and I seem to hear music and sweet singing, as I've heard papa say the angels in heaven sing. (*Pause.*) Are you there now, Madame Vine?

MME. V. Yes darling?

WIL. I cannot see you or hear your voice. I cannot hear the singing of those voices in the shining garden. There!—there! (*Points up and falls back, pause.*)

MME. V. Ah! the sweet young face is calm as—as—if—in death. His little heart has ceased to beat for ev—. Oh! no! not for ever! Speak to me, Willie! (*Throws off her disguise.*) This cannot be death so soon; speak to me, your broken-hearted mother. Oh! Willie! my own darling! my own—my—

(JOYCE *enters* L. D.)

JOY. Oh, Madame Vine, what is this? (*She starts up and faces* JOYCE.)

MME. V. Oh! My child is dead! (JOYCE *starts back in amazement.*)

JOY. My dear Lady Isabel! Not!—not dead?

ISA. No. Oh, would that I were dead. I recovered by a miracle, and returned, the shattered wreck you see me here prematurely aged, crippled, broken-hearted. Oh, that I had died and had been spared this agony. Oh! my boy!—my boy! (*Sobbing on body of child.*)

JOY. Do—do come away lady! Mr. Carlyle is coming with his wife, for the love of heaven come away! If they find you here, thus—

ISA. I care not now, oh, my Willie!

JOY. Oh, my dear lady, you ought not to have come here.

ISA. (*lifting up her haggard face*). I could not stay longer away from my children. Think you it has been no punishment to me being here, to see *him, my* husband, once, the—the—husband of another, it was killing me; and now to see my boy close his eyes for ever on this world and me. (*Music p.p. to curtain.*)

JOY. Oh, come, my dear lady, I hear their voices. They will be here in a moment, and you will be discovered—(*Trying to drag her away.*)

ISA. (*breaks from* JOYCE). Let them come! I care not for my life's sands will soon be run. Oh, Willie, my child dead, dead, dead! and he never knew me, never called me mother! (*Falling sobbing across the body as* CARLYLE *and* BARBARA *enter* L. D.)

RING.

ACT IV

SCENE I: *A lane or street in the suburbs of East Lynne, 1st Grooves.*

COR. (R. H., *meeting* DILL R. H.). What's the news Mr. Dill? And is it really true that young Dick is in town here, disguised as a sailor? Joyce tells me his disappearance is made clear.

DIL. We hope that it will soon be made remarkably clear, now the mysterious Thorne is found (here at West Lynne) in the person of the villain Levison.

COR. What! that wretch. And to think that he should have the barefaced assurance to come to Lynne, after the reception he met with on his previous visit.

DIL. Well, yes, one would think that the ducking in a stinking pond to which he was treated on that occasion would have cooled his courage.

COR. His what?

DIL. Well, his impudence.

COR. How could he think of being elected for the very place where his name is execrated, and his presence provokes the just indignation of the whole town.

DIL. Well, he is a government nominee, and that party has great influence down here you know.

COR. But surely the government would not allow such a villain as Levison to sit in Parliament.

DIL. I don't know; they care very little about the moral character of a man whose vote, and influence, may help to keep the party in office.

COR. And that brazenfaced young baggage, Afy Hallijohn, has come flaunting about here again, the young Jezebel!

DIL. Ah, yes; and from Richard's information I was forced to subpoena her to give evidence before the magistrates, and by a severe cross examination, elicited *from her* the important admission that Levison (under the *alias* of THORNE) *was in the cottage* the very night her father was shot.

COR. Oh, the young wretch! Why couldn't she say so before? Why, as I live, here comes Richard—(*Looks off* R. H.) What does he mean by parading himself in this imprudent way, with a—a warrant for his arrest still out?

DIL. He can now walk about in the broad light of day, for the proofs of his innocence are so overwhelming, that he can enter a court of justice without fear.

COR. Who is that fellow with him, that looks like a polar bear?

DIL. Otway Bethell, who has returned to England only within the last few days; on his evidence the magistrates have issued a warrant for the arrest of Sir Francis Levison, *alias* Thorne.

COR. Jubilate! Then there is some hope of the villain being hanged at last.

DIL. Well, it will go very hard with him; he will, at any rate suffer a lengthened term of imprisonment.

COR. Imprisonment! bah! hang him at once. (*Exit* R. *with* DILL.)

(*Groans outside* L. H., "Duck him," "Down with him," &c., "Put him in the horsepond," &c. LEVISON *hurries on* L. H. *alarmed.*)

LEV. They mean mischief, I must hasten back to London, *there* I shall be safe from their threatened vengeance. (*Going* R. *is met by* RICHD. HARE, *dressed as a Sailor.*)

RIC. But not from mine. Now villain I can meet you face to face, without fear, you have more than once escaped me, when I was powerless to *prove* your villainy, but *now* you escape me not. (*Seizes* LEVISON.)

LEV. Madman! Take your hands from me, or I will denounce you to the officers of justice.

(DILL *and* OFFICERS* *from* R. H.)

RIC. They are here to take charge of you. Officers, do your duty.

LEV. Stand off fellows, dare you lay hands on me.

DIL. Come, come, resistance is useless, here is the necessary warrant for your arrest.

LEV. My arrest! for what?

DIL. For the murder of George Hallijohn in Lynne Wood. Your quondam mistress, Afy, has confessed that you were there, and Mr. Otway Bethell has deposed that he saw you come from the cottage just after the fatal shot was fired.

LEV. Bethell! He is in Norway—has been there—or some where abroad, for years.

DIL. He has returned to give evidence against you.

(*Enter* BETHELL R. H., *fur coat, &c., see novel.*)

BET. Yes, and I would have returned years ago, had I known another was suffering for your crime.

LEV. Ha, betrayed! and by *you,* whom I—

DIL. Had bribed! Don't have any hesitation to say the word; we know all.

BET. With the money you paid me for my silence I left England the day after the murder, little thinking that an innocent man might be accused of the crime which you had committed; but hearing that poor Dick Hare has been allowed by you to lie under this terrible accusation, I hastened to make a tardy reparation by telling all I knew.

LEV. Scoundrel!

BET. I should have been had I not spoken the truth, and so put justice on the track of one who is a scoundrel and a coward. (LEVISON *appears terrified by his position.*)

LEV. (*aside*). What devil prompted me to come down here to provoke my Nemesis—my destruction. (*Assumes an air of bravado, and turns to* RICHARD.) Richard Hare, you are premature in your triumph; we have yet to see whether the liberty and life of an English baronet are to be endangered by the assertions of an outlawed bankrupt, like your friend, Mr. Otway Bethell. (*Exit with officers* L. H. AFY HALLIJOHN *enters* R., *speaks to* RICHARD *as he goes* L. *with* DILL *and* BETHELL.)

AFY. Ah, good day, Mr. Richard; why surely you're not going to pass an old friend in that way.

RIC. I have so many friends I can scarcely find time for them all individually.

---

*N.B. *Officers in plain clothes, not comic policemen.*

AFY. But you might for *me*. Have you forgotten old days?

RIC. I am not likely to forget them.

AFY. I feel sure you had not. My heart told me you—

RIC. Your *what,* Miss Hallijohn?

AFY. My heart; when you went away on that dreadful night, I thought I should have died.

RIC. It was not your fault that *I* didn't. (DILL *and* BETHELL *exit* L. H.)

AFY. Oh, and now to meet you again! Oh! (*Gushing.*)

RIC. Don't be a fool, Afy. I was young and foolish; but I am older and wiser now. How's Mr. Jiffin?

AFY. Mr. Jiffin! Oh, is it possible you think I could ever bemean myself to a man who sells cheese and cuts up bacon. That's Lynne all over; nothing but scandal and invention from week's end to week's end. But to think that *you* should believe—

RIC. I was thinking how lucky you were to get a man so well off, and so respectable.

AFY. Would you—could you bear to see me stoop to Jiffin?

RIC. Could I? Certainly. Why not? I don't know what ridiculous notions you may have in your head, but the sooner you get rid of them the better. I was foolish once, but you cured me of my folly very effectually. Henceforth we are strangers.

AFY. Oh, can you speak such words to me? (*Sobs hysterically.*)

RIC. It *won't do,* Afy, it *won't* do.

AFY. Oh, oh, o-oh! and is this my reward after waiting for you all these years, pining and breaking my heart for you. I'm so ill, I—I shall faint; I know I shall faint. Oh! (*Business.*)

RIC. I'm sorry I can't stay to catch you. Had you not better faint nearer Mr. Jiffin's shop door? he will be enchanted to bear so lovely a burden in his arms. Good day.

(*Crosses* L. OLD HARE *and* DILL *enter* L. H. HARE *greets* DICK *warmly.*)

AFY. (*recovers immediately*). Oh, the brute! the unfeeling beast! I'll go and be overcome by the heat near Jiffin's door. I'll marry the old wretch out of spite, yes, that I will; he's as soft as one of his own cheeses, and will jump at the chance. He's an old fool, but he'll do for a husband. (*Exit* R. H. HARE *and* RICHARD *come* C.)

HAR. Oh, Dick, my dear boy, can you forgive me for my unnatural cruelty towards you?

RIC. Freely, dear dad, freely. We will forget the miserable past in our newly-found happiness.

HAR. But I can never forgive myself. I—I might have hunted my own son to death.

DIL. (*advances*). I am loth to disturb a family greeting, but remember, Justice, there is a meeting of the magistrates at—

HAR. They must meet without me for the future. A man who undertakes the administration of justice should have more wisdom than I have, and less conceited obstinacy. I've been an old fool, Dill, I *have,* so don't contradict me, Dill.

DIL. I was not going to contradict you in *that* admission.

HAR. Come, my boy, come to the home from which you have too long been banished—unjustly banished, and where a fond mother is longing to embrace you. Ah, Dill, you'll find Old Dick Hare a changed man now, I'm so happy, so thankful, and so humble.

DIL. That will be a change, indeed, ha, ha. (*Exit* R. H. *Eight bars of plaintive music before scene is changed.*)

SCENE II: *Bedroom, same as last scene of third act, with different furniture. Pale orange sunlight through window, casting a warm hue on Isabel's face as she reclines in large chair by bed,* C. JOYCE *and* CORNELIA *discovered by* LADY ISABEL. *Music p.p.*

ISA. Only for a minute I have prayed Joyce to bring him to me, and she will not, only for one little fleeting minute, to *hear him* say, "I forgive you."

COR. Go, Joyce, request your master to come to me.

JOY. Oh, ma'am! will it be well for him to see her?

COR. (*putting* JOYCE *to door* L. H.). Tell him I wish to see him. (*Exit* JOYCE L. H.) My poor child, had I any part in sending you away from your home?

ISA. Oh, no, no! I was not very happy with you; but that was not the cause of—of—Oh! forgive me, Miss Carlyle.

COR. Forgive me my poor girl. I might have made your home happier, and I wish—oh how I wish I had.

(CARLYLE *enters* L. H. D. *with* JOYCE.)

CAR. Is Madame Vine worse?

COR. She wishes to see you alone. (*Going* L. H. CARLYLE *crosses to* L. C.)

JOY. (*to* CORNELIA). Oh, ma'am! won't you tell him. (CORNELIA *gently puts* JOYCE *off* L. H. *and exits. They shut him in alone with her; he walks gently to the bed, &c.*)

CAR. I am grieved Madame Vine that you—

ISA. Archibald! oh, do not leave me; do not turn from me! (*She puts out her trembling hand and catches his &c.*)

CAR. Isabel! were—were—you—Madame Vine!

ISA. I did not die, I recovered as by a miracle; though when I wrote that letter, I was given up as past all hope of recovery, I was so changed, nobody knew me, and I came here as Madame Vine to see my children and you—I could not stay away, I could not die without your forgiveness—oh! do not turn from me—bear with me a little, only a *little* while!

CAR. Oh, Isabel! why, oh why did you leave me?

ISA. I thought you were false to me; that your love was given to another, and in my mad jealousy I listened to the tempter who whispered to me of revenge!

CAR. My poor, darling, how could you have been so deceived, knowing me as you should have known me; loving you so tenderly as I did. There was not a thought wherein falsehood to you ever found a place. Oh! how could you deem me false to *you,* who were my world?

ISA. I was mad! I must have been. I have not known one moment's peace since I became a guilty creature, in the sin that wrecked me—see, Archibald! see what it has done for me! (*Tossing up her grey hair and holding out her attenuated wrists.*) My sin was great, but my punishment has been still greater. Think what torture it has been—what it has been for me to bear, living in the same house with—with—your wife; seeing your love for her—love that once was *mine.* Oh, think what agony to watch dear Willie, and see him fading day by day, and not be able to say "he is my child as well as yours!"

CAR. Why did you come back to endure——

ISA. I could not live away from you and my children; the longing for them was killing me. I never thought to stay here to die; but death is coming on me now, as with a leap—and my life is ebbing fast —(*The orange sunlight gradually fades out of the room, leaving her face deathly white, when the warm hue of lime-light is off.*) Oh! say, in mercy, say that you forgive me, that you forget and forgive.

CAR. I have already *forgiven;* but you were too dear for me ever, to forget how happy I was in your love. I cannot forget the blow that crushed me, and well-nigh killed me, then.

ISA. Try and forget the dreadful time; let your thoughts go back only to those days when you first knew me—here—a happy innocent girl, with my dear father. Ah, how gentle you were with me when *he* died! Oh, that the past could be blotted out, that I might die with a pure conscience, as I *might* have died then!

CAR. For your sake, as for mine, *I* wish the dark past could be blotted out.

ISA. Let what I *am* be erased from your memory, think of me (if you can) as the innocent, trusting girl whom you made your wife. Say one word of love to me before I pass away! Oh, Archibald, my heart is breaking for one last word of love.

CAR. As mine was when you left me!

ISA. You forgive me?

CAR. May God bless you, and so deal with me, as I forgive you, Isabel, dear Isabel, my first, *first* love, who once was as *light* and *life* to me! (*Music tremo to curtain, "Then you'll remember me."*)

ISA. Be kind and loving to Lucy and little Archie. Do not let their mother's sin be visited on them!

CAR. Never, never! They are dear to me as you *once* were!

ISA. Aye, as I once was, and as I might—alas—I might have been, even now. Ah, is this death? 'Tis hard to part! Farewell, dear Archibald! my husband once, and loved now in death, as I never loved before! Farewell, until eternity! Think of me sometimes, keep one little corner in your heart for me—your poor—erring—lost Isabel! (*Dies.*)

Slow curtain.

H. M. S. PINAFORE

No wonder William S. Gilbert was amused by melodrama: at the age of two he was kidnaped in Naples and ransomed for £25. No wonder he made fun of The Establishment: he failed to get a commission in the Royal Artillery, was tangled for years in red tape as a clerk (in the Privy Council office, Education Department), failed as a courtroom lawyer and succeeded as a satirist (in *Fun, The Piccadilly Annual,* and *Punch*—until Mark Lemon refused his "Yarn of the Nancy Bell" as "too cannibalistic"). And with all this, he ran to conventional sentiment: he drowned trying to save a young lady, just like the dashing young man in the melodrama.

He came along in the 1860's just at the time that Planché was finally giving out. There was not much promise in *Dulcamara; or, The Little Duck and the Great Quack* (1866), an extravaganza whose very title warns of the bad puns that littered it, and Gilbert floundered for years in what Planché called "jungles of jingles and sloughs of slang" but finally began to write more disciplined comedy. *Pygmalion and Galatea* (1871), for no reason imaginable, earned him £40,000. *Engaged* (1877), with which it is interesting to compare *The Importance of Being Earnest,* was charming. So, to a lesser extent, was *Sweethearts* (1874). But when Gilbert met Arthur Sullivan, though Gilbert was already the leading comic dramatist of the London stage, great things really began to happen. Dr. Sullivan (who the Queen herself had predicted would be "the Mozart of England") was a leading composer and conductor and very serious about both his music and his close friends among the younger members of The Royal Family Itself. However, he needed money to keep up his social position. Gilbert showed him how to make about £8,000 a year. They were to quarrel and create for years to come, to become the most famous and successful collaborators in the English theatre since Beaumont and Fletcher. They became, indeed, part of the British heritage, along with Shakespeare and Sherlock Holmes, the Bible and Scrooge. Their first collaboration, *Thespis; or, The Gods Grown Old* (1871), was not a success. For a while it seemed that Mr. Gilbert and Sir Arthur Sullivan (recently knighted for uplifting British music with the oratorio *The Light of the World* and the hymn *Onward, Christian Soldiers*) would separate. But Richard D'Oyly Carte got them together for *Trial by Jury* (1875), and they were on their way. They followed up with *The Sorcerer* (1877) and by the end of that year were working on what was to be their greatest success: *H. M. S. Pinafore.*

H. M. S. Pinafore was made out of a half dozen of Gilbert's *Bab Ballads* (1869), that little gem of Victorian humor that distills the very essence of Gilbertian topsy-turveydom. "Literature has many a solemn masterpiece," wrote Sir Max Beerbohm, "that one would without a qualm barter for that absurd and riotous one." *Pinafore* uses every device of the *Black-Ey'd Susan* variety, every cliché of melodrama (including the exchanged babies that keep turning up in the damnedest places, from *The Gondoliers* to handbags at Victoria Station), every Gilbertian pun and paradox. It laughs at every obviously ridiculous situation and personage, but happily. (Gilbert's sadism, activated by elderly spinsters, is fortunately not in evidence in this particular comedy.) There was never a one who didn't love it. Well, hardly ever. Queen Victoria said: "We are not amused." The reaction of Mr. W. H. Smith, a publisher who had somehow contrived to "rise to the top of the tree" and become First Lord of the Admiralty, is not recorded.

The first London production was immediately greeted with sneers: "studied absurdity . . . frothy . . . destined soon to subside into nothingness." Talk about the dangers of prophecy! In New York *H. M. S. Pinafore* was hailed as "one of the neatest, brightest, funniest operatic burlesques in any language . . . sparkling music . . . destined to be famous." News of the American reception stirred interest in Britain and the London company eventually ran for seven hundred nights, an unheard-of success for any kind of musical theatre. By the spring of 1879 there were eight different companies of *H. M. S. Pinafore* in New York City alone. Eventually some ninety companies were touring the United States with it, and it was presented on a real ship in Madison Square

Garden. (This was repeated at Jones Beach, New York, in 1935.) Today there are Gilbert and Sullivan societies all over the world, and, in addition to the standard performances by the D'Oyly Carte company, there are thousands of productions each year in schools and colleges, in little theatres and community theatres, by amateurs and professionals in everything from tents and church halls to the New York City Center for the Performing Arts.

Gilbert did much for the Victorian theatre with his light comedies and farces and his tyrannical supervision of production and rehearsals, for (following Robertson) he agreed with Régnier (François Tousez, 1807-1885) that "an actor deprives me of all that he does not add to the part I have written" but was determined that what was added should be strictly controlled and wholy germane. Gilbert's chief contribution, however, was undeniably that made in partnership with Sullivan, of which *H. M. S. Pinafore* is the very best and most enduring example. Do not, however, mistake this comic opera's popularity for proof that the average Victorian had the view of himself which we have today. Heed this brilliant analysis from Hesketh Pearson's *Gilbert and Sullivan* (1935):

> It must be repeated that the qualities of wariness and daring were mixed in his [Gilbert's] nature in about equal proportions; and also, it may be added, stupidity and insight. He was a typical Briton with a streak of genius, possibly the only known example. He could see through a thing, but he could not see round it. He was visited with sudden flashes of reality, but he was not gifted with a steady vision. He had acute perceptions, but no guiding philosophy. He was a respectable man who made fun of respectability, a sentimentalist who laughed at sentiment, a patriot who ridiculed patriotism. Again and again, at the bidding of some powerful intuition, he exposed a social or national absurdity, but as often as not he failed to see the point of his exposure, and fell back upon a piece of conventional clap-trap which was equally typical of him. His sudden exhibitions of daring and insight, coupled with his native caution and conventionality, made his work uneven and incalculable, and it was Sullivan's music that rendered it wholly palatable to the Victorians. The Englishman is perhaps the only man in the world who can laugh at himself; add music to the satire and he brings the house down, for music removes the sting of reality.

H. M. S. PINAFORE

OR,

THE LASS THAT LOVED A SAILOR

An Entirely Original Nautical Comic Opera

IN TWO ACTS

by

Sir William S. Gilbert

First produced in London (by Mr. R. D'Oyly Carte) at the Opéra Comique Theatre, on Saturday, May 25, 1878, with the following cast:

The Rt. Hon. Sir JOSEPH PORTER, K. C. B., *First Lord of the Admiralty*	Mr. George Grosmith
Captain CORCORAN, *Commanding H. M. S. Pinafore*	Mr. R. Barrington
RALPH RACKSTRAW, *Able Seamen*	Mr. George Power
DICK DEADEYE, *Able Seamen*	Mr. R. Temple
BILL BOBSTAY, *Boatswain's Mate*	Mr. F. Clifton
BOB BECKET, *Carpenter's Mate*	Mr. Dymott
TOM TUCKER, *Midshipmate*	———
Sergeant of Marines	———
JOSEPHINE, *Captain Corcoran's Daughter*	Miss Emma Howson
HEBE, *Sir Joseph Porter's First Cousin*	Miss Jessie Bond
MRS. CRIPPS (*Little Buttercup*), *A Portsmouth Bumboat [provisions] Woman*	Miss Everard

The First Lord of the Admiralty's Sisters, Cousins, and Aunts
Sailors and Marines

SCENE: *The Quarter-deck of Her Majesty's Ship "Pinafore," off Portsmouth*

Act I: Noon

Act II: Night

ACT I

SCENE: *Quarter-deck of H. M. S. Pinafore. View of Portsmouth in distance.* SAILORS, *led by* BOATSWAIN, *discovered cleaning brass-work, splicing rope, etc.*

CHORUS

We sail the ocean blue,
And our saucy ship's a beauty;
We're sober men, and true,
And attentive to our duty.
When the balls whistle free o'er the bright blue sea,
We stand to our guns all day;
When at anchor we ride on the Portsmouth tide,
We have plenty of time to play.

(*Enter* LITTLE BUTTERCUP, *with large basket on her arm.*)

RECITATIVE

Hail, men-o'-war's men—safeguards of your nation,
Here is an end, at last, of all privation;
You've got your pay—spare all you can afford
To welcome Little Buttercup on board.

Because of the lack of copyright protection, a pirated version of H. M. S. Pinafore *was presented at the Standard Theatre, New York, January 17, 1879, under John Duff. The authorized version was given at the Fifth Avenue Theatre, New York, December 1, 1879, Arthur Sullivan conducting. For their next production Gilbert and Sullivan tried to avoid notices such as that which appeared in an American newspaper: "At present there are forty-two companies playing* Pinafore *about the country. Companies formed after six p.m. yesterday are not included." Or, at least, if they were going to be so popular they thought they ought to be prosperous as well. They came to America and rushed to completion* The Pirates of Penzance. *On December 30, 1879,* The Pirates *was given a token performance (for British copyright) at the Bijou Theatre, Paignton. It certainly could not have included the overture, which Sullivan wrote during the night of December 30/31. The next day the "first" performance (for American copyright) was given at the Fifth Avenue Theatre, New York. When the vogue was firmly established, Richard D'Oyly Carte built the Savoy Theatre, London (1881, the first public building in England lighted by electricity), to house the Gilbert and Sullivan operettas.*

ARIA

For I'm called Little Buttercup, dear Little Buttercup,
  Though I could never tell why,
But still I'm called Buttercup, poor Little Buttercup,
  Sweet Little Buttercup, I.
I've snuff, and tobaccy, and excellent jacky;
  I've scissors, and watches, and knives;
I've ribbons and laces to set off the faces
  Of pretty young sweethearts and wives.
I've treacle and toffee and excellent coffee,
  Soft tommy and succulent chops;
I've chickens and conies and pretty polonies,
  And excellent peppermint drops.
Then buy of your Buttercup—dear Little Buttercup,
  Sailors should never be shy;
So buy of your Buttercup—poor Little Buttercup,
  Come, of your Buttercup buy!

BOATSWAIN. Ay, Little Buttercup—and well called—for you're the rosiest, the roundest, and the reddest beauty in all Spithead.

BUTTERCUP. Red, am I? and round—and rosy! Maybe, for I have dissembled well! But hark ye, my merry friend—hast ever thought that beneath a gay and frivolous exterior there may lurk a cankerworm which is slowly but surely eating its way into one's very heart?

BOATSWAIN. No, my lass, I can't say I've ever thought that.

(*Enter* DICK DEADEYE. *He pushes through* SAILORS.)

DICK. *I* have thought it often. (*All recoil from him.*)

BUTTERCUP. Yes, you look like it! What's the matter with the man? Isn't he well?

BOATSWAIN. Don't take no heed of *him;* that's only poor Dick Deadeye.

DICK. I say—it's a beast of a name, ain't it—Dick Deadeye?

BUTTERCUP. It's not a nice name.

DICK. I'm ugly too, ain't I?

BUTTERCUP. You are certainly plain.

DICK. And I'm three-cornered too, ain't I?

BUTTERCUP. You are rather triangular.

DICK. Ha! ha! That's it. I'm ugly, and they hate me for it; for you all hate me, don't you?

BOATSWAIN (*crossing*). Well, Dick, we wouldn't go for to hurt any fellow-creature's feelings, but you can't expect a chap with such a name as Dick Deadeye to be a popular character—now, can you?

DICK. No.

BOATSWAIN. It's asking too much, ain't it?

DICK. It is. From such a face and form as mine the noblest sentiments sound like the black utterances of a depraved imagination. It is human nature—I am resigned.

RECITATIVE

BUTTERCUP (*looking down hatchway*).
But, tell me—who's the youth whose faltering feet
With difficulty bear him on his course?

BOATSWAIN (*crossing*).
That is the smartest lad in all the fleet—Ralph Rackstraw!

BUTTERCUP.
Ha! that name! Remorse! remorse!

(*Enter* RALPH *from hatchway.*)

MADRIGAL.—RALPH

The nightingale
Loved the pale moon's bright ray,
And told his tale
In his own melodious way!
He sang "Ah, well-a-day!"

ALL. He sang "Ah, well-a-day!"

The lowly vale
For the mountain vainly sighed;
To his humble wail
The echoing hills replied.
They sang "Ah, well-a-day!"

ALL. They sang "Ah, well-a-day!"

RECITATIVE

I know the value of a kindly chorus,
But choruses yield little consolation,
When we have pain and trouble too before us!
I love—and love, alas, above my station!

BUTTERCUP (*aside*). He loves—and loves a lass above his station!
ALL (*aside*). Yes, yes, the lass is much above his station!

BALLAD.—RALPH

A maiden fair to see,
The pearl of minstrelsy,
  A bud of blushing beauty;
For whom proud nobles sigh,
And with each other vie,
  To do her menial's duty.

ALL. To do her menial's duty.

A suitor, lowly born,
With hopeless passion torn,
  And poor beyond concealing.
Has dared for her to pine
At whose exalted shrine
  A world of wealth is kneeling.

ALL. A world of wealth is kneeling!

Unlearnèd he in aught
Save that which love has taught.
  (For love had been his tutor)
Oh, pity, pity me—
Our captain's daughter she,
  And I that lowly suitor!

ALL. And he that lowly suitor!

(*Exit* LITTLE BUTTERCUP.)

BOATSWAIN. Ah, my poor lad, you've climbed too high: our worthy captain's child won't have nothin' to say to a poor chap like you. Will she, lads?
DICK. No, no, captains' daughters don't marry foremast hands.
ALL (*recoiling from him*). Shame! shame!
BOATSWAIN (*crossing*). Dick Deadeye, them sentiments o' yourn are a disgrace to our common natur'.

RALPH. But it's a strange anomaly, that the daughter of a man who hails from the quarter-deck may not love another who lays out on the fore-yard arm. For a man is but a man, whether he hoists his flag at the maintruck or his slacks on the maindeck.

DICK. Ah, it's a queer world!

RALPH. Dick Deadeye, I have no desire to press hardly on you, but such a revolutionary sentiment is enough to make an honest sailor shudder.

BOATSWAIN (*who has gone on poop-deck, returns*). My lads, our gallant captain has come on deck; let us greet him as so brave an officer and so gallant a seaman deserves.

RECITATIVE

CAPTAIN. My gallant crew, good morning.

ALL (*saluting*). Sir, good morning!

CAPTAIN. I hope you're all well.

ALL (*as before*). Quite well; and you, sir?

CAPTAIN. I am in reasonable health, and happy
To meet you all once more.

ALL (*as before*). You do us proud, sir!

SONG.—CAPTAIN

CAPTAIN.
I am the Captain of the Pinafore!
ALL.
And a right good captain, too!
CAPTAIN.
You're very, very good,
And be it understood
I command a right good crew.
ALL.
We're very, very good,
And be it understood
He commands a right good crew.
CAPTAIN.
Though related to a peer,
I can hand, reef, and steer,

And ship a selvagee;
I am never known to quail
At the fury of a gale,
And I'm never, never sick at sea!
ALL. What, never?
CAPTAIN. No, never!
ALL. What, *never?*
CAPTAIN. Hardly ever!
ALL.
He's hardly ever sick at sea!
Then give three cheers, and one cheer more,
For the hardy Captain of the Pinafore!
CAPTAIN.
I do my best to satisfy you all—
ALL.
And with you we're quite content.
CAPTAIN.
You're exceedingly polite,
And I think it only right
To return the compliment.
ALL.
We're exceedingly polite,
And he thinks it's only right
To return the compliment.
CAPTAIN.
Bad language or abuse,
I never, never use,
Whatever the emergency;
Though, "bother it", I may
Occasionally say,
I never use a big, big D—
ALL. What, never?
CAPTAIN. No, never!
ALL. What, *never?*
CAPTAIN. Hardly ever!
ALL.
Hardly ever swears a big, big D—
Then give three cheers, and one cheer more,
For the well-bred Captain of the Pinafore!
(*After song exeunt all but* CAPTAIN.)

(*Enter* LITTLE BUTTERCUP.)

RECITATIVE

BUTTERCUP.
Sir, you are sad. The silent eloquence
Of yonder tear that trembles on your eyelash
Proclaims a sorrow far more deep than common;
Confide in me—fear not—I am a mother!
CAPTAIN.
Yes, Little Buttercup, I'm sad and sorry—
My daughter, Josephine, the fairest flower
That ever blossomed on ancestral timber,
Is sought in marriage by Sir Joseph Porter,
Our Admiralty's First Lord, but for some reason,
She does not seem to tackle kindly to it.
BUTTERCUP (*with emotion*).
Ah, poor Sir Joseph! Ah, I know too well
The anguish of a heart that loves but vainly!
But see, here comes your most attractive daughter.
I go—Farewell! (*Exit.*)
CAPTAIN (*looking after her*).
A plump and pleasing person!

(*Enter* JOSEPHINE *on poop. She comes down, twining some flowers which she carries in a small basket.*)

BALLAD.—JOSEPHINE

Sorry her lot who loves too well,
Heavy the heart that hopes but vainly,
Sad are the sighs that own the spell
Uttered by eyes that speak too plainly;
Heavy the sorrow that bows the head
When love is alive and hope is dead!
Sad is the hour when sets the sun—
Dark is the night to earth's poor daughters,
When to the ark the wearied one
Flies from the empty waste of waters!
Heavy the sorrow that bows the head
When love is alive and hope is dead!

CAPTAIN. My child, I grieve to see that you are a prey to melancholy. You should look your best to-day, for Sir Joseph Porter, K.C.B., will be here this afternoon to claim your promised hand.

JOSEPHINE. Ah, father, your words cut me to the quick. I can esteem —reverence—venerate Sir Joseph, for he is a great and good man; but oh, I cannot love him! My heart is already given.

CAPTAIN (*aside*). It is, then, as I feared. (*Aloud.*) Given? And to whom? Not to some gilded lordling?

JOSEPHINE. No, father—the object of my love is no lordling. Oh, pity me, for he is but a humble sailor on board your own ship!

CAPTAIN. Impossible!

JOSEPHINE. Yes, it is true—too true.

CAPTAIN. A common sailor? Oh, fie!

JOSEPHINE. I blush for the weakness that allows me to cherish such a passion. I hate myself when I think of the depth to which I have stooped in permitting myself to think tenderly of one so ignobly born, but I love him! I love him! I love him! (*Weeps.*)

CAPTAIN. Come, my child, let us talk this over. In a matter of the heart I would not coerce my daughter—I attach but little value to rank or wealth, but the line must be drawn somewhere. A man in that station may be brave and worthy, but at every step he would commit solecisms that society would never pardon.

JOSEPHINE. Oh, I have thought of this night and day. But fear not, father. I have a heart, and therefore I love; but I am your daughter, and therefore I am proud. Though I carry my love with me to the tomb, he shall never, never know it.

CAPTAIN. You *are* my daughter, after all. But see, Sir Joseph's barge approaches, manned by twelve trusty oarsmen and accompanied by the admiring crowd of female relatives that attend him wherever he goes. Retire, my daughter, to your cabin—take this, his photograph, with you —it may help to bring you to a more reasonable frame of mind.

JOSEPHINE. My own thoughtful father. (*Exit* JOSEPHINE.)

BARCAROLLE (*without*).

Over the bright blue sea
Comes Sir Joseph Porter, K.C.B.,
Wherever he may go
Bang-bang the loud nine-pounders go!
Shout o'er the bright blue sea
For Sir Joseph Porter, K.C.B.

(*During this the* CREW *have entered on tiptoe, listening attentively to the song.*)

CHORUS OF SAILORS

We sail the ocean blue,
And our saucy ship's a beauty;
We're sober men, and true,
And attentive to our duty.
We're smart and sober men,
And quite devoid of fe-ar,
In all the Royal N,
None are so smart as we are.

(*Enter* SIR JOSEPH'S *Female* RELATIVES. *They dance round stage.*)

RELATIVES.
Gaily tripping,
Lightly skipping,
Flock the maidens to the shipping.
SAILORS.
Flags and guns and pennants dipping
All the ladies love the shipping.
RELATIVES.
Sailors sprightly
Always rightly
Welcome ladies so politely.
SAILORS.
Ladies who can smile so brightly,
Sailors welcome most politely.

(*Enter* SIR JOSEPH *with* COUSIN HEBE.)

CAPTAIN (*from poop*).
Now give three cheers, I'll lead the way.
ALL.
Hurrah! hurrah! hurrah! hurrah! (*Repeat.*)

SONG.—SIR JOSEPH

I am the monarch of the sea,
The Ruler of the Queen's Navee,
Whose praise Great Britain loudly chants.

COUSIN HEBE.
And we are his sisters, and his cousins, and his aunts!
RELATIVES.
And we are his sisters, and his cousins, and his aunts!
SIR JOSEPH.
When at anchor here I ride,
My bosom swells with pride,
And I snap my fingers at a foeman's taunts.
COUSIN HEBE.
And so do his sisters, and his cousins, and his aunts!
ALL.
And so do his sisters, and his cousins, and his aunts!
SIR JOSEPH.
But when the breezes blow,
I generally go below,
And seek the seclusion that a cabin grants!
COUSIN HEBE.
And so do his sisters, and his cousins, and his aunts!
ALL.
And so do his sisters, and his cousins, and his aunts!
His sisters and his cousins,
Whom he reckons up by dozens,
And his aunts!

SONG.—SIR JOSEPH

When I was a lad I served a term
As officer boy to an attorney's firm.
I cleaned the windows and I swept the floor,
And I polished up the handle of the big front door.
I polished up that handle so carefullee
That now I am the Ruler of the Queen's Navee!
CHORUS.—He polished, etc.

As office boy I made such a mark
That they gave me the post of a junior clerk.
I served the writs with a smile so bland,
And I copied all the letters in a big round hand—
I copied all the letters in a hand so free,
That now I am the Ruler of the Queen's Navee.
CHORUS.—He copied, etc.

In serving writs I made such a name
That an articled clerk I soon became;
I wore clean collars and a brand-new suit
For the pass examination at the Institute.
  And that pass examination did so well for me,
  That now I am the Ruler of the Queen's Navee!
    CHORUS.—And that pass examination, etc.

Of legal knowledge I acquired such a grip
That they took me into the partnership,
And that junior partnership, I ween,
Was the only ship that I ever had seen.
  But that kind of ship so suited me,
  That now I am the Ruler of the Queen's Navee!
    CHORUS.—But that kind, etc.

I grew so rich that I was sent
By a pocket borough into Parliament.
I always voted at my party's call,
And I never thought of thinking for myself at all.
  I thought so little, they rewarded me
  By making me the Ruler of the Queen's Navee!
    CHORUS.—He thought so little, etc.

Now, landsmen all, whoever you may be,
If you want to rise to the top of the tree,
If your soul isn't fettered to an office stool,
Be careful to be guided by this golden rule—
  Stick close to your deck and never go to sea,
  And you all may be Rulers of the Queen's Navee!
    CHORUS.—Stick close, etc.

SIR JOSEPH. You've a remarkably fine crew, Captain Corcoran.

CAPTAIN. It *is* a fine crew, Sir Joesph.

SIR JOSEPH (*examining a very small midshipman*). A British sailor is a splendid fellow, Captain Corcoran.

CAPTAIN. A splendid fellow indeed, Sir Joseph.

SIR JOSEPH. I hope you treat your crew kindly, Captain Corcoran.

CAPTAIN. Indeed, I hope so, Sir Joseph.

SIR JOSEPH. Never forget that they are the bulwarks of England's greatness, Captain Corcoran.

CAPTAIN. So I have always considered them, Sir Joseph.

SIR JOSEPH. No bullying, I trust—no strong language of any kind, eh?

CAPTAIN. Oh, never, Sir Joseph.

SIR JOSEPH. What, *never?*

CAPTAIN. Hardly ever, Sir Joseph. They are an excellent crew, and do their work thoroughly without it.

SIR JOSEPH (*reprovingly*). Don't patronize them, sir—pray, don't patronize them.

CAPTAIN. Certainly not, Sir Joseph.

SIR JOSEPH. That you are their captain is an accident of birth. I cannot permit these noble fellows to be patronized because an accident of birth has placed you above them and them below you.

CAPTAIN. I am the last person to insult a British sailor, Sir Joseph.

SIR JOSEPH. You are the last person who did, Captain Corcoran. Desire that splendid seaman to step forward.

CAPTAIN. Ralph Rackstraw, come here.

SIR JOSEPH (*sternly*). If what?

CAPTAIN. I beg your pardon—

SIR JOSEPH. If you *please.*

CAPTAIN. Oh yes, of course. If you *please.* (RALPH *steps forward.*)

SIR JOSEPH. You're a remarkably fine fellow.

RALPH. Yes, your honour.

SIR JOSEPH. And a first-rate seaman, I'll be bound.

RALPH. There's not a smarter topman in the navy, your honour, though I say it who shouldn't.

SIR JOSEPH. Not at all. Proper self-respect, nothing more. Can you dance a hornpipe?

RALPH. No, your honour.

SIR JOSEPH. That's a pity: all sailors should dance hornpipes. I will teach you one this evening, after dinner. Now, tell me—don't be afraid—how does your captain treat you, eh?

RALPH. A better captain don't walk the deck, your honour.

ALL. Hear!

SIR JOSEPH. Good. I like to hear you speak well of your commanding officer; I dare say he don't deserve it, but still it does you credit. Can you sing?

RALPH. I can hum a little, your honour.

SIR JOSEPH. Then hum this at your leisure. (*Giving him* MS. *music.*) It is a song that I have composed for the use of the Royal Navy. It is designed to encourage independence of thought and action in the lower branches of the service, and to teach the principle that a British sailor is any man's equal, excepting mine. Now, Captain Corcoran, a word with you in your cabin, on a tender and sentimental subject.

CAPTAIN. Ay, ay, Sir Joseph. Boatswain, in commemoration of this joyous occupation, see that extra grog is served out to the ship's company at one bell.

BOATSWAIN. Beg pardon. If what, your honour?

CAPTAIN. If what? I don't think I understand you.

BOATSWAIN. If you *please,* your honour.

CAPTAIN. What!

SIR JOSEPH. The gentleman is quite right. If you *please.*

CAPTAIN (*stamping his foot impatiently*). If you *please!*

SIR JOSEPH.

For I hold that on the seas
The expression, "If you please,"
A particularly gentlemanly tone implants.

COUSIN HEBE.

And so do his sisters, and his cousins, and his aunts!

ALL.

And so do his sisters, and his cousins, and his aunts!

(*Exeunt* CAPTAIN *and* SIR JOSEPH *into cabin.*)

BOATSWAIN. Ah! Sir Joseph's a true gentleman: courteous and considerate to the very humblest.

RALPH. True, Boatswain: but we are not the very humblest. Sir Joseph has explained our true position to us. As he says, a British seaman is any man's equal excepting his; and if Sir Joseph says that, is it not our duty to believe him?

ALL. Well spoke! well spoke!

DICK. You're on a wrong tack, and so is he. He means well, but he don't know. When people have to obey other people's orders, equality's out of the question.

ALL (*recoiling*). Horrible! horrible!

BOATSWAIN. Dick Deadeye, if you go for to infuriate this here ship's company too far, I won't answer for being able to hold 'em in. I'm shocked! that's what I am—shocked!

RALPH (*coming forward*). Messmates, my mind's made up. I'll speak to the captain's daughter, and tell her, like an honest man, of the honest love I have for her.

ALL. Hurrah!

RALPH. Is not my love as good as another's? Is not my heart as true as another's? Have I not hands and eyes and ears and limbs like another?

ALL. Ay, ay.

RALPH. True, I lack birth—

BOATSWAIN. You've a berth on board this very ship.

RALPH. Well said—I had forgotten that. Messmates, what do you say? do you approve my determination?

ALL. We do.

DICK. *I* don't.

BOATSWAIN. What is to be done with this here hopeless chap? Let us sing him the song that Sir Joseph has kindly composed for us. Perhaps it will bring this here miserable creetur to a proper state of mind.

GLEE.—RALPH, BOATSWAIN, BOATSWAIN'S MATE, AND CHORUS

A British tar is a soaring soul,
As free as a mountain bird!
His energetic fist should be ready to resist
A dictatorial word.
His nose should pant and his lip should curl,
His cheeks should flame and his brow should furl,
His bosom should heave and his heart should glow,
And his fist be ever ready for a knockdown blow.
CHORUS.—His nose should pant, etc.

His eyes should flash with an inborn fire,
His brow with scorn be wrung;
He never should bow down to a domineering frown,
Or the tang of a tyrant tongue.
His foot should stamp and his throat should growl,
His hair should twirl and his face should scowl,
His eyes should flash and his breast protrude,
And this should be his customary attitude! (*Pose.*)
CHORUS.—His foot should stamp, etc.

(*All strike attitude and then dance off to hornpipe down hatchway, excepting* RALPH, *who remains, leaning pensively against bulwark.*)

(*Enter* JOSEPHINE *from cabin.*)

JOSEPHINE. It is useless—Sir Joseph's attentions nauseate me. I know that he is a truly great and good man, but to me he seems tedious, fretful, and dictatorial. Yet his must be a mind of no common order, or he would not dare to teach my dear father to dance a hornpipe on the cabin table. (*Sees* RALPH.) Ralph Rackstraw! (*Overcome by emotion.*)

RALPH. Ay, lady—no other than poor Ralph Rackstraw!

JOSEPHINE (*aside*). How my head beats! (*Aloud.*) And why poor, Ralph?

RALPH. I am poor in the essence of happiness, lady—rich only in never-ending unrest. In me there meet a combination of antithetical elements which are at eternal war with one another. Driven hither by objective influences—thither by subjective emotions—wafted one moment into blazing day by mocking hope—plunged the next into the Cimmerian darkness of tangible despair, I am but a living ganglion of irreconcilable antagonisms. I hope I make myself clear, lady?

JOSEPHINE. Perfectly. (*Aside.*) His simple eloquence goes to my heart. Oh, if I dared—but no, the thought is madness! (*Aloud.*) Dismiss these foolish fancies, they torture you but needlessly. Come, make one effort.

RALPH (*aside*). I will—one. (*Aloud.*) Josephine!

JOSEPHINE (*indignantly*). Sir!

RALPH. Ay, even though Jove's armoury were launched at the head of the audacious mortal whose lips, unhallowed by relationship, dared to breathe that precious word, yet would I breathe it once, and then perchance be silent evermore. Josephine, in one brief breath I will concentrate the hopes, the doubts, the anxious fears of six weary months. Josephine, I am a British sailor, and I love you!

JOSEPHINE. Sir, this audacity! (*Aside.*) Oh, my heart, my heart! (*Aloud.*) This unwarrantable presumption on the part of a common sailor! (*Aside.*) Common! oh, the irony of the word! (*Aloud.*) Oh, sir, you forget the disparity in our ranks.

RALPH. I forget nothing, haughty lady. I love you desperately, my life is in thy hand—I lay it at your feet! Give me hope, and what I lack in education and polite accomplishments, that I will endeavour to acquire. Drive me to despair, and in death alone I shall look for consolation. I am proud, and cannot stoop to implore. I have spoken, and I wait your word!

JOSEPHINE. You shall not wait long. Your proffered love I haughtily reject. Go, sir, and learn to cast your eyes on some village maiden in your own poor rank—they should be lowered before your captain's daughter!

DUET.—JOSEPHINE AND RALPH

JOSEPHINE.
Refrain, audacious tar,
  Your suit from pressing,
Remember what you are,
  And whom addressing!
Proud lords to seek my hand
  In throngs assemble,
The loftiest in the land
  Bow down and tremble! (*Aside.*)
I'd laugh my rank to scorn
  In union holy,
Were he more highly born
  Or I more lowly!
RALPH.
Proud lady, have your way,
  Unfeeling beauty!
You speak and I obey,
  It is my duty!
I am the lowliest tar
  That sails the water.
And you, proud maiden, are
  My captain's daughter! (*Aside.*)
My heart with anguish torn
  Bows down before her,
She laughs my love to scorn,
  Yet I adore her.
(*Repeat refrain ensemble, then exit* JOSEPHINE *into cabin.*)

RECITATIVE.—RALPH

Can I survive this overbearing
Or live a life of mad despairing,
My proffered love despised, rejected?
No, no, it's not to be expected!
(*Calling off.*) Messmates, ahoy!
  Come here! Come here!

(*Enter* SAILORS, HEBE, *and* RELATIVES.)

ALL.

Ay, ay, my boy,
  What cheer, what cheer?
    Now tell us, pray,
    Without delay,
    What does she say—
  What cheer, what cheer?

RALPH (*to* COUSIN HEBE).

The maiden treats my suit with scorn,
  Rejects my humble love, my lady;
She says I am ignobly born,
  And cuts my hopes adrift, my lady.

ALL. Oh, cruel one!

DICK.

She spurns your suit? Oho! Oho!
I told you so, I told you so.

SAILORS *and* RELATIVES.

Shall we/they submit?
Are we/they but slaves?
  Love comes alike to high and low—
Britannia's sailors rule the waves,
  And shall they stoop to insult? No!

DICK.

You must submit, you are but slaves;
  A lady she! Oho! Oho!
You lowly toilers of the waves,
  She spurns you all—I told you so! (*Goes off.*)

RALPH (*drawing a pistol*).

My friends, my leave of life I'm taking,
For oh, for oh, my heart is breaking.
When I am gone, oh, prithee tell
The maid that, as I died, I loved her well! (*Loading it.*)

ALL (*turning away, weeping*).

Of life, alas! his leave he's taking,
For, ah! his faithful heart is breaking.
When he is gone we'll surely tell
The maid that, as he died, he loved her well.

(*During chorus he has loaded pistol.*)

RALPH.

Be warned, my messmates all

Who love in rank above you—
For Josephine I fall!

(*Puts pistol to his head. All the* SAILORS *stop their ears.*)

(*Enter* JOSEPHINE.)

JOSEPHINE.
Ah! stay your hand! I love you!

ALL.
Ah! stay your hand—she loves you!

RALPH (*incredulously*). Loves me?

JOSEPHINE. Loves you!

ALL.
Yes, yes—ah, yes—she loves you!

ENSEMBLE

SAILORS AND RELATIVES, AND JOSEPHINE

Oh, joy! oh, rapture unforeseen!
For now the sky is all serene;
The god of day—the orb of love,
Has hung his ensign high above,
The sky is all a-blaze.
With wooing words and loving song,
We'll chase the lagging hours along.
And if I find/we find the maiden coy,
I'll/We'll murmur forth decorous joy
In dreamy roundelays!

DICK DEADEYE.
He thinks he's won his Josephine,
But though the sky is now serene,
A frowning thunderbolt above
May end their ill-assorted love
Which now is all a-blaze.
Our captain, ere the day is gone,
Will be extremely down upon
The wicked men who art employ
To make his Josephine his coy
In many various ways.

JOSEPHINE. This very night,
HEBE. With bated breath
RALPH. And muffled oar—
JOSEPHINE. Without a light,
HEBE. As still as death,
RALPH. We'll steal ashore.
JOSEPHINE. A clergyman
RALPH. Shall make us one
BOATSWAIN. At half-past ten,
JOSEPHINE. And then we can
RALPH. Return, for none
BOATSWAIN. Can part us then!
ALL. This very night, etc.

(DICK *appears at hatchway.*)

DICK.
Forbear, nor carry out the scheme you've planned,
She is a lady—you a foremast hand!
Remember, she's your gallant captain's daughter.
And you the meanest slave that crawls the water.
ALL.
Back, vermin, back,
Nor mock us!
Back, vermin, back,
You shock us!
Let's give three cheers for the sailor's bride
Who casts all thought of rank aside—
Who gives up house and fortune too
For the honest love of a sailor true!
For a British tar is a soaring soul
As free as a mountain bird!
His energetic fist should be ready to resist
A dictatorial word!
His foot should stamp and his throat should growl,
His hair should twirl and his face should scowl,
His eyes should flash and his breast protrude,
And this should be his customary attitude. (*Pose.*)
(*General Dance.*)

ACT II

Same Scene. Night. Moonlight.

(CAPTAIN *discovered singing on poop-deck, and accompanying himself on a mandolin.* LITTLE BUTTERCUP *seated on quarter-deck, near gun, gazing sentimentally at him.*)

SONG.—CAPTAIN

Fair moon, to thee I sing,
Bright regent of the heavens;
Say, why is everything
Either at sixes or at sevens?
I have lived hitherto
Free from breath of slander,
Beloved by all my crew—
A really popular commander.
But now my kindly crew rebel;
My daughter to a tar is partial;
Sir Joseph storms, and, sad to tell,
He threatens a court martial!
Fair moon, to thee I sing,
Bright regent of the heavens;
Say, why is everything
Either at sixes or at sevens?

BUTTERCUP. How sweetly he carols forth his melody to the unconscious moon! Of whom is he thinking? Of some high-born beauty? It may be! (*Sighing.*) Who is poor Little Buttercup that she should expect his glance to fall on one so lowly! And yet if he knew—(CAPTAIN *has come down from poop-deck.*)

CAPTAIN. Ah! Little Buttercup, still on board? That is not quite right, little one. It would have been more respectable to have gone on shore at dusk.

BUTTERCUP. True, dear Captain—but the recollection of your sad pale face seemed to chain me to the ship. I would fain see you smile before I go.

CAPTAIN. Ah! Little Buttercup, I fear it will be long before I recover my accustomed cheerfulness, for misfortunes crowd upon me, and all my old friends seem to have turned against me!

BUTTERCUP. Oh no—do not say "all", dear Captain. That were unjust to one, at least.

CAPTAIN. True, for you are staunch to me. (*Aside.*) If ever I gave my heart again, methinks it would be to such a one as this! (*Aloud.*) I am deeply touched by your innocent regard for me, and were we differently situated, I think I could have returned it. But as it is, I fear I can never be more to you than a friend.

BUTTERCUP (*change of manner*). I understand! You hold aloof from me because you are rich and lofty—and I, poor and lowly. But take care! The poor bumboat woman has gipsy blood in her veins, and she can read destinies. There is a change in store for you!

CAPTAIN. A change!

BUTTERCUP. Ay—be prepared!

DUET.—LITTLE BUTTERCUP AND CAPTAIN

BUTTERCUP.

Things are seldom what they seem:
Skim milk masquerades as cream;
Highlows pass as patent leathers;
Jackdaws strut in peacocks' feathers.

CAPTAIN (*puzzled*).

Very true.
So they do.

BUTTERCUP.

Black sheep dwell in every fold;
All that glitters is not gold;
Storks turn out to be but logs;
Bulls are but inflated frogs.

CAPTAIN (*puzzled*).

So they be,
Frequentlee.

BUTTERCUP.

Drops the wind and stops the mill;
Turbot is ambitious brill;
Gild the farthing if you will,
But it is a farthing still.

CAPTAIN (*puzzled*).

Yes, I know
That is so.
Though to catch your drift I'm striving,
It is shady—it is shady;
I don't see at what you're driving,
Mystic lady—mystic lady,
(*Aside.*)
Stern conviction's o'er me stealing,
That the mystic lady's dealing
In oracular revealing.
BUTTERCUP (*aside*).
Stern conviction's o'er him stealing,
That the mystic lady's dealing
In oracular revealing.
BOTH. Yes, I know
That is so!
CAPTAIN.
Though I'm anything but clever,
I could talk like that for ever:
Once a cat was killed by care;
Only brave deserve the fair.
BUTTERCUP. Very true,
So they do.
CAPTAIN.
Wink is often good as nod;
Spoils the child who spares the rod;
Thirsty lambs run foxy dangers;
Dogs are found in many mangers.
BUTTERCUP. Frequentlee,
I agree.
CAPTAIN.
Paw of cat the chestnut snatches;
Worn-out garments show new patches;
Only count the chick that hatches;
Men are grown up catchy-catchies.
BUTTERCUP. Yes, I know
That is so.
(*Aside.*)
Though to catch my drift he's striving,
I'll dissemble—I'll dissemble;

When he sees at what I'm driving,
  Let him tremble—let him tremble!

ENSEMBLE

Though a mystic tone I/you borrow,
I shall/You will learn the truth with sorrow,
Here to-day and gone to-morrow;
      Yes, I know
      That is so!
        (*At the end exit* LITTLE BUTTERCUP, *melodramatically.*)

CAPTAIN. Incomprehensible as her utterances are, I nevertheless feel that they are dictated by a sincere regard for me. But to what new misery is she referring? Time alone can tell!

(*Enter* SIR JOSEPH.)

SIR JOSEPH. Captain Corcoran, I am much disappointed with your daughter. In fact, I don't think she will do.

CAPTAIN. She won't do, Sir Joseph!

SIR JOSEPH. I'm afraid not. The fact is, that although I have urged my suit with as much eloquence as is consistent with an official utterance, I have done so hitherto without success. How do you account for this?

CAPTAIN. Really, Sir Joseph, I hardly know. Josephine is, of course, sensible of your condescension.

SIR JOSEPH. She naturally would be.

CAPTAIN. But perhaps your exalted rank dazzles her.

SIR JOSEPH. You think it does?

CAPTAIN. I can hardly say; but she is a modest girl, and her social position is far below your own. It may be that she feels she is not worthy of you.

SIR JOSEPH. That is really a very sensible suggestion, and displays more knowledge of human nature than I had given you credit for.

CAPTAIN. See, she comes. If your lordship would kindly reason with her, and assure her, officially, that it is a standing rule at the Admiralty that love levels all ranks, her respect for an official utterance might induce her to look upon your offer in its proper light.

SIR JOSEPH. It is not unlikely. I will adopt your suggestion. But soft, she is here. Let us withdraw, and watch our opportunity.

(*Enter* JOSEPHINE *from cabin.* SIR JOSEPH *retires up and watches her.*)

SCENA.—JOSEPHINE

The hours creep on apace,
My guilty heart is quaking!
Oh that I might retract
The step that I am taking.
Its folly it were easy to be showing,
What I am giving up and whither going.

On the one hand, papa's luxurious home,
Hung with ancestral armour and old brasses,
Carved oak and tapestry from distant Rome,
Rare "blue and white" Venetian finger-glasses,
Rich Oriental rugs, luxurious sofa pillows,
And everything that isn't old, from Gillow's.
And on the other, a dark dingy room
In some back street, with stuffy children crying,
Where organs yell, and clacking housewives fume,
And clothes are hanging out all day a-drying;
With one cracked looking-glass to see your face in,
And dinner served up in a pudding basin!

A simple sailor, lowly born,
Unlettered and unknown,
Who toils for bread from early morn
Till half the night has flown!
No golden rank can he impart—
No wealth of house or land—
No fortune save his trusty heart
And honest brown right hand!
And yet he is so wondrous fair
That love for one so passing rare,
So peerless in his manly beauty,
Were little else than solemn duty!
Oh, god of love, and god of reason, say,
Which of you twain shall my poor heart obey!

SIR JOSEPH (*coming forward*). Madam, it has been represented to me that you are appalled by my exalted rank; I desire to convey to you, officially, my assurance that if your hesitation is attributable to that circumstance, it is uncalled for.

JOSEPHINE. Oh! then your lordship is of opinion that married happiness is *not* inconsistent with discrepancy in rank?

SIR JOSEPH. I am officially of that opinion.

JOSEPHINE. That the high and the lowly may be truly happy together, provided that they truly love one another?

SIR JOSEPH. Madam, I desire to convey to you, officially, my opinion that love is a platform upon which all ranks meet.

JOSEPHINE. I thank you, Sir Joseph. I *did* hesitate, but I will hesitate no longer. (*Aside.*) He little thinks how eloquently he has pleaded his rival's cause!

(CAPTAIN *has entered; during this speech he comes forward.*)

TRIO.—SIR JOSEPH, CAPTAIN, AND JOSEPHINE

CAPTAIN.
Never mind the why and wherefore,
Love can level ranks, and therefore,
Though his lordship's station's mighty,
Though stupendous be his brain,
Though your tastes are mean and flighty
And your fortune poor and plain—

CAPTAIN *and* SIR JOSEPH.
Ring the merry bells on board ship,
Rend the air with warbling wild,
For the union of his/my lordship
With a humble captain's child!

CAPTAIN.
For a humble captain's daughter—

JOSEPHINE (*aside*).
For a gallant captain's daughter—

SIR JOSEPH.
And a lord who rules the water—

JOSEPHINE (*aside*).
And a *tar* who ploughs the water!

ALL.
Let the air with joy be laden,
Rend with songs the air above,
For the union of a maiden
With the man who owns her love!

SIR JOSEPH.
Never mind the why and wherefore,
Love can level ranks, and therefore,
Though your nautical relation (*alluding to* CAPTAIN)
In my set could scarcely pass—
Though you occupy a station
In the lower middle class—
CAPTAIN *and* SIR JOSEPH.
Ring the merry bells on board ship,
Rend the air with warbling wild,
For the union of his/my lordship
With a humble captain's child!
SIR JOSEPH.
For a humble captain's daughter—
JOSEPHINE (*aside*).
For a gallant captain's daughter—
CAPTAIN.
And a lord who rules the water—
JOSEPHINE (*aside*).
And a *tar* who ploughs the water!
ALL.
Let the air with joy be laden,
Fill with songs the air above,
For the union of a maiden
With the man who owns her love!
JOSEPHINE.
Never mind the why and wherefore,
Love can level ranks, and therefore
I admit its jurisdiction;
Ably have you played your part;
You have carried firm conviction
To my hesitating heart.
CAPTAIN *and* SIR JOSEPH.
Ring the merry bells on board ship,
Rend the air with warbling wild,
For the union of his/my lordship
With a humble captain's child!
CAPTAIN *and* SIR JOSEPH.
For a humble captain's daughter—
JOSEPHINE (*aside*).
For a gallant captain's daughter—

CAPTAIN *and* SIR JOSEPH.
And a lord who rules the water—
JOSEPHINE (*aside*).
And a *tar* who ploughs the water!
(*Aloud.*)
Let the air with joy be laden—
CAPTAIN *and* SIR JOSEPH.
Ring the merry bells on board ship—
JOSEPHINE.
For the union of a maiden—
CAPTAIN *and* SIR JOSEPH.
For the union with his lordship.
ALL.
Rend with songs the air above
For the man who owns her love!

(*Exit* JOSEPHINE.)

CAPTAIN. Sir Joseph, I cannot express to you my delight at the happy result of your eloquence. Your argument was unanswerable.

SIR JOSEPH. Captain Corcoran, it is one of the happiest characteristics of this glorious country that official utterances are invariably regarded as unanswerable. (*Exit* SIR JOSEPH *into cabin.*)

CAPTAIN. At last my fond hopes are to be crowned. My only daughter is to be the bride of a Cabinet Minister. The prospect is Elysian.

(*During this speech* DICK DEADEYE *has entered.*)

DICK. Captain.

CAPTAIN. Deadeye! You here? Don't! (*Recoiling from him.*)

DICK. Ah, don't shrink from me, Captain. I'm unpleasant to look at, and my name's agin me, but I ain't as bad as I seem.

CAPTAIN. What would you with me?

DICK (*mysteriously*). I'm come to give you warning.

CAPTAIN. Indeed! Do you propose to leave the Navy, then?

DICK. No, no, you misunderstand me; listen.

DUET.—CAPTAIN AND DICK DEADEYE

DICK.
Kind Captain, I've important information,
Sing hey, the kind commander that you are!
About a certain intimate relation;
Sing hey, the merry maiden and the tar!
BOTH.
The merry maiden and the tar!

CAPTAIN.
Good fellow, in conundrums you are speaking,
Sing hey, the mystic sailor that you are!
The answer to them vainly I am seeking;
Sing hey, the merry maiden and the tar!
BOTH.
The merry maiden and the tar!

DICK.
Kind Captain, your young lady is a-sighing,
Sing hey, the simple captain that you are!
This very night with Rackstraw to be flying;
Sing hey, the merry maiden and the tar!
BOTH.
The merry maiden and the tar!

CAPTAIN.
Good fellow, you have given timely warning,
Sing hey, the thoughtful sailor that you are!
I'll talk to Master Rackstraw in the morning;
Sing hey, the cat-o'-nine-tails and the tar! (*Producing a "cat".*)
BOTH.
The merry cat-o'-nine-tails and the tar!

CAPTAIN. Dick Deadeye, I thank you for your warning; I will at once take means to arrest their flight. This boat-cloak will afford me ample disguise. So! (*Envelopes himself in a mysterious cloak, holding it before his face.*)

DICK. Ha! ha! They are foiled—foiled—foiled!

(*Enter* CREW *on tiptoe, with* RALPH *and* BOATSWAIN, *meeting* JOSEPHINE, *who enters from cabin on tiptoe, with bundle of necessaries, and accompanied by* LITTLE BUTTERCUP. *The* CAPTAIN, *shrouded in his boat-cloak, watches them unnoticed.*)

ENSEMBLE

Carefully on tiptoe stealing,
Breathing gently as we may,
Every step with caution feeling,
We will softly steal away.

(CAPTAIN *stamps—chord.*)

ALL (*much alarmed*).
Goodness me!
Why, what was that?
DICK. Silent be,
It was the cat!
ALL (*reassured*).
It was—it was the cat!
CAPTAIN (*producing cat-o'-nine-tails*).
They're right, it was the cat!

Pull ashore, in fashion steady,
Hymen will defray the fare,
For a clergyman is ready
To unite the happy pair!

(*Stamp as before, and chord.*)

ALL. Goodness me!
Why, what was that?
DICK. Silent be,
Again the cat!
ALL. It was again that cat!
CAPTAIN (*aside*).
They're right, it was the cat!

(*Throwing off cloak.*) Hold! (*All start.*)
Pretty daughter of mine,
I insist upon knowing
Where you may be going
With these sons of the brine;
For my excellent crew,
Though foes they could thump any,
Are scarcely fit company,
My daughter, for you.
CREW.
Now, hark at that, do!
Though foes we could thump any,
We are scarcely fit company
For a lady like you!

RALPH.

Proud officer, that haughty lip uncurl!
  Vain man, suppress that supercilious sneer,
For I have dared to love your matchless girl,
  A fact well known to all my messmates here!

CAPTAIN. Oh, horror!

RALPH *and* JOSEPHINE.

I,/He, humble, poor, and lowly born,
  The meanest in the port division—
The butt of epauletted scorn—
  The mark of quarter-deck derision—
Have/Has dared to raise my/his wormy eyes
  Above the dust to which you'd mould me,/him,
In manhood's glorious pride to rise.
I am/He is an Englishman—behold me!/him!

ALL. He is an Englishman!

BOATSWAIN.

He is an Englishman!
  For he himself has said it,
  And it's greatly to his credit,
That he is an Englishman!

ALL.

That he is an Englishman!

BOATSWAIN.

For he might have been a Roosian,
A French, or Turk, or Proosian,
Or perhaps Itali-an!

ALL.

Or perhaps Itali-an!

BOATSWAIN.

But in spite of all temptations
To belong to other nations,
  He remains an Englishman!

ALL. Hurrah!

For the true-born Englishman!

CAPTAIN (*trying to repress his anger*).

In uttering a reprobation
  To any British tar,
  I try to speak with moderation.
    But you have gone too far.

I'm very sorry to disparage
A humble foremast lad,
But to seek your captain's child in marriage,
Why, damme, it's too bad!
(*During this* COUSIN HEBE *and* FEMALE RELATIVES *have entered.*)
ALL (*shocked*). Oh!
CAPTAIN. Yes, damme, it's too bad!
CAPTAIN *and* DICK DEADEYE. Yes, damme, it's too bad.
(*During this* SIR JOSEPH *has appeared on poop-deck. He is horrified at the bad language.*)
HEBE.
Did you hear him—did you hear him?
Oh, the monster overbearing!
Don't go near him—don't go near him—
He is swearing—he is swearing.
SIR JOSEPH (*with impressive dignity*).
My pain and my distress
I find it is not easy to express;
My amazement—my surprise—
You may learn from the expression of my eyes!
CAPTAIN.
My lord, one word—the facts are known before you;
The word was injudicious, I allow—
But hear my explanation, I implore you,
And you will be indignant, too, I vow!
SIR JOSEPH.
I will hear of no defence,
Attempt none if you're sensible.
That word of evil sense
Is wholly indefensible.
Go, ribald, get you hence
To your cabin with celerity.
This is the consequence
Of ill-advised asperity!
(*Exit* CAPTAIN, *disgraced, followed by* JOSEPHINE.)
ALL.
Behold the consequence
Of ill-advised asperity!
SIR JOSEPH.
For I'll teach you all, ere long,

To refrain from language strong.
For I haven't any sympathy for ill-bred taunts!

HEBE.

No more have his sisters, nor his cousins, nor his aunts.

ALL.

For he is an Englishman, etc.

SIR JOSEPH. Now, tell me, my fine fellow—for you *are* a fine fellow—

RALPH. Yes, your honour.

SIR JOSEPH. How came your captain so far to forget himself? I am quite sure you had given him no cause for annoyance.

RALPH. Please your honour, it was thus wise. You see, I'm only a topman—a mere foremast hand—

SIR JOSEPH. Don't be ashamed of that. Your position as a topman is a very exalted one.

RALPH. Well, your honour, love burns as brightly in the foksle as it does on the quarter-deck, and Josephine is the fairest bud that ever blossomed upon the tree of a poor fellow's wildest hopes. (*Enter* JOSEPHINE; *she rushes to* RALPH'S *arms.* SIR JOSEPH *horrified.*) She's the figurehead of my ship of life—the bright beacon that guides me into my port of happiness—the rarest, the purest gem that ever sparkled on a poor but worthy fellow's trusting brow.

ALL. Very pretty.

SIR JOSEPH. Insolent sailor, you shall repent this outrage. Seize him! (*Two* MARINES *seize him and handcuff him.*)

JOSEPHINE. Oh, Sir Joseph, spare him, for I love him tenderly.

SIR JOSEPH. Away with him. I will teach this presumptuous mariner to discipline his affections. Have you such a thing as a dungeon on board?

ALL. We have!

SIR JOSEPH. Then load him with chains and take him there at once!

OCTETTE

RALPH.

Farewell, my own!
Light of my life, farewell!
For crime unknown
I go to a dungeon cell.

ALL.
For crime, etc.
JOSEPHINE.
In the meantime, farewell!
And all alone
  Rejoice in your dungeon cell!
ALL.
And all, etc.
SIR JOSEPH.
A bone, a bone
  I'll pick with this sailor fell;
Let him be shown
  At once to his dungeon cell.
ALL.
Let him, etc.
BOATSWAIN, DICK, *and* HEBE.
He'll hear no tone
  Of the maiden he loves so well!
No telephone
  Communicates with his cell!
ALL.
No telephone, etc.
BUTTERCUP (*mysteriously*).
But when is known
  The secret I have to tell,
Wide will be thrown
  The door of his dungeon cell.
ALL.
Wide will be thrown
  The door of his dungeon cell!

(*All repeat respective verses, ensemble. At the end* RALPH *is led off in custody.*)

SIR JOSEPH. Josephine, I cannot tell you the distress I feel at this most painful revelation. I desire to express to you, officially, that I am hurt. You, whom I honoured by seeking in marriage—you, the daughter of a captain in the Royal Navy!

BUTTERCUP. Hold! *I* have something to say to that!

SIR JOSEPH. You?

BUTTERCUP. Yes, I!

SONG.—BUTTERCUP

A many years ago,
When I was young and charming,
As some of you may know
I practised baby-farming.
ALL.
Now this is most alarming!
When she was young and charming,
She practised baby-farming,
A many years ago.

BUTTERCUP.
Two tender babes I nussed:
One was of low condition,
The other, upper crust,
A regular patrician.
ALL (*explaining to each other*).
Now, this is the position:
One was of low condition,
The other a patrician,
A many years ago.

BUTTERCUP.
Oh, bitter is my cup!
However could I do it?
I mixed those children up,
And not a creature knew it!
ALL.
However could you do it?
Some day, no doubt, you'll rue it,
Although no creature knew it,
So many years ago.

BUTTERCUP.
In time each little waif
Forsook his foster-mother.
The well-born babe was Ralph—
Your captain was the other!
ALL.
They left their foster-mother.

The one was Ralph, our brother—
Our captain was the other,
A many years ago.

SIR JOSEPH. Then I am to understand that Captain Corcoran and Ralph were exchanged in childhood's happy hour—that Ralph is really the Captain, and the Captain is Ralph?

BUTTERCUP. That is the idea I intended to convey.

SIR JOSEPH. You have done it very well. Let them appear before me, at once!

(RALPH *enters as Captain;* CAPTAIN *as a common sailor.* JOSEPHINE *rushes to his arms.*)

JOSEPHINE. My father—a common sailor!

CAPTAIN. It is hard, is it not, my dear?

SIR JOSEPH. This is a very singular occurrence; I congratulate you both. (*To* RALPH.) Desire that remarkably fine seaman to step forward.

RALPH. Corcoran, come here.

CAPTAIN. If what? If you *please.*

SIR JOSEPH. Perfectly right. If you *please.*

RALPH. Oh. If you *please.* (CAPTAIN *steps forward.*)

SIR JOSEPH (*to* CAPTAIN). You are an extremely fine fellow.

CAPTAIN. Yes, your honour.

SIR JOSEPH. So it seems that you were Ralph, and Ralph was you.

CAPTAIN. So it seems, your honour.

SIR JOSEPH. Well, I need not tell you that after this change in your condition, a marriage with your daughter will be out of the question.

CAPTAIN. Don't say that, your honour—love levels all ranks.

SIR JOSEPH. It does to a considerable extent, but it does not level them as much as that. (*Handing* JOSEPHINE *to* RALPH.) Here—take her, sir, and mind you treat her kindly.

RALPH *and* JOSEPHINE.
Oh, bliss! oh, rapture!

SIR JOSEPH.
Sad my lot, and sorry,
What shall I do? I cannot live alone!

ALL.
What will he do? he cannot live alone!

HEBE.
Fear nothing—while I live I'll not desert you.
I'll soothe and comfort your declining days.

SIR JOSEPH.
No, don't do that.

HEBE. Yes, but indeed I'd rather.

SIR JOSEPH (*resigned*).

To-morrow morn our vows shall all be plighted,
Three loving pairs on the same day united!

DUET.—RALPH AND JOSEPHINE

Oh! joy! oh, rapture unforeseen!
The clouded sky is now serene;
The god of day—the orb of love,
Has hung his ensign high above,
The sky is all ablaze.

With wooing words and loving song,
We'll chase the lagging hours along;
And if he finds/I find the maiden coy,
We'll murmur forth decorous joy,
In dreamy roundelays.

CAPTAIN.

For he is the Captain of the Pinafore.

ALL.

And a right good captain too!

CAPTAIN.

And though before my fall
I was Captain of you all,
I'm a member of the crew.

ALL.

Although before his fall, etc.

CAPTAIN.

I shall marry with a wife
In my own rank of life! (*Turning to* BUTTERCUP.)
And you, my love, are she.
I must wander to and fro,
But wherever I may go,
I shall never be untrue to thee!

ALL. What, never?

CAPTAIN. No, never!

ALL. What, *never?*

CAPTAIN. Hardly ever!

ALL.

Hardly ever be untrue to thee.

Then give three cheers, and one cheer more,
For the faithful seamen of the Pinafore.
BUTTERCUP.
For he loves Little Buttercup, dear Little Buttercup,
I'm sure I shall never know why;
But still he loves Buttercup, poor Little Buttercup,
Sweet Little Buttercup, ay!
ALL. For he loves, etc.
SIR JOSEPH.
I'm the monarch of the sea,
And when I've married thee (*To* HEBE.)
I'll be true to the devotion that my love implants.
HEBE.
Then good-bye to his sisters, and his cousins, and his aunts,
Especially his cousins,
Whom he reckons up by dozens,
His sisters, and his cousins, and his aunts!
ALL.
For he is an Englishman,
And he himself hath said it,
And it's greatly to his credit
That he is an Englishman!
Curtain

THE COUNTESS CATHLEEN

Critic William Archer, producer Jack Thomas Grein, and dramatist Bernard Shaw (*The Quintessence of Ibsenism*) did much to bring to bear upon the faltering English theatre the influence of the greatest playwright of the nineteenth century, Henrik Ibsen (1828-1906). One of the least obvious of the Norwegian genius' effects was the foundation of the Irish theatre, a theatre that achieved world-wide recognition not only for the realistic comedy of J. M. Synge (1871-1909) but also for the intensely poetic and dramatic, spiritual and symbolic plays of W. B. Yeats (1865–1939). Yeats, while inspired by Ibsen's idea of a national theatre, diametrically opposed almost everything else about Ibsen.

The ideals of the Irish theatre as explained by Yeats in "The Irish Dramatic Movement" (*Plays and Controversies,* 1923) and by Lady [Augusta] Gregory in *Our Irish Theatre* (1914) were clear-cut: a modern Irish drama, written by native dramatists on native subjects; a national, not narrowly political drama; a drama, however poetical, in touch with reality; a drama creating its own classics and playing them in repertory, with Irish actors, professional or amateur; a drama sufficiently subsidized to be free of the tyranny of the box office until an audience could be created for a revolutionary new theatre, thoroughly fresh subject matter, a new style of acting and production.

The new theatre suffered, as did the new republic later, from

"Troubles," but it lived. "We went on giving them what we thought good," wrote Lady Gregory in retrospect, "until it became popular." Yeats wanted something else: "I want not a theatre, but the theatre's antiself." He turned his back on "popular" theatre—and it turned its back on him, so that he is now very seldom played, even at the Abbey Theatre.

In plays that commented critically upon human experience, whether recorded in golden legends newly minted or observed in simple modern life humorously described, the founders of the movement all made use of Irish traditions, some preserved in the ancient manuscripts that industrious Germans were beginning to translate, some still vital in the lives of the people of the West who continued to speak their ancient and beautiful language. Lady Gregory, Edward Martyn, and Synge used "the language of the folk" and drew their inspiration from the life of the peasantry. Yeats used older materials, as Ibsen had done for *Peer Gynt* (1867). Yeats harkened back to an earlier world of primitive emotions and more vivid coloration but always retained—however distant his setting, mystical his tone, or enigmatic his message—an immediacy and current significance. He chose grand old themes and gave them new political importance. He was not only patriotically reshaping the stirring tales of his country's heroic past; he spoke directly to the descendants of Cuchulain and Deirdre, of Cathleen ni Houlihan. In his lecture on "The Irish Literary Tradition" (Folkways Records FL 9825) Frank O'Connor asserts that Yeats'

> renaissance is firmly established in the circumstances and politics of his day. Yeats's great achievement was the creation of a theatre in which the sagas of the old aristocrats and the stories of the Irish-speaking country people found a common meeting place.

Though he wanted his plays to relate to life, Yeats made them consciously "literary." In the traditions of the 1890's, he embraced "pure poetry"; in the traditions of the French symbolists, he stylized his language. Later he was to turn (at Ezra Pound's suggestion) to the Nōh plays of Japan; but from the beginning his simplicity was self-conscious, and his severe form always enclosed an unabashedly romantic content. Out of disparate elements, however, he was able to fashion a system that at its best united literature and theatre to make drama. Others could not. "Read Edward Martyn and A. E. [George Russell]," warns Eric Bentley, "read the verse plays of Bridges and Masefield and

Sturge Moore and Gordon Bottomley and you will quickly lose interest in the Irish Renaissance, the revival of poetic drama, and perhaps life itself." Yet Yeats, says Bentley, was "the only considerable verse playwright in English for several hundred years."

Certainly one of the things we find in Yeats and sadly miss in the verse dramas of his contemporaries is a sense of grandeur. The old poet in *The King's Threshold* (1904) claims that "those that make rhymes have a power from beyond the world," and in the best plays of Yeats we feel that spiritual force. He is, writes G. Wilson Knight in *The Golden Labyrinth,*

> deliberately concerned with the spiritual. . . . Yeats believes in heroism and the supernatural; for him poetry is the right means of approach; and his central dramatic quest looks accordingly for some type of super-hero symbolizing the incarnate imagination.

Frank O'Connor puts it more straightforwardly and helps to explain why we chose the story of the Countess Cathleen's heroic self-sacrifice and only half-unexpected reward to represent him and this movement, for

> the characteristic type of the Abbey Theatre play was the miracle play. The first play Yeats ever wrote, *Countess Cathleen,* was a play about a woman who, in order to save the lives of people during a famine, sells her soul to the devil and at the end of the play you realize that a miracle has taken place and that in fact she is saved. And all the Abbey Theatre plays have this peculiar quality. You see, there's always the possibility of divine intervention, and in these plays death itself is treated as though it were only another form of illumination.

Countess Cathleen is intended to be one of Yeats' "more heroic or grotesque types that, keeping always an appropriate distance from life, would seem images of those profound emotions that exist only in solitude and silence." She is an early creation of a dramatist who, says O'Connor, "according to most critics, never could write a play" (for Bentley's praise is as unorthodox as it is justified) but who knew enough about his craft to write comments this perceptive about the essence of drama:

What attracts me to drama is that it is, in the most obvious way, what all the arts are upon a last analysis. A farce and a tragedy are alike in this, that they are a moment of intense life. An action is taken out of all other actions; it is reduced to its simplest form, or at any rate to as simple a form as it can be brought to without our losing the sense of its place in the world. The characters that are involved in it are freed from everything that is not a part of that action; and whether it is, as in the less important kinds of drama, a mere bodily activity, a hair-breadth escape or the like, or as it is in the more important kinds, an activity of the soul of the characters, it is an energy, an eddy of life purified from everything but itself. The dramatist must picture life in action, with an unpre-occupied mind, as the musician pictures her in sound and the sculptor in form.

THE COUNTESS CATHLEEN

by

William Butler Yeats

"THE SORROWFUL ARE DUMB FOR THEE"

—Lament of Morian Shehone for Miss Mary Bourke

TO

MAUD GONNE

PERSONS IN THE PLAY

SHEMUS RUA, *a Peasant*
MARY, *his Wife*
TEIGUE, *his Son*
ALEEL, *a Poet*
The Countess CATHLEEN
OONA, *her Foster-Mother*
Two Demons disguised as Merchants
Peasants, Servants, Angelical Beings

The Scene is laid in Ireland and in old times

SCENE I

A room with lighted fire, and a door into the open air, through which one sees, perhaps, the trees of a wood, and these trees should be painted in flat colour upon a gold or diapered sky. The walls are of one colour. The scene should have the effect of missal painting. MARY, *a woman of forty years or so, is grinding a quern.*

First published in The Countess Kathleen [sic] and Various Legends and Lyrics *in 1892, the year in which Yeats and others founded the Irish Literary Society (Dublin). In the Preface to the first edition of his* Collected Plays *(1934) Yeats wrote: "Those who think of producing any particular play should seek for it in* Plays and Controversies, Plays *and* Wheels and Butterflies. *The Note on* The Countess Cathleen, *for instance, in* Plays and Controversies *contains a simplified version of the last scene, and when I have known of appropriate music for some play I have given it in a Note or Appendix."*

MARY. What can have made the grey hen flutter so?
(TEIGUE, *a boy of fourteen, is coming in with turf, which he lays beside the hearth.*)
TEIGUE. They say that now the land is famine-struck
The graves are walking.
MARY. What can the hen have heard?
TEIGUE. And that is not the worst; at Tubber-vanach
A woman met a man with ears spread out,
And they moved up and down like a bat's wing.
MARY. What can have kept your father all this while?
TEIGUE. Two nights ago, at Carrick-orus churchyard,
A herdsman met a man who had no mouth,
Nor eyes, nor ears; his face a wall of flesh;
He saw him plainly by the light of the moon.
MARY. Look out, and tell me if your father's coming.
(TEIGUE *goes to door.*)
TEIGUE. Mother!
MARY. What is it?
TEIGUE. In the bush beyond,
There are two birds—if you can call them birds—
I could not see them rightly for the leaves—
But they've the shape and colour of horned owls,
And I'm half certain they've a human face.
MARY. Mother of God, defend us!
TEIGUE. They're looking at me.
What is the good of praying? father says.
God and the Mother of God have dropped asleep.
What do they care, he says, though the whole land
Squeal like a rabbit under a weasel's tooth?
MARY. You'll bring misfortune with your blasphemies
Upon your father, or yourself, or me.
Would God that he were home—ah, there he is. (SHEMUS *comes in.*)
What was it kept you in the wood? You know
I cannot get all sorts of accidents
Out of my mind till you are home again.
SHEMUS. I'm in no mood to listen to your clatter.
Although I tramped the woods for half a day,
I've taken nothing, for the very rats,
Badgers, and hedgehogs seem to have died of drought,
And there was scarce a wind in the parched leaves.
TEIGUE. Then you have brought no dinner.

SHEMUS. After that
I sat among the beggars at the cross-roads,
And held a hollow hand among the others.

MARY. What, did you beg?

SHEMUS. I had no chance to beg,
For when the beggars saw me they cried out
They would not have another share their alms,
And hunted me away with sticks and stones.

TEIGUE. You said that you would bring us food or money.

SHEMUS. What's in the house?

TEIGUE. A bit of mouldy bread.

MARY. There's flour enough to make another loaf.

TEIGUE. And when that's gone?

MARY. There is the hen in the coop.

SHEMUS. My curse upon the beggars, my curse upon them!

TEIGUE. And the last penny gone.

SHEMUS. When the hen's gone,
What can we do but live on sorrel and dock,
And dandelion, till our mouths are green?

MARY. God, that to this hour has found bit and sup,
Will cater for us still.

SHEMUS. His kitchen's bare.
There were five doors that I looked through this day
And saw the dead and not a soul to wake them.

MARY. Maybe He'd have us die because He knows,
When the ear is stopped and when the eye is stopped,
That every wicked sight is hid from the eye,
And all fool talk from the ear! (*A stringed instrument without.*)

SHEMUS. Who's passing there?
And mocking us with music?

TEIGUE. A young man plays it.
There's an old woman and a lady with him.

SHEMUS. What is the trouble of the poor to her?
Nothing at all or a harsh radishy sauce
For the day's meat.

MARY. God's pity on the rich!
Had we been through as many doors, and seen
The dishes standing on the polished wood
In the wax candle light, we'd be as hard,
And there's the needle's eye at the end of all.

SHEMUS. My curse upon the rich!
TEIGUE. They're coming here.
SHEMUS. Then down upon that stool, down quick, I say,
And call up a whey face and a whining voice,
And let your head be bowed upon your knees.
MARY. Had I but time to put the place to rights!
(CATHLEEN, OONA, *and* ALEEL *enter.*)
CATHLEEN. God save all here. There is a certain house,
An old grey castle with a kitchen garden,
A cider orchard and a plot for flowers,
Somewhere among these woods.
MARY. We know it, lady.
A place that's set among impassable walls
As though world's trouble could not find it out.
CATHLEEN. It may be that we are that trouble, for we—
Although we've wandered in the wood this hour—
Have lost it too, yet I should know my way,
For I lived all my childhood in that house.
MARY. Then you are Countess Cathleen?
CATHLEEN. And this woman,
Oona, my nurse, should have remembered it,
For we were happy for a long time there.
OONA. The paths are overgrown with thickets now,
Or else some change has come upon my sight.
CATHLEEN. And this young man, that should have known the woods—
Because we met him on their border but now,
Wandering and singing like a wave of the sea—
Is so wrapped up in dreams of terrors to come
That he can give no help.
MARY. You have still some way,
But I can put you on the trodden path
Your servants take when they are marketing.
But first sit down and rest yourself awhile,
For my old fathers served your fathers, lady,
Longer than books can tell—and it were strange
If you and yours should not be welcome here.
CATHLEEN. And it were stranger still were I ungrateful
For such kind welcome—but I must be gone,
For the night's gathering in.
SHEMUS. It is a long while

Since I've set eyes on bread or on what buys it.
CATHLEEN. So you are starving even in this wood,
Where I had thought I would find nothing changed.
But that's a dream, for the old worm o' the world
Can eat its way into what place it pleases. (*She gives money.*)
TEIGUE. Beautiful lady, give me something too;
I fell but now, being weak with hunger and thirst,
And lay upon the threshold like a log.
CATHLEEN. I gave for all and that was all I had.
But look, my purse is empty. I have passed
By starving men and women all this day,
And they have had the rest; but take the purse,
The silver clasps on't may be worth a trifle.
And if you'll come to-morrow to my house
You shall have twice the sum. (ALEEL *begins to play.*)
SHEMUS (*muttering*). What, music, music!
CATHLEEN. Ah, do not blame the finger on the string;
The doctors bid me fly the unlucky times
And find distraction for my thoughts, or else
Pine to my grave.
SHEMUS. I have said nothing, lady.
Why should the like of us complain?
OONA. Have done.
Sorrows that she's but read of in a book
Weigh on her mind as if they had been her own.
(OONA, MARY, *and* CATHLEEN *go out.*
ALEEL *looks defiantly at* SHEMUS.)
ALEEL (*singing*). Were I but crazy for love's sake
I know who'd measure out his length,
I know the heads that I should break,
For crazy men have double strength.
I know—all's out to leave or take,
Who mocks at music mocks at love;
Were I but crazy for love's sake,
No need to pick and choose.
(*Snapping his fingers in* SHEMUS' *face.*)
Enough!
I know the heads that I should break.
(*He takes a step towards the door and then turns again.*)
Shut to the door before the night has fallen,

For who can say what walks, or in what shape
Some devilish creature flies in the air; but now
Two grey horned owls hooted above our heads.

(*He goes out, his singing dies away.* MARY *comes in.* SHEMUS *has been counting the money.*)

SHEMUS. So that fool's gone.

TEIGUE. He's seen the horned owls too.
There's no good luck in owls, but it may be
That the ill luck's to fall upon his head.

MARY. You never thanked her ladyship.

SHEMUS. Thank her
For seven halfpence and a silver bit?

TEIGUE. But for this empty purse?

SHEMUS. What's that for thanks,
Or what's the double of it that she promised,
With bread and flesh and every sort of food
Up to a price no man has heard the like of
And rising every day?

MARY. We have all she had;
She emptied out the purse before our eyes.

SHEMUS (*to* MARY, *who has gone to close the door*). Leave that door open.

MARY. When those that have read books,
And seen the seven wonders of the world,
Fear what's above or what's below the ground,
It's time that poverty should bolt the door.

SHEMUS. I'll have no bolts, for there is not a thing
That walks above the ground or under it
I had not rather welcome to this house
Than any more of mankind, rich or poor.

TEIGUE. So that they brought us money.

SHEMUS. I heard say
There's something that appears like a white bird,
A pigeon or a seagull or the like,
But if you hit it with a stone or a stick
It clangs as though it has been made of brass,
And that if you dig down where it was scratching
You'll find a crock of gold.

TEIGUE. But dream of gold
For three nights running, and there's always gold.

SHEMUS. You might be starved before you've dug it out.
TEIGUE. But maybe if you called, something would come.
They have been seen of late.
MARY. Is it call devils?
Call devils from the wood, call them in here?
SHEMUS. So you'd stand up against me, and you'd say
Who or what I am to welcome here. (*He hits her.*)
That is to show who's master.
TEIGUE. Call them in.
MARY. God help us all!
SHEMUS. Pray, if you have a mind to.
It's little that the sleepy ears above
Care for your words; but I'll call what I please.
TEIGUE. There is many a one, they say, had money from them.
SHEMUS (*at door*). Whatever you are that walk the woods at night,
So be it that you have not shouldered up
Out of a grave—for I'll have nothing human—
And have free hands, a friendly trick of speech,
I welcome you. Come, sit beside the fire.
What matter if your head's below your arms
Or you've a horse's tail to whip your flank,
Feathers instead of hair, that's all but nothing.
Come, share what bread and meat is in the house,
And stretch your heels and warm them in the ashes.
And after that, let's share and share alike
And curse all men and women. Come in, come in.
What, is there no one there? (*Turning from door.*)
And yet they say
They are as common as the grass, and ride
Even upon the book in the priest's hand.

(TEIGUE *lifts one arm slowly and points towards the door and begins moving backward.* SHEMUS *turns, he also sees something and begins moving backward.* MARY *does the same. A man dressed as an Eastern merchant comes in carrying a small carpet. He unrolls it and sits cross-legged at one end of it. Another man dressed in the same way follows, and sits at the other end. This is done slowly and deliberately. When they are seated they take money out of embroidered purses at their girdles and begin arranging it on the carpet.*)

TEIGUE. You speak to them.
SHEMUS. No, you.
TEIGUE. 'Twas you that called them.

SHEMUS (*coming nearer*). I'd make so bold, if you would pardon it,
To ask if there's a thing you'd have of us.
Although we are but poor people, if there is,
Why, if there is—

FIRST MERCHANT. We've travelled a long road,
For we are merchants that must tramp the world,
And now we look for supper and a fire
And a safe corner to count money in.

SHEMUS. I thought you were . . . but that's no matter now—
There had been words between my wife and me
Because I said I would be master here,
And ask in what I pleased or who I pleased,
And so . . . but that is nothing to the point,
Because it's certain that you are but merchants.

FIRST MERCHANT. We travel for the Master of all merchants.

SHEMUS. Yet if you were that I had thought but now
I'd welcome you no less. Be what you please
And you'll have supper at the market rate.
That means that what was sold for but a penny
Is now worth fifty.

FIRST MERCHANT (*arranging money*). Our Master bids us pay
So good a price that all who deal with us
Shall eat, drink, and be merry.

SHEMUS (*to* MARY). Bestir yourself,
Go kill and draw the fowl, while Teigue and I
Lay out the plates and make a better fire.

MARY. I will not cook for you.

SHEMUS. Not cook! not cook!
Do not be angry. She wants to pay me back
Because I struck her in that argument.
But she'll get sense again. Since the dearth came
We rattle one on another as though we were
Knives thrown into a basket to be cleaned.

MARY. I will not cook for you, because I know
In what unlucky shape you sat but now
Outside this door.

TEIGUE. It's this, your honours:
Because of some wild words my father said
She thinks you are not of those who cast a shadow.

SHEMUS. I said I'd make the devils of the wood

Welcome, if they'd a mind to eat and drink;
But it is certain that you are men like us.
FIRST MERCHANT. It's strange that she should think we cast no shadow,
For there is nothing on the ridge of the world
That's more substantial than the merchants are
That buy and sell you.
MARY. If you are not demons,
And seeing what great wealth is spread out there,
Give food or money to the starving poor.
FIRST MERCHANT. If we knew how to find deserving poor
We'd do our share.
MARY. But seek them patiently.
FIRST MERCHANT. We know the evils of mere charity.
MARY. Those scruples may befit a common time.
I had thought there was a pushing to and fro,
At times like this, that overset the scale
And trampled measure down.
FIRST MERCHANT. But if already
We'd thought of a more prudent way than that?
SECOND MERCHANT. If each one brings a bit of merchandise,
We'll give him such a price he never dreamt of.
MARY. Where shall the starving come at merchandise?
FIRST MERCHANT. We will ask nothing but what all men have.
MARY. Their swine and cattle, fields and implements
Are sold and gone.
FIRST MERCHANT. They have not sold all yet.
For there's a vaporous thing—that may be nothing,
But that's the buyer's risk—a second self,
They call immortal for a story's sake.
SHEMUS. They come to buy our souls?
TEIGUE. I'll barter mine.
Why should we starve for what may be but nothing?
MARY. Teigue and Shemus—
SHEMUS. What can it be but nothing?
What has God poured out of His bag but famine?
Satan gives money.
TEIGUE. Yet no thunder stirs.
FIRST MERCHANT. There is a heap for each. (SHEMUS *goes to take money.*)
But, no, not yet,

For there's a work I have to set you to.

SHEMUS. So, then, you're as deceitful as the rest,
And all that talk of buying what's but a vapour
Is fancy bread. I might have known as much,
Because that's how the trick-o'-the-loop man talks.

FIRST MERCHANT. That's for the work, each has its separate price;
But neither price is paid till the work's done.

TEIGUE. The same for me.

MARY. O God, why are You still?

FIRST MERCHANT. You've but to cry aloud at every cross-road,
At every house door, that we buy men's souls
And give so good a price that all may live
In mirth and comfort till the famine's done,
Because we are Christian men.

SHEMUS. Come, let's away.

TEIGUE. I shall keep running till I've earned the price.

SECOND MERCHANT (*who has risen and gone towards fire*). Stop; you must have proof behind the words,
So here's your entertainment on the road.

(*He throws a bag of money on the ground.*)

Live as you please; our Master's generous.

(TEIGUE *and* SHEMUS *have stopped.* TEIGUE *takes the money. They go out.*)

MARY. Destroyers of souls, God will destroy you quickly.
You shall at last dry like dry leaves and hang
Nailed like dead vermin to the doors of God.

SECOND MERCHANT. Curse to your fill, for saints will have their dreams.

FIRST MERCHANT. Though we're but vermin that our Master sent
To overrun the world, he at the end
Shall pull apart the pale ribs of the moon
And quench the stars in the ancestral night.

MARY. God is all-powerful.

SECOND MERCHANT. Pray, you shall need Him.
You shall eat dock and grass, and dandelion,
Till that low threshold there becomes a wall,
And when your hands can scarcely drag your body
We shall be near you. (MARY *faints.*)

(*The* FIRST MERCHANT *takes up the carpet, spreads it before the fire and stands in front of it warming his hands.*)

FIRST MERCHANT. Our faces go unscratched.
Wring the neck o' that fowl, scatter the flour,
And look if there is bread upon the shelves.
We'll turn the fowl upon the spit and roast it,
And eat the supper we were bidden to,
Now that the house is quiet, praise our Master,
And stretch and warm our heels among the ashes.

SCENE II

FRONT SCENE: *A wood with perhaps distant view of turreted house at one side, but all in flat colour, without light and shade and against a diapered or gold background.*

(COUNTESS CATHLEEN *comes in leaning upon* ALEEL'S *arm,* OONA *follows them.*)

CATHLEEN (*stopping*). Surely this leafy corner, where one smells
The wild bee's honey, has a story too?

OONA. There is the house at last.

ALEEL. A man, they say,
Loved Maeve the Queen of all the invisible host,
And died of his love nine centuries ago.
And now, when the moon's riding at the full,
She leaves her dancers lonely and lies there
Upon that level place, and for three days
Stretches and sighs and wets her long pale cheeks.

CATHLEEN. So she loves truly.

ALEEL. No, but wets her cheeks,
Lady, because she has forgot his name.

CATHLEEN. She'd sleep that trouble away—though it must be
A heavy trouble to forget his name—
If she had better sense.

OONA. Your own house, lady.

ALEEL. She sleeps high up on wintry Knocknarea
In an old cairn of stones; while her poor women
Must lie and jog in the wave if they would sleep—
Being water-born—yet if she cry their names
They run up on the land and dance in the moon
Till they are giddy and would love as men do,

And be as patient and as pitiful.
But there is nothing that will stop in their heads,
They've such poor memories, though they weep for it.
O yes, they weep; that's when the moon is full.

CATHLEEN. Is it because they have short memories
They live so long?

ALEEL. What's memory but the ash
That chokes our fires that have begun to sink?
And they've a dizzy, everlasting fire.

OONA. There is your own house, lady.

CATHLEEN. Why, that's true,
And we'd have passed it without noticing.

ALEEL. A curse upon it for a meddlesome house!
Had it but stayed away I would have known
What Queen Maeve thinks on when the moon is pinched;
And whether now—as in the old days—the dancers
Set their brief love on men.

OONA. Rest on my arm.
These are no thoughts for any Christian ear.

ALEEL. I am younger, she would be too heavy for you.

(*He begins taking his lute out of the bag.* CATHLEEN, *who has turned towards* OONA, *turns back to him.*)

This hollow box remembers every foot
That danced upon the level grass of the world,
And will tell secrets if I whisper to it.

(*Sings.*)

Lift up the white knee;
Hear what they sing,
Those young dancers
That in a ring
Raved but now
Of the hearts that broke
Long, long ago
For their sake.

OONA. New friends are sweet.

ALEEL. But the dance changes,
Lift up the gown,
All the sorrow
Is trodden down.

OONA. The empty rattle-pate! Lean on this arm,

That I can tell you is a christened arm,
And not like some, if we are to judge by speech.
But as you please. It is time I was forgot.
Maybe it is not on this arm you slumbered
When you were as helpless as a worm.

ALEEL. Stay with me till we come to your own house.

CATHLEEN (*sitting down*). When I am rested I will need no help.

ALEEL. I thought to have kept her from remembering
The evil of the times for full ten minutes;
But now when seven are out you come between.

OONA. Talk on; what does it matter what you say,
For you have not been christened?

ALEEL. Old woman, old woman,
You robbed her of three minutes' peace of mind,
And though you live unto a hundred years,
And wash the feet of beggars and give alms,
And climb Cro-Patrick, you shall not be pardoned.

OONA. How does a man who never was baptized
Know what Heaven pardons?

ALEEL. You are a sinful woman.

OONA. I care no more than if a pig had grunted.

(*Enter* CATHLEEN'S STEWARD.)

STEWARD. I am not to blame, for I had locked the gate.
The forester's to blame. The men climbed in
At the east corner where the elm-tree is.

CATHLEEN. I do not understand you. Who has climbed?

STEWARD. Then God be thanked, I am the first to tell you.
I was afraid some other of the servants—
Though I've been on the watch—had been the first,
And mixed up truths and lies, your ladyship.

CATHLEEN (*rising*). Has some misfortune happened?

STEWARD. Yes, indeed.
The forester that let the branches lie
Against the wall's to blame for everything,
For that is how the rogues got into the garden.

CATHLEEN. I thought to have escaped misfortune here.
Has any one been killed?

STEWARD. O no, not killed.
They have stolen half a cart-load of green cabbage.

CATHLEEN. But maybe they were starving.

STEWARD. That is certain.
To rob or starve, that was the choice they had.
CATHLEEN. A learned theologian has laid down
That starving men may take what's necessary,
And yet be sinless.
OONA. Sinless and a thief!
There should be broken bottles on the wall.
CATHLEEN. And if it be a sin, while faith's unbroken
God cannot help but pardon. There is no soul
But it's unlike all others in the world,
Nor one but lifts a strangeness to God's love
Till that's grown infinite, and therefore none
Whose loss were less than irremediable
Although it were the wickedest in the world.
(*Enter* TEIGUE *and* SHEMUS.)
STEWARD. What are you running for? Pull off your cap.
Do you not see who's there?
SHEMUS. I cannot wait.
I am running to the world with the best news
That has been brought it for a thousand years.
STEWARD. Then get your breath and speak.
SHEMUS. If you'd my news
You'd run as fast and be as out of breath.
TEIGUE. Such news, we shall be carried on men's shoulders.
SHEMUS. There's something every man has carried with him
And thought no more about than if it were
A mouthful of the wind; and now it's grown
A marketable thing!
TEIGUE. And yet it seemed
As useless as the paring of one's nails.
SHEMUS. What sets me laughing when I think of it,
Is that a rogue who's lain in lousy straw,
If he but sell it, may set up his coach.
TEIGUE (*laughing*). There are two gentlemen who buy men's souls.
CATHLEEN. O God!
TEIGUE. And maybe there's no soul at all.
STEWARD. They're drunk or mad.
TEIGUE. Look at the price they give. (*Showing money.*)
SHEMUS (*tossing up money*). 'Go cry it all about the world', they said.
' "Money for souls, good money for a soul." '

CATHLEEN. Give twice and thrice and twenty times their money,
And get your souls again. I will pay all.
SHEMUS. Not we! not we! For souls—if there are souls—
But keep the flesh out of its merriment.
I shall be drunk and merry.
TEIGUE. Come, let's away. (*He goes.*)
CATHLEEN. But there's a world to come.
SHEMUS. And if there is,
I'd rather trust myself into the hands
That can pay money down than to the hands
That have but shaken famine from the bag. (*He goes out* R. *lilting.*)
'There's money for a soul, sweet yellow money.
There's money for men's souls, good money, money.'
CATHLEEN (*to* ALEEL). Go call them here again, bring them by force,
Beseech them, bribe, do anything you like; (ALEEL *goes.*)
And you too follow, add your prayers to his.
(OONA, *who has been praying, goes out.*)
Steward, you know the secrets of my house.
How much have I?
STEWARD. A hundred kegs of gold.
CATHLEEN. How much have I in castles?
STEWARD. As much more.
CATHLEEN. How much have I in pasture?
STEWARD. As much more.
CATHLEEN. How much have I in forests?
STEWARD. As much more.
CATHLEEN. Keeping this house alone, sell all I have,
Go barter where you please, but come again
With herds of cattle and with ships of meal.
STEWARD. God's blessing light upon your ladyship.
You will have saved the land.
CATHLEEN. Make no delay. (*He goes* L.)
(ALEEL *and* OONA *return.*)
CATHLEEN. They have not come; speak quickly.
ALEEL. One drew his knife
And said that he would kill the man or woman
That stopped his way; and when I would have stopped him
He made this stroke at me; but it is nothing.
CATHLEEN. You shall be tended. From this day for ever
I'll have no joy or sorrow of my own.

OONA. Their eyes shone like the eyes of birds of prey.
CATHLEEN. Come, follow me, for the earth burns my feet
Till I have changed my house to such a refuge
That the old and ailing, and all weak of heart,
May escape from beak and claw; all, all, shall come
Till the walls burst and the roof fall on us.
From this day out I have nothing of my own. (*She goes.*)
OONA (*taking* ALEEL *by the arm and as she speaks bandaging his wound*).
She has found something now to put her hand to,
And you and I are of no more account
Than flies upon a window-pane in the winter. (*They go out.*)

SCENE III

Hall in the house of COUNTESS CATHLEEN. *At the left an oratory with steps leading up to it. At the right a tapestried wall, more or less repeating the form of the oratory, and a great chair with its back against the wall. In the centre are two or more arches through which one can see dimly the trees of the garden.* CATHLEEN *is kneeling in front of the altar in the oratory; there is a hanging lighted lamp over the altar.* ALEEL *enters.*

ALEEL. I have come to bid you leave this castle and fly
Out of these woods.
(CATHLEEN *rises from the altar and comes into the hall.*)
CATHLEEN. What evil is there here
That is not everywhere from this to the sea?
ALEEL. They who have sent me walk invisible.
CATHLEEN. So it is true what I have heard men say,
That you have seen and heard what others cannot.
ALEEL. I was asleep in my bed, and while I slept
My dream became a fire; and in the fire
One walked and he had birds about his head.
CATHLEEN. I have heard that one of the old gods walked so.
ALEEL. It may be that he is angelical;
And, lady, he bids me call you from these woods.
And you must bring but your old foster-mother,
And some few serving-men, and live in the hills,

Among the sounds of music and the light
Of waters, till the evil days are done.
For here some terrible death is waiting you,
Some unimagined evil, some great darkness
That fable has not dreamt of, nor sun nor moon
Scattered.

CATHLEEN. No, not angelical.

ALEEL. This house
You are to leave with some old trusty man,
And bid him shelter all that starve or wander
While there is food and house-room.

CATHLEEN. He bids me go
Where none of mortal creatures but the swan
Dabbles, and there you would pluck the harp, when the trees
Had made a heavy shadow about our door,
And talk among the rustling of the reeds,
When night hunted the foolish sun away
With stillness and pale tapers. No—no—no!
I cannot. Although I weep, I do not weep
Because that life would be most happy, and here
I find no way, no end. Nor do I weep
Because I had longed to look upon your face,
But that a night of prayer has made me weary.

ALEEL (*prostrating himself before her*). Let Him that made mankind, the angels and devils
And dearth and plenty, mend what He has made,
For when we labour in vain and eye still sees,
Heart breaks in vain.

CATHLEEN. How would that quiet end?

ALEEL. How but in healing?

CATHLEEN. You have seen my tears,
And I can see your hand shake on the floor.

ALEEL (*faltering*). I thought but of healing. He was angelical.

CATHLEEN (*turning away from him*). No, not angelical, but of the old gods,
Who wander about the world to waken the heart—
The passionate, proud heart—that all the angels,
Leaving nine heavens empty, would rock to sleep.

(*She goes to the oratory door;* ALEEL *holds his clasped hands towards her for a moment hesitatingly, and then lets them fall beside him.*)

CATHLEEN. Do not hold out to me beseeching hands.

This heart shall never waken on earth. I have sworn,
By her whose heart the seven sorrows have pierced,
To pray before this altar until my heart
Has grown to Heaven like a tree, and there
Rustled its leaves, till Heaven has saved my people.

ALEEL (*who has risen*). When one so great has spoken of love to one
So little as I, though to deny him love,
What can he but hold out beseeching hands,
Then let them fall beside him, knowing how greatly
They have overdared?

(*He goes towards the door of the hall. The* COUNTESS CATHLEEN *takes a few steps towards him.*)

CATHLEEN. If the old tales are true,
Queens have wed shepherds and kings beggar-maids;
God's procreant waters flowing about your mind
Have made you more than kings or queens; and not you
But I am the empty pitcher.

ALEEL. Being silent,
I have said all, yet let me stay beside you.

CATHLEEN. No, no, not while my heart is shaken. No,
But you shall hear wind cry and water cry,
And curlew cry, and have the peace I longed for.

ALEEL. Give me your hand to kiss.

CATHLEEN. I kiss your forehead.
And yet I send you from me. Do not speak;
There have been women that bid men to rob
Crowns from the Country-under-Wave or apples
Upon a dragon-guarded hill, and all
That they might sift the hearts and wills of men,
And trembled as they bid it, as I tremble
That lay a hard task on you, that you go,
And silently, and do not turn your head.
Good-bye; but do not turn your head and look;
Above all else, I would not have you look. (ALEEL *goes.*)
I never spoke to him of his wounded hand,
And now he is gone. (*She looks out.*)
I cannot see him, for all is dark outside.
Would my imagination and my heart
Were as little shaken as this holy flame!

(*She goes slowly into the oratory. The distant sound of an alarm bell. The two* MERCHANTS *enter hurriedly.*)

SECOND MERCHANT. They are ringing the alarm, and in a moment
They'll be upon us.

FIRST MERCHANT (*going to a door at the side*). Here is the Treasury.
You'd my commands to put them all to sleep.

SECOND MERCHANT. Some angel or else her prayers protected them.

(*Goes into the Treasury and returns with bags of treasure.* FIRST MERCHANT *has been listening at the oratory door.*)

FIRST MERCHANT. She has fallen asleep.

(SECOND MERCHANT *goes out through one of the arches at the back and stands listening. The bags are at his feet.*)

SECOND MERCHANT. We've all the treasure now,
So let's away before they've tracked us out.

FIRST MERCHANT. I have a plan to win her.

SECOND MERCHANT. You have time enough
If you would kill her and bear off her soul
Before they are upon us with their prayers;
They search the Western Tower.

FIRST MERCHANT. That may not be.
We cannot face the heavenly host in arms.
Her soul must come to us of its own will;
But being of the ninth and mightiest Hell,
Where all are kings, I have a plan to win it.
Lady, we've news that's crying out for speech.

(CATHLEEN *wakes and comes to door of oratory.*)

CATHLEEN. Who calls?

FIRST MERCHANT. Lady, we have brought news.

CATHLEEN. What are you?

FIRST MERCHANT. We are merchants, and we know the book of the world
Because we have walked upon its leaves; and there
Have read of late matters that much concern you;
And noticing the castle door stand open,
Came in to find an ear.

CATHLEEN. The door stands open
That no one who is famished or afraid
Despair of help or of a welcome with it.
But you have news, you say.

FIRST MERCHANT. We saw a man
Heavy with sickness in the bog of Allen,
Whom you had bid buy cattle. Near Fair Head
We saw your grain ships lying all becalmed

In the dark night; and not less still than they,
Burned all their mirrored lanthorns in the sea.
CATHLEEN. Thanks be to God there's money in the house
That can buy grain from those who have stored it up
To prosper on the hunger of the poor.
But you've been far and know the signs of things,
When will this famine end?
FIRST MERCHANT. Day copies day,
And there's no sign of change, nor can it change,
With the wheat withered and the cattle dead.
CATHLEEN. And heard you of the demons who buy souls?
FIRST MERCHANT. There are some men who hold they have wolves' heads,
And say their limbs—dried by the infinite flame—
Have all the speed of storms; others, again,
Say they are gross and little; while a few
Will have it they seem much as mortals are,
But tall and brown and travelled—like us, lady—
Yet all agree a power is in their looks
That makes men bow, and flings a casting-net
About their souls, and that all men would go
And barter those poor vapours, were it not
You bribe them with the safety of your gold.
CATHLEEN. Praise God that I am wealthy! Why do they sell?
FIRST MERCHANT. As we came in at the great door we saw
Your porter sleeping in his niche—a soul
Too little to be worth a hundred pence,
And yet they buy it for a hundred crowns.
But for a soul like yours, I heard them say,
They would give five hundred thousand crowns and more.
CATHLEEN. How can a heap of crowns pay for a soul?
Is the green grave so terrible a thing?
FIRST MERCHANT. Some sell because the money gleams, and some
Because they are in terror of the grave,
And some because their neighbours sold before,
And some because there is a kind of joy
In casting hope away, in losing joy,
In ceasing all resistance, in at last
Opening one's arms to the eternal flames,
In casting all sails out upon the wind;
To this—full of the gaiety of the lost—

Would all folk hurry if your gold were gone.

CATHLEEN. There is a something, Merchant, in your voice
That makes me fear. When you were telling how
A man may lose his soul and lose his God
Your eyes were lighted up, and when you told
How my poor money serves the people, both—
Merchants, forgive me—seemed to smile.

FIRST MERCHANT. I laugh
To think that all these people should be swung
As on a lady's shoe-string,—under them
The glowing leagues of never-ending flame.

CATHLEEN. There is a something in you that I fear;
A something not of us; were you not born
In some most distant corner of the world?

(*The* SECOND MERCHANT, *who has been listening at the door, comes forward, and as he comes a sound of voices and feet is heard.*)

SECOND MERCHANT. Away now—they are in the passage—hurry,
For they will know us, and freeze up our hearts
With Ave Marys, and burn all our skin
With holy water.

FIRST MERCHANT. Farewell; for we must ride
Many a mile before the morning come;
Our horses beat the ground impatiently.

(*They go out. A number of* PEASANTS *enter by other door.*)

FIRST PEASANT. Forgive us, lady, but we heard a noise.

SECOND PEASANT. We sat by the fireside telling vanities.

FIRST PEASANT. We heard a noise, but though we have searched the house
We have found nobody.

CATHLEEN. You are too timid,
For now you are safe from all the evil times,
There is no evil that can find you here.

OONA (*entering hurriedly*). Ochone! The treasure-room is broken in.
The door stands open, and the gold is gone.

(PEASANTS *raise a lamentable cry.*)

CATHLEEN. Be silent. (*The cry ceases.*) Have you seen nobody?

OONA. Ochone!
That my good mistress should lose all this money!

CATHLEEN. Let those among you not too old to ride
Get horses and search all the country round.
I'll give a farm to him who finds the thieves.

(*A man with keys at his girdle has come in while she speaks. There is a general murmur of* 'The porter! the porter!')

PORTER. Demons were here. I sat beside the door
In my stone niche, and two owls passed me by,
Whispering with human voices.

OLD PEASANT. God forsakes us.

CATHLEEN. Old man, old man, He never closed a door
Unless one opened. I am desolate
Because of a strange thought that's in my heart;
But I have still my faith; therefore be silent;
For surely He does not forsake the world,
But stands before it modelling in the clay
And moulding there His image. Age by age
The clay wars with His fingers and pleads hard
For its old, heavy, dull and shapeless ease;
But sometimes—though His hand is on it still—
It moves awry and demon hordes are born.

(PEASANTS *cross themselves.*)

Yet leave me now, for I am desolate.
I hear a whisper from beyond the thunder.

(*She comes from the oratory door.*)

Yet stay an instant. When we meet again
I may have grown forgetful. Oona, take
These two—the larder and the dairy keys. (*To the* PORTER.)
But take you this. It opens the small room
Of herbs for medicine, every kind of herb.
The book of cures is on the upper shelf.

PORTER. Why do you do this, lady; did you see
Your coffin in a dream?

CATHLEEN. Ah, no, not that.
But I have come to a strange thought. I have heard
A sound of wailing in unnumbered hovels,
And I must go down, down—I know not where—
Pray for all men and women mad from famine;
Pray, you good neighbours.

(*The* PEASANTS *all kneel.* COUNTESS CATHLEEN *ascends the steps to the door of the oratory, and turning round stands there motionless for a little, and then cries in a loud voice:*)

Mary, Queen of angels,
And all you clouds on clouds of saints, farewell!

SCENE IV

FRONT SCENE: *A wood near the Castle, as in Scene II. A group of* PEASANTS *pass.*

FIRST PEASANT. I have seen silver and copper, but not gold.
SECOND PEASANT. It's yellow and it shines.
FIRST PEASANT. It's beautiful.
The most beautiful thing under the sun,
That's what I've heard.
THIRD PEASANT. I have seen gold enough.
FOURTH PEASANT. I would not say that it's so beautiful.
FIRST PEASANT. But doesn't a gold piece glitter like the sun?
That's what my father, who'd seen better days,
Told me when I was but a little boy—
So high—so high, it's shining like the sun,
Round and shining, that is what he said.
SECOND PEASANT. There's nothing in the world it cannot buy.
FIRST PEASANT. They've bags and bags of it.

(*They go out. The two* MERCHANTS *follow silently. Then* ALEEL *passes over the stage singing.*)

ALEEL. Impetuous heart be still, be still,
Your sorrowful love can never be told,
Cover it up with a lonely tune.
He who could bend all things to His will
Has covered the door of the infinite fold
With the pale stars and the wandering moon.

SCENE V

The house of SHEMUS RUA. *There is an alcove at the back with curtains; in it a bed, and on the bed is the body of* MARY *with candles round it. The two* MERCHANTS *while they speak put a large book upon a table, arrange money, and so on.*

FIRST MERCHANT. Thanks to that lie I told about her ships
And that about the herdsman lying sick,
We shall be too much thronged with souls to-morrow.

SECOND MERCHANT. What has she in her coffers now but mice?
FIRST MERCHANT. When the night fell and I had shaped myself
Into the image of the man-headed owl,
I hurried to the cliffs of Donegal,
And saw with all their canvas full of wind
And rushing through the parti-coloured sea
Those ships that bring the woman grain and meal.
They're but three days from us.
SECOND MERCHANT. When the dew rose
I hurried in like feathers to the east,
And saw nine hundred oxen driven through Meath
With goads of iron. They're but three days from us.
FIRST MERCHANT. Three days for traffic.
(PEASANTS *crowd in with* TEIGUE *and* SHEMUS.)
SHEMUS. Come in, come in, you are welcome.
That is my wife. She mocked at my great masters,
And would not deal with them. Now there she is;
She does not even know she was a fool,
So great a fool she was.
TEIGUE. She would not eat
One crumb of bread bought with our masters' money,
But lived on nettles, dock, and dandelion.
SHEMUS. There's nobody could put into her head
That death is the worst thing can happen us,
Though that sounds simple, for her tongue grew rank
With all the lies that she had heard in chapel.
Draw to the curtain. (TEIGUE *draws it.*) You'll not play the fool
While these good gentlemen are there to save you.
SECOND MERCHANT. Since the drought came they drift about in a throng,
Like autumn leaves blown by the dreary winds.
Come, deal—come, deal.
FIRST MERCHANT. Who will come deal with us?
SHEMUS. They are out of spirit, sir, with lack of food,
Save four or five. Here, sir, is one of these;
The others will gain courage in good time.
MIDDLE-AGED MAN. I come to deal—if you give honest price.
FIRST MERCHANT (*reading in a book*). 'John Maher, a man of substance, with dull mind,

And quiet senses and unventurous heart.
The angels think him safe.' Two hundred crowns,
All for a soul, a little breath of wind.

MIDDLE-AGED MAN. I ask three hundred crowns. You have read there
That no mere lapse of days can make me yours.

FIRST MERCHANT. There is something more writ here—'Often at night
He is wakeful from a dread of growing poor,
And thereon wonders if there's any man
That he could rob in safety.'

A PEASANT. Who'd have thought it?
And I was once alone with him at midnight.

ANOTHER PEASANT. I will not trust my mother after this.

FIRST MERCHANT. There is this crack in you—two hundred crowns.

A PEASANT. That's plenty for a rogue.

ANOTHER PEASANT. I'd give him nothing.

SHEMUS. You'll get no more—so take what's offered you.

(*A general murmur, during which the* MIDDLE-AGED MAN *takes money, and slips into background, where he sinks on to a seat.*)

FIRST MERCHANT. Has no one got a better soul than that?
If only for the credit of your parishes,
Traffic with us.

A WOMAN. What will you give for mine?

FIRST MERCHANT (*reading in book*). 'Soft, handsome, and still young'—not much, I think.
'It's certain that the man she's married to
Knows nothing of what's hidden in the jar
Between the hour-glass and the pepper-pot.'

THE WOMAN. The scandalous book!

FIRST MERCHANT. 'Nor how when he's away
At the horse-fair the hand that wrote what's hid
Will tap three times upon the window-pane.'

THE WOMAN. And if there is a letter, that is no reason
Why I should have less money than the others.

FIRST MERCHANT. You're almost safe. I give you fifty crowns.

(*She turns to go.*)

A hundred, then.

SHEMUS. Woman, have sense—come, come.
Is this a time to haggle at the price?
There, take it up. There, take it up. That's right.

(*She takes them and goes into the crowd.*)

FIRST MERCHANT. Come, deal, deal, deal. It is but for charity
We buy such souls at all; a thousand sins
Made them our Master's long before we came.

(ALEEL *enters.*)

ALEEL. Here, take my soul, for I am tired of it.
I do not ask a price.

SHEMUS. Not ask a price?
How can you sell your soul without a price?
I would not listen to his broken wits.
His love for Countess Cathleen has so crazed him
He hardly understands what he is saying.

ALEEL. The trouble that has come on Countess Cathleen,
The sorrow that is in her wasted face,
The burden in her eyes, have broke my wits,
And yet I know I'd have you take my soul.

FIRST MERCHANT. We cannot take your soul, for it is hers.

ALEEL. No, but you must. Seeing it cannot help her I have grown tired of it.

FIRST MERCHANT. Begone from me,
I may not touch it.

ALEEL. Is your power so small?
And must I bear it with me all my days?
May you be scorned and mocked!

FIRST MERCHANT. Drag him away.
He troubles me.

(TEIGUE *and* SHEMUS *lead* ALEEL *into the crowd.*)

SECOND MERCHANT. His gaze has filled me, brother,
With shaking and a dreadful fear.

FIRST MERCHANT. Lean forward
And kiss the circlet where my Master's lips
Were pressed upon it when he sent us hither;
You shall have peace once more.

(SECOND MERCHANT *kisses the gold circlet that is about the head of the* FIRST MERCHANT.)

I, too, grow weary,
But there is something moving in my heart
Whereby I know that what we seek the most
Is drawing near—our labour will soon end.
Come, deal, deal, deal, deal, deal; are you all dumb?
What, will you keep me from our ancient home,
And from the eternal revelry?

SECOND MERCHANT. Deal, deal.

SHEMUS. They say you beat the woman down too low.

FIRST MERCHANT. I offer this great price: a thousand crowns
For an old woman who was always ugly.

(*An old* PEASANT WOMAN *comes forward, and he takes up a book and reads:*)

There is but little set down here against her.
'She has stolen eggs and fowl when times were bad,
But when the times grew better has confessed it;
She never missed her chapel of a Sunday
And when she could, paid dues.' Take up your money.

OLD WOMAN. God bless you, sir. (*She screams.*) O, sir, a pain went through me!

FIRST MERCHANT. That name is like a fire to all damned souls.

(*Murmur among the* PEASANTS, *who shrink back from her as she goes out.*)

A PEASANT. How she screamed out!

SECOND PEASANT. And maybe we shall scream so.

THIRD PEASANT. I tell you there is no such place as Hell.

FIRST MERCHANT. Can such a trifle turn you from your profit?
Come, deal; come, deal.

MIDDLE-AGED MAN. Master, I am afraid.

FIRST MERCHANT. I bought your soul, and there's no sense in fear
Now the soul's gone.

MIDDLE-AGED MAN. Give me my soul again.

WOMAN (*going on her knees and clinging to* MERCHANT). And take this money too, and give me mine.

SECOND MERCHANT. Bear bastards, drink or follow some wild fancy;
For cryings out and sighs are the soul's work,
And you have none. (*Throws the* WOMAN *off.*)

PEASANT. Come, let's away.

ANOTHER PEASANT. Yes, yes.

ANOTHER PEASANT. Come quick; if that woman had not screamed
I would have lost my soul.

ANOTHER PEASANT. Come, come away.

(*They turn to door, but are stopped by shouts of* 'Countess Cathleen! Countess Cathleen!')

CATHLEEN (*entering*). And so you trade once more?

FIRST MERCHANT. In spite of you.
What brings you here, saint with the sapphire eyes?

CATHLEEN. I come to barter a soul for a great price.
SECOND MERCHANT. What matter, if the soul be worth the price?
CATHLEEN. The people starve, therefore the people go
Thronging to you. I hear a cry come from them
And it is in my ears by night and day,
And I would have five hundred thousand crowns
That I may feed them till the dearth go by.
FIRST MERCHANT. It may be the soul's worth it.
CATHLEEN. There is more:
The souls that you have bought must be set free.
FIRST MERCHANT. We know of but one soul that's worth the price.
CATHLEEN. Being my own it seems a priceless thing.
SECOND MERCHANT. You offer us——
CATHLEEN. I offer my own soul.
A PEASANT. Do not, do not, for souls the like of ours
Are not precious to God as your soul is.
O, what would Heaven do without you, lady?
ANOTHER PEASANT. Look how their claws clutch in their leathern gloves.
FIRST MERCHANT. Five hundred thousand crowns; we give the price.
The gold is here; the souls even while you speak
Have slipped out of our bond, because your face
Has shed a light on them and filled their hearts.
But you must sign, for we omit no form
In buying a soul like yours.
SECOND MERCHANT. Sign with this quill.
It was a feather growing on the cock
That crowed when Peter dared deny his Master,
And all who use it have great honour in Hell.
(CATHLEEN *leans forward to sign.*)
ALEEL (*rushing forward and snatching the pen from her*). Leave all things to the Builder of the Heavens.
CATHLEEN. I have no thoughts; I hear a cry—a cry.
ALEEL (*casting the pen on the ground*). I have seen a vision under a green hedge,
A hedge of hips and haws—men yet shall hear
The archangels rolling Satan's empty skull
Over the mountain-tops.
FIRST MERCHANT. Take him away.

(TEIGUE *and* SHEMUS *drag him roughly away so that he falls upon the floor among the* PEASANTS. CATHLEEN *picks up parchment and signs, then turns towards the* PEASANTS.)

CATHLEEN. Take up the money, and now come with me;
When we are far from this polluted place
I will give everybody money enough.

(*She goes out, the* PEASANTS *crowding round her and kissing her dress.* ALEEL *and the two* MERCHANTS *are left alone.*)

SECOND MERCHANT. We must away and wait until she dies,
Sitting above her tower as two grey owls,
Waiting as many years as may be, guarding
Our precious jewel; waiting to seize her soul.

FIRST MERCHANT. We need but hover over her head in the air,
For she has only minutes. When she signed
Her heart began to break. Hush, hush, I hear
The brazen door of Hell move on its hinges,
And the eternal revelry float hither
To hearten us.

SECOND MERCHANT. Leap feathered on the air
And meet them with her soul caught in your claws.

(*They rush out.* ALEEL *crawls into the middle of the room. The twilight has fallen and gradually darkens as the scene goes on. There is a distant muttering of thunder and a sound of rising storm.*)

ALEEL. The brazen door stands wide, and Balor comes
Borne in his heavy car, and demons have lifted
The age-weary eyelids from the eyes that of old
Turned gods to stone; Barach, the traitor, comes
And the lascivious race, Cailitin,
That cast a Druid weakness and decay
Over Sualtim's and old Dectora's child;
And that great king Hell first took hold upon
When he killed Naoise and broke Deirdre's heart;
And all their heads are twisted to one side,
For when they lived they warred on beauty and peace
With obstinate, crafty, sidelong bitterness.

(OONA *enters.*)

Crouch down, old heron, out of the blind storm.

OONA. Where is the Countess Cathleen? All this day
Her eyes were full of tears, and when for a moment
Her hand was laid upon my hand it trembled,

And now I do not know where she is gone.

ALEEL. Cathleen has chosen other friends than us,
And they are rising through the hollow world.
Demons are out, old heron.

OONA. God guard her soul!

ALEEL. She's bartered it away this very hour,
As though we two were never in the world.

(*He points downward.*)

First, Orchil, her pale, beautiful head alive,
Her body shadowy as vapour drifting
Under the dawn, for she who awoke desire
Has but a heart of blood when others die;
About her is a vapoury multitude
Of women alluring devils with soft laughter;
Behind her a host heat of the blood made sin,
But all the little pink-white nails have grown
To be great talons.

(*He seizes* OONA *and drags her into the middle of the room and points downward with vehement gestures. The wind roars.*)

They begin a song
And there is still some music on their tongues.

OONA (*casting herself face downwards on the floor*). O Maker of all, protect her from the demons,
And if a soul must needs be lost, take mine.

(ALEEL *kneels beside her, but does not seem to hear her words. The* PEASANTS *return. They carry the* COUNTESS CATHLEEN *and lay her upon the ground before* OONA *and* ALEEL. *She lies there as if dead.*)

OONA. O that so many pitchers of rough clay
Should prosper and the porcelain break in two!

(*She kisses the hands of* CATHLEEN.)

A PEASANT. We were under the tree where the path turns,
When she grew pale as death and fainted away.
And while we bore her hither cloudy gusts
Blackened the world and shook us on our feet.
Draw the great bolt, for no man has beheld
So black, bitter, blinding, and sudden a storm.

(*One who is near the door draws the bolt.*)

CATHLEEN. O, hold me, and hold me tightly, for the storm
Is dragging me away.

(OONA *takes her in her arms. A woman begins to wail.*)

PEASANTS. Hush!

OTHER PEASANTS. Hush!

PEASANT WOMEN. Hush!

OTHER PEASANT WOMEN. Hush!

CATHLEEN (*half rising*). Lay all the bags of money in a heap,
And when I am gone, old Oona, share them out
To every man and woman; judge, and give
According to their needs.

A PEASANT WOMAN. And will she give
Enough to keep my children through the dearth?

ANOTHER PEASANT WOMAN. O Queen of Heaven, and all you blessed saints,
Let us and ours be lost so she be shriven.

CATHLEEN. Bend down your faces, Oona and Aleel;
I gaze upon them as the swallow gazes
Upon the nest under the eave, before
She wander the loud waters. Do not weep
Too great a while, for there is many a candle
On the High Altar though one fall. Aleel,
Who sang about the dancers of the woods
That know not the hard burden of the world,
Having but breath in their kind bodies, farewell!
And farewell, Oona, you who played with me,
And bore me in your arms about the house
When I was but a child and therefore happy,
Therefore happy, even like those that dance.
The storm is in my hair and I must go. (*She dies.*)

OONA. Bring me the looking-glass.

(*A woman brings it to her out of the inner room.* OONA *holds it over the lips of* CATHLEEN. *All is silent for a moment. And then she speaks in a half scream;*)

O, she is dead!

A PEASANT. She was the great white lily of the world.

ANOTHER PEASANT. She was more beautiful than the pale stars.

AN OLD PEASANT WOMAN. The little plant I loved is broken in two.

(ALEEL *takes looking-glass from* OONA *and flings it upon the floor so that it is broken in many pieces.*)

ALEEL. I shatter you in fragments, for the face
That brimmed you up with beauty is no more:
And die, dull heart, for she whose mournful words

Made you a living spirit has passed away
And left you but a ball of passionate dust.
And you, proud earth and plumy sea, fade out!
For you may hear no more her faltering feet,
But are left lonely amid the clamorous war
Of angels upon devils.

(*He stands up; almost every one is kneeling, but it has grown so dark that only confused forms can be seen.*)

And I who weep
Call curses on you, Time and Fate and Change,
And have no excellent hope but the great hour
When you shall plunge headlong through bottomless space.

(*A flash of lightning followed immediately by thunder.*)

A PEASANT WOMAN. Pull him upon his knees before his curses
Have plucked thunder and lightning on our heads.

ALEEL. Angels and devils clash in the middle air,
And brazen swords clang upon brazen helms.

(*A flash of lightning followed immediately by thunder.*)

Yonder a bright spear, cast out of a sling,
Has torn through Balor's eye, and the dark clans
Fly screaming as they fled Moytura of old.

(*Everything is lost in darkness.*)

AN OLD MAN. The Almighty wrath at our great weakness and sin
Has blotted out the world and we must die.

(*The darkness is broken by a visionary light. The* PEASANTS *seem to be kneeling upon the rocky slope of a mountain, and vapour full of storm and ever-changing light is sweeping above them and behind them. Half in the light, half in the shadow, stand armed angels. Their armour is old and worn, and their drawn swords dim and dinted. They stand as if upon the air in formation of battle and look downward with stern faces. The* PEASANTS *cast themselves on the ground.*)

ALEEL. Look no more on the half-closed gates of Hell,
But speak to me, whose mind is smitten of God,
That it may be no more with mortal things,
And tell of her who lies there.

(*He seizes one of the angels.*)

Till you speak
You shall not drift into eternity.

THE ANGEL. The light beats down; the gates of pearl are wide;
And she is passing to the floor of peace,

And Mary of the seven times wounded heart
Has kissed her lips, and the long blessed hair
Has fallen on her face; The Light of Lights
Looks always on the motive, not the deed,
The Shadow of Shadows on the deed alone.

(ALEEL *releases the* ANGEL *and kneels.*)

OONA. Tell them who walk upon the floor of peace
That I would die and go to her I love;
The years like great black oxen tread the world,
And God the herdsman goads them on behind,
And I am broken by their passing feet.

(*A sound of far-off horns seems to come from the heart of the light. The vision melts away, and the forms of the kneeling* PEASANTS *appear faintly in the darkness.*)

The End

THE SECOND MRS. TANQUERAY

This ambitious play, which William Archer received with a compliment that today sounds ambiguous (he said it was a drama "which Dumas might sign without a blush"), caused a sensation in 1893. Barrett Clark explained why:

> Ibsen was a new name in England; his plays were beginning to be translated, discussed, produced. The Independent Theater, under J. T. Grein, had produced "Ghosts" in 1891, and invoked a storm of invective from the press ["an open drain; a loathsome sore unbandaged; a dirty deed done publicly," "noisome corruption," "garbage and offal," "maunderings of nookshotten Norwegians," "if any repetition of this outrage be attempted, the authorities will doubtless wake from their lethargy," "lugubrious diagnosis of sordid impropriety"]; Bernard Shaw was hurling thunderbolts at the British public in the columns of the *Saturday Review;* Henry Arthur Jones was lecturing on the "Renascence of the Drama." It was the day of the New Woman. And Pinero wrote a powerful play around a woman with a past; five years previously, it is safe to say that the play would not have been successful. As it was, the time was ripe.

From the beginning some critics saw that the "tremendous awakening effect" of *The Second Mrs. Tanqueray,* sounding what has been called the first note of modern English drama, was false, that the machinery creaked, that the problems of this problem play were stage problems only, that the superiority of this drama over others bespoke not so much the genius of the author but the dismal lack of talent among his competitors—that this outstanding success was, in fact, only the youngest horse in a glue factory. True, Paula Tanqueray was a striking character (though one critic said "there is no cheaper subject for the character draughtsman than the ill-tempered sensual woman seen from the point of view of the conventional man"), but novelists such as Lord Lytton, Anthony Trollope, and Charles Reade had done much better much earlier.

> The theatre was not ready for that class of work then [wrote Bernard Shaw in 1895]: it is now; and accordingly Mr. Pinero . . . who has never written a line from which it could be guessed that he is a contemporary of Ibsen, Tolstoi, Meredith, or Sarah Grand, finds himself . . . hailed as a man of new ideas, of daring originality, of supreme literary distinction, and even—which is perhaps oddest—of consummate stage craft.

Shaw then exposed the "naïve machinery" of the exposition: "two whole acts wasted on sham parts," the clumsy device of the confidant (Cayley Drummle), the badly motivated exits and entrances and unmotivated confessions and explanations, and the fact that the characters, "having been given a passable air of being human beings," are then manipulated to produce "the requisite jar—a pitilessly disagreeable jar—and that is all."

Then, to clinch matters, came Granville-Barker, Galsworthy, and a small horde of dramatists more grimly realistic and more unwaveringly earnest than Pinero. But in his time Pinero was breaking new ground; he departed radically from the plays that had built his reputation. In comparison with the exposition of *East Lynne* (see Lord Mount Severn's first speech and indeed all of the Prologue), the two analytical acts that begin *The Second Mrs. Tanqueray* are light-years ahead. We are in full drama, as the French say, very quickly; and the public had not yet seen what could be done by the genius who wrote *Hedda Gabler* (1890), in which, as William Archer stated in his epoch-making book on *Play-Making* (1912), the vivid action of the present is firmly rooted in "facts and relations of the past, which are elicited under circumstances of high dramatic tension." Archer found Pinero's exposition quite credible and creditable:

> *The Second Mrs. Tanqueray* requires an unusual amount of preliminary retrospect. We have to learn the history of Aubrey Tanqueray's first marriage, with the mother of Ellean, as well as the history of Paula Ray's past life. The mechanism employed to this end has been much criticized, but seems to me admirable. Aubrey gives a farewell dinner-party to his intimate friends, Misquith and Jayne. Cayley Drummle, too, is expected, but has not arrived when the play opens. Without naming the lady, Aubrey announces to his guests his approaching marriage. He proposes to go out with them, and has one or two notes to write before doing so. Moreover, he is not sorry to give them an opportunity to talk over the announcement he has made; so he retires to a side-table in the same room, to do his writing. Misquith and Jayne exchange a few speeches in an undertone, and then Cayley Drummle comes in, bringing the story of George Orreyed's marriage to the unmentionable Miss Hervey. This story is so unpleasant to Tanqueray that, to get out of the conversation, he returns to his writing; but still he cannot help listening to Cayley's comments on George Orreyed's "disappearance"; and at last the situation becomes so intolerable to him that he purposely leaves the room, bidding the other two "Tell Cayley the news." [Shaw says that "he is compelled to get up and go ignominiously into the next room 'to write some letters' when something has to be said behind his back."] The technical manipulation of all this seems to me to be above reproach —dramatically effective and yet life-like in every detail. If one were bound to raise an objection, it would be to the coincidence which brings to Cayley's knowledge, on one and the same evening, two such exactly similar misalliances in his own circle of acquaintance. But these are just the coincidences that do constantly happen. Everyone knows that life is full of them.

Today we are not likely to praise Pinero for realistic criticism of life. The dialogue (of which he was so proud that he would not permit a syllable to be changed), like the problems which he used it to discuss, is stagey. But he and Henry Arthur Jones (who in 1895 wrote the following statement) were leaders in

> a steadfast and growing attempt to treat the great realities of our modern life upon our stage, to bring our drama into relation with our literature, our religion, our art, and our science, and to make it reflect the main movements of our national thought and character. That anything great or permanent was accomplished I am last to claim; all was crude, confused, tentative, aspiring. But there was *life* in it.

There is life yet in *The Second Mrs. Tanqueray.* We are not likely to remark, as did Brigham Young (stalking out of a performance of this play accompanied by his many wives), "I won't stand such a damned row being made about one woman," for Paula, even without Mrs. Patrick Campbell's irresistible charm, is fascinating.

THE SECOND MRS. TANQUERAY

by

Sir Arthur Wing Pinero

A program in The Theatre Collection, New York Public Library, dated April 21, 1893, gives the following cast for this play which opened at The St. James's Theatre on Saturday, May 27, of that year:

AUBREY TANQUERAY	George Alexander
Sir GEORGE ORREYED, *Bart.*	A. Vane-Tempest
Captain HUGH ARDALE	Ben Webster
CAYLEY DRUMMLE	H. V. Esmond
FRANK MISQUITH, Q.C., M.P.	H. H. Vincent
GORDON JAYNE, M.D.	A. Bromley-Davenport
MORSE [*Tanqueray's man servant*]	Alfred Holles
Lady ORREYED	Miss Laura Graves
Mrs. CORTELYON	Miss Granville
PAULA [RAY]	Mrs. Patrick Campbell
ELLEAN [TANQUERAY]	Miss Maude Millett

Servants

TIME: *The Present Day* [1893]

The Scene of the First Act is laid at MR. TANQUERAY'*s rooms, No. 2 x, The Albany* [London], *in the month of November; the occurrences of the succeeding Acts take place at his house, "Highercoombe," near Willowmere, Surrey, during the early part of the following year.*

ACT I

AUBREY TANQUERAY'S *chambers in the Albany—a richly and tastefully decorated room, elegantly and luxuriously furnished: on the right a large pair of doors opening into another room, on the left at the further end of the room a small door leading to a bed-chamber. A circular table is laid for a dinner for four persons, which has now reached the stage of dessert and coffee. Everything in the apartment suggests wealth and refinement. The fire is burning brightly.*

(AUBREY TANQUERAY, MISQUITH, *and* JAYNE *are seated at the dinner table.* AUBREY *is forty-two, handsome, winning in manner, his speech and bearing retaining some of the qualities of young manhood.* MISQUITH *is about forty-seven, genial and portly.* JAYNE *is a year or two* MISQUITH'S *senior; soft-speaking and precise—in appearance a type of the prosperous town physician.* MORSE, AUBREY'S *servant, places a little cabinet of cigars and the spirit-lamp on the table beside* AUBREY, *and goes out.*)

MISQUITH. Aubrey, it is a pleasant yet dreadful fact to contemplate, but it's nearly fifteen years since I first dined with you. You lodged in Piccadilly in those days, over a hat-shop. Jayne, I met you at that dinner, and Cayley Drummle.

JAYNE. Yes, yes. What a pity it is that Cayley isn't here to-night.

AUBREY. Confound the old gossip! His empty chair has been staring us in the face all through dinner. I ought to have told Morse to take it away.

MISQUITH. Odd, his sending no excuse.

AUBREY. I'll walk round to his lodgings later on and ask after him.

MISQUITH. I'll go with you.

JAYNE. So will I.

AUBREY (*opening the cigar-cabinet*). Doctor, it's useless to tempt you, I know. Frank—(MISQUITH *and* AUBREY *smoke.*) I particularly wished Cayley Drummle to be one of us to-night. You two fellows and Cayley are my closest, my best friends—

MISQUITH. My dear Aubrey!

JAYNE. I rejoice to hear you say so.

AUBREY. And I wanted to see the three of you round this table. You can't guess the reason.

MISQUITH. You desired to give us a most excellent dinner.

JAYNE. Obviously.

AUBREY (*hesitatingly*). Well—I—(*glancing at the clock*)—Cayley won't turn up now.

JAYNE. H'm, hardly.

AUBREY. Then you two shall hear it. Doctor, Frank, this is the last time we are to meet in these rooms.

JAYNE. The last time?

MISQUITH. You're going to leave the Albany?

AUBREY. Yes. You've heard me speak of a house I built in the country years ago, haven't you?

MISQUITH. In Surrey.

AUBREY. Well, when my wife died I cleared out of that house and let it. I think of trying the place again.

MISQUITH. But you'll go raving mad if ever you find yourself down there alone.

AUBREY. Ah, but I shan't be alone, and that's what I wanted to tell you. I'm going to be married.

JAYNE. Going to be married?

MISQUITH. Married?

AUBREY. Yes—to-morrow.

JAYNE. To-morrow?

MISQUITH. You take my breath away! My dear fellow, I—I—of course, I congratulate you.

JAYNE. And—and—so do I—heartily.

AUBREY. Thanks—thanks. (*There is a moment or two of embarrassment.*)

MISQUITH. Er—ah—this is an excellent cigar.

JAYNE. Ah—um—your coffee is remarkable.

AUBREY. Look here; I dare say you two old friends think this treatment very strange, very unkind. So I want you to understand me. You know a marriage often cools friendships. What's the usual course of things? A man's engagement is given out, he is congratulated, complimented upon his choice; the church is filled with troops of friends, and he goes away happily to a chorus of good wishes. He comes back, sets up house in town or country, and thinks to resume the old associations, the old companionships. My dear Frank, my dear good doctor, it's very seldom that it can be done. Generally, a worm has begun to eat its way into those hearty, unreserved, pre-nuptial friendships; a damnable constraint sets in and acts like a wasting disease; and so, believe me, in nine cases out of ten a man's marriage severs for him more close ties than it forms.

MISQUITH. Well, my dear Aubrey, I earnestly hope—

AUBREY. I know what you're going to say, Frank. I hope so, too. In the meantime let's face dangers. I've reminded you of the *usual* course of things, but my marriage isn't even the conventional sort of marriage likely to satisfy society. Now, Cayley's a bachelor, but you two men have wives. By the bye, my love to Mrs. Misquith and to Mrs. Jayne when you get home—don't forget that. Well, your wives may not —like—the lady I'm going to marry.

JAYNE. Aubrey, forgive me for suggesting that the lady you are going to marry may not like our wives—mine at least; I beg your pardon, Frank.

AUBREY. Quite so; then I must go the way my wife goes.

MISQUITH. Come, come, pray don't let us anticipate that either side will be called upon to make such a sacrifice.

AUBREY. Yes, yes, let us anticipate it. And let us make up our minds to have no slow bleeding to death of our friendship. We'll end a pleasant chapter here to-night, and after to-night start afresh. When my wife and I settle down at Willowmere it's possible that we shall all come together. But if this isn't to be, for Heaven's sake let us recognize that it is simply because it *can't* be, and not wear hypocritical faces and suffer and be wretched. Doctor, Frank—(*holding out his hands, one to* MISQUITH, *the other to* JAYNE)—good luck to all of us!

MISQUITH. But—but—do I understand we are to ask nothing? Not even the lady's name, Aubrey?

AUBREY. The lady, my dear Frank, belongs to the next chapter, and in that her name is Mrs. Aubrey Tanqueray.

JAYNE (*raising his coffee-cup*). Then, in an old-fashioned way, I propose a toast. Aubrey, Frank, I give you "The Next Chapter!" (*They drink the toast, saying, "The Next Chapter!"*)

AUBREY. Doctor, find a comfortable chair; Frank, you too. As we're going to turn out by and by, let me scribble a couple of notes now while I think of them.

MISQUITH AND JAYNE. Certainly—yes, yes.

AUBREY. It might slip my memory when I get back. (AUBREY *sits at a writing-table at the other end of the room, and writes.*)

JAYNE (*to* MISQUITH *in a whisper*). Frank—(MISQUITH *quietly leaves his chair, and sits nearer to* JAYNE.) What is all this? Simply a morbid crank of Aubrey's with regard to ante-nuptial acquaintances?

MISQUITH. H'm! Did you notice *one* expression he used?

JAYNE. Let me think—

MISQUITH. "My marriage is not even the conventional sort of marriage likely to satisfy society."

JAYNE. Bless me, yes! What does that suggest?

MISQUITH. That he has a particular rather than a general reason for anticipating estrangement from his friends, I'm afraid.

JAYNE. A horrible *mésalliance!* A dairy-maid who has given him a glass of milk during a day's hunting, or a little anæmic shop-girl! Frank, I'm utterly wretched!

MISQUITH. My dear Jayne, speaking in absolute confidence, I have never been more profoundly depressed in my life.

(MORSE *enters.*)

MORSE (*announcing*). Mr. Drummle.

(CAYLEY DRUMMLE *enters briskly. He is a neat little man of about five-and-forty, in manner bright, airy, debonair, but with an undercurrent of seriousness.* MORSE *retires.*)

DRUMMLE. I'm in disgrace; nobody realizes that more thoroughly than I do. Where's my host?

AUBREY (*who has risen*). Cayley.

DRUMMLE (*shaking hands with him*). Don't speak to me till I have tendered my explanation. A harsh word from anybody would unman me. (MISQUITH *and* JAYNE *shake hands with* DRUMMLE.)

AUBREY. Have you dined?

DRUMMLE. No—unless you call a bit of fish, a cutlet, and a pancake dining.

AUBREY. Cayley, this is disgraceful.

JAYNE. Fish, a cutlet, and a pancake will require a great deal of explanation.

MISQUITH. Especially the pancake. My dear friend, your case looks miserably weak.

DRUMMLE. Hear me! hear me!

JAYNE. Now then!

MISQUITH. Come!

AUBREY. Well!

DRUMMLE. It so happens that to-night I was exceptionally early in dressing for dinner.

MISQUITH. For which dinner—the fish and cutlet?

DRUMMLE. For *this* dinner, of course—really, Frank! At a quarter to eight, in fact, I found myself trimming my nails, with ten minutes to spare. Just then enter my man with a note—would I hasten, as fast as cab could carry me, to old Lady Orreyed in Bruton Street?—"sad trouble." Now, recollect, please, I had ten minutes on my hands, old Lady Orreyed was a very dear friend of my mother's, and was in some distress.

AUBREY. Cayley, come to the fish and cutlet!

MISQUITH AND JAYNE. Yes, yes, and the pancake!

DRUMMLE. Upon my word! Well, the scene in Bruton Street beggars description; the women servants looked scared, the men drunk; and there was poor old Lady Orreyed on the floor of her boudoir like Queen Bess among her pillows.

AUBREY. What's the matter?

DRUMMLE (*to everybody*). You know George Orreyed?

MISQUITH. Yes.

JAYNE. I've met him.

DRUMMLE. Well, he's a thing of the past.

AUBREY. Not dead!

DRUMMLE. Certainly, in the worst sense. He's married Mabel Hervey.

MISQUITH. What!

DRUMMLE. It's true—this morning. The poor mother showed me his letter—a dozen curt words, and some of those ill-spelt.

MISQUITH (*walking up to the fireplace*). I'm very sorry.

JAYNE. Pardon my ignorance—who *was* Mabel Hervey?

DRUMMLE. You don't—? Oh, of course not. Miss Hervey—Lady Orreyed, as she now is—was a lady who would have been, perhaps has been, described in the reports of the Police or the Divorce Court as an actress. Had she belonged to a lower stratum of our advanced civilization she would, in the event of judicial inquiry, have defined her calling with equal justification as that of a dressmaker. To do her justice, she is a type of a class which is immortal. Physically, by the strange caprice of creation, curiously beautiful; mentally, she lacks even the strength of deliberate viciousness. Paint her portrait, it would symbolize a creature perfectly patrician; lance a vein of her superbly-modelled arm, you would get the poorest *vin ordinaire!* Her affections, emotions, impulses, her very existence—a burlesque! Flaxen, five-and-twenty, and feebly frolicsome; anybody's, in less gentle society I should say everybody's, property! That, doctor, was Miss Hervey who is the new Lady Orreyed. Dost thou like the picture?

MISQUITH. Very good, Cayley! Bravo!

AUBREY (*laying his hand on* DRUMMLE'S *shoulder*). You'd scarcely believe it, Jayne, but none of us really know anything about this lady, our gay young friend here, I suspect, least of all.

DRUMMLE. Aubrey, I applaud your chivalry.

AUBREY. And perhaps you'll let me finish a couple of letters which Frank and Jayne have given me leave to write. (*Returning to the writing-*

table.) Ring for what you want, like a good fellow! (AUBREY *resumes his writing.*)

MISQUITH (*to* DRUMMLE). Still, the fish and the cutlet remain unexplained.

DRUMMLE. Oh, the poor old woman was so weak that I insisted upon her taking some food, and felt there was nothing for it but to sit down opposite her. The fool! the blackguard!

MISQUITH. Poor Orreyed! Well, he's gone under for a time.

DRUMMLE. For a time! My dear Frank, I tell you he has absolutely ceased to be. (AUBREY, *who has been writing busily, turns his head towards the speakers and listens. His lips are set, and there is a frown upon his face.*) For all practical purposes you may regard him as the late George Orreyed. To-morrow the very characteristics of his speech, as we remember them, will have become obsolete.

JAYNE. But surely, in the course of years, he and his wife will outlive—

DRUMMLE. No, no, doctor, don't try to upset one of my settled beliefs. You may dive into many waters, but there is *one* social Dead Sea—!

JAYNE. Perhaps you're right.

DRUMMLE. Right! Good God! I wish you could prove me otherwise! Why, for years I've been sitting, and watching and waiting.

MISQUITH. You're in form to-night, Cayley. May we ask where you've been in the habit of squandering your useful leisure?

DRUMMLE. Where? On the shore of that same sea.

MISQUITH. And, pray, what have you been waiting for?

DRUMMLE. For some of my best friends to come up. (AUBREY *utters a half-stifled exclamation of impatience; then he hurriedly gathers up his papers from the writing-table. The three men turn to him.*) Eh?

AUBREY. Oh, I—I'll finish my letters in the other room if you'll excuse me for five minutes. Tell Cayley the news. (*He goes out.*)

DRUMMLE (*hurrying to the door*). My dear fellow, my jabbering has disturbed you! I'll never talk again as long as I live!

MISQUITH. Close the door, Cayley. (DRUMMLE *shuts the door.*)

JAYNE. Cayley—

DRUMMLE (*advancing to the dinner table*). A smoke, a smoke, or I perish! (*Selects a cigar from the little cabinet.*)

JAYNE. Cayley, marriages are in the air.

DRUMMLE. Are they? Discover the bacillus, doctor, and destroy it.

JAYNE. I mean, among our friends.

DRUMMLE. Oh, Nugent Warrinder's engagement to Lady Alice Tring. I've heard of that. They're not to be married till the spring.

JAYNE. Another marriage that concerns us a little takes place to-morrow.

DRUMMLE. Whose marriage?

JAYNE. Aubrey's.

DRUMMLE. Aub—! (*Looking towards* MISQUITH.) Is it a joke?

MISQUITH. No.

DRUMMLE (*looking from* MISQUITH *to* JAYNE). To whom?

MISQUITH. He doesn't tell us.

JAYNE. We three were asked here to-night to receive the announcement. Aubrey has some theory that marriage is likely to alienate a man from his friends, and it seems to me he has taken the precaution to wish us good-bye.

MISQUITH. No, no.

JAYNE. Practically, surely.

DRUMMLE (*thoughtfully*). Marriage in general, does he mean, or *this* marriage?

JAYNE. That's the point. Frank says—

MISQUITH. No, no, no; I feared it suggested—

JAYNE. Well, well. (*To* DRUMMLE.) What do you think of it?

DRUMMLE (*after a slight pause*). Is there a light there? (*Lighting his cigar.*) He—wraps the lady—in mystery—you say?

MISQUITH. Most modestly.

DRUMMLE. Aubrey's—not—a very—young man.

JAYNE. Forty-three.

DRUMMLE. Ah! *L'âge critique!*

MISQUITH. A dangerous age—yes, yes.

DRUMMLE. When you two fellows go home, do you mind leaving me behind here?

MISQUITH. Not at all.

JAYNE. By all means.

DRUMMLE. All right. (*Anxiously.*) Deuce take it, the man's second marriage mustn't be another mistake! (*With his head bent he walks up to the fireplace.*)

JAYNE. You knew him in his short married life, Cayley. Terribly unsatisfactory, wasn't it?

DRUMMLE. Well—(*looking at the door*) I quite closed that door?

MISQUITH. Yes. (*Settles himself on the sofa;* JAYNE *is seated in an arm-chair.*)

DRUMMLE (*smoking with his back to the fire*). He married a Miss Herriott; that was in the year eighteen—confound dates—twenty years ago. She was a lovely creature—by Jove, she was; by religion a Roman Catholic. She was one of your cold sort, you know—all marble arms and black velvet. I remember her with painful distinctness as the only woman who ever made me nervous.

MISQUITH. Ha, ha!

DRUMMLE. He loved her—to distraction, as they say. Jupiter, how fervently that poor devil courted her! But I don't believe she allowed him even to squeeze her fingers. She *was* an iceberg! As for kissing, the mere contact would have given him chapped lips. However, he married her and took her away, the latter greatly to my relief.

JAYNE. Abroad, you mean?

DRUMMLE. Eh? Yes. I imagine he gratified her by renting a villa in Lapland, but I don't know. After a while they returned, and then I saw how woefully Aubrey had miscalculated results.

JAYNE. Miscalculated—?

DRUMMLE. He had reckoned, poor wretch, that in the early days of marriage she would thaw. But she didn't. I used to picture him closing his doors and making up the fire in the hope of seeing her features relax. Bless her, the thaw never set in! I believe she kept a thermometer in her stays and always registered ten degrees below zero. However, in time a child came—a daughter.

JAYNE. Didn't that—?

DRUMMLE. Not a bit of it; it made matters worse. Frightened at her failure to stir up in him some sympathetic religious belief, she determined upon strong measures with regard to the child. He opposed her for a miserable year or so, but she wore him down, and the insensible little brat was placed in a convent, first in France, then in Ireland. Not long afterwards the mother died, strangely enough, of fever, the only warmth, I believe, that ever came to that woman's body.

MISQUITH. Don't, Cayley!

JAYNE. The child is living, we know.

DRUMMLE. Yes, if you choose to call it living. Miss Tanqueray—a young woman of nineteen now—is in the Loretto convent at Armagh. She professes to have found her true vocation in a religious life, and within a month or two will take final vows.

MISQUITH. He ought to have removed his daughter from the convent when the mother died.

DRUMMLE. Yes, yes, but absolutely at the end there was reconciliation between husband and wife, and she won his promise that the child should complete her conventual education. He reaped his reward. When he attempted to gain his girl's confidence and affection he was too late; he found he was dealing with the spirit of the mother. You remember his visit to Ireland last month?

JAYNE. Yes.

DRUMMLE. That was to wish his girl good-bye.

MISQUITH. Poor fellow!

DRUMMLE. He sent for me when he came back. I think he must have had a lingering hope that the girl would relent—would come to life, as it were—at the last moment, for, for an hour or so, in this room, he was terribly shaken. I'm sure he'd clung to that hope from the persistent way in which he kept breaking off in his talk to repeat one dismal word, as if he couldn't realize his position without dinning this damned word into his head.

JAYNE. What word was that?

DRUMMLE. Alone—alone.

(AUBREY *enters.*)

AUBREY. A thousand apologies!

DRUMMLE (*gayly*). We are talking about you, my dear Aubrey. (*During the telling of the story,* MISQUITH *has risen and gone to the fire, and* DRUMMLE *has thrown himself full-length on the sofa.* AUBREY *now joins* MISQUITH *and* JAYNE.)

AUBREY. Well, Cayley, are you surprised?

DRUMMLE. Surp—! I haven't been surprised for twenty years.

AUBREY. And you're not angry with me?

DRUMMLE. Angry! (*Rising.*) Because you considerately withhold the name of a lady with whom it is now the object of my life to become acquainted? My dear fellow, you pique my curiosity, you give zest to my existence! And as for a wedding, who on earth wants to attend that familiar and probably draughty function? Ugh! My cigar's out.

AUBREY. Let's talk about something else.

MISQUITH (*looking at his watch*). Not to-night, Aubrey.

AUBREY. My dear Frank!

MISQUITH. I go up to Scotland to-morrow, and there are some little matters—

JAYNE. I am off too.

AUBREY. No, no.

JAYNE. I must: I have to give a look to a case in Clifford Street on my way home.

AUBREY (*going to the door*). Well! (MISQUITH *and* JAYNE *exchange looks with* DRUMMLE. *Opening the door and calling.*) Morse, hats and coats! I shall write to you all next week from Genoa or Florence. Now, doctor, Frank, remember, my love to Mrs. Misquith and to Mrs. Jayne!

(MORSE *enters with hats and coats.*)

MISQUITH *and* JAYNE. Yes, yes—yes, yes.

AUBREY. And your young people! (*As* MISQUITH *and* JAYNE *put on their coats there is the clatter of careless talk.*)

JAYNE. Cayley, I meet you at dinner on Sunday.

DRUMMLE. At the Stratfields'. That's very pleasant.

MISQUITH (*putting on his coat with* AUBREY'S *aid*). Ah-h!

AUBREY. What's wrong?

MISQUITH. A twinge. Why didn't I go to Aix in August?

JAYNE (*shaking hands with* DRUMMLE). Good-night, Cayley.

DRUMMLE. Good-night, my dear doctor!

MISQUITH (*shaking hands with* DRUMMLE). Cayley, are you in town for long?

DRUMMLE. Dear friend, I'm nowhere for long. Good-night.

MISQUITH. Good-night. (AUBREY, JAYNE, *and* MISQUITH *go out, followed by* MORSE; *the hum of talk is continued outside.*)

AUBREY. A cigar, Frank.

MISQUITH. No, thank you.

AUBREY. Going to walk, doctor?

JAYNE. If Frank will.

MISQUITH. By all means.

AUBREY. It's a cold night. (*The door is closed.* DRUMMLE *remains standing with his coat on his arm and his hat in his hand.*)

DRUMMLE (*to himself, thoughtfully*). Now then! What the devil—

(AUBREY *returns.*)

AUBREY (*eyeing* DRUMMLE *a little awkwardly*). Well, Cayley?

DRUMMLE. Well, Aubrey? (AUBREY *walks up to the fire and stands looking into it.*)

AUBREY. You're not going, old chap?

DRUMMLE (*sitting*). No.

AUBREY (*after a slight pause, with a forced laugh*). Hah, Cayley, I never thought I should feel—shy—with you.

DRUMMLE. Why do you?

AUBREY. Never mind.

DRUMMLE. Now, I can quite understand a man wishing to be married in the dark, as it were.

AUBREY. You can?

DRUMMLE. In your place I should very likely adopt the same course.

AUBREY. You think so?

DRUMMLE. And if I intended marrying a lady not prominently in society, as I presume you do—as I presume you do—

AUBREY. Well?

DRUMMLE. As I presume you do, I'm not sure that *I* should tender her for preliminary dissection at afternoon tea-tables.

AUBREY. No?

DRUMMLE. In fact, there is probably only one person—were I in your position to-night—with whom I should care to chat the matter over.

AUBREY. Who's that?

DRUMMLE. Yourself, of course. (*Going to* AUBREY *and standing beside him.*) Of course, yourself, old friend.

AUBREY (*after a pause*). I must seem a brute to you, Cayley. But there are some acts which are hard to explain, hard to defend—

DRUMMLE. To defend—

AUBREY. Some acts which one must trust to time to put right. (DRUMMLE *watches him for a moment, then takes up his hat and coat.*)

DRUMMLE. Well, I'll be moving.

AUBREY. Cayley! Confound you and your old friendship! Do you think I forget it? Put your coat down! Why did you stay behind here? Cayley, the lady I am going to marry is the lady—who is known as—Mrs. Jarman. (*There is a pause.*)

DRUMMLE (*in a low voice*). Mrs. Jarman! are you serious? (*He walks to the fireplace, where he leans upon the mantelpiece uttering something like a groan.*)

AUBREY. As you've got this out of me I give you leave to say all you care to say. Come, we'll be plain with each other. You know Mrs. Jarman?

DRUMMLE. I first met her at—what does it matter?

AUBREY. Yes, yes, everything! Come!

DRUMMLE. I met her at Homburg, two—three seasons ago.

AUBREY. Not as Mrs. Jarman?

DRUMMLE. No.

AUBREY. She was then—?

DRUMMLE. Mrs. Dartry.

AUBREY. Yes. She has also seen you in London, she says.

DRUMMLE. Certainly.

AUBREY. In Alford Street. Go on.

DRUMMLE. Please!

AUBREY. I insist.

DRUMMLE (*with a slight shrug of the shoulders*). Some time last year I was asked by a man to sup at his house, one night after the theater.

AUBREY. Mr. Selwyn Ethurst—a bachelor.

DRUMMLE. Yes.

AUBREY. You were surprised therefore to find Mr. Ethurst aided in his cursed hospitality by a lady.

DRUMMLE. I was unprepared.

AUBREY. The lady you had known as Mrs. Dartry? (DRUMMLE *inclines his head silently.*) There is something of a yachting cruise in the Mediterranean, too, is there not?

DRUMMLE. I joined Peter Jarman's yacht at Marseilles, in the Spring, a month before he died.

AUBREY. Mrs. Jarman was on board?

DRUMMLE. She was a kind hostess.

AUBREY. And an old acquaintance?

DRUMMLE. Yes.

AUBREY. You have told your story.

DRUMMLE. With your assistance.

AUBREY. I have put you to the pain of telling it to show you that this is not the case of a blind man entrapped by an artful woman. Let me add that Mrs. Jarman has no legal right to that name; that she is simply Miss Ray—Miss Paula Ray.

DRUMMLE (*after a pause*). I should like to express my regret, Aubrey, for the way in which I spoke of George Orreyed's marriage.

AUBREY. You mean you compare Lady Orreyed with Miss Ray? (DRUMMLE *is silent.*) Oh, of course! To you, Cayley, all women who have been roughly treated, and who dare to survive by borrowing a little of our philosophy, are alike. You see in the crowd of the ill-used only one pattern; you can't detect the shades of goodness, intelligence, even nobility there. Well, how should you? The crowd is dimly lighted! And, besides, yours is the way of the world.

DRUMMLE. My dear Aubrey, I *live* in the world.

AUBREY. The name we give our little parish of St. James's.

DRUMMLE (*laying a hand on* AUBREY'S *shoulder*). And you are quite prepared, my friend, to forfeit the esteem of your little parish?

AUBREY. I avoid mortification by shifting from one parish to another. I give up Pall Mall for the Surrey hills; leave off varnishing my boots, and double the thickness of the soles.

DRUMMLE. And your skin—do you double the thickness of that also?

AUBREY. I know you think me a fool, Cayley—you needn't infer that I'm a coward into the bargain. No! I know what I'm doing, and I do it deliberately, defiantly. I'm alone: I injure no living soul by the step I'm going to take; and so you can't urge the one argument which might restrain me. Of course, I don't expect you to think compassionately, fairly even, of the woman whom I—whom I am drawn to—

DRUMMLE. My dear Aubrey, I assure you I consider Mrs.—Miss Jarman—Mrs. Ray—Miss Ray—delightful. But I confess there is a form of chivalry which I gravely distrust, especially in a man of—our age.

AUBREY. Thanks. I've heard you say that from forty till fifty a man is at heart either a stoic or a satyr.

DRUMMLE (*protestingly*). Ah! now—

AUBREY. I am neither. I have a temperate, honorable affection for Mrs. Jarman. She has never met a man who has treated her well—I intend to treat her well. That's all. And in a few years, Cayley, if you've not quite forsaken me, I'll prove to you that it's possible to rear a life of happiness, of good repute, on a—miserable foundation.

DRUMMLE (*offering his hand*). Do prove it!

AUBREY (*taking his hand*). We have spoken too freely of—of Mrs. Jarman. I was excited—angry. Please forget it!

DRUMMLE. My dear Aubrey, when we next meet I shall remember nothing but my respect for the lady who bears your name.

(MORSE *enters, closing the door behind him carefully.*)

AUBREY. What is it?

MORSE (*hesitatingly*). May I speak to you, sir? (*In an undertone.*) Mrs. Jarman, sir.

AUBREY (*softly to* MORSE). Mrs. Jarman! Do you mean she is at the lodge in her carriage?

MORSE. No, sir—here. (AUBREY *looks towards* DRUMMLE, *perplexed.*) There's a nice fire in your—in that room, sir. (*Glancing in the direction of the door leading to the bedroom.*)

AUBREY (*between his teeth, angrily*). Very well. (MORSE *retires.*)

DRUMMLE (*looking at his watch*). A quarter to eleven—horrible! (*Taking up his hat and coat.*) Must get to bed—up late every night this week. (AUBREY *assists* DRUMMLE *with his coat.*) Thank you. Well, good-night, Aubrey. I feel I've been dooced serious, quite out of keeping with myself; pray overlook it.

AUBREY (*kindly*). Ah, Cayley!

DRUMMLE (*putting on a neck-handkerchief*). And remember that, after all, I'm merely a spectator in life; nothing more than a man at a play, in fact; only, like the old-fashioned play goer, I love to see certain characters happy and comfortable at the finish. You understand?

AUBREY. I think I do.

DRUMMLE. Then, for as long as you can, old friend, will you—keep a stall for me?

AUBREY. Yes, Cayley.

DRUMMLE (*gayly*). Ah, ha! Good-night! (*Bustling to the door.*) Don't bother! I'll let myself out! Good-night! God bless yer! (*He goes out;* AUBREY *follows him.* MORSE *enters by the other door, carrying some unopened letters, which after a little consideration he places on the mantelpiece against the clock.* AUBREY *returns.*)

AUBREY. Yes?

MORSE. You hadn't seen your letters that came by the nine o'clock post, sir; I've put 'em where they'll catch your eye by and by.

AUBREY. Thank you.

MORSE (*hesitatingly*). Gunter's cook and waiter have gone, sir. Would you prefer me to go to bed?

AUBREY (*frowning*). Certainly not.

MORSE. Very well, sir. (*He goes out.*)

AUBREY (*opening the upper door*). Paula! Paula!

(PAULA *enters and throws her arms round his neck. She is a young woman of about twenty-seven: beautiful, fresh, innocent-looking. She is in superb evening dress.*)

PAULA. Dearest!

AUBREY. Why have you come here?

PAULA. Angry?

AUBREY. Yes—no. But it's eleven o'clock.

PAULA (*laughing*). I know.

AUBREY. What on earth will Morse think?

PAULA. Do you trouble yourself about what servants *think*?

AUBREY. Of course.

PAULA. Goose! They're only machines made to wait upon people—and to give evidence in the Divorce Court. (*Looking round.*) Oh, indeed! A snug little dinner!

AUBREY. Three men.

PAULA (*suspiciously*). Men?

AUBREY. Men.

PAULA (*penitently*). Ah! (*Sitting at the table.*) I'm so hungry.

AUBREY. Let me get you some game pie, or some—

PAULA. No, no, hungry for this. What beautiful fruit! I love fruit when it's expensive. (*He clears a space on the table, places a plate before her, and helps her to fruit.*) I haven't dined, Aubrey dear.

AUBREY. My poor girl! Why?

PAULA. In the first place, I forgot to order any dinner, and my cook, who has always loathed me, thought he'd pay me out before he departed.

AUBREY. The beast!

PAULA. That's precisely what I—

AUBREY. No, Paula!

PAULA. What I told my maid to call him. What next will you think of me?

AUBREY. Forgive me. You must be starved.

PAULA (*eating fruit*). I didn't care. As there was nothing to eat, I sat in my best frock, with my toes on the dining-room fender, and dreamt, oh, such a lovely dinner party.

AUBREY. Dear lonely little woman!

PAULA. It was perfect. I saw you at the end of a very long table, opposite me, and we exchanged sly glances now and again over the flowers. We were host and hostess, Aubrey, and had been married about five years.

AUBREY (*kissing her hand*). Five years.

PAULA. And on each side of us was the nicest set imaginable—you know, dearest, the sort of men and women that can't be imitated.

AUBREY. Yes, yes. Eat some more fruit.

PAULA. But I haven't told you the best part of my dream.

AUBREY. Tell me.

PAULA. Well, although we had been married only such a few years, I seemed to know by the look on their faces that none of our guests had ever heard anything—anything—anything peculiar about the fascinating hostess.

AUBREY. That's just how it will be, Paula. The world moves so quickly. That's just how it will be.

PAULA (*with a little grimace*). I wonder! (*Glancing at the fire.*) Ugh! Do throw another log on.

AUBREY (*mending the fire*). There. But you mustn't be here long.

PAULA. Hospitable wretch! I've something important to tell you. No, stay where you are. (*Turning from him, her face averted.*) Look here, that was my dream, Aubrey; but the fire went out while I was dozing, and I woke up with a regular fit of the shivers. And the result of it all was that I ran upstairs and scribbled you a letter.

AUBREY. Dear baby!

PAULA. Remain where you are. (*Taking a letter from her pocket.*) This is it. I've given you an account of myself, furnished you with a list of my adventures since I—you know. (*Weighing the letter in her hand.*) I wonder if it would go for a penny. Most of it you're acquainted with; *I've* told you a good deal, haven't I?

AUBREY. Oh, Paula!

PAULA. What I haven't told you I dare say you've heard from others. But in case they've omitted anything—the dears—it's all here.

AUBREY. In Heaven's name, why must you talk like this to-night?

PAULA. It may save discussion by and by, don't you think? (*Holding out the letter.*) There you are.

AUBREY. No, dear, no.

PAULA. Take it. (*He takes the letter.*) Read it through after I've gone, and then—read it again, and turn the matter over in your mind finally. And if, even at the very last moment, you feel you—oughtn't to go to church with me, send a messenger to Pont Street, any time before eleven to-morrow, telling me that you're afraid, and I—I'll take the blow.

AUBREY. Why, what—what do you think I am?

PAULA. That's it. It's because I know you're such a dear good fellow that I want to save you the chance of ever feeling sorry you married me. I really love you so much, Aubrey, that to save you that, I'd rather you treated me as—as the others have done.

AUBREY (*turning from her with a cry*). Oh!

PAULA (*after a slight pause*). I suppose I've shocked you. I can't help it if I have. (*She sits with assumed languor and indifference. He turns to her, advances, and kneels by her.*)

AUBREY. My dearest, you don't understand me. I—I can't bear to hear you always talking about—what's done with. I tell you I'll never remember it; Paula, can't you dismiss it? Try. Darling, if we promise each other to forget, to forget, we're bound to be happy. After all, it's a mechanical matter; the moment a wretched thought enters your head, you quickly think of something bright—it depends on one's will. Shall I burn this, dear? (*Referring to the letter he holds in his hand.*) Let me, let me!

PAULA (*with a shrug of the shoulders*). I don't suppose there's much that's new to you in it,—just as you like. (*He goes to the fire and burns the letter.*)

AUBREY. There's an end of it. (*Returning to her.*) What's the matter?

PAULA (*rising coldly*). Oh, nothing! I'll go and put my cloak on.

AUBREY (*detaining her*). What *is* the matter?

PAULA. Well, I think you might have said, "You're very generous, Paula," or at least, "Thank you, dear," when I offered to set you free.

AUBREY (*catching her in his arms*). Ah!

PAULA. Ah! ah! Ha! ha! It's all very well, but you don't know what it cost me to make such an offer. I do so want to be married.

AUBREY. But you never imagined—?

PAULA. Perhaps not. And yet I *did* think of what I'd do at the end of our acquaintance if you had preferred to behave like the rest. (*Taking a flower from her bodice.*)

AUBREY. Hush!

PAULA. Oh, I forgot!

AUBREY. What would you have done when we parted?

PAULA. Why, killed myself.

AUBREY. Paula, dear!

PAULA. It's true. (*Putting the flower in his buttonhole.*) Do you know, I feel certain I should make away with myself if anything serious happened to me.

AUBREY. Anything serious! What, has nothing ever been serious to you, Paula?

PAULA. Not lately; not since a long while ago. I made up my mind then to have done with taking things seriously. If I hadn't, I—However, we won't talk about that.

AUBREY. But now, now, life will be different to you, won't it—quite different? Eh, dear?

PAULA. Oh, yes, now. Only, Aubrey, mind you keep me always happy.

AUBREY. I will try to.

PAULA. I know I couldn't swallow a second big dose of misery. I know that if ever I felt wretched again—truly wretched—I should take a leaf out of Connie Tirlemont's book. You remember? They found her—(*With a look of horror.*)

AUBREY. For God's sake, don't let your thoughts run on such things!

PAULA (*laughing*). Ha, ha, how scared you look! There, think of the time! Dearest, what will my coachman say? My cloak! (*She runs off, gayly, by the upper door.* AUBREY *looks after her for a moment, then he walks up to the fire and stands warming his feet at the bars. As he does so he raises his head and observes the letters upon the mantelpiece. He takes one down quickly.*)

AUBREY. Ah! Ellean! (*Opening the letter and reading.*) "My dear father,

—A great change has come over me. I believe my mother in Heaven has spoken to me, and counseled me to turn to you in your loneliness. At any rate, your words have reached my heart, and I no longer feel fitted for this solemn life. I am ready to take my place by you. Dear father, will you receive me?—ELLEAN."

(PAULA *re-enters, dressed in a handsome cloak. He stares at her as if he hardly realized her presence.*)

PAULA. What are you staring at? Don't you admire my cloak?

AUBREY. Yes.

PAULA. Couldn't you wait till I'd gone before reading your letters?

AUBREY (*putting the letter away*). I beg your pardon.

PAULA. Take me downstairs to the carriage. (*Slipping her arm through his.*) How I tease you! To-morrow! I'm so happy! (*They go out.*)

ACT II

A morning-room in AUBREY TANQUERAY'S *house, "Highercoombe," near Willowmere, Surrey—a bright and prettily furnished apartment of irregular shape, with double doors opening into a small hall at the back, another door on the left, and a large recessed window through which is obtained a view of extensive grounds. Everything about the room is charming and graceful. The fire is burning in the grate, and a small table is tastefully laid for breakfast. It is a morning in early spring, and the sun is streaming in through the window.*

(AUBREY *and* PAULA *are seated at breakfast, and* AUBREY *is silently reading his letters. Two servants, a man and a woman, hand dishes and then retire. After a little while* AUBREY *puts his letters aside and looks across to the window.*)

AUBREY. Sunshine! Spring!

PAULA (*glancing at the clock*). Exactly six minutes.

AUBREY. Six minutes?

PAULA. Six minutes, Aubrey dear, since you made your last remark.

AUBREY. I beg your pardon: I was reading my letters. Have you seen Ellean this morning?

PAULA (*coldly*). Your last observation but one was about Ellean.

AUBREY. Dearest, what shall I talk about?

PAULA. Ellean breakfasted two hours ago, Morgan tells me, and then went out walking with her dog.

AUBREY. She wraps up warmly, I hope; this sunshine is deceptive.

PAULA. I ran about the lawn last night, after dinner, in satin shoes. Were you anxious about me?

AUBREY. Certainly.

PAULA (*melting*). Really.

AUBREY. You make me wretchedly anxious; you delight in doing incautious things. You are incurable.

PAULA. Ah, what a beast I am! (*Going to him and kissing him, then glancing at the letters by his side.*) A letter from Cayley?

AUBREY. He is staying very near here, with Mrs.——Very near here.

PAULA. With the lady whose chimneys we have the honor of contemplating from our windows?

AUBREY. With Mrs. Cortelyon—Yes.

PAULA. Mrs. Cortelyon! The woman who might have set the example of calling on me when we first threw out roots in this deadly-lively soil! Deuce take Mrs. Cortelyon!

AUBREY. Hush! my dear girl!

PAULA (*returning to her seat*). Oh, I know she's an old acquaintance of yours—and of the first Mrs. Tanqueray. And she joins the rest of 'em in slapping the second Mrs. Tanqueray in the face. However, I have my revenge—she's six-and-forty, and I wish nothing worse to happen to any woman.

AUBREY. Well, she's going to town, Cayley says here, and his visit's at an end. He's coming over this morning to call on you. Shall we ask him to transfer himself to us? Do say yes.

PAULA. Yes.

AUBREY (*gladly*). Ah, ha! old Cayley.

PAULA (*coldly*). He'll amuse *you*.

AUBREY. And you too.

PAULA. Because you find a companion, shall I be boisterously hilarious?

AUBREY. Come, come! He talks London, and you know you like that.

PAULA. London! London or Heaven! which is farther from me!

AUBREY. Paula!

PAULA. Oh! Oh, I am so bored, Aubrey!

AUBREY (*gathering up his letters and going to her, leaning over her shoulder*). Baby, what can I do for you?

PAULA. I suppose, nothing. You have done all you can for me.

AUBREY. What do you mean?

PAULA. You have married me. (*He walks away from her thoughtfully, to the writing table. As he places his letters on the table he sees an addressed letter, stamped for the post, lying on the blotting-book; he picks it up.*)

AUBREY (*in an altered tone*). You've been writing this morning before breakfast?

PAULA (*looking at him quickly, then away again*). Er—that letter.

AUBREY (*with the letter in his hand*). To Lady Orreyed. Why?

PAULA. Why not? Mabel's an old friend of mine.

AUBREY. Are you—corresponding?

PAULA. I heard from her yesterday. They've just returned from the Riviera. She seems happy.

AUBREY (*sarcastically*). That's good news.

PAULA. Why are you always so cutting about Mabel? She's a kind-hearted girl. Everything's altered; she even thinks of letting her hair go back to brown. She's Lady Orreyed. She's married to George. What's the matter with her?

AUBREY (*turning away*). Oh!

PAULA. You drive me mad sometimes with the tone you take about things! Great goodness, if you come to that, George Orreyed's wife isn't a bit worse than yours! (*He faces her suddenly.*) I suppose I needn't have made that observation.

AUBREY. No, there was scarcely a necessity. (*He throws the letter on to the table, and takes up the newspaper.*)

PAULA. I am very sorry.

AUBREY. All right, dear.

PAULA (*trifling with the letter*). I—I'd better tell you what I've written. I meant to do so, of course. I—I've asked the Orreyeds to come and stay with us. (*He looks at her, and lets the paper fall to the ground in a helpless way.*) George was a great friend of Cayley's; I'm sure *he* would be delighted to meet them here.

AUBREY (*laughing mirthlessly*). Ha, ha, ha! They say Orreyed has taken to tippling at dinner. Heavens above!

PAULA. Oh! I've no patience with you! You'll kill me with this life! (*She selects some flowers from a vase on the table, cuts and arranges them, and fastens them in her bodice.*) What is my existence, Sunday to Saturday? In the morning, a drive down to the village, with the groom, to give my orders to the tradespeople. At lunch, you and Ellean. In the afternoon, a novel, the newspapers; if fine, another drive—*if* fine! Tea—you and Ellean. Then two hours of dusk; then dinner—you and Ellean. Then a game of Bésique, you and I, while Ellean reads a religious book in a dull corner. Then a yawn from me, another from you, a sigh from Ellean; three figures suddenly rise—"Good-night, good-night, good-night!" (*Imitating a kiss.*) "God bless you!" Ah!

AUBREY. Yes, yes, Paula—yes, dearest—that's what it is *now*. But by and by, if people begin to come round us—

PAULA. Hah! That's where we've made the mistake, my friend Aubrey! (*Pointing to the window.*) Do you believe these people will *ever* come round us? Your former crony, Mrs. Cortelyon? Or the grim old vicar, or that wife of his whose huge nose is positively indecent? Or the Ullathornes, or the Gollans, or Lady William Petres? I know better! And when the young ones gradually take the place of the old, there will still remain the sacred tradition that the dreadful person who lives at the top of the hill is never, under any circumstances, to be called upon! And so we shall go on here, year in and year out, until the sap is run out of our lives, and we're stale and dry and withered from sheer, solitary respectability. Upon my word, I wonder we didn't see that we should have been far happier if we'd gone in for the devil-may-care, café-living sort of life in town! After all, *I* have a set, and you might have joined it. It's true, I did want, dearly, dearly, to be a married woman, but where's the pride in being a married woman among married women who are—married! If—(*Seeing that* AUBREY'S *head has sunk into his hands.*) Aubrey! My dear boy! You're not—crying?

(*He looks up, with a flushed face.* ELLEAN *enters, dressed very simply for walking. She is a low-voiced, grave girl of about nineteen, with a face somewhat resembling a Madonna. Towards* PAULA *her manner is cold and distant.*)

AUBREY (*in an undertone*). Ellean!

ELLEAN. Good-morning, papa. Good-morning, Paula. (PAULA *puts her arms round* ELLEAN *and kisses her.* ELLEAN *makes little response.*)

PAULA. Good-morning. (*Brightly.*) We've been breakfasting this side of the house, to get the sun. (*She sits at the piano and rattles at a gay melody. Seeing that* PAULA'S *back is turned to them,* ELLEAN *goes to* AUBREY *and kisses him; he returns the kiss almost furtively. As they separate, the servants re-enter, and proceed to carry out the breakfast table.*)

AUBREY (*to* ELLEAN). I guess where you've been: there's some gorse clinging to your frock.

ELLEAN (*removing a sprig of gorse from her skirt*). Rover and I walked nearly as far as Black Moor. The poor fellow has a thorn in his pad; I am going upstairs for my tweezers.

AUBREY. Ellean! (*She returns to him.*) Paula is a little depressed—out of sorts. She complains that she has no companion.

ELLEAN. I am with Paula nearly all the day, papa.

AUBREY. Ah, but you're such a little mouse. Paula likes cheerful people about her.

ELLEAN. I'm afraid I am naturally rather silent; and it's so difficult to seem to be what one is not.

AUBREY. I don't wish that, Ellean.

ELLEAN. I will offer to go down to the village with Paula this morning—shall I?

AUBREY (*touching her hand gently*). Thank you—do.

ELLEAN. When I've looked after Rover, I'll come back to her. (*She goes out;* PAULA *ceases playing, and turns on the music-stool, looking at* AUBREY.)

PAULA. Well, have you and Ellean had your little confidence?

AUBREY. Confidence?

PAULA. Do you think I couldn't feel it, like a pain between my shoulders?

AUBREY. Ellean is coming back in a few minutes to be with you. (*Bending over her.*) Paula, Paula dear, is this how you keep your promise?

PAULA. Oh! (*Rising impatiently, and crossing swiftly to the settee, where she sits; moving restlessly.*) I *can't* keep my promise; I *am* jealous; it won't be smothered. I see you looking at her, watching her; your voice drops when you speak to her. I know how fond you are of that girl, Aubrey.

AUBREY. What would you have? I've no other home for her. She is my daughter.

PAULA. She is your saint. Saint Ellean!

AUBREY. You have often told me how good and sweet you think her.

PAULA. Good!—Yes! Do you imagine *that* makes me less jealous? (*Going to him and clinging to his arm.*) Aubrey, there are two sorts of affection—the love for a woman you respect, and the love for the woman you—love. She gets the first from you: I never can.

AUBREY. Hush, hush! you don't realize what you say.

PAULA. If Ellean cared for me only a little, it would be different. I shouldn't be jealous then. Why doesn't she care for me?

AUBREY. She—she—she will, in time.

PAULA. You can't say that without stuttering.

AUBREY. Her disposition seems a little unresponsive; she resembles her mother in many ways; I can see it every day.

PAULA. She's marble. It's a shame. There's not the slightest excuse; for all she knows, I'm as much a saint as she—only married. Dearest, help me to win her over!

AUBREY. Help you?

PAULA. You can. Teach her that it is her duty to love me; she hangs on to every word you speak. I'm sure, Aubrey, that the love of a nice woman who believed me to be like herself would do me a world of good. You'd get the benefit of it as well as I. It would soothe me; it would make me less horribly restless; it would take this—this—mischievous feeling from me. (*Coaxingly.*) Aubrey!

AUBREY. Have patience; everything will come right.

PAULA. Yes, if you help me.

AUBREY. In the meantime you will tear up your letter to Lady Orreyed, won't you?

PAULA (*kissing his hand*). Of course I will—anything!

AUBREY. Ah, thank you, dearest! (*Laughing.*) Why, good gracious! —ha, ha!—just imagine "Saint Ellean" and that woman side by side!

PAULA (*going back with a cry*). Ah!

AUBREY. What?

PAULA (*passionately*). It's Ellean you're considering, not me! It's all Ellean with you! Ellean! Ellean!

(ELLEAN *re-enters.*)

ELLEAN. Did you call me, Paula? (*Clenching his hands,* AUBREY *turns away and goes out.*) Is papa angry?

PAULA. I drive him distracted, sometimes. There, I confess it!

ELLEAN. Do you? Oh, why do you!

PAULA. Because I—because I'm jealous.

ELLEAN. Jealous?

PAULA. Yes—of you. (ELLEAN *is silent.*) Well, what do you think of that?

ELLEAN. I knew it; I've seen it. It hurts me dreadfully. What do you wish me to do? Go away?

PAULA. Leave us! (*Beckoning her with a motion of the head.*) Look here! (ELLEAN *goes to* PAULA *slowly and unresponsively.*) You can cure me of my jealousy very easily. Why don't you—like me?

ELLEAN. What do you mean by—like you? I don't understand.

PAULA. Love me.

ELLEAN. Love is not a feeling that is under one's control. I shall alter as time goes on, perhaps. I didn't begin to love my father deeply till a few months ago, and then I obeyed my mother.

PAULA. Ah, yes, you dream things, don't you—see them in your sleep? You fancy your mother speaks to you?

ELLEAN. When you have lost your mother it is a comfort to believe that she is dead only to this life, that she still watches over her child. I do believe that of my mother.

PAULA. Well, and so you haven't been bidden to love *me?*

ELLEAN (*after a pause, almost inaudibly*). No.

PAULA. Dreams are only a hash-up of one's day-thoughts, I suppose you know. Think intently of anything, and it's bound to come back to you at night. I don't cultivate dreams myself.

ELLEAN. Ah, I knew you would only sneer!

PAULA. I'm not sneering; I'm speaking the truth. I say that if you cared for me in the daytime I should soon make friends with those nightmares of yours. Ellean, why don't you try to look on me as your second mother? Of course there are not many years between us, but I'm ever so much older than you—in experience. I shall have no children of my own, I know that; it would be a real comfort to me if you would make me feel we belonged to each other. Won't you? Perhaps you think I'm odd—not nice. Well, the fact is I've two sides to my nature, and I've let the one almost smother the other. A few years ago I went through some trouble, and since then I haven't shed a tear. I believe if you put your arms around me just once I should run upstairs and have a good cry. There, I've talked to you as I've never talked to a woman in my life. Ellean, you seem to fear me. Don't! Kiss me! (*With a cry, almost of despair,* ELLEAN *turns from* PAULA *and sinks on to the settee, covering her face with her hands.*)

PAULA (*indignantly*). Oh! Why is it! How dare you treat me like this? What do you mean by it? What do you mean?

(*A* SERVANT *enters.*)

SERVANT. Mr. Drummle, ma'am.

(CAYLEY DRUMMLE, *in riding-dress, enters briskly. The* SERVANT *retires.*)

PAULA (*recovering herself*). Well, Cayley!

DRUMMLE (*shaking hands with her cordially*). How are you? (*Shaking hands with* ELLEAN, *who rises.*) I saw you in the distance an hour ago, in the gorse near Stapleton's.

ELLEAN. I didn't see you, Mr. Drummle.

DRUMMLE. My dear Ellean, it is my experience that no charming young lady of nineteen ever does see a man of forty-five. (*Laughing.*) Ha, ha!

ELLEAN (*going to the door*). Paula, papa wishes me to drive down to the village with you this morning. Do you care to take me?

PAULA (*coldly*). Oh, by all means. Pray tell Watts to balance the cart for three. (ELLEAN *goes out.*)

DRUMMLE. How's Aubrey?

PAULA. Very well—when Ellean's about the house.

DRUMMLE. And you? I needn't ask.

PAULA (*walking away to the window*). Oh, a dog's life, my dear Cayley, mine.

DRUMMLE. Eh?

PAULA. Doesn't that define a happy marriage? I'm sleek, well-kept, well-fed, never without a bone to gnaw and fresh straw to lie upon. (*Gazing out of the window.*) Oh, dear me!

DRUMMLE. H'm! Well, I heartily congratulate you on your kennel. The view from the terrace here is superb.

PAULA. Yes; I can see London.

DRUMMLE. London! Not quite so far, surely?

PAULA. *I* can. Also the Mediterranean, on a fine day. I wonder what Algiers looks like this morning from the sea! (*Impulsively.*) Oh, Cayley, do you remember those jolly times on board Peter Jarman's yacht when we lay off—? (*Stopping suddenly, seeing* DRUMMLE *staring at her.*) Good gracious! What are we talking about!

(AUBREY *enters.*)

AUBREY (*to* DRUMMLE). Dear old chap! Has Paula asked you?

PAULA. Not yet.

AUBREY. We want you to come to us, now that you're leaving Mrs. Cortelyon—at once, to-day. Stay a month, as long as you please—eh, Paula?

PAULA. As long as you can possibly endure it—do, Cayley.

DRUMMLE (*looking at* AUBREY). Delighted. (*To* PAULA.) Charming of you to have me.

PAULA. My dear man, you're a blessing. I must telegraph to London for more fish! A strange appetite to cater for! Something to do, to do, to do! (*She goes out in a mood of almost childish delight.*)

DRUMMLE (*eyeing* AUBREY). Well?

AUBREY (*with a wearied, anxious look*). Well, Cayley?

DRUMMLE. How are you getting on?

AUBREY. My position doesn't grow less difficult. I told you, when I met you last week, of this feverish, jealous attachment of Paula's for Ellean?

DRUMMLE. Yes. I hardly know why, but I came to the conclusion that you don't consider it an altogether fortunate attachment.

AUBREY. Ellean doesn't respond to it.

DRUMMLE. These are early days. Ellean will warm towards your wife by and by.

AUBREY. Ah, but there's the question, Cayley!

DRUMMLE. What question?

AUBREY. The question which positively distracts me. Ellean is so different from—most women; I don't believe a purer creature exists out of heaven. And I—I ask myself, am I doing right in exposing her to the influence of poor Paula's light, careless nature?

DRUMMLE. My dear Aubrey!

AUBREY. That shocks you! So it does me. I assure you I long to urge my girl to break down the reserve which keeps her apart from Paula, but somehow I can't do it—well, I don't do it. How can I make you understand? But when you come to us you'll understand quickly enough. Cayley, there's hardly a subject you can broach on which poor Paula hasn't some strange, out-of-the-way thought to give utterance to; some curious, warped notion. They are not mere worldly thoughts—unless, good God! they belong to the little hellish world which our blackguardism has created: no, her ideas have too little calculation in them to be called worldly. But it makes it more dreadful that such thoughts should be ready, spontaneous; that expressing them has become a perfectly natural process; that her words, acts even, have almost lost their proper significance for her, and seem beyond her control. Ah, and the pain of listening to it all from the woman one loves, the woman one hoped to make happy and contented, who is really and truly a good woman, as it were, maimed! Well, this is my burden, and I shouldn't speak to you of it but for my anxiety about Ellean. Ellean! What is to be her future? It is in my hands; what am I to do? Cayley, when I remember how Ellean comes to me, from another world I always think, —when I realize the charge that's laid on me, I find myself wishing, in a sort of terror, that my child were safe under the ground!

DRUMMLE. My dear Aubrey, aren't you making a mistake?

AUBREY. Very likely. What is it?

DRUMMLE. A mistake, not in regarding your Ellean as an angel, but in believing that, under any circumstances, it would be possible for her to go through life without getting her white robe—shall we say, a little dusty at the hem? Don't take me for a cynic. I am sure there are many women upon earth who are almost divinely innocent; but being on earth, they must send their robes to the laundry occasionally. Ah, and it's right that they should have to do so, for what can they learn from the checking of their little washing-bills but lessons of charity? Now I see but two courses open to you for the disposal of your angel

AUBREY. Yes?

DRUMMLE. You must either restrict her to a paradise which is, like every earthly paradise, necessarily somewhat imperfect, or treat her as an ordinary flesh-and-blood young woman, and give her the advantages of that society to which she properly belongs.

AUBREY. Advantages?

DRUMMLE. My dear Aubrey, of all forms of innocence mere ignorance is the least admirable. Take my advice, let her walk and talk and suffer and be healed with the great crowd. Do it, and hope that she'll some day meet a good, honest fellow who'll make her life complete, happy, secure. Now you see what I'm driving at.

AUBREY. A sanguine programme, my dear Cayley! Oh, I'm not pooh-poohing it. Putting sentiment aside, of course I know that a fortunate marriage for Ellean would be the best—perhaps the only—solution of my difficulty. But you forget the danger of the course you suggest.

DRUMMLE. Danger?

AUBREY. If Ellean goes among men and women, how can she escape from learning, sooner or later, the history of—poor Paula's—old life?

DRUMMLE. H'm! You remember the episode of the Jeweler's Son in the Arabian Nights? Of course you don't. Well, if your daughter lives, she *can't* escape—what you're afraid of. (AUBREY *gives a half-stifled exclamation of pain.*) And when she does hear the story, surely it would be better that she should have some knowledge of the world to help her to understand it.

AUBREY. To understand!

DRUMMLE. To understand, to—philosophize.

AUBREY. To philosophize?

DRUMMLE. Philosophy is toleration, and it is only one step from toleration to forgiveness.

AUBREY. You're right, Cayley; I believe you always are. Yes, yes. But, even if I had the courage to attempt to solve the problem of Ellean's future in this way, I—I'm helpless.

DRUMMLE. How?

AUBREY. What means have I now of placing my daughter in the world I've left?

DRUMMLE. Oh, some friend—some woman friend.

AUBREY. I have none; they're gone.

DRUMMLE. You're wrong there; I know one—

AUBREY (*listening*). That's Paula's cart. Let's discuss this again.

DRUMMLE (*going up to the window and looking out*). It isn't the dog-cart. (*Turning to* AUBREY.) I hope you'll forgive me, old chap.

AUBREY. What for?

DRUMMLE. Whose wheels do you think have been cutting ruts in your immaculate drive?

(A SERVANT *enters.*)

SERVANT (*to* AUBREY). Mrs. Cortelyon, sir.

AUBREY. Mrs. Cortelyon! (*After a short pause.*) Very well. (*The* SERVANT *withdraws.*) What on earth is the meaning of this?

DRUMMLE. Ahem! While I've been our old friend's guest, Aubrey, we have very naturally talked a good deal about you and yours.

AUBREY. Indeed, have you?

DRUMMLE. Yes; and Alice Cortelyon has arrived at the conclusion that it would have been far kinder had she called on Mrs. Tanqueray long ago. She's going abroad for Easter before settling down in London for the season, and I believe she has come over this morning to ask for Ellean's companionship.

AUBREY. Oh, I see! (*Frowning.*) Quite a friendly little conspiracy, my dear Cayley!

DRUMMLE. Conspiracy! Not at all, I assure you. (*Laughing.*) Ha, ha!

(ELLEAN *enters from the hall with* MRS. CORTELYON, *a handsome, good-humored, spirited woman of about forty-five.*)

ELLEAN. Papa—

MRS. CORTELYON (*to* AUBREY, *shaking hands with him heartily*). Well, Aubrey, how are you? I've just been telling this great girl of yours that I knew her when she was a sad-faced, pale baby. How is Mrs. Tanqueray? I have been a bad neighbor, and I'm here to beg forgiveness. Is she indoors?

AUBREY. She's upstairs putting on a hat, I believe.

MRS. CORTELYON (*sitting comfortably*). Ah! (*She looks round;* DRUMMLE *and* ELLEAN *are talking together in the hall.*) We used to be very frank with each other, Aubrey. I suppose the old footing is no longer possible, eh?

AUBREY. If so, I'm not entirely to blame, Mrs. Cortelyon.

MRS. CORTELYON. Mrs. Cortelyon? H'm! No, I admit it. But you must make some little allowance for me, *Mr. Tanqueray*. Your first wife and I, as girls, were like two cherries on one stalk, and then I was the confidential friend of your married life. That post, perhaps, wasn't altogether a sinecure. And now—well, when a woman gets to my age I suppose she's a stupid, prejudiced, conventional creature. However, I've got over it and—(*giving him her hand*)—I hope you'll be enormously happy and let me be a friend once more.

AUBREY. Thank you, Alice.

MRS. CORTELYON. That's right. I feel more cheerful than I've done for weeks. But I suppose it would serve me right if the second Mrs. Tanqueray showed me the door. Do you think she will?

AUBREY (*listening*). Here is my wife. (MRS. CORTELYON *rises, and* PAULA *enters, dressed for driving; she stops abruptly on seeing* MRS. CORTELYON.) Paula, dear, Mrs. Cortelyon has called to see you. (PAULA *starts, looks at* MRS. CORTELYON *irresolutely, then after a slight pause barely touches* MRS. CORTELYON'S *extended hand.*)

PAULA (*whose manner now alternates between deliberate insolence and assumed sweetness*). Mrs.——? What name, Aubrey?

AUBREY. Mrs. Cortelyon.

PAULA. Cortelyon? Oh, yes, Cortelyon.

MRS. CORTELYON (*carefully guarding herself throughout against any expression of resentment*). Aubrey ought to have told you that Alice Cortelyon and he are very old friends.

PAULA. Oh, very likely he has mentioned the circumstance. I have quite a wretched memory.

MRS. CORTELYON. You know we are neighbors, Mrs. Tanqueray.

PAULA. Neighbors? Are we really? Won't you sit down? (*They both sit.*) Neighbors! That's most interesting!

MRS. CORTELYON. Very near neighbors. You can see my roof from your windows.

PAULA. I fancy I *have* observed a roof. But you have been away from home; you have only just returned.

MRS. CORTELYON. I? What makes you think that?

PAULA. Why, because it is two months since we came to Highercoombe, and I don't remember your having called.

MRS. CORTELYON. Your memory is now terribly accurate. No, I've not been away from home, and it is to explain my neglect that I am here, rather unceremoniously, this morning.

PAULA. Oh, to explain—quite so. (*With mock solicitude.*) Ah, you've been very ill; I ought to have seen that before.

MRS. CORTELYON. Ill!

PAULA. You look dreadfully pulled down. We poor women show illness so plainly in our faces, don't we?

AUBREY (*anxiously*). Paula dear, Mrs. Cortelyon is the picture of health.

MRS. CORTELYON (*with some asperity*). I have never *felt* better in my life.

PAULA (*looking around innocently*). Have I said anything awkward? Aubrey, tell Mrs. Cortelyon how stupid and thoughtless I always am!

MRS. CORTELYON (*to* DRUMMLE, *who is now standing close to her*). Really, Cayley—! (*He soothes her with a nod and smile and a motion of his finger to his lip.*) Mrs. Tanqueray, I am afraid my explanation will not be quite so satisfactory as either of those you have just helped me to. You may have heard—but, if you have heard, you have doubtless forgotten—that twenty years ago, when your husband first lived here, I was a constant visitor at Highercoombe.

PAULA. Twenty years ago—fancy! I was a naughty little child then.

MRS. CORTELYON. Possibly. Well, at that time, and till the end of her life, my affections were centered upon the lady of this house.

PAULA. Were they? That was very sweet of you. (ELLEAN *approaches* MRS. CORTELYON, *listening intently to her.*)

MRS. CORTELYON. I will say no more on that score, but I must add this: when, two months ago, you came here, I realized, perhaps for the first time, that I was a middle-aged woman, and that it had become impossible for me to accept without some effort a breaking-in upon many tender associations. There, Mrs. Tanqueray, that is my confession. Will you try to understand it and pardon me?

PAULA (*watching* ELLEAN,—*sneeringly*). Ellean dear, you appear to be very interested in Mrs. Cortelyon's reminiscences; I don't think I can do better than make you my mouthpiece—there is such sympathy between us. What do you say—can we bring ourselves to forgive Mrs. Cortelyon for neglecting us for two weary months?

MRS. CORTELYON (*to* ELLEAN, *pleasantly*). Well, Ellean? (*With a little cry of tenderness* ELLEAN *impulsively sits beside* MRS. CORTELYON *and takes her hand.*) My dear child!

PAULA (*in an undertone to* AUBREY). Ellean isn't so very slow in taking to Mrs. Cortelyon!

MRS. CORTELYON (*to* PAULA *and* AUBREY). Come, this encourages me to broach my scheme. Mrs. Tanqueray, it strikes me that you two good people are just now excellent company for each other, while Ellean would perhaps be glad of a little peep into the world you are anxious to avoid. Now, I'm going to Paris to-morrow for a week or two before settling down in Chester Square, so—don't gasp, both of you!—if this girl is willing, and you have made no other arrangements for her, will you let her come with me to Paris, and afterwards remain with me in town during the season? (ELLEAN *utters an exclamation of surprise.* PAULA *is silent.*) What do you say?

AUBREY. Paula—Paula dear. (*Hesitatingly.*) My dear Mrs. Cortelyon, this is wonderfully kind of you; I am really at a loss to—eh, Cayley?

DRUMMLE (*watching* PAULA *apprehensively*). Kind! Now I must say I don't think so! I begged Alice to take *me* to Paris, and she declined! I am thrown over for Ellean! Ha! ha!

MRS. CORTELYON (*laughing*). What nonsense you talk, Cayley! (*The laughter dies out.* PAULA *remains quite still.*)

AUBREY. Paula dear.

PAULA (*slowly collecting herself*). One moment. I—I don't quite—(*To* MRS. CORTELYON.) You propose that Ellean leaves Highercoombe almost at once, and remains with you some months?

MRS. CORTELYON. It would be a mercy to me. You can afford to be generous to a desolate old widow. Come, Mrs. Tanqueray, won't you spare her?

PAULA. Won't *I* spare her. (*Suspiciously.*) Have you mentioned your plan to Aubrey—before I came in?

MRS. CORTELYON. No; I had no opportunity.

PAULA. Nor to Ellean?

MRS. CORTELYON. Oh, no.

PAULA (*looking about her in suppressed excitement*). This hasn't been discussed at all, behind my back?

MRS. CORTELYON. My dear Mrs. Tanqueray!

PAULA. Ellean, let us hear your voice in the matter!

ELLEAN. I should like to go with Mrs. Cortelyon—

PAULA. Ah!

ELLEAN. That is, if—if—

PAULA. If—what?

ELLEAN (*looking towards* AUBREY, *appealingly*). Papa!

PAULA (*in a hard voice*). Oh, of course—I forgot. (*To* AUBREY.) My dear Aubrey, it rests with you, naturally, whether I am—to lose—Ellean.

AUBREY. Lose Ellean! (*Advancing to* PAULA.) There is no question of losing Ellean. You would see Ellean in town constantly when she returned from Paris; isn't that so, Mrs. Cortelyon?

MRS. CORTELYON. Certainly.

PAULA (*laughing softly*). Oh, I didn't know I should be allowed that privilege.

MRS. CORTELYON. Privilege, my dear Mrs. Tanqueray!

PAULA. Ha, ha! that makes all the difference, doesn't it?

AUBREY (*with assumed gayety*). All the difference? I should think so! (*To* ELLEAN, *laying his hand upon her head tenderly.*) And you are quite certain you wish to see what the world is like on the other side of Black Moor!

ELLEAN. If you are willing, papa, I am quite certain.

AUBREY (*looking at* PAULA *irresolutely, then speaking with an effort*). Then I—I am willing.

PAULA (*rising and striking the table lightly with her clenched hand*). That decides it! (*There is a general movement. Excitedly to* MRS. CORTELYON, *who advances towards her.*) When do you want her?

MRS. CORTELYON. We go to town this afternoon at five o'clock, and sleep to-night at Bayliss's. There is barely time for her to make her preparations.

PAULA. I will undertake that she is ready.

MRS. CORTELYON. I've a great deal to scramble through at home too, as you may guess. Good-bye!

PAULA (*turning away*). Mrs. Cortelyon is going. (PAULA *stands looking out of the window, with her back to those in the room.*)

MRS. CORTELYON (*to* DRUMMLE). Cayley—

DRUMMLE (*to her*). Eh?

MRS. CORTELYON. I've gone through it, for the sake of Aubrey and his child, but I—I feel a hundred. Is that a mad-woman?

DRUMMLE. Of course; all jealous women are mad. (*He goes out with* AUBREY.)

MRS. CORTELYON (*hesitatingly, to* PAULA). Good-bye, Mrs. Tanqueray. (PAULA *inclines her head with the slightest possible movement, then resumes her former position.* ELLEAN *comes from the hall and takes* MRS. CORTELYON *out of the room. After a brief silence,* PAULA *turns with a fierce cry, and hurriedly takes off her coat and hat, and tosses them upon the settee.*)

PAULA. Who's that? Oh! Oh! Oh! (*She drops into the chair as* AUBREY *returns; he stands looking at her.*)

AUBREY. I—you have altered your mind about going out.

PAULA. Yes. Please to ring the bell.

AUBREY (*touching the bell*). You are angry about Mrs. Cortelyon and Ellean. Let me try to explain my reasons—

PAULA. Be careful what you say to me just now! I have never felt like this—except once—in my life. Be careful what you say to me!

(*A* SERVANT *enters.*)

PAULA (*rising*). Is Watts at the door with the cart?

SERVANT. Yes, ma'am.

PAULA. Tell him to drive down to the post-office directly with this. (*Picking up the letter which has been lying upon the table.*)

AUBREY. With that?

PAULA. Yes. My letter to Lady Orreyed. (*Giving the letter to the* SERVANT, *who goes out.*)

AUBREY. Surely you don't wish me to countermand any order of yours to a servant. Call the man back—take the letter from him!

PAULA. I have not the slightest intention of doing so.

AUBREY. I must, then. (*Going to the door. She snatches up her hat and coat and follows him.*) What are you going to do?

PAULA. If you stop that letter, I walk out of the house. (*He hesitates, then leaves the door.*)

AUBREY. I am right in believing that to be the letter inviting George Orreyed and his wife to stay here, am I not?

PAULA. Oh, yes—quite right.

AUBREY. Let it go; I'll write to him by and by.

PAULA (*facing him*). You dare!

AUBREY. Hush, Paula!

PAULA. Insult me again and, upon my word, I'll go straight out of the house!

AUBREY. Insult you?

PAULA. Insult me! What else is it? My God! what else is it? What do you mean by taking Ellean from me?

AUBREY. Listen—!

PAULA. Listen to *me!* And how do you take her? You pack her off in the care of a woman who has deliberately held aloof from me, who's thrown mud at me! Yet this Cortelyon creature has only to put foot here once to be entrusted with the charge of the girl you know I dearly want to keep near me!

AUBREY. Paula dear! hear me—!

PAULA. Ah! of course, of course! I can't be so useful to your daughter as such people as this; and so I'm to be given the go-by for any town friend of yours who turns up and chooses to patronize us! Hah! Very well, at any rate, as you take Ellean from me you justify my looking for companions where I can most readily find 'em.

AUBREY. You wish me to fully appreciate your reason for sending that letter to Lady Orreyed?

PAULA. Precisely—I do.

AUBREY. And could you, after all, go back to associates of that order? It's not possible!

PAULA (*mockingly*). What, not after the refining influence of these intensely respectable surroundings? (*Going to the door.*) We'll see!

AUBREY. Paula!

PAULA (*violently*). We'll see! (*She goes out. He stands still looking after her.*)

ACT III

The drawing-room at "Highercoombe." Facing the spectator are two large French windows, sheltered by a verandah, leading into the garden; on the right is a door opening into a small hall. The fire-place, with a large mirror above it, is on the left-hand side of the room, and higher up in the same wall are double doors recessed. The room is richly furnished, and everything betokens taste and luxury. The windows are open, and there is moonlight in the garden.

(LADY ORREYED, *a pretty, affected doll of a woman, with a mincing voice and flaxen hair, is sitting on the ottoman, her head resting against the drum, and her eyes closed.* PAULA, *looking pale, worn, and thoroughly unhappy, is sitting at a table. Both are in sumptuous dinner-gowns.*)

LADY ORREYED (*opening her eyes*). Well, I never! I dropped off! (*Feeling her hair.*) Just fancy! Where are the men?

PAULA (*icily*). Outside, smoking.

(*A* SERVANT *enters with coffee, which he hands to* LADY ORREYED. SIR GEORGE ORREYED *comes in by the window. He is a man of about thirty-five, with a low forehead, a receding chin, a vacuous expression, and an ominous redness about the nose.*)

LADY ORREYED (*taking coffee*). Here's Dodo.

SIR GEORGE. I say, the flies under the verandah make you swear. (*The* SERVANT *hands coffee to* PAULA, *who declines it, then to* SIR GEORGE, *who takes a cup.*) Hi! wait a bit! (*He looks at the tray searchingly, then puts back his cup.*) Never mind. (*Quietly to* LADY ORREYED.) I say, they're dooced sparin' with their liqueur, ain't they? (*The* SERVANT *goes out at window.*)

PAULA (*to* SIR GEORGE). Won't you take coffee, George?

SIR GEORGE. No, thanks. It's gettin' near time for a whiskey and potass. (*Approaching* PAULA, *regarding* LADY ORREYED *admiringly.*) I say, Birdie looks rippin' to-night, don't she?

PAULA. Your wife?

SIR GEORGE. Yaas—Birdie.

PAULA. Rippin'?

SIR GEORGE. Yaas.

PAULA. Quite—quite rippin'. (*He moves round to the settee.* PAULA *watches him with distaste, then rises and walks away.* SIR GEORGE *falls asleep on the settee.*)

LADY ORREYED. Paula love, I fancied you and Aubrey were a little more friendly at dinner. You haven't made it up, have you?

PAULA. We? Oh, no. We speak before others, that's all.

LADY ORREYED. And how long do you intend to carry on this game, dear?

PAULA (*turning away impatiently*). I really can't tell you.

LADY ORREYED. Sit down, old girl; don't be so fidgety. (PAULA *sits on the upper seat of the ottoman, with her back to* LADY ORREYED.) Of course, it's my duty, as an old friend, to give you a good talking-to—(PAULA *glares at her suddenly and fiercely*)—but really I've found one gets so many smacks in the face through interfering in matrimonial squabbles that I've determined to drop it.

PAULA. I think you're wise.

LADY ORREYED. However, I must say that I do wish you'd look at marriage in a more solemn light—just as I do, in fact. It is such a beautiful thing—marriage, and if people in our position don't respect it, and set a good example by living happily with their husbands, what can you expect from the middle classes? When did this sad state of affairs between you and Aubrey actually begin?

PAULA. Actually, a fortnight and three days ago; I haven't calculated the minutes.

LADY ORREYED. A day or two before Dodo and I turned up—arrived.

PAULA. Yes. One always remembers one thing by another; we left off speaking to each other the morning I wrote asking you to visit us.

LADY ORREYED. Lucky for you I was able to pop down, wasn't it, dear?

PAULA (*glaring at her again*). Most fortunate.

LADY ORREYED. A serious split with your husband without a pal on the premises—I should say, without a friend in the house—would be most unpleasant.

PAULA (*turning to her abruptly*). This place must be horribly doleful for you and George just now. At least you ought to consider him before me. Why didn't you leave me to my difficulties?

LADY ORREYED. Oh, we're quite comfortable, dear, thank you—both of us. George and me are so wrapped up in each other, it doesn't matter where we are. I don't want to crow over you, old girl, but I've got a perfect husband. (SIR GEORGE *is now fast asleep, his head thrown back and his mouth open, looking hideous.*)

PAULA (*glancing at* SIR GEORGE). So you've given me to understand.

LADY ORREYED. Not that we don't have our little differences. Why, we fell out only this very morning. You remember the diamond and ruby tiara Charley Prestwick gave poor dear Connie Tirlemont years ago, don't you?

PAULA. No, I do not.

LADY ORREYED. No? Well, it's in the market. Benjamin of Piccadilly has got it in his shop window, and I've set my heart on it.

PAULA. You consider it quite necessary?

LADY ORREYED. Yes; because what I say to Dodo is this—a lady of my station must smother herself with hair ornaments. It's different with you, love—people don't look for so much blaze from you, but I've got rank to keep up; haven't I?

PAULA. Yes.

LADY ORREYED. Well, that was the cause of the little set-to between I and Dodo this morning. He broke two chairs, he was in such a rage. I forgot they're your chairs; do you mind?

PAULA. No.

LADY ORREYED. You know, poor Dodo can't lose his temper without smashing something; if it isn't a chair, it's a mirror; if it isn't that, it's china—a bit of Dresden for choice. Dear old pet! he loves a bit of Dresden when he's furious. He doesn't really throw things *at* me, dear; he simply lifts them up and drops them, like a gentleman. I expect our room upstairs will look rather wrecky before I get that tiara.

PAULA. Excuse the suggestion; perhaps your husband can't afford it.

LADY ORREYED. Oh, how dreadfully changed you are, Paula! Dodo can always mortgage something, or borrow of his ma. What *is* coming to you!

PAULA. Ah! (*She sits at the piano and touches the keys.*)

LADY ORREYED. Oh, yes, do play! That's the one thing I envy you for.

PAULA. What shall I play?

LADY ORREYED. What was that heavenly piece you gave us last night, dear?

PAULA. A bit of Schubert. Would you like to hear it again?

LADY ORREYED. You don't know any comic songs, do you?

PAULA. I'm afraid not.

LADY ORREYED. I leave it to you. (PAULA *plays.* AUBREY *and* CAYLEY DRUMMLE *appear outside the window; they look into the room.*)

AUBREY (*to* DRUMMLE). You can see her face in that mirror. Poor girl, how ill and wretched she looks.

DRUMMLE. When are the Orreyeds going?

AUBREY (*entering the room*). Heaven knows!

DRUMMLE (*following* AUBREY). But *you're* entertaining them; what's it to do with heaven?

AUBREY. Do you know, Cayley, that even the Orreyeds serve a useful purpose? My wife actually speaks to me before our guests—think of that! I've come to rejoice at the presence of the Orreyeds!

DRUMMLE. I dare say; we're taught that beetles are sent for a benign end.

AUBREY. Cayley, talk to Paula again to-night.

DRUMMLE. Certainly, if I get the chance.

AUBREY. Let's contrive it. George is asleep; perhaps I can get that doll out of the way. (*As they advance into the room,* PAULA *abruptly ceases playing and finds interest in a volume of music.* SIR GEORGE *is now nodding and snoring apoplectically.*) Lady Orreyed, whenever you feel inclined for a game of billiards I'm at your service.

LADY ORREYED (*jumping up*). Charmed, I'm sure! I really thought you had forgotten poor little me. Oh, look at Dodo!

AUBREY. No, no, don't wake him; he's tired.

LADY ORREYED. I must, he looks so plain. (*Rousing* SIR GEORGE.) Dodo! Dodo!

SIR GEORGE (*stupidly*). 'Ullo!

LADY ORREYED. Dodo dear, you were snoring.

SIR GEORGE. Oh, I say, you could 'a' told me that by and by.

AUBREY. You want a cigar, George; come into the billiard-room. (*Giving his arm to* LADY ORREYED.) Cayley, bring Paula. (AUBREY *and* LADY ORREYED *go out.*)

SIR GEORGE (*rising*). Hey, what! Billiard-room! (*Looking at his watch.*) How goes the—? Phew! 'Ullo, 'Ullo! Whiskey and potass! (*He goes rapidly after* AUBREY *and* LADY ORREYED. PAULA *resumes playing.*)

PAULA (*after a pause*). Don't moon about after me, Cayley; follow the others.

DRUMMLE. Thanks, by and by. (*Sitting.*) That's pretty.

PAULA (*after another pause, still playing*). I wish you wouldn't stare so.

DRUMMLE. Was I staring? I'm sorry. (*She plays a little longer, then stops suddenly, rises, and goes to the window, where she stands looking out.* DRUMMLE *moves from the ottoman to the settee.*) A lovely night.

PAULA (*startled*). Oh! (*Without turning to him.*) Why do you hop about like a monkey?

DRUMMLE. Hot rooms play the deuce with the nerves. Now, it would have done you good to have walked in the garden with us after dinner and made merry. Why didn't you?

PAULA. You know why.

DRUMMLE. Ah, you're thinking of the—difference between you and Aubrey?

PAULA. Yes, I *am* thinking of it.

DRUMMLE. Well, so am I. How long—?

PAULA. Getting on for three weeks.

DRUMMLE. Bless me, it must be! And this would have been such a night to have healed it! Moonlight, the stars, the scent of flowers; and yet enough darkness to enable a kind woman to rest her hand for an instant on the arm of a good fellow who loves her. Ah, ha! It's a wonderful power, dear Mrs. Aubrey, the power of an offended woman! Only realize it! Just that one touch—the mere tips of her fingers—and, for herself and another, she changes the color of the whole world.

PAULA (*turning to him calmly*). Cayley, my dear man, you talk exactly like a very romantic old lady. (*She leaves the window and sits playing with the knick-knacks on the table.*)

DRUMMLE (*to himself*). H'm, that hasn't done it! Well—ha, ha!—I accept the suggestion.—An old woman, eh?

PAULA. Oh, I didn't intend—

DRUMMLE. But why not? I've every qualification—well, almost. And I confess it would have given this withered bosom a throb of grandmotherly satisfaction if I could have seen you and Aubrey at peace before I take my leave to-morrow.

PAULA. To-morrow, Cayley!

DRUMMLE. I must.

PAULA. Oh, this house is becoming unendurable.

DRUMMLE. You're very kind. But you've got the Orreyeds.

PAULA (*fiercely*). The Orreyeds! I—I hate the Orreyeds! I lie awake at night, hating them!

DRUMMLE. Pardon me, I've understood that their visit is, in some degree, owing to—hem—your suggestion.

PAULA. Heavens! that doesn't make me like them better. Somehow or another, I—I've outgrown these people. This woman—I used to think her "jolly!"—sickens me. I can't breathe when she's near me: the whiff of her handkerchief turns me faint! And she patronizes me by the hour, until I—I feel my nails growing longer with every word she speaks!

DRUMMLE. My dear lady, why on earth don't you say all this to Aubrey?

PAULA. Oh, I've been such an utter fool, Cayley!

DRUMMLE (*soothingly*). Well, well, mention it to Aubrey!

PAULA. No, no, you don't understand. What do you think I've done?

DRUMMLE. Done! What, *since* you invited the Orreyeds?

PAULA. Yes; I must tell you—

DRUMMLE. Perhaps you'd better not.

PAULA. Look here! I've intercepted some letters from Mrs. Cortelyon and Ellean to—him. (*Producing three unopened letters from the bodice of her dress.*) There are the accursed things! From Paris—two from the Cortelyon woman, the other from Ellean!

DRUMMLE. But why—why?

PAULA. I don't know. Yes, I do! I saw letters coming from Ellean to her father; not a line to me—not a line. And one morning it happened I was downstairs before he was, and I spied this one lying with his heap on the breakfast table, and I slipped it into my pocket—out of malice, Cayley, pure deviltry! And a day or two afterwards I met Elwes the postman at the Lodge, and took the letters from him, and found these others amongst 'em. I felt simply fiendish when I saw them—fiendish! (*Returning the letters to her bodice.*) And now I carry them about with me, and they're scorching me like a mustard plaster!

DRUMMLE. Oh, this accounts for Aubrey not hearing from Paris lately!

PAULA. That's an ingenious conclusion to arrive at! Of course it does! (*With an hysterical laugh.*) Ha, ha!

DRUMMLE. Well, well! (*Laughing.*) Ha, ha, ha!

PAULA (*turning upon him*). I suppose it *is* amusing!

DRUMMLE. I beg pardon.

PAULA. Heaven knows I've little enough to brag about! I'm a bad lot, but not in mean tricks of this sort. In all my life this is the most caddish thing I've done. How am I to get rid of these letters—that's what I want to know? How am I to get rid of them?

DRUMMLE. If I were you I should take Aubrey aside and put them into his hands as soon as possible.

PAULA. What! and tell him to his face that I—! No, thank you. I suppose *you* wouldn't like to—

DRUMMLE. No, no; I won't touch 'em!

PAULA. And you call yourself my friend?

DRUMMLE (*good-humoredly*). No, I don't!

PAULA. Perhaps I'll tie them together and give them to his man in the morning.

DRUMMLE. That won't avoid an explanation.

PAULA (*recklessly*). Oh, then he must miss them—

DRUMMLE. And trace them.

PAULA (*throwing herself upon the ottoman*). I don't care!

DRUMMLE. I know you don't; but let me send him to you now, may I?

PAULA. Now! What do you think a woman's made of? I couldn't stand it, Cayley. I haven't slept for nights; and last night there was thunder, too! I believe I've got the horrors.

DRUMMLE (*taking the little hand-mirror from the table*). You'll sleep well enough when you deliver those letters. Come, come, Mrs. Aubrey—a good night's rest! (*Holding the mirror before her face.*) It's quite time. (*She looks at herself for a moment, then snatches the mirror from him.*)

PAULA. You brute, Cayley, to show me that!

DRUMMLE. Then—may I? Be guided by a fr—a poor old woman! May I?

PAULA. You'll kill me, amongst you!

DRUMMLE. What do you say?

PAULA (*after a pause*). Very well. (*He nods his head and goes out rapidly. She looks after him for a moment, and calls "Cayley! Cayley!" Then she again produces the letters, deliberately, one by one, fingering them with aversion. Suddenly she starts, turning her head towards the door.*) Ah!

(AUBREY *enters quickly.*)

AUBREY. Paula!

PAULA (*handing him the letters, her face averted*). There! (*He examines the letters, puzzled, and looks at her enquiringly.*) They are many days old. I stole them, I suppose to make you anxious and unhappy. (*He looks at the letters again, then lays them aside on the table.*)

AUBREY (*gently*). Paula, dear, it doesn't matter.

PAULA (*after a short pause*). Why—why do you take it like this?

AUBREY. What did you expect?

PAULA. Oh, but I suppose silent reproaches are really the severest. And then, naturally, you are itching to open your letters. (*She crosses the room as if to go.*)

AUBREY (*with a gesture of despair*). Oh, Paula! (*Going up to the window, and standing with his back to the room.*)

PAULA (*to herself*). A few—years ago! (*She walks slowly towards the door, then suddenly drops upon the ottoman in a paroxysm of weeping.*) O God! A few years ago!

AUBREY (*going to her*). Paula!

PAULA (*sobbing*). Oh, don't touch me!

AUBREY. Paula!

PAULA. Oh, go away from me! (*He goes back a few steps, and after a little while she becomes calmer and rises unsteadily; then in an altered tone.*) Look here—! (*He advances a step; she checks him with a quick gesture.*) Look here! Get rid of these people—Mabel and her husband—as soon as possible! I—I've done with them!

AUBREY (*in a whisper*). Paula!

PAULA. And then—then—when the time comes for Ellean to leave Mrs. Cortelyon, give me—give me another chance! (*He advances again, but she shrinks away.*) No, no! (*She goes out by the door on the right. He sinks onto the settee, covering his eyes with his hands. There is a brief silence, then a* SERVANT *enters.*)

SERVANT. Mrs. Cortelyon, sir, with Miss Ellean. (AUBREY *rises to meet* MRS. CORTELYON, *who enters, followed by* ELLEAN, *both being in travelling dresses. The* SERVANT *withdraws.*)

MRS. CORTELYON (*shaking hands with* AUBREY). Oh, my dear Aubrey!

AUBREY. Mrs. Cortelyon! (*Kissing* ELLEAN.) Ellean dear!

ELLEAN. Papa, is all well at home?

MRS. CORTELYON. We're shockingly anxious.

AUBREY. Yes, yes, all's well. This is quite unexpected. (*To* MRS. CORTELYON.) You've found Paris insufferably hot?

MRS. CORTELYON. Insufferably hot! Paris is pleasant enough. We've had no letter from you!

AUBREY. I wrote to Ellean a week ago.

MRS. CORTELYON. Without alluding to the subject I had written to you upon.

AUBREY (*thinking*). Ah, of course—

MRS. CORTELYON. And since then we've both written, and you've been absolutely silent. Oh, it's too bad!

AUBREY (*picking up the letters from the table*). It isn't altogether my fault. Here are the letters—

ELLEAN. Papa!

MRS. CORTELYON. They're unopened.

AUBREY. An accident delayed their reaching me till this evening. I'm afraid this has upset you very much.

MRS. CORTELYON. Upset me!

ELLEAN (*in an undertone to* MRS. CORTELYON). Never mind. Not now, dear—not to-night.

AUBREY. Eh?

MRS. CORTELYON (*to* ELLEAN, *aloud*). Child, run away and take your things off. She doesn't look as if she'd journeyed from Paris to-day.

AUBREY. I've never seen her with such a color. (*Taking* ELLEAN'S *hands.*)

ELLEAN (*to* AUBREY, *in a faint voice*). Papa, Mrs. Cortelyon has been so very, very kind to me, but I—I have come home. (*She goes out.*)

AUBREY. Come home! (*To* MRS. CORTELYON.) Ellean returns to us then?

MRS. CORTELYON. That's the very point I put to you in my letters, and you oblige me to travel from Paris to Willowmere on a warm day to settle it. I think perhaps it's right that Ellean should be with you just now, although I—My dear friend, circumstances are a little altered.

AUBREY. Alice, you're in some trouble.

MRS. CORTELYON. Well—yes, I *am* in trouble. You remember pretty little Mrs. Brereton who was once Caroline Ardale?

AUBREY. Quite well.

MRS. CORTELYON. She's a widow now, poor thing. She has the *entresol* of the house where we've been lodging in the Avenue de Friedland. Caroline's a dear chum of mine; she formed a great liking for Ellean.

AUBREY. I'm very glad.

MRS. CORTELYON. Yes, it's nice for her to meet her mother's friends. Er—that young Hugh Ardale the papers were full of some time ago—he's Caroline Brereton's brother, you know.

AUBREY. No, I didn't know. What did he do? I forget.

MRS. CORTELYON. Checked one of those horrid mutinies at some far-away station in India. Marched down with a handful of his men and a few faithful natives, and held the place until he was relieved. They gave him his company and a V.C. for it.

AUBREY. And he's Mrs. Brereton's brother?

MRS. CORTELYON. Yes. He's with his sister—*was,* rather—in Paris. He's home—invalided. Good gracious, Aubrey, why don't you help me out? Can't you guess what has occurred?

AUBREY. Alice!

MRS. CORTELYON. Young Ardale—Ellean!

AUBREY. An attachment?

MRS. CORTELYON. Yes, Aubrey. (*After a little pause.*) Well, I suppose I've got myself into sad disgrace. But really I didn't foresee anything of this kind. A serious, reserved child like Ellean, and a boyish, high-spirited soldier—it never struck me as being likely. (AUBREY *paces to and fro thoughtfully.*) I did all I could directly Captain Ardale spoke—wrote to you at once. Why on earth don't you receive your letters promptly, and when you do get them why can't you open them? I endured the anxiety till last night, and then made up my mind—home! Of course, it has worried me terribly. My head's bursting. Are there any salts about? (AUBREY *fetches a bottle from the cabinet and hands it to her.*) We've had one of those hateful smooth crossings that won't let you be properly indisposed.

AUBREY. My dear Alice, I assure you I've no thought of blaming you.

MRS. CORTELYON. That statement always precedes a quarrel.

AUBREY. I don't know whether this is the worst or the best luck. How will my wife regard it? Is Captain Ardale a good fellow?

MRS. CORTELYON. My dear Aubrey, you'd better read up the accounts of his wonderful heroism. Face to face with death for a whole week; always with a smile and a cheering word for the poor helpless souls depending on him! Of course it's that that has stirred the depths of your child's nature. I've watched her while we've been dragging the story out of him, and if angels look different from Ellean at that moment, I don't desire to meet any, that's all!

AUBREY. If you were in my position—? But you can't judge.

MRS. CORTELYON. Why, if I had a marriageable daughter of my own, and Captain Ardale proposed for her, naturally I should cry my eyes out all night—but I should thank Heaven in the morning.

AUBREY. You believe so thoroughly in him?

MRS. CORTELYON. Do you think I should have only a headache at this minute if I didn't! Look here, you've got to see me down the lane; that's the least you can do, my friend. Come into my house for a moment and shake hands with Hugh.

AUBREY. What, is he here?

MRS. CORTELYON. He came through with us, to present himself formally to-morrow. Where are my gloves? (AUBREY *fetches them from the ottoman.*) Make my apologies to Mrs. Tanqueray, please. She's well, I hope? (*Going towards the door.*) I can't feel sorry she hasn't seen me in this condition.

(ELLEAN *enters.*)

ELLEAN (*to* MRS. CORTELYON). I've been waiting to wish you good-night. I was afraid I'd missed you.

MRS. CORTELYON. Good-night, Ellean.

ELLEAN (*in a low voice, embracing* MRS. CORTELYON). I can't thank you. Dear Mrs. Cortelyon!

MRS. CORTELYON (*her arms round* ELLEAN, *in a whisper to* AUBREY). Speak a word to her. (MRS. CORTELYON *goes out.*)

AUBREY (*to* ELLEAN). Ellean, I'm going to see Mrs. Cortelyon home. Tell Paula where I am; explain, dear. (*Going to the door.*)

ELLEAN (*her head drooping*). Yes. (*Quickly.*) Father! You are angry with me—disappointed?

AUBREY. Angry? No.

ELLEAN. Disappointed?

AUBREY (*smiling and going to her and taking her hand*). If so, it's only because you've shaken my belief in my discernment. I thought you took after your poor mother a little, Ellean; but there's a look on your face to-night, dear, that I never saw on hers—never, never.

ELLEAN (*leaning her head on his shoulder*). Perhaps I ought not to have gone away.

AUBREY. Hush! You're quite happy?

ELLEAN. Yes.

AUBREY. That's right. Then, as you are quite happy, there is something I particularly want you to do for me, Ellean.

ELLEAN. What is that?

AUBREY. Be very gentle with Paula. Will you?

ELLEAN. You think I have been unkind.

AUBREY (*kissing her upon the forehead*). Be very gentle with Paula. (*He goes out, and she stands looking after him; then, as she turns thoughtfully from the door, a rose is thrown through the window and falls at her feet. She picks up the flower wonderingly and goes to the window.*)

ELLEAN (*starting back*). Hugh!

(HUGH ARDALE, *a handsome young man of about seven-and-twenty, with a boyish face and manner, appears outside the window.*)

HUGH. Nelly! Nelly dear!

ELLEAN. What's the matter?

HUGH. Hush! Nothing. It's only fun. (*Laughing.*) Ha, ha, ha! I've found out that Mrs. Cortelyon's meadow runs up to your father's plantation; I've come through a gap in the hedge.

ELLEAN. Why, Hugh?

HUGH. I'm miserable at The Warren: it's so different from the Avenue de Friedland. Don't look like that! Upon my word I meant just to peep at your home and go back, but I saw figures moving about here, and came nearer, hoping to get a glimpse of you. Was that your father? (*He enters the room.*)

ELLEAN. Yes.

HUGH. Isn't this fun! A rabbit ran across my foot while I was hiding behind that old yew.

ELLEAN. You must go away; it's not right for you to be here like this.

HUGH. But it's only fun, I tell you. You take everything so seriously. Do wish me good-night.

ELLEAN. We have said good-night.

HUGH. In the hall at The Warren, before Mrs. Cortelyon and a man-servant. Oh, it's so different from the Avenue de Friedland!

ELLEAN (*giving him her hand hastily*). Good-night, Hugh!

HUGH. Is that all? We might be the merest acquaintances. (*He momentarily embraces her, but she releases herself.*)

ELLEAN. It's when you're like this that you make me feel utterly miserable. (*Throwing the rose from her angrily.*) Oh!

HUGH. I've offended you now, I suppose?

ELLEAN. Yes.

HUGH. Forgive me, Nelly. Come into the garden for five minutes; we'll stroll down to the plantation.

ELLEAN. No, no.

HUGH. For two minutes—to tell me you forgive me.

ELLEAN. I forgive you.

HUGH. Evidently. I shan't sleep a wink to-night after this. What a fool I am! Come down to the plantation. Make it up with me.

ELLEAN. There is somebody coming into this room. Do you wish to be seen here?

HUGH. I shall wait for you behind that yew-tree. You must speak to me, Nelly!

(*He disappears.* PAULA *enters.*)

PAULA. Ellean!

ELLEAN. You—you are very surprised to see me, Paula, of course.

PAULA. Why are you here? Why aren't you with—your friend?

ELLEAN. I've come home—if you'll have me. We left Paris this morning; Mrs. Cortelyon brought me back. She was here a minute or two ago; papa has gone with her to The Warren. He asked me to tell you.

PAULA. There are some people staying with us that I'd rather you didn't meet. It was hardly worth your while to return for a few hours.

ELLEAN. A few hours?

PAULA. Well, when do you go to London?

ELLEAN. I don't think I go to London, after all.

PAULA (*eagerly*). You—you've quarreled with her?

ELLEAN. No, no, no, not that; but—Paula! (*In an altered tone.*) Paula!

PAULA (*startled*). Eh! (ELLEAN *goes deliberately to* PAULA *and kisses her.*) Ellean!

ELLEAN. Kiss me.

PAULA. What—what's come to you?

ELLEAN. I want to behave differently to you in the future. Is it too late?

PAULA. Too—late! (*Impulsively kissing* ELLEAN *and crying.*) No—no—no! No—no!

ELLEAN. Paula, don't cry.

PAULA (*wiping her eyes*). I'm a little shaky; I haven't been sleeping. It's all right,—talk to me.

ELLEAN. There is something I want to tell you—

PAULA. Is there—is there? (*They sit together on the ottoman,* PAULA *taking* ELLEAN'S *hand.*)

ELLEAN. Paula, in our house in the Avenue de Friedland, on the floor below us, there was a Mrs. Brereton. She used to be a friend of my mother's. Mrs. Cortelyon and I spent a great deal of our time with her.

PAULA (*suspiciously*). Oh! (*Letting* ELLEAN'S *hand fall.*) Is this lady going to take you up in place of Mrs. Cortelyon?

ELLEAN. No, no. Her brother is staying with her—*was* staying with her. Her brother—(*Breaking off in confusion.*)

PAULA. Well?

ELLEAN (*almost inaudibly*). Paula—(*She rises and walks away,* PAULA *following her.*)

PAULA (*taking hold of her*). You're not in love! (ELLEAN *looks at* PAULA *appealingly.*) Oh, *you* in love! You! Oh, this is why you've come home! Of course, you can make friends with me now! You'll leave us for good soon, I suppose; so it doesn't much matter being civil to me for a little while!

ELLEAN. Oh, Paula!

PAULA. Why, how you have deceived us—all of us! We've taken you for a cold-blooded little saint. The fools you've made of us! Saint Ellean, Saint Ellean!

ELLEAN. Ah, I might have known you'd only mock me!

PAULA (*her tone changing*). Eh?

ELLEAN. I—I can't talk to you. (*Sitting on the settee.*) You do nothing else but mock and sneer, nothing else.

PAULA. Ellean dear! Ellean! I didn't mean it. I'm so horribly jealous, it's a sort of curse on me. (*Kneeling beside* ELLEAN *and embracing her.*)

My tongue runs away with me. I'm going to alter, I swear I am. I've made some good resolutions, and as God's above me, I'll keep them! If you are in love, if you do ever marry, that's no reason why we shouldn't be fond of each other. Come, you've kissed me of your own accord—you can't take it back. Now we're friends again, aren't we? Ellean, dear! I want to know everything, everything. Ellean, dear, Ellean!

ELLEAN. Paula, Hugh has done something that makes me very angry. He came with us from Paris to-day, to see papa. He is staying with Mrs. Cortelyon and—I ought to tell you—

PAULA. Yes, yes. What?

ELLEAN. He has found his way by The Warren meadow through the plantation up to this house. He is waiting to bid me good-night. (*Glancing towards the garden.*) He is—out there.

PAULA. Oh!

ELLEAN. What shall I do?

PAULA. Bring him in to see me! Will you?

ELLEAN. No, no.

PAULA. But I'm dying to know him. Oh, yes, you must. I shall meet him before Aubrey does. (*Excitedly running her hands over her hair.*) I'm so glad. (ELLEAN *goes out by the window.*) The mirror—mirror. What a fright I must look! (*Not finding the hand-glass on the table, she jumps onto the settee, and surveys herself in the mirror over the mantelpiece, then sits quietly down and waits.*) Ellean! Just fancy! Ellean!

(*After a pause* ELLEAN *enters by the window with* HUGH.)

ELLEAN. Paula, this is Captain Ardale—Mrs. Tanqueray. (PAULA *rises and turns, and she and* HUGH *stand staring blankly at each other for a moment or two; then* PAULA *advances and gives him her hand.*)

PAULA (*in a strange voice, but calmly*). How do you do?

HUGH. How do you do?

PAULA (*to* ELLEAN). Mr. Ardale and I have met in London, Ellean. Er—Captain Ardale now?

HUGH. Yes.

ELLEAN. In London?

PAULA. They say the world's very small, don't they?

HUGH. Yes.

PAULA. Ellean, dear, I want to have a little talk about you to Mr. Ardale—Captain Ardale—alone. (*Putting her arms around* ELLEAN, *and leading her to the door.*) Come back in a little while. (ELLEAN *nods to* PAULA *with a smile and goes out, while* PAULA *stands watching her at the open door.*) In a little while—in a little—(*Closing the door and then taking a seat facing* HUGH.) Be quick! Mr. Tanqueray has only gone down to The Warren with Mrs. Cortelyon. What is to be done?

HUGH (*blankly*). Done?

PAULA. Done—done. Something must be done.

HUGH. I understood that Mr. Tanqueray had married a Mrs.—Mrs.—

PAULA. Jarman?

HUGH. Yes.

PAULA. I'd been going by that name. You didn't follow my doings after we separated.

HUGH. No.

PAULA (*sneeringly*). No.

HUGH. I went out to India.

PAULA. What's to be done?

HUGH. Damn this chance!

PAULA. Oh, my God!

HUGH. Your husband doesn't know, does he?

PAULA. That you and I—?

HUGH. Yes.

PAULA. No. He knows about others.

HUGH. Not about me. How long were we—?

PAULA. I don't remember, exactly.

HUGH. Do you—do you think it matters?

PAULA. His—his daughter. (*With a muttered exclamation he turns away, and sits with his head in his hands.*) What's to be done?

HUGH. I wish I could think.

PAULA. Oh! Oh! What happened to that flat of ours in Ethelbert Street?

HUGH. I let it.

PAULA. All that pretty furniture?

HUGH. Sold it.

PAULA. I came across the key of the escritoire the other day in an old purse! (*Suddenly realizing the horror and hopelessness of her position, and starting to her feet with an hysterical cry of rage.*) What am I maundering about?

HUGH. For God's sake, be quiet! Do let me think.

PAULA. This will send me mad! (*Suddenly turning and standing over him.*) You—you beast, to crop up in my life again like this!

HUGH. I always treated you fairly.

PAULA (*weakly*). Oh! I beg your pardon—I know you did—I—(*She sinks onto the settee crying hysterically.*)

HUGH. Hush!

PAULA. She kissed me to-night! I'd won her over! I've had such a fight to make her love me! and now—just as she's beginning to love me, to bring this on her!

HUGH. Hush, hush! Don't break down!

PAULA (*sobbing*). You don't know! I—I haven't been getting on well in my marriage. It's been my fault. The life I used to lead spoilt me completely. But I'd made up my mind to turn over a new leaf from to-night. From to-night!

HUGH. Paula—

PAULA. Don't you call me that!

HUGH. Mrs. Tanqueray, there is no cause for you to despair in this way. It's all right, I tell you—it *shall* be all right.

PAULA (*shivering*). What are we to do?

HUGH. Hold our tongues.

PAULA. Eh? (*Staring vacantly.*)

HUGH. The chances are a hundred to one against any one ever turning up who knew us when we were together. Besides, no one would be such a brute as to split on us. If anybody did do such a thing we should have to lie! What are we upsetting ourselves like this for, when we've simply got to hold our tongues?

PAULA. You're as mad as I am.

HUGH. Can you think of a better plan?

PAULA. There's only one plan possible—let's come to our senses!—Mr. Tanqueray must be told.

HUGH. Your husband! What, and I lose Ellean! I lose Ellean!

PAULA. You've got to lose her.

HUGH. I won't lose her; I can't lose her!

PAULA. Didn't I read of your doing any number of brave things in India? Why, you seem to be an awful coward!

HUGH. That's another sort of pluck altogether; I haven't this sort of pluck.

PAULA. Oh, I don't ask *you* to tell Mr. Tanqueray. That's my job.

HUGH (*standing over her*). You—you—you'd better! You—

PAULA (*rising*). Don't bully me! I intend to.

HUGH (*taking hold of her; she wrenches herself free*). Look here, Paula. I never treated you badly—you've owned it. Why should you want to pay me out like this? You don't know how I love Ellean!

PAULA. Yes, that's just what I *do* know.

HUGH. I say you don't! She's as good as my own mother. I've been downright honest with her, too. I told her, in Paris, that I'd been a bit wild at one time, and, after a damned wretched day, she promised to forgive me because of what I'd done since in India. She's behaved like an angel to me! Surely I oughtn't to lose her, after all, just because I've been like other fellows! No; I haven't been half as rackety as a hundred men we could think of. Paula, don't pay me out for nothing; be fair to me, there's a good girl—be fair to me!

PAULA. Oh, I'm not considering you at all! I advise you not to stay here any longer: Mr. Tanqueray is sure to be back soon.

HUGH (*taking up his hat*). What's the understanding between us, then? What have we arranged to do?

PAULA. I don't know what you're going to do; I've got to tell Mr. Tanqueray.

HUGH. By God, you shall do nothing of the sort! (*Approaching her fiercely.*)

PAULA. You shocking coward!

HUGH. If you dare! (*Going up to the window.*) Mind! If you dare!

PAULA (*following him*). Why, what would you do?

HUGH (*after a short pause, sullenly*). Nothing. I'd shoot myself—that's nothing. Good-night.

PAULA. Good-night. (*He disappears. She walks unsteadily to the ottoman, and sits; and as she does so her hand falls upon the little silver mirror, which she takes up, staring at her own reflection.*)

ACT IV

The Drawing-room at "Highercoombe," the same evening.

(PAULA *is still seated on the ottoman, looking vacantly before her, with the little mirror in her hand.* LADY ORREYED *enters.*)

LADY ORREYED. There you are! You never came into the billiard-room. Isn't it maddening—Cayley Drummle gives me sixty out of a hundred, and beats me. I must be out of form, because I know I play remarkably well for a lady. Only last month—(PAULA *rises.*) Whatever is the matter with you, old girl?

PAULA. Why?

LADY ORREYED (*staring*). It's the light, I suppose. (PAULA *replaces the mirror on the table.*) By Aubrey's bolting from the billiard-table in that fashion I thought perhaps—

PAULA. Yes; it's all right.

LADY ORREYED. You've patched it up? (PAULA *nods.*) Oh, I am jolly glad—! I mean—

PAULA. Yes, I know what you mean. Thanks, Mabel.

LADY ORREYED (*kissing* PAULA). Now take my advice; for the future—

PAULA. Mabel, if I've been disagreeable to you while you've been staying here, I—I beg your pardon. (*Walking away and sitting down.*)

LADY ORREYED. You disagreeable, my dear? I haven't noticed it. Dodo and me both consider you make a first-class hostess; but then you've had such practice, haven't you? (*Dropping on the ottoman and gaping.*) Oh, talk about being sleepy—

PAULA. Why don't you—!

LADY ORREYED. Why, dear, I must hang about for Dodo. You may as well know it; he's in one of his moods.

PAULA (*under her breath*). Oh—!

LADY ORREYED. Now, it's not his fault; it was deadly dull for him while we were playing billiards. Cayley Drummle did ask him to mark, but I stopped that; it's so easy to make a gentleman look like a billiard-marker. This is just how it always is; if poor old Dodo has nothing to do, he loses count, as you may say.

PAULA. Hark!

(SIR GEORGE ORREYED *enters, walking slowly and deliberately; he looks pale and watery-eyed.*)

SIR GEORGE (*with mournful indistinctness*). I'm 'fraid we've lef' you a grea' deal to yourself to-night, Mrs. Tanqueray. Attra'tions of billiards. I apol'gise. I say, where's ol' Aubrey?

PAULA. My husband has been obliged to go out to a neighbor's house.

SIR GEORGE. I want his advice on a rather pressing matter connected with my family—my family. (*Sitting.*) To-morrow will do just as well.

LADY ORREYED (*to* PAULA). This is the mood I hate so—driveling about his precious family.

SIR GEORGE. The fact is, Mrs. Tanqueray, I am not easy in my min' 'bout the way I am treatin' my poor ol' mother.

LADY ORREYED (*to* PAULA). Do you hear that? That's *his* mother, but *my* mother he won't so much as look at!

SIR GEORGE. I shall write to Bruton Street firs' thing in the morning.

LADY ORREYED (*to* PAULA). Mamma has stuck to me through everything—well, you know!

SIR GEORGE. I'll get ol' Aubrey to figure out a letter. I'll drop line to Uncle Fitz too—dooced shame of the ol' feller to chuck me over in this manner. (*Wiping his eyes.*) All my family have chucked me over.

LADY ORREYED (*rising*). Dodo!

SIR GEORGE. Jus' because I've married beneath me, to be chucked over! Aunt Lydia, the General, Hooky Whitgrave, Lady Sugnall—my own dear sister!—all turn their backs on me. It's more than I can stan'!

LADY ORREYED (*approaching him with dignity*). Sir George, wish Mrs. Tanqueray good-night at once, and come upstairs. Do you hear me?

SIR GEORGE (*rising angrily*). Wha—!

LADY ORREYED. Be quiet!

SIR GEORGE. You presoom to order me about!

LADY ORREYED. You're making an exhibition of yourself!

SIR GEORGE. Look 'ere—!

LADY ORREYED. Come along, I tell you! (*He hesitates, utters a few inarticulate sounds, then snatches up a fragile ornament from the table and is about to dash it on the ground.* LADY ORREYED *retreats, and* PAULA *goes to him.*)

PAULA. George! (*He replaces the ornament.*)

SIR GEORGE (*shaking* PAULA'S *hand*). Good ni', Mrs. Tanqueray.

LADY ORREYED (*to* PAULA). Good-night, darling. Wish Aubrey good-night for me. Now, Dodo? (*She goes out.*)

SIR GEORGE (*to* PAULA). I say, are you goin' to sit up for ol' Aubrey?

PAULA. Yes.

SIR GEORGE. Shall I keep you comp'ny?

PAULA. No, thank you, George.

SIR GEORGE. Sure?

PAULA. Yes, sure.

SIR GEORGE (*shaking hands*). Good-night again.

PAULA. Good-night. (*She turns away. He goes out steadying himself carefully.* DRUMMLE *appears outside the window, smoking.*)

DRUMMLE (*looking into the room and seeing* PAULA). My last cigar. Where's Aubrey?

PAULA. Gone down to The Warren to see Mrs. Cortelyon home.

DRUMMLE (*entering the room*). Eh? Did you say Mrs. Cortelyon?

PAULA. Yes. She has brought Ellean back.

DRUMMLE. Bless my soul! Why?

PAULA. I—I'm too tired to tell you, Cayley. If you stroll along the lane you'll meet Aubrey. Get the news from him.

DRUMMLE (*going up to the window*). Yes, yes. (*Returning to* PAULA.) I don't want to bother you, only—the anxious old woman, you know. Are you and Aubrey—?

PAULA. Good friends again?

DRUMMLE (*nodding*). Um.

PAULA (*giving him her hand*). Quite, Cayley, quite.

DRUMMLE (*retaining her hand*). That's capital. As I'm off so early to-morrow morning, let me say now—thank you for your hospitality. (*He bends over her hand gallantly, then goes out by the window.*)

PAULA (*to herself*). "Are you and Aubrey—?" "Good friends again?" "Yes." "Quite, Cayley, quite."

(*There is a brief pause, then* AUBREY *enters hurriedly, wearing a light overcoat and carrying a cap.*)

AUBREY. Paula dear! Have you seen Ellean?

PAULA. I found her here when I came down.

AUBREY. She—she's told you?

PAULA. Yes, Aubrey.

AUBREY. It's extraordinary, isn't it! Not that somebody should fall in love with Ellean, or that Ellean herself should fall in love. All that's natural enough and was bound to happen, I suppose, sooner or later. But this young fellow! You know his history?

PAULA. His history?

AUBREY. You remember the papers were full of his name a few months ago?

PAULA. Oh, yes.

AUBREY. The man's as brave as a lion, there's no doubt about that; and, at the same time, he's like a big good-natured school-boy, Mrs. Cortelyon says. Have you ever pictured the kind of man Ellean would marry some day?

PAULA. I can't say that I have.

AUBREY. A grave, sedate fellow I've thought about—hah! She has fallen in love with the way in which Ardale practically laid down his life to save those poor people shut up in the Residency. (*Taking off his coat.*) Well, I suppose if a man can do that sort of thing, one ought to be content. And yet—(*Throwing his coat on the settee.*) I should have met him to-night, but he'd gone out. Paula dear, tell me how you look upon this business.

PAULA. Yes, I will—I must. To begin with, I—I've seen Mr. Ardale.

AUBREY. Captain Ardale?

PAULA. Captain Ardale.

AUBREY. Seen him?

PAULA. While you were away he came up here, through our grounds, to try to get a word with Ellean. I made her fetch him in and present him to me.

AUBREY (*frowning*). Doesn't Captain Ardale know there's a lodge and a front door to this place? Never mind! What is your impression of him?

PAULA. Aubrey, do you recollect my bringing you a letter—a letter giving you an account of myself—to the Albany late one night—the night before we got married?

AUBREY. A letter?

PAULA. You burnt it; don't you know?

AUBREY. Yes; I know.

PAULA. His name was in that letter.

AUBREY (*going back from her slowly, and staring at her*). I don't understand.

PAULA. Well—Ardale and I once kept house together. (*He remains silent, not moving.*) Why don't you strike me? Hit me in the face—I'd rather you did! Hurt me! hurt me!

AUBREY (*after a pause*). What did you—and this man—say to each other—just now?

PAULA. I—hardly—know.

AUBREY. Think!

PAULA. The end of it all was that I—I told him I must inform you of—what had happened . . . he didn't want me to do that . . . I declared that I would . . . he dared me to. (*Breaking down.*) Let me alone!—oh!

AUBREY. Where was my daughter while this went on?

PAULA. I—I had sent her out of the room . . . that is all right.

AUBREY. Yes, yes—yes, yes. (*He turns his head towards the door.*)

PAULA. Who's that?

(*A* SERVANT *enters with a letter.*)

SERVANT. The coachman has just run up with this from The Warren, sir. (AUBREY *takes the letter.*) It's for Mrs. Tanqueray, sir; there's no answer. (*The* SERVANT *withdraws.* AUBREY *goes to* PAULA *and drops the letter into her lap; she opens it with uncertain hands.*)

PAULA (*reading it to herself*). It's from—him. He's going away—or gone—I think. (*Rising in a weak way.*) What does it say? I never could make out his writing. (*She gives the letter to* AUBREY, *and stands near him, looking at the letter over his shoulder as he reads.*)

AUBREY (*reading*). "I shall be in Paris by to-morrow evening. Shall wait there, at Meurice's, for a week, ready to receive any communication you or your husband may address to me. Please invent some explanation to Ellean. Mrs. Tanqueray, for God's sake, do what you can for me." (PAULA *and* AUBREY *speak in low voices, both still looking at the letter.*)

PAULA. Has he left The Warren, I wonder, already?

AUBREY. That doesn't matter.

PAULA. No; but I can picture him going quietly off. Very likely he's walking on to Bridgeford or Cottering to-night, to get the first train in the morning. A pleasant stroll for him.

AUBREY. We'll reckon he's gone, that's enough.

PAULA. That isn't to be answered in any way?

AUBREY. Silence will answer that.

PAULA. He'll soon recover his spirits, I know.

AUBREY. You know. (*Offering her the letter.*) You don't want this, I suppose?

PAULA. No.

AUBREY. It's done with—done with. (*He tears the letter into small pieces. She has dropped the envelope; she searches for it, finds it, and gives it to him.*)

PAULA. Here!

AUBREY (*looking at the remnants of the letter*). This is no good; I must burn it.

PAULA. Burn it in your room.

AUBREY. Yes.

PAULA. Put it in your pocket for now.

AUBREY. Yes. (*He does so.* ELLEAN *enters, and they both turn, guiltily, and stare at her.*)

ELLEAN (*after a short silence, wonderingly*). Papa—

AUBREY. What do you want, Ellean?

ELLEAN. I heard from Willis that you had come in; I only want to wish you good-night. (PAULA *steals away, without looking back.*)What's the matter? Ah! Of course, Paula has told you about Captain Ardale?

AUBREY. Well?

ELLEAN. Have you and he met?

AUBREY. No.

ELLEAN. You are angry with him; so was I. But to-morrow when he calls and expresses his regret—to-morrow—

AUBREY. Ellean—Ellean!

ELLEAN. Yes, papa.

AUBREY. I—I can't let you see this man again. (*He walks away from her in a paroxysm of distress; then after a moment or two, he returns to her and takes her to his arms.*) Ellean! my child!

ELLEAN (*releasing herself*). What has happened, papa? What is it?

AUBREY (*thinking out his words deliberately*). Something has occurred, something has come to my knowledge, in relation to Captain Ardale, which puts any further acquaintanceship between you two out of the question.

ELLEAN. Any further acquaintanceship . . . out of the question?

AUBREY. Yes. (*Advancing to her quickly, but she shrinks from him.*)

ELLEAN. No, no—I am quite well. (*After a short pause.*) It's not an hour ago since Mrs. Cortelyon left you and me together here; you had nothing to urge against Captain Ardale then.

AUBREY. No.

ELLEAN. You don't know each other; you haven't even seen him this evening, Father!

AUBREY. I have told you he and I have not met.

ELLEAN. Mrs. Cortelyon couldn't have spoken against him to you just now. No, no, no; she's too good a friend to both of us. Aren't you going to give me some explanation? You can't take this position towards me—towards Captain Ardale—without affording me the fullest explanation.

AUBREY. Ellean, there are circumstances connected with Captain Ardale's career which you had better remain ignorant of. It must be sufficient for you that I consider these circumstances render him unfit to be your husband.

ELLEAN. Father!

AUBREY. You must trust me, Ellean; you must try to understand the depth of my love for you and the—the agony it gives me to hurt you. You must trust me.

ELLEAN. I will, father; but you must trust me a little too. Circumstances connected with Captain Ardale's career?

AUBREY. Yes.

ELLEAN. When he presents himself here to-morrow, of course you will see him and let him defend himself?

AUBREY. Captain Ardale will not be here to-morrow.

ELLEAN. Not! You have stopped his coming here?

AUBREY. Indirectly—yes.

ELLEAN. But just now he was talking to me at that window! Nothing had taken place then! And since then nothing can have—! Oh! Why—you have heard something against him from Paula.

AUBREY. From—Paula!

ELLEAN. She knows him.

AUBREY. She has told you so?

ELLEAN. When I introduced Captain Ardale to her she said she had met him in London. Of course! It is Paula who has done this!

AUBREY (*in a hard voice*). I—I hope you—you'll refrain from rushing at conclusions. There's nothing to be gained by trying to avoid the main point, which is that you must drive Captain Ardale out of your thoughts. Understand that! You're able to obtain comfort from your religion, aren't you? I'm glad to think that's so. I talk to you in a harsh way, Ellean, but I feel your pain almost as acutely as you do. (*Going to the door.*) I—I can't say anything more to you to-night.

ELLEAN. Father! (*He pauses at the door.*) Father, I'm obliged to ask you this; there's no help for it—I've no mother to go to. Does what you have heard about Captain Ardale concern the time when he led a wild, a dissolute life in London?

AUBREY (*returning to her slowly and staring at her*). Explain yourself!

ELLEAN. He has been quite honest with me. One day—in Paris—he confessed to me—what a man's life is—what his life had been.

AUBREY (*under his breath*). Oh!

ELLEAN. He offered to go away, not to approach me again.

AUBREY. And you—you accepted his view of what a man's life is?

ELLEAN. As far as *I* could forgive him, I forgave him.

AUBREY (*with a groan*). Why, when was it you left us? It hasn't taken you long to get your robe "just a little dusty at the hem!"

ELLEAN. What do you mean?

AUBREY. Hah! A few weeks ago my one great desire was to keep you ignorant of evil.

ELLEAN. Father, it is impossible to be ignorant of evil. Instinct, common instinct, teaches us what is good and bad. Surely I am none the worse for knowing what is wicked and detesting it!

AUBREY. Detesting it! Why, you love this fellow!

ELLEAN. Ah, you don't understand! I have simply judged Captain Ardale as we all pray to be judged. I have lived in imagination through that one week in India when he deliberately offered his life back to God to save those wretched, desperate people. In his whole career I see now nothing but that one week; those few hours bring him nearer the saints, I believe, than fifty uneventful years of mere blamelessness would have done! And so, father, if Paula has reported anything to Captain Ardale's discredit—

AUBREY. Paula—!

ELLEAN. It must be Paula; it can't be anybody else.

AUBREY. You—you'll please keep Paula out of the question. Finally, Ellean, understand me—I have made up my mind. (*Again going to the door.*)

ELLEAN. But wait—listen! I have made up my mind also.

AUBREY. Ah! I recognize your mother in you now!

ELLEAN. You need not speak against my mother because you are angry with me!

AUBREY. I—I hardly know what I'm saying to you. In the morning—in the morning—(*He goes out. She remains standing, and turns her head to listen. Then after a moment's hesitation she goes softly to the window, and looks out under the verandah.*)

ELLEAN (*in a whisper*). Paula! Paula!

(PAULA *appears outside the window and steps into the room; her face is white and drawn, her hair is a little disordered.*)

PAULA (*huskily*). Well?

ELLEAN. Have you been under the verandah all the while—listening?

PAULA. No—no.

ELLEAN. You *have* overheard us—I see you have. And it *is* you who have been speaking to my father against Captain Ardale. Isn't it? Paula, why don't you own it or deny it?

PAULA. Oh, I—I don't mind owning it; why should I?

ELLEAN. Ah! You seem to have been very, very eager to tell your tale.

PAULA. No, I wasn't eager, Ellean. I'd have given something not to have had to do it. I wasn't eager.

ELLEAN. Not! Oh, I think you might safely have spared us all for a little while.

PAULA. But, Ellean, you forget I—I am your stepmother. It was my—my duty—to tell your father what I—what I knew—

ELLEAN. What you knew! Why, after all, what can you know? You can only speak from gossip, report, hearsay! How is it possible that you—! (*She stops abruptly. The two women stand staring at each other for a moment; then* ELLEAN *backs away from* PAULA *slowly.*) Paula!

PAULA. What—what's the matter?

ELLEAN. You—you knew Captain Ardale in London!

PAULA. Why—what do you mean?

ELLEAN. Oh! (*She makes for the door, but* PAULA *catches her by the wrist.*)

PAULA. You shall tell me what you mean!

ELLEAN. Ah! (*Suddenly, looking fixedly into* PAULA'*s face.*) You know what I mean.

PAULA. You accuse me!

ELLEAN. It's in your face!

PAULA (*hoarsely*). You—you think I'm—that sort of creature, do you?

ELLEAN. Let me go!

PAULA. Answer me! You've always hated me! (*Shaking her.*) Out with it!

ELLEAN. You hurt me!

PAULA. You've always hated me! You shall answer me!

ELLEAN. Well, then, I have always—always—

PAULA. What?

ELLEAN. I have always known what you were!

PAULA. Ah! Who—who told you?

ELLEAN. Nobody but yourself. From the first moment I saw you I knew you were altogether unlike the good women I'd left; directly I saw you I knew what my father had done. You've wondered why I've turned from you! There—that's the reason! Oh, but this is a horrible way for the truth to come home to every one! Oh!

PAULA. It's a lie! It's all a lie! (*Forcing* ELLEAN *down upon her knees.*) You shall beg my pardon for it. (ELLEAN *utters a loud shriek of terror.*) Ellean, I'm a good woman! I swear I am! I've always been a good woman! You dare to say I've ever been anything else! It's a lie! (*Throwing her off violently.*)

(AUBREY *re-enters.*)

AUBREY. Paula! (PAULA *staggers back as* AUBREY *advances. Raising* ELLEAN.) What's this? What's this?

ELLEAN (*faintly*). Nothing. It—it's my fault. Father, I—I don't wish to see Captain Ardale again. (*She goes out,* AUBREY *slowly following her to the door.*)

PAULA. Aubrey, she—she guesses.

AUBREY. Guesses?

PAULA. About me—and Ardale.

AUBREY. About you—and Ardale?

PAULA. She says she suspected my character from the beginning . . . that's why she's always kept me at a distance . . . and now she sees through—(*She falters; he helps her to the ottoman, where she sits.*)

AUBREY (*bending over her*). Paula, you must have said something—admitted something—

PAULA. I don't think so. It—it's in my face.

AUBREY. What?

PAULA. She tells me so. She's right! I'm tainted through and through; anybody can see it, anybody can find it out. You said much the same to me to-night.

AUBREY. If she has got this idea into her head we must drive it out, that's all. We must take steps to—What shall we do? We had better—better—What—what? (*Sitting and staring before him.*)

PAULA. Ellean! So meek, so demure! You've often said she reminded you of her mother. Yes, I know now what your first marriage was like.

AUBREY. We must drive this idea out of her head. We'll do something. What shall we do?

PAULA. She's a regular woman, too. She could forgive *him* easily enough—but *me!* That's just a woman!

AUBREY. What *can* we do?

PAULA. Why, nothing! She'd have no difficulty in following up her suspicions. Suspicions! You should have seen how she looked at me! (*He buries his head in his hands. There is silence for a time, then she rises slowly, and goes and sits beside him.*) Aubrey.

AUBREY. Yes.

PAULA. I'm very sorry. (*Without meeting her eyes, he lays his hand on her arm for a moment.*)

AUBREY. Well, we must look things straight in the face. (*Glancing around.*) At any rate, we've done with this.

PAULA. I suppose so. (*After a brief pause.*) Of course, she and I can't live under the same roof any more. You know she kissed me to-night, of her own accord.

AUBREY. I asked her to alter towards you.

PAULA. That was it, then.

AUBREY. I—I'm sorry I sent her away.

PAULA. It was my fault; I made it necessary.

AUBREY. Perhaps now she'll propose to return to the convent—well, she must.

PAULA. Would you like to keep her with you and—and leave me?

AUBREY. Paula—!

PAULA. You needn't be afraid I'd go back to—what I was. I couldn't.

AUBREY. S—sh, for God's sake! We—you and I—we'll get out of this place . . . what a fool I was to come here again!

PAULA. You lived here with your first wife!

AUBREY. We'll get out of this place and go abroad again, and begin afresh?

PAULA. Begin afresh?

AUBREY. There's no reason why the future shouldn't be happy for us—no reason that I can see—

PAULA. Aubrey!

AUBREY. Yes.

PAULA. You'll never forget this, you know.

AUBREY. This?

PAULA. To-night, and everything that's led up to it. Our coming here, Ellean, our quarrels—cat and dog!—Mrs. Cortelyon, the Orreyeds, this man! What an everlasting nightmare for you!

AUBREY. Oh, we can forget it, if we choose.

PAULA. That was always your cry. How *can* one do it!

AUBREY. We'll make our calculations solely for the future, talk about the future, think about the future.

PAULA. I believe the future is only the past again, entered through another gate.

AUBREY. That's an awful belief.

PAULA. To-night proves it. You must see now that, do what we will, go where we will, you'll be continually reminded of—what I was. I see it.

AUBREY. You're frightened to-night; meeting this man has frightened you. But that sort of thing isn't likely to recur. The world isn't quite so small as all that.

PAULA. Isn't it! The only great distances it contains are those we carry within ourselves—the distances that separate husbands and wives, for instance. And so it'll be with us. You'll do your best—oh, I know that—you're a good fellow. But circumstances will be too strong for you in the end, mark my words.

AUBREY. Paula—!

PAULA. Of course I'm pretty now—I'm pretty still—and a pretty woman, whatever else she may be, is always—well, endurable. But even now I notice that the lines of my face are getting deeper; so are the hollows about my eyes. Yes, my face is covered with little shadows that usen't to be there. Oh, I know I'm "going off." I hate paint and dye and those messes, but by and by, I shall drift the way of the others; I shan't be able to help myself. And then, some day—perhaps very suddenly, under a queer, fantastic light at night or in the glare of the morning—that horrid, irresistible truth that physical repulsion forces on men and women will come to you, and you'll sicken at me.

AUBREY. I—!

PAULA. You'll see me then, at last, with other people's eyes; you'll see me just as your daughter does now, as all wholesome folks see women like me. And I shall have no weapon to fight with—not one serviceable little bit of prettiness left me to defend myself with! A worn-out creature—broken up, very likely, some time before I ought to be—my hair bright, my eyes dull, my body too thin or too stout, my cheeks raddled and ruddled—a ghost, a wreck, a caricature, a candle that gutters, call such an end what you like! Oh, Aubrey, what shall I be able to say to you then? And this is the future you talk about! I know it—I know it! (*He is still sitting staring forward; she rocks herself to and fro as if in pain.*) Oh, Aubrey! Oh! Oh!

AUBREY. Paula—! (*Trying to comfort her.*)

PAULA. Oh, and I wanted so much to sleep to-night! (*Laying her head upon his shoulder. From the distance, in the garden, there comes the sound of* DRUMMLE'S *voice; he is singing as he approaches the house.*) That's Cayley, coming back from The Warren. (*Starting up.*) He doesn't know, evidently. I—I won't see him! (*She goes out quickly.* DRUMMLE'S *voice comes nearer.* AUBREY *rouses himself and snatches up a book from a table, making a pretence of reading.*)

(*After a moment or two,* DRUMMLE *appears at the window and looks in.*)

DRUMMLE. Aha! my dear chap!

AUBREY. Cayley?

DRUMMLE (*coming into the room*). I went down to The Warren after you.

AUBREY. Yes?

DRUMMLE. Missed you. Well—I've been gossiping with Mrs. Cortelyon. Confound you, I've heard the news!

AUBREY. What have you heard?

DRUMMLE. What have I heard! Why—Ellean and young Ardale! (*Looking at* AUBREY *keenly.*) My dear Aubrey! Alice is under the impression that you are inclined to look on the affair favorably.

AUBREY (*rising and advancing to* DRUMMLE). You've not—met—Captain Ardale?

DRUMMLE. No. Why do you ask? By the by, I don't know that I need tell you—but it's rather strange. He's not at The Warren to-night.

AUBREY, No?

DRUMMLE. He left the house half an hour ago, to stroll about the lanes; just now a note came from him, a scribble in pencil simply telling Alice that she would receive a letter from him to-morrow. What's the matter? There's nothing very wrong, is there? My dear chap, pray forgive me, if I'm asking too much.

AUBREY. Cayley, you—you urged me to send her away!

DRUMMLE. Ellean! Yes, yes. But—but—by all accounts this is quite an eligible young fellow. Alice has been giving me the history—

AUBREY. Curse him! (*Hurling his book to the floor.*) Curse him! Yes, I do curse him—him and his class! Perhaps I curse myself, too, in doing it. He has only led "a man's life"—just as I, how many of us have done! The misery he has brought on me and mine it's likely enough we, in our time, have helped to bring on others by this leading "a man's life"! But I do curse him for all that. My God, *I've* nothing more to fear—I've paid *my* fine! And so I can curse him in safety. Curse him! Curse him!

DRUMMLE. In Heaven's name, tell me what's happened?

AUBREY (*gripping* DRUMMLE'S *arm*). Paula! Paula!

DRUMMLE. What?

AUBREY. They met to-night here. They—they—they're not strangers to each other.

DRUMMLE. Aubrey!

AUBREY. Curse him! My poor, wretched wife! My poor, wretched wife!

(*The door opens and* ELLEAN *appears. The two men turn to her. There is a moment's silence.*)

ELLEAN. Father . . . father . . . !

AUBREY. Ellean?

ELLEAN. I—I want you. (*He goes to her.*) Father . . . go to Paula! (*He looks into her face, startled.*) Quickly—quickly! (*He passes her to go out; she seizes his arm, with a cry.*) No, no; don't go! (*He shakes her off and goes.* ELLEAN *staggers back towards* DRUMMLE.)

DRUMMLE (*to* ELLEAN). What do you mean? What do you mean?

ELLEAN. I—I went to her room—to tell her I was sorry for something I had said to her. And I *was* sorry—I *was* sorry. I heard the fall. I—I've seen her. It's horrible.

DRUMMLE. She—she has—!

ELLEAN. Killed—herself? Yes—yes. So, everybody will say. But I know—I helped to kill her. If I'd only been merciful! (*She faints upon the ottoman. He pauses for a moment irresolutely—then he goes to the door, opens it, and stands looking out.*)

THE IMPORTANCE OF BEING EARNEST

"Tragedy," writes Eric Bentley, "begins with calamity and ends in beauty, reconciliation, and hope; comedy begins with laughter and ends in judgment, reproof, and perhaps bitterness." *The Importance of Being Earnest* is not merely a farce, its "trivial comedy" is "for serious people," and it makes, though ever so entertainingly, some trenchant comments on social conditions. It is quite as concerned with important human values as is the work of Henry Arthur Jones or any other very earnest and eminent Victorian. We laugh in surprise or embarrassment or delight at the puns and the paradoxes and the preposterous, persistent plot. The shimmering surface of the wit, however, like the surface of a dancing brook, should not blind us with its sparkle to the depth or direction of the play. The work is in earnest. The clichés, turned upside down, suddenly reveal the truth. This is a play by a moralist who is demanding a revaluation of values; by an unconventional man with a vested interest in exploding priggishness, hypocrisy, and even convention; by a sentimental cynic who writes satire because he thinks he perceives the difference between things as they are and things as they ought to be. Because he attacks with a rapier instead of with a battle-axe, Wilde is sometimes dismissed as superficial, insincere. But people have been killed with a poisoned hatpin who never would have stood still for an attack by bad Sir Brian Botany wielding his mace "with great big nobs on." Wilde is un-English, that's all.

That Wilde would like to be an accepted part of that very society he so subtly excoriates is as clear in his art as it was in his life. He says somewhere that "the two things that every artist must avoid are modernity of form and modernity of subject-matter," yet he coolly takes a bead and fires at contemporary targets: modern attitudes toward marriage and love, art and aesthetics, philosophy and philanthropy, The Establishment and the disestablished aristocracy, the good, the true, and the beautiful. Wilde's is a timely (and universal) comment on life itself as he demonstrates that exaggeration, selection, and overemphasis are the essence of art and that the truth is this: what we take as fact is only opinion, what we call truth is merely misconception, and nature is false. As in the world of Gilbert, Things Are Seldom What They Seem. The most solid-seeming things are really hollow. The apparently flippant remarks are painfully profound. The face is removed to reveal the mask—and the mask in its complex simplicity is the real reality. The people who are the most serious in this joke we live are the most ludicrous. The parody of a melodrama is itself a melodrama as surely as nature imitates art.

The satire is never vicious in Wilde because quintessentially it is a valentine. *That's* the truth. Or at least that's as true as anything ought to be in polite society, and, of course, "a truth in art is that whose contradictory is also true." The disquietingly comforting fact is that society is going to worry, as we do with valentines, more about who sent it than what it says. We may even ignore what it says. *The Importance of Being Earnest* is going to be seen and read by some who are more fascinated by Wilde than wisdom, who are quite as oblivious to anything that concerns them as the dreadnought Lady Bracknell is to everything that does not concern her. To them Wilde's method of multiplying his personalities will seem to be insincerity or schizophrenia; his taking life by the throat, escapism. They may attack their attacker, defending their wayward ways by turning Lady Bracknell's words against their author: "Never speak disrespectfully of Society. . . . Only people who can't get into it do that." People who turn on Wilde as an outsider will fail to see books in running brooks, eternity in a grain of salt, and the epitome of Victorian England in three-volume novels "of more than usually revolting sentimentality" and the Army lists of "the last forty years." ("These delightful records should have been my constant study.")

Wilde's real crime was that he told people the truth about himself and themselves—and The Truth is hardly what one should tell to a nice, sweet, refined Society. Wilde was accused of being flip when actually he was earnest. Wilde was accused of lying. The fact is that he was an artist who was only *posing* as a liar. "Oh, that's nonsense, Algy. You never talk anything but nonsense," Society chides, amused but a little exasperated. And Algernon shrewdly replies, "Nobody ever does."

Perhaps Wilde would have been gratified to be misunderstood; amused to see those who were most needful of his criticism, most critical of him. Perhaps that was Wilde's revenge upon the society that made him the victim of that most Victorian of all sentimental predicaments, unrequited love.

THE IMPORTANCE OF BEING EARNEST

A TRIVIAL COMEDY FOR SERIOUS PEOPLE

by

Oscar Wilde

TO ROBERT BALDWIN ROSS
IN APPRECIATION AND AFFECTION

First presented Thursday, February 14, 1895, at George Alexander's St. James's Theatre, with the following cast:

JOHN WORTHING, J.P. *of the Manor House, Woolton, Hertfordshire*	Mr. George Alexander
ALGERNON MONCRIEFF (*his Friend*)	Mr. Allan Aynesworth
REV. CANON CHASUBLE, D.D. (*Rector of Woolton*)	Mr. H. H. Vincent
MERRIMAN (*Butler to Mr. Worthing*)	Mr. Frank Dyall
LANE (*Mr. Moncrieff's Man-servant*)	Mr. F. Kinsey Peile
LADY BRACKNELL	Miss Rose Leclercq
HON. GWENDOLEN FAIRFAX (*her Daughter*)	Miss Irene Vanbrugh
CECILY CARDEW (*John Worthing's Ward*)	Miss Evelyn Millard
MISS PRISM (*her Governess*)	Mrs. George Canninge

Time—The Present

ACT I *Algernon Moncrieff's Rooms in [Half-Moon Street, W.] Piccadilly*

ACT II *The Garden at the Manor House, Woolton*

ACT III *Morning-Room at the Manor House, Woolton*

At the first production the play was preceded by a one-act curtain-raiser, In the Season, *by Langdon E. Mitchell, with Mr. Herbert Waring, Mr. Arthur Royston, and Miss Elliott Page.*

FIRST ACT

SCENE: *Morning-room in Algernon's flat in Half-Moon Street. The room is luxuriously and artistically furnished. The sound of a piano is heard in the adjoining room.*

(LANE *is arranging afternoon tea on the table, and after the music has ceased,* ALGERNON *enters.*)

ALGERNON. Did you hear what I was playing, Lane?

LANE. I didn't think it polite to listen, sir.

ALGERNON. I'm sorry for that, for your sake. I don't play accurately—any one can play accurately—but I play with wonderful expression. As far as the piano is concerned, sentiment is my forte. I keep science for Life.

LANE. Yes, sir.

ALGERNON. And, speaking of the science of Life, have you got the cucumber sandwiches cut for Lady Bracknell?

LANE. Yes, sir. (*Hands them on a salver.*)

ALGERNON (*inspects them, takes two, and sits down on the sofa*). Oh! . . . by the way, Lane, I see from your book that on Thursday night, when Lord Shoreman and Mr. Worthing were dining with me, eight bottles of champagne are entered as having been consumed.

LANE. Yes, sir; eight bottles and a pint.

ALGERNON. Why is it that at a bachelor's establishment the servants invariably drink the champagne? I ask merely for information.

LANE. I attribute it to the superior quality of the wine, sir. I have often observed that in married households the champagne is rarely of a first-rate brand.

ALGERNON. Good heavens! Is marriage so demoralizing as that?

LANE. I believe it *is* a very pleasant state, sir. I have had very little experience of it myself up to the present. I have only been married once. That was in consequence of a misunderstanding between myself and a young person.

ALGERNON (*languidly*). I don't know that I am much interested in your family life, Lane.

LANE. No, sir; it is not a very interesting subject. I never think of it myself.

ALGERNON. Very natural, I am sure. That will do, Lane, thank you.

LANE. Thank you, sir. (LANE *goes out.*)

ALGERNON. Lane's views on marriage seem somewhat lax. Really, if the lower orders don't set us a good example, what on earth is the use of them? They seem, as a class, to have absolutely no sense of moral responsibility.

(*Enter* LANE.)

LANE. Mr. Ernest Worthing.

(*Enter* JACK. LANE *goes out.*)

ALGERNON. How are you, my dear Ernest? What brings you up to town?

JACK. Oh, pleasure, pleasure! What else should bring one anywhere? Eating as usual, I see, Algy!

ALGERNON (*stiffly*). I believe it is customary in good society to take some slight refreshment at five o'clock. Where have you been since last Thursday?

JACK (*sitting down on the sofa*). In the country.

ALGERNON. What on earth do you do there?

JACK (*pulling off his gloves*). When one is in town one amuses oneself. When one is in the country one amuses other people. It is excessively boring.

ALGERNON. And who are the people you amuse?

JACK (*airily*). Oh, neighbours, neighbours.

ALGERNON. Got nice neighbours in your part of Shropshire?

JACK. Perfectly horrid! Never speak to one of them.

ALGERNON. How immensely you must amuse them! (*Goes over and takes sandwich.*) By the way, Shropshire is your county, is it not?

JACK. Eh? Shropshire? Yes, of course. Hallo! Why all these cups? Why cucumber sandwiches? Why such reckless extravagance in one so young? Who is coming to tea?

ALGERNON. Oh! merely Aunt Augusta and Gwendolen.

JACK. How perfectly delightful!

ALGERNON. Yes, that is all very well; but I am afraid Aunt Augusta won't quite approve of your being here.

JACK. May I ask why?

ALGERNON. My dear fellow, the way you flirt with Gwendolen is perfectly disgraceful. It is almost as bad as the way Gwendolen flirts with you.

JACK. I am in love with Gwendolen. I have come up to town expressly to propose to her.

ALGERNON. I thought you had come up for pleasure? . . . I call that business.

JACK. How utterly unromantic you are!

ALGERNON. I really don't see anything romantic in proposing. It is very romantic to be in love. But there is nothing romantic about a definite proposal. Why, one may be accepted. One usually is, I believe. Then the excitement is all over. The very essence of romance is uncertainty. If ever I get married, I'll certainly try to forget the fact.

JACK. I have no doubt about that, dear Algy. The Divorce Court was specially invented for people whose memories are so curiously constituted.

ALGERNON. Oh! there is no use speculating on the subject. Divorces are made in Heaven—(JACK *puts out his hand to take a sandwich.* ALGERNON *at once interferes.*) Please don't touch the cucumber sandwiches. They are ordered specially for Aunt Augusta. (*Takes one and eats it.*)

JACK. Well, you have been eating them all the time.

ALGERNON. That is quite a different matter. She is my aunt. (*Takes plate from below.*) Have some bread and butter. The bread and butter is for Gwendolen. Gwendolen is devoted to bread and butter.

JACK (*advancing to table and helping himself*). And very good bread and butter it is too.

ALGERNON. Well, my dear fellow, you need not eat as if you were going to eat it all. You behave as if you were married to her already. You are not married to her already, and I don't think you ever will be.

JACK. Why on earth do you say that?

ALGERNON. Well, in the first place, girls never marry the men they flirt with. Girls don't think it right.

JACK. Oh, that is nonsense!

ALGERNON. It isn't. It is a great truth. It accounts for the extraordinary number of bachelors that one sees all over the place. In the second place, I don't give my consent.

JACK. Your consent!

ALGERNON. My dear fellow, Gwendolen is my first cousin. And before I allow you to marry her, you will have to clear up the whole question of Cecily. (*Rings bell.*)

JACK. Cecily! What on earth do you mean? What do you mean, Algy, by Cecily! I don't know any one of the name of Cecily.

(*Enter* LANE.)

ALGERNON. Bring me that cigarette case Mr. Worthing left in the smoking-room the last time he dined here.

LANE. Yes, sir. (LANE *goes out.*)

JACK. Do you mean to say you have had my cigarette case all this time? I wish to goodness you had let me know. I have been writing frantic letters to Scotland Yard about it. I was very nearly offering a large reward.

ALGERNON. Well, I wish you would offer one. I happen to be more than usually hard up.

JACK. There is no good offering a large reward now that the thing is found.

(*Enter* LANE *with the cigarette case on a salver.* ALGERNON *takes it at once.* LANE *goes out.*)

ALGERNON. I think that is rather mean of you, Ernest, I must say. (*Opens case and examines it.*) However, it makes no matter, for, now that I look at the inscription inside, I find that the thing isn't yours after all.

JACK. Of course it's mine. (*Moving to him.*) You have seen me with it a hundred times, and you have no right whatsoever to read what is written inside. It is a very ungentlemanly thing to read a private cigarette case.

ALGERNON. Oh! it is absurd to have a hard and fast rule about what one should read and what one shouldn't. More than half of modern culture depends on what one shouldn't read.

JACK. I am quite aware of the fact, and I don't propose to discuss modern culture. It isn't the sort of thing one should talk of in private. I simply want my cigarette case back.

ALGERNON. Yes; but this isn't your cigarette case. This cigarette case is a present from someone of the name of Cecily, and you said you didn't know anyone of that name.

JACK. Well, if you want to know, Cecily happens to be my aunt.

ALGERNON. Your aunt!

JACK. Yes. Charming old lady she is, too. Lives at Tunbridge Wells. Just give it back to me, Algy.

ALGERNON (*retreating to back of sofa*). But why does she call herself little Cecily if she is your aunt and lives at Tunbridge Wells? (*Reading.*) 'From little Cecily with her fondest love.'

JACK (*moving to sofa and kneeling upon it*). My dear fellow, what on earth is there in that? Some aunts are tall, some aunts are not tall. That is a matter that surely an aunt may be allowed to decide for herself. You seem to think that every aunt should be exactly like your aunt! That is absurd. For Heaven's sake give me back my cigarette case. (*Follows* ALGERNON *round the room.*)

ALGERNON. Yes. But why does your aunt call you her uncle? 'From little Cecily, with her fondest love to her dear Uncle Jack.' There is no objection, I admit, to an aunt being a small aunt, but why an aunt, no matter what her size may be, should call her own nephew her uncle, I can't quite make out. Besides, your name isn't Jack at all; it is Ernest.

JACK. It isn't Ernest; it's Jack.

ALGERNON. You have always told me it was Ernest. I have introduced you to every one as Ernest. You answer to the name of Ernest. You look as if your name was Ernest. You are the most earnest-looking person I ever saw in my life. It is perfectly absurd your saying that your name isn't Ernest. It's on your cards. Here is one of them. (*Taking it from case.*) 'Mr. Ernest Worthing, B.4, The Albany.' I'll keep this as a proof that your name is Ernest if ever you attempt to deny it to me, or to Gwendolen, or to any one else. (*Puts the card in his pocket.*)

JACK. Well, my name is Ernest in town and Jack in the country, and the cigarette case was given to me in the country.

ALGERNON. Yes, but that does not account for the fact that your small Aunt Cecily, who lives at Tunbridge Wells, calls you her dear uncle. Come, old boy, you had much better have the thing out at once.

JACK. My dear Algy, you talk exactly as if you were a dentist. It is very vulgar to talk like a dentist when one isn't a dentist. It produces a false impression.

ALGERNON. Well, that is exactly what dentists always do. Now, go on! Tell me the whole thing. I may mention that I have always suspected you of being a confirmed and secret Bunburyist; and I am quite sure of it now.

JACK. Bunburyist? What on earth do you mean by a Bunburyist?

ALGERNON. I'll reveal to you the meaning of that incomparable expression as soon as you are kind enough to inform me why you are Ernest in town and Jack in the country.

JACK. Well, produce my cigarette case first.

ALGERNON. Here it is. (*Hands cigarette case.*) Now produce your explanation, and pray make it improbable. (*Sits on sofa.*)

JACK. My dear fellow, there is nothing improbable about my explanation at all. In fact it's perfectly ordinary. Old Mr. Thomas Cardew, who adopted me when I was a little boy, made me in his will guardian to his granddaughter, Miss Cecily Cardew. Cecily, who addresses me as her uncle from motives of respect that you could not possibly appreciate, lives at my place in the country under the charge of her admirable governess, Miss Prism.

ALGERNON. Where is that place in the country, by the way?

JACK. That is nothing to you, dear boy. You are not going to be invited. . . . I may tell you candidly that the place is not in Shropshire.

ALGERNON. I suspected that, my dear fellow! I have Bunburyed all over Shropshire on two separate occasions. Now, go on. Why are you Ernest in town and Jack in the country?

JACK. My dear Algy, I don't know whether you will be able to understand my real motives. You are hardly serious enough. When one is placed in the position of guardian, one has to adopt a very high moral tone on all subjects. It's one's duty to do so. And as a high moral tone can hardly be said to conduce very much to either one's health or one's happiness, in order to get up to town I have always pretended to have a younger brother of the name of Ernest, who lives in the Albany, and gets into the most dreadful scrapes. That, my dear Algy, is the whole truth pure and simple.

ALGERNON. The truth is rarely pure and never simple. Modern life would be very tedious if it were either, and modern literature a complete impossibility!

JACK. That wouldn't be at all a bad thing.

ALGERNON. Literary criticism is not your forte, my dear fellow. Don't try it. You should leave that to people who haven't been at a University. They do it so well in the daily papers. What you really are is a Bunburyist. I was quite right in saying you were a Bunburyist. You are one of the most advanced Bunburyists I know.

JACK. What on earth do you mean?

ALGERNON. You have invented a very useful younger brother called Ernest, in order that you may be able to come up to town as often as you like. I have invented an invaluable permanent invalid called Bunbury, in order that I may be able to go down into the country whenever I choose. Bunbury is perfectly invaluable. If it wasn't for Bunbury's extraordinary bad health, for instance, I wouldn't be able to dine with you at Willis's to-night, for I have been really engaged to Aunt Augusta for more than a week.

JACK. I haven't asked you to dine with me anywhere to-night.

ALGERNON. I know. You are absurdly careless about sending out invitations. It is very foolish of you. Nothing annoys people so much as not receiving invitations.

JACK. You had much better dine with your Aunt Augusta.

ALGERNON. I haven't the smallest intention of doing anything of the kind. To begin with, I dined there on Monday, and once a week is quite enough to dine with one's own relations. In the second place, whenever I do dine there I am always treated as a member of the family, and sent down with either no woman at all, or two. In the third place, I know perfectly well whom she will place me next to, to-night. She will place me next Mary Farquhar, who always flirts with her own husband across the dinner-table. That is not very pleasant. Indeed, it is not even decent . . . and that sort of thing is enormously on the increase. The amount of women in London who flirt with their own husbands is perfectly scandalous. It looks so bad. It is simply washing one's clean linen in public. Besides, now that I know you to be a confirmed Bunburyist I naturally want to talk to you about Bunburying. I want to tell you the rules.

JACK. I'm not a Bunburyist at all. If Gwendolen accepts me, I am going to kill my brother, indeed I think I'll kill him in any case. Cecily is a little too much interested in him. It is rather a bore. So I am going to get rid of Ernest. And I strongly advise you to do the same with Mr. . . . with your invalid friend who has the absurd name.

ALGERNON. Nothing will induce me to part with Bunbury, and if you ever get married, which seems to me extremely problematic, you will be very glad to know Bunbury. A man who marries without knowing Bunbury has a very tedious time of it.

JACK. That is nonsense. If I marry a charming girl like Gwendolen, and she is the only girl I ever saw in my life that I would marry, I certainly won't want to know Bunbury.

ALGERNON. Then your wife will. You don't seem to realize, that in married life three is company and two is none.

JACK (*sententiously*). That, my dear young friend, is the theory that the corrupt French Drama has been propounding for the last fifty years.

ALGERNON. Yes; and that the happy English home has proved in half the time.

JACK. For heaven's sake, don't try to be cynical. It's perfectly easy to be cynical.

ALGERNON. My dear fellow, it isn't easy to be anything nowadays. There's such a lot of beastly competition about. (*The sound of an electric bell is heard.*) Ah! that must be Aunt Augusta. Only relatives, or creditors, ever ring in that Wagnerian manner. Now, if I get her out of the way for ten minutes, so that you can have an opportunity for proposing to Gwendolen, may I dine with you to-night at Willis's?

JACK. I suppose so, if you want to.

ALGERNON. Yes, but you must be serious about it. I hate people who are not serious about meals. It is so shallow of them.

(*Enter* LANE.)

LANE. Lady Bracknell and Miss Fairfax.

(ALGERNON *goes forward to meet them. Enter* LADY BRACKNELL *and* GWENDOLEN.)

LADY BRACKNELL. Good afternoon, dear Algernon, I hope you are behaving very well.

ALGERNON. I'm feeling very well, Aunt Augusta.

LADY BRACKNELL. That's not quite the same thing. In fact the two things rarely go together. (*Sees* JACK *and bows to him with icy coldness.*)

ALGERNON (*to* GWENDOLEN). Dear me, you are smart!

GWENDOLEN. I am always smart! Am I not, Mr. Worthing?

JACK. You're quite perfect, Miss Fairfax.

GWENDOLEN. Oh! I hope I am not that. It would leave no room for developments, and I intend to develop in many directions. (GWENDOLEN *and* JACK *sit down together in the corner.*)

LADY BRACKNELL. I'm sorry if we are a little late, Algernon, but I was obliged to call on dear Lady Harbury. I hadn't been there since her poor husband's death. I never saw a woman so altered; she looks quite twenty years younger. And now I'll have a cup of tea, and one of those nice cucumber sandwiches you promised me.

ALGERNON. Certainly, Aunt Augusta. (*Goes over to tea-table.*)

LADY BRACKNELL. Won't you come and sit here, Gwendolen?

GWENDOLEN. Thanks, mamma, I'm quite comfortable where I am.

ALGERNON (*picking up empty plate in horror*). Good heavens! Lane! Why are there no cucumber sandwiches? I ordered them specially.

LANE (*gravely*). There were no cucumbers in the market this morning, sir. I went down twice.

ALGERNON. No cucumbers!

LANE. No, sir. Not even for ready money.

ALGERNON. That will do, Lane, thank you.

LANE. Thank you, sir. (*Goes out.*)

ALGERNON. I am greatly distressed, Aunt Augusta, about there being no cucumbers, not even for ready money.

LADY BRACKNELL. It really makes no matter, Algernon. I had some crumpets with Lady Harbury, who seems to me to be living entirely for pleasure now.

ALGERNON. I hear her hair has turned quite gold from grief.

LADY BRACKNELL. It certainly has changed its colour. From what cause I, of course, cannot say. (ALGERNON *crosses and hands tea.*) Thank you. I've quite a treat for you to-night, Algernon. I am going to send you down with Mary Farquhar. She is such a nice woman, and so attentive to her husband. It's delightful to watch them.

ALGERNON. I am afraid, Aunt Augusta, I shall have to give up the pleasure of dining with you to-night after all.

LADY BRACKNELL (*frowning*). I hope not, Algernon. It would put my table completely out. Your uncle would have to dine upstairs. Fortunately he is accustomed to that.

ALGERNON. It is a great bore, and, I need hardly say, a terrible disappointment to me, but the fact is I have just had a telegram to say that my poor friend Bunbury is very ill again. (*Exchanges glances with* JACK.) They seem to think I should be with him.

LADY BRACKNELL. It is very strange. This Mr. Bunbury seems to suffer from curiously bad health.

ALGERNON. Yes; poor Bunbury is a dreadful invalid.

LADY BRACKNELL. Well, I must say, Algernon, that I think it is high time that Mr. Bunbury made up his mind whether he was going to live or to die. This shilly-shallying with the question is absurd. Nor do I in any way approve of the modern sympathy with invalids. I consider it morbid. Illness of any kind is hardly a thing to be encouraged in others. Health is the primary duty of life. I am always telling that to your poor uncle, but he never seems to take much notice . . . as far as any improvement in his ailment goes. I should be much obliged if you would ask Mr. Bunbury, from me, to be kind enough not to have a relapse on Saturday, for I rely on you to arrange my music for me. It is my last reception, and one wants something that will encourage conversation, particularly at the end of the season when every one has practically said whatever they had to say, which, in most cases, was probably not much.

ALGERNON. I'll speak to Bunbury, Aunt Augusta, if he is still conscious, and I think I can promise you he'll be all right by Saturday. Of course the music is a great difficulty. You see, if one plays good music, people don't listen, and if one plays bad music people don't talk. But I'll run over the programme I've drawn out, if you will kindly come into the next room for a moment.

LADY BRACKNELL. Thank you, Algernon. It is very thoughtful of you. (*Rising, and following* ALGERNON.) I'm sure the programme will be delightful, after a few expurgations. French songs I cannot possibly allow. People always seem to think that they are improper, and either look shocked, which is vulgar, or laugh, which is worse. But German sounds a thoroughly respectable language, and, indeed I believe is so. Gwendolen, you will accompany me.

GWENDOLEN. Certainly, mamma. (LADY BRACKNELL *and* ALGERNON *go into the music-room,* GWENDOLEN *remains behind.*)

JACK. Charming day it has been, Miss Fairfax.

GWENDOLEN. Pray don't talk to me about the weather, Mr. Worthing. Whenever people talk to me about the weather, I always feel quite certain that they mean something else. And that makes me so nervous.

JACK. I do mean something else.

GWENDOLEN. I thought so. In fact, I am never wrong.

JACK. And I would like to be allowed to take advantage of Lady Bracknell's temporary absence. . . .

GWENDOLEN. I would certainly advise you to do so. Mamma has a way of coming back suddenly into a room that I have often had to speak to her about.

JACK (*nervously*). Miss Fairfax, ever since I met you I have admired you more than any girl . . . I have ever met since . . . I met you.

GWENDOLEN. Yes, I am quite well aware of the fact. And I often wish that in public, at any rate, you had been more demonstrative. For me you have always had an irresistible fascination. Even before I met you I was far from indifferent to you. (JACK *looks at her in amazement.*) We live, as I hope you know, Mr. Worthing, in an age of ideals. The fact is constantly mentioned in the more expensive monthly magazines, and has reached the provincial pulpits, I am told; and my ideal has always been to love some one of the name of Ernest. There is something in that name that inspires absolute confidence. The moment Algernon first mentioned to me that he had a friend called Ernest, I knew I was destined to love you.

JACK. You really love me, Gwendolen?

GWENDOLEN. Passionately!

JACK. Darling! You don't know how happy you've made me.

GWENDOLEN. My own Ernest!

JACK. But you don't really mean to say that you couldn't love me if my name wasn't Ernest?

GWENDOLEN. But your name is Ernest.

JACK. Yes, I know it is. But supposing it was something else? Do you mean to say you couldn't love me then?

GWENDOLEN (*glibly*). Ah! that is clearly a metaphysical speculation, and like most metaphysical speculations has very little reference at all to the actual facts of real life, as we know them.

JACK. Personally, darling, to speak quite candidly, I don't much care about the name of Ernest. . . . I don't think the name suits me at all.

GWENDOLEN. It suits you perfectly. It is a divine name. It has music of its own. It produces vibrations.

JACK. Well, really, Gwendolen, I must say that I think there are lots of other much nicer names. I think Jack, for instance, a charming name.

GWENDOLEN. Jack? . . . No, there is very little music in the name Jack, if any at all, indeed. It does not thrill. It produces absolutely no vibrations. . . . I have known several Jacks, and they all, without exception, were more than usually plain. Besides, Jack is a notorious domesticity for John! And I pity any woman who is married to a man called John. She would probably never be allowed to know the entrancing pleasure of a single moment's solitude. The only really safe name is Ernest.

JACK. Gwendolen, I must get christened at once—I mean we must get married at once. There is no time to be lost.

GWENDOLEN. Married, Mr. Worthing?

JACK (*astounded*). Well . . . surely. You know that I love you, and you led me to believe, Miss Fairfax, that you were not absolutely indifferent to me.

GWENDOLEN. I adore you. But you haven't proposed to me yet. Nothing has been said at all about marriage. The subject has not even been touched on.

JACK. Well . . . may I propose to you now?

GWENDOLEN. I think it would be an admirable opportunity. And to spare you any possible disappointment, Mr. Worthing, I think it only fair to tell you quite frankly beforehand that I am fully determined to accept you.

JACK. Gwendolen!

GWENDOLEN. Yes, Mr. Worthing, what have you got to say to me?

JACK. You know what I have got to say to you.

GWENDOLEN. Yes, but you don't say it.

JACK. Gwendolen, will you marry me? (*Goes on his knees.*)

GWENDOLEN. Of course I will, darling. How long you have been about it! I am afraid you have had very little experience in how to propose.

JACK. My own one, I have never loved any one in the world but you.

GWENDOLEN. Yes, but men often propose for practice. I know my brother Gerald does. All my girl-friends tell me so. What wonderfully blue eyes you have, Ernest! They are quite, quite blue. I hope you will always look at me just like that, especially when there are other people present.

(*Enter* LADY BRACKNELL.)

LADY BRACKNELL. Mr. Worthing! Rise, sir, from this semi-recumbent posture. It is most indecorous.

GWENDOLEN. Mamma! (*He tries to rise; she restrains him.*) I must beg you to retire. This is no place for you. Besides, Mr. Worthing has not quite finished yet.

LADY BRACKNELL. Finished what, may I ask?

GWENDOLEN. I am engaged to Mr. Worthing, mamma. (*They rise together.*)

LADY BRACKNELL. Pardon me, you are not engaged to any one. When you do become engaged to some one, I, or your father, should his health permit him, will inform you of the fact. An engagement should come on a young girl as a surprise, pleasant or unpleasant, as the case may be. It is hardly a matter that she could be allowed to arrange for herself. . . . And now I have a few questions to put to you, Mr. Worthing. While I am making these inquiries, you, Gwendolen, will wait for me below in the carriage.

GWENDOLEN (*reproachfully*). Mamma!

LADY BRACKNELL. In the carriage, Gwendolen! (GWENDOLEN *goes to the door. She and* JACK *blow kisses to each other behind* LADY BRACKNELL'S *back.* LADY BRACKNELL *looks vaguely about as if she could not understand what the noise was. Finally turns round.*) Gwendolen, the carriage!

GWENDOLEN. Yes, mamma. (*Goes out, looking back at* JACK.)

LADY BRACKNELL (*sitting down*). You can take a seat, Mr. Worthing. (*Looks in her pocket for note-book and pencil.*)

JACK. Thank you, Lady Bracknell, I prefer standing.

LADY BRACKNELL (*pencil and note-book in hand*). I feel bound to tell you that you are not down on my list of eligible young men, although I have the same list as the dear Duchess of Bolton has. We work together, in fact. However, I am quite ready to enter your name, should your answers be what a really affectionate mother requires. Do you smoke?

JACK. Well, yes, I must admit I smoke.

LADY BRACKNELL. I am glad to hear it. A man should always have an occupation of some kind. There are far too many idle men in London as it is. How old are you?

JACK. Twenty-nine.

LADY BRACKNELL. A very good age to be married at. I have always been of opinion that a man who desires to get married should know either everything or nothing. Which do you know?

JACK (*after some hesitation*). I know nothing, Lady Bracknell.

LADY BRACKNELL. I am pleased to hear it. I do not approve of anything that tampers with natural ignorance. Ignorance is like a delicate exotic fruit; touch it and the bloom is gone. The whole theory of modern education is radically unsound. Fortunately in England, at any rate, education produces no effect whatsoever. If it did, it would prove a serious danger to the upper classes, and probably lead to acts of violence in Grosvenor Square. What is your income?

JACK. Between seven and eight thousand a year.

LADY BRACKNELL (*makes a note in her book*). In land, or in investments?

JACK. In investments, chiefly.

LADY BRACKNELL. That is satisfactory. What between the duties expected of one during one's lifetime, and the duties exacted from one after one's death, land has ceased to be either a profit or a pleasure. It gives one position, and prevents one from keeping it up. That's all that can be said about land.

JACK. I have a country house with some land, of course, attached to it, about fifteen hundred acres, I believe; but I don't depend on that for my real income. In fact, as far as I can make out, the poachers are the only people who make anything out of it.

LADY BRACKNELL. A country house! How many bedrooms? Well, that point can be cleared up afterwards. You have a town house, I hope? A girl with a simple, unspoiled nature, like Gwendolen, could hardly be expected to reside in the country.

JACK. Well, I own a house in Belgrave Square, but it is let by the year to Lady Bloxham. Of course, I can get it back whenever I like, at six months' notice.

LADY BRACKNELL. Lady Bloxham? I don't know her.

JACK. Oh, she goes about very little. She is a lady considerably advanced in years.

LADY BRACKNELL. Ah, nowadays that is no guarantee of respectability of character. What number in Belgrave Square?

JACK. 149.

LADY BRACKNELL (*shaking her head*). The unfashionable side. I thought there was something. However, that could easily be altered.

JACK. Do you mean the fashion, or the side?

LADY BRACKNELL (*sternly*). Both, if necessary, I presume. What are your politics?

JACK. Well, I am afraid I really have none. I am a Liberal Unionist.

LADY BRACKNELL. Oh, they count as Tories. They dine with us. Or come in the evening, at any rate. Now to minor matters. Are your parents living?

JACK. I have lost both my parents.

LADY BRACKNELL. To lose one parent, Mr. Worthing, may be regarded as a misfortune; to lose both looks like carelessness. Who was your father? He was evidently a man of some wealth. Was he born in what the Radical papers call the purple of commerce, or did he rise from the ranks of the aristocracy?

JACK. I am afraid I really don't know. The fact is, Lady Bracknell, I said I had lost my parents. It would be nearer the truth to say that my parents seem to have lost me. . . . I don't actually know who I am by birth. I was . . . well, I was found.

LADY BRACKNELL. Found!

JACK. The late Mr. Thomas Cardew, an old gentleman of a very charitable and kindly disposition, found me, and gave me the name of Worthing, because he happened to have a first-class ticket for Worthing in his pocket at the time. Worthing is a place in Sussex. It is a seaside resort.

LADY BRACKNELL. Where did the charitable gentleman who had a first-class ticket for this seaside resort find you?

JACK (*gravely*). In a hand-bag.

LADY BRACKNELL. A hand-bag?

JACK (*very seriously*). Yes, Lady Bracknell. I was in a hand-bag—a somewhat large, black leather hand-bag, with handles to it—an ordinary hand-bag in fact.

LADY BRACKNELL. In what locality did this Mr. James, or Thomas, Cardew come across this ordinary hand-bag?

JACK. In the cloak-room at Victoria Station. It was given to him in mistake for his own.

LADY BRACKNELL. The cloak-room at Victoria Station?

JACK. Yes. The Brighton line.

LADY BRACKNELL. The line is immaterial. Mr. Worthing, I confess I feel somewhat bewildered by what you have just told me. To be born, or at any rate bred, in a hand-bag, whether it had handles or not, seems to me to display a contempt for the ordinary decencies of family life that reminds one of the worst excesses of the French Revolution. And

I presume you know what that unfortunate movement led to? As for the particular locality in which the hand-bag was found, a cloak-room at a railway station might serve to conceal a social indiscretion—has probably, indeed, been used for that purpose before now—but it could hardly be regarded as an assured basis for a recognized position in good society.

JACK. May I ask you then what you would advise me to do? I need hardly say I would do anything in the world to ensure Gwendolen's happiness.

LADY BRACKNELL. I would strongly advise you, Mr. Worthing, to try and acquire some relations as soon as possible, and to make a definite effort to produce at any rate one parent, of either sex, before the season is quite over.

JACK. Well, I don't see how I could possibly manage to do that. I can produce the hand-bag at any moment. It is in my dressing-room at home. I really think that should satisfy you, Lady Bracknell.

LADY BRACKNELL. Me, sir! What has it to do with me? You can hardly imagine that I and Lord Bracknell would dream of allowing our only daughter—a girl brought up with the utmost care—to marry into a cloak-room, and form an alliance with a parcel. Good morning, Mr. Worthing! (LADY BRACKNELL *sweeps out in majestic indignation.*)

JACK. Good morning! (ALGERNON, *from the other room, strikes up the Wedding March.* JACK *looks perfectly furious, and goes to the door.*) For goodness' sake don't play that ghastly tune, Algy! How idiotic you are!

(*The music stops and* ALGERNON *enters cheerily.*)

ALGERNON. Didn't it go off all right, old boy? You don't mean to say Gwendolen refused you? I know it is a way she has. She is always refusing people. I think it is most ill-natured of her.

JACK. Oh, Gwendolen is as right as a trivet. As far as she is concerned, we are engaged. Her mother is perfectly unbearable. Never met such a Gorgon. . . . I don't really know what a Gorgon is like, but I am quite sure that Lady Bracknell is one. In any case, she is a monster, without being a myth, which is rather unfair. . . . I beg your pardon, Algy, I suppose I shouldn't talk about your own aunt in that way before you.

ALGERNON. My dear boy, I love hearing my relations abused. It is the only thing that makes me put up with them at all. Relations are simply a tedious pack of people, who haven't got the remotest knowledge of how to live, nor the smallest instinct about when to die.

JACK. Oh, that is nonsense!

ALGERNON. It isn't!

JACK. Well, I won't argue about the matter. You always want to argue about things.

ALGERNON. That is exactly what things were originally made for.

JACK. Upon my word, if I thought that, I'd shoot myself. . . . (*A pause.*) You don't think there is any chance of Gwendolen becoming like her mother in about a hundred and fifty years, do you, Algy?

ALGERNON. All women become like their mothers. That is their tragedy. No man does. That's his.

JACK. Is that clever?

ALGERNON. It is perfectly phrased! and quite as true as any observation in civilized life should be.

JACK. I am sick to death of cleverness. Everybody is clever nowadays. You can't go anywhere without meeting clever people. The thing has become an absolute public nuisance. I wish to goodness we had a few fools left.

ALGERNON. We have.

JACK. I should extremely like to meet them. What do they talk about?

ALGERNON. The fools? Oh! about the clever people, of course.

JACK. What fools.

ALGERNON. By the way, did you tell Gwendolen the truth about your being Ernest in town, and Jack in the country?

JACK (*in a very patronizing manner*). My dear fellow, the truth isn't quite the sort of thing one tells to a nice, sweet, refined girl. What extraordinary ideas you have about the way to behave to a woman!

ALGERNON. The only way to behave to a woman is to make love to her, if she is pretty, and to someone else, if she is plain.

JACK. Oh, that is nonsense.

ALGERNON. What about your brother? What about the profligate Ernest?

JACK. Oh, before the end of the week I shall have got rid of him. I'll say he died in Paris of apoplexy. Lots of people die of apoplexy, quite suddenly, don't they?

ALGERNON. Yes, but it's hereditary, my dear fellow. It's a sort of thing that runs in families. You had much better say a severe chill.

JACK. You are sure a severe chill isn't hereditary, or anything of that kind?

ALGERNON. Of course it isn't!

JACK. Very well, then. My poor brother Ernest is carried off suddenly, in Paris, by a severe chill. That gets rid of him.

ALGERNON. But I thought you said that . . . Miss Cardew was a little too much interested in your poor brother Ernest? Won't she feel his loss a good deal?

JACK. Oh, that is all right. Cecily is not a silly romantic girl, I am glad to say. She has got a capital appetite, goes for long walks, and pays no attention at all to her lessons.

ALGERNON. I would rather like to see Cecily.

JACK. I will take very good care you never do. She is excessively pretty, and she is only just eighteeen.

ALGERNON. Have you told Gwendolen yet that you have an excessively pretty ward who is only just eighteen?

JACK. Oh! one doesn't blurt these things out to people. Cecily and Gwendolen are perfectly certain to be extremely great friends. I'll bet you anything you like that half an hour after they have met, they will be calling each other sister.

ALGERNON. Women only do that when they have called each other a lot of other things first. Now, my dear boy, if we want to get a good table at Willis's, we really must go and dress. Do you know it is nearly seven?

JACK (*irritably*). Oh! it always is nearly seven.

ALGERNON. I'm hungry.

JACK. I never knew you when you weren't. . . .

ALGERNON. What shall we do after dinner? Go to a theatre?

JACK. Oh no! I loathe listening.

ALGERNON. Well, let us go to the Club?

JACK. Oh, no! I hate talking.

ALGERNON. Well, we might trot round to the Empire at ten?

JACK. Oh, no! I can't bear looking at things. It is so silly.

ALGERNON. Well, what shall we do?

JACK. Nothing!

ALGERNON. It is awfully hard work doing nothing. However, I don't mind hard work where there is no definite object of any kind.

(*Enter* LANE.)

LANE. Miss Fairfax.

(*Enter* GWENDOLEN. LANE *goes out.*)

ALGERNON. Gwendolen, upon my word!

GWENDOLEN. Algy, kindly turn your back. I have something very particular to say to Mr. Worthing.

ALGERNON. Really, Gwendolen, I don't think I can allow this at all.

GWENDOLEN. Algy, you always adopt a strictly immoral attitude towards life. You are not quite old enough to do that. (ALGERNON *retires to the fire-place.*)

JACK. My own darling!

GWENDOLEN. Ernest, we may never be married. From the expression on mamma's face I fear we never shall. Few parents nowadays pay any regard to what their children say to them. The old-fashioned respect for the young is fast dying out. Whatever influence I ever had over mamma, I lost at the age of three. But although she may prevent us from becoming man and wife, and I may marry someone else, and marry often, nothing that she can possibly do can alter my eternal devotion to you.

JACK. Dear Gwendolen!

GWENDOLEN. The story of your romantic origin, as related to me by mamma, with unpleasing comments, has naturally stirred the deeper fibres of my nature. Your Christian name has an irresistible fascination. The simplicity of your character makes you exquisitely incomprehensible to me. Your town address at the Albany I have. What is your address in the country?

JACK. The Manor House, Woolton, Hertfordshire. (ALGERNON, *who has been carefully listening, smiles to himself, and writes the address on his shirt-cuff. Then picks up the Railway Guide.*)

GWENDOLEN. There is a good postal service, I suppose? It may be necessary to do something desperate. That of course will require serious consideration. I will communicate with you daily.

JACK. My own one!

GWENDOLEN. How long do you remain in town?

JACK. Till Monday.

GWENDOLEN. Good! Algy, you may turn round now.

ALGERNON. Thanks, I've turned round already.

GWENDOLEN. You may also ring the bell.

JACK. You will let me see you to your carriage, my own darling?

GWENDOLEN. Certainly.

JACK (*to* LANE, *who now enters*). I will see Miss Fairfax out.

LANE. Yes, sir. (JACK *and* GWENDOLEN *go off.*) (LANE *presents several letters on a salver to* ALGERNON. *It is to be surmised that they are bills, as* ALGERNON, *after looking at the envelopes, tears them up.*)

ALGERNON. A glass of sherry, Lane.

LANE. Yes, sir.

ALGERNON. To-morrow, Lane, I'm going Bunburying.

LANE. Yes, sir.

ALGERNON. I shall probably not be back till Monday. You can put up my dress clothes, my smoking jacket, and all the Bunbury suits. . . .

LANE. Yes, sir. (*Handing sherry.*)

ALGERNON. I hope to-morrow will be a fine day, Lane.

LANE. It never is, sir.

ALGERNON. Lane, you're a perfect pessimist.

LANE. I do my best to give satisfaction, sir.

(*Enter* JACK. LANE *goes off.*)

JACK. There's a sensible, intellectual girl! the only girl I ever cared for in my life. (ALGERNON *is laughing immoderately.*) What on earth are you so amused at?

ALGERNON. Oh, I'm a little anxious about poor Bunbury, that is all.

JACK. If you don't take care, your friend Bunbury will get you into a serious scrape some day.

ALGERNON. I love scrapes. They are the only things that are never serious.

JACK. Oh, that's nonsense, Algy. You never talk anything but nonsense.

ALGERNON. Nobody ever does. (JACK *looks indignantly at him, and leaves the room.* ALGERNON *lights a cigarette, reads his shirt-cuff, and smiles.*)

Act Drop

SECOND ACT

SCENE: *Garden at the Manor House. A flight of grey stone steps leads up to the house. The garden, an old-fashioned one, full of roses. Time of year, July. Basket chairs, and a table covered with books, are set under a large yew-tree.*

(MISS PRISM *discovered seated at the table.* CECILY *is at the back, watering flowers.*)

MISS PRISM (*calling*). Cecily, Cecily! Surely such a utilitarian occupation as the watering of flowers is rather Moulton's duty than yours? Especially at a moment when intellectual pleasures await you. Your German grammar is on the table. Pray open it at page fifteen. We will repeat yesterday's lesson.

CECILY (*coming over very slowly*). But I don't like German. It isn't at all a becoming language. I know perfectly well that I look quite plain after my German lesson.

MISS PRISM. Child, you know how anxious your guardian is that you should improve yourself in every way. He laid particular stress on your German, as he was leaving for town yesterday. Indeed, he always lays stress on your German when he is leaving for town.

CECILY. Dear Uncle Jack is so very serious! Sometimes he is so serious that I think he cannot be quite well.

MISS PRISM (*drawing herself up*). Your guardian enjoys the best of health, and his gravity of demeanour is especially to be commended in one so comparatively young as he is. I know no one who has a higher sense of duty and responsibility.

CECILY. I suppose that is why he often looks a little bored when we three are together.

MISS PRISM. Cecily! I am surprised at you. Mr. Worthing has many troubles in his life. Idle merriment and triviality would be out of place in his conversation. You must remember his constant anxiety about that unfortunate young man, his brother.

CECILY. I wish Uncle Jack would allow that unfortunate young man, his brother, to come down here sometimes. We might have a good influence over him, Miss Prism. I am sure you certainly would. You know German, and geology, and things of that kind influence a man very much. (CECILY *begins to write in her diary.*)

MISS PRISM (*shaking her head*). I do not think that even I could produce any effect on a character that according to his own brother's admission is irretrievably weak and vacillating. Indeed I am not sure that I would desire to reclaim him. I am not in favour of this modern mania for turning bad people into good people at a moment's notice. As a man sows so let him reap. You must put away your diary, Cecily. I really don't see why you should keep a diary at all.

CECILY. I keep a diary in order to enter the wonderful secrets of my life. If I didn't write them down, I should probably forget all about them.

MISS PRISM. Memory, my dear Cecily, is the diary that we all carry about with us.

CECILY. Yes, but it usually chronicles the things that have never happened, and couldn't possibly have happened. I believe that Memory is responsible for nearly all the three-volume novels that Mudie sends us.

MISS PRISM. Do not speak slightingly of the three-volume novel, Cecily. I wrote one myself in earlier days.

CECILY. Did you really, Miss Prism? How wonderfully clever you are! I hope it did not end happily? I don't like novels that end happily. They depress me so much.

MISS PRISM. The good ended happily, and the bad unhappily. That is what Fiction means.

CECILY. I suppose so. But it seems very unfair. And was your novel ever published?

MISS PRISM. Alas! no. The manuscript unfortunately was abandoned. (CECILY *starts.*) I used the word in the sense of lost or mislaid. To your work, child, these speculations are profitless.

CECILY (*smiling*). But I see dear Dr. Chasuble coming up through the garden.

MISS PRISM (*rising and advancing*). Dr. Chasuble! This is indeed a pleasure.

(*Enter* CANON CHASUBLE.)

CHASUBLE. And how are we this morning? Miss Prism, you are, I trust, well?

CECILY. Miss Prism has just been complaining of a slight headache. I think it would do her so much good to have a short stroll with you in the Park, Dr. Chasuble.

MISS PRISM. Cecily, I have not mentioned anything about a headache.

CECILY. No, dear Miss Prism, I know that, but I felt instinctively that you had a headache. Indeed I was thinking about that, and not about my German lesson, when the Rector came in.

CHASUBLE. I hope, Cecily, you are not inattentive.

CECILY. Oh, I am afraid I am.

CHASUBLE. That is strange. Were I fortunate enough to be Miss Prism's pupil, I would hang upon her lips. (MISS PRISM *glares.*) I spoke metaphorically.—My metaphor was drawn from bees. Ahem! Mr. Worthing, I suppose, has not returned from town yet?

MISS PRISM. We do not expect him till Monday afternoon.

CHASUBLE. Ah yes, he usually likes to spend his Sunday in London. He is not one of those whose sole aim is enjoyment, as, by all accounts, that unfortunate young man his brother seems to be. But I must not disturb Egeria and her pupil any longer.

MISS PRISM. Egeria? My name is Laetitia, Doctor.

CHASUBLE (*bowing*). A classical allusion merely, drawn from the Pagan authors. I shall see you both no doubt at Evensong?

MISS PRISM. I think, dear Doctor, I will have a stroll with you. I find I have a headache after all, and a walk might do it good.

CHASUBLE. With pleasure, Miss Prism, with pleasure. We might go as far as the schools and back.

MISS PRISM. That would be delightful. Cecily, you will read your Political Economy in my absence. The chapter on the Fall of the Rupee you may omit. It is somewhat too sensational. Even these metallic problems have their melodramatic side.

(*Goes down the garden with* DR. CHASUBLE.)

CECILY (*picks up books and throws them back on table*). Horrid Political Economy! Horrid Geography! Horrid, horrid German!

(*Enter* MERRIMAN *with a card on a salver.*)

MERRIMAN. Mr. Ernest Worthing has just driven over from the station. He has brought his luggage with him.

CECILY (*takes the card and reads it*). 'Mr. Ernest Worthing, B.4, The Albany, W.' Uncle Jack's brother! Did you tell him Mr. Worthing was in town?

MERRIMAN. Yes, Miss. He seemed very much disappointed. I mentioned that you and Miss Prism were in the garden. He said he was anxious to speak to you privately for a moment.

CECILY. Ask Mr. Ernest Worthing to come here. I suppose you had better talk to the housekeeper about a room for him.

MERRIMAN. Yes, Miss. (MERRIMAN *goes off.*)

CECILY. I have never met any really wicked person before. I feel rather frightened. I am so afraid he will look just like every one else.

(*Enter* ALGERNON, *very gay and debonair.*)

He does!

ALGERNON (*raising his hat*). You are my little cousin Cecily, I'm sure.

CECILY. You are under some strange mistake. I am not little. In fact, I believe I am more than usually tall for my age. (ALGERNON *is rather taken aback.*) But I am your cousin Cecily. You, I see from your card, are Uncle Jack's brother, my cousin Ernest, my wicked cousin Ernest.

ALGERNON. Oh! I am not really wicked at all, cousin Cecily. You mustn't think that I am wicked.

CECILY. If you are not, then you have certainly been deceiving us all in a very inexcusable manner. I hope you have not been leading a double life, pretending to be wicked and being really good all the time. That would be hypocrisy.

ALGERNON (*looks at her in amazement*). Oh! Of course I have been rather reckless.

CECILY. I am glad to hear it.

ALGERNON. In fact, now you mention the subject, I have been very bad in my own small way.

CECILY. I don't think you should be so proud of that, though I am sure it must have been very pleasant.

ALGERNON. It is much pleasanter being here with you.

CECILY. I can't understand how you are here at all. Uncle Jack won't be back till Monday afternoon.

ALGERNON. That is a great disappointment. I am obliged to go up by the first train on Monday morning. I have a business appointment that I am anxious . . . to miss!

CECILY. Couldn't you miss it anywhere but in London?

ALGERNON. No: the appointment is in London.

CECILY. Well, I know, of course, how important it is not to keep a business engagement, if one wants to retain any sense of the beauty of life, but still I think you had better wait till Uncle Jack arrives. I know he wants to speak to you about your emigrating.

ALGERNON. About my what?

CECILY. Your emigrating. He has gone up to buy your outfit.

ALGERNON. I certainly wouldn't let Jack buy my outfit. He has no taste in neckties at all.

CECILY. I don't think you will require neckties. Uncle Jack is sending you to Australia.

ALGERNON. Australia! I'd sooner die.

CECILY. Well, he said at dinner on Wednesday night, that you would have to choose between this world, the next world, and Australia.

ALGERNON. Oh, well! The accounts I have received of Australia and the next world are not particularly encouraging. This world is good enough for me, cousin Cecily.

CECILY. Yes, but are you good enough for it?

ALGERNON. I'm afraid I'm not that. That is why I want you to reform me. You might make that your mission, if you don't mind, Cousin Cecily.

CECILY. I'm afraid I've no time, this afternoon.

ALGERNON. Well, would you mind my reforming myself this afternoon?

CECILY. It is rather Quixotic of you. But I think you should try.

ALGERNON. I will. I feel better already.

CECILY. You are looking a little worse.

ALGERNON. That is because I am hungry.

CECILY. How thoughtless of me. I should have remembered that when one is going to lead an entirely new life, one requires regular and wholesome meals. Won't you come in?

ALGERNON. Thank you. Might I have a buttonhole first? I have never any appetite unless I have a buttonhole first.

CECILY. A Maréchal Niel? (*Picks up scissors.*)

ALGERNON. No, I'd sooner have a pink rose.

CECILY. Why? (*Cuts a flower.*)

ALGERNON. Because you are like a pink rose, Cousin Cecily.

CECILY. I don't think it can be right for you to talk to me like that. Miss Prism never says such things to me.

ALGERNON. Then Miss Prism is a short-sighted old lady. (CECILY *puts the rose in his buttonhole.*) You are the prettiest girl I ever saw.

CECILY. Miss Prism says that all good looks are a snare.

ALGERNON. They are a snare that every sensible man would like to be caught in.

CECILY. Oh, I don't think I would care to catch a sensible man. I shouldn't know what to talk to him about.

(*They pass into the house.* MISS PRISM *and* DR. CHASUBLE *return.*)

MISS PRISM. You are too much alone, dear Dr. Chasuble. You should get married. A misanthrope I can understand—a womanthrope, never!

CHASUBLE (*with a scholar's shudder*). Believe me, I do not deserve so neologistic a phrase. The precept as well as the practice of the Primitive Church was distinctly against matrimony.

MISS PRISM (*sententiously*). That is obviously the reason why the Primitive Church has not lasted up to the present day. And you do not seem to realize, dear Doctor, that by persistently remaining single, a man converts himself into a permanent public temptation. Men should be more careful; this very celibacy leads weaker vessels astray.

CHASUBLE. But is a man not equally attractive when married?

MISS PRISM. No married man is ever attractive except to his wife.

CHASUBLE. And often, I've been told, not even to her.

MISS PRISM. That depends on the intellectual sympathies of the woman. Maturity can always be depended on. Ripeness can be trusted. Young women are green. (DR. CHASUBLE *starts.*) I spoke horticulturally. My metaphor was drawn from fruits. But where is Cecily?

CHASUBLE. Perhaps she followed us to the schools.

(*Enter* JACK *slowly from the back of the garden. He is dressed in the deepest mourning, with crepe hatband and black gloves.*)

MISS PRISM. Mr. Worthing!

CHASUBLE. Mr. Worthing?

MISS PRISM. This is indeed a surprise. We did not look for you till Monday afternoon.

JACK (*shakes* MISS PRISM'S *hand in a tragic manner*). I have returned sooner than I expected. Dr. Chasuble, I hope you are well?

CHASUBLE. Dear Mr. Worthing, I trust this garb of woe does not betoken some terrible calamity?

JACK. My brother.

MISS PRISM. More shameful debts and extravagance?

CHASUBLE. Still leading his life of pleasure?

JACK (*shaking his head*). Dead!

CHASUBLE. Your brother Ernest dead?

JACK. Quite dead.

MISS PRISM. What a lesson for him! I trust he will profit by it.

CHASUBLE. Mr. Worthing, I offer you my sincere condolence. You have at least the consolation of knowing that you were always the most generous and forgiving of brothers.

JACK. Poor Ernest! He had many faults, but it is a sad, sad blow.

CHASUBLE. Very sad indeed. Were you with him at the end?

JACK. No. He died abroad; in Paris, in fact. I had a telegram last night from the manager of the Grand Hotel.

CHASUBLE. Was the cause of death mentioned?

JACK. A severe chill, it seems.

MISS PRISM. As a man sows, so shall he reap.

CHASUBLE (*raising his hand*). Charity, dear Miss Prism, charity! None of us are perfect. I myself am peculiarly susceptible to draughts. Will the interment take place here?

JACK. No. He seems to have expressed a desire to be buried in Paris.

CHASUBLE. In Paris! (*Shakes his head.*) I fear that hardly points to any very serious state of mind at the last. You would no doubt wish me to make some slight allusion to this tragic domestic affliction next Sunday. (JACK *presses his hand convulsively.*) My sermon on the meaning of the manna in the wilderness can be adapted to almost any occasion, joyful, or, as in the present case, distressing. (*All sigh.*) I have preached it at harvest celebrations, christenings, confirmations, on days of humiliation and festal days. The last time I delivered it was in the Cathedral, as a charity sermon on behalf of the Society for the Prevention of Discontent among the Upper Orders. The Bishop, who was present, was much struck by some of the analogies I drew.

JACK. Ah! that reminds me, you mentioned christenings I think,

Dr. Chasuble? I suppose you know how to christen all right? (DR. CHASUBLE *looks astounded.*) I mean, of course, you are continually christening, aren't you?

MISS PRISM. It is, I regret to say, one of the Rector's most constant duties in this parish. I have often spoken to the poorer classes on the subject. But they don't seem to know what thrift is.

CHASUBLE. But is there any particular infant in whom you are interested, Mr. Worthing? Your brother was, I believe, unmarried, was he not?

JACK. Oh yes.

MISS PRISM (*bitterly*). People who live entirely for pleasure usually are.

JACK. But it is not for any child, dear Doctor. I am very fond of children. No! the fact is, I would like to be christened myself, this afternoon, if you have nothing better to do.

CHASUBLE. But surely, Mr. Worthing, you have been christened already?

JACK. I don't remember anything about it.

CHASUBLE. But have you any grave doubts on the subject?

JACK. I certainly intend to have. Of course I don't know if the thing would bother you in any way, or if you think I am a little too old now.

CHASUBLE. Not at all. The sprinkling, and, indeed, the immersion of adults is a perfectly canonical practice.

JACK. Immersion!

CHASUBLE. You need have no apprehensions. Sprinkling is all that is necessary, or indeed I think advisable. Our weather is so changeable. At what hour would you wish the ceremony performed?

JACK. Oh, I might trot round about five if that would suit you.

CHASUBLE. Perfectly, perfectly! In fact I have two similar ceremonies to perform at that time. A case of twins that occurred recently in one of the outlying cottages on your own estate. Poor Jenkins the carter, a most hard-working man.

JACK. Oh! I don't see much fun in being christened along with other babies. It would be childish. Would half-past five do?

CHASUBLE. Admirably! Admirably! (*Takes out watch.*) And now, dear Mr. Worthing, I will not intrude any longer into a house of sorrow. I would merely beg you not to be too much bowed down by grief. What seem to us bitter trials are often blessings in disguise.

MISS PRISM. This seems to me a blessing of an extremely obvious kind.

(*Enter* CECILY *from the house.*)

CECILY. Uncle Jack! Oh, I am pleased to see you back. But what horrid clothes you have got on. Do go and change them.

MISS PRISM. Cecily!

CHASUBLE. My child! my child. (CECILY *goes towards* JACK; *he kisses her brow in a melancholy manner.*)

CECILY. What is the matter, Uncle Jack? Do look happy! You look as if you had a toothache, and I have got such a surprise for you. Who do you think is in the dining-room? Your brother!

JACK. Who?

CECILY. Your brother Ernest. He arrived about half an hour ago.

JACK. What nonsense! I haven't got a brother.

CECILY. Oh, don't say that. However badly he may have behaved to you in the past he is still your brother. You couldn't be so heartless as to disown him. I'll tell him to come out. And you will shake hands with him, won't you, Uncle Jack? (*Runs back into the house.*)

CHASUBLE. These are very joyful tidings.

MISS PRISM. After we had all been resigned to his loss, his sudden return seems to me peculiarly distressing.

JACK. My brother is in the dining-room? I don't know what it all means. I think it is perfectly absurd.

(*Enter* ALGERNON *and* CECILY *hand in hand. They come slowly up to* JACK.)

JACK. Good heavens! (*Motions* ALGERNON *away.*)

ALGERNON. Brother John, I have come down from town to tell you that I am very sorry for all the trouble I have given you, and that I intend to lead a better life in the future. (JACK *glares at him and does not take his hand.*)

CECILY. Uncle Jack, you are not going to refuse your own brother's hand?

JACK. Nothing will induce me to take his hand. I think his coming down here disgraceful. He knows perfectly well why.

CECILY. Uncle Jack, do be nice. There is some good in everyone. Ernest has just been telling me about his poor invalid friend Mr. Bunbury whom he goes to visit so often. And surely there must be much good in one who is kind to an invalid, and leaves the pleasures of London to sit by a bed of pain.

JACK. Oh! he has been talking about Bunbury, has he?

CECILY. Yes, he has told me all about poor Mr. Bunbury, and his terrible state of health.

JACK. Bunbury! Well, I won't have him talk to you about Bunbury or about anything else. It is enough to drive one perfectly frantic.

ALGERNON. Of course I admit that the faults were all on my side. But I must say that I think that Brother John's coldness to me is peculiarly painful. I expected a more enthusiastic welcome, especially considering it is the first time I have come here.

CECILY. Uncle Jack, if you don't shake hands with Ernest I will never forgive you.

JACK. Never forgive me?

CECILY. Never, never, never!

JACK. Well, this is the last time I shall ever do it. (*Shakes hands with* ALGERNON *and glares.*)

CHASUBLE. It's pleasant, is it not, to see so perfect a reconciliation? I think we might leave the two brothers together.

MISS PRISM. Cecily, you will come with us.

CECILY. Certainly, Miss Prism. My little task of reconciliation is over.

CHASUBLE. You have done a beautiful action to-day, dear child.

MISS PRISM. We must not be premature in our judgements.

CECILY. I feel very happy. (*They all go off except* JACK *and* ALGERNON.)

JACK. You young scoundrel, Algy, you must get out of this place as soon as possible. I don't allow any Bunburying here.

(*Enter* MERRIMAN.)

MERRIMAN. I have put Mr. Ernest's things in the room next to yours, sir. I suppose that is all right?

JACK. What?

MERRIMAN. Mr. Ernest's luggage, sir. I have unpacked it and put it in the room next to your own.

JACK. His luggage?

MERRIMAN. Yes, sir. Three portmanteaus, a dressing-case, two hat-boxes, and a large luncheon-basket.

ALGERNON. I am afraid I can't stay more than a week this time.

JACK. Merriman, order the dog-cart at once. Mr. Ernest has been suddenly called back to town.

MERRIMAN. Yes, sir. (*Goes back into the house.*)

ALGERNON. What a fearful liar you are, Jack. I have not been called back to town at all.

JACK. Yes, you have.

ALGERNON. I haven't heard any one call me.

JACK. Your duty as a gentleman calls you back.

ALGERNON. My duty as a gentleman has never interfered with my pleasures in the smallest degree.

JACK. I can quite understand that.

ALGERNON. Well, Cecily is a darling.

JACK. You are not to talk of Miss Cardew like that. I don't like it.

ALGERNON. Well, I don't like your clothes. You look perfectly ridiculous in them. Why on earth don't you go up and change? It is perfectly childish to be in deep mourning for a man who is actually staying for a whole week with you in your house as a guest. I call it grotesque.

JACK. You are certainly not staying with me for a whole week as a guest or anything else. You have got to leave . . . by the four-five train.

ALGERNON. I certainly won't leave you so long as you are in mourning. It would be most unfriendly. If I were in mourning you would stay with me, I suppose. I should think it very unkind if you didn't.

JACK. Well, will you go if I change my clothes?

ALGERNON. Yes, if you are not too long. I never saw anybody take so long to dress, and with such little result.

JACK. Well, at any rate, this is better than being always over-dressed as you are.

ALGERNON. If I am occasionally a little over-dressed, I make up for it by being always immensely over-educated.

JACK. Your vanity is ridiculous, your conduct an outrage, and your presence in my garden utterly absurd. However, you have got to catch the four-five, and I hope you will have a pleasant journey back to town. This Bunburying, as you call it, has not been a great success for you. (*Goes into the house.*)

ALGERNON. I think it has been a great success. I'm in love with Cecily, and that is everything.

(*Enter* CECILY *at the back of the garden. She picks up the can and begins to water the flowers.*)

But I must see her before I go, and make arrangements for another Bunbury. Ah, there she is.

CECILY. Oh, I merely came back to water the roses. I thought you were with Uncle Jack.

ALGERNON. He's gone to order the dog-cart for me.

CECILY. Oh, is he going to take you for a nice drive?

ALGERNON. He's going to send me away.

CECILY. Then have we got to part?

ALGERNON. I am afraid so. It's a very painful parting.

CECILY. It is always painful to part from people whom one has known for a very brief space of time. The absence of old friends one can endure with equanimity. But even a momentary separation from any one to whom one has just been introduced is almost unbearable.

ALGERNON. Thank you.

(*Enter* MERRIMAN.)

MERRIMAN. The dog-cart is at the door, sir. (ALGERNON *looks appealingly at* CECILY.)

CECILY. It can wait, Merriman . . . for . . . five minutes.

MERRIMAN. Yes, miss. (*Exit* MERRIMAN.)

ALGERNON. I hope, Cecily, I shall not offend you if I state quite frankly and openly that you seem to me to be in every way the visible personification of absolute perfection.

CECILY. I think your frankness does you great credit, Ernest. If you will allow me, I will copy your remarks into my diary. (*Goes over to table and begins writing in diary.*)

ALGERNON. Do you really keep a diary? I'd give anything to look at it. May I?

CECILY. Oh no. (*Puts her hand over it.*) You see, it is simply a very young girl's record of her own thoughts and impressions, and consequently meant for publication. When it appears in volume form I hope you will order a copy. But pray, Ernest, don't stop. I delight in taking down from dictation. I have reached 'absolute perfection.' You can go on. I am quite ready for more.

ALGERNON (*somewhat taken aback*). Ahem! Ahem!

CECILY. Oh, don't cough, Ernest. When one is dictating one should speak fluently and not cough. Besides, I don't know how to spell a cough. (*Writes as* ALGERNON *speaks.*)

ALGERNON (*speaking very rapidly*). Cecily, ever since I first looked upon your wonderful and incomparable beauty, I have dared to love you wildly, passionately, devotedly, hopelessly.

CECILY. I don't think that you should tell me that you love me wildly, passionately, devotedly, hopelessly. Hopelessly doesn't seem to make much sense, does it?

ALGERNON. Cecily.

(*Enter* MERRIMAN.)

MERRIMAN. The dog-cart is waiting, sir.

ALGERNON. Tell it to come round next week, at the same hour.

MERRIMAN (*looks at* CECILY, *who makes no sign*). Yes, sir. (MERRIMAN *retires.*)

CECILY. Uncle Jack would be very much annoyed if he knew you were staying on till next week, at the same hour.

ALGERNON. Oh, I don't care about Jack. I don't care for anybody in the whole world but you. I love you, Cecily. You will marry me, won't you?

CECILY. You silly boy! Of course. Why, we have been engaged for the last three months.

ALGERNON. For the last three months?

CECILY. Yes, it will be exactly three months on Thursday.

ALGERNON. But how did we become engaged?

CECILY. Well, ever since dear Uncle Jack first confessed to us that he had a younger brother who was very wicked and bad, you of course have formed the chief topic of conversation between myself and Miss Prism. And of course a man who is much talked about is always very attractive. One feels there must be something in him, after all. I daresay it was foolish of me, but I fell in love with you, Ernest.

ALGERNON. Darling. And when was the engagement actually settled?

CECILY. On the 14th of February last. Worn out by your entire ignorance of my existence, I determined to end the matter one way or the other, and after a long struggle with myself I accepted you under this dear old tree here. The next day I bought this little ring in your name, and this is the little bangle with the true lover's knot I promised you always to wear.

ALGERNON. Did I give you this? It's very pretty, isn't it?

CECILY. Yes, you've wonderfully good taste, Ernest. It's the excuse I've always given for your leading such a bad life. And this is the box in which I keep all your dear letters. (*Kneels at table, opens box, and produces letters tied up with blue ribbon.*)

ALGERNON. My letters! But, my own sweet Cecily, I have never written you any letters.

CECILY. You need hardly remind me of that, Ernest. I remember only too well that I was forced to write your letters for you. I wrote always three times a week, and sometimes oftener.

ALGERNON. Oh, do let me read them, Cecily?

CECILY. Oh, I couldn't possibly. They would make you far too conceited. (*Replaces box.*) The three you wrote me after I had broken off the engagement are so beautiful, and so badly spelled, that even now I can hardly read them without crying a little.

ALGERNON. But was our engagement ever broken off?

CECILY. Of course it was. On the 22nd of last March. You can see the entry if you like. (*Shows diary.*) 'To-day I broke off my engagement with Ernest. I feel it is better to do so. The weather still continues charming.'

ALGERNON. But why on earth did you break it off? What had I done? I had done nothing at all. Cecily, I am very much hurt indeed to hear you broke it off. Particularly when the weather was so charming.

CECILY. It would hardly have been a really serious engagement if it hadn't been broken off at least once. But I forgave you before the week was out.

ALGERNON (*crossing to her, and kneeling*). What a perfect angel you are, Cecily.

CECILY. You dear romantic boy. (*He kisses her, she puts her fingers through his hair.*) I hope your hair curls naturally, does it?

ALGERNON. Yes, darling, with a little help from others.

CECILY. I am so glad.

ALGERNON. You'll never break off our engagement again, Cecily?

CECILY. I don't think I could break it off now that I have actually met you. Besides, of course, there is the question of your name.

ALGERNON. Yes, of course. (*Nervously.*)

CECILY. You must not laugh at me, darling, but it had always been a girlish dream of mine to love some one whose name was Ernest. (ALGERNON *rises,* CECILY *also.*) There is something in that name that seems to inspire absolute confidence. I pity any poor married woman whose husband is not called Ernest.

ALGERNON. But, my dear child, do you mean to say you could not love me if I had some other name?

CECILY. But what name?

ALGERNON. Oh, any name you like—Algernon—for instance . . .

CECILY. But I don't like the name of Algernon.

ALGERNON. Well, my own dear, sweet, loving little darling, I really can't see why you should object to the name of Algernon. It is not at all a bad name. In fact, it is rather an aristocratic name. Half of the chaps who get into the Bankruptcy Court are called Algernon. But seriously, Cecily . . . (*moving to her*) if my name was Algy, couldn't you love me?

CECILY (*rising*). I might respect you, Ernest, I might admire your character, but I fear that I should not be able to give you my undivided attention.

ALGERNON. Ahem! Cecily! (*Picking up hat.*) Your Rector here is, I suppose, thoroughly experienced in the practice of all the rites and ceremonials of the Church?

CECILY. Oh, yes. Dr. Chasuble is a most learned man. He has never written a single book, so you can imagine how much he knows.

ALGERNON. I must see him at once on a most important christening—I mean on most important business.

CECILY. Oh!

ALGERNON. I shan't be away more than half an hour.

CECILY. Considering that we have been engaged since February the 14th, and that I only met you to-day for the first time, I think it is rather hard that you should leave me for so long a period as half an hour. Couldn't you make it twenty minutes?

ALGERNON. I'll be back in no time. (*Kisses her and rushes down the garden.*)

CECILY. What an impetuous boy he is! I like his hair so much. I must enter his proposal in my diary.

(*Enter* MERRIMAN.)

MERRIMAN. A Miss Fairfax has just called to see Mr. Worthing. On very important business, Miss Fairfax states.

CECILY. Isn't Mr. Worthing in his library?

MERRIMAN. Mr. Worthing went over in the direction of the Rectory some time ago.

CECILY. Pray ask the lady to come out here; Mr. Worthing is sure to be back soon. And you can bring tea.

MERRIMAN. Yes, Miss. (*Goes out.*)

CECILY. Miss Fairfax! I suppose one of the many good elderly women who are associated with Uncle Jack in some of his philanthropic work in London. I don't quite like women who are interested in philanthropic work. I think it is so forward of them.

(*Enter* MERRIMAN.)

MERRIMAN. Miss Fairfax.

(*Enter* GWENDOLEN. *Exit* MERRIMAN.)

CECILY (*advancing to meet her*). Pray let me introduce myself to you. My name is Cecily Cardew.

GWENDOLEN. Cecily Cardew? (*Moving to her and shaking hands.*) What a very sweet name! Something tells me that we are going to be great friends. I like you already more than I can say. My first impressions of people are never wrong.

CECILY. How nice of you to like me so much after we have known each other such a comparatively short time. Pray sit down.

GWENDOLEN (*still standing up*). I may call you Cecily, may I not?

CECILY. With pleasure!

GWENDOLEN. And you will always call me Gwendolen, won't you?

CECILY. If you wish.

GWENDOLEN. Then that is all quite settled, is it not?

CECILY. I hope so. (*A pause. They both sit down together.*)

GWENDOLEN. Perhaps this might be a favourable opportunity for my mentioning who I am. My father is Lord Bracknell. You have never heard of papa, I suppose?

CECILY. I don't think so.

GWENDOLEN. Outside the family circle, papa, I am glad to say, is entirely unknown. I think that is quite as it should be. The home seems to me to be the proper sphere for the man. And certainly once a man begins to neglect his domestic duties he becomes painfully effeminate, does he not? And I don't like that. It makes men so very attractive. Cecily, mamma, whose views on education are remarkably strict, has brought me up to be extremely short-sighted; it is part of her system; so do you mind my looking at you through my glasses?

CECILY. Oh! not at all, Gwendolen. I am very fond of being looked at.

GWENDOLEN (*after examining* CECILY *carefully through a lorgnette*). You are here on a short visit, I suppose.

CECILY. Oh no! I live here.

GWENDOLEN (*severely*). Really? Your mother, no doubt, or some female relative of advanced years, resides here also?

CECILY. Oh no! I have no mother, nor, in fact, any relations.

GWENDOLEN. Indeed?

CECILY. My dear guardian, with the assistance of Miss Prism, has the arduous task of looking after me.

GWENDOLEN. Your guardian?

CECILY. Yes, I am Mr. Worthing's ward.

GWENDOLEN. Oh! it is strange he never mentioned to me that he had a ward. How secretive of him! He grows more interesting hourly. I am not sure, however, that the news inspires me with feelings of unmixed delight. (*Rising and going to her.*) I am very fond of you, Cecily; I have liked you ever since I met you! But I am bound to state that now that I know that you are Mr. Worthing's ward, I cannot help expressing a wish you were—well, just a little older than you seem to be—and not quite so very alluring in appearance. In fact, if I may speak candidly——

CECILY. Pray do! I think that whenever one has anything unpleasant to say, one should always be quite candid.

GWENDOLEN. Well, to speak with perfect candour, Cecily, I wish that you were fully forty-two, and more than usually plain for your age. Ernest has a strong upright nature. He is the very soul of truth and honour. Disloyalty would be as impossible to him as deception. But even men of the noblest possible moral character are extremely susceptible to the influence of the physical charms of others. Modern, no less than Ancient History, supplies us with many most painful examples of what I refer to. If it were not so, indeed, History would be quite unreadable.

CECILY. I beg your pardon, Gwendolen, did you say Ernest?

GWENDOLEN. Yes.

CECILY. Oh, but it is not Mr. Ernest Worthing who is my guardian. It is his brother—his elder brother.

GWENDOLEN (*sitting down again*). Ernest never mentioned to me that he had a brother.

CECILY. I am sorry to say they have not been on good terms for a long time.

GWENDOLEN. Ah! that accounts for it. And now that I think of it I have never heard any man mention his brother. The subject seems distasteful to most men. Cecily, you have lifted a load from my mind. I was growing almost anxious. It would have been terrible if any cloud had come across a friendship like ours, would it not? Of course you are quite, quite sure that it is not Mr. Ernest Worthing who is your guardian?

CECILY. Quite sure. (*A pause.*) In fact, I am going to be his.

GWENDOLEN (*inquiringly*). I beg your pardon?

CECILY (*rather shy and confidingly*). Dearest Gwendolen, there is no reason why I should make a secret of it to you. Our little county newspaper is sure to chronicle the fact next week. Mr. Ernest Worthing and I are engaged to be married.

GWENDOLEN (*quite politely, rising*). My darling Cecily, I think there must be some slight error. Mr. Ernest Worthing is engaged to me. The announcement will appear in the *Morning Post* on Saturday at the latest.

CECILY (*very politely, rising*). I am afraid you must be under some misconception. Ernest proposed to me exactly ten minutes ago. (*Shows diary.*)

GWENDOLEN (*examines diary through her lorgnette carefully*). It is very curious, for he asked me to be his wife yesterday afternoon at 5:30. If you would care to verify the incident, pray do so. (*Produces diary of her own.*) I never travel without my diary. One should always have something sensational to read in the train. I am so sorry, dear Cecily, if it is any disappointment to you, but I am afraid I have the prior claim.

CECILY. It would distress me more than I can tell you, dear Gwendolen, if it caused you any mental or physical anguish, but I feel bound to point out that since Ernest proposed to you he clearly has changed his mind.

GWENDOLEN (*meditatively*). If the poor fellow has been entrapped into any foolish promise I shall consider it my duty to rescue him at once, and with a firm hand.

CECILY (*thoughtfully and sadly*). Whatever unfortunate entanglement my dear boy may have got into, I will never reproach him with it after we are married.

GWENDOLEN. Do you allude to me, Miss Cardew, as an entanglement? You are presumptuous. On an occasion of this kind it becomes more than a moral duty to speak one's mind. It becomes a pleasure.

CECILY. Do you suggest, Miss Fairfax, that I entrapped Ernest into an engagement? How dare you? This is no time for wearing the shallow mask of manners. When I see a spade I call it a spade.

GWENDOLEN (*satirically*). I am glad to say that I have never seen a spade. It is obvious that our social spheres have been widely different.

(*Enter* MERRIMAN, *followed by the footman. He carries a salver, table cloth, and plate stand.* CECILY *is about to retort. The presence of the servants exercises a restraining influence, under which both girls chafe.*)

MERRIMAN. Shall I lay tea here as usual, Miss?

CECILY (*sternly, in a calm voice*). Yes, as usual. (MERRIMAN *begins to clear table and lay cloth. A long pause.* CECILY *and* GWENDOLEN *glare at each other.*)

GWENDOLEN. Are there many interesting walks in the vicinity, Miss Cardew?

CECILY. Oh! yes! a great many. From the top of one of the hills quite close one can see five counties.

GWENDOLEN. Five counties! I don't think I should like that; I hate crowds.

CECILY (*sweetly*). I suppose that is why you live in town? (GWENDOLEN *bites her lip, and beats her foot nervously with her parasol.*)

GWENDOLEN (*looking round*). Quite a well-kept garden this is, Miss Cardew.

CECILY. So glad you like it, Miss Fairfax.

GWENDOLEN. I had no idea there were any flowers in the country.

CECILY. Oh, flowers are as common here, Miss Fairfax, as people are in London.

GWENDOLEN. Personally I cannot understand how anybody manages to exist in the country, if anybody who is anybody does. The country always bores me to death.

CECILY. Ah! This is what the newspapers call agricultural depression, is it not? I believe the aristocracy are suffering very much from it just at present. It is almost an epidemic amongst them, I have been told. May I offer you some tea, Miss Fairfax?

GWENDOLEN (*with elaborate politeness*). Thank you. (*Aside.*) Detestable girl! But I require tea!

CECILY (*sweetly*). Sugar?

GWENDOLEN (*superciliously*). No, thank you. Sugar is not fashionable any more. (CECILY *looks angrily at her, takes up the tongs and puts four lumps of sugar into the cup.*)

CECILY (*severely*). Cake or bread and butter?

GWENDOLEN (*in a bored manner*). Bread and butter, please. Cake is rarely seen at the best houses nowadays.

CECILY (*cuts a very large slice of cake and puts it on the tray*). Hand that to Miss Fairfax. (MERRIMAN *does so, and goes out with footman.* GWENDOLEN *drinks the tea and makes a grimace. Puts down cup at once, reaches out her hand to the bread and butter, looks at it, and finds it is cake. Rises in indignation.*)

GWENDOLEN. You have filled my tea with lumps of sugar, and though I asked most distinctly for bread and butter, you have given me cake. I am known for the gentleness of my disposition, and the extraordinary sweetness of my nature, but I warn you, Miss Cardew, you may go too far.

CECILY (*rising*). To save my poor, innocent, trusting boy from the machinations of any other girl there are no lengths to which I would not go.

GWENDOLEN. From the moment I saw you I distrusted you. I felt that you were false and deceitful. I am never deceived in such matters. My first impressions of people are invariably right.

CECILY. It seems to me, Miss Fairfax, that I am trespassing on your valuable time. No doubt you have many other calls of a similar character to make in the neighbourhood.

(*Enter* JACK.)

GWENDOLEN (*catching sight of him*). Ernest! My own Ernest!

JACK. Gwendolen! Darling! (*Offers to kiss her.*)

GWENDOLEN (*drawing back*). A moment! May I ask if you are engaged to be married to this young lady? (*Points to* CECILY.)

JACK (*laughing*). To dear little Cecily! Of course not! What could have put such an idea into your pretty little head?

GWENDOLEN. Thank you. You may! (*Offers her cheek.*)

CECILY (*very sweetly*). I knew there must be some misunderstanding, Miss Fairfax. The gentleman whose arm is at present round your waist is my guardian, Mr. John Worthing.

GWENDOLEN. I beg your pardon?

CECILY. This is Uncle Jack.

GWENDOLEN (*receding*). Jack! Oh!

(*Enters* ALGERNON.)

CECILY. Here is Ernest.

ALGERNON (*goes straight over to* CECILY *without noticing anyone else*). My own love! (*Offers to kiss her.*)

CECILY (*drawing back*). A moment, Ernest! May I ask you—are you engaged to be married to this young lady?

ALGERNON (*looking round*). To what young lady? Good heavens! Gwendolen!

CECILY. Yes: to good heavens, Gwendolen, I mean to Gwendolen.

ALGERNON (*laughing*). Of course not! What could have put such an idea into your pretty little head?

CECILY. Thank you (*Presenting her cheek to be kissed.*) You may. (ALGERNON *kisses her.*)

GWENDOLEN. I felt there was some slight error, Miss Cardew. The gentleman who is now embracing you is my cousin, Mr. Algernon Moncrieff.

CECILY (*breaking away from Algernon*). Algernon Moncrieff! Oh! (*The two girls move towards each other and put their arms round each other's waists as if for protection.*)

CECILY. Are you called Algernon?

ALGERNON. I cannot deny it.

CECILY. Oh!

GWENDOLEN. Is your name really John?

JACK (*standing rather proudly*). I could deny it if I liked. I could deny anything if I liked. But my name certainly is John. It has been John for years.

CECILY (*to* GWENDOLEN). A gross deception has been practiced on both of us.

GWENDOLEN. My poor wounded Cecily!

CECILY. My sweet wronged Gwendolen!

GWENDOLEN (*slowly and seriously*). You will call me sister, will you not? (*They embrace.* JACK *and* ALGERNON *groan and walk up and down.*)

CECILY (*rather brightly*). There is just one question I would like to be allowed to ask my guardian.

GWENDOLEN. An admirable idea! Mr. Worthing, there is just one question I would like to be permitted to put to you. Where is your brother Ernest? We are both engaged to be married to your brother Ernest, so it is a matter of some importance to us to know where your brother Ernest is at present.

JACK (*slowly and hesitatingly*). Gwendolen—Cecily—it is very painful for me to be forced to speak the truth. It is the first time in my life that I have ever been reduced to such a painful position, and I am really quite inexperienced in doing anything of the kind. However, I will tell you quite frankly that I have no brother Ernest. I have no brother at all. I never had a brother in my life, and I certainly have not the smallest intention of ever having one in the future.

CECILY (*surprised*). No brother at all?

JACK (*cheerily*). None!

GWENDOLEN (*severely*). Had you never a brother of any kind?

JACK (*pleasantly*). Never. Not even of any kind.

GWENDOLEN. I am afraid it is quite clear, Cecily, that neither of us is engaged to be married to anyone.

CECILY. It is not a very pleasant position for a young girl suddenly to find herself in. Is it?

GWENDOLEN. Let us go into the house. They will hardly venture to come after us there.

CECILY. No, men are so cowardly, aren't they? (*They retire into the house with scornful looks.*)

JACK. This ghastly state of things is what you call Bunburying, I suppose?

ALGERNON. Yes, and a perfectly wonderful Bunbury it is. The most wonderful Bunbury I have ever had in my life.

JACK. Well, you've no right whatsoever to Bunbury here.

ALGERNON. That is absurd. One has a right to Bunbury anywhere one chooses. Every serious Bunburyist knows that.

JACK. Serious Bunburyist? Good heavens!

ALGERNON. Well, one must be serious about something, if one wants to have any amusement in life. I happen to be serious about Bunburying. What on earth you are serious about I haven't got the remotest idea. About everything, I should fancy. You have such an absolutely trivial nature.

JACK. Well, the only small satisfaction I have in the whole of this wretched business is that your friend Bunbury is quite exploded. You won't be able to run down to the country quite so often as you used to do, dear Algy. And a very good thing too.

ALGERNON. Your brother is a little off colour, isn't he, dear Jack? You won't be able to disappear to London quite so frequently as your wicked custom was. And not a bad thing either.

JACK. As for your conduct towards Miss Cardew, I must say that your taking in a sweet, simple, innocent girl like that is quite inexcusable. To say nothing of the fact that she is my ward.

ALGERNON. I can see no possible defence at all for your deceiving a brilliant, clever, thoroughly experienced young lady like Miss Fairfax. To say nothing of the fact that she is my cousin.

JACK. I wanted to be engaged to Gwendolen, that is all. I love her.

ALGERNON. Well, I simply wanted to be engaged to Cecily. I adore her.

JACK. There is certainly no chance of your marrying Miss Cardew.

ALGERNON. I don't think there is much likelihood, Jack, of you and Miss Fairfax being united.

JACK. Well, that is no business of yours.

ALGERNON. If it was my business, I wouldn't talk about it. (*Begins to eat muffins.*) It is very vulgar to talk about one's business. Only people like stockbrokers do that, and then merely at dinner parties.

JACK. How you can sit there, calmly eating muffins when we are in this horrible trouble, I can't make out. You seem to me to be perfectly heartless.

ALGERNON. Well, I can't eat muffins in an agitated manner. The butter would probably get on my cuffs. One should always eat muffins quite calmly. It is the only way to eat them.

JACK. I say it's perfectly heartless your eating muffins at all, under the circumstances.

ALGERNON. When I am in trouble, eating is the only thing that consoles me. Indeed, when I am in really great trouble, as any one who knows me intimately will tell you, I refuse everything except food and drink. At the present moment I am eating muffins because I am unhappy. Besides, I am particularly fond of muffins. (*Rising.*)

JACK (*rising*). Well, there is no reason why you should eat them all in that greedy way. (*Takes muffins from Algernon.*)

ALGERNON (*offering tea-cake*). I wish you would have tea-cake instead. I don't like tea-cake.

JACK. Good heavens! I suppose a man may eat his own muffins in his own garden.

ALGERNON. But you have just said it was perfectly heartless to eat muffins.

JACK. I said it was perfectly heartless of you, under the circumstances. That is a very different thing.

ALGERNON. That may be. But the muffins are the same. (*He seizes the muffin-dish from* JACK.)

JACK. Algy, I wish to goodness you would go.

ALGERNON. You can't possibly ask me to go without having some dinner. It's absurd. I never go without my dinner. No one ever does, except vegetarians and people like that. Besides I have just made arrangements with Dr. Chasuble to be christened at a quarter to six under the name of Ernest.

JACK. My dear fellow, the sooner you give up that nonsense the better. I made arrangements this morning with Dr. Chasuble to be christened myself at 5:30, and I naturally will take the name of Ernest. Gwendolen would wish it. We can't both be christened Ernest. It's absurd. Besides, I have a perfect right to be christened if I like. There is no evidence at all that I have ever been christened by anybody. I should think it extremely probable I never was, and so does Dr. Chasuble. It is entirely different in your case. You have been christened already.

ALGERNON. Yes, but I have not been christened for years.

JACK. Yes, but you have been christened. That is the important thing.

ALGERNON. Quite so. So I know my constitution can stand it. If you are not quite sure about your ever having been christened, I must say I think it rather dangerous your venturing on it now. It might make you very unwell. You can hardly have forgotten that someone very closely connected with you was very nearly carried off this week in Paris by a severe chill.

JACK. Yes, but you said yourself that a severe chill was not hereditary.

ALGERNON. It usen't to be, I know—but I daresay it is now. Science is always making wonderful improvements in things.

JACK (*picking up the muffin-dish*). Oh, that is nonsense; you are always talking nonsense.

ALGERNON. Jack, you are at the muffins again! I wish you wouldn't. There are only two left. (*Takes them.*) I told you I was particularly fond of muffins.

JACK. But I hate tea-cake.

ALGERNON. Why on earth then do you allow tea-cake to be served up for your guests? What ideas you have of hospitality!

JACK. Algernon! I have already told you to go. I don't want you here. Why don't you go!

ALGERNON. I haven't quite finished my tea yet! and there is still one muffin left. (JACK *groans, and sinks into a chair.* ALGERNON *continues eating.*)

Act Drop

THIRD ACT

SCENE: *Drawing-room at the Manor House.*

(GWENDOLEN *and* CECILY *are at the window, looking out into the garden.*)

GWENDOLEN. The fact that they did not follow us at once into the house, as any one else would have done, seems to me to show that they have some sense of shame left.

CECILY. They have been eating muffins. That looks like repentance.

GWENDOLEN (*after a pause*). They don't seem to notice us at all. Couldn't you cough?

CECILY. But I haven't got a cough.

GWENDOLEN. They're looking at us. What effrontery!

CECILY. They're approaching. That's very forward of them.

GWENDOLEN. Let us preserve a dignified silence.

CECILY. Certainly. It's the only thing to do now.

(*Enter* JACK *followed by* ALGERNON. *They whistle some dreadful popular air from a British Opera.*)

GWENDOLEN. This dignified silence seems to produce an unpleasant effect.

CECILY. A most distasteful one.

GWENDOLEN. But we will not be the first to speak.

CECILY. Certainly not.

GWENDOLEN. Mr. Worthing, I have something very particular to ask you. Much depends on your reply.

CECILY. Gwendolen, your common sense is invaluable. Mr. Moncrieff, kindly answer me the following question. Why did you pretend to be my guardian's brother?

ALGERNON. In order that I might have an opportunity of meeting you.

CECILY (*to* GWENDOLEN). That certainly seems a satisfactory explanation, does it not?

GWENDOLEN. Yes, dear, if you can believe him.

CECILY. I don't. But that does not affect the wonderful beauty of his answer.

GWENDOLEN. True. In matters of grave importance, style, not sincerity, is the vital thing. Mr. Worthing, what explanation can you offer to me for pretending to have a brother? Was it in order that you might have an opportunity of coming up to town to see me as often as possible?

JACK. Can you doubt it, Miss Fairfax?

GWENDOLEN. I have the gravest doubts upon the subject. But I intend to crush them. This is not the moment for German scepticism. (*Moving to* CECILY.) Their explanations appear to be quite satisfactory, especially Mr. Worthing's. That seems to me to have the stamp of truth upon it.

CECILY. I am more than content with what Mr. Moncrieff said. His voice alone inspires one with absolute credulity.

GWENDOLEN. Then you think we should forgive them?

CECILY. Yes. I mean no.

GWENDOLEN. True! I had forgotten. There are principles at stake that one cannot surrender. Which of us should tell them? The task is not a pleasant one.

CECILY. Could we not both speak at the same time?

GWENDOLEN. An excellent idea! I nearly always speak at the same time as other people. Will you take the time from me?

CECILY. Certainly. (GWENDOLEN *beats time with uplifted finger.*)

GWENDOLEN *and* CECILY (*speaking together*). Your Christian names are still an insuperable barrier. That is all!

JACK *and* ALGERNON (*speaking together*). Our Christian names! Is that all? But we are going to be christened this afternoon.

GWENDOLEN (*to* JACK). For my sake you are prepared to do this terrible thing?

JACK. I am.

CECILY (*to* ALGERNON). To please me you are ready to face this fearful ordeal?

ALGERNON. I am!

GWENDOLEN. How absurd to talk of the equality of the sexes! Where questions of self-sacrifice are concerned, men are infinitely beyond us.

JACK. We are. (*Clasps hands with* ALGERNON.)

CECILY. They have moments of physical courage of which we women know absolutely nothing.

GWENDOLEN (*to* JACK). Darling!

ALGERNON (*to* CECILY). Darling! (*They fall into each other's arms.*)

(*Enter* MERRIMAN. *When he enters he coughs loudly, seeing the situation.*)

MERRIMAN. Ahem! Ahem! Lady Bracknell.

JACK. Good heavens!

(*Enter* LADY BRACKNELL. *The couples separate in alarm. Exit* MERRIMAN.)

LADY BRACKNELL. Gwendolen! What does this mean?

GWENDOLEN. Merely that I am engaged to be married to Mr. Worthing, mamma.

LADY BRACKNELL. Come here. Sit down. Sit down immediately. Hesitation of any kind is a sign of mental decay in the young, of physical weakness in the old. (*Turns to* JACK.) Apprised, sir, of my daughter's sudden flight by her trusty maid, whose confidence I purchased by means of a small coin, I followed her at once by a luggage train. Her unhappy father is, I am glad to say, under the impression that she is attending a more than usually lengthy lecture by the University Extension Scheme on the Influence of a Permanent Income on Thought. I do not propose to undeceive him. Indeed I have never undeceived him on any question. I would consider it wrong. But of course, you will clearly understand that all communication between yourself and my daughter must cease immediately from this moment. On this point, as indeed on all points, I am firm.

JACK. I am engaged to be married to Gwendolen, Lady Bracknell!

LADY BRACKNELL. You are nothing of the kind, sir. And now as regards Algernon! . . . Algernon!

ALGERNON. Yes, Aunt Augusta.

LADY BRACKNELL. May I ask if it is in this house that your invalid friend Mr. Bunbury resides?

ALGERNON (*stammering*). Oh! No! Bunbury doesn't live here. Bunbury is somewhere else at present. In fact, Bunbury is dead.

LADY BRACKNELL. Dead! When did Mr. Bunbury die? His death must have been extremely sudden.

ALGERNON (*airily*). Oh! I killed Bunbury this afternoon. I mean poor Bunbury died this afternoon.

LADY BRACKNELL. What did he die of?

ALGERNON. Bunbury? Oh, he was quite exploded.

LADY BRACKNELL. Exploded! Was he the victim of a revolutionary outrage? I was not aware that Mr. Bunbury was interested in social legislation. If so, he is well punished for his morbidity.

ALGERNON. My dear Aunt Augusta, I mean he was found out! The doctors found out that Bunbury could not live, that is what I mean—so Bunbury died.

LADY BRACKNELL. He seems to have had great confidence in the opinion of his physicians. I am glad, however, that he made up his mind at the last to some definite course of action, and acted under proper medical advice. And now that we have finally got rid of this Mr. Bunbury, may I ask, Mr. Worthing, who is that young person whose hand my nephew Algernon is now holding in what seems to me a peculiarly unnecessary manner?

JACK. That lady is Miss Cecily Cardew, my ward. (LADY BRACKNELL *bows coldly to* CECILY.)

ALGERNON. I am engaged to be married to Cecily, Aunt Augusta.

LADY BRACKNELL. I beg your pardon?

CECILY. Mr. Moncrieff and I are engaged to be married, Lady Bracknell.

LADY BRACKNELL (*with a shiver, crossing to the sofa and sitting down*). I do not know whether there is anything peculiarly exciting in the air of this particular part of Hertfordshire, but the number of engagements that go on seems to me considerably above the proper average that statistics have laid down for our guidance. I think some preliminary inquiry on my part would not be out of place. Mr. Worthing, is Miss Cardew at all connected with any of the larger railway stations in London? I merely desire information. Until yesterday I had no idea that there were any families or persons whose origin was a Terminus. (JACK *looks perfectly furious, but restrains himself.*)

JACK (*in a cold, clear voice*). Miss Cardew is the granddaugher of the late Mr. Thomas Cardew of 149 Belgrave Square, S.W.; Gervase Park, Dorking, Surrey; and the Sporran, Fifeshire, N.B.

LADY BRACKNELL. That sounds not unsatisfactory. Three addresses always inspire confidence, even in tradesmen. But what proof have I of their authenticity?

JACK. I have carefully preserved the Court Guides of the period. They are open to your inspection, Lady Bracknell.

LADY BRACKNELL (*grimly*). I have known strange errors in that publication.

JACK. Miss Cardew's family solicitors are Messrs. Markby, Markby, and Markby.

LADY BRACKNELL. Markby, Markby, and Markby? A firm of the very highest position in their profession. Indeed I am told that one of the Mr. Markby's is occasionally to be seen at dinner parties. So far I am satisfied.

JACK (*very irritably*). How extremely kind of you, Lady Bracknell! I have also in my possession, you will be pleased to hear, certificates of Miss Cardew's birth, baptism, whooping cough, registration, vaccination, confirmation, and the measles; both the German and the English variety.

LADY BRACKNELL. Ah! A life crowded with incident, I see; though perhaps somewhat too exciting for a young girl. I am not myself in favour of premature experiences. (*Rises, looks at her watch.*) Gwendolen! the time approaches for our departure. We have not a moment to lose. As a matter of form, Mr. Worthing, I had better ask you if Miss Cardew has any little fortune?

JACK. Oh! about a hundred and thirty thousand pounds in the Funds. That is all. Good-bye, Lady Bracknell. So pleased to have seen you.

LADY BRACKNELL (*sitting down again*). A moment, Mr. Worthing. A hundred and thirty thousand pounds! And in the Funds! Miss Cardew seems to me a most attractive young lady, now that I look at her. Few girls of the present day have any really solid qualities, any of the qualities that last, and improve with time. We live, I regret to say, in an age of surfaces. (*To* CECILY.) Come over here, dear. (CECILY *goes across.*) Pretty child! your dress is sadly simple, and your hair seems almost as Nature might have left it. But we can soon alter all that. A thoroughly experienced French maid produces a really marvellous result in a very brief space of time. I remember recommending one to young Lady Lancing, and after three months her own husband did not know her.

JACK. And after six months nobody knew her.

LADY BRACKNELL (*glares at Jack for a few moments. Then bends, with a practiced smile, to* CECILY). Kindly turn round, sweet child. (CECILY *turns completely round.*) No, the side view is what I want. (CECILY *presents her profile.*) Yes, quite as I expected. There are distinct social possibilities in your profile. The two weak points in our age are its want of principle and its want of profile. The chin a little higher, dear. Style largely depends on the way the chin is worn. They are worn very high, just at present. Algernon!

ALGERNON. Yes, Aunt Augusta!

LADY BRACKNELL. There are distinct social possibilities in Miss Cardew's profile.

ALGERNON. Cecily is the sweetest, dearest, prettiest girl in the whole world. And I don't care twopence about social possibilities.

LADY BRACKNELL. Never speak disrespectfully of Society, Algernon. Only people who can't get into it do that. (*To* CECILY.) Dear child, of course you know that Algernon has nothing but his debts to depend upon. But I do not approve of mercenary marriages. When I married Lord Bracknell I had no fortune of any kind. But I never dreamed for a moment of allowing that to stand in my way. Well, I suppose I must give my consent.

ALGERNON. Thank you, Aunt Augusta.

LADY BRACKNELL. Cecily, you may kiss me!

CECILY (*kisses her*). Thank you, Lady Bracknell.

LADY BRACKNELL. You may also address me as Aunt Augusta for the future.

CECILY. Thank you, Aunt Augusta.

LADY BRACKNELL. The marriage, I think, had better take place quite soon.

ALGERNON. Thank you, Aunt Augusta.

CECILY. Thank you, Aunt Augusta.

LADY BRACKNELL. To speak frankly, I am not in favour of long engagements. They give people the opportunity of finding out each other's character before marriage, which I think is never advisable.

JACK. I beg your pardon for interrupting you, Lady Bracknell, but this engagement is quite out of the question. I am Miss Cardew's guardian, and she cannot marry without my consent until she comes of age. That consent I absolutely decline to give.

LADY BRACKNELL. Upon what grounds, may I ask? Algernon is an extremely, I may also say an ostentatiously, eligible young man. He has nothing, but he looks everything. What more can one desire?

JACK. It pains me very much to have to speak frankly to you, Lady Bracknell, about your nephew, but the fact is that I do not approve at all of his moral character. I suspect him of being untruthful. (ALGERNON *and* CECILY *look at him in indignant amazement.*)

LADY BRACKNELL. Untruthful! My nephew Algernon? Impossible! He is an Oxonian.

JACK. I fear there can be no possible doubt about the matter. This afternoon during my temporary absence in London on an important question of romance, he obtained admission to my house by means of the false pretence of being my brother. Under an assumed name he drank, I've just been informed by my butler, an entire pint bottle of my Perrier-Jouet, Brut, '89; wine I was specially reserving for myself. Continuing his disgraceful deception, he succeeded in the course of the afternoon in alienating the affections of my only ward. He subsequently stayed to tea, and devoured every single muffin. And what makes his conduct all the more heartless is, that he was perfectly well aware from the first that I have no brother, that I never had a brother, and that I don't intend to have a brother, not even of any kind. I distinctly told him so myself yesterday afternoon.

LADY BRACKNELL. Ahem! Mr. Worthing, after careful consideration I have decided entirely to overlook my nephew's conduct to you.

JACK. That is very generous of you, Lady Bracknell. My own decision, however, is unalterable. I decline to give my consent.

LADY BRACKNELL (*to* CECILY). Come here, sweet child. (CECILY *goes over.*) How old are you, dear?

CECILY. Well, I am really only eighteen, but I always admit to twenty when I go to evening parties.

LADY BRACKNELL. You are perfectly right in making some slight alteration. Indeed, no woman should ever be quite accurate about her age. It looks so calculating. . . . (*In a meditative manner.*) Eighteen, but admitting to twenty at evening parties. Well, it will not be very long before you are of age and free from the restraints of tutelage. So I don't think your guardian's consent is, after all, a matter of any importance.

JACK. Pray excuse me, Lady Bracknell, for interrupting you again, but it is only fair to tell you that according to the terms of her grandfather's will Miss Cardew does not come legally of age till she is thirty-five.

LADY BRACKNELL. That does not seem to me to be a grave objection. Thirty-five is a very attractive age. London society is full of women of the very highest birth who have, of their own free choice, remained thirty-five for years. Lady Dumbleton is an instance in point. To my own knowledge she has been thirty-five ever since she arrived at the age of forty, which was many years ago now. I see no reason why our dear Cecily should not be even still more attractive at the age you mention than she is at present. There will be a large accumulation of property.

CECILY. Algy, could you wait for me till I was thirty-five?

ALGERNON. Of course I could, Cecily. You know I could.

CECILY. Yes, I felt it instinctively, but I couldn't wait all that time. I hate waiting even five minutes for anybody. It always makes me rather cross. I am not punctual myself, I know, but I do like punctuality in others, and waiting, even to be married, is quite out of the question.

ALGERNON. Then what is to be done, Cecily?

CECILY. I don't know, Mr. Moncrieff.

LADY BRACKNELL. My dear Mr. Worthing, as Miss Cardew states positively that she cannot wait till she is thirty-five—a remark which I am bound to say seems to me to show a somewhat impatient nature —I would beg of you to reconsider your decision.

JACK. But my dear Lady Bracknell, the matter is entirely in your own hands. The moment you consent to my marriage with Gwendolen, I will most gladly allow your nephew to form an alliance with my ward.

LADY BRACKNELL (*rising and drawing herself up*). You must be quite aware that what you propose is out of the question.

JACK. Then a passionate celibacy is all that any of us can look forward to.

LADY BRACKNELL. That is not the destiny I propose for Gwendolen. Algernon, of course, can choose for himself. (*Pulls out her watch.*) Come, dear (GWENDOLEN *rises*), we have already missed five, if not six, trains. To miss any more might expose us to comment on the platform.

(*Enter* DR. CHASUBLE.)

CHASUBLE. Everything is quite ready for the christenings.

LADY BRACKNELL. The christenings, sir! Is not that somewhat premature?

CHASUBLE (*looking rather puzzled, and pointing to* JACK *and* ALGERNON). Both these gentlemen have expressed a desire for immediate baptism.

LADY BRACKNELL. At their age? The idea is grotesque and irreligious! Algernon, I forbid you to be baptized. I will not hear of such excesses. Lord Bracknell would be highly displeased if he learned that that was the way in which you wasted your time and money.

CHASUBLE. Am I to understand then that there are to be no christenings at all this afternoon?

JACK. I don't think that, as things are now, it would be of much practical value to either of us, Dr. Chasuble.

CHASUBLE. I am grieved to hear such sentiments from you, Mr. Worthing. They savour of the heretical views of the Anabaptists, views that I have completely refuted in four of my unpublished sermons. However, as your present mood seems to be one peculiarly secular, I will return to the church at once. Indeed, I have just been informed by the pew-opener that for the last hour and a half Miss Prism has been waiting for me in the vestry.

LADY BRACKNELL (*starting*). Miss Prism! Did I hear you mention a Miss Prism?

CHASUBLE. Yes, Lady Bracknell. I am on my way to join her.

LADY BRACKNELL. Pray allow me to detain you for a moment. This matter may prove to be one of vital importance to Lord Bracknell and myself. Is this Miss Prism a female of repellent aspect, remotely connected with education?

CHASUBLE (*somewhat indignantly*). She is the most cultivated of ladies, and the very picture of respectability.

LADY BRACKNELL. It is obviously the same person. May I ask what position she holds in your household?

CHASUBLE (*severely*). I am a celibate, madam.

JACK (*interposing*). Miss Prism, Lady Bracknell, has been for the last three years Miss Cardew's esteemed governess and valued companion.

LADY BRACKNELL. In spite of what I hear of her, I must see her at once. Let her be sent for.

CHASUBLE (*looking off*). She approaches; she is nigh.

(*Enter* MISS PRISM *hurriedly*.)

MISS PRISM. I was told you expected me in the vestry, dear Canon. I have been waiting for you there for an hour and three-quarters. (*Catches sight of* LADY BRACKNELL, *who has fixed her with a stony glare.* MISS PRISM *grows pale and quails. She looks anxiously round as if desirous to escape.*)

LADY BRACKNELL (*in a severe, judicial voice*). Prism! (MISS PRISM *bows her head in shame.*) Come here, Prism! (MISS PRISM *approaches in a humble manner.*) Prism! Where is that baby? (*General consternation. The Canon starts back in horror.* ALGERNON *and* JACK *pretend to be anxious to shield* CECILY *and* GWENDOLEN *from hearing the details of a terrible public scandal.*) Twenty-eight years ago, Prism, you left Lord Bracknell's house, Number 104, Upper Grosvenor Square, in charge of a perambulator that contained a baby of the male sex. You never returned. A few weeks later, through the elaborate investigations of the Metropolitan police, the perambulator was discovered at midnight standing by itself in a remote corner of Bayswater. It contained the manuscript of a three-volume novel of more than usually revolting sentimentality. (MISS PRISM *starts in involuntary indignation.*) But the baby was not there. (*Every one looks at* MISS PRISM.) Prism! Where is that baby? (*A pause.*)

MISS PRISM. Lady Bracknell, I admit with shame that I do not know. I only wish I did. The plain facts of the case are these. On the morning of the day you mention, a day that is for ever branded on my memory, I prepared as usual to take the baby out in its perambulator. I had also with me a somewhat old, but capacious hand-bag in which I had intended to place the manuscript of a work of fiction that I had written during my few unoccupied hours. In a moment of mental abstraction, for which I can never forgive myself, I deposited the manuscript in the bassinette and placed the baby in the hand-bag.

JACK (*who has been listening attentively*). But where did you deposit the hand-bag?

MISS PRISM. Do not ask me, Mr. Worthing.

JACK. Miss Prism, this is a matter of no small importance to me. I insist on knowing where you deposited the hand-bag that contained that infant.

MISS PRISM. I left it in the cloak-room of one of the larger railway stations in London.

JACK. What railway station?

MISS PRISM (*quite crushed*). Victoria. The Brighton line. (*Sinks into a chair.*)

JACK. I must retire to my room for a moment. Gwendolen, wait here for me.

GWENDOLEN. If you are not too long, I will wait here for you all my life. (*Exit* JACK *in great excitement.*)

CHASUBLE. What do you think this means, Lady Bracknell?

LADY BRACKNELL. I dare not even suspect, Dr. Chasuble. I need hardly tell you that in families of high position strange coincidences are not supposed to occur. They are hardly considered the thing. (*Noises heard overhead as if some one was throwing trunks about. Every one looks up.*)

CECILY. Uncle Jack seems strangely agitated.

CHASUBLE. Your guardian has a very emotional nature.

LADY BRACKNELL. This noise is extremely unpleasant. It sounds as if he was having an argument. I dislike arguments of any kind. They are always vulgar, and often convincing.

CHASUBLE (*looking up*). It has stopped now. (*The noise is redoubled.*)

LADY BRACKNELL. I wish he would arrive at some conclusion.

GWENDOLEN. This suspense is terrible. I hope it will last.

(*Enter* JACK *with a hand-bag of black leather in his hand.*)

JACK (*rushing over to* MISS PRISM). Is this the hand-bag, Miss Prism? Examine it carefully before you speak. The happiness of more than one life depends on your answer.

MISS PRISM (*calmly*). It seems to be mine. Yes, here is the injury it received through the upsetting of a Gower Street omnibus in younger and happier days. Here is the stain on the lining caused by the explosion of a temperance beverage, an incident that occurred at Leamington. And here, on the lock, are my initials. I had forgotten that in an extravagant mood I had had them placed there. The bag is undoubtedly mine. I am delighted to have it so unexpectedly restored to me. It has been a great inconvenience being without it all these years.

JACK (*in a pathetic voice*). Miss Prism, more is restored to you than this hand-bag. I was the baby you placed in it.

MISS PRISM (*amazed*). You?

JACK (*embracing her*). Yes . . . mother!

MISS PRISM (*recoiling in indignant astonishment*). Mr. Worthing. I am unmarried!

JACK. Unmarried! I do not deny that is a serious blow. But after all, who has the right to cast a stone against one who has suffered? Cannot repentance wipe out an act of folly? Why should there be one law for men, and another for women? Mother, I forgive you. (*Tries to embrace her again.*)

MISS PRISM (*still more indignant*). Mr. Worthing, there is some error. (*Pointing to* LADY BRACKNELL.) There is the lady who can tell you who you really are.

JACK (*after a pause*). Lady Bracknell, I hate to seem inquisitive, but would you kindly inform me who I am?

LADY BRACKNELL. I am afraid that the news I have to give you will not altogether please you. You are the son of my poor sister, Mrs. Moncrieff, and consequently Algernon's elder brother.

JACK. Algy's elder brother! Then I have a brother after all. I knew I had a brother! I always said I had a brother! Cecily—how could you have ever doubted that I had a brother? (*Seizes hold of* ALGERNON.) Dr. Chasuble, my unfortunate brother. Miss Prism, my unfortunate brother. Gwendolen, my unfortunate brother. Algy, you young scoundrel, you will have to treat me with more respect in the future. You have never behaved to me like a brother in all your life.

ALGERNON. Well, not till to-day, old boy, I admit. I did my best, however, though I was out of practice. (*Shakes hands.*)

GWENDOLEN (*to* JACK). My own! But what own are you? What is your Christian name, now that you have become some one else?

JACK. Good heavens! . . . I had quite forgotten that point. Your decision on the subject of my name is irrevocable, I suppose?

GWENDOLEN. I never change, except in my affections.

CECILY. What a noble nature you have, Gwendolen!

JACK. Then the question had better be cleared up at once. Aunt Augusta, a moment. At the time when Miss Prism left me in the hand-bag, had I been christened already?

LADY BRACKNELL. Every luxury that money could buy, including christening, had been lavished on you by your fond and doting parents.

JACK. Then I was christened! That is settled. Now, what name was I given? Let me know the worst.

LADY BRACKNELL. Being the eldest son you were naturally christened after your father.

JACK (*irritably*). Yes, but what was my father's Christian name?

LADY BRACKNELL (*meditatively*). I cannot at the present moment recall what the General's Christian name was. But I have no doubt he had one. He was eccentric, I admit. But only in later years. And that was the result of the Indian climate, and marriage, and indigestion, and other things of that kind.

JACK. Algy! Can't you recollect what our father's Christian name was?

ALGERNON. My dear boy, we were never even on speaking terms. He died before I was a year old.

JACK. His name would appear in the Army Lists of the period, I suppose, Aunt Augusta?

LADY BRACKNELL. The General was essentially a man of peace, except in his domestic life. But I have no doubt his name would appear in any military directory.

JACK. The Army Lists of the last forty years are here. These delightful records should have been my constant study. (*Rushes to bookcase and tears the books out.*) M. Generals . . . Mallam, Maxbohm, Magley—what ghastly names they have—Markby, Migsby, Mobbs, Moncrieff! Lieutenant 1840, Captain, Lieutenant-Colonel, Colonel, General 1869, Christian names, Ernest John. (*Puts book very quietly down and speaks quite calmly.*) I always told you, Gwendolen, my name was Ernest, didn't I? Well, it is Ernest after all. I mean it naturally is Ernest.

LADY BRACKNELL. Yes, I remember now that the General was called Ernest. I knew I had some particular reason for disliking the name.

GWENDOLEN. Ernest! My own Ernest! I felt from the first that you could have no other name!

JACK. Gwendolen, it is a terrible thing for a man to find out suddenly that all his life he has been speaking nothing but the truth. Can you forgive me?

GWENDOLEN. I can. For I feel that you are sure to change.

JACK. My own one!

CHASUBLE (*to* MISS PRISM). Laetitia! (*Embraces her.*)

MISS PRISM (*enthusiastically*). Frederick! At last!

ALGERNON. Cecily! (*Embraces her.*) At last!

JACK. Gwendolen! (*Embraces her.*) At last!

LADY BRACKNELL. My nephew, you seem to be displaying signs of triviality.

JACK. On the contrary, Aunt Augusta, I've now realized for the first time in my life the vital Importance of Being Earnest.

TABLEAU

CURTAIN

MICHAEL AND HIS LOST ANGEL

Once upon a time Ben Jonson's plays were more popular and more highly regarded than those of Shakespeare, for their structure was more precise and their dialogue, full of contemporary references and the everyday matter of life, more realistic; but by the end of the seventeenth century Jonson was "dated." In introducing a selection from Henry Arthur Jones' drama of manners *Mrs. Dane's Defence* (1900), Allardyce Nicoll speaks of the realistic dramatist's problem (*Readings from British Drama*):

> . . . one of the weaknesses of realism is that the concrete facts of life which it reflects are frequently destroyed in a succeeding age, either by the operation of law or by that of the social conscience. The greater artist, however, usually succeeds in portraying these facts in a way which makes them of universal significance, or in stressing, instead of the external facts of life, the emotions and the thoughts of the characters. Jonson frequently achieves that universal significance, despite his "realism." Shakespeare, of course, surpassed even Jonson, despite his romanticism (or because of it).

In the best plays of Jones the dialogue is naturalistic, not natural, and a permanent significance is achieved through the selective processes of art which suggest the universal from the particular. Perhaps the most lasting of Jones' "serious" plays is *Michael and his Lost Angel* (1896).

The career of Henry Arthur Jones really began when he saw his first play, at the age of eighteen, but it was not until he was twenty-seven that he saw the first of his own plays produced. After having written a number of trifling pieces, he was catapulted to fame in 1882 when his melodrama *The Silver King* (written in collaboration[1]) was produced in London. Produced in the United States in 1883, twice filmed, long played in repertory, *The Silver King* was universally praised. Even the great Sir Henry Irving had but a slight reservation about it:

> Henry Irving went to see 'The Silver King,' [Jones tells us] and you know Irving's love for dark, mysterious and gloomy scenes. He criticized one special scene. 'Wasn't that scene a little light, my boy?' 'Well, you see, it's eleven in the morning.' 'I should have had an eclipse,' said Irving.

Jones' two greatest commercial failures were *Michael and his Lost Angel* and *The Tempter* (1893). Though he always had a soft spot in his heart for *The Silver King* as the turning point in his career ("I had a wife and two children, and about £300 between me and the workhouse, and night after night I used to think 'Good God! Will it come off?' "), *Michael and his Lost Angel* was his proudest creation. It ran for only ten nights in London and eleven (with Viola Allen) in New York. Sir Johnston Forbes-Robertson disliked the very title of the play (even before the piece opened, *Truth* called its title "as silly as it was objectionable"). Mrs. Patrick Campbell, who had been cast as Audrie, resigned her part a few days before the opening and had to be replaced by Marion Terry, who was not right for it. "Most of the leading critics condemned

---

1. *For the disputes over the authorship of the play (of which Jones in a* Nineteenth Century *article of 1883 called himself the "joint author") see pp. 42 ff. of Doris Arthur Jones'* Taking the Curtain Call: The Life and Letters of Henry Arthur Jones *(1930). Henry Herman claimed the lion's share of the work, but Jones credited him with much less in a letter to the editor of the* Era *(September 12, 1885) which Miss Arthur Jones quotes. The actor-manager Wilson Barrett later claimed a large share of the credit and in 1904 Jones wrote Barrett a nasty letter—Max Beerbohm called it "a masterpiece of cruelty"—in which he assured him: "I am sure it will give you great satisfaction to know that you will be quite safe in posing as the author of* The Silver King,*" but the next year the matter was arbitrated (by Sir Squire Bancroft, Sir Charles Wyndham, and Ben Greet, all celebrated actor-managers) and, says Miss Arthur Jones, "The award refuted in the clearest terms Mr. Barrett's claim to authorship."*

the play," Jones' daughter records, but Bernard Shaw in the *Saturday Review* wrote this:

> One of the greatest comforts of criticizing the work of Mr. Henry Arthur Jones is that the critic can go straight to the subject-matter without troubling about the dramatic construction. [In 1947 Shaw had changed his mind and lumped Jones with Pinero, Carton, Grundy, and Wilde, authors of "constructed" plays manufactured in the style of Scribe. "Plays manufactured on this plan, and called 'well-made plays,' " he said in the London *Observer*, "I compared to cats'-cradles, clockwork mice, mechanical rabbits, and the like." But in 1896 he was saying of Jones:] In the born writer the style is the man; and with the born dramatist, the play is the subject. Mr. Jones's plays grow; they are not cut out of bits of paper and stuck together. . . . Mr. Jones's technical skill is taken as a matter of course. . . . When I respond to the appeal of Mr. Jones's art by throwing myself sympathetically into his characteristic attitude of mind, I am conscious of no shortcomings in *Michael and his Lost Angel*. It then seems to me to be a genuinely sincere and moving play, feelingly imagined, written with knowledge as to the man and insight as to the woman by an author equipped not only with the experience of an adept playwright, and a kindly and humorous observer's sense of contemporary manners, but with that knowledge of spiritual history in which Mr. Jones's nearest competitors seem so stupendously deficient. Its art is in vital contact with the most passionate religious movement of its century, as fully quickened art always has been. . . . I unhesitatingly class Mr. Jones as first, and eminently first, among the surviving fittest of his own generation of playwrights. . . .

Shaw went on to some animadversions about the last act ("only saved from being a sorry business by the man's plucking a sort of courage out of abandonment, and by a humorous piteousness in the dying woman, who, whilst submitting, out of sheer feebleness of character, to Michael's attitude, is apologetically conscious of having no sincere conviction of sin") and concluded that the play had been badly acted at the Lyceum:

> The public see the play as it is acted, not as it ought to be acted. The sooner Mr. Jones publishes it, the better for his reputation. . . .

> The melancholy truth of the matter is that the English stage got a good play [he means the Forbes-Robertson and Frederick Harrison management had], and was completely and ignominiously beaten by it.

Jones had sold the play outright and had less than complete control over the production, though he insisted that "I will not have the text altered." He refused to cut some lines Mrs. Campbell thought were profane ("I must just titivate a cherub's nose, or hang a garland on an apostle's toe"), and, when told she might reconsider resigning from the cast if asked very nicely by the author, said "I'll see her damned first." His preference had always been for Sir Henry Irving and Ellen Terry to play Michael and Audrie anyway, but Irving had not liked the script, and Forbes-Robertson knew that he was a second choice. After getting bad reviews, Forbes-Robertson withdrew the production, over the author's strong objections. That was 1896. In 1920 Forbes-Robertson was writing to Henry Arthur Jones and declining to produce his "strong and interesting play" *The Divine Gift* though rendering it this compliment: "It has, if I may say so, the fearless truth of your finest work, *Michael and his Lost Angel*."

MICHAEL AND HIS LOST ANGEL

A PLAY IN FIVE ACTS

by

Henry Arthur Jones

DRAMATIS PERSONAE

THE REVEREND MICHAEL FEVERSHAM
SIR LYOLF FEVERSHAM
EDWARD LASHMAR (*Father Hilary*)
ANDREW GIBBARD
THE REVEREND MARK DOCWRAY
WITHYCOMBE
AUDRIE LESDEN
ROSE GIBBARD
MRS. CANTELO
FANNY CLOVER

Villagers, Congregation of St. Decuman's parish, Choristers, Priests, a Nun

ACT I *A Spring morning. The vicarage parlor at Cleveheddon.*

ACT II *Four months later: a Wednesday evening in September. The Shrine on St. Decuman's Island in the Bristol Channel.*

ACT III *The following Friday morning. The vicarage parlor as in Act I.*

ACT IV *An autumn evening, a year later. The chancel of St. Decuman, the minster church at Cleveheddon.*

ACT V *A summer evening, ten months later. The reception hall of the monastery of San Salvatore, Majano, Italy.*

English première at the Lyceum Theatre, London, January 15, 1896, starring Johnstone Forbes-Robertson and Marion Terry. Opened at the Empire Theatre, New York, January 13, 1896, starring Henry Miller and Viola Allen.

ACT I

SCENE: *The Vicarage parlor at Clevebeddon. An old-fashioned comfortable room in an old English house. A large window, with low broad sill, takes up nearly all the back of the stage, showing to the right a part of Clevebeddon Minster in ruins. To the left a stretch of West Country landscape. A door, right, leading to house. A fireplace, right. A door, left. Table with chairs, right. A portrait of* MICHAEL'S *mother hangs on wall at a height of about nine feet. It is a very striking painting of a lady about twenty-eight, very delicate and spirituelle. Time.—A fine spring morning.*

(*Discover at the window, looking off right, with face turned away from audience, and in an attitude of strained attention to something outside,* ANDREW GIBBARD. *Enter* FANNY CLOVER, *the vicarage servant, showing in the* REVEREND MARK DOCWRAY, *a middle-aged clergyman.*)

FANNY. Mr. Feversham is over to the church, sir, but he'll be back directly. (*Exit.*)

MARK. Andrew—(ANDREW *turns round, an odd, rather seedy, carelessly-dressed man, a little over forty, rather gaunt, longish hair, an intelligent face with something slightly sinister about it. He shows signs of great recent sorrow and distress.*)

MARK. Andrew, what is it?

ANDREW. I'd rather not tell you, Mr. Docwray.

MARK. Nothing has happened to Mr. Feversham?

ANDREW. No.

MARK. Come! Come! What's the matter?

ANDREW. My daughter—

MARK. What ails her? Where is she?

ANDREW. Over at the church.

MARK. What is she doing?

ANDREW. Making a public confession.

MARK. Public confession—of what?

ANDREW. You'll be sure to hear all about it, so I may as well tell you myself. Perhaps it was my fault, perhaps I neglected her. All my time is given to Mr. Feversham in the library here. While I was buried in my work, and sometimes staying here half the night with Mr. Feversham, a scoundrel ruined my girl. Of course my only thought was to hide it. Was I wrong?

MARK. Go on. Tell me all.

ANDREW. Well, right or wrong, I sent her away to the other end of England. Her child only lived a few weeks. And I brought her back home thinking it was all hushed up.

MARK. But it became known?

ANDREW. Yes. Little by little, things began to leak out. Well, you may blame me, if you like—I lied about it; and the more lies I told, the more I had to tell to cover them. Mr. Feversham heard of it and questioned us. Like a fool I lied to him. It wasn't like lying, it was like murdering the truth to tell lies to him. And she had to lie, too. Of course he believed us and defended us against everybody. And then we daredn't tell him the truth.

MARK. Go on. What else?

ANDREW. There's nothing else. It all had to come out at last.

MARK. What did Mr. Feversham do?

ANDREW. He persuaded us that we could never be right with ourselves, or right with our neighbors, or right with our God, till we had unsaid all our lies, and undone our deceit. So we've confessed it this morning.

MARK. In church? In public?

ANDREW. Yes. I wouldn't have minded it for myself. But was it necessary for her—for Rose? Was it bound to be in public before all her companions, before all who had watched her grow up from a child?

MARK. You may be sure Mr. Feversham wouldn't have urged it unless he had felt it to be right and necessary.

ANDREW. I wouldn't have done it for anybody else in the world. I feel almost as if I were quits with him for all his favors to me.

MARK. You mustn't speak like this. Remember all he has done for you.

ANDREW. Oh, I don't forget it. I don't forget that I was his scout's son, and that he educated me and made me his friend and companion and helper—there isn't a crumb I eat or a thread I wear that I don't owe to him. I don't forget it. But after this morning, I feel it isn't I who am in Mr. Feversham's debt—it's he who is in my debt. (*A penitential hymn, with organ accompaniment, is sung in church outside.*)

ANDREW (*looking off*). It's over. They're coming out.

MARK. Why aren't you there, in church, by her side?

ANDREW. I was. I went to church with her. I stood up first and answered all his questions, and then I stood aside, and it was her turn. I saw her step forward, and I noticed a little twitch of her lip like her mother used to have, and then—I couldn't bear it any longer—I came away. I know it was cowardly, but I couldn't stay. (*Looking off.*) Hark! They're coming! She's coming with the sister who is going to take her away.

MARK. Take her away?

ANDREW. Mr. Feversham thinks it better for her to be away from the gossip of the village, so he has found a home for her with some sisters in London. She's going straight off there. Perhaps it's best. I don't know. (ROSE GIBBARD, *sobbing, with her face in her hands, passes the window from right to left, supported by an Anglican sister. The* REVEREND MICHAEL FEVERSHAM *follows them and passes window. A crowd of villagers come up to the window and look in. A moment or two later,* ROSE GIBBARD *enters left, supported by the sister.* ROSE *is a pretty, delicate girl of about twenty, with rather refined features and bearing.*)

ANDREW (*holding out his arms to her*). Bear up, my dear. Don't cry! It breaks my heart to see you.

(*Enter the* REVEREND MICHAEL FEVERSHAM, *about forty; pale, strong, calm, ascetic, scholarly face, with much sweetness and spirituality of expression; very dignified, gentle manners, calm, strong, persuasive voice, rarely raised above an ordinary speaking tone. His whole presence and bearing denote great strength of character, great dignity, great gentleness, and great self-control. The villagers gather round the outside of the window and look in with mingled curiosity, rudeness, and respect.* MICHAEL *goes up to left window, opens it. The villagers draw back a little.*)

MICHAEL (*speaking in a very calm voice*). Those of you who are filled with idle foolish curiosity, come and look in. (*They fall back.*) Those of you who have been moved by the awful lesson of this morning, go to your homes, ponder it in your hearts, so that all your actions and all your thoughts from this time forth may be as open as the day, as clear as crystal, as white as snow. (*They all go away gradually.* MICHAEL *comes away from the window, leaving it open, goes to* MARK.)

MICHAEL. Mark! (*Cordial handshake.*) You've come to stay, I hope?

MARK. A few days. You have a little business here? (*Glancing at the group of* ROSE, ANDREW, *and* Sister.)

MICHAEL. It's nearly finished. Leave me with them for a few moments.

MARK. I'll get rid of the dust of my journey and come back to you. (*Exit* MARK. MICHAEL *turns towards* ROSE *with great tenderness.*)

MICHAEL. Poor child! (*She comes towards him with evident effort; the* Sister *brings a chair and she sinks into it, sobbing.*)

MICHAEL (*bending over her with great tenderness*). I know what you have suffered this morning. I would willingly have borne it for you, but that would not have made reparation to those whom you have deceived, or given you peace in your own soul. (*She continues sobbing.*) Hush! Hush! All the bitterness is past! Look only to the future! Think of the happy newness and whiteness of your life from this moment! Think of the delight of waking in the morning and knowing that you have nothing to hide! Be sure you have done right to own your sin. There won't be a softer pillow in England to-night than the one your head rests upon. (*She becomes quieter.* MICHAEL *turns to the* Sister.) Watch over her very carefully. Keep her from brooding. Let her be occupied constantly with work. And write to me very often to tell me how she is. (*Turns to* ROSE.) The carriage is ready. It's time to say good-bye.

ROSE. Good-bye, sir. Thank you for all your kindness. I've been very wicked—

MICHAEL. Hush! That is all buried now.

ROSE. Good-bye, father. (*Throws her arms round* ANDREW'S *neck, clings to him, sobs convulsively for some moments in a paroxysm of grief.* MICHAEL *watches them for some moments.*)

MICHAEL (*intercepts, gently separates them*). It's more than she can bear. Say good-bye, and let her go.

ANDREW (*breaking down*). Good-bye, my dear! (*Kissing her.*) Good-bye —I—I—I—(*Tears himself away, goes up to window, stands back to audience.*)

MICHAEL (*to* ROSE). No more tears! Tears are for evil and sin, and yours are all past! Write to me and tell me how you get on, and how you like the work. It will bring you great peace—great peace. Why, you are comforted already—I think I see one of your old happy smiles coming. What do you think, sister, isn't that the beginning of a smile?

SISTER. Yes, sir. I think it is.

ROSE. Good-bye, sir—thank you for all your goodness. I—I—(*Beginning to sob again.*)

MICHAEL. No, no, you are forgetting. I must see a little smile before you go. Look, Andrew. (ANDREW *turns round.*) For your father's sake. When you have gone you will like him to remember that the last time he saw your face it wore a smile. That's brave! Good-bye! Good-bye! (ROSE *with great effort forces a smile and goes off with the* Sister. *A moment or two later she is seen to pass the window sobbing in the* Sister's *arms.*)

ANDREW. Look! Oh, sir, was it bound to be in public, before everybody who knew her?

MICHAEL. Believe me, Andrew, if my own sister, if my own child had been in your daughter's place, I would have counseled her to act as your daughter has done.

ANDREW. She'll never hold up her head again.

MICHAEL. Would you rather that she held up her head in deceit and defiance, or that she held it down in grief and penitence? Think what you and she have endured this last year, the deceit, the agony, the shame, the guilt!

ANDREW. I can't think of anything except her standing up in the church. I shall never forget it.

MICHAEL. Tell me you know I would willingly have spared you and her if it had been possible.

ANDREW. Then it wasn't possible?

MICHAEL. I have done to you this morning as I would wish to be done by if I had followed a course of continued deception.

ANDREW. Ah, sir, it's easy for you to talk. You aren't likely to be tempted, so you aren't likely to fall.

MICHAEL. I trust not! I pray God to keep me. But if ever I did, I should think him my true friend who made me confess and rid my soul of my guilt. And you think me your true friend, don't you, Andrew? (*Holding out hand.*) Won't you shake hands with me? (ANDREW *takes* MICHAEL'S *hand reluctantly, shakes it half-heartedly; is going off at door.*)

MICHAEL (*calls*). Andrew, it will be very lonely in your own house now your daughter has gone. Come and live with me here. There is the large visitors' room. Take it for your own, and make this your home. You will be nearer to our work, and you will be nearer to me, my friend.

(MARK *enters.*)

MARK (*at door*). Am I interrupting?

MICHAEL. No. Come in. My little talk with Andrew is finished. (*To* ANDREW.) Say you know I have done what is right and best for you and her.

ANDREW. You've done what you thought was best for us, sir. I've never doubted that. I can't see anything straight or clear this morning. (*Exit.*)

MARK. You've had a painful business here?

MICHAEL. Terrible! But I was bound to go through with it. The whole village was talking of it. I believed in her innocence and defended her to the last. So when the truth came out I daren't hush it up. I should have been accused of hiding sin in my own household. But that poor child! My heart bled for her! Don't let us speak any more of it. Tell me about yourself and the work in London.

MARK. You must come and join us there. (MICHAEL *shakes his head.*)

MICHAEL. I couldn't live there. Every time I go up for a day or two I come back more and more sickened and frightened and disheartened. Besides, you forget my Eastern studies. They are my real work. I couldn't pursue them in the hurry and fever of London.

MARK. How are you getting on with the Arabic translations?

MICHAEL. Slowly but surely. Andrew is invaluable to me. In spite of his bringing up, he has the true instincts of the scholar.

MARK. Well, you know best. But we want you in London. You'd soon raise the funds for restoring the Minster.

MICHAEL (*shakes his head*). I can't go round with the hat.

MARK. How's the work getting on?

MICHAEL. Very slowly. I'm afraid I shall never live to finish it. By the by, I received fifty pounds anonymously only yesterday.

MARK. Have you any idea where it came from?

MICHAEL. No. The Bank advised me that it had been paid to my credit by a reader of my "Hidden Life," who desired to remain anonymous.

MARK. The book is having an enormous influence. Nothing else is talked about. And it has gained you one very rich proselyte—this Mrs. Lesden. She's living here, isn't she?

MICHAEL. Yes. Curious woman—

MARK. Have you seen much of her?

MICHAEL. I called, of course. I've met her once or twice at dinner. She has called here three or four times, and wasted several good hours for me.

MARK. How wasted?

MICHAEL. Kept me from my work. I wish the woman would take herself back to London.

MARK. Why?

MICHAEL. Her frivolity and insincerity repel me. No—not insincerity. I recall that. For she said one or two things that seemed to show a vein of true, deep feeling. But on the whole I dislike her—I think I dislike her very much.

MARK. Why?

MICHAEL. She comes regularly to church—

MARK. Surely there's no very great harm in that—

MICHAEL. No; but I don't know whether she's mocking, or criticizing, or worshiping; or whether she's merely bored, and thinking that my surplice is not enough starched, or starched too much.

MARK. She's very rich, and would be an immense help to our movement. I should try and cultivate her.

MICHAEL. I can't cultivate people. What do you think of her?

MARK. A very clever society woman, all the more clever that she was not born in society.

MICHAEL. What do you know of her?

MARK. Merely what I wrote you in my letter. That she was the only daughter of an Australian millionaire. Her great-grandfather, I believe, was an Australian convict. She was sent to England to be educated, went back to Australia, married, lost her husband and father, came back to England a widow, took a house in Mayfair, entertained largely, gave largely to charities, read your book, "The Hidden Life," came down to see the country round here, made up her mind to live here, and wanted an introduction to you—which I gave her.

(*Enter* FANNY, *announcing* SIR LYOLF FEVERSHAM, *an English country gentleman, about sixty-five, a little old-fashioned in manners and dress. Exit* FANNY.)

SIR LYOLF. Michael—Mr. Docwray! Glad to see you. You're talking business, or rather religion, which is your business. Am I in the way?

MICHAEL. No, we're not talking business. We're discussing a woman.

SIR LYOLF. Aren't women nine tenths of a parson's business? (MICHAEL *looks a little shocked.*) Excuse me, my dear boy. (*To* MARK.) I quite believe in all Michael is doing. I accept all his new doctrines, I'm prepared to go all lengths with him, on condition that I indulge the latent old Adam in me with an occasional mild joke at his expense. But (*with great feeling*) he knows how proud I am of him, and how thankful I am to God for having given me a son who is shaping religious thought throughout England to-day, and who (*with a change to sly humor*) will never be a bishop—not even an archdeacon—I don't believe he'll be so much as a rural dean. What about this woman you were discussing? I'll bet—(*coughs himself up*)—I should say, I'll wager—(MICHAEL *looks shocked,* SIR LYOLF *shrugs his shoulders at* MARK, *proceeds in a firm voice*)—without staking anything, I will wager I know who the lady is—Mrs. Lesden? Am I right?

MICHAEL. Yes.

SIR LYOLF. Well, I haven't heard your opinion of her. But I'll give you mine—without prejudice—(*with emphasis*) very queer lot.

MARK. Michael had just said she was a curious creature.

MICHAEL. I don't understand her.

SIR LYOLF. When you don't understand a woman, depend upon it there's something not quite right about her.

MICHAEL. She seems to have immense possibilities of good and evil.

SIR LYOLF. Nonsense. There are all sorts of men, but, believe me, there are only two sorts of women—good and bad.

MICHAEL. You can't divide women into two classes like that.

SIR LYOLF. But I do—sheep and goats. Sheep on the right hand—goats on the left.

MICHAEL (*shaking his head*). Women's characters have greater subtlety than you suppose.

SIR LYOLF. Subtlety is the big cant word of our age. Depend upon it, there's nothing in subtlety. It either means hair-splitting or it means downright evil. The devil was the first subtle character we meet with in history.

MICHAEL. And he has still something to do with the shaping of character in this world.

SIR LYOLF. I don't doubt it. And I think he has very likely something to do with the shaping of Mrs. Lesden's.

MICHAEL. Hasn't he something to do with the shaping of all our characters? Don't all our souls swing continually between heaven and hell?

SIR LYOLF. Well, the woman whose soul swings continually between heaven and hell is not the woman whom I would choose to sit at my fireside or take the head of my table. Though I don't say I wouldn't ask her to dinner occasionally. That reminds me, how long are you staying, Mr. Docwray?

MARK. Only till Friday.

SIR LYOLF. You'll dine with me to-morrow evening?

MARK. Delighted.

SIR LYOLF. You too, Michael. I'll ask the Standerwicks, and (*suddenly*) suppose I ask this lady?

MICHAEL. Mrs. Lesden? I would rather you didn't.

SIR LYOLF. Why not? If her soul is swinging between heaven and hell, it would only be kind of you to give it a jog towards heaven.

MICHAEL. Very well—ask her. But I would rather you didn't speak lightly of—

SIR LYOLF. Of her soul?

MICHAEL. Of any one's soul?

SIR LYOLF. I won't—even of a woman's. But I wish they wouldn't swing about. Women's souls oughtn't to swing anywhere, except towards heaven. Ah, Michael, you must let me have my fling. Remember when I was a boy, religion was a very simple, easy-going affair. Parson—clerk—old three-decker pulpit—village choir. What a village choir! I suppose it was all wrong—but they were very comfortable old days.

MICHAEL. Religion is not simple—or easy-going.

SIR LYOLF. No. Subtlety again. I want a plain "yes" or "no," a plain black or white, a plain right or wrong, and none of our teachers or preachers is prepared to give it to me. Oh dear! This world has grown too subtle for me! I'll step over to Island House and ask Mrs. Lesden to dinner to-morrow.

MARK. I'll come with you and pay my respects to her. You don't mind, Michael?

MICHAEL. Not at all. I want to set Andrew to work at once to keep him from dwelling on his trouble.

SIR LYOLF. I didn't come to the church this morning. I felt it would be too painful. (*Glancing up at portrait.*) What would she have said about it?

MICHAEL. I think she approves what I have done.

SIR LYOLF (*looks at portrait, sighs, turns away*). Come, Mr. Docwray. I can't say I like this Mrs. Lesden of yours—I wonder why I'm going to ask her to dinner. (*Exit.*)

MARK (*who has been looking intently at portrait*). What a wonderful portrait that is of your mother! It seems as if she were alive!

MICHAEL. She is. (*Exit* MARK *after* SIR LYOLF.)

MICHAEL (*goes up steps, takes portrait into his hand*). Yes, I have acted faithfully to my people, have I not? Whisper to me that I have done right to restore to this wandering father and child the blessing of a transparent life, a life without secrecy and without guile! Whisper to me that in this morning's work I have done what is well pleasing to my God, and to you.

(AUDRIE LESDEN, *about thirty, in a very fashionable morning dress, enters at back of window in the opposite direction to that in which* SIR LYOLF *and* MARK *have gone off. At first she seems to be watching them off. When she gets to the open window, she turns and sees* MICHAEL *with the portrait in his hand.* MICHAEL *very reverently kisses the portrait and places it on table; as he does so he sees her.*)

MICHAEL. Mrs. Lesden!

AUDRIE. Wasn't that Sir Lyolf who just went out?

MICHAEL. Yes. I'll call him back—

AUDRIE. Please don't.

MICHAEL. But he wishes to speak to you.

AUDRIE. I don't wish to speak to him.

MICHAEL. Why not?

AUDRIE. I wish to speak to you.

MICHAEL. About what?

AUDRIE. About my soul, about your soul, and about other people's souls. (*Leaning a little in at the window. He remains silent, and reserved. All through the early part of the scene his demeanor is cold, constrained, and a little impatient. A pause.*) I know you make it a rule always to see people about their souls.

MICHAEL (*very coldly*). If they are really in need of spiritual advice.

AUDRIE. I think I'm in need of spiritual advice. (*A pause. He stands cold, irresponsive.*) Did you see me in church?

MICHAEL. Yes.

AUDRIE. The whole thing was delightfully novel. (*He frowns.*) Do you mean to repeat this morning's scene?

MICHAEL. Scene?

AUDRIE. It was a "scene," you know. I felt terribly distressed for the poor girl. And yet I envied her.

MICHAEL. Envied her?

AUDRIE (*leaning a little more in at the window*). You must allow she was the heroine of the occasion, though you were certainly very impressive yourself, and did your part very well. Still, after all, it's the man who is to be hanged who is the central figure in the proceedings. And the poor little creature looked exquisitely pathetic and graceful, and so sweetly innocent—quite good enough to go to heaven right away, I thought. A Sunday-school teacher told me once that it is nearly always the good girls who are betrayed. Is that so?

MICHAEL (*coldly*). You came to speak to me about yourself.

AUDRIE. So I did. Do you know when I saw that girl standing there and looking so interesting, I felt I wouldn't mind making a public confession myself—if you thought it would benefit the parish—and if you would allow me to wear a special dress for the occasion? (MICHAEL *turns round quickly as if about to speak angrily to her, stops, remains silent.*)

AUDRIE (*musingly*). I suppose one couldn't confess in anything except black or white. It couldn't be done in red and yellow—or blue. Pale grey might do. (*Pause.*) What do you think? (MICHAEL *does not reply.*)

AUDRIE (*leaning a little more in at the window, in a much lower and subtler tone*). Don't you find it an exquisite pleasure to feel your sense of power over your people, especially over us poor women?

MICHAEL. When you come to me you are neither man nor woman—you are only a soul in sin and distress.

AUDRIE. Oh, no! I won't be an "it." I insist on being a woman, though I don't mind *having* a soul—and in sin and distress, too. And I would save it—only I always think it's such a selfish piece of business, saving one's soul,—don't you?—so unkind to all one's neighbors? (*He stands half-bored, half-angry. A little pause.*) Do you know what I was thinking in church this morning?

MICHAEL. No.

AUDRIE. I was comparing the delights of three different professions, —the soldier's, the doctor's, and the priest's. What a glorious joy it must be to ride to meet a man who is riding to kill you—*and to kill him!* But I'd rather be a doctor, and play with life and death. To have a man in your power, to see him lying tossing on his bed, and to think, "This may cure him, or it may kill him. Shall I risk it? At any rate, if he dies, I shall have learnt so much. I will risk it! And—he dies—No, he lives! I've saved him." Wouldn't you like to be a doctor?

MICHAEL. No.

AUDRIE. That's because you know what far greater joy it is to be a priest. (*He turns very angrily.*) To play with people's souls—

MICHAEL. Play!

AUDRIE. You do play with our souls, don't you? They're in your hands. To think, "This man, or say, this woman, has an immortal soul. She is vain, silly, deceitful, foolish, perhaps wicked, perhaps horribly wicked. She'll lose her soul and be eternally lost. But if I were to struggle with her for it, rebuke her, teach her, plead with her, entreat her, guide her—who knows—she's not wholly bad—I might save her? Is she worth saving? The worse she is, the greater will be my reward and honor for having saved her. Shall I do it? This woman's soul is in my keeping! I can choose for her eternal life or eternal death. What shall I do? Shall I save her, or let her be lost?"

MICHAEL (*coming eagerly to the window*). Do you mean that?

AUDRIE. Mean what?

MICHAEL. That your soul is in my keeping.

AUDRIE. Not at all. I meant nothing except that thoughts like these must constantly stray through a priest's mind. Don't they? (*Long pause.*) Why don't you speak?

MICHAEL (*cold, stern*). I have nothing to say. (*Pause.*)

AUDRIE (*taking out purse, takes out two notes*). Oh! I was forgetting—

I've brought you a little contribution for the restoration of your Minster. (*Putting notes on window-sill.* MICHAEL *stands cold, angry.*)

AUDRIE. Won't you take it?

MICHAEL. Thank you. No.

AUDRIE. I think you're a little rude to me. I came as a heart-stricken penitent; you wouldn't accept me in that character. Then I came as a pious donor. You wouldn't accept me in that. You've kept me outside here—you haven't even asked me in.

MICHAEL (*very sternly*). Come in! (*She looks up, uncertain as to his intentions. Same cold, stern voice.*) Please to come in. That way—the outer door is open. (*She goes off, he goes to door left, opens it, she comes in.*)

MICHAEL (*the moment she has entered closes door decisively, then turns round on her very sternly*). What brings you to this village, to my church, to my house? Why are you here? Come to me as a penitent, and I will try to give you peace! Come to me as a woman of the world, and I will tell you "The friendship of the world is enmity with God. It always has been so, it always will be. The Church has no need of you, of your pretended devotions, of your gifts, of your presence at her services. Go your way back to the world, and leave her alone." But you come neither as a penitent, nor as a woman of the world. You come like—like some bad angel, to mock, and hint, and question; and suggest. How dare you play with sacred things? How dare you!

AUDRIE (*in a very low, quiet, amused voice*). I do not think it seemly or becoming in a clergyman to give way to temper. If any one had asked me I should have said it was impossible in you. (*He stands stern, cold, repellent.*)

(*Enter* ANDREW.)

MICHAEL. What is it, Andrew?

ANDREW. I thought you were disengaged. (*Going.*)

MICHAEL. So I am. I'll come to you at once. (*Exit* ANDREW.)

MICHAEL (*to* AUDRIE). You are right. It is unseemly to give way to temper, and perhaps you won't think me rude if I guard myself against it in future by asking you not to call upon me until I can be of real service to you. Good-morning.

AUDRIE. Mr. Feversham, Mr. Feversham. (MICHAEL *turns.*) I've been very rude and troublesome. I beg your pardon. Please forgive me.

MICHAEL. Certainly. Pray say no more.

AUDRIE. I saw you kissing that portrait as I stood at the window. It is your mother?

MICHAEL. Yes.

AUDRIE. What a good woman she must have been! Don't think because I am bad—

MICHAEL. Are you bad?

AUDRIE. Didn't you say I was? I don't know whether I'm bad or good, but I know that no woman longs to be good more than I do—sometimes.

MICHAEL. Do you indeed?

AUDRIE (*impulsively*). Let me kiss that portrait! (*Leaning forward to do it.*)

MICHAEL (*peremptorily*). No. (*Intercepts and stops her.*)

AUDRIE. Why not?

MICHAEL. I'd rather you didn't.

AUDRIE. You don't think I'm good enough.

MICHAEL. I cannot allow you.

AUDRIE. Who painted it?

MICHAEL. A young Italian. My mother's brother is a Catholic priest, and at that time he was living at Rome. My mother went there for her health when I was three years old. This young Italian saw her and asked permission to paint her. She came home and died of consumption. Then my uncle sent this portrait to my father with the news that the young painter had also died of consumption.

AUDRIE. How strange! And you've had it ever since?

MICHAEL. I was only a child when it came. I fell into the habit of saying my prayers before it. So when I first left home my father gave it to me; it has been with me ever since, at Eton, and Oxford, and in my different curacies.

AUDRIE. Won't you let me kiss it before I go? (*Leaning towards it.*)

MICHAEL (*preventing her*). I'd rather you did not.

AUDRIE. Why not?

MICHAEL. I have a strange belief about that picture. I'll hang it up.

AUDRIE (*a little intercepting him*). No. Let me look at it. Let me hold it in my hands. I won't kiss it without your permission. (*She takes it and looks at it intently.*) Tell me—what is your strange belief about it?

MICHAEL. My mother was a deeply religious woman, and before my birth she consecrated me to this service as Hannah consecrated Samuel. When she was dying she said to me, "I'm not leaving you. I shall watch over you every moment of your life. There's not a word, or a deed, or a thought of yours but I shall know it. You won't see me, but I shall be very near you. Sometimes my hands will be upon your head, but you won't know it; sometimes my arms will be round you, but you won't feel them; sometimes my lips will be on your face, but you won't know that I have kissed you. Remember you are watched by the dead."

AUDRIE. And you believe that you are watched by the dead?

MICHAEL. Yes.

AUDRIE. And that she is with us now—in this room?

MICHAEL. Yes.

AUDRIE. She is your good angel.

MICHAEL. She is my good angel.

AUDRIE. I can understand why you did not wish me to kiss her. (MICHAEL *makes a movement to take the picture.*)

AUDRIE (*retains it*). No. Yes, I feel she must be in this room.

MICHAEL. Why?

AUDRIE. I was full of silly wicked thoughts when I came—she has taken them away.

MICHAEL. Ah, if I dared hope that you would really change!

AUDRIE. Perhaps I will. (*Very imploringly.*) Do let me kiss this sweet face. (*Pause.*)

MICHAEL. No—at least not now; not yet. Please give it back to me. (*He takes it.*) I'll hang it up. (*He takes it to steps.*) Will you hold it for a moment? (*She comes to steps, holds it while he mounts, gives it to him.*)

AUDRIE. What a wonderful thought that is, that we are watched by the dead. It never occurred to me before. I wonder what a spirit is like? (*He hangs up the picture.*) Now she is quite out of my reach. (*He comes down steps.*) Won't you take that money for rebuilding the Minster! It's there on the window-sill. (*He goes and takes it.*) Thank you.

MICHAEL. Thank you.

AUDRIE. Then I'm not to call again? Not even about my soul?

MICHAEL. I'm going over to the Island for some time, and shall only be back on Sundays.

AUDRIE. Saint Decuman's Island. You've built yourself a house over there, haven't you?

MICHAEL. The shrine was neglected and decayed. I restored it and built myself a couple of rooms round it. I've a few books, and just food and drink. I go over there sometimes for work and meditation.

AUDRIE. And yours is the only house on the island?

MICHAEL. Yes.

AUDRIE. Isn't it awfully lonely there?

MICHAEL (*glancing at picture*). I'm never alone.

AUDRIE. No, you have your millions and millions of good and bad angels, besides hundreds of cheap excursionists.

MICHAEL. Yes, in the summer, but they only stay a few hours.

AUDRIE. I can see the smoke from your chimney quite plainly in the evening from my drawing-room windows. How far is it across?

MICHAEL. About four miles.

AUDRIE. I shall get Hannaford to row me over some day. Don't look alarmed. I won't come when you are there. I should frighten all your good angels away. (MICHAEL *shows a little impatience.*) You want to get rid of me. (*Going, suddenly turns.*) If I come to you as a penitent, you won't send me away?

MICHAEL. Not if I can be of service to you.

AUDRIE. I seem to have changed my nature since I came into this room.

MICHAEL. How?

AUDRIE. I don't know. I wonder how many natures I have and how often I can change them.

MICHAEL. I wish you wouldn't speak like that.

AUDRIE. I won't. (*Very seriously.*) You said just now that I was playing with sacred things. I am, or I was until you spoke about her. (*With warning.*) Don't let me play with your soul.

MICHAEL. I don't understand you.

AUDRIE. You may do me good, but I am far more likely to do you harm.

MICHAEL. How?

AUDRIE. I'm not nearly so good a woman as you are a man.

MICHAEL. But perhaps I may influence you for good.

AUDRIE. Do you think that you can have any influence on my soul without my having an equal influence on yours?

MICHAEL. Action and reaction are equal and opposite. You think that law prevails in the spiritual world as well as in the material world?

AUDRIE. I'm sure it does. So let me go.

MICHAEL (*suddenly, with great feeling*). Oh, if I could save you!

AUDRIE. You can if you will. I would try so hard if you would only help me. But you don't believe that I can.

MICHAEL. What makes you say that?

AUDRIE. You called me a bad angel—and you don't think me good enough to kiss her. (*Sidling up to the steps; he makes a deprecating movement to prevent her, but she takes no notice.*) If you knew it would give me a splendid impulse to goodness, would you refuse me? (*She watches him very closely; he watches her, half deprecating, half consenting; she goes up a step or two; he again makes a deprecating gesture, but does not stop her.*) Can't you see what an awful effect it would have on me if you thought me worthy to be in the company of your good angel? It would be almost a sacrament! (*Going up steps. He makes a stronger gesture of deprecation.*) Ah, you think I'm not worthy—

MICHAEL. No, no—

AUDRIE (*on top of steps, very seductively*). Do save me. I'm worth saving. (*Whispers.*) I may kiss her? I may? I may? (*He does not reply. She very reverently kisses the picture on the wall, turns round, comes down slowly to him.*) Your bad angel has kissed your good angel. (*A mock curtsy to him. Exit softly.* MICHAEL *stands troubled.*)

(*Four months pass between Acts I and II.*)

ACT II

SCENE: *The Shrine on Saint Decuman's Island in the Bristol Channel. A living-room built round the shrine of the Saint, a fine piece of decayed Decorated Gothic now in the back wall of the room. A large fireplace down right. A door above fireplace. A door left; two windows, one on each side of the shrine, show the sea with the horizon line and the sky above. A bookcase; a table; old oaken paneling, about seven feet high, all round the room, and above them whitewashed walls. Red brick floor. Everything very rude and simple, and yet tasteful, as if it had been done by the village mason and carpenter under* MICHAEL'S *direction. Time, a September evening.*

(*Discover* ANDREW GIBBARD *packing a portmanteau, and* EDWARD LASHMAR (FATHER HILARY), *a Catholic priest, about sixty, very dignified and refined.*

(*Enter* WITHYCOMBE, *an old boatman.*)

WITHYCOMBE. Now, gentlemen, if yu'me ready to start! If you daunt come sune, us shall lose the tide down.

FATHER HILARY. I'm quite ready, Withycombe, as soon as I have said "Good-bye" to Mr. Feversham.

WITHYCOMBE. Mr. Feversham ain't coming along with us, then?

ANDREW. No, he stays on the island all the week, and you are to fetch him on Saturday morning.

WITHYCOMBE. Saturday morning. To-day's Wednesday. Right you are. Well and good. Saturday morning. Yu 'me coming on to Saint Margaret's along with us, Mr. Gibbard?

ANDREW. Yes—we can find some accommodation there for the night, can't we?

WITHYCOMBE. Well, I warn ye 'tis rough.

FATHER HILARY. Rougher than my Master had on his first coming here?

WITHYCOMBE. Well, I waun't say that, but so fur as I can judge, 'tis about as rough.

FATHER HILARY. Then it will do for me. Where is Mr. Feversham?

WITHYCOMBE. A few minutes agone he wor watching the excursion steamer back to Lowburnham.

FATHER HILARY. Will you find him and tell him that I am waiting to start?

WITHYCOMBE. Right you are, sir. Well and good. (*Exit.*)

FATHER HILARY. Andrew—have you noticed any change in Mr. Feversham lately?

ANDREW. Change, Father?

FATHER HILARY. He seems so restless and disturbed, so unlike himself.

ANDREW. Does he?

FATHER HILARY. It's six years since I was in England. But he was always so calm and concentrated. Has he any trouble, do you know?

ANDREW. He hasn't spoken of any.

FATHER HILARY. No. But you're with him constantly. Surely you must have seen the difference in him.

ANDREW. Yes. He has changed.

FATHER HILARY. How long has he been like this?

ANDREW. The last four months.

FATHER HILARY. Do you know of any reason for it?

ANDREW. He's coming!

(*Enter* MICHAEL.)

MICHAEL. You're ready to start, Uncle Ned?

FATHER HILARY. Yes. You won't change your mind and come with us?

MICHAEL. No, I must stay here. (*Glancing at books, restlessly.*) I want to be alone. I couldn't be of any service to you over at Saint Margaret's?

FATHER HILARY. There is the legend that connects her with Saint Decuman—I suppose no more is to be learned of that than we already know?

MICHAEL. No. The fisher people only know what they have learned from the guide books.

ANDREW (*standing with portmanteau*). Have you anything more to take to the boat, Father?

FATHER HILARY. No, that's all, Andrew.

ANDREW. Then I'll take it down and wait for you there. (*Exit* ANDREW *with portmanteau.*)

FATHER HILARY. Then this is good-bye, Michael?

MICHAEL. Unless you'll stay over the Sunday at Cleveheddon?

FATHER HILARY. No, I've done my work in England, and I must be back among my people. I wanted to see the shrines on these two sister islands again before I died. I shall leave Saint Margaret's to-morrow morning, get back to Cleveheddon, take the afternoon train up to London, and leave for Italy on Friday morning. You'll come and see me at Majano?

MICHAEL. When I can.

FATHER HILARY. This winter?

MICHAEL. No, not this winter. I shall be at work at once on the restorations now I've got all the money.

FATHER HILARY. Strange that it should all come so soon within two or three months.

MICHAEL. Yes, and from such different quarters of England—a thousand one day from Manchester—five hundred the next from some unheard-of village—and then the last great final gift last week.

FATHER HILARY. It looks as if it all came from one giver?

MICHAEL. Yes, I had thought of that.

FATHER HILARY. You don't know of any one?

MICHAEL. I've one or two suspicions. However, the great fact is that I have it all, and can set my architects to work.

FATHER HILARY. Michael—I was asking Andrew just now, there is something troubling you?

MICHAEL. No—no. What makes you think that?

FATHER HILARY. You are not yourself. (*Pause.*) Is it anything where I can be of help?

MICHAEL. There is nothing. (*Pause.*) There has been something. But it is past. (FATHER HILARY *looks grave.*) You need have no fear for me. (*Holding out hand.*)

FATHER HILARY (*takes his hand, holds it for a long while, looks gravely at him*). If you should ever need a deeper peace than you can find within or around you, come to me in Italy.

MICHAEL. But I am at peace now. (*Restlessly, pushing his hand through hair, then a little querulously.*) I am at peace now. (FATHER HILARY *shakes his head.*) You think you can give me that deeper peace?

FATHER HILARY. I know I can.

MICHAEL. I may come to you some day. (WITHYCOMBE *puts his head in at door.*)

WITHYCOMBE. Now, sir, if yu plaise, we 'me losing the tide—us shan't get to Margaret's avore supper-time.

FATHER HILARY. I'm coming, Withycombe.

MICHAEL. Withycombe, you'll come and fetch me on Saturday morning.

WITHYCOMBE. Saturday morning, twelve o'clock sharp, I'm here. Right you are, Mr. Feversham. Well and good. (*Exit.*)

FATHER HILARY. Good-bye.

MICHAEL. Good-bye, Uncle Ned. (*Very hearty hand-shake. Exit* FATHER HILARY. MICHAEL *goes to door, stands looking a few seconds, comes in, turns to his books.*)

(*Reënter* FATHER HILARY.)

MICHAEL. What is it?

FATHER HILARY. I don't like leaving you. Come with me to-night to Margaret's.

MICHAEL. Shall I? Perhaps it would be best—wait a minute.

WITHYCOMBE (*voice heard off*). Now, Mr. Lashmar, if you plaise, sir —we 'me losing the tide.

MICHAEL. Don't wait, I'm safe here. Good-bye.

FATHER HILARY (*slowly and regretfully*). Good-bye. (*Exit slowly.* MICHAEL *watches* FATHER HILARY *off; stays at door for some time, waves his hand, then closes door.*)

MICHAEL. Now I shall be at peace! (*Takes out letter from his pocket.*) Her letter! I will not read it! (*Puts it back in pocket, kneels and lights the fire.*) Why did you come into my life? I did not seek you! You came unbidden, and before I was aware of it you had unlocked the holiest places of my heart. Your skirts have swept through all the gateways of my being. There is a fragrance of you in every cranny of me. You possess me! (*Rises.*) No! No! No! I will not yield to you! (*Takes up book, seats himself at fire, reads a moment or two.*) You are there in the fire! Your image plays in the shadows—Oh, my light and my fire, will you burn me up with love for you? (*Rises, sighs.*) I'm mad! (*Pause, very resolutely.*) I will be master of myself—I will be servant to none save my work and my God! (*Seats himself resolutely, reads a moment or two, then drops book on knees.*) The wind that blows round here may perhaps play round her brow, the very breath that met my lips as I stood at the door may meet hers on the shore yonder. (*Rises, flings book on table, goes to window; takes out letter again, holds it undecidedly.*) Why shouldn't I read it? Every stroke of it is graven on my heart.—(*Opens it.*) "Dear keeper of souls in this parish, I have thought so much of our talk last night. I'm inclined to think that I have a soul after all, but it is a most uncomfortable possession. I believe if someone gave me an enormous impulse I might make a saint or a martyr, or anything that's divine. And I believe there is one man living who could give me that impulse." "One man living who could give me that impulse—" "But I hope he won't. Frankly, you may save me at too great cost to yourself. So trouble yourself no further about me. But if after this, you still think my wandering, dangling soul worth a moment of your ghostly care, come and lunch with me to-morrow, and I will give you the sweet plain butter-cakes that you love, on the old blue china. And that our salvation may not be too easy, I will tempt you with one sip of the ancient Johannisburg." And I went—yes, I went. "But for your own sake—I speak with all a woman's care for your earthly and heavenly welfare—I would rather you did not come. Let it be so. Let this be farewell. Perhaps our souls may salute each other in aimless vacancy hereafter, and I will smile as sweet a smile as I can without lips or cheeks to smile with, when I remember as I pass you in the shades that I saved you from your bad angel, Audrie Lesden. P.S. Be wise and let me go." I cannot! I cannot! Yet if I do not—what remains for me? Torture, hopeless love, neglected duty, work cast aside and spoilt, all my life disordered and wrecked! Oh, if I could be wise—I will! I will tear out this last one dear sweet thought of her. (*Goes to fire, tears up the letter in little pieces, watches them burn.*) It's done! I've conquered! Now I shall be at peace. (*Seats himself resolutely at table, reads. A little tap at the door; he shows surprise; the tap is repeated; he rises, goes to door, opens it. At that moment* AUDRIE'S *face appears at the right-hand window for a moment. He looks out, stays there a moment or two, closes door, seats himself again at table, reads. The tap is repeated; he rises,* AUDRIE *appears at door, he shows a moment of intense delight which he quickly subdues.*)

AUDRIE. May I come in? (*Pause.*) You are busy—I'll go—

MICHAEL. No—(*She stops on threshold.*) Come in.

(*She enters. He stands motionless at table. Sunset without. It gradually grows darker.*)

MICHAEL. What brings you here?

AUDRIE. You did not expect me. You aren't accustomed to entertain angels unawares—even bad ones.

MICHAEL (*his voice thick and a little hoarse*). Your boat, your companions?

AUDRIE. I have no boat, and no companions.

MICHAEL (*horrified, delighted*). You're alone?

AUDRIE. Quite alone.

MICHAEL. How did you come here?

AUDRIE. By the simplest and most prosaic means in the world. This morning I took the train to Lowburnham to do some shopping. As I was coming back to the station, a boy put this little handbill into my hand. (*Showing a little yellow handbill.*) Afternoon excursion to Saint Decuman's and Saint Margaret's Isles. I had an impulse—I obeyed it. I telegraphed to Cleveheddon for a boat to meet me here at six—(*takes out watch*)—it only wants ten minutes—and took the excursion steamer. They all landed here for half an hour. I hid myself till after the steamer had gone. Then I came up here to your cottage. I heard some voices, so I hid again—who was here?

MICHAEL. Only my secretary and my uncle Ned.

AUDRIE. The Catholic priest. I saw a boat leaving—it was they?

MICHAEL. Yes.

AUDRIE. They're not coming back?

MICHAEL. No.

AUDRIE. You're annoyed with me for coming?

MICHAEL. No, but wasn't it a little—imprudent?

AUDRIE. Oh, I must do mad things sometimes, just to preserve my general balance of sanity. Besides, my boat will be here in ten minutes. (*Pause.*)

AUDRIE. How strange we should be here alone!

MICHAEL. The only two beings on this island—we two!

AUDRIE. And our two souls.

MICHAEL. I wish you wouldn't jest with sacred things.

AUDRIE. I won't. (*Suddenly, impulsively.*) I want to be good! Help me to be good! You think I'm foolish and light and frivolous! Well, perhaps I am, but when I'm with you I'm capable of anything, anything—except being an ordinary, average, good woman.

MICHAEL. But isn't that all that is required of a woman?

AUDRIE. Perhaps. It's rather a damnable heritage, isn't it? And I'm not a barn-door fowl.

MICHAEL. What are you?

AUDRIE. Just what you like to make of me. Don't think I'm flattering you. Don't think I'm bold and unwomanly. I'm only speaking the truth. You have changed me. I'm ready to do anything, believe anything, suffer anything that you bid me! To-night I'm on a pinnacle! I shall either be snatched up to the skies, or tumble into the abyss. Which will it be, I wonder?

MICHAEL (*after a struggle, in a calm voice*). Neither, I trust. I hope you will take your boat back in ten minutes, have a good passage across, a comfortable dinner from your pretty blue china, and a sound night's rest. And to-morrow you will wake and forget this rather imprudent freak.

AUDRIE. Oh, you won't tread the clouds with me! Very well! Down to the earth we come. I can be as earthy as the very clay itself. But I thought you wanted me to be spiritual.

MICHAEL. I want you to be sincere, to be yourself.

AUDRIE. Very well. Tell me how. You are my ghostly father.

MICHAEL. No, you've never allowed me to be a priest to you.

AUDRIE. I've never allowed you?

MICHAEL. And I've never dared.

AUDRIE. Why not?

MICHAEL. Because you've never allowed me to forget that I am a man.

AUDRIE. Very well. Don't be a priest to me—at least not now. Tell me some one thing that you would wish me to do, and I'll do it!

MICHAEL. In that letter you wrote me—

AUDRIE. Did you keep it?

MICHAEL. No, I destroyed it.

AUDRIE. Destroyed it!

MICHAEL. In that letter you said it would be better for us if we did not meet again—

AUDRIE. No. I said it would be better for *you* if we did not meet again.

MICHAEL. Better for me?

AUDRIE. Yes, and worse for me. I came here to-night to warn you—

MICHAEL. Against what?

AUDRIE. Myself. I've done something that may endanger your peace for ever.

MICHAEL. What do you mean?

AUDRIE. Sometimes I laugh at it, sometimes I'm frightened. I daren't tell you what I've done. I'll go. (*Goes to door, opens it.*)

MICHAEL. No. (*Stops her.*) Mrs. Lesden, what have you done against me? You don't mean your gifts to the Minster?

AUDRIE. My gifts—what gifts?

MICHAEL. During the last four months I've constantly received large sums for the restoration of the Minster, and last week a very large sum was sent me, enough to carry out all the work just as I wished.

AUDRIE. Well?

MICHAEL. It was you who sent it all.

AUDRIE. I must see if my boatman has come.

MICHAEL (*stopping her*). No. Why did you send the money—so many different sums from so many different places?

AUDRIE. Because that gave me dozens of pleasures instead of one, in sending it. And I thought it would give you dozens of pleasures instead of one, in receiving it.

MICHAEL. I knew it was you! How glad I am to owe it all to you! Words couldn't tell you how grateful I am.

AUDRIE. And yet you wouldn't walk the clouds with me for a few minutes?

MICHAEL. You know that I would do anything in my power for your best, your heavenly welfare.

AUDRIE. I don't think I care much for my heavenly welfare just at this moment. You tumbled me off my pinnacle, and here I am stuck in the mud. (*Looking off at the open door.*) Look! That boat is half-way to Saint Margaret's.

MICHAEL. Yes, they sleep there to-night.

AUDRIE. What a queer-looking man your secretary is. Is he quite trustworthy?

MICHAEL. Quite. Why?

AUDRIE. I caught him looking at you in a very strange way a week or two back.

MICHAEL. He's devoted to me.

AUDRIE. I'm glad of that. How far is it to Saint Margaret's?

MICHAEL. Three miles.

AUDRIE. Do you believe the legend about Saint Decuman and Saint Margaret?

MICHAEL. That they loved each other?

AUDRIE. Yes, on separate islands, and never met.

MICHAEL. They denied themselves love here that they might gain heavenly happiness hereafter.

AUDRIE. Now that their hearts have been dust all these hundreds of years, what good is it to them that they denied themselves love?

MICHAEL. You think—

AUDRIE. I think a little love on this earth is worth a good many paradises hereafter. It's a cold world, hereafter. It chills me to the bone when I think of it! (*Shivers a little and comes away from the door.*) I'm getting a little cold.

MICHAEL (*placing chair*). Sit by the fire. (*She sits near fire, which is blazing up; he goes and closes door.*)

AUDRIE (*putting on some logs*). Do I know you well enough to make your fire for you?

MICHAEL. I hope so. (*She sits; he stands above her for some seconds, watching her keenly; a long pause.*)

AUDRIE. You were looking at me. What were you thinking of?

MICHAEL. I was wondering what memories are stored in that white forehead.

AUDRIE. Memories? (*Long sigh.*) A few bright ones, and many sad ones.

MICHAEL. Your past life was not happy?

AUDRIE (*with a little shudder of recollection*). No. And yours? Tell me—

MICHAEL. What?

AUDRIE. Something about your past life, something you've never told to a living creature.

MICHAEL. When I was twenty—

AUDRIE. Stay—what were you like when you were twenty? (*Shuts her eyes, puts her hand over them.*) Now I can see you when you were twenty.

MICHAEL. Is there any one with me?

AUDRIE. No, I can't see her. What was she like? Fair or dark?

MICHAEL. Fair, with changing gray eyes that could be serious or merry as she pleased, and fine clear features, and the sweetest provoking mouth—

AUDRIE. I hate her. Who was she?

MICHAEL. Miss Standerwick's niece. She stayed there all the summer that year.

AUDRIE. Was that a happy summer?

MICHAEL. The happiest I have ever known—till this.

AUDRIE. Ah!

MICHAEL. I used to go to evening church and follow them home, and wait outside till I could see the candle in her window. When it went out I used to walk home.

AUDRIE. Across those fields where we walked the other night?

MICHAEL. Yes.

AUDRIE. I'll never walk that way again. Go on.

MICHAEL. One night as I was waiting, she came out suddenly. I couldn't speak for trembling. At last I found my tongue, and we talked about silly commonplace things. When she was going in I dared to breathe, "Give me one kiss." She didn't answer. I just touched her cheek with my lips, and I whispered, "Good-night, Nelly." She said, "Good-night, Mike."

AUDRIE. She called you Mike?

MICHAEL. I was called Mike when I was a boy.

AUDRIE. And your next meeting?

MICHAEL. She was called away early the next morning to her father's deathbed. Her mother went abroad. I never saw her again. Tell me something about your past life.

AUDRIE. Can you see me when I was eight? I was a pretty little brown maid, and I set all aflame the heart of a cherub aged ten, with strong fat legs and curly red hair. His sister was my dearest friend. He spent all his pocket-money in buying sugar-plums for me, and gave them to her to give to me. She ate them herself, and slandered me to him, for she said I was false. He kicked her on the nose, and was sent far—far away to school. This was the first tragedy of my life. Now tell me some more of your life. You have had other romances, darker, deeper ones?

MICHAEL. Nothing that I dare show. I have told you of the one love of my youth. And you—Have you had darker, deeper romances?

AUDRIE. I was unhappy without romance. I would show you all my heart, all my thoughts, all my life, if I could do it as one shows a picture, and let it speak for itself. I wonder if you'd condemn me—

MICHAEL. Condemn you!

AUDRIE. I don't think you would. You have never guessed—

MICHAEL. Guessed—

AUDRIE. What a world there is within one's self that one never dares speak of! I wish to hide nothing from you. I would have you know me through and through for just the woman that I am, just that and no other, because, don't you see—I don't want to cheat you of a farthing's-worth of esteem on false pretenses—I want you to like me, Audrie Lesden, and not some myth of your imagination. But if you were armed with all the tortures of hell for plucking the truth about myself from my lips, I should still hide myself from you. So, guess, guess, guess, grand inquisitor—what is here (*tapping her forehead*) and here (*putting her hand on her heart*). You'll never guess one thousandth part of the truth!

MICHAEL. But tell me something in your past life that you have never told to another creature.

AUDRIE. I have two great secrets—one is about yourself, one is about another man.

MICHAEL. Myself? Another man?

AUDRIE. My husband.

MICHAEL. You said you had been unhappy.

AUDRIE. I married as thousands of girls do, carelessly, thoughtlessly. I was married for my money. No one had ever told me that love was sacred.

MICHAEL. Nobody ever does tell us that, till we hear it from our own hearts.

AUDRIE. I suppose it was my own fault. I was very well punished.

MICHAEL. How long were you married?

AUDRIE. Two years.

MICHAEL. And then your husband died?

AUDRIE. He went away from me. I never saw him again—alive. (*Passionately.*) And there's an end of him!

MICHAEL. I won't ask you what that secret is. I would wish you to keep it sacred. But your secret about myself? Surely I may ask that?

AUDRIE. I have sold you to the devil.

MICHAEL. What?

AUDRIE. I have sold myself, too.

MICHAEL. Still jesting?

AUDRIE. No, I did it in real, deep earnest.

MICHAEL. I don't understand you.

AUDRIE. Six months ago I was tired, gnawed to the very heart with ennui, and one hot restless night I happened to take up your book, "The Hidden Life." It came to me—oh, like a breath of the purest, freshest air in a fevered room. I thought I should like to know you. I got up early, took the first morning train down here, looked about the place, saw the Island House was to let, and rented it for three years.

MICHAEL. Well?

AUDRIE. I got Mr. Docwray to give me an introduction to you. You annoyed me, you were so cold and priestlike. Each time I saw you, you piqued and angered me more and more. I longed to get some power over you. At last one day after you had been so frozen and distant a little black imp jumped into my brain and whispered to me. I said to the devil, "Give this sculptured saint to me, and I'll give both our souls to you."

MICHAEL. But you didn't mean it?

AUDRIE. Yes. I said it with all my heart, and I bit my arm—look—(*Showing her arm.*) I made the teeth meet. There's the mark. If there is a devil, he heard me.

MICHAEL. And you think he has given me to you?

AUDRIE. The next time I saw you, you let me kiss your mother's portrait.

MICHAEL. Ah!

AUDRIE. But you don't really believe there is a devil? Why don't you speak? Why don't you laugh at me and tell me it's all nonsense? I haven't really given the devil power over your soul?

MICHAEL. No devil has any power over any soul of man until the man himself first gives him entrance and consent.

AUDRIE. And you haven't! Say you don't care for me.

MICHAEL. How can I say that?

AUDRIE. You must! I'm not strong enough to leave you of my own free will. I shall hang about you, worry you, tease you, tempt you, and at last, destroy you. Don't let me do it! Beat me away from you, insult me, do something to make me hate you! Make me leave you!

MICHAEL. When I love you with all my being?

AUDRIE (*shows great delight*). And you dare go on? It's an awful delight to think that a man would dare to risk hell for one! There aren't many men who would dare lose this world for the woman they love—how many men are there that would dare to lose the other?

MICHAEL. We must lose this world, for I am vowed away from all earthly things. But why should we lose the other? Why should we not make our love the lever to raise our souls? You do love me?

AUDRIE. Love is hardly the word. It is more like—if a man could create a dog, and be her master, friend, father, and God, I think she would feel towards him something of what I feel towards you. You have first made me know what love is, what life is. You have changed me thoroughly—no, you have changed half of me thoroughly—one half is still worthless, silly, capricious, hollow, worldly, and bad—that's my old self. She is gradually withering up under your influence, that old Audrie Lesden. The other half is looking out of my eyes at you now! Look! do you see the new Audrie Lesden that is your daughter and your creature? Aren't you proud of her?

MICHAEL. I shall be proud of her when she is full grown and dares to leave me of her own free will, because she loves me, and because I am vowed to Heaven!

AUDRIE. Do I tempt you? I'll go. You love me. That's enough, or it should be enough. I'll get back to London to-morrow, and strangle the new Audrie. Then the old Audrie will come back again, and live the old weary, dry, empty life—and grow old and wrinkled and heartless and perhaps—rouged—

MICHAEL. Why do you tear me so? What do you want of me here or hereafter? Take it! It's yours—

AUDRIE. You dare go on—now you know?

MICHAEL. Yes.

AUDRIE. Ah! I thought it was only women who dared hell for love. I won't take your sacrifice—I will leave you.

MICHAEL. You will? Yes, it must be so! My work, my vows—I cannot, may not taste of earthly love. Oh, it's cruel to dash the cup from my lips! (*Pause; then very calmly.*) You are right! I feel that we are choosing heaven or hell for both our souls this night! Help me to choose heaven for you, and I'll help you to choose heaven for me.

AUDRIE. Good-bye, my love, for ever. Be brave—and very cold to me, now. Be like marble—and death.

MICHAEL (*takes her hand; a very long pause; then speaks very calmly*). It is victory, isn't it? We have conquered? I'll go down to the bay and see if your boat has come. (*By this time it is dark outside.*)

AUDRIE. Half past six. I shall have a cold, dark voyage.

MICHAEL. And it is just a little rough. But Hannaford is a careful boatman.

AUDRIE. It's not Hannaford who is coming for me. I telegraphed for Withycombe.

MICHAEL (*pause—very pale and cold*). Withycombe? But you always employ Hannaford.

AUDRIE. Yes; and I did write out one telegram to him, and then I thought I should like to go back in the boat that always takes you. So I tore up the telegram to Hannaford, and telegraphed to Withycombe.

MICHAEL. Withycombe?

AUDRIE. Yes, what's the matter?

MICHAEL. He lives alone. When he goes out, he locks up his cottage. Your telegram will wait at the post office.

AUDRIE. Why?

MICHAEL. Withycombe has gone over to Saint Margaret's with Gibbard and my uncle. They stay there the night.

AUDRIE. Your own boat?

MICHAEL. I had it towed back last week, so that I couldn't be tempted to come to you.

AUDRIE. Then—

MICHAEL (*looks at her*). No boat will come to-night. (*Looks at her more intently.*) No boat will come to-night! (*They stand looking at each other.*)

(*Two nights and a day—from Wednesday evening to Friday morning —pass between Acts II and III.*)

ACT III

SCENE: *The Vicarage parlor, as in first act. Morning.*

(*Enter* MICHAEL, *haggard, troubled, with self-absorbed expression, the expression of a man trying to realize that he has committed a great and irrevocable sin; he stands for some moments helpless, dreamy, as if unconscious of his whereabouts; then looks round; his eyes fall upon his mother's picture, he shudders a little, shows intense pain. At length he goes up the steps, takes the picture down, places it on the floor with its face against the wall, carefully avoiding all the while to look at it. He then moves to table in the same dreamy, helpless, self-absorbed state, sits, looks in front of him. Enter* ANDREW, *comes up behind him.*)

MICHAEL. Oh, Andrew—Well?

ANDREW (*coming up to him*). I want to consult you on that passage in the Arabic—if you can spare the time.

MICHAEL. Bring the manuscripts here. (MICHAEL *unconsciously looks at his hands.*) What are you looking at?

ANDREW. Nothing. Your hands are blistered?

MICHAEL. I did a little rowing—the other day. Bring the manuscripts. (ANDREW *goes to door.*) Andrew—(ANDREW *stops*)—I was very restless—did you hear me stirring in the night?

ANDREW. Stirring?

MICHAEL. Yes, I couldn't sleep. I got up about one and went out—walked about for some hours—it was nearly light when I came in again. Did you hear me?

ANDREW (*pauses, then answers*). No. (*Is about to go off at right door when* FANNY *enters left. He stops.*)

FANNY. Mrs. Lesden wishes to see you for a minute or two about one of her cottagers. (ANDREW *watches* MICHAEL *keenly, but unobtrusively.*)

MICHAEL (*after a little start of surprise, in a tone of affected carelessness*). Show her in. (*Exit* ANDREW, *right. Exit* FANNY, *left.* MICHAEL *rises, shows great perturbation, walks about, watches the door for her entrance.*)

(*Reënter* FANNY, *left, showing in* AUDRIE.)

FANNY. Mrs. Lesden. (*Exit* FANNY. MICHAEL *and* AUDRIE *stand looking at each other for some seconds; then he goes to her, takes her hand, kisses it with great reverence, motions her to a chair; she sits. He holds out to her the palms of his hands with a rueful smile, shows they are much blistered as if with rowing.*)

AUDRIE. Poor hands!

MICHAEL. I'm not used to rowing. (*Pause.*)

AUDRIE. I didn't thank you.

MICHAEL. Thank me!

AUDRIE (*pause*). Wasn't it a terrible voyage, terrible and delightful? But we ought to have been drowned together!

MICHAEL. Oh, don't say that—in sin! To be lost in sin!

AUDRIE. I'd rather be lost with you than saved with any one else.

MICHAEL. You mustn't speak like this—

AUDRIE. It won't be right, you know, unless we are lost or saved together, will it?

MICHAEL. Hush! Hush! (*Pause.*)

AUDRIE. You're sorry?

MICHAEL. No. And you?

AUDRIE. No. Is all safe, do you think?

MICHAEL. Yes, I believe so.

AUDRIE. Didn't that strange secretary of yours think it curious that you came back on Thursday instead of Saturday?

MICHAEL. No. I explained that when Withycombe brought me your telegram I thought it better to return at once in case you had started to come, and had been somehow lost.

AUDRIE. Let us go carefully through it all as it happened, to make sure. To-day is Friday. On Wednesday I telegraphed to Withycombe to be at the landing-place at Saint Decuman's with a boat at six o'clock in the evening to bring me back home from there.

MICHAEL. Yes.

AUDRIE. But being a strange creature and quite unaccountable for my actions, I changed my mind, and instead of coming to Saint Decuman's I went up to London, stayed there all day yesterday, and returned by the night mail, reaching home at seven this morning.

MICHAEL. Yes.

AUDRIE. Meantime Withycombe has gone to Saint Margaret's with your uncle, stays there Wednesday night and does not get my telegram till his return home yesterday afternoon. He consults my servants, who know nothing of my whereabouts, consults Mr. Gibbard, who advises him to go to Saint Decuman's and see if I am there. He reaches Saint Decuman's last evening. You are surprised when he shows you the telegram—you explain that I'm not there, that I haven't been there, that you've seen nothing of me. (*Very tenderly.*) Dear, I felt so sorry for you when I heard you blundering and stammering through your tale to Withycombe.

MICHAEL. Why?

AUDRIE. I knew the pain and shame it caused you to say what wasn't true. I wished I could have told all the lies for you.

MICHAEL. No, no. Isn't the truth dear to you?

AUDRIE. Not in comparison with you. Besides, I shall be let off my fibs and little sins very cheaply, much more cheaply than you'll be, great serious person.

MICHAEL. You grieve me to the heart when you speak like this—

AUDRIE (*penitent*). I won't! I won't! I'll be very good and quite serious. Where were we? Well, you explain to Withycombe that I have never been to Saint Decuman's, and at the same time you also change your mind and return with him last evening instead of staying till Saturday.

MICHAEL. You've seen Withycombe and told him you went to London?

AUDRIE. Yes.

MICHAEL. He suspects nothing?

AUDRIE. No, I made it all quite clear to him.

MICHAEL. And your servants?

AUDRIE. They're used to my absences. They think nothing of it.

MICHAEL. Then all is safe. The matter will never be heard of again—except—

AUDRIE. Except?

MICHAEL. In our two hearts, and in the High Court where such cases are tried. (*With an inclination of the head and finger towards heaven.*)

AUDRIE. Don't preach, and—don't regret.

MICHAEL. I won't—only how strange it all is!

AUDRIE. What?

MICHAEL (*in a quiet, calm voice throughout, smiling a little*). How men try to make their religion square with their practice! I was hard, cruelly hard, on that poor little girl of Andrew's. I was sure it was for the good of her soul that she should stand up and confess in public. But now it comes to my own self, I make excuses; I hide, and cloak, and equivocate, and lie—what a hypocrite I am!

AUDRIE. Ah, you're sorry!

MICHAEL. No, I'm strangely happy and—dazed. I feel nothing, except my great joy, and a curious bitter amusement in tracing it all out.

AUDRIE. Tracing what out?

MICHAEL. The hundred little chances, accidents as we call them, that gave us to each other. Everything I did to avoid you threw me at your feet. I felt myself beginning to love you. I wrote urgently to Uncle Ned in Italy, thinking I'd tell him and that he would save me. He came—I couldn't tell him of you, but his coming kept Withycombe from getting your telegram. I went to Saint Decuman's to escape from you. You were moved to come to me. I sent away my own boat to put the sea between us, and so I imprisoned you with me. Six years ago I used all my influence to have the new lighthouse built on Saint Margaret's Isle instead of Saint Decuman's, so that I might keep Saint Decuman's lonely for myself and prayer. I kept it lonely for myself and *you*. It was what we call a chance I didn't go to Saint Margaret's with Andrew and my uncle. It was what we call a chance that you telegraphed to my boatman instead of your own. If any one thing had gone differently—

AUDRIE (*shaking her head*). We couldn't have missed each other in this world. It's no use blaming chance or fate, or whatever it is.

MICHAEL. I blame nothing. I am too happy. Besides, Chance? Fate? I had the mastery of all these things. They couldn't have conquered me if my own heart hadn't first yielded. You mustn't stay here. (*Turning towards her with great tenderness.*) Oh, I'm glad that no stain rests upon you through me—

AUDRIE. Don't trouble about me. I have been thinking of you. Your character?

MICHAEL. My character! My character! My character!

AUDRIE (*glances up at the place where the portrait had hung*). Where is she? (*He points to the picture on the floor.*)

MICHAEL. I daren't look at her. I must hide it until—

AUDRIE. Until?

MICHAEL. Until we have done what we can to atone for this.

AUDRIE. What?

MICHAEL. Repent, confess, submit to any penance that may be enjoined us. And then if and when it shall be permitted us—marriage.

AUDRIE. Marriage?

MICHAEL. Retirement from all who know us, and lifelong consecration of ourselves to poverty and good works, so that at the last we may perhaps win forgiveness for what we have done.

AUDRIE. Marriage?

(*Reënter* ANDREW *with manuscripts.*)

ANDREW. I beg pardon. I thought Mrs. Lesden had gone. (*Puts manuscripts on table and is going off.*)

AUDRIE. I am just going, Mr. Gibbard.

ANDREW (*turns and speaks to her*). I met a stranger on the beach yesterday evening. He inquired for you and the way to your house.

AUDRIE. Indeed.

ANDREW. He asked a great many questions about you.

AUDRIE. What questions?

ANDREW. How you lived in this quiet place, and who were your friends, and where you were yesterday.

AUDRIE. Did he give his name?

ANDREW. I didn't ask for it. I suppose he's staying in the place. I saw him at the door of the George later in the evening.

AUDRIE. One of my London friends, I suppose. What did you reply to his questions?

ANDREW. I told him Mr. Feversham was one of your friends, but as I didn't know where you were yesterday, of course I couldn't tell him, could I? (*Looks at her, exit.*)

AUDRIE. Did you notice that?

MICHAEL. Notice what?

AUDRIE. The look that man gave me as he went out. Does he suspect us?

MICHAEL. Impossible.

AUDRIE. I feel sure he does. Send for him and question him at once. I'll go.

(*Enter* FANNY *with a letter.*)

FANNY. For you, ma'am. (*Gives letter to* AUDRIE, *who glances at it, shows a sharp, frightened surprise, instantly concealed, and then stands motionless.*) The gentleman's waiting for an answer.

AUDRIE (*in a very quiet, cold voice*). I'll come at once. (*Exit* FANNY.)

MICHAEL. What's the matter?

AUDRIE. Nothing. Question that man. Find out if he knows anything. I'll come back as soon as I can. (*Exit, without opening letter.*)

MICHAEL (*follows her to door, closes it after her, then goes to right door, calls*). Andrew. (*Reënter* ANDREW.) What is this passage you're in difficulty about?

ANDREW (*comes to him with old manuscripts*). What's the matter?

MICHAEL. My head is dizzy this morning.

ANDREW. Didn't you say you couldn't sleep?

MICHAEL. What time did you get back from Saint Margaret's yesterday?

ANDREW. About twelve.

MICHAEL. You saw my uncle off by the afternoon train?

ANDREW. Yes.

MICHAEL. And then? (ANDREW *does not reply*.) You were surprised to see me coming back with Withycombe instead of staying till Saturday?

ANDREW. No.

MICHAEL. Withycombe's message about the telegram a little disturbed me. (*A little pause, watching* ANDREW.) I thought perhaps Mrs. Lesden might have started to come to Saint Decuman's (*pause, still watching* ANDREW), and been lost on the way.

ANDREW. Did you?

MICHAEL. She is such a strange, flighty creature, that I should scarcely be surprised at anything she took it into her head to do.

ANDREW (*looking him full in the face*). She went up to London, didn't she?

MICHAEL (*wincing a little*). Yes.

ANDREW. And came back through the night by the mail?

MICHAEL. Yes. Why do you look at me like that?

ANDREW. I beg your pardon. Is there any other question you'd like to ask me?

MICHAEL. Question? About what?

ANDREW. About Mrs. Lesden—or anything that's troubling you.

MICHAEL. Troubling me? I'm not troubled about anything.

ANDREW. Oh! I thought perhaps you were. (*Going*.)

MICHAEL. Andrew. (ANDREW *stops*.) I've been thinking about—about Rose.

ANDREW. Have you?

MICHAEL. Perhaps I was wrong in urging her to confess.

ANDREW. It isn't much good thinking that now, is it?

MICHAEL. No, except to ask you to forgive me, and to say that you don't cherish any ill-feeling against me on that account.

ANDREW. I forgive you, and I don't cherish any ill-feeling against you on that or any account.

MICHAEL. I may trust you entirely, Andrew?

ANDREW. If you doubt it—try me.

MICHAEL. Try you?

ANDREW. Didn't I tell you to ask me any question you like?

MICHAEL (*alarmed*). What do you mean? (*Pause, looks at* ANDREW.) Enough. I trust you absolutely—(*looks at him*)—in everything.

ANDREW. You may. (*Is again going.*)

MICHAEL. No, Andrew, nothing has occurred—I was afraid—it seemed so strange—this telegram business. What are you thinking about me?

ANDREW. Take care, sir. Don't betray yourself to anybody but me.

MICHAEL. Betray myself?

ANDREW. You're a worse bungler at lying than I was. Don't look like that, or other people will guess. Don't give way. You're safe. Nobody but me suspects anything. Your character is quite safe—her character is quite safe. They're both in my keeping.

MICHAEL (*stares helplessly at him*). How did you know?

ANDREW. I've suspected for some time past—

MICHAEL. You were wrong. There was nothing to suspect. It was a chance, an accident—there was no intention to deceive. What made you guess?

ANDREW. When Withycombe brought the telegram to me I guessed something was wrong. I heard you go out in the middle of the night. I followed you down to the beach; I saw you put off; I waited for you to come back. I was on the top of the cliff just above you when you landed with her. I saw you come on here, and I watched her take the road to the station, and saw her come back to her home as if she had come in by the early morning train.

MICHAEL. What are you going to do?

ANDREW. Nothing. Don't I owe everything I am and everything I have in this world to you? I shall never breathe a word of what I know to a living soul.

MICHAEL. Thank you, Andrew. Thank you. And you'll be sure above all that she is safe—

ANDREW. As safe as if I were in the grave. You go your way, just the same as if I didn't know.

MICHAEL. Andrew.

ANDREW (*comes back*). Sir—

MICHAEL (*breaking down*). I was harsh and cruel to Rose. I punished her more than she deserved. I was a hard, self-righteous priest! I hadn't been tempted myself then. Send for her to come home again! Comfort her and give her the best place in your heart. Write at once. Let her come back to-morrow! Oh, what weak, wretched Pharisees we are! What masks of holiness we wear! What whited sepulchres we are! Send for her! Make up to her for all she has suffered! Let me ask her pardon! Oh, Andrew, have pity on me! Forgive me, forgive me! (*Bending his head in tears.* ANDREW *steals out of the room. A long pause.* AUDRIE *appears at window in the same place as in Act I, looks in, sees him, taps the window, he goes up to it*).

AUDRIE. Let me in, quickly. I want to speak to you. (*He goes to door, opens it; a moment later she enters.*)

MICHAEL. Well?

AUDRIE. Why didn't you take my warning? Why didn't you beat me, drive me, hound me away from you as I told you?

MICHAEL. What now?

AUDRIE. Say you'll forgive me before I tell you! No, don't forgive me!

MICHAEL. I don't understand you. Is anything discovered?

AUDRIE. What does that matter? Oh, don't hate me. If you say one unkind word to me I shall kill myself. Read the letter which came here to me just now. (*He takes the letter wonderingly.*)

MICHAEL. Whom did it come from?

AUDRIE. My husband.

MICHAEL. Your husband? (*She nods.*) Your husband! He is alive? (*She nods.*)

AUDRIE (*with a laugh*). Didn't I tell you I should ruin you body and soul? (*He stands overwhelmed.*) Why do you stand there? Why don't you do something? (*Laughing at him.*) I say, ghostly father, we make a pretty pair, you and I, don't we? What shall we do? Confess in white sheets and candles together, you and I? Why don't you do something—(*Laughing at him.*) And you stand there like a stone saint. (*Comes up to him.*) Kill me and have done with me!

MICHAEL. You said your husband died after two years.

AUDRIE. I said I never saw him again—alive. I thought then that I never should.

MICHAEL. But—you believed he was dead. You believed he was dead—(*She does not reply.*) You didn't know the night before last that your husband was living?

AUDRIE. Don't I tell you to kill me and have done with it.

MICHAEL (*horrified*). You knew he was living?

AUDRIE (*very imploringly*). I love you, I love you. Say one word to me! Say one word to me! Say you forgive me.

MICHAEL. I forgive you. (*Stands overwhelmed*). Take this letter—(*Offering it.*)

AUDRIE. I didn't mean to do this. Do make excuses for me. We lived unhappily together. When I came into all my money I bargained with him that we would never see each other again. It was a fair bargain —a contract. He went away to America—I gave out he was dead. From that time to this I have never had a thought of his return. He was dead to me. He has no right to come and spoil my life. Read that letter from him.

MICHAEL. No—take it. (*Gives the letter back.*)

AUDRIE. Tell me what to do.

MICHAEL. I am not fit to advise you.

AUDRIE. What can we do?

MICHAEL. I don't know. We're in a blind alley with our sin. There's no way out of this.

AUDRIE. I shall defy him.

MICHAEL. No.

AUDRIE. Yes. A bargain's a bargain. I shall go back and defy him. I'll never see him again. But then—what then? What will you do?

MICHAEL. Don't think of me.

AUDRIE. Speak to me. Say one word. Oh, it has been on the tip of my tongue so many times to tell you all, but I couldn't bear to lose your love, so I deceived you. (*He walks about perplexed. She goes to him very gently and coaxingly.*) Say you aren't sorry—say that deep down in your inmost heart you aren't sorry for what is past!

MICHAEL. Sorry? No. God forgive me. I'm not sorry. I can't be sorry. I wish I could.

AUDRIE (*coming to him*). Ah, now I know you love me! If you only dare be as bold as I dare—

MICHAEL. Bold?

AUDRIE. We love each other. Our loves and lives are in our own hands.

MICHAEL (*repulses her, braces himself to stern resolve, very coldly and commandingly*). Listen! These are perhaps the last words I shall ever speak to you. The past is past. There's no way out of that. But the future is in our power. Can't you see, woman, that we are half-way down the precipice? We'll go no further. From this moment we part; I toil back to repentance and peace one way, you toil back another. So far as God will give me grace I'll never think of you from this moment—I'll spend all my life in putting a gulf between you and me. You do the same—ask only one thing for yourself and me, that we may forget each other.

AUDRIE (*looks at him, smiles, sighs, then as she is going off*). I was right about man's love. You are all cowards. There's not one of you that doesn't think first of his comfort, or his pocket, or his honor, or his skin, or his soul, and second of the woman he thinks he loves. Forget you? (*A little laugh.*) Do you think that possible? Do you think I was jesting with you when I gave myself to you? Forget you? (*A little laugh.*) My memory is good for such trifles. Forget you?

MICHAEL (*with a wild revulsion*). Oh, take me where you will! I have no guide but you! Heaven, hell, wherever you go, I shall follow. Be sure of that. But won't you be my better angel, now I've lost her: If you love me as you say, you can yet be the master influence of my life, you can yet save yourself through me, and me through you. Won't you make our love a monument for good? Dearest of all, I'm at your feet—I think you come from heaven, and I'm all obedience to you. You are my angel. Lead me—Lead me, not back to sin—Lead me towards heaven—You can even now!

AUDRIE. What do you wish me to do?

MICHAEL. Go back to your duty and to deep repentance. Have strength, dearest. These are not idle words—duty, purity, holiness. They mean something. Love is nothing without them. Have courage to tread the hard road. Leave me.

AUDRIE. If I leave you now, shall we meet one day—hereafter?

MICHAEL. Yes.

AUDRIE. You're sure? You do believe it?

MICHAEL. With all my heart.

AUDRIE. And you'll stay here and carry on your work, restore the Minster, and let me think that I'm helping you.

MICHAEL. I can't do that now.

AUDRIE. Yes.

MICHAEL. No.

AUDRIE. Yes.

MICHAEL. But with that money—your money!

AUDRIE. Many churches are built with sinners' money. Do this for me.

MICHAEL. If I dared—if it would come to good—You know how dear a hope it has been to me all my life through.

AUDRIE. Do it, because I ask it. You will?

MICHAEL. And you'll leave me, leave this place, because I ask it. You will?

AUDRIE. I love you. I obey you. (*She comes to him.*)

MICHAEL. No, I daren't come near to you. You'll go? (*He opens the door; she passes out, reënters.*)

AUDRIE. Listen to this. Whatever happens, I shall never belong to anybody but you. You understand? (MICHAEL *bows his head.*) I shall never belong to anybody but you, Mike. (*She goes out again. He closes door, goes up to window. She passes. He watches her off, stays there some moments.*)

(*Reënter* ANDREW. MICHAEL *comes from window; the two men stand looking at each other.*)

ANDREW. You won't begin work this morning, I suppose?

MICHAEL (*firmly*). Yes. (*Goes to table, motions* ANDREW *to one chair, seats himself opposite. They take up the manuscripts.*) Where is the place?

ANDREW. Fifty-first Psalm, verse three. (MICHAEL *winces, turns over the manuscript.*) Have you found it? What are you looking at?

MICHAEL (*gets up suddenly*). I can't bear it.

ANDREW. Can't bear what? (MICHAEL *stands looking at him with terror.*)

ANDREW (*rises, comes to him*). Don't I tell you that all is safe. I shan't blab. Nobody shall ever know.

MICHAEL. But *you* know!

ANDREW. I shall never remind you of it.

MICHAEL. But you do, you do. Your presence reminds me.

ANDREW. Shall I leave you now and come again by and by.

MICHAEL (*with an effort*). No, stay. (*Points to seat.* ANDREW *seats himself.*) You've sent for Rose to come home?

ANDREW. No.

MICHAEL. No?

ANDREW. I don't want to have her in this place where everybody knows about her.

MICHAEL. Won't you send for her, Andrew—to please me?

ANDREW. She's well enough where she is. (*Pointing to the manuscripts.*) Shall we go on?

MICHAEL. What ought I to do, Andrew?

ANDREW. Don't you know what you ought to do?

MICHAEL. What?

ANDREW. Mete out to yourself the same measure you meted to others.

MICHAEL. Confess—in public. I can't! I can't! I daren't. I'm a coward, a weak, miserable coward! Don't judge me harshly, Andrew! Don't be hard on me! (*Covering his face with his hands.*)

ANDREW (*cold, firm*). Come, sir! shall we get on with our work? (*Reading manuscript.*) "For I acknowledge my transgressions, and my sin is ever before me." (MICHAEL *uncovers his face and sits staring at* ANDREW, *who sits cold and grim on the other side of the table.*)

(*A year passes between Acts III and IV.*)

ACT IV

SCENE: *The Chancel of the Minster church of Saint Decuman at Clevehedon, a beautiful building of Decorated Gothic architecture with signs of recent restoration. The altar and reredos, approached by steps, face the audience, who take up the same position towards it as spectators in the nave would do. Behind the altar a long vista of columns, arches, roof, and stained-glass windows. An organ is built in left wall of the chancel at a considerable height. On both sides of the chancel are handsome high carved oak stalls. A large open place in front of the altar steps is flanked on each side by the transepts, which run to right and left of spectators and are filled with chair seats so far as can be seen. A small door in the north wall of the left transept leads to the organ loft. The whole church is most lavishly decorated with banners, hangings, scrolls, and large frescoes, and is smothered with flowers as if in readiness for a church festival. Large brass candlesticks on altar with lighted candles. Time, about nine on an autumn night.*

(*An organ voluntary is being played as curtain rises. Enter* MICHAEL *from transept. He has aged much, is very pale and emaciated. The voluntary ceases and the organ boy, a lad about fifteen, comes from small door in wall of left transept.*)

WALTER (*carelessly*). Good-night, sir.

MICHAEL (*stopping him, puts his hand on the boy's head*). Good-bye, Walter. (*Pause, still detaining him, with considerable feeling.*) Good-bye, my dear lad. (*Sighs, moves away from him. The boy shows slight respectful surprise and exits along transept. The Organist with keys enters from the little door, looks round the church admiringly.*)

ORGANIST. Everything ready for the ceremony to-morrow?

MICHAEL. Yes, I think, everything.

ORGANIST. I was just putting the finishing touches to my music.

How beautiful the church looks! You must be very proud and happy now your work is complete.

MICHAEL. Not quite complete. I've to put the finishing touches to my part—to-morrow.

(ANDREW *enters rather suddenly from transept.*)

ANDREW. Can I speak to you for a moment?

ORGANIST. Good-night. (*Going.*)

MICHAEL (*detains him*). Thank you for all you have done for me, and for the church, and for her services. (*Shakes hands warmly. Exit the Organist by transept.*) Well?

ANDREW. I thought you'd like to know—Mrs. Lesden has come back to Cleveheddon, and she has brought a lady friend with her.

MICHAEL. I know.

ANDREW. You've seen her? (MICHAEL *looks at him with great dignity.*) I beg your pardon.

MICHAEL. I've not seen her.

ANDREW. I beg your pardon. It's no business of mine. (*Going.*)

MICHAEL (*quietly*). Yes, it is business of yours.

ANDREW. What do you mean?

MICHAEL. Haven't you made it the chief business of your life all this last year?

ANDREW. How? I've kept my word. I've never reminded you of it.

MICHAEL. You've never allowed me to forget it for a single moment. Every time you've spoken to me, or looked at me, or crossed the room, or passed the window, every time I've heard your step on the stairs, or your voice speaking to the servants, you've accused me. If you had been in my place I would have been very kind to you, Andrew.

ANDREW. How did you treat my girl?

MICHAEL. I did what I thought was best for her soul.

ANDREW. Then why don't you do what is best for your own soul?

MICHAEL. I shall. (ANDREW *looks at* MICHAEL *in startled inquiry.*)

(*Enter by transept* DOCWRAY *and* SIR LYOLF. SIR LYOLF *is in evening dress under summer overcoat.* DOCWRAY *points out the decorations to* SIR LYOLF.)

ANDREW. Why have you sent for Rose to come back to Cleveheddon?

MICHAEL. I wish her to be present at the services to-morrow. She is almost due. Go to the station and meet her. Bring her to me here. (SIR LYOLF *and* DOCWRAY *saunter up towards* MICHAEL *and* ANDREW. ANDREW *stands perplexed.*)

MICHAEL (*firmly, to* ANDREW). Bring her to me here. (ANDREW *goes off through transept, turns to look at* MICHAEL *before he goes off.*)

SIR LYOLF. You didn't turn up at dinner?

MICHAEL. I was too busy.

SIR LYOLF. All prepared for to-morrow?

MICHAEL. Yes, I think.

SIR LYOLF. So it seems Mrs. Lesden has come down from town.

MICHAEL. So I understand.

SIR LYOLF (MICHAEL *is listening intently*). I thought we had seen the last of her when the long-lost husband returned and took her off to London. By the way, what has become of her husband?

MARK. He has gone back to South America. (MICHAEL *is listening intently.*)

SIR LYOLF. Gone back to South America?

MARK. He only stayed three weeks in England. It is said that she has pensioned him off—he is to keep to his hemisphere, and she is to keep to hers.

SIR LYOLF. I don't like it!

MARK. Don't like what?

SIR LYOLF. I don't like women who pension off their husbands to live in South America.

MICHAEL. Do you see much of her in town?

MARK. Not much. About every two months she sweeps into church in a whirlwind of finery and perfume, gives me a ridiculously large sum for the offertory, makes some most irreverent joke, or else pretends to be deeply religious—

MICHAEL. Pretends?

MARK. What can it be but pretense? Look at her life this last year.

MICHAEL. What of it?

MARK. It has been one continual round of gayety and excitement except when she was ill.

MICHAEL. She has been ill?

MARK. Yes, and no wonder.

MICHAEL. Why?

MARK. She goes everywhere, gives the most extravagant parties, mixes with the fastest, emptiest, London set. And she has taken for her companion a silly, flighty little woman, Mrs. Cantelo.

SIR LYOLF. I don't like it! Why has she come back to Cleveheddon just now?

MARK. To be present at the dedication service to-morrow, I suppose.

SIR LYOLF. Michael—

MICHAEL. Well?

SIR LYOLF. You know that everybody is asking where all the money came from for these magnificent restorations?

MICHAEL. It was sent to me anonymously. The giver wishes to remain unknown.

SIR LYOLF. Yes! Yes! That's what you've told us. But of course you know who it is?

MICHAEL. I mustn't speak of it.

SIR LYOLF. Forgive me.

MICHAEL. Let's say no more. I'm glad you came here to-night. I've been very much perplexed by a confession that has been made to me recently. A priest—you know him, Mark—he is to be present to-morrow—a priest some time ago discovered one of his people in a course of lying and deception, and insisted upon a very severe penalty from the man. And now the priest tells me, that in order to save one very dear to him, he himself has lately been practising exactly the same course of lying and deception. He came to me for advice. I said, "You must pay exactly the same penalty that you demanded from your parishioner." But he objects—he says it will bring disgrace on his family, and disgrace on our cloth. He urged all manner of excuses, but I wouldn't listen to him. He wishes to be present at the dedication service to-morrow. I've refused him. Have I done right?

SIR LYOLF. Yes, I should say so.

MARK. Was it a just penalty?

MICHAEL. Yes, I believe so—the just, the only penalty, in my opinion. Have I done right?

MARK. Yes, certainly.

MICHAEL. I'm glad you both think that. To-morrow before the dedication service begins, I shall stand where I'm standing now and confess that I have been guilty of deadly sin and deceit. Then I shall go out from this place and never return. (*They come away from him, staring at him in speechless surprise for some moments.*)

SIR LYOLF. But—Good Heaven!—what have you done?

MICHAEL (*after a long pause*). Guess.

SIR LYOLF. But you won't proclaim yourself?

MICHAEL. Yes.

SIR LYOLF. But your career—your reputation—your opportunities of doing good—

MARK. Have you thought what this will mean to you, to us, to the church?

MICHAEL. I have thought of nothing else for many months past.

SIR LYOLF. Surely there must be some way to avoid a public declaration. (MICHAEL *shakes his head.*) You know I don't speak for myself. My day is nearly done, but you're in the full vigor of life, with a great reputation to sustain and increase. Don't do this—for my sake, for your own sake, for the sake of Heaven, don't do it!

MICHAEL. I must.

MARK. What are the circumstances?

MICHAEL. I can't tell you. I wouldn't have told you so much except that I knew I might trust both of you never to hint or whisper anything against—against any but myself. If you should guess—as most likely you will—the name of my companion in sin, it will never cross your lips? I may ask that of you?

SIR LYOLF. You know you may.

MARK. Of course we shall say nothing.

SIR LYOLF. But—but—(*Sits down overwhelmed.*)

MARK. Can't we talk this over further? Have you considered everything?

MICHAEL. Everything. I have known for many months that this must come. I have tried to palter and spare myself, but each time the conviction has returned with greater and greater force, "You must do it there, and then, and in that way."

MARK. But you've repented?

MICHAEL. Most deeply. I have fasted and prayed. I have worn a hair shirt close to my skin. But my sin remains. It isn't rooted out of my heart. I can't get rid of its image.

MARK. Its image?

MICHAEL (*in same calm, tranquil, matter-of-fact tone*). I believe that every sin has its exact physical image. That just as man is the expression of the thought of God, so our own thoughts and desires and aims, both good and bad, have somewhere or other their exact material counterpart, their embodiment. The image of my sin is a reptile, a greyish-green reptile, with spikes, and cold eyes without lids. It's more horrible than any creature that was ever seen. It comes and sits in my heart and watches me with those cold eyes that never shut, and never sleep, and never pity. At first it came only very seldom; these last few months it has scarcely left me day or night, only at night it's deadlier and more distorted and weighs more upon me. It's not fancy. Mark, I know, I know, that if I do not get rid of my sin, my hell will be to have that thing sitting beside me for ever and ever, watching me with its cold eyes. But (*hopefully*) I shall be rid of it after to-morrow.

MARK. My poor fellow!

SIR LYOLF (*rising, coming back to* MICHAEL). Michael, can't you postpone this? Can't it be at some other time? Not in the very hour which should be the proudest and happiest of your life?

MICHAEL. There is no other hour, no other way. (*Looks at them both, takes both their hands affectionately.*) Tell me (*very piteously*) that you neither of you love me the less,—or at least say that you love me a little still, after what I've told you.

SIR LYOLF. Don't you know?

MARK. How can you ask that? (ANDREW *and* ROSE *appear in the transept.*)

MICHAEL (*to* ANDREW). One moment, Andrew. (*To his father.*) I've a word or two to say to Andrew.

SIR LYOLF. Come and stay the night with me and let us talk this over.

MICHAEL. No, I must be alone to-night. Good-night, dear Mark. (MARK *wrings his hand.*)

SIR LYOLF. You are resolved to go through with this? It must be? (MICHAEL *bows his head.*) I can't be here to-morrow. I couldn't face it. But (*with great affection*) I shan't be far away when you want me. (*Very warm handshake.*) Come, Mr. Docwray. (*Exeunt* SIR LYOLF *and* DOCWRAY *by transept.*)

ANDREW (*bringing* ROSE *to* MICHAEL). I've brought her. (ROSE *is in an Anglican sister's dress; she is very pale and her manner is subdued. She comes slowly and reverently to* MICHAEL, *and is going to bend to him. He takes her hands and raises her.*)

MICHAEL. No. You mustn't bend to me. I've sent for you, Rose, to ask your pardon.

ROSE. My pardon?

MICHAEL. I made you pass through a terrible ordeal last year. Will you forgive me?

ROSE. What should I forgive? You were right. You said it would bring me great peace. And so it has—great peace.

MICHAEL. And you wouldn't undo that morning's work?

ROSE. No. It seems I died that morning and left all my old life in a grave. This is quite a new life. I wouldn't change it.

MICHAEL. Andrew, do you hear that?

ANDREW. Yes.

MICHAEL. I was right, then? I was right? You are happy?

ROSE. Yes, I am happy—at least, I'm peaceful, and peace is better than happiness, isn't it?

MICHAEL. Yes, peace is best! Peace is best! I shall find it too, some day. Andrew, she has forgiven me. Can't you forgive me? We may never see each other again on this side the grave. Don't let us part in anger!

ANDREW. Part?

MICHAEL. As soon as I can arrange my affairs I shall leave Cleveheddon.

ANDREW. But your work?

MICHAEL. My work is ended. I'll see that you and Rose are sufficiently provided for. (*Taking their hands, trying to join them;* ANDREW *holds aloof.*)

ANDREW. No. I can't take any favor from you.

MICHAEL. It's no favor. I've trained you to a special work which has unfitted you for everything else. It is my duty to provide for your old age.

ANDREW. I can't take any favor from you.

MICHAEL. Old comrade (*leaning on* ANDREW'S *shoulder;* ANDREW *draws away*), old comrade (*draws* ANDREW *to him*), we had many happy days together in the summer of our life. Now the autumn has come, now the winter is coming, I'm setting out on a cold, dark journey. Won't you light a little flame in our old lamp of friendship to cheer me on my way? You'll take my gift—you'll take it, and make a home for her?

ANDREW (*bursts out*). You'll break my heart with your kindness! I don't deserve it! I was a half-bred, starving dog. You took me in, and, like the hound I am, I turned and bit the hand that fed me. Let me be! Let me be!

MICHAEL. Rose, speak to him.

ROSE. Father, you are grieving Mr. Feversham.

ANDREW. I'll do whatever you tell me. But don't forgive me.

MICHAEL. Take him home, Rose. I parted you. Let me think I have restored you to each other. (*Joining them.*)

ANDREW (*to* MICHAEL). I can't say anything to-night. I never was good enough to black your shoes. I can't thank you. I can't speak. Good-night. Come, Rose! (MICHAEL *shakes* ROSE'S *hand very tenderly. Exeunt* ROSE *and* ANDREW *by transept.* MICHAEL *watches them off, goes to altar.*)

MICHAEL (*alone*). One thing more and all is done. (*Looking round the church.*) And I must give you up! Never enter your doors, never lead my people through you in chariots of fire, never make you the very presence-chamber of God to my soul and their souls who were committed to me! Oh, if I had been worthy! (*A little pause. A woman's laugh is heard in the transept opposite to that by which* ANDREW *and* ROSE *have gone off.* MICHAEL *withdraws to the side of chancel, where he is seen by the audience, during the following scene, but is hidden from* AUDRIE *and* MRS. CANTELO.)

(AUDRIE *enters from transept in magnificent evening dress, cloak, and jewelry, and carrying a large basket of roses. Her features are much paler and sharpened, and she shows a constant restlessness and excitement.*)

AUDRIE (*looks round, calls out*). Somebody is here? (*Pause, calls out.*) Somebody is here? No? (*Speaks down transept.*) You may come in, Milly.

(MILLY CANTELO, *a fashionable little woman, enters at transept, looking admiringly round the church.*)

AUDRIE. There's nobody here except (*raising her voice*) a stone saint (*pointing up to carved figure*), and he can't hear, because he has only stone ears, and he can't feel, because he has only a stone heart. (MICHAEL *shows intense feeling.*)

MILLY (*looking round*). Isn't it gorgeous?

AUDRIE. H'm—yes—(*Raises her voice.*) I can't bear that stone saint. Look how hard and lifeless he is. In a well-regulated world there would be no room for angels or devils, or stone saints, or any such griffins.

MILLY. Audrie, you are queer to-night. You'll be ill again.

AUDRIE. I hope so.

MILLY. What's the matter with you?

AUDRIE. Life's the matter with me, I think. I've got it badly, and I don't know how to cure myself.

MILLY. I wish you wouldn't talk nonsense, and run about on silly errands in the dark.

AUDRIE. I won't for long. When my head is tightly bandaged in a white cloth, I can't talk any more nonsense, can I? And when my feet are comfortably tucked up in my final nightgown I can't run after stone saints in the dark, can I?

MILLY. Oh, you give me the creeps. I can't imagine why you wanted to come out to-night.

AUDRIE. To decorate the church.

MILLY. Don't you think it's decorated enough?

AUDRIE (*looking*). No, it wants a few more touches. I must just titivate a cherub's nose, or hang a garland on an apostle's toe, just to show my deep, deep devotion—

MILLY. Your deep, deep devotion.

AUDRIE. My deep, deep love, my deep, deep worship, my deep, deep remembrance.

MILLY. Of what?

AUDRIE. The church, of course.

MILLY. What a heap of money all this must have cost! Who gave it all?

AUDRIE. I gave two hundred pounds when I lived here last year.

MILLY. I wonder who gave all the rest?

AUDRIE. I wonder!

MILLY. Mr. Feversham must have some very devoted friends.

AUDRIE. So it seems.

MILLY. Did you know him very well when you lived here?

AUDRIE. Not very well.

MILLY. What sort of a man is he?

AUDRIE. Oh, a very cold, distant man—a good deal of the priest about him, and as much feeling as that stone figure up there.

MILLY. You didn't like him?

AUDRIE. Oh, I liked him well enough. But I don't think he cared much for me. I dare say he has forgotten all about me by this time. Milly—(*Bursts into tears.*)

MILLY. What is it?

AUDRIE. I'm not well to-night. I oughtn't to have come here. Milly—I never forget anybody. If I had once loved you I should love you for ever. If you were wicked, or unfortunate, or unfaithful, it would make no difference to me. Kiss me, Milly—say you believe me.

MILLY. You know I do, darling.

AUDRIE (*very passionately*). I can be constant, Milly—I can! Constant in my friendship, constant in my love! Oh, Milly, I'm the most wretched woman in the world!

MILLY. You're hysterical, dear.

AUDRIE. No, I'm forsaken. Nobody loves me! (*Sobbing. Gesture from* MICHAEL.)

MILLY. Poor Audrie!

AUDRIE. Let me be a few minutes by myself. I want to be quite alone. Go home and wait for me there.

MILLY. I don't like leaving you.

AUDRIE (*getting her off at transept*). Yes—go, dear. I shall be better soon. Do leave me.

MILLY. You won't be long?

AUDRIE. No—I'll come soon. (*Accompanying her along transept. Exit* MILLY *by transept.* AUDRIE *stands listening.* MICHAEL *comes forward a step or two.*)

AUDRIE (*in the transept*). Are you there? (*He comes forward; she goes towards him; they stand for a moment or two looking at each other.*)

AUDRIE. Are you deaf? I thought it was only your memory that was gone.

MICHAEL. Why have you come here?

AUDRIE. Mayn't I come into my own church? And such a sinner as I am?

MICHAEL. Forgive me. You know how welcome I would make you —if I dared.

AUDRIE. Then you don't dare? Then I'm not welcome?

MICHAEL (*troubled*). Yes! Yes! Very welcome! The Church owes much to you.

AUDRIE. I think she does, for she has robbed me of your love. Why have you sent back all my letters unopened?

MICHAEL. Can't you guess what it cost me to return them? (*Pause.*) What have you been doing all this last year?

AUDRIE. Doing? Eating my heart. Racing through my life to get to the end of it. Skipping and chatting from Hyde Park Corner to the Inferno by a new short cut. What have you been doing?

MICHAEL. Trying to repent and to forget.

AUDRIE. Ah, well—I haven't been wasting my time quite so foolishly as you after all.

MICHAEL. Will you never be serious?

AUDRIE. Yes—soon.

MICHAEL. You've been ill?

AUDRIE. Oh, my dear spiritual doctor, you don't know how ill I've been. I get up every morning without hope, I drag through the day without hope, I go to this thing and that, to this party, to that reception, to the theater, to church, to a pigeon-shooting match, to the park, to Ascot, to Henley—here, there, everywhere, all without hope.

MICHAEL. What is it you want?

AUDRIE. I want to live again! I've never lived but those few months when we were learning to love each other! I want to feel that fierce breeze on my cheek that blew us together! Do you remember when we stood on the cliff hand in hand? And we shrieked and laughed down the wind like mad children? Do you remember?

MICHAEL. No.

AUDRIE. No? Nor the wonderful pale sunrise, with the lemon and green lakes of light, and then the path of diamonds all across the sea? Don't you remember?

MICHAEL. No.

AUDRIE. How strange you don't remember! Oh, my God, if I could forget!

MICHAEL (*apart from her*). Oh, my God, if I could forget! (*A long pause. He comes to her.*) I have one awful thought—I am bound to you —There is but one of us—I never felt it more than at this moment— And yet the awful thought comes to me—if by any decree we should be put asunder hereafter—if we should be parted then!

AUDRIE. Don't you dread being parted now—now this moment? Don't you dread being unhappy here—here on this earth?

MICHAEL. I will not think of that. I have vowed!

AUDRIE. You don't love me! You don't love me! You don't love me!

MICHAEL. If I had ten thousand worlds I'd sell them all and buy your soul. But I will keep the vow I have vowed. You are the holiest thing on earth to me. I will keep you white and stainless from me.

AUDRIE. You'll never forget me.

MICHAEL. I have forgotten you.

AUDRIE. You'll never forget me.

MICHAEL (*in the same cold tone, going up the altar steps*). I have forgotten you. (*Stands with his back to her for a few moments.*)

AUDRIE (*with a gesture of resignation*). You'll let me put a bunch or two of flowers about the church before I go?

MICHAEL. If I asked you not—

AUDRIE. I should obey you.

MICHAEL. I do ask you not—

AUDRIE. Very well. It's hard lines that I mayn't decorate my own church.

MICHAEL. I have another request to make—a favor to beg of you.

AUDRIE. It's done, whatever it is. But make it some great thing— something very hard and desperate, that I may show you there's nothing I would not do if you ask it.

MICHAEL. It's something very simple. I'm going to ask you not to be present at the dedication service to-morrow.

AUDRIE. But I came on purpose—

MICHAEL. I beg you not. I have a strong reason. You won't come?

AUDRIE. Not if you wish me to stay away. Shall I see you after tomorrow?

MICHAEL. After to-morrow I leave Cleveheddon for ever.

AUDRIE. Where are you going?

MICHAEL. I don't know.

AUDRIE. It doesn't matter, I shall find you out.

MICHAEL. You'll follow me?

AUDRIE. Yes—all over this world, and the ten thousand others. I shall follow you. You'll find me always with you, clawing at your heart. Au revoir. (*Takes up her basket of roses; going out with them by transept, stops.*) Do let me put some flowers on the altar—just to remind you. Your memory is so bad, you know. (*He raises his hand very quietly and turns his back on her. She stands very quiet and hopeless for a few seconds, then takes up the basket of flowers, goes a step or two towards transept, turns.*) I'm going to be very ill after this. (*He stands at altar in an attitude of prayer, his back to her.*) Do you hear. I'm going to be very ill? There's a little string in my heart—I've just heard it snap. (*Pause.*) If I were dying and I sent for you, would you come?

MICHAEL (*after a long pause, very quietly*). Yes. (*Pause.*)

AUDRIE. And that's all? And that's all? (*He stands unmoved at altar, his back to her. She takes a large red rose out of the basket, throws it towards him; it falls on the white marble altar steps.*) There's a flower for to-morrow! Do put it on the altar for me! You won't? You won't? (*No answer.*) It is hard to be turned out of my own church—It is hard—(*Exit* AUDRIE *by transept with the basket of flowers. A sob is heard,* MICHAEL *turns round. A door is heard to close. He puts out the altar lights, throws himself on altar steps. The curtains fall.*

(*The falling of the curtains signifies the passing of the night. A peal of joyous church bells followed by organ music and singing. The curtain rises and discovers the church in broad daylight and filled with worshipers.* ANDREW *and* ROSE *are at the corner in prominent positions.* AUDRIE'S *flower is lying on the altar steps. A processional hymn is being sung. A procession of surpliced priests file up the aisle and take their places in the chancel, walking over* AUDRIE'S *rose.* MICHAEL *follows at the end of the procession; as he reaches the altar steps, he turns, very pale and cold, and speaks in a low, calm voice.*)

MICHAEL. Before this service begins and this church is reconsecrated I have a duty to perform to my people. (*Great attention of all.*) I have often insisted in this place on the necessity of a life of perfect openness before God and man. I have taught you that your lives should be crystal clear, that your hearts should be filled with sunlight, so that no foul thing may hide therein. I have enforced that with others, because I believe with my heart and soul that it is the foundation of all wholesome and happy human life. I stand here to affirm it to-day in the presence of God and you all. I stand here to affirm it against myself as I formerly affirmed it against another. I stand here to own to you that while I have been vainly preaching to you, my own life has been polluted with deceit and with deadly sin. I can find no repentance and no peace till I have freely acknowledged to you all that I am not worthy to continue my sacred office, not worthy to be the channel of grace to you. It was the dearest wish of my life to restore this beautiful temple, and to be Heaven's vicar here. I have raised it again, but I may not enter. I dare not enter. I have sinned—as David sinned. I have broken the sanctity of the marriage vow. It is my just sentence to go forth from you, not as your guide, your leader, your priest; but as a broken sinner, humbled in the dust before the Heaven he has offended. I bid you all farewell. I ask your pardon for having dared to continue in my office knowing I had profaned and desecrated it. It now remains for me to seek the pardon of Heaven. Let the service continue without me. Let no one leave his place. Pray for me all of you! I have need of your prayers! Pray for me! (*He comes down from the altar steps amidst the hushed and respectful surprise of the congregation, who all turn to look at him as he passes.* ROSE *makes a very slight gesture of sympathy as he passes her.* ANDREW *stands with hands over his eyes.* MICHAEL *passes out by transept, his head bowed, his lips moving in prayer as he goes off.*)

(*Ten months pass between Acts IV and V.*)

ACT V

SCENE: *Reception room of the Monastery of San Salvatore at Majano, in Italy. A simply furnished room in an old Italian building. At back right an open door approached by a flight of steps, at back left a large window; a mass of masonry divides the window and door. A door down stage, left. The portrait of* MICHAEL'S *mother hangs on the wall. Time, a summer evening.*

(*Discover* FATHER HILARY *reading. Enter* SIR LYOLF *up the steps and by door at back.*)

FATHER HILARY. Well?

SIR LYOLF. I've been to see her again. I can't get her out of my mind.

FATHER HILARY. How is she this evening?

SIR LYOLF. In the very strangest state, laughing, crying, jesting, fainting, and chattering like a magpie. I believe she's dying.

FATHER HILARY. Dying?

SIR LYOLF. Yes. It seems she had a kind of malarial fever a month or two ago and wasn't properly treated. I wish there was a good English doctor in the place. And I wish Michael was here.

FATHER HILARY. Be thankful that he is away.

SIR LYOLF. But if he finds out that she has been here, that she has sent again and again for him, and that we have hidden it from him—and that she has died?

FATHER HILARY. He mustn't know it until he can bear to hear it. We must consider him first. Think what he must have suffered all these months. Now that at last he is learning to forget her, now that he is finding peace, how wrong, how cruel it would be to reopen his wounds!

SIR LYOLF. She said he promised to come to her if she sent for him. She begged so hard. She has come from England with the one hope of seeing him. I felt all the while that I was helping to crush the life out of her.

FATHER HILARY. What did you tell her?

SIR LYOLF. That he had gone away alone for a few days in the mountains. That we didn't exactly know where to find him, but that he might come back at any time, and that I would bring him to her the moment he returned.

FATHER HILARY. Well, what more can we do?

SIR LYOLF. Nothing now, I suppose. I wish we had sent after him when she came last week. We could have found him before this. Besides, she doesn't believe me.

FATHER HILARY. Doesn't believe you?

SIR LYOLF. She thinks that Michael is here with us, and that we are hiding it from him. I wish he'd come back.

FATHER HILARY. If she is passing away, better it should all be over before he returns.

SIR LYOLF. I don't like parting them at the last. She loves him, Ned, she loves him.

FATHER HILARY. Remember it's a guilty love.

SIR LYOLF. Yes, I know.

FATHER HILARY. Remember what it has already cost him.

SIR LYOLF. Yes, I know. But love is love, and whether it comes from heaven, or whether it comes from the other place, there's no escaping it. I believe it always comes from heaven! (FATHER HILARY *shakes his head.*)

SIR LYOLF. I'm getting my morals mixed up in my old age, I suppose. But, by God, she loves him, Ned, she loves him—Who's that? (FATHER HILARY *looks out of window, makes a motion of silence.*)

FATHER HILARY. Hush! He's come back.

SIR LYOLF. I must tell him.

FATHER HILARY. Let us sound him first, and see what his feelings are. Then we can judge whether it will be wise to let him know.

(*Enter up steps and by door* MICHAEL *in a traveling cloak. He enters very listlessly. He has an expression of settled pensiveness and resignation, almost despair. He comes up very affectionately to his father, shakes hands, does the same to* FATHER HILARY. *Then he sits down without speaking.*)

SIR LYOLF. Have you come far to-day, Michael?

MICHAEL. No, only from Casalta. I stayed there last night.

SIR LYOLF. You are back rather sooner that you expected?

MICHAEL. I had nothing to keep me away. One place is the same as another.

FATHER HILARY. And about the future? Have you made up your mind?

MICHAEL. Yes. I had really decided before I went away, but I wanted this week alone to be quite sure of myself, to be quite sure that I was right in taking this final step, and that I should never draw back. (*To* FATHER HILARY.) You remember at Saint Decuman's Isle, two years ago, you said you could give me a deeper peace than I could find within or around me?

FATHER HILARY. And I can. And I will.

MICHAEL. Give me that peace. I need it. When can I be received?

FATHER HILARY. When I have prepared you.

MICHAEL. Let it be soon. Let it be soon. (*To his father.*) This is a blow to you—

SIR LYOLF. You know best. I wish you could have seen your way to stay in your own Church.

MICHAEL. I was an unfaithful steward and a disobedient son to her. She is well rid of me. (*To* FATHER HILARY.) You are sure you can give me that peace—

FATHER HILARY. If you'll but give me your will entirely, and let me break it in pieces. On no other condition. Come and talk to me alone. (*Trying to lead him off left.*)

SIR LYOLF. No—(*Goes to* MICHAEL.) Michael, you are at peace now, aren't you? (MICHAEL *looks at him.*)

FATHER HILARY. He will be soon. Leave him to me.

SIR LYOLF. No. I must know the truth from him.

FATHER HILARY. You're wrong to torture him.

SIR LYOLF (*to* MICHAEL). You are at peace now—at least, you are gaining peace, you are forgetting the past?

FATHER HILARY. He will. He shall. Say no more. (*To* MICHAEL.) Come with me,—I insist!

SIR LYOLF. No. Michael, before you take this last step answer me one question—I have a reason for asking. Tell me this truly. If by any chance some one in England—some one who was dear to you—

MICHAEL. Oh, don't speak of her—(*Turns away, hides his head for a minute, turns round with a sudden outburst.*) Yes, speak of her! Speak of her! I haven't heard her name for so long! Let me hear it again—Audrie! Audrie!

FATHER HILARY (*sternly to* SIR LYOLF). Do you hear? Let him alone. Don't torment him by dragging up the past. He has buried it.

MICHAEL. No! No! No! Why should I deceive you? Why should I deceive myself? All this pretended peace is no peace! There is no peace for me without her, either in this world or the next!

FATHER HILARY. Hush! Hush! How dare you speak so!

MICHAEL. I must. The live agony of speech is better than the dead agony of silence, the eternal days and nights without her! Forget her? I can't forget! Look! (*Takes out a faded red rose.*)

SIR LYOLF. What is it?

MICHAEL. A flower she threw me in church the last time I saw her. And I wouldn't take it! I sent her away! I sent her away! And her flower was trampled on. The next night I got up in the middle of the night and went over to the church and found it on the altar steps. I've kept it ever since. (*To his father.*) Talk to me about her. I want somebody to talk to me about her. Tell me something you remember of her—some little speech of hers.—Do talk to me about her.

SIR LYOLF. My poor fellow!

MICHAEL. I can't forget. The past is always with me! I live in it! It's my life. You think I'm here in this place with you—I've never been here. I'm living with her two years ago. I have no present, no future. I've only the past when she was with me. Give me the past! Oh! give me back only one moment of the past, one look, one word from her—and then take all that remains of me and do what you like with it. Oh! (*Goes back to bench, sits.*)

SIR LYOLF (*to* FATHER HILARY). You see! I must tell him—

FATHER HILARY. No, not while he's in this mad state. Let's quiet him first.

SIR LYOLF. Then we'll take him to her!

FATHER HILARY. When he is calmer.

SIR LYOLF. Take care it isn't too late.

FATHER HILARY (*goes to* MICHAEL, *puts his hand on* MICHAEL'S *shoulder*). This is weakness. Be more brave. Control yourself!

MICHAEL. Have I not controlled myself? Who trained and guided himself with more care than I? Who worked as I worked, prayed as I prayed, kept watch over himself, denied himself, sacrificed himself as I did? And to what end? Who had higher aims and resolves than I? They were as high as heaven, and they've tumbled all round me! Look at my life, the inconsequence, the inconsistency, the futility, the foolishness of it all. What a patchwork of glory and shame! Control myself? Why? Let me alone! Let me drift! What does it matter where I go? I'm lost in the dark! One way is as good as another! (*The vesper bell heard off at some little distance.*)

FATHER HILARY. You've wandered away from the road, and now you complain that the maps are wrong. Get back to the highway, and you'll find that the maps are right.

MICHAEL. Forgive me, Uncle Ned—I'm ashamed of this. I shall get over it. I'll talk with you by and by. I will submit myself. I will be ruled. Father, come to me. You nursed me yourself night after night when I was delirious with the fever. I was a child then. I'm a child now. Talk to me about her. Talk to me about Audrie! (AUDRIE'S *face, wasted and hectic, appears just over the doorstep, coming up the steps at back; during the following conversation she raises herself very slowly and with great difficulty up the steps, leaning on the wall.*) I've heard nothing of her. Where do you think she is? In England? I think I could be patient, I think I could bear my life if I knew for certain that all was well with her. If I could know that she is happy—No, she isn't happy—I know that.

SIR LYOLF. Michael, I've had some news of her.

MICHAEL. News! Good? Bad? Quick! Tell me.

SIR LYOLF. You can bear it?

MICHAEL. She's dead? And I never went to her! I never went to her! She won't forgive me!

SIR LYOLF. She's not dead.

MICHAEL. What then?

SIR LYOLF. You promised you'd go to her if she sent for you.

MICHAEL. Yes.

SIR LYOLF. She has sent for you. (*Sees her entering.*)

MICHAEL. She's dying? (*She has gained the door, just enters, leaning back against the post.* MICHAEL'S *back is towards her.*)

AUDRIE. I'm afraid I am. (MICHAEL *looks at her, utters a wild cry of joy, then looks at her more closely, realizes she is dying, goes to her, kisses her, bursts into sobs.*)

AUDRIE (*putting her hand on his head*). Don't cry. I'm past crying for. Help me there. (*Points to seat.*) (*He seats her; looks at her with great anxiety.*)

AUDRIE (*laughing, a little weak feeble laugh, and speaking feebly with pause between each word*). Don't pull—that—long—face. You'll—make me—laugh—if you—do. And I want to be—serious now.

MICHAEL. But you're dying!

AUDRIE (*with a sigh*). Yes. Can't help it. Sir Lyolf, pay—coachman—(*taking out purse feebly*) outside—No, perhaps—better—wait—or bring another sort—of—carriage. But no mutes—no feathers—no mummery.

SIR LYOLF. I'll send him away. You'll stay with us now?

AUDRIE (*nods*). So sorry—to intrude. Won't be very long about it. (*Exit* SIR LYOLF *by door and steps;* MICHAEL *is standing with hands over eyes.*)

FATHER HILARY (*coming to* AUDRIE). Can I be of any service, any comfort to you?

AUDRIE. No, thanks. I've been dreadfully wicked—doesn't much—matter, eh? Can't help it now. Haven't strength to feel sorry. So sorry I can't feel sorry.

FATHER HILARY. There is forgiveness—

AUDRIE. Yes, I know. Not now. Want to be with him. (*Indicating* MICHAEL.)

(SIR LYOLF *reënters by steps.*)

SIR LYOLF. Come, Ned—

AUDRIE (*to* FATHER HILARY). Come back again—in—few minutes. I shall want you. I've been dreadfully wicked. But I've built a church—and—(*feverishly*) I've loved him—with all my heart—and a little bit over. (*Exeunt* SIR LYOLF *and* FATHER HILARY, *door left.*)

AUDRIE (*motioning* MICHAEL). Why didn't you come when I sent for you?

MICHAEL. I've only known this moment. Why didn't you send before?

AUDRIE. I sent you hundreds—of messages—from my heart of hearts. Didn't you get them?

MICHAEL. Yes—every one.

AUDRIE. I've crawled all over Europe after you. And you aren't worth it—Yes, you are. You wouldn't come—

MICHAEL. Yes—anywhere—anywhere—take me where you will.

AUDRIE. You know—he's dead. I'm free.

MICHAEL. Is it so? But it's too late.

AUDRIE. Yes. Pity! Not quite a well-arranged world, is it? Hold my hand. We're not to be parted?

MICHAEL. No.

AUDRIE. Sure?

MICHAEL. Quite sure. You're suffering?

AUDRIE. No—that's past—(*Shuts her eyes. He watches her.*) Very comfortable—very happy—just like going into a delicious faint—(*Sighs.*) Do you remember—beautiful sunrise—diamonds on the sea—

MICHAEL. Yes, I remember—all—every moment! And the wind that blew us together when we stood on the cliff! Oh! we were happy then—I remember all! All! All!

AUDRIE. So glad your memory's good at last. (*A vesper hymn heard off at some distance.*) Pity to die on such a lovely evening—not quite well-arranged world? But we were happy—if the next world has anything as good it won't be much amiss. I'm going. Fetch—priest—(MICHAEL *is going to door left; she calls him back.*) No. No time to waste. Don't leave me. We shan't be parted?

MICHAEL. No! No! No! No!

AUDRIE (*gives a deep sigh of content, then looks up at his mother's picture*). She's there? (MICHAEL *nods.*) She'll forgive me! (*Blows a little kiss to the picture.*) But I'm your angel—I'm leading you—

MICHAEL. Yes. Where?

AUDRIE. I don't know. Don't fuss about it. "Le bon Dieu nous pardonnera: c'est son métier"*—(*Closes her eyes.*) Not parted? (*Looks up at him.*)

MICHAEL. No! No! No! No!

AUDRIE. You won't keep me waiting too long? (*Looks up at him, a long deep sigh of content.*) Hold my hand—Tight! tight! Oh! don't look so solemn—(*Begins to laugh, a ripple of bright, feeble laughter, growing louder and stronger, a little outburst, then a sudden stop, as she drops dead.* MICHAEL *kisses her lips, her face, her hands, her dress.*)

(*Enter* FATHER HILARY.)

MICHAEL. Take me! I give my life, my will, my soul, to you! Do what you please with me! I'll believe all, do all, suffer all—only—only persuade me that I shall meet her again! (*Throws himself on her body.*)

["God will forgive us: it is His trade"—Heinrich Heine on his deathbed* (1856).]

DRAMATIC SEQUELS

St. John Hankin was, like the *fin-de-siècle* poseurs, rather cynical on the surface and profoundly moralistic underneath, a fact which is abundantly obvious in the best known of his seven plays, *The Cassilis Engagement* (1907) and *The Return of the Prodigal* (1905). In the latter comedy he goes out of his way to avoid a conventional ending. The fate of Eustace Jackson "the ne'er-do-well" is a surprise: Eustace, unrepentant, simply forces his righteous father, a textile manufacturer, to purchase peace and respectability by paying his son £250 a year to go away and not make trouble for the family. Mr. Jackson, with no alternative, pays up and when sentiment threatens to intrude ("You may write occasionally, just to let us know how you are") Eustace snaps it off like a lily-stalk:

> EUSTACE (*smiles grimly, then hands back check*). Make it three hundred, Father—and I won't write. (MR. JACKSON *is about to protest angrily, then recognizing the uselessness of that proceeding, says nothing, but waves check contemptuously away.* EUSTACE, *still smiling, pockets it.*) No? Well have it your own way. . . .

And he walks out, refusing to shake hands with his elder brother, as the father *leans his head on the mantelpiece with a sigh* and the curtain falls.

Hankin was equally original in the new endings he provided in his *Dramatic Sequels,* which included irreverent additions to, among others, *The Lady of Lyons, Caste,* and *The Second Mrs. Tanqueray.* The rationale of *Dramatic Sequels* was this:

Plays end too soon. They never show
The whole of what I want to know.

The curtain falls and I'm perplexed
With doubts about what happened next.

Did HAMLET's father haunt no more
The battlements of Elsinore?

Does LADY TEAZLE never call
At LADY SNEERWELL's now at all?

Was BENEDICK's a happy marriage?
And will the MELNOTTES keep a carriage?

Will AUBREY take to wife one day
Another MRS. TANQUERAY?

DRAMATIC SEQUELS
by

St. John Hankin

When Lord Lytton provided the conventional "happy ending" for The Lady of Lyons *by reuniting Pauline, née Deschappelles, to the devoted Claude Melnotte, promoting the latter to the rank of Colonel in the French army, he seems not to have troubled his head as to the divergent social ideas of the happy pair, nor as to how the vulgar and purse-proud family of Deschappelles and the humbler Melnottes would get on together. The sequel throws a lurid light on these points. In writing it great pains have been taken to make the blank verse, wherever possible, as bad as Lord Lytton's.*

IN THE LYONS DEN

SCENE: *The drawing-room of* CLAUDE MELNOTTE'S *house.* PAULINE *is sitting by the fire,* CLAUDE *leaning with his back against the mantelpiece.* JAMES, *a man-servant in livery, enters with a card on a salver.*

PAULINE (*reading card*). Mrs. Smith! Not at home, James.

CLAUDE (*who can never quite get out of his habit of speaking in blank verse*). Why are you not at home to Mrs. Smith?

PAULINE. My dear Claude, that woman! Mr. Smith kept a greengrocer's shop. 'Tis true he made a great deal of money by his contracts to supply the armies of the Republic with vegetables, but they are not gentlepeople!

CLAUDE (*in his most Byronic manner*). What is it makes a gentleman, Pauline? Is it to have a cousin in the Peerage—

PAULINE. Partly that, dear.

CLAUDE (*refusing to be interrupted*). Or is it to be honest, simple, kind—

PAULINE. But I have no reason for believing Mr. Smith to have been more honest than the general run of army contractors.

CLAUDE (*continuing*). Gentle in speech and action as in name?
Oh, it is this that makes a gentleman!
And Mr. Smith, although he kept a shop,
May very properly be so described.

PAULINE. Yes, I know, dear. Everybody calls himself a gentleman nowadays, even the boy who cleans the boots. But I am not going to give in to these unhealthy modern ideas, and I am not going to visit Mrs. Smith. She is not in Society.

CLAUDE (*off again on his high horse*). What is Society? All noble men—

PAULINE (*objecting*). But Mr. Smith isn't a *nobleman*, Claude.

CLAUDE. . . . And women, in whatever station born,
These, only these, make up "Society."

PAULINE (*patiently*). But that's such a dreadful misuse of words, dear. When one talks of "Society," one does not mean good people, or unselfish people, or high-minded people, but people who keep a carriage and give dinner-parties. Those are the only things which really matter socially.

CLAUDE. Pauline, Pauline, what dreadful sentiments!
They show a worldly and perverted mind.
I grieve to think my wife should utter them!

PAULINE (*very sweetly*). I wish, Claude, you'd try and give up talking in blank verse. It's very bad form. And it's very bad verse, too. Try and break yourself of it.

CLAUDE (*off again*). All noble thoughts, Pauline—

PAULINE. No, no, no, Claude. I really can't have this ranting. Byronics are quite out of fashion.

CLAUDE (*relapsing gloomily into prose*). You may laugh at me, Pauline, but you know I'm right.

PAULINE. Of course you're right, dear. Much too right for this wicked world. That's why I never can take your advice on any subject. You're so unpractical.

CLAUDE (*breaking out again*). The world, the world, oh, how I hate this world!

PAULINE. Now that's silly of you, dear. There's nothing like making the best of a bad thing. By the way, Claude, didn't you say Mrs. Melnotte was coming to call this afternoon?

CLAUDE. Yes. Dear mother, how nice it will be to see her again!

PAULINE. It will be charming, of course. . . . I do hope no one else will call at the same time. Perhaps I'd better tell James we are not at home to anyone except Mrs. Melnotte.

CLAUDE. Oh no, don't do that. My mother will enjoy meeting our friends.

PAULINE. No doubt, dear. But will our friends enjoy meeting your mother? (*Seeing him about to burst forth again.*) Oh yes, Claude, I know what you are going to say. But, after all, Lyons is a very purse-proud, vulgar place. You know how *my* mother can behave on occasions! And if Mrs. Melnotte happens to be here when any other people call it may be very unpleasant. I really think I had better say we are not at home to anyone else. (*Rises to ring the bell.*)

CLAUDE. Pauline, I forbid you! Sit down at once. If my family are not good enough for your friends, let them drop us and be hanged to them.

PAULINE. Claude, don't storm. It's so vulgar. And there's not the least occasion for it either. I only thought it would be pleasanter for all our visitors—your dear mother among the number—if we avoided all chance of disagreeable scenes. But there, dear, you've no *savoir faire,* and I'm afraid we shall never get into Society. It's very sad.

CLAUDE (*touched by her patience*). I am sorry, my dear. I ought to have kept my temper. But I wish you weren't so set upon getting into Society. Isn't it a little snobbish?

PAULINE (*wilfully misunderstanding him*). It's dreadfully snobbish, dear; the most snobbish sort of Society I know. All provincial towns are like that. But it's the only Society there is here, you know, and we must make the best of it.

CLAUDE. My poor Pauline! (*Kissing her.*)

PAULINE (*gently*). But you know, Claude, social distinctions do exist. Why not recognise them? And the late Mr. Melnotte *was* a gardener!

CLAUDE. He was—an excellent gardener.

PAULINE. One of the Lower Classes.

CLAUDE. In a Republic there are no Lower Classes.

PAULINE (*correcting him*). In a Republic there are no Higher Classes. And class distinctions are more sharply drawn than ever in consequence.

CLAUDE. So much the worse for the Republic.

PAULINE (*shocked*). Claude, I begin to think you are an anarchist.

CLAUDE. I? (*Proudly.*) I am a colonel in the French army.

PAULINE. But not a *real* colonel, Claude. Only a Republican colonel.

CLAUDE (*sternly*). I rose from the ranks in two years by merit.

PAULINE. I know, dear. Real colonels only rise by interest. (CLAUDE *gasps.*)

JAMES (*opening the door and showing in a wizened old lady in rusty black garments and a bonnet slightly awry*). Mrs. Melnotte. (PAULINE *goes forward to greet her.*)

MRS. MELNOTTE (*not seeing her*). Ah, my dear son (*runs across the room to* CLAUDE *before the eyes of the deeply scandalised* JAMES, *and kisses him repeatedly*), how glad I am to see you again! And your grand house! And your fine servants! In livery, too! (PAULINE *shudders, and so does* JAMES. *The latter goes out.*)

CLAUDE. My dearest mother! (*Kisses her.*)

MRS. MELNOTTE (*beaming on* PAULINE). How do you do, my dear? Let me give my Claude's wife a kiss. (*Does so in resounding fashion.*)

PAULINE (*as soon as she has recovered from the warmth of this embrace*). How do you do, Mrs. Melnotte? Won't you sit down?

MRS. MELNOTTE. Thank you kindly, my dear. I don't mind if I do. (*A ring is heard outside, followed by the sound of someone being admitted.* PAULINE *looks anxiously towards the door.*)

PAULINE (*to herself*). A visitor! How unlucky! I wonder who it is?

JAMES (*throwing open the door*). Mrs. Deschappelles.

PAULINE. Great heavens, my mother! (*Falls back, overwhelmed, into her chair.*)

MRS. DESCHAPPELLES (*in her most elaborate manner*). My dear child, you are unwell. My coming has been a shock to you. But there, a daughter's affection, Claude—(*shaking hands with him*)—how wonderful it is!

PAULINE. Dear mother, we are delighted to see you.

MRS. DESCHAPPELLES. Of course I ought to have called before. I have been meaning to come ever since you returned from your honeymoon. But I have so many visits to pay; and you have been back only ten weeks!

PAULINE. I quite understand, mother dear.

MRS. DESCHAPPELLES. And, as I always say to your poor father, "When one is a leader of Society, one has so many engagements." I am sure *you* find that.

PAULINE. I have hardly begun to receive visits yet.

MRS. DESCHAPPELLES. No, dear? But then it's different with *you*. When you married Colonel Melnotte, of course you gave up all *social* ambitions.

MRS. MELNOTTE. I am sure no one could wish for a better, braver husband than my Claude.

MRS. DESCHAPPELLES (*turning sharply round and observing* MRS. MELNOTTE *for the first time*). I beg your pardon? (*Icily.*)

MRS. MELNOTTE (*bravely*). I said no one could have a better husband than Claude.

MRS. DESCHAPPELLES (*dumbfounded, appealing to* PAULINE). Who—who is this *person?*

PAULINE (*nervously*). I think you have met before, mother. This is Mrs. Melnotte.

MRS. DESCHAPPELLES (*insolently*). Oh! the gardener's wife.

CLAUDE (*melodramatic at once*). Yes. The gardener's wife and my mother!

MRS. DESCHAPPELLES (*impatiently*). Of course, I know the unfortunate relationship between you, Claude. You need not thrust it down my throat. You know how unpleasant it is to me.

PAULINE (*shocked at this bad taste*). Mother!

MRS. DESCHAPPELLES. Oh yes, it is. As I was saying to your poor father only yesterday: "Of course, Claude is all right. He is an officer now, and all officers are supposed to be gentlemen. But his relatives are impossible, quite impossible!"

CLAUDE (*furiously*). This insolence is intolerable. Madame Deschappelles—

MRS. MELNOTTE (*intervening*). Claude, Claude, don't be angry. Remember who she is.

CLAUDE (*savagely*). I remember well enough. She is Madame Deschappelles, and her husband is a successful tradesman. He was an English shop-boy, and his proper name was Chapel. He came over to France, grew rich, put a "de" before his name, and now gives himself airs like the other *parvenus.*

MRS. DESCHAPPELLES. Monster!

PAULINE. My dear Claude, how wonderfully interesting!

MRS. MELNOTTE (*rising*). My son, you must not forget your manners. Mrs. Deschappelles is Pauline's mother. I will go away now, and leave you to make your apologies to her. (CLAUDE *tries to prevent her going.*) No, no, I will go, really. Good-bye, my son; good-bye, dear Pauline. (*Kisses her and goes out.*)

MRS. DESCHAPPELLES. If that woman imagines that I am going to stay here after being insulted by you as I have been, she is much mistaken. Please ring for my carriage. (CLAUDE *rings.*) As for you, Pauline, I always told you what would happen if you insisted on marrying beneath you, and now you see I'm right.

PAULINE (*quietly*). You seem to forget, mamma, that papa was practically a bankrupt when I married, and that Claude paid his debts.

MRS. DESCHAPPELLES. I forget nothing. And I do not see that it makes the smallest difference. I am not blaming your poor father for having his debts paid by Colonel Melnotte; I am blaming you for marrying him. Good-bye. (*She sweeps out in a towering passion.*)

PAULINE. Sit down, Claude, and don't glower at me like that. It's not my fault if mamma does not know how to behave.

CLAUDE (*struggling with his rage*). That's true, that's true.

PAULINE. Poor mamma, her want of breeding is terrible! I have always noticed it. But that story about Mr. Chapel explains it all. Why didn't you tell it to me before?

CLAUDE. I thought it would pain you.

PAULINE. Pain me? I am delighted with it! Why, it explains everything. It explains *me.* It explains *you,* even. A Miss Chapel might marry *anyone.* Don't frown, Claude; laugh. We shall never get into Society in Lyons, but, at least, we shall never have another visit from mamma. The worst has happened. We can now live happily ever afterwards.

Curtain.

Most people, in their day, have wept tears of relief at the ending of T. W. Robertson's comedy Caste, *when the Hon. George D'Alroy—not dead, poor chap!—falls into the arms of his wife, Esther, while his father-in-law, Eccles, bestows a drunken benediction upon him before starting for Jersey, and his sister-in-law, Polly, and her adored plumber, Gerridge, embrace sympathetically in the background. In these circumstances it seems hardly kind to add a further act to this harrowing drama. But the writer of sequels, like Nemesis, is inexorable. If the perusal of the following scene prevents any young subaltern from emulating D'Alroy and marrying a ballet-dancer with a drunken father it will not have been written in vain.*

THE VENGEANCE OF CASTE

SCENE: *The dining-room of the* D'ALROYS' *house in the suburbs. Dinner is just over, and* GEORGE D'ALROY, *in a seedy coat and carpet slippers, is sitting by the fire smoking a pipe. On the other side of the fire sits* ESTHER, *his wife, darning a sock.*

ESTHER. Tired, George?

GEORGE. Yes.

ESTHER. Had a bad day in the City?

GEORGE. Beastly! I believe I'm the unluckiest beggar in the world. Every stock I touch goes down.

ESTHER. Why don't you give up speculating if you're so unlucky?

GEORGE (*hurt*). I don't speculate, dear. I invest.

ESTHER. Why don't you give up investing then? It makes a dreadful hole in our income.

GEORGE. One must do *something* for one's living.

ESTHER (*sighing*). What a pity it is you left the army!

GEORGE. I had to. The regiment wouldn't stand your father. He was always coming to the mess-room when he was drunk, and asking for me. So the Colonel said I'd better send in my papers.

ESTHER (*gently*). Not *drunk,* George.

GEORGE. The Colonel said so. And he was rather a judge.

ESTHER (*unable to improve upon her old phrase*). Father is a very eccentric man, but a very good man, when you know him.

GEORGE (*grimly*). If you mean by "eccentric" a man who is always drunk and won't die, he is—most eccentric!

ESTHER. Hush, dear! After all, he's my father.

GEORGE. That's my objection to him.

ESTHER. I'm afraid you must have lost a *great* deal of money today!

GEORGE. Pretty well. But I've noticed that retired military men who go into the City invariably do lose money.

ESTHER. Why do they go into the City, then?

GEORGE (*gloomily*). Why, indeed? (*There is a short pause.* GEORGE *stares moodily at the fire.*)

ESTHER. I had a visit from your mother to-day.

GEORGE. How was she?

ESTHER. Not very well. She has aged sadly in the last few years. Her hair is quite white now.

GEORGE (*half to himself*). Poor mother, poor mother!

ESTHER. She was very kind. She asked particularly after you, and she saw little George. (*Gently.*) I think she is getting more reconciled to our marriage.

GEORGE. Do you really, dear? (*Looks at her curiously.*)

ESTHER. Yes; and I think it's such a good thing. How strange it is that people should attach such importance to class distinctions!

GEORGE. Forgive me, dear, but if you think it strange that the Marquise de St. Maur does not consider Mr. Eccles and the Gerridges wholly desirable connections, I am afraid I cannot agree with you.

ESTHER. Of course papa is a very eccentric man—

GEORGE. My dear Esther, Mr. Eccles made his hundred and fifty-sixth appearance in the police court last week. The fact was made the subject of jocular comment in the cheaper evening papers. The sentence was five shillings or seven days.

ESTHER. Poor papa felt his position acutely.

GEORGE. Not half so acutely as I did. I paid the five shillings. If he had only consented to remain in Jersey!

ESTHER. But you know Jersey didn't suit him. He was never well there.

GEORGE. He was never sober there. That was the only thing that was the matter with him. No, my love, let us look facts in the face. You are a dear little woman, but your father is detestable, and there is not the slightest ground for hope that my mother will ever be "reconciled" to our marriage as long as she retains her reason.

ESTHER. I suppose father *is* rather a difficulty.

GEORGE. Yes. He and the Gerridges, between them, have made us impossible socially.

ESTHER. What's the matter with the Gerridges?

GEORGE. Nothing, except that you always ask them to all our dinner-parties. And as gentlepeople have a curious prejudice against sitting down to dinner with a plumber and glazier, it somewhat narrows our circle of acquaintance.

ESTHER. But Sam isn't a working plumber now. He has a shop of his own—quite a large shop. And their house is just as good as ours. The furniture is better. Sam bought Polly a new carpet for the drawing-room only last week. It cost fourteen pounds. And *our* drawing-room carpet is dreadfully shabby.

GEORGE. I'm glad they're getting on so well. (*With a flicker of hope.*) Do you think there's any chance, as they grow more prosperous, of their "dropping" us?

ESTHER (*indignantly*). How can you think of such a thing!

GEORGE (*sighing*). I was afraid not.

ESTHER (*enthusiastically*). Why, Sam is as kind as can be, and so is Polly. And you know how fond they are of little George.

GEORGE. Poor child, yes. He has played with their children ever since he could toddle. And what is the result? A Cockney accent that is indescribable.

ESTHER. What does it matter about his accent so long as he is a good boy, and grows up to be a good man?

GEORGE. Ethically, my dear, not at all. But practically, it matters a great deal. Is causes me intense physical discomfort. And I think it is killing my mother.

ESTHER. George!

GEORGE. Moreover, when the time comes for him to go to a Public School he will probably be very unhappy in consequence.

ESTHER. Why?

GEORGE. Merely irrational prejudice. Public School boys dislike deviations from the normal. And to them—happily—a pronounced Cockney accent represents the height of abnormality.

ESTHER (*sadly*). In spite of our marriage, I'm afraid you're still a worshipper of caste. I thought you turned your back on all that when you married me.

GEORGE. So I did, dear, so I did. But I don't want to commit my son to the same hazardous experiment.

ESTHER. Ah, George, you don't really love me or you wouldn't talk like that.

GEORGE. My dear, I love you to distraction. That's exactly the difficulty. I am torn between my devotion to you and my abhorrence of your relations. When your father returned from Jersey, and took a lodging close by us, nothing but the warmth of my affection prevented me from leaving you for ever. He is still here, and so am I. What greater proof could you have of the strength of my attachment?

ESTHER. Poor father! he could not bear to be away from us. And he has grown so fond of little George! (GEORGE *shudders.*) Father has a good heart.

GEORGE. I wish he had a stronger head. (*This remark is prompted by the sound of* MR. ECCLES *entering the front door and having a tipsy altercation with the maid.*)

MAID (*announcing*). Mr. Eccles.

ECCLES (*joyously*). Evening—hic—me children. Bless you, bless you!

ESTHER. Good-evening, father.

ECCLES. Won't you—hic—speak to yer old father-in-law, Georgie? (GEORGE *says nothing.*) Ah, pride, pride, cruel pride! You come before a fall, *you* do! (*Lurches heavily against the table, and subsides into a chair.*) Funny, that! Almost—hic—seemed as if the proverb was a-coming true that time!

GEORGE (*sternly*). How often have I told you, Mr. Eccles, not to come to this house except when you're sober!

ECCLES (*raising his voice in indignant protest*). Shober—hic—perfectly shober! Shober as a—hic—judge!

GEORGE. I'm afraid I can't argue with you as to the precise stage of intoxication in which you find yourself. You had better go home at once.

ECCLES. Do you hear that—Esh—ter? Do you hear that—hic—me child?

ESTHER. Yes, father. I think you had better go home. You're not very well to-night.

ECCLES (*rising unsteadily from his chair*). Allri—Esh—ter. I'm goin'. Good-ni—Georgie.

GEORGE (*with the greatest politeness*). Good-night, Mr. Eccles. If you could possibly manage to fall down and damage yourself seriously on the way home, I should be infinitely obliged.

ECCLES (*beginning to weep*). There's words to address to a loving—hic—farrer-in-law. There's words—— (*Lurches out.*)

ESTHER. I think, George, you had better see him home. It's not safe for him to be alone in that state.

GEORGE (*savagely*). Safe! I don't want him to be safe. Nothing would give me greater satisfaction than to hear he had broken his neck.

ESTHER (*gently*). But he might meet a policeman, George.

GEORGE. Ah! that's another matter. Perhaps I'd better see the beast into a cab.

ESTHER (*sighing*). Ah, you never understood poor father! (*A crash is heard from the hall as* ECCLES *lurches heavily and upsets the hat-stand.* GEORGE *throws up his hands in despair at the wreck of the hall furniture—or, perhaps, at the obtuseness of his wife's last remark—and goes out to call a cab.*

Curtain.

After the second Mrs. Tanqueray killed herself at the end of the play which bears her name, it might be supposed that her husband would be content with his two successive failures in matrimony, and not tempt a third. But Aubrey, as his second marriage shows, was nothing if not courageous in matrimonial affairs, and we have therefore every reason to believe that he did marry again, while we have small ground for hoping that he chose his third wife with any greater wisdom than he chose the other two. That is the impression conveyed by the following pathetic scene.

THE THIRD MRS. TANQUERAY

SCENE: *The dining-room of* AUBREY TANQUERAY'S *country house, Highercombe, in Surrey. A lean* BUTLER *is standing at the sideboard.* AUBREY *and* CAYLEY DRUMMLE *enter and go up to warm themselves at the fire, which burns feebly. The time is an evening in March, five years after the events of Mr. Pinero's play, and* CAYLEY *looks quite five years stouter.* AUBREY *does not.*

CAYLEY. It's quite shocking, Aubrey, that you should have been married nearly a year, and that I should not yet have had the pleasure of making Mrs. Tanqueray's acquaintance. I am dying to know her.

AUBREY. My fault, my dear Cayley.

CAYLEY. Entirely. Your weddings are always so furtive. (*Pokes the fire resolutely, in the hope of producing something approaching a cheerful blaze.*)

AUBREY. Well, you'll see her to-night. I hoped she would be able to dine at home, but she had promised to address a Temperance meeting in the village. (CAYLEY *looks dubious.*) However, she'll be back at ten. Meanwhile, you'll have to be contented with a bachelor dinner. (*They go to the table and sit down.*)

CAYLEY (*unfolding serviette*). Experience has taught me, my dear Aubrey, that bachelor dinners are apt to be particularly well worth eating. No doubt it is to make up for the absence of more charming society.

AUBREY (*doubtfully*). I hope it will prove so in this case.

CAYLEY. I feel sure of it. I remember your cook of old.

AUBREY. I'm afraid it won't be *that* cook.

CAYLEY (*in horror*). You haven't parted with him?

AUBREY. Yes. He left soon after my marriage. There was some small error in his accounts, which Mrs. Tanqueray discovered. So, of course, we had to dismiss him.

CAYLEY (*eagerly*). Do you happen to have his address?

AUBREY. I dare say Mrs. Tanqueray has, if you wish to know it. (FOOTMAN *hands soup.*)

CAYLEY. I shall be eternally indebted to her.

AUBREY. Why?

CAYLEY. I shall engage him at once. (*Begins to eat his soup, frowns, and then puts down his spoon.*) But I'm afraid you'll want him back yourself.

AUBREY. No. My wife is most particular about the character of her servants.

CAYLEY. Ah! I'm more particular about the character of my soup. (*His hand goes out instinctively towards his sherry-glass. As he is about to raise it he sees that it is empty, and refrains.*)

AUBREY. Cayley, you ought to marry. Then you'd realise that there are more important things in the world than soup.

CAYLEY. Of course there are, my dear fellow. There's the fish and the joint. (*Fish of an unattractive kind is handed to him. He takes some.*)

AUBREY. Sybarite! (CAYLEY *looks at his fish dubiously, then leaves it untasted.*)

CAYLEY. You are quite wrong. A simple cut of beef or mutton, well cooked, is quite enough for me.

BUTLER (*to* CAYLEY). Lemonade, sir?

CAYLEY. Eh, what? No, thank you.

AUBREY. Ah, Cayley. What will you drink? (CAYLEY'S *face brightens visibly.*) I'm afraid I can't offer you any wine. (*It falls again.*) My wife never allows alcohol at her table. But there are various sorts of mineral waters. You don't mind?

CAYLEY (*grimly*). Not at all, my dear fellow, not at all. Which brand of mineral water do you consider most—ah—stimulating?

AUBREY (*laughing mirthlessly*). I'm afraid, Cayley, you're not a convert to Temperance principles yet. That shows you have never heard my wife speak.

CAYLEY (*emphatically*). Never! Temperance meetings are not in my line. (FOOTMAN *removes his plate.*)

AUBREY. Perhaps some of the other movements in which she is interested would appeal to you more. (*With a touch of happy pride.*) As you may know, my wife is a vice-president of the Anti-Vaccination Society, and of the Woman's Home Rule Union. Indeed, she is in great request on all public platforms.

CAYLEY (*with simulated enthusiasm*). I feel sure of that, my dear Aubrey. (FOOTMAN *hands* CAYLEY *some rice pudding.* CAYLEY *puts up his eyeglass, and eyes it curiously.*) What is this?

FOOTMAN. Rice pudding, sir. (CAYLEY *drops spoon hastily.*)

AUBREY (*politely*). You're eating nothing, Cayley.

CAYLEY (*with some concern*). Aubrey, have I *slept* through the joint? I have no recollection of eating it. If, in a moment of abstraction, I refused it, may I change my mind?

AUBREY (*sternly*). My wife never has *meat* at her table on Fridays.

CAYLEY (*peevishly*). My dear fellow, I wish you'd thought of mentioning it before I came down. Then I might have had a more substantial luncheon. Where's that rice pudding? (*Helps himself. There is a rather constrained silence.*)

AUBREY. It's really very good of you to have come down to see us, Cayley.

CAYLEY (*pulling himself together*). Very good of you to say so, my dear chap. (*Tackles his rice pudding manfully.*)

AUBREY. My wife and I can so seldom get any man to drop in to dinner nowadays.

CAYLEY (*giving up his struggle with rice pudding in despair*). I suppose so.

AUBREY. In fact, we see very little society now.

CAYLEY (*sententiously*). Society only likes people who feed it, my dear Aubrey. You ought to have kept that cook.

AUBREY (*meditatively*). So my daughter said.

CAYLEY. Ellean? Is she with you now?

AUBREY. No. She is in Ireland. After making that remark she went back to her convent.

CAYLEY (*heartily*). Sensible girl! I like Ellean.

AUBREY. She and my wife did not get on, somehow. It was very unfortunate, as it was mainly on Ellean's account that I thought it right to marry again.

CAYLEY (*with polite incredulity*). Indeed?

AUBREY. Yes. You see, it is so difficult for a girl of Ellean's retiring disposition to meet people and make friends when she has no mother to chaperon her. And if she meets no one, how is she to get married? Dessert, Cayley?

CAYLEY (*after surveying a rather unattractive assortment of apples and walnuts*). No, thanks. As you were saying—

AUBREY. So I thought if I could meet with a really suitable person, someone with whom she would be in sympathy, someone she would look upon as a sort of second mother—

CAYLEY (*correcting him*). Third, Aubrey.

AUBREY (*ignoring the interruption*)—it would make home more comfortable for her.

CAYLEY (*laughing*). I like your idea of *comfort,* Aubrey! But I should have thought you could have adopted some less extreme measure for providing Ellean with a chaperon? You have neighbours. Mrs. Cortelyon, for instance?

AUBREY (*stiffly*). Mrs. Cortelyon's chaperonage was not very successful on the last occasion.

CAYLEY. No, no; to be sure. Young Ardale. I was forgetting.

AUBREY. Unhappily the whole scheme was a failure. Ellean conceived a violent aversion for Mrs. Tanqueray almost directly we came home, and a week later—I remember it was directly after dinner—she announced her intention of leaving the house for ever.

CAYLEY (*the thought of his dinner still rankling*). Poor girl! No doubt she's happier in her convent. (BUTLER *enters with coffee.* CAYLEY *takes some.*)

AUBREY. I am sorry I can't ask you to smoke, Cayley, but my wife has a particular objection to tobacco. She is a member of the Anti-Tobacco League, and often speaks at its meetings.

CAYLEY (*annoyed*). Really, my dear fellow, if I may neither eat, drink, nor smoke, I don't quite see why you asked me down.

AUBREY (*penitently*). I suppose I ought to have thought of that. The fact is, I have got so used to these little deprivations that now I hardly notice them. Of course, it's different with you.

CAYLEY. I should think it was!

AUBREY (*relenting*). If you *very* much want to smoke, I dare say it might be managed. If we have this window wide open, and you sit by it, a cigarette might not be noticed.

CAYLEY (*shortly*). Thanks. (*Takes out cigarette, and lights it, as soon as* AUBREY *has made the elaborate arrangements indicated above.*)

AUBREY (*politely*). I hope you won't find it cold.

CAYLEY (*grimly*). England in March is always cold. (*Sneezes violently.*)

But, perhaps, if you ring for my overcoat, I may manage to survive the evening.

AUBREY. Certainly. What is it like?

CAYLEY. I've no idea. It's an ordinary sort of coat. Your man will know it if you ring for him.

AUBREY (*hesitating*). I'd rather fetch it for you myself, if you don't mind. I should not like Parkes to see that you were smoking. It would set such a bad example.

CAYLEY (*throwing his cigarette on to the lawn in a rage, and closing the window with a shiver*). Don't trouble. I'll smoke in the train. By the way, what time *is* my train?

AUBREY. Your train?

CAYLEY. Yes. I must get back to town, my dear fellow.

AUBREY. Nonsense! You said you'd stay a week.

CAYLEY. Did I? Then I didn't know what I was saying. I must get back to-night.

AUBREY. But you brought a bag.

CAYLEY. Only to dress, Aubrey. By the way, will you tell your man to pack it?

AUBREY. You can't go to-night. The last train leaves at nine-thirty. It's nine-fifteen now.

CAYLEY (*jumping up*). Then I must start at once. Send my bag after me.

AUBREY. You've not a chance of catching it.

CAYLEY (*solemnly*). My dear old friend, I shall return to town to-night if I have to walk!

AUBREY (*detaining him*). But my wife? You haven't even made her acquaintance yet. She'll think it so strange.

CAYLEY. Not half so strange as I have thought her dinner. (*Shaking himself free.*) No, Aubrey, this is really good-bye. I like you very much, and it cuts me to the heart to have to drop your acquaintance; but nothing in the world would induce me to face another dinner such as I have had to-night!

AUBREY. Cayley!

CAYLEY (*making for the door*). And nothing in the world would induce me to be introduced to the third Mrs. Tanqueray. (*Exit hurriedly.*)

Curtain.

BIOGRAPHICAL AND BIBLIOGRAPHICAL NOTES

Dion Boucicault (Dionysius Lardner Bourcicault, or Boursiquot, 1822?–1890) was house dramatist for Charles Kean and a prolific author of plays that exploited all the devices of the theatre and all the emotions of the audience with appeals to the gallery and inventive stage and dramatic machinery. Whether he was adapting from the French of Eugène Scribe or writing his own peculiar kind of Irish comedy, Boucicault had an unerring eye for the public taste. He began at Covent Garden with *London Assurance* (1841)—"that despicable mass of inanity," Poe called it. Boucicault was nineteen. The play was a hit, a palpable hit. For *Dot* (New York 1859, London 1862) he introduced a wagon stage. For historical romances like *Louis XI* (1855, from the French of Casimir Delavigne) he filled the limelit Princess' stage with glittering costumes. He ran two hundred nights in London with *Flying Scud; or, A Four-Legged Fortune* (1866), capitalizing on the appeal of the equestrian drama and staging a horse race in four acts and seventeen scenes. He was ahead of his time with the detective drama of *Mercy Dodd; or, Presumptive Evidence* (1869), which featured a complicated exterior/interior set and a "sensation scene" where the balcony collapses under the struggling Sir Bertie Buckthorne and Bobby Saker. He used multiple sets, transparencies, fires, floods. His characters might come on dragging a train or riding in one. He had one character called "Zulu, The Female Cartridge." In *The Octoroon* (1859) he wrote the first serious dramatic treatment of the Negro. His version of Washington Irving's *Rip van Winkle* was expanded and played for a generation by Joseph Jefferson. *The Corsican Brothers* (1852) was the standard romantic melodrama throughout the nineteenth century and has several times been brought to the screen in the twentieth. A musical version of *The Poor of New York* (1857) played off Broadway successfully in 1964. Boucicault, a shrewd playwright and a fabulously successful actor-manager, divided his time between Britain and America. With his wife, Agnes Kelly Robertson (1833–1916), he acted his own plays of Irish life "in a style which was a sort of bridge between the conventional Stage Irishman and that which the Abbey Theatre was later to make popular" (Downer). *The Colleen Bawn* (1860), *Arragh-na-Pogue* (1864), and *The Shaughraun* (New York, 1864, and London, 1875) were hits. On the latter he cleared $800,000 profit.

These Irish plays relied on the "due admixture of the Maiden-in-Distress, the Patriot-in-danger-of-his-life, and the cowardly Informer, who have furnished forth many score plays since first the Red-Coats were seen on the Emerald Isle." Several of his children, including the actor-manager Dionysius George Boucicault (1859–1929), were also on the stage. Dion Boucicault's pieces, variously counted as between fifty and three hundred, all share an unmistakable theatricality, keen observation, clever construction, and technical innovation.

Nicoll credits him with "the cultivation of naturalistically conceived scenes allied to melodramatic excitement." *London Assurance* (2 editions, 1841) was in Lacy's and Dicks' collections and in Montrose J. Moses' *Representative British Dramas* (1918). See articles in the *Theatre* (November, 1879), the *Saturday Review* (1886), the *Critic* (1886), the *North American Review* (1889), and the *Athenaeum* (obituary, September 27, 1890). Townsend Walsh surveyed *The Career of Dion Boucicault* (1915). For the years Boucicault spent in the United States (1876–1890), consult Arthur Hobson Quinn's *History of the American Drama* (2 vols., 1923–1927), etc.

Sir William Schwenck Gilbert (1836–1911) is forever linked with Sir Arthur Sullivan as the librettist of the Savoy operas: *Trial by Jury* (1875), *The Sorcerer* (1877), *H. M. S. Pinafore* (1878), *The Pirates of Penzance* (1880), *Patience* (1881), *Iolanthe* (1882), *Princess Ida* (1884), *The Mikado* (1885), *Ruddigore* (1887), *The Yeoman of the Guard* (1888), *Utopia Limited* (1813), and the overly ambitious opera *The Grand Duke* (1896). Like so many other playwrights of his period, Gilbert dabbled in both law and journalism, contributing to *Punch* and other humorous papers. His *Bab Ballads* were collected in 1869, and together with *More Bab Ballads* (1873) and *Songs of a Savoyard* were issued in one volume in 1898. Some say he began his theatrical career with a farce, *Uncle's Baby* (Lyceum, 1863), but in any case it was T. W. Robertson who really launched him by commissioning *Ruy Blas,* a burlesque (1866). Gilbert collaborated on *Robinson Crusoe; or, The Injun Bride and The Injured Wife* (1867), a burlesque for the Haymarket. Then he wrote a number of musical and spectacular entertainments of the quality and approach of *Robert the Devil; or, The Nun, The Dun and the Son of a Gun* (1868) and the "Fairy comedy" *The Palace of Truth* (1870). The author of pantomimes and farces and of dramatic sketches for the popular entertainers Mr. and Mrs. German Reed, Gilbert suddenly achieved real success with a pseudoclassical romance, *Pygmalion and Galatea* (1871). Before meeting Sullivan, Gilbert wrote a series of comedies for Marie Litton at the Court Theatre. Of his straight plays—including *The Wicked World* (1873), *Charity* and *Sweethearts* (1874), *Broken Hearts* (1875), and *Dan'l Druce* (1876)—only *Engaged* (1877) is readable. *Pinafore*'s parody of nautical melodrama and its social satire is a much better sample of Gilbert's peculiarly urbane talent for what he called true humor: "a grave and quasi-respectful treatment of the ludicrous." He also wrote the words for some eighteen other operas and musical plays set by composers other than Sullivan. *The Original Plays of W. S. Gilbert* were issued in four series, 1876–1911. The comic operas, first collected in 1890 and 1896, are obtainable in *The Savoy Operas* (1926) and many other editions. A bibliography of Gilbert was published by T. Searle (1931) and H. B. Grimsditch lists thirty-six articles about Gilbert in the *Cambridge Bibliography of English Literature,* III: 612–13. Gilbert and Sullivan, of course, particularly as presented in the tradition of D'Oyly Carte, are practically a cult.

Commentaries include Isaac Goldberg's *The Story of Gilbert and Sullivan* (1929), Hesketh Pearson's *Gilbert and Sullivan, A Biography* (1935) and *Gilbert: His Life and Strife* (1957), C. L. Purdy's *Gilbert and Sullivan, Masters of Mirth and Melody* (1946), Audrey Williamson's *Gilbert and Sullivan Opera: A New Assessment* (1953), Raymond Mander and Joe Mitchenson's *Pictorial History of Gilbert and Sullivan* (1961), and Reginald Allen, "William Schwenck Gilbert: An Anniversary Survey," *Theatre Notebook,* XV (1961), 118–128. Recently Jane W. Stedman edited *Gilbert Before Sullivan: Six Comic Plays* (1966).

St. John Emile Clavering Hankin (1869–1909) was a refreshingly bitter draught after the sticky and saccharine sentimentality of some Victorian plays. He particularly despised romance and *Zwei Seelen und ein Gedanke / Zwei Herzen und ein Schlag!*[1] He introduced into the typical Edwardian setting, the drawing-rooms of the middle or lower-upper classes, some useful (if self-consciously straightforward) commentary on domestic debt and doubt. His plays include *The Two Mr. Wetherbys* (1903), *The Return of the Prodigal* (1905), *The Charity that Began at Home* (1906), *The Cassilis Engagement* (1907), and *The Last of the De Mullins* (1908).

Hankin was particularly effective when produced with care at the Court Theatre by Harley Granville-Barker, but today he appears a trifle artificial, more brittle than Noel Coward, less solid than Somerset Maugham. In comparison with the truly intellectual drama of Shaw, his plays pale. Moreover, *Dramatic Sequels* (1926), though not in the

---

[1] *Two minds with but a single thought, / Two hearts that beat as one!*

same league with the work of other theatre personalities who also wrote about the stage (Henry Arthur Jones, Harley Granville-Barker, St. John Ervine, Ashley Dukes, W. Somerset Maugham and the rest) is not without point. In the "tamer and primmer and less intellectual" Edwardian period he was an important playwright, and in the views he reflects of the previous age he is of amusement and interest to us.

His *Dramatic Works* (3 vols., 1912) were introduced by John Drinkwater. (*Thompson,* an unproduced play, was finished by George Calderon and published separately in 1913.) Hankin received notice in his own time in P. P. Howe's *Dramatic Portraits,* Charlton Andrews' *The Drama Today,* Mario Borsa's *The English Stage of Today,* J. M. Kennedy's *English Literature, 1880–1905,* Desmond McCarthy's *The Court Theatre,* and Archibald Henderson's *The Changing Drama.* Barrett H. Clark's *The British and American Drama of Today* (1915) also lists magazine articles on Hankin.

Douglas William Jerrold (1803–1857) was carried on stage as a baby by Edmund Kean in *Pizarro.* His father, Samuel Jerrold, was an actor who managed the Sheerness Theatre. Douglas Jerrold's interest in the stage may have begun when he served as a midshipman from 1813 to 1815 with James Stanfield, the marine painter and scene designer, or it may have developed later when, as a printer's devil, he began contributing to periodicals. His theatrical career commenced with *The Duelists* (1821, later called *More Frightened than Hurt*) and spectaculars at Sadler's Wells. After many minor entertainments at the Coburg Theatre and elsewhere he suddenly gained a phenomenal run of four hundred nights with *Black-Ey'd Susan* (1829) at the Surrey. Nautical sequels such as *The Mutiny at the Nore* (1830) and *The Press Gang* (1830) were less successful, but *The Rent Day* (1832) was notable. After that he turned to writing for the *Athenaeum, Blackwood's,* and other journals, and 1835 marked his theatrical height (two comedies, two burlettas, and a tragedy, all forgotten), though he wrote for the stage on and off for years after. *Retired from Business* (1851) and *A Heart of Gold* (1854), once popular, are representative of his later work. He co-managed the Strand Theatre in 1836 and acted as well as wrote, but journalism finally occupied most of his time. Thackeray contributed to one of Jerrold's many journals. In his spare time Jerrold wrote novels like *St. Giles and St. James* (1851). From 1841 he was (as "Q") a constant contributor to *Punch,* and there he wrote his series—so popular that they were translated into five languages—of *Mrs. Caudle's Curtain Lectures* (1846); Harold Orel's *The*

World of Victorian Humor (1961) prints some and adds that "he despised hypocrisy and injustice" and "detested being called a wit, a person who, according to his definition, did not take life seriously." Jerrold was notorious for his sarcastic wit which "carried a heart-stain away on its blade." Samuel Carter Hall described it in his *Retrospect of a Long Life* (1883) as

> ever biting, bitter, and caustic, and careless as distinguishing friend from foe . . . calculated to give somebody pain.

The works we know today, however, exhibit none of the bitterness which caused Jerrold, when confronted in the street by a man who asked "What's going on?" to reply "I am," and do so. His melodramas of *Fifteen Years of a Drunkard's Life* (1827) and most of his fifty or sixty plays are forgotten along with his acerbity. *Black-Ey'd Susan* remains. His son William Blanchard Jerrold edited his works (4 vols., 1863–1864) and another son, Walter C. Jerrold, wrote *Douglas Jerrold: Dramatist and Wit* (2 vols., 1914) and *Douglas Jerrold and 'Punch'* (1910). He figures largely in books about his friends Dickens (for example, T. Edgar Pemberton's *Charles Dickens and The Stage,* 1888), Macready, Edmund Hodgson Yates, George Hodder, and others, and in histories of *Punch* by Marion Harry Spielmann (1895) and R. G. G. Price (1957), *Pictures from Punch* (4 vols., 1904), etc. Lewis Melville hailed "The Centenary of Douglas Jerrold," *Temple Bar,* CXXVII (January, 1903), 22–29. *Black-Ey'd Susan* "established the pattern of nautical melodrama" (Rowell).

Henry Arthur Jones (1851–1929) not only wrote plays but advanced literary drama, fought censorship, raised public taste, and begged authors to print, to achieve what Archer crusaded for in *English Dramatists of To-day* (1882); "a body of playwrights, however small, whose works are not only acted but printed and *read.*" An unlikely candidate for these Herculean tasks, the son of a Welsh tenant farmer, he left school at the age of twelve and until 1879 was a traveler for a Bradford firm. He did not see a play until he was eighteen, but then he attended the theatre as often as he could and studied technique until he was a master. He wrote more than a dozen plays before *The Silver King* (a collaboration, 1882) made him famous. His fame made influential *The Renascence of the English Drama* (1895), *Foundations of a National Drama* (1913), and *The Theatre of Ideas* (1915), which stressed the drama's potential for social reform. He deplored Ibsen's plays as being morbid examinations of disease, despair, and vice, but (with Henry Herman) he adapted *A Doll's House* as *Breaking a Butterfly* (1884) and faced real problems in *The Middleman* and *Wealth* (both 1884). *The Case of Rebellious Susan* (1894) relied heavily on its stars Sir Charles Wyndham and Mary Moore, but the ideas in his plays were appealing too—*The Silver King* got Matthew Arnold and other intellectuals back into the theatre. *Michael and His Lost Angel* was an artistic triumph and a commercial failure; Jones was deeply hurt, though *Mrs. Dane's Defence* (1900) restored his popularity. Jones, unalterably Victorian, resisted Ibsenism, quarreled with Shaw, and at last was *passé.* It was some comfort that, if the public disliked his proudest work, *Michael and His Lost Angel,* they hailed *The Silver King.* That, his publishers happily informed him, had played somewhere every single week since its première in 1882. Working within commercial limitations, as all real dramatists must, Jones had made significant advances; he had helped to build those thinking audiences that finally turned away from him to attend plays by Ibsen and Shaw.

Of his comedies *The Masqueraders* (1894), *The Liars* (1897), *Dolly Reforming Herself* (1908), and the "Marie Tempestuous" play of *Mary Goes First* (1913) are best. Clayton Hamilton edited *Representative Plays* (4 vols., 1926). Doris Arthur Jones published a disarming *Life and Letters of Henry Arthur Jones* (1930). See also P. Shorey's *Henry Arthur Jones* (1925) and Richard A. Cordell's *Henry Arthur Jones and the Modern Drama* (1932). To the many articles listed in the *Cambridge Bibliography of English Literature,* III: 615, add Marjorie Northend, "Henry Arthur Jones and the Development of the Modern English Drama," *Review of English Studies,* XVIII (1942), 448–63.

Leopold David Lewis (1828–1890) was stagestruck. A leading actor helped him to a great hit, *The Bells.* He also wrote *The Wandering Jew* (1873), *Give a Dog a Bad Name* (1876), and *Foundlings; or, The Ocean of Life* (1881), all produced at the Adelphi but never published, and a three-volume prose item called *A Peal of Many Bells* (1880). With Arthur Thompson he wrote in its entirety *The Mask. A Humorous and Fantastic Review* (February to December, 1868). Sir Henry Irving's personal copy of *The Bells,* sold for £100 in London in 1965, shows how extensively that star adapted the "property" to his own unusual talents. *The Bells* brought the Lyceum prosperity and Irving fame. Bateman, the manager, had given up his idea of abandoning the Lyceum, scrapped plans for a desperate American tour, and taken a chance on Irving's ability to turn *The Bells'* melodramatic tableaux into a moneymaker; Irving made the play become an apparent masterpiece, a tingling theatrical experience. "Any author would be fortunate," said Bulwer-Lytton (who himself had benefited much from Macready's help), "who obtained his [Irving's] assistance in some character worthy of his powers." The production owed its tremendous run (over 150 performances) to the actor-manager, not the author. Irving often revived it and probably had no greater single triumph except his record-smashing, controversial *Hamlet.*

There is as little scholarship on Leopold Lewis as on George L. Aiken, the forgotten actor who dramatized the novel and gave to America one of its greatest hits, *Uncle Tom's Cabin* (1856). Look to biographies of Irving—Percy Fitzgerald (1906), Austin Brereton (2 vols., 1908), etc.—for details, along with *Personal Reminiscences of Sir Henry Irving* (2 vols., 1906) by his secretary Abraham (Bram) Stoker (author of *Dracula*), and the writings of the actor himself, whose talents lit up the stage and whose knighthood glorified his profession.

Edward George Earle Lytton Bulwer-Lytton, Lord Lytton (1803–1873), author of *The Last Days of Pompeii* (anon., 1834), was born in London. He wrote a prize poem at Cambridge in 1825 and thereafter combined literature with politics. "He was the most accomplished and industrious man of letters of his age," wrote T. H. S. Escott, "the most polished of novelists, and the only dramatist of his generation whose name can be mentioned in the same breath with Sheridan." Some were less impressed. Carlyle called him "a poor fribble," and Mrs. Carlyle, that critic on the hearth, dismissed Bulwer-Lytton as "a lanthorn-jawed quack." Considering his busy politics, the bulk if not the quality of his showy, shallow work is astonishing: his novels were collected in forty-three volumes (1859–1863), and his *Poetical* and *Dramatic Works* (1852–1854) filled five more.

His plays include *The Duchess de la Vallière* (1836), *The Lady of Lyons* (1838), *Richelieu* (1839), *The Sea Captain* (1839; also known as *The Rightful Heir* and *The Birth-Right*), *Money* (1840), and *Not So Bad As We Seem* (1851). His *Collected Works* appeared in thirty-seven volumes (1873–1875), T. Cooper wrote his biography (1873), and his son edited his autobiography (1883). See E. B. Burgum's *The Literary Career of Edward Bulwer, Lord Lytton* (1924), P. J. Cooke's pamphlet of 1894 on "Bulwer Lytton's Plays," and Dewey Gauzel on *The Lady of Lyons,* "Bulwer and His *Lady,*" *Modern Philology,* LVII (1960), 41–52. Older articles include: Edward L.

Bulwer-Lytton, "Bulwer-Lytton as Dramatist and Novelist," *Temple Bar,* XXXVII (May, 1873), 233–245; Percy Fitzgerald, "Lady of Lyons," *Gentleman's Magazine,* n.s. XLIII (August, 1889), 136–141; "Bibliography, Lord Lytton," by the Library School, The Pratt Institute (Brooklyn, N. Y.) *Bulletin* for 1893, pp. 629–631; Francis Gribble, "The Art of Lord Lytton," *Fortnightly Review,* LXXIX (n.s. LXXIII) (May 1, 1903), 838–847; Edwin W. Bowen, "Bulwer-Lytton Forty Years After," *Sewanee Review,* XXVI (1918), 92–111; and André Maurois, "The Bulwer-Lyttons," *Southwest Review,* XVI (1930), 75–107. Michael Sadleir's *Bulwer: A Panorama* (1931), has a bibliography. Lord Lytton depended upon the actor to vivify his pretentious verse and disguise inadequacies of characterization and plot, so consult Macready's *Diaries* (edited by W. Toynbee, 2 vols., 1912), etc.

T. A. Palmer (fl. 1861) rates no mention in standard reference books but was once popular in the Provinces. Lacy published six acting editions of his plays, and French three more. His conscious carpentry (with dates of production) comprised *Too Late to Save* (1861), *Brought to Light* (1868), *Among the Relics* (1869), *Hard Hands and Happy Hearts* (1869), *Rely on My Discretion* (1870), *Insured at Lloyd's* (1870), *A Dodge for a Dinner* (1872), *Florence* (1872), *The Last Life* (1874), *East Lynne* (1874), *Moral Suasion* (1875), *An Appeal to the Feelings* (1875), *Fascinating Fellows* (1876), *Cremorne* (1876, also known as *Seeing Life*), *Memories* (1878), *Roasting a Rogue* (1882), and *Woman's Rights* (1882). He used one of Mrs. S. C. Hall's stories of Irish life for *The Last Life* and Mrs. Henry Wood's novel to make *East Lynne,* a classic example of dramatization in an era when everything from *The Castle of Otranto* to *Oliver Twist* reached the boards.

Sir Arthur Wing Pinero (1855–1934), of Portuguese extraction, was the best dramatic craftsman of his time and, said William Archer, "the regenerator of the English drama." He built farces and fantasies, light comedies and serious social dramas. *The Magistrate* (1885) typifies his frivolous farces, *Sweet Lavender* (1888) his soppy sentimentality. He began with *Two Hundred Pounds a Year* (1877) and, after juvenalia, hit his stride in farce with *The Schoolmistress* (1886), *Dandy Dick* (1887), *The Cabinet Minister* (1890), and *The Amazons* (1893). With *The Profligate* (1889) he began his "unpleasant" plays. These culminated in *The Second Mrs. Tanqueray,* a bourgeois tragedy that convinced the jaded public that the drama of ideas, realistically treated and steadily viewed, had arrived. Pinero (having acted in Irving's company and elsewhere) knew how to write actable scenes and speakable dialogue. He was lucky in his cast in this and its sequel, *The Notorious Mrs. Ebbsmith* (1895). Theatrically superb were *The Benefit of the Doubt* (1895), *Trelawney of the 'Wells'* (1898), *The Gay Lord Quex* (1899), and *Iris* (1901). Pinero was the English Scribe. He approached Ibsenism in *Mid-Channel* (1909) and was knighted that year. Some call *The Thunderbolt* (1908) his serious zenith, but he is better known for thesis plays, however shallow his arguments, than for the later works which concentrated on character. He sparked "polite controversy," says *The Oxford Companion to the Theatre,* "but where he shocked his countrymen he shocked them within the range of their pleasure." When times changed he did not. After the outbreak of World War I he wrote little of consequence, and his last play, *A Cold June* (1932), received disrespectful reviews. His favorite theme, the double standard, and his "usual judgement on the erring woman," which Gerald Weales describes as "death after dishonor," were sadly old hat. Now it is chic to underestimate him; a Pinero revival must be in the offing.

Clayton Hamilton edited *The Social Plays of Arthur Wing Pinero* (4 vols., 1917–1922). An incomplete edition of his *Works* (1907) in fifteen volumes has notes by M. C. Salaman. Hamilton has also edited Pinero's study of *Robert Louis Stevenson as a Dramatist* (1914). See H. H. Fyfe's *Arthur Wing Pinero, Playwright* (1902), W. Stöcker's *Pinero's Dramen: Studien über Motive, Charaktere und Technik* (1911), and Wilbur D. Dunkel's *Sir Arthur Pinero: A Critical Biography with Letters* (1941).

Thomas William Robertson (1829–1871), eldest of twenty-two theatrical children, debuted at five and at fifteen was touring the Lincoln circuit in the family tradition. (His sister became the famous actress Dame Madge Kendal.) At nineteen he was in London, at twenty-two his *A Night's Adventure* ran four nights. Rights to his *Castles in the Air* (1854) brought £3, but that equaled his week's salary as prompter at the Olympic Theatre under Madame Vestris and Charles Matthews. Original dramas paid poorly but there was cash in plagiarizing or in translating French plays, so Robertson, partly educated in France, adapted D'Ennery, Labiche, and Scribe for Thomas Hailes Lacy, the agent and theatrical publisher. With Elizabeth Burton, a "walking lady" (bit player) whom he married in 1856, Robertson toured the Provinces and Ireland. Eventually he decided to live by writing and translating. While his wife acted he ground out sketches, humorous articles, and adaptations from the French. E. A. Sothern scored with his *David Garrick* (1863), from the *Sullivan* of

Mélesville (Anne-Honoré-Joseph Duveyrier), and Robertson was encouraged to try a new approach: his personal knowledge of *la vie de Bohème* led to the sprightly, satirical piece *Society* (1865). The Haymarket rejected it as "Rubbish!" Marie Wilton at the tiny, tatty Prince of Wales' Theatre ("the Dust Hole") said, "It is better to be dangerous than to be dull," and took it with the encouragement of Robertson's longtime friend, playwright Henry James Byron. So life among the middle class, in Fleet Street, in Parliament, was shown; it began the school of realistic comedies that were long on character and short on plot. *Society* was still a little old-fashioned and included such clichés as mistaken paternity, bought notes, arrest for debt, the loved and the unloved suitor, and the usorious Jew. But Robertson gradually rejected the armamentarium of cheap melodrama and turned from tortuous plots to plays about subjects, not mere circumstances: *Ours* (1866), *Caste* (1867), *Play* (1868), *School* (1869), *Home* (1869), *Birth* (1870), *War* (1871). *Caste* (1867) was the high point of Robertson's career, immeasurably distant from *The Half-Caste; or, The Poison'd Pearl* (1856). Greater than his stage-managing, which provided practicable sets and properties and all sorts of effects minutely described in the stage directions, was his real achievement: writing plays that could stand realistic acting and setting. He is perhaps more famous for being the first real stage-manager, establishing the dramatist-director tradition in which Pinero and Gilbert triumphed. Gilbert wrote:

> Robertson showed how to give life and variety and order to the scene by breaking it up with all sorts of incidents and delicate by-play. I have been at many of his rehearsals and learnt a great deal from them.

So did actors like Sir Squire Bancroft, dramatists like Tom Taylor, and generations of theatre folk who followed, in London, in the Provinces (where *Caste*'s was one of the first London companies to tour), and even in America.

The Principal Dramatic Works.... With a Memoir by His Son were edited by T. W. S. Robertson (2 vols., 1889). T. E. Pemberton published *The Life and Writings of T. W. Robertson* (1893). Robertson's centenary produced articles by F. Rahill, "Mid-Victorian Regisseur," *Theatre Arts,* XIII (1929), 838–844, and H. Dale, "Tom Robertson: A Centenary Criticism," *Contemporary Review,* CXXXV (1929), 356–361. Bernard Shaw speaks of *Caste* in the *Saturday Review,* LXXXIII (1897), 685. See also C. F. Armstrong's *Shakespeare to Shaw* (1913) and Pinero's chapter in

The Eighteen-Seventies (edited by Harley Granville-Barker, 1929). Tom Wrench, the struggling young playwright in Pinero's *Trelawney of the 'Wells'* (1898), is a fictional portrait of Robertson.

Percy Bysshe Shelley (1792–1822), whom Leigh Hunt compared to the angel in Milton who bore a reed "tipt with fire," was born in Sussex and educated at Eton and University College, Oxford. At school he published *Zastrozzi* (1810) and at college *St. Irvyne* (1811), two Gothic romances which forecast *The Cenci* (1819), the best known of his several poetic dramas. He was expelled from Oxford in his first year (1811) because of a tract proposing atheism. Shelley quickly married Harriet Westbrook, aged sixteen. The marriage lasted three years. In 1816 he married Mary Godwin, daughter of William Godwin, philosopher of anarchical views on political justice. Shelley himself, claiming that the poets were the unacknowledged legislators of the world, was caught up in political matters all his life. Love of freedom informs many of his famous lyrical works: *Queen Mab* (1813), *Alastor* (1816), *Prometheus Unbound* (1820), *Epipsychidion* and *Adonais* (1821), and *Hellas* (1822). When he was drowned while sailing at Spezzia (July 8, 1822), Shelley left unfinished a drama about Charles I and *The Triumph of Life,* a long allegory in *terza rima.*

Shelley's *Works* were edited by his wife (1847), by Roger Ingpen and Walter E. Peck (10 vols., 1926–1930), and by others; the *Poems* in single volumes by E. Dowden (1893), G. E. Woodberry (1908), and T. Hutchinson (1919); *The Essays and Letters* by E. Rhys (1886); the *Letters* by Frederick L. Jones (2 vols., 1964); and the lyrical and dramatic poems separately by C. H. Herford (1918). The standard life is by Newman I. White (2 vols., 1940). Specialized biographies include Kenneth Neill Cameron's *The Young Shelley* (1950), C. Cline's *Byron, Shelley, and Their Pisan Circle* (1952), Ivan Roe's *Shelley. The Last Phase* (1953), and Newman White's *The Examination of the Shelley Legend* (1951). Less scholarly are Edward J. Trelawney's two memoirs (1858 and 1878). C. H. Grabo's *A Newton Among Poets* (1930) and *The Magic Plant* (1936) top a long list which includes Carlos Baker's *Shelley's Major Poetry* (1948), Joseph Barrell's *Shelley and The Thought of His Time* (1947), Richard Fogle's *The Imagery of Keats and Shelley* (1949), A. M. Hughes' *The Nascent Mind of Shelley* (1947), F. A. Lea's *Shelley and the Romantic Revolution* (1945), J. A. Notopoulas' *The Platonism of Shelley* (1949), and Glenn O'Malley's *Shelley and Synesthesia* (1964). H. S. Salt's *A Shelley Primer* (1887) and Ernest Bernbaum's *A Guide Through the Romantic Movement* (1930) are still useful. G. E. Woodberry edited *The Cenci* (1909); articles on it include Sara Watson's on *Othello* and *The Cenci, PMLA,* LV (1940), 611; K. G. Pfeiffer, "Landor's Critique," *Studies in Philology,* XXXIX (1942), 670; K. N. Cameron and Horst Frenz, "The Stage History of *The Cenci,*" *PMLA,* LX (1945), 1080–1105; B. O. States, Jr., "Addendum: The Stage History," *PMLA,* LXXVI (1957), 633–644; Robert F. Whitman, "Beatrice's 'Pernicious Mistake' in *The Cenci,*" *PMLA,* LXXIV (1958), 249–253; Paul Smith, "Restless Casuistry: Shelley's Composition of *The Cenci,*" *Keats-Shelley Journal,* XIII (1964), 77–85; and Shaw's "Shaming the Devil about Shelley," *Selected Non-Dramatic Writings of Bernard Shaw,* ed. Dan H. Laurence (1965), 315 ff.

The Cenci's stageableness has always been debated. For recent exchanges see the correspondence between B. O. States and Marcel in *PMLA,* LXV (1960), 147–49. Representative of the period, *The Cenci* is uncharacteristic of the poet, says Graham Hough in *The Romantic Poets* (2nd edition, 1957):

> The story, a horrible one of incest and revenge, seems very little related to the main lines of Shelley's thought; the dramatic structure in extremely weak and disordered; and most of its striking passages are derivative, mostly from Shakespeare and Webster, as Shelley never is elsewhere. It appears from the preface that he is extremely conscious of attempting what is for him an unusual kind of composition . . . only a diversion from the main line of Shelley's work.

Oscar Fingal O'Flahertie Wills Wilde (1856–1900), with Swift, Sheridan, and Shaw, was another Irish genius in English literature. At Oxford, where he won the Newdigate Prize for "Ravenna" and took a First in Classics, his pose and his poetry began to attract attention. As "An ultra-poetical, super aesthetical, / Out-of-the-way young man" he was pilloried in *Patience* and in *The Green Carnation* (1894), where he appeared wearing "the arsenic flower of an exquisite life" and preaching: "Despise the normal and flee from everything that is hallowed by custom as you would flee from the seven deadly virtues." He toured the United States in 1882, passing through customs in New York with "I have nothing to declare except my genius," and presented two plays: *Vera; or, The Nihilists* at Union Square (1883) and *The Duchess of Padua* (played as *Guido Ferranti*) on Broadway (1891). *Vera* failed. Wilde made his name with conversation, epigrams, notoriety ("There is only one thing in the world worse than being talked about, and that is not being talked about"), poetry and prose (*The Picture of Dorian Gray,* 1891, etc.).

Then immense success greeted his light comedies: *Lady Windemere's Fan* (1892), *A Woman of No Importance* (1893), *An Ideal Husband* (1895), and *The Importance of Being Earnest* (1895), the best English comedy in a century. His poetic play *Salomé* (1893, first written in French) was shocking. It was banned in England, played in Paris by Sarah Bernhardt in 1894, made into an opera by Richard Strauss. Suddenly Wilde, a married man with two sons, was accused of being a homosexual and involved with Lord Alfred Douglas. He sued the boy's father (the Marquis of Queensberry) for criminal libel, lost, and was then tried and convicted of sexual offenses. Sentenced to two years at hard labor, he wrote *De Profundis* (1905) in jail and then went to France, visited Naples (where he wrote *The Ballad of Reading Gaol,* published 1898), and finished his life in exile as "Sebastian Melmoth," a name borrowed from a romantic novel. He changed his religion (to Roman Catholicism) but not his wit: "I suppose that I shall have to die beyond my means."

The real talent in his plays (he said that he put his genius into his life) shines in the stylish comedies which prove that "in matters of grave importance, style, not sincerity, is the vital thing."

Wilde's *Works* were edited by Robert Ross (1914) and his wit and his scandal have attracted R. H. Sherard, André Gide, Lord Alfred Douglas, Holbrook Jackson, the Comtesse de Brémont, Bernard Shaw, André Maurois, Arthur Ransome, Arthur Symonds, G. Renier, P. Braybrooke, Hesketh Pearson, etc. His scintillating *Letters* were collected by Rupert Hart-Davis (1961). See William Archer's *Play-Making* (1912); Frances Winwar in *Oscar Wilde and the Yellow 'Nineties* (1940); E. Roditi's *Oscar Wilde* (1947); A. H. Nethercot, "Oscar Wilde and the Devil's Advocate," *PMLA,* LIX (1944), 833–850; and Arthur Ganz, "The Meaning of *The Importance of Being Earnest,*" *Modern Drama,* VI (1962), 42–52, and (for a minority report) Mary McCarthy, "The Unimportance of Being Oscar," *Theatre Chronicles, 1937–1962* (1963), pp. 106–110.

William Butler Yeats (1865–1939), a most productive poet, also served Ireland in politics (as a senator) and tried to make the Irish proud of their heritage. A founder of "The Irish Dramatic Movement," he was the first president of the national theatre and encouraged writing on Irish themes. He defended J. M. Synge against his countrymen, and inspired, directed, and wrote plays as well. The earliest used Celtic legend: *The Countess Cathleen* (1892), *The Land of Heart's Desire* (1894), and *Shadowy Waters* (1897, 1906). More intensely poetic were *The Hour-Glass* (1903, 1912), *The King's Threshold* (1903), and *The Unicorn from* *the Stars* (with Lady Gregory, 1907), while peasant themes served for *Cathleen ni Houlihan* (1902) and *The Pot of Broth* (1902). Unfortunately his plays on Cuchulain and other legends and myths fall outside our chronological limits here: *On Baile's Strand* (1904) is a masterpiece second only to Synge's *Riders to the Sea. Deirdre* (1906), *The Golden Helmet* (1908), and *The Green Helmet* (1910) were followed by "Four Plays for Dancers" (1916–1917). Yeats adapted Sophocles' *King Oedipus* and produced his original stage works right up to *Purgatory* (1938). The last plays are sometimes mystical and obscure—Yeats, after all, dabbled with Rosicrucianism, The Golden Dawn, Madame Blavatsky, and Blake, and wrote *A Vision* (1925, 1937)—but in the early dramas he held to the maxim that Lady Gregory taught him from Aristotle: "To think like a wise man but to express oneself like the common people." His best work sprang from common Irish life ("mad Ireland hurt you into poetry"—W. H. Auden[1]), but it has passed into the "general memory" of mankind.

Collected Poetry appeared in 1933, *Collected Plays* in 1935, *Nine One-Act Plays* in 1937. Volume VIII of the *Collected Works* (1908) has A. Wade's bibliography and A. J. A. Symonds compiled a *Bibliography of First Editions* (1924). *Plays and Controversies* (1924) has useful material. *The Countess Kathleen and Various Legends and Lyrics* was printed in English (1892, 1912, 1929), and in Polish (1912), Italian (1914), and German (1933). Beginners use John Unterecker's *Reader's Guide to William Butler Yeats* (1959) and find criticism and a long bibliography in *The Permanence of Yeats* (1961), edited by James Hall and Martin Steinmann. See Leonard E. Nathan's *The Tragic Drama of William Butler Yeats* and Curtis B. Bradford's *Yeats at Work* (both 1965). Our century's greatest poet wrote an *Autobiography* (1916) and Richard Ellman wrote *Yeats: The Man and the Masks* (1948), but master the poetry itself and you will concur in Eliot's judgment that Yeats was "one of those few whose history is the history of their own time, who are a part of the consciousness of an age which cannot be understood without them."

---

1. "In Memory of W. B. Yeats," copyright © 1940 by W. H. Auden.
Reprinted from *The Collected Poetry of W. H. Auden*, by permission of Random House, Inc.

BIBLIOGRAPHY

Nineteenth-century plays are often available in print nowhere but in the cheap series published by Cumberland (*Cumberland's British Theatre,* to about 1860), Dicks (*Dicks's Standard Plays,* 1883–1908), Duncombe (*Duncombe's Edition,* ending about 1853), Lacy (*Lacy's Acting Edition,* from 1851 on), and French (*French's Acting Edition,* continuing Lacy and still being issued).

For selected readings on the authors and the plays in this volume, see the biographical notes beginning on page 681. This list had to omit the colorful and informative memoirs and biographies of playwrights and players, and references to the many dramatic periodicals and collections of plays published in the period. For those see the *Cambridge Bibliography of English Literature,* III: 580–628, and the bibliography of George Rowell's *The Victorian Theatre* (1956). Also useful is the bibliography in an American counterpart of this present book, Richard Moody's *Dramas from the American Theatre, 1762–1909* (1966).

Agate, James, ed. *The English Dramatic Critics, 1660–1932: An Anthology.* London, 1932.

Archer, William. *English Dramatists of To-day.* London, 1882.

———. *The Old Drama and the New.* London, 1923.

———. *Play-Making: A Manual of Craftsmanship.* London, 1912.

———. *The Theatrical 'World'.* 5 vols. London, 1893–1897.

Armstrong, C. F. *From Shakespeare to Shaw.* London, 1913.

Arnold, Matthew. *Letters of an Old Playgoer,* ed. Brander Matthews. New York, 1919.

Arvin, Neil Cole. *Eugène Scribe and the French Theatre, 1815–1860.* Cambridge, Mass., 1924.

Bailey, J. O. *British Plays of the Nineteenth Century: An Anthology to Illustrate the Evolution of the Drama.* New York, 1966.

Baker, Blanch M. *Dramatic Bibliography.* New York, 1933.

Baker, George Pierce. *Dramatic Technique.* Boston, 1919.

Baker, W. T. *The Manchester Stage: 1800–1900.* London, 1903.

Balmforth, Ramsden. *The Problem-Play.* New York, 1928.

Bates, Alfred, ed. *The Drama.* 22 vols. London, 1913.

Baugh, Albert C., et al. *A Literary History of England.* New York, 1948.

Beerbohm, Sir Max. *Around the Theatres.* 2 vols. New York, 1930.

Beers, H. A. "The English Drama of To-day," *North American Review,* CLXXX (1905), 746–757.

Bergholz, H. *Die Neugestaltung des modernen englischer Theatres, 1870–1930.* Berlin, 1933.

Booth, Michael R. "The Acting of Melodrama," *University of Toronto Quarterly,* XXXIV (1964), 31–48.

Bradbrook, Muriel C. *English Dramatic Form: A History of Its Development.* London, 1965.

Brandes, Georg. *Main Currents in*

Nineteenth Century Literature. 5 vols. London, 1906.

Brereton, A. *Dramatic Notes.* London, 1881–1882.

Broadbent, R. J. *A History of Pantomime.* London, 1901.

Brown, Calvin Smith. *The Later English Drama.* New York, 1898.

Brunetière, Ferdinand. *The Law of the Drama.* New York, 1914.

Bunn, Alfred. *The Stage.* 3 vols. London, 1840.

Byrne, Dawson. *The Story of Ireland's National Theatre.* Dublin, 1929.

Campbell, Lily B. *A History of Costuming on the English Stage Between 1660 and 1823.* University of Wisconsin Studies, II, 1918.

Chandler, F. W. *Aspects of Modern Drama.* New York, 1914.

Child, H. "Nineteenth-Century Drama," *Cambridge History of English Literature,* Vol. XIII, London, 1916, pp. 203–305.

"Clarence, R." See Eldridge, H. J.

Clark, Barrett H. *European Theories of the Drama, with a Supplement on the American Drama.* New York, 1947.

Clinton-Baddeley, V. C. *The Burlesque Tradition in the English Theatre After 1660.* London, 1952.

"Cole, John William." *The Life and Theatrical Times of Charles Kean.* London, 1860.

Cook, Dutton. *On the Stage.* 2 vols. London, 1883.

Cordell, Richard A. *Henry Arthur Jones and the Modern Drama.* New York, 1932.

Craig, Edward Gordon. *The Art of the Theatre.* Edinburgh, 1905.

Cunliffe, J. W. *Modern English Playwrights.* London, 1927.

Darton, F. J. Harvey. *Vincent Crummles: His Theatre and His Times.* London, 1926.

Decker, C. R. "Ibsen's Literary Reputation and Victorian Taste," *Studies in Philology,* XXXII (1935), 632–645.

Dibdin, J. C. *The Annals of the Edinburgh Stage.* London, 1888.

Dickens, Charles. "The Amusements of the People," *Household Words,* 30 March, 30 April, 1850.

Dickinson, Thomas H. *The Contemporary Drama of England.* London, 1925.

Disher, Maurice Willson. *Blood and Thunder.* London, 1949.

———. *Clowns and Pantomimes.* London, 1925.

———. *Melodrama.* London, 1954.

———. *Winkles and Champagne.* London, 1938.

Donoghue, Dennis. *The Third Voice* [verse drama]. New York, 1966.

Downer, Alan S. *The British Drama: A Handbook and Brief Chronicle.* New York, 1950.

———. "Players and the Painted Stage: Nineteenth Century Acting," *PMLA,* LXI (1946), 522–576.

Drinkwater, John, ed. *The Eighteen-Sixties.* Cambridge, 1932.

Dubech, Lucien J. de Montbrial and Hélène Dorn-Monval. *Histoire Général illustrée du Théâtre,* 5 vols. Paris, 1931–1934.

Dukes, Ashley. *Modern Dramatists.* London, 1911.

———. *The Scene Is Changed.* London, 1942.

———. *The Youngest Drama.* London, 1924.

Eldredge, H. J. *'The Stage' Cyclopedia.* London, 1909.

Eliot, T. S. *Poetry and Drama.* Cambridge, Mass., 1951.

Ellehauge, Martin. "Initial Stages in the Development of the English Problem-Play: The Savoy Opera," *Englische Studien,* CXVI (1932), 373–401.

———. *Striking Figures Amongst Modern English Dramatists.* Copenhagen, 1931.

Erle, T. W. *Letters from a Theatrical Scene-Painter.* London, 1880.

Evans, Bertrand. *Gothic Drama from Walpole to Shelley.* Berkeley, 1947.

Filon, Augustin. *The English Stage, Being an Account of the Victorian Drama,* trans. Frederic Whyte. London, 1897.

Firkins, Ina Ten Eyck. *Index to Plays, 1800–1926.* New York, 1927.

Fitzgerald, P. H. *A New History of the English Stage (1660–1842),* 2 vols. London, 1882.

Fornelli, G. *Tendenze e Motivi nel Dramma inglese moderno e contemporaneo.* Firenze, [1930].

Frank, M. A. *Ibsen in England.* London, 1919.

Freytag, Gustavo. *Technique of the Drama,* trans. Elias J. MacEwan. Chicago, 1895.

"G. M. G." *The Stage Censor: An Historical Sketch, 1544–1907.* London, 1908.

Gamble, William Burt. *The Development of Scenic Art and Stage Machinery* (bibliography), rev. New York, 1928.

Ganzel, Dewey. "Patent Wrongs and Patent Theatres: Drama and the Law in the Early Nineteenth Century," *PMLA,* LXXXVI (1961), 384–396.

Gassner, John. *Masters of the Drama,* 2nd ed. New York, 1945.

[Genest, John]. *Some Account of the English Stage, From 1660 to 1830.* 10 vols. Bath, 1832.

Gilder, Rosamond and George Freedley. *Theatre Collections in Libraries and Museums,* rev. New York, 1964.

Goldman, E. *The Social Significance of Modern Drama.* London, 1914.

Granville-Barker, Harley. *The Eighteen-Seventies.* Cambridge, 1929.

———. *The Study of Drama.* New York, 1934.

Gregory, Lady [Augusta]. *Our Irish Theatre.* New York, 1913.

Grein, J. T. *Dramatic Criticism.* 3 vols. London, 1899–1903.

Grundy, Sydney. *The Play of the Future, by A Playwright of the Past.* London, 1914.

Hamilton, Clayton. *The Theory of the Theatre.* London, 1910.

———. and L. Baylis. *The Old Vic.* London, 1926.

Hanratty, Jerome. "Melodrama—Then and Now: Some Possible Lessons from the 19th Century," *Review of English Literature,* IV, ii (1963), 108–114.

Hartnoll, Phyllis, ed. *The Oxford Companion to the Theatre.* London, 1957.

Hastings, Charles. *The Theatre.* London, 1901.

Hazlitt, William. *A View of the English Stage* (1818), ed. William Archer and R. W. Lowe. London, 1895.

Henderson, Archibald. *The Changing Drama.* London, 1914.

Hogarth, G. *Memoirs of the Musical Drama.* London, 1838.

Hollingshead, J. *Gaiety Chronicles.* London, 1890.

Horne, Richard Hengist. *A New*

Spirit of the Age. 2 vols. London, 1844.

Houssaye, Arsène. *La Comédie Française, 1680–1880.* Paris, 1880.

Howe, P. P. *Dramatic Portraits.* London, 1913.

Hudson, Lynton. *The English Stage, 1850–1950.* London, 1951.

Huneker, James G. *Iconoclasts: A Book of Dramatists.* London, 1905.

Hunt, Leigh. *Critical Essays on the Performers of the London Theatres.* London, 1807.

Irving, Sir Henry. *The Stage.* London, 1878.

Jackson, Holbrook. *The Eighteen-Nineties.* London, 1923.

James, Henry. *The Scenic Art; Notes on Acting and the Drama: 1872–1901.* New York, 1957.

Jones, F. M. *On the Causes of the Decline of the Drama.* Edinburgh, 1834.

Jones, Henry Arthur. *The Foundations of a National Drama.* New York, 1912.

———. *The Renascence of the English Drama.* New York, 1895.

———. *The Theatre of Ideas.* London, 1915.

Jones, Stephen. *Biographia Dramatica.* 3 vols. London, 1812.

Joseph, B. L. *The Tragic Actor... from Burbage to Irving.* London, 1959.

Kendal, Dame Madge. *The Drama.* London, 1884.

Knight, J. *The History of the English Stage During the Reign of Victoria.* London, 1901.

Laver, James. *Drama: Its Costume and Decor.* London, 1951.

Lawrence, W. J. *Old Theatre Days and Ways.* London, 1935.

Lennox, Lord William. *Plays, Players, and Playhouses.* 2 vols. London, 1881.

Lewes, G. H. *On Actors and Acting.* London, 1875.

Lowe, Robert W. *A Bibliographical Account of English Theatrical Literature.* London, 1888.

Mantzius, Karl. *A History of Theatrical Art,* trans. L. von Cossel. 6 vols. London, 1903–21.

Martin, Sir Theodore. *Essays on the Drama.* London, 1874.

Matthews, Brander. *French Dramatists of the Nineteenth Century.* New York, 1905.

———. and Laurence Hutton, eds. *Actors and Actresses... David Garrick to the Present Time.* 5 vols. New York, 1886.

Maude, Cyril. *The Haymarket Theatre.* London, 1903.

Mears, Richard McM. "Serious Verse Drama in England, 1812–1850." Unpubl. diss., University of North Carolina, 1954.

Meisel, Martin. *Shaw and the Nineteenth Century Theatre.* New York, 1966.

Meredith, George. *An Essay on Comedy and the Use of the Comic Spirit.* London, 1897.

Miller, Anna I. *The Independent Theatre in Europe.* London, 1931.

Morgan, A. E. *Tendencies of Modern English Drama.* London, 1923.

Morley, Henry. *The Journal of a London Playgoer, 1851–1866.* London, 1891.

Morris, M. *Essays in Theatrical Criticism.* London, 1882.

Moses, Montrose J. *Representative British Drama, Victorian and Modern.* Boston, 1931.

Nag, U. C. "The English Theatre of the Romantic Revival," *Nineteenth Century,* CIV (1928), 384–398.

Nagler, A. M. *Sources of Theatrical History.* New York, 1952.

Newton, H. Chance. *Crime and the Drama, or, Dark Deeds Dramatized.* London, 1927.
Nicholson, W. *The Struggle for a Free Stage.* London, 1906.
Nicoll, Allardyce. *British Drama.* London, 1935.
———. *The English Theatre: A Short History.* London, 1936.
———. *Early Nineteenth Century Drama* and *Later Nineteenth Century Drama. A History of English Drama, 1600–1900,* Vols. III and IV. Cambridge, 1959.
———. *The Theory of Drama.* London, 1931.
Odell, G. C. D. *Shakespeare from Betterton to Irving.* 2 vols. New York, 1920.
O'Neill, J. J. *A Bibliographical Account of Irish Theatrical Literature.* Dublin, 1920.
Pallette, D. B. "The English Actor's Fight for Respectability," *Theatre Annual* (1948–1949), 27–34.
Palmer, J. *The Censor and the Theatres.* London, 1913.
Pawley, Frederic. *Theatre Architecture: A Brief Bibliography.* New York, 1932.
Peacock, Ronald. *Art of the Drama.* London, corrected 1960.
———. *The Poet in the Theatre.* New York, 1960.
Pearson, Hesketh. *The Last Actor-Managers.* London, 1950.
Pellizzi, C. *English Drama, the Last Great Phase,* trans. Rowan Williams. London, 1935.
Perry, Henry Ten Eyck. *Masters of Dramatic Comedy and Their Social Themes.* Cambridge, Mass., 1939.
Phelps, William Lyon. *Essays on Modern Dramatists.* London, 1921.
[Purnell, Thomas]. *Dramatists of the Present Day.* London, 1871.
Reynolds, Ernest. *Early Victorian Drama, 1830–70.* Cambridge, 1936.
Rice, Charles. *The London Theatre in the Eighteen-Thirties,* ed. A. C. Sprague and Bertram Shuttleworth. London, 1950.
Robinson, Lennox, ed. *The Irish Theatre.* London, 1939.
Rowell, George. *The Victorian Theatre.* London, 1956.
Russell, Sir Edward. *The Theatre and Things Said About It.* Liverpool, 1911.
Ryan, R. *Dramatic Table Talk.* 3 vols. London, 1825–1830.
Saintsbury, George. *A History of Nineteenth Century Literature.* New York, 1896.
Saintsbury, H. A., and Cecil Palmer, eds. *We Saw Him Act: A Symposium on the Art of Sir Henry Irving.* London, 1939.
Sawyer, Maynard. *The Comedy of Manners from Sheridan to Maugham.* Philadelphia, 1931.
Schelling, Felix E. *English Drama.* London, 1914.
Schlegel, August Wilhelm. *Lectures on Dramatic Art and Literature,* trans. John Black, rev. Rev. A. J. W. Morrison. London, 1909.
Scott, Clement William. *The Drama of Yesterday and Today.* 2 vols. London, 1899.
———. *From 'The Bells' to 'King Arthur'...1871 to1895.* London, 1896.
Scott, Harold. *The Early Doors: Origins of the Music-Hall.* London, 1948.
Sellier, W. *Kotzebue in England.* Leipzig, 1901.
Sharp, R. F. *A Short History of the*

English Stage to 1908. London, 1909.

Shaw, Desmond. *London Nights of Long Ago.* London, 1927.

Shaw, George Bernard. *Dramatic Opinions and Essays.* 2 vols. New York, 1907.

———. *The Quintessence of Ibsenism.* rev. ed. London, 1913.

Sherson, E. *London's Lost Theatre of the Nineteenth Century.* London, 1925.

Short, E., and A. Compton-Rickett. *Ring up the Curtain.* London, 1938.

Southern, Richard. *Changeable Scenery.* London, 1952.

Spectacles à travers les âges, ed. anon.; prefaces by Denys Amiel and Henri Fescourt. 3 vols. Paris, 1931–1932.

Spence, E. F. *Our Stage and Its Critics.* London, 1910.

Stahl, E. *Das englische Theatre im 19. Jahrhundert.* München, 1914.

Stoakes, J. P. "English Melodrama: Forerunner of Modern Social Drama," *Florida State University Studies,* III (1951), 53–62.

Stratman, Carl J., C.S.U., "English Tragedy: 1819-1823," *Philological Quarterly,* XLI (1962), 465–74.

Stuart, Charles Douglas and A. J. Park. *The Variety Stage: A History of the Music Halls.* London, 1895.

Syles, L. D. *Essays in Dramatic Criticism.* London, 1898.

Taylor, Tom. *The Theatre in England: Some of Its Shortcomings and Possibilities.* London, 1871.

Thackeray, T. J. *On Theatrical Emancipation and the Rights of Dramatic Authors.* London, 1832.

Thorndike, Ashley Horace. *English Comedy.* New York, 1929.

———. *Tragedy.* New York and Boston, 1908.

Thorp, Willard. "The Stage Adventures of Some Gothic Novels," *PMLA,* XLIII (1928), 476–486.

Thouless, P. *Modern Poetic Drama.* Oxford, 1934.

Tompkins, F. G. *A Brief View of the English Drama.* London, 1840.

Vardac, A. N. *Stage to Screen.* Cambridge, Mass., 1949.

Waitzkin, L. *The Witch of Wych Street* [Madame Vestris]. Cambridge, Mass., 1933.

Walkley, A. B. *Drama and Life.* London, 1907.

———. *Frames of Mind.* London, 1899.

———. *Playhouse Impressions.* London, 1892.

Ward, A. C., ed. *Specimens of English Dramatic Criticism: XVII–XX Centuries.* London, 1945.

Ward, Sir Alphonsus W., and A. R. Walter, eds. *The Cambridge History of English Literature,* vols. V and VI. New York, 1910.

Watson, Ernest Bradlee. *Sheridan to Robertson.* Cambridge, Mass., 1926.

West, E. J. "The London Stage, 1870–1890," *University of Colorado Studies,* Series B, II (1943), 31–84.

White, H. A. *Sir Walter Scott's Novels on the Stage.* New Haven, 1927.

Wilson, A. E. *The Lyceum.* London, 1952.

———. *Penny Plain, Twopence Coloured.* London, 1932.

Williams, M. *Some London Theatres Past and Present.* London, 1883.

Witkowski, Georg. *The German Drama of the Nineteenth Century,* trans. L. E. Horning. New York, 1909.

Wyndham, H. S. *Annals of the Covent Garden Theatre, 1732–1897.* 2 vols. London, 1906.

Wynne, A. *The Growth of English Drama.* Oxford, 1914.

ADDENDUM TO THE 1988 EDITION

Alastair Fowler's *A History of English Literature* (1987) expresses a popular view when it says that "theatre flourished in the Victorian period—at least in the sense that it attracted mass audiences to farces and popular melodramas" but "Victorian theatre offered little that could be called dramatic literature, however, until the 1880s."

Now, in the 1980's, we see that (as Richard Kelly is quoted below as saying) "it is fashionable to sneer at Victorian drama"; but some scholarly work continues. The following notes update reports on individual plays and on nineteenth-century British drama in general.

THE CENCI

Adams, Charles L. "The Structure of *The Cenci*," *Drama Survey* 4 (1965), 139 - 148.

Brophy, Robert . *"Rappacini's Daughter, The Cenci* and the Cenci Legend," *American Literature* 42 (1970), 241 - 244.

Curran, Stuart. *Shelley's Cenci: Scorpions Ringed with Fire.* Princeton University Press, 1970.

Davison, Richard A. "A Websterian Echo in *The Cenci*," *American Notes & Queries* 6 (1967), 53 - 54.

Delmar, P. Jay. "Evil and Character in Shelley's *The Cenci*," *Massachusetts Studies in English* 6:1-2 (1977), 37 - 48.

Dewsnapp, Mary Anne Caporraletti. "Idiosyncrasy and Spirit: Five Tragedies of the English Romantic Period," *Dissertation Abstracts* 39 (1979), 6104A.

Duerksen, Roland A. *The Cenci.* Bobbs-Merrill, 1970.

Gottleib, Erika. "Cosmic Allegory in *The Cenci*," *Aligarh Journal of English Studies* 3 (1978), 24 - 43.

Hornby, Richard. *Script into Performance: A Structuralist View of Play Production.* University of Texas Press, 1977.

Jacoben, Sally-Ann H. "Shelley's Idea of Tragedy and the Structure of *The Cenci*," *Dissertation Abstracts* 39 (1978), 2929A.

Johnson, Betty F. "Shelley's *Cenci* and *Mrs. Warren's Profession*," *Shaw* 15 (1972), 26 - 34.

LaBelle, Maurice M. "Artaud's Use of Shelley's *The Cenci...*," *Revue de Litterature Comparée* 46 (1972), 128 - 134.

Lemoncelli, Ronald L. "Cenci as Corrupt Dramatic Poet," *English Language Notes* 16 (1978) 103 - 117.

Miller, Sarah M. "Irony in Shelley's *The Cenci*," *University of Mississippi Studies in English* 9 (1968), 23 - 35.

Milne, Fred. L. "Shelley's *The Cenci:* I.iii.55-69," *Explicator* 35:2 (1976), 30 - 31.

______ . "Shelley's *The Cenci:* The Ice Motif and the Ninth Circle of Dante's Hell," *Tennessee Studies in Literature* 22 (1977), 117 - 132.

Otten, Terry. *The Deserted Stage: The Search for Dramatic Form in Nineteenth-Century England,* Ohio

University Press, 1972.

Rickert, Alfred E. "Two Views of *The Cenci:* Shelley and Artaud," *Ball State University Forum* 14:1 (1973), 31 - 35.

Sims-Gunsenhauser, William D. "Conflict of the Inner Life in Goethe's *Iphegenie* and Shelley's Cenci," Neophilologus 63 (1979), 95 - 107.

Smith, Paul. "Restless Casuistry: Shelley's Composition of *The Cenci,*" *Keats-Shelley Journal* 13 (1964), 77 - 85.

Steffan, Truman G. "Seven Accounts of the Cenci and Shelley's Drama," *Studies in English Literature* 9 (1968), 23 - 25.

Thorn, Arline R. "Shelley's *The Cenci* as Tragedy," *Costerus* 9 (1973), 219 - 228.

Turner, Justin G. *"The Cenci,* Shelley *vs.* the Truth," *American Book Collector* 22:4 (1972), 5 - 9.

Twitchell, James B. "Shelley's Use of Vampirism in *The Cenci,*" *Tennessee Studies in Literature* 24 (1979), 120 - 133.

Warren, John W. *"The Cenci* Tragedy: Heroism Restored," *Tennessee Philological Bulletin* 9:1 (1972), 3 - 13.

White, Henry. "Beatrice Cenci and Shelley's Avenger," *Essays in Literature* 5 (1978) 27 - 38.

Wilson, James D. "Beatrice Cenci and Shelley's Vision of Moral Responsibility," *Ariel* 9:3 (1978), 75 - 89.

BLACK-EY'D SUSAN

Atkinson, Colin B. " The Plays of Douglas Jerrold," *Dissertation Abstracts* 32 (1972), 5772A.

Burgess, Anthony. *Mrs. Caudle's Curtain Lectures.* London: Harvill Press, 1974.

Dobryzcka, Irena. "English Nineteenth Century Melodrama: Themes and Techniques," *Kwartalnik Neofilologiczny* 22 (1975), 395 - 406.

Doyle, Walter E. "Through the Domestic Drama Darkly: Douglas Jerrold and Early Nineteenth-Century Minor Drama," *Victorian Institute Journal* 9 (1980 - 1981), 83 - 98.

James, Louis *et al.* "Was Jerrold's Black Eyed Susan More Popular than Wordsworth's Lucy?", *Popular Drama: Aspects of Popular Entertainment in Theatre, Film and Television 1800-1976.* Cambridge University Press, 1980.

Kelly, Richard M. "Douglas Jerrold: Author and Journalist," *Dissertation Abstracts* 26 (1965), 1022 - 1023.

______. "Mrs. Caudle, A Victorian Curtain Lecturer," *University of Toronto Quarterly* 38 (1969), 295 - 309.

______. *Douglas Jerrold.* New York: Twayne's English Authors Series (# 146), 1972. (Now from G. K. Hall, Boston.).

______. "Jerrold, Douglas William," *Great Writers of the English Language: Dramatists.* London: St. James' Press and New York: St. Martin's Press, 1979, 317 - 320.

Kunde, Arnold J. "A Structural Analysis of Douglas William Jerrold's Melodramas," *Dissertation Abstracts* 33 (1973), 4579A.

Morgan, Paula M. "E. L. Davenport and *Black-Eyed Susan,*" *Princeton University Library Chronicle* 48:1 (Autumn, 1986), 21 - 37.

Worth, Christopher. *From Picture to Stage: Douglas Jerrold's THE RENT DAY.* Amsterdam: Rodopi, 1984.

THE LADY OF LYONS

Lord Lytton's 10 plays (of which *Lady of Lyons* was the second, 1838) have been generally ignored, except for passing mention in surveys of the nineteenth-century drama and melodrama, in favor of his nearly 30 novels. The latter are covered in such studies as S. B. Liljegren (*Bulwer-Lytton's Novels and Isis Unveiled,* 1957), Keith Hollingsworth (*The Newgate Novel 1830 - 1847,* 1963), and Allen Conrad Christensen *(The Fiction of New Regions,* 1977). In the fifth edition (1985) of the *Oxford Companion to English Literature,* Margaret Drabble gives *The Lady of Lyons* only "a romantic comedy by* Bulwer-Lytton." However, Curtis Dahl on Bulwer-Lytton in *Great Writers of the English Language: Novelists* (1979), p. 187, grants "his plays *The Lady of Lyons* and *Richelieu,* written for the great actor-manager Macready, held the boards into the twentieth century, and still have vitality," though not enough to warrant inclusion in *Great Writers of the English Language: Dramatists* (1979), unfortunately.

Julian Price Avis' unpublished dissertation "The Melodramatic Mode, and Melodrama as Social Criticism..." (1981) deals with Bulwer-Lytton's novels, not his plays.

LONDON ASSURANCE

Robert Hogan (who wrote on *The Irish Literary Theatre* with James Kilroy, etc.) published *Boucicault* (1969) and wrote the entry on him in *Great Writers of the English Language: Dramatists* (1979), 81, which is the most convenient source now listing Boucicault's 128 plays and other works (the novel *Foul Play* with Charles Reade, several times produced as a play, and *The Story of Ireland* 1881 and *The Art of Acting* 1926).

The Colleen Bawn, Arragh-na-Pogue and *The Shaughraun* were edited by David Krause (1964), *London Assurance* by Ronald Eyre (1971). *The Corsican Brothers* (1852, from Dumas *père* is in Michael Booth's *English Plays of the Nineteenth Century II* (1969). Boucicault's career is also part of the history of the American stage and his *Rip Van Winkle* was edited by Arthur Hobson Quinn in *Representative American Plays* (1917). *The Octoroon* (and Joseph Jefferson's *Rip Van Winkle* are in Myron Matlaw's anthology *The Black Crook and Other Nineteenth-Century American Plays* (1967), and *The Octoroon* is also found in Lee Jacobus' *Longmans Anthology of American Drama* (1982), etc.

Articles neglect *London Assurance* – an opportunity for scholars! – and tend to address themselves to Boucicault's melodramas rather than his comedies and to stress Ireland and America over London:

Basta, Samira. "The French Influence on Dion Boucicault's Sensation Drama," *Literary Interrelations: Ireland, England and the World,* Tubingen, 1987.

Cave, Richard A. "The Presentation of English and Irish Characters in Boucicault's Irish Melodramas," *Literary Interrelations....*

Davis, Jim. "The Importance of Being Caleb: The Influence of Boucicault's Dot on the Comic Styles of J. L. Toole and Joseph Jefferson," *The Dickensian* 82:1 (Spring 1986), 27 - 32.

Galassi, Frank S. "Slavery and Melodrama: Boucicault's *The Octoroon,*" *Markham Review* 6 (1977), 77 - 80.

Gargano, James W. "Tableaux of Renunciation: Wharton's Use of *The Shaugraun* in *The Age of Innocence,*" *Studies in American Fiction* 15:1 (Spring 1987), 1 - 11.

Harrison, A. Cleveland. "Boucicault's Formula: Illusion Equals Pleasure," *Educational Theatre Journal* 21 (1969), 299 - 309.

Johnson, Stephen. "Joseph Jefferson's *Rip Van Winkle,*" *Drama Review* 26:1 (Spring 1982), 3 - 20.

LaCasse, Don. "Edwin Booth on Dion Boucicault, Playwriting, and Play Production: A Previously Unpublished Letter," *Theatre Survey* 21:2 (1980), 181 - 184.

Nelson, James Malcolm. "From Rory and Paddy to Boucicault's Myles, Shaun and Conn: The Irishman on the London Stage, 1830 - 1860," *Eire/Ireland* 13:3 (1978), 79 - 105. See also 21:1, 135 - 138.

Richardson, Gary A. "Boucicault's *The Octoroon* and American Law," *Theatre Journal* 34:2 (1982), 155 - 164.

Steele, William P. *The Character of Melodrama: An Examination Through Dion Boucicault's THE POOR OF NEW YORK....* University of Maine Press, 1968. Includes text of the play.

Warren, Lisa Cooper. "Boucicault and Melodrama Onstage: The Evidence from Nineteenth-Century Advertising Illustrations for Staging, Blocking, and Costuming," *Dissertation Abstracts* 45:3 (1984), 685A - 686A.

Watt, Stephen. "Boucicault and Whitbread: The Dublin Stage at the End of the Nineteenth Century," *Eire/Ireland* 18:3 (1983), 23 - 53.

William Hunter Kendal [Grimstone] and Madge [Margaret Sholto Robertson] Kendal starred in a revival of *London Assurance* (1877). It is time for another revival, in my opinion.

CASTE

Robertson is now regarded largely for his stagecraft (Maynard Savin, *Robertson, His Plays and Stagecraft,* 1950) but other angles are covered in articles such as these:

Barrett, Daniel. "Freedom of Memory *v.* Copyright Law: The American Premiere of *Caste,*" *Theatre Research Annual* 8:1 (Spring 1983), 43 - 52.

Fitzgerald, Barry. *The World Behind the Scenes.* London, 1881.

Kaplan, Joel H. " 'Have We No Chairs?' Pinero's Trelawny and the Myth of Tom Robertson," *Essays in Theatre* 4:2 (May 1986), 119 - 133.

Robertson's *Principal Dramatic Works*

(1889) contain only some of his nearly 50 dramatic works. He also wrote a novel (*David Garrick,* 1865, as well as adapting a work by Anne H. J. Duveyrier on the subject for the stage: *David Garrick* of 1864, called *Sullivan* 1873) and edited (with E. P. Hingston) *Artemus Ward's Panorama* (1869). Seek him, therefore, also in non-theatrical contexts.

For the Theatre part, memoirs of Victorian theatre and surveys of Robertson's period. Examples:

Bancroft, Sir Squire and Lady. *Recollections of Sixty Years.* London, 1909.

Pinero, Sir Arthur Wing. "The Theatre of the 'Seventies," *The Eighteen Seventies* (ed. Harley Granville Barker), London, 1929, 135 - 163.

THE BELLS

Lewis was a very minor writer, though author of a major hit. Scholars tend to write about melodrama in general, or Sir Henry Irving's playing of it, not about Lewis, but a few modern references can be found such as Jim Davis' "Jingle without 'The Bells' " in *The Dickensian* 81:3 (1985), 175 - 180.

Lewis' melodrama needs to be seen in the context of others such as those included in J. O. Bailey's *British Plays of the Nineteenth Century* (1966): Thomas Holcroft's *A Tale of Mystery* (1802), John Baldwin Buckstone's *Luke the Labourer* (1826), Douglas Jerrold's *The Rent Day* (1832), Dion Boucicault's *After Dark* (1868), Mrs. Henry Wood's *East Lynne* (1862), and Henry Arthur Jones' *The Silver King* (1882).

Lewis doesn't even make the index of Michael Booth's *English Melodrama* (1965) but see pp. 49, 83, 160, 176 - 177 for *The Bells.* Also such articles on melodrama as:

Coolidge, Archibald C., Jr. "Dickens and the Philosophical Basis of Melodrama," *Victorian Newsletter* 20 (Fall 1961), 1 - 5.

Thompson, A. R. "Melodrama and Tragedy," *PMLA 43 (September 1928),* 810 - 835.

EAST LYNNE

Goubert, Dennis. "Did Tolstoy Read *East Lynne?" , Slavonic and East European Review* 58 (1980), 22 - 39.

Jackson, Barry. "Barnstorming Days," *Studies in English Theatre History,* 1952.

Loesberg, Jonathan. "The Ideology of Narrative Form in Sensation Fiction," *Representations* 13 (Winter, 1986), 115 - 138.

Rahill, Frank. *World of Melodrama.* Pennsylvania State University Press, 1967.

Steele, William P. *The Character of Melodrama.* Universtiy of Maine Press, 1968.

Sterner, Mark H. "The Changing Status of Women in Late Victorian Drama," *Within the Dramatic Spectrum.* University Press of America, 1986.

H.M.S. PINAFORE

Asimov, Isaac. *The Annotated Gilbert and Sullivan* and other standard G&S sources should be consulted.

Bordman, Gerald. *American Operetta: From HMS Pinafore to Sweeney Todd.* Oxford University Press, 1981.

Eden, David. *Gilbert and Sullivan: The Creative Conflict.* Fairleigh Dickinson University Press, 1986.

Godwin, A. H. *Gilbert & Sullivan: A Critical Appreciation of the Savoy Operas.* Associated Faculty Press, 1969 (reprint of 1926 edition).

Williamson, Audrey. *Gilbert & Sullivan Opera.* Marion Boyars Publishers, revised edition 1983.

Wilson, Robin and Frederick Lloyd. *Gilbert & Sullivan: the Official D'Oyley Carte Picture History.* Alfred A. Knopf, 1984.

THE COUNTESS CATHLEEN

Bramsback, Birgit. *Folklore and W. B. Yeats: The Function of Folklore in Three Early Plays.* Uppsala University Press, 1984.

Cardullo, Bert. "Notes toward a Production of W. B. Yeats's *The Countess Cathleen,*" *Canadian Journal of Irish Studies* 11:2 (December 1985), 49 - 67.

Patsch, Sylvia M. *The Countess Cathleen*....University of Innsbruck Press, 1974.

Ranganathan, Sudha. "Rabindrath Tagore's *Malini* and W. B. Yeats's *The Countess Cathleen,*" *Osmania Journal of English Studies* 9:1 (1972), 51 - 54.

Smith, Peter Alderson. "Grown to Heaven Like a Tree: The Scenery of *The Countess Cathleen,*" *Eire/Ireland: A Journal of Irish Studies* 14:3 (1979), 65 - 82. See also 17:2 (1982), 141 - 146.

Smythe, Colin. "*The Countess Cathleen:* A Note," *Yeats Annual* 3 (1985), 193 - 197.

THE SECOND MRS. TANQUERAY

The critical biography (with letters) by Wilbur D. Dunkel (1941) was replaced by a *Pinero* by Walter Lazenby (1972) but recent articles are few. Two of them are:

Kaplan, Joel H. "Pinero Redivivus: A Review Essay," *Essays in Theatre* 6:1 (November 1987), 61 - 66.

Nethercot, Arthur C. "*Mrs. Warren's Profession* and *The Second Mrs. Tanqueray,*" *Shaw: The Annual of Bernard Shaw Studies* 13 (1970), 26 - 28.

There are reviews of modern productions of his most lasting play, *Trelawny of the "Wells"*, in theatrical history sources.

The cruelty in P. P. Howe's *Dramatic Portraits* was not as bad for Pinero as recent neglect. When Clayton Hamilton edited his *Social Plays* in 4 volumes (1917 - 1922), Pinero was considered an important dramatist. Today he is not, not even in a time when "the woman with a past" might be thought to attract feminist critical attention. But as I write (1988) the Roundabout Theatre in New York City is about to stage Pinero's *Dandy Dick.*

THE IMPORTANCE OF BEING EARNEST

Publication on Wilde is extensive and includes Richard Ellmann's biography

(1988) and reviews of productions of this play. Articles and dissertations include:

Barth, Adolf. "Oscar Wilde's 'Comic Refusal'...." *Archiv* 216 (1979), 120 - 128.

Berggren, Ruth Harriet. "Oscar Wilde's *The Importance of Being Earnest:* A Critical Edition of the Four-Act Version (Volumes I and II)," *Dissertation Abstracts* 45:2 (1984), 524A.

Bose, Tirthankar. "Oscar Wilde's Game of Being Earnest," *Modern Drama* 21 (1978), 81 - 86.

Dobrin, David N. "Stoppard's *Travesties,*" *Explicator* 40:1 (1981), 63 - 64.

Donaldson, Ian. "The Ledger of the Lost-and-Stolen Office: Parody in Dramatic Comedy," *Southern Review* 13:1 (March, 1980), 41 - 52.

Fineman, Joel. "The Significance of Literature: *The Importance of Being Earnest,*" *October* 15 (1980), 79 - 90.

Glavin, John. "Deadly Earnest And Earnest Revived: Wilde's Four-Act Play," *Nineteenth-Century Studies* 1 (1987), 13 - 24.

Jordan, Robert J. "Satire and Fantasy in Wilde's *The Importance of Being Earnest,*" *Ariel* 1:3 (1970), 101 - 109.

Kaplan, Joel H. "Earnest Worthing's London Address...," *Canadian Journal of Irish Studies* 11:1 (1985), 53 - 54.

Mikhail, E. H. "The Four-Act Version of *The Importance of Being Earnest,*" *Modern Drama* 11 (1968), 263 - 266.

Mullini, Roberta. *"Cortesia e 'onesta'* in *The Importance of Being Earnest,*" *Spicilegio Moderno* 12 (1979), 149 - 158.

Paglia, Camille. "Oscar Wilde and the English Epicene," *Raritan* 4:3 (1985), 85 - 109.

Parker, David. "Oscar Wilde's Great Farce: *The Importance of Being Earnest,*" *Modern Language Quarterly* 35 (1974), 173 - 186.

Sammells, Neil. "Earning Liberties: *Travesties* and *The Importance of Being Earnest,*" *Modern Drama* 29:3 (1986), 376 - 387.

Spinninger, Dennis J. "Profiles and Principles: The Sense of the Absurd in *The Importance of Being Earnest,* [Evansville, Illinois] *Papers on Language and Literature* 12 (1976), 49 - 72.

Stone, Geoffrey. "Serious Bunburyism: The Logic of *The Importance of Being Earnest,*" *Essays in Criticism* 26 (1976), 28 - 41.

Takahashi, Yasunari. *"Nonsene a Taisetsu: Majime ga Taisetsu o yumo,"* *Eigo Seinen* 124 (1978), 53 - 56.

Wadleigh, Paul C. *"Earnest* at St. James's Theatre," *Quarterly Journal of Speech* 52 (1966), 58 - 62.

MICHAEL AND HIS LOST ANGEL

Carlson, Susan L. "Two Genres and their Women: The Problem Play and the Comedy of Manners in the Edwardian Theatre," *Midwest Quarterly* 26:4 (Summer 1985), 413 - 424.

Domeraski, Regina. "The World Divided: The Plays of Henry Arthur Jones," *Dissertation Abstracts* 41 (1980), 4607A.

Habicht, Werner. "Henry Arthur Jones: *Michael and His Lost Angel,*" *Festschrift* article in *AN* 71-1-73 (1976), 334 - 346.

Perez Petit, Victor. *"Dos dramaturogos*

ingleses: Henry-Arthur Jones y Arthur Wing Pinero," *Revista Nacional* (Uruguay, 1965), 5 - 25.

Preussner, Alanna Sue. "The Minister's Wooing: Temptation and the Sentimental Tradition in Five British and American Works of the Late Nineteenth Century," *Dissertation Abstracts* 40 (1980) 4610A.

Simon, Elliott M. *The Problem Play in British Drama 1890-1914.* Salzburg, 1978.

Taylor, John Russell. *The Rise and Fall of the Well Made Play.* London, 1967.

Wallis, Bruce. *"Michael and His Lost Angel:* Archetypal Conflict and Victorian Life," *Victorian Newsletter* 56 (1979), 20 - 26.

Wearing, J. P. "Henry Arthur Jones: An Annotated Bibliography of Writings about Him," *English Literature in Transition (1880 - 1920)* 22 (1979), 160 - 228.

DRAMATIC SEQUELS

There has not been much of use on Hankin since G. Engel's *Hankin als Dramatiker* (1931), which includes a bibliography. A dissertation on "St. John Hankin's Dramatic Esthetic: Its Theory and Practice" (1974) by Sister M. De Chantal Whelan is unpublished. There is an article by Harr Lane on Hankin's play *The Cassilis Engagement* in *English Studies in Canada* 8:4 (1982), 437 - 451 and an estimate of Hankin by William M. Tydeman (University College of North Wales) in *Great Writers of the English Language: Dramatists* (1979), 270 - 271. Read Hankin's own work (in which he tries "to represent life, not argue about it") in *Plays* (1923). Introduction to these two (revised) volumes by John Drinkwater.

NINETEENTH-CENTURY BRITISH DRAMA: SOME NEW STUDIES AND RECENT REPRINTS

Baker, M. *The Rise of the Victorian Actor.* Croom, 1978. Rowman & Littlefield.

Booth, Michael R., ed. *Hiss the Villain: Six English and American Melodramas.* Ayer Publications, 1972.

Conolly, L. W. and J. P. Wearing, *English Drama and Theatre, 1800-1900....* Gale Publishers, 1978.

Darbyshire, Alfred. *Art of the Victorian Stage.* Ayer reprint of 1907 publication.

Davies, Robertson. *The Personal Art....* (1961), reprinted Darby Books (1983). Partly on Victorian Theatre.

Disher, M. Willson. *Blood and Thunder.* Haskell Books, 1974. Mid-Victorian melodrama.

Emeljanow, Victor. *Victorian Popular Dramatists.* Twayne's English Authors Series, G. K. Hall, 1987.

Esslin, Marin. *Illustrated Encyclopedia of World Drama.* Thames & Hudson, 1977.

Filon, Augustin. *The English Stage...* Ayer reprint of 1897 publication.

Foulkes, Richard, Ed. *Shakespeare & the Victorian Stage.* Cambridge University Press, 1986.

Fryckstedt, Monica C. *Geraldine Jewsbury's ATHENAEUM Reviews....* Uppsala University Press, 1986. Coronet Paperbacks.

Glasstone, B. *Victorian and Edwardian*

Theatres. Thames & Hudson, 1975.

Grein, J. T. *Dramatic Criticism.* Benjamin Blom (1968) reprint of 5 vols. published 1897 - 1904.

Hogg, James. *Robert Browning and the Victorian Theatre, II.* Salzburg Studies in English Literature, 1977. Acting versions of *Strafford, A Blot on the 'Scutcheon, Colombe's Birthday.*

Howard, Diana. *London Theatres and Music Halls, 1850-1950.* Library Association, 1970.

Huberman, Jeffrey. *Late Victorian Farce.* UMI Research Press, 1986.

Hughes, Samuel C. *Pre-Victorian Drama in Dublin.* Burt Franklin reprint (1970) of 1904 publication.

Kendal, Dame Madge [Margaret]. *The Drama.* Garland reprint, 1986.

Kesler, K. *Theatrical Costume....* Gale Research, 1979. "Guide to information Sources."

Knight, Joseph A. *A History of The Stage during the Victorian Era.* Garland reprint (1986) of the 1901 publication.

Lennox, William P. *Plays, Players & Playhouses at Home & Abroad with Anecdotes of the Drama & the Stage.* Garland reprint 1986 of the original two-volume work.

Litto, Fredric M. *American Dissertations on the Drama and Theatre.* Kent State University Press, 1969.

MacCallum, Mungo W. *The Dramatic Monologue in the Victorian Period.* Folcroft Library reprint (1974) of 1925 publication.

Mander, Raymond and Mitchenson, Joe. *British Music Hall.* Gentry Books revised edition, 1974. See also Roy Busby's illustrated *British Music Hall,* Elek, 1976. And Mander & Mitchenson's *Lost Theatres of London,* new edition New English Library, 1976.

Mayer, David. *Harlequin in His Element.* Oxford University Press, 1969. British pantomime 1806 - 1836.

McGhee, Richard D. *Marriage, Duty, and Desire in Victorian Poetry and Drama.* University of Kansas Press, 1980.

Mullin, Donald, ed. *Victorian Actors and Actresses in Review....* Greenwood Press, 1983. Theatrical reviews of the US and UK stage 1837 -1901.

_______ . *Victorian Plays: A Record of Significant Productions on the London Stage, 1837 - 1901.* Greenwood Press, 1987.

Neville, Henry. *The Stage: Its Past and Present in Relation to Fine Art.* Garland reprint 1986, Victorian Muse Series.

Nicoll, Allardyce. *World Drama From Aeschylus to Anouilh.* Harrap, second edition 1976

Purnell, Thomas. *Dramatists of the Present Day.* Garland reprint (1985) of 1871 publication.

Reynolds, Ernest. *Early Victorian Drama, 1830 - 1870.* Benjamin Blom reprint (1965) of 1936 publication.

Richards, K. and P. Thompson. *Essays in Nineteenth-Century British Theatre.* Methuen, 1971.

Robinson, Henry Crabbe. *The London Theatre, 1811 - 1866.* The Society for Theatre Research (1966) published memoirs of this notable figure (1775 - 1867) famous for his posthumously printed *Diaries* and *Letters* and important friends.

Roose-Evans, James. *London Theatres from the Globe to the National.* Phaidon, 1977.

Rowell, George. *Victorian Dramatic Criticism.* Methuen (1971) anthology.

______. *Queen Victoria Goes to the Theatre.* Elek, 1978.

______. *The Victorian Theatre....* Cambridge University Press, 1979. This second edition defines the period as 1792 - 1914.

______. *Theatre in the Age of Irving.* Basil Blackwell, 1981.

Scott, Clement. *The Drama of Yesterday and Today.* Garland has reprinted the two-volume 1899 publication in Victorian Muse Series.

Sharma, Virendra. *Studies in Victorian Drama....* Salzburg Studies in English Literature, 1979. Browning's and Tennyson's poetic dramas, etc.

Southern, Richard. *The Victorian Theatre.* David & Charles, 1970. Pictorial survey.

Speaight, George. *Punch and Judy: A History.* Studio Vista, 1970.

Stirling, A. M. *Victorian Sidelights....* Norwood Editions reprint (1954) of "The Papers of the Late Mrs. Adams-Acton." Victorian Age Series.

Styan, J. L. *Drama, Stage and Audience.* Cambridge University Press, 1975.

Thomas, James. *The Art of the Actor-Manager: Wilson Barrett and the Victorian Theatre.* Theatre and Dramatic Studies Series. UMI Research Press, 1984.

Tolles, Winton. *Tom Taylor and the Victorian Drama.* AMS reprint of 1940 book on the author of *Masks and Faces, Our American Cousin, The Ticket-of-Leave Man,* etc.

Trewin, J. C. Revised A. Nicoll's *British Drama.* Harper & Row, sixth edition, 1979.

Vinson, James, ed. *Reference Guide to English Literature.* St. James Press' 8-volume set has as Vol. 3 *The Romantic and Victorian Periods.*

Walkley, A. B. *Drama and Life.* Books for Libraries (1969) reprint of 1907 publication.

Wilson, A. E. *The Story of Pantomime.* Home and Van Thal, 1949.